In Memory of

CHARLES ERBES
GIVEN BY
FRIENDS OF LIBRARY

KEN SCHULTZ'S

ESSENTIALS OF
FISHING

Also by Ken Schultz

Bass Madness: Big Money, Big Mouths, and Big Dreams at the Bassmaster Classic

Ken Schultz's Field Guide to Freshwater Fish

Ken Schultz's Field Guide to Saltwater Fish

Spectacular Fishing

Ken Schultz's North American Fishing

Ken Schultz's Fishing Encyclopedia: Worldwide Angling Guide

Successful Bass Fishing

The Ultimate Book of Freshwater Fishing

Greatest Fishing Locales of North America: The World Atlas of Saltwater Fishing

The Complete Book of Sportfishing

The Complete Book of Freshwater Fishing

The Art of Trolling

Bass Fishing Fundamentals

KEN SCHULTZ'S
ESSENTIALS OF
FISHING

The Only Guide You Need to Catch Freshwater and Saltwater Fish

KEN SCHULTZ

Fish illustrations by David Kiphuth

Essentials is a condensation of *Ken Schultz's Fishing Encyclopedia: Worldwide Angling Guide* with new material added.

WILEY

John Wiley & Sons, Inc.

Published by John Wiley & Sons, Inc., Hoboken, New Jersey
Published simultaneously in Canada

Design by Forty-five Degree Design, LLC

For general information about our other products and services, please contact our Customer Care Department within the United States at (800) 762-2974, outside the United States at (317) 572-3993 or fax (317) 572-4002.

Wiley also publishes its books in a variety of electronic formats. Some content that appears in print may not be available in electronic books. For more information about Wiley products, visit our web site at www.wiley.com.

Library of Congress Cataloging-in-Publication Data:

Schultz, Ken.
   Ken Schultz's essentials of fishing / Ken Schultz.
      p. cm.
   Includes index.
   ISBN 978-0-470-44431-3 (cloth)
      1. Fishing—Encyclopedias. I. Title.
  SH411.S34 2009
  799.103—dc22

                             2009006820

Printed in the United States of America

10 9 8 7 6 5 4 3 2 1

Contents

PART FOUR
Techniques

PART FIVE
Practical Matters

Introduction

I once worked for an editor at *Field & Stream* who eschewed articles about the basic elements of fishing because, in his eyes, it was stuff everyone knew. I disagreed, and always felt that not only were we writing to a constant influx of new anglers who did not know many basic things, or who were misinformed, but that we were writing to many people with years of experience who had never received good tutelage in the fundamental skills and techniques that make for more productive and more enjoyable angling.

Knot tying, line care, fish preparation, and species behavior are topics that immediately come to mind as being prone to widespread lack of understanding. And there are many more. Often, when speaking with anglers, I've discovered that they lack a fundamental knowledge about some key aspect of fishing, which may have hindered their efforts or detracted from maximum success or angling enjoyment. "I never knew that" has been a common response to my explanation or demonstration.

As a writer, I've often been disappointed to learn that something I've written extensively about, such as the difference between test and class lines and the vagaries of line strength and labeling, still has not been absorbed by a majority of anglers. Obviously that's too much to expect and not everyone is so deeply engaged in all aspects of sportfishing.

But even the most avid anglers can get a lot twisted around. Just the other day I had a conversation with a longtime angler about saltwater sportfish that were good to eat. "I don't like bluefish, though," the fellow offered. "They don't taste good."

Bluefish are one of my favorite sportfish to catch and to eat, but since they are delicate and spoil quickly, they require particular care. I told him this, and he was surprised to learn that when I have offered smoked bluefish to guests, it gets gobbled up in a hurry as if they were starving. And the kicker is that many of them, like this fellow, profess to dislike bluefish, but in reality they are just not knowledgeable about the proper care, handling, and cooking of bluefish.

Now, you don't need to know how an internal combustion engine works to drive a car. I don't, and I don't care to know. Similarly, I don't need to know how a fishing rod is manufactured to know what a good rod is or how to fight and land a strong fish with it.

Essentials of Fishing does not get down to the level of how fishing gear is made. Rather, it focuses on the key elements of *all* aspects of the art of angling that are important to making you a more knowledgeable, more well-rounded, and more successful angler.

To do this, the book is segmented into five fundamental topics, beginning with Part One, Fish, which provides succinct, pertinent details about all of the major North American sportfish pursued by anglers in freshwater and saltwater. This is an impressive and diverse array of creatures. When you read about each of them, you'll realize how unique their habits and habitats are and begin to understand why fishing for one is not like fishing for the other. You'll also appreciate the angler's broad and varied "playing field."

Species information was placed first because I believe that you need a basic understanding of your quarries before you pick up your tools. The species profiles are followed by Part Two, Tools, because the angler's equipment is also varied and, logically, you have to know what tools you need and how to use them properly.

I'm sure that you probably got a new cell phone and started using it without reading the manual and learning about all of its features. I do like gear that is intuitive and doesn't require a PhD to use, and fishing tackle looks a lot simpler than many things do. Still, you really should take time to learn how to properly use the equipment, which is why the information in Part Two is so in-depth. By using and/or properly adjusting some of the features on a reel, for example, you'll be able to cast farther, control strong fish better, and be more proficient overall. It's best to start out this way.

Part Three, Basic Skills, and Part Four, Techniques, are where the rubber meets the road. Mastery of the foundation-building details discussed in Part Three and the more advanced knowledge found in Part Four, is what fundamentally makes anglers more adept at the catching part of the fishing game. When you apply these skills and techniques to various situations, you become multidimensional and your efforts are more directed and less haphazard. That's when good luck becomes less of an explanation and bad luck becomes less of an excuse.

The final part, Practical Matters, deals in-depth with topics that most books, magazines, and Web sites don't get into in a substantive way, perhaps because, like my old editor, they think everyone knows it (safety), or perhaps because they are uncomfortable talking about it (ethics and etiquette). While most people know something about a practical matter like catch and release, nowhere else will you find such a detailed review of the pros and cons and do's and don'ts, which I feel are essential knowledge in present-day angling.

Because *Essentials of Fishing* is a distillation and enhancement of my *Fishing Encyclopedia*, which has been widely praised and which is used all over the world, it contains the most important and practical knowledge that I can offer on the full gamut of sportfishing activities, in a straightforward manner and presentation.

The illustrations and photos have been selected not only because they are appropriate complements to the text, but also because they visually reflect the diversity that exists in the people, places, gear, and circumstances of the sportfishing world. I sincerely hope that this entire package becomes your go-to source for credible and indispensable angling information.

PART ONE

Fish

1

Anatomy and Physiology

The term "fish" is applied to a class of animals that, according to various scientific estimates, includes between 21,000 and 25,000 extremely diverse species.

Fish can be roughly defined (and there are a few exceptions) as cold-blooded creatures that have backbones, live in water, and have gills. The gills enable fish to "breathe" underwater, without drawing oxygen from the atmosphere. This is the primary difference between fish and all other vertebrates. Although such vertebrates as whales and turtles live in water, they cannot breathe underwater. No other vertebrate but the fish is able to live without breathing air. One family of fish, the lungfish, is able to breathe air when mature, and actually loses its functional gills.

Scientifically, fish are divided into four groups, or families: the hagfish, the lampreys, cartilaginous fish, and bony fish. The hagfish and lampreys lack jaws, and as such they are known as jawless fish; there are 32 species of hagfish and forty species of lamprey. The cartilaginous fish and the bony fish have jaws. The bony fish are by far the most common, making up over 95 percent of the world's fish species. Cartilaginous fish, including sharks, rays, and skates, are the second largest group, numbering some 700 species. Various

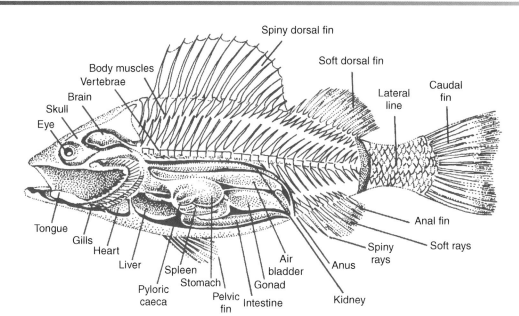

Anatomy of a Perch

species of cartilaginous and bony fish are the object of angling attention and thus the focus of this section.

Body

The body of a fish is particularly adapted to aquatic life. It is equipped with fins for the purpose of locomotion. Scales and mucus protect the body and keep it streamlined. The skeleton features a long backbone that can produce the side-to-side movements needed for forward propulsion in water. Since water is eight hundred times denser than air, fish must be extremely strong to move in their environment. They respond to this condition by being mostly muscle. Thus muscles make up 40 to 65 percent of a fish's body weight.

Many fish have air or gas bladders (sometimes called swim bladders) that allow them to float at a desired depth. They also have gills, their underwater breathing apparatus, located in the head. Most fish have only one gill cover, although some, like sharks, have gill slits, some as many as seven. The gills are the most fragile part of the fish; anglers should avoid touching the gills on fish that they plan on releasing.

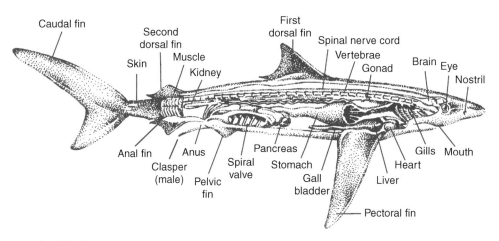

Anatomy of a Shark

The limbs of fish come in the form of fins, membranes that extend from the body and are supported by spines or rays. Because the number of rays is usually constant within a species, a ray count is often used by scientists to determine the species of a fish. Each of the fins on a fish has a distinct name.

Moving from the head toward the tail, the first fins are the pectoral fins. They are used for balance and maneuvering in many species, and in a few for propulsion. Farther down the underside of the fish are the pelvic fins, located beneath the belly and used for balance. On the back is the dorsal fin. Some fish have more than one dorsal fin; in this case the dorsal fins are numbered, with the fin closest to the head called the first dorsal fin, and so on. Behind the dorsal fin there is occasionally a smaller, fleshy fin called the adipose fin. Behind the pelvic fins and the anus on the underside is the anal fin. The last fin, usually called the tail, is known scientifically as the caudal fin. It is the most important fin for locomotion: By moving it from side to side, a fish is able to gather forward momentum.

The scales of a fish form the main protection for the body. They are kept for the fish's entire life; as a fish grows, the scales get larger rather than regenerating.

Scales are divided into several types. The majority of fish have ctenoid or cycloid scales. Ctenoid scales are serrated on one edge and feel rough when rubbed the wrong way (such as on largemouth bass). Cycloid scales are entirely smooth, like the scales of trout. A minority of fish have other types of scales: Sharks have more primitive placoid scales, which are spiny; sturgeon have ganoid scales, which form armored ridges along parts of the body. Some species, like catfish, have no scales at all.

Scales can be used to determine the age of a fish. A scale will develop rings showing annual growth, much like the rings of a tree.

Many fish also have a covering of mucus that helps streamline their body and prevent infections. This covering will rub off onto a person's hands; it is the slimy substance that you can feel on your hands after holding a fish. Since the loss of mucus is detrimental to the fish, it is better to wet your hands before handling a fish that will be released, in order to minimize the amount of mucus removed. Also be careful not to harm a fish by holding it too tightly.

The skeletal and muscular systems of fish work together to maximize swimming power, the serially repeated vertebrae and muscle structure creating the shimmering, undulating movements that allow a fish to swim quickly. This structure is evident in a filleted fish, where the muscles show themselves in their interlocking pattern. The highly muscular nature of fish is the reason why they make such good eating, and why they are such a high-yield food source.

Bony fish have developed an organ called an air bladder, which acts as a kind of flotation device. A fish's body is naturally a bit denser than water, but the air bladder, filled with gas, increases the fish's ability to float. Fish can change the depth at which they float by varying the amount of gas in their air bladder, allowing them to float at any depth they desire without expending any effort. Fish that do not have air bladders, such as sharks, must continually move in order to prevent themselves from sinking.

Like virtually all animals, fish need oxygen to survive. However, a fish can get all the oxygen it needs from water by use of its gills. Water entering through the mouth is forced over the gills, which extract oxygen. In order to breathe, fish must

Scale Types

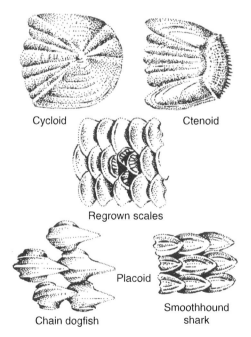

Cycloid   Ctenoid

Regrown scales

Placoid

Chain dogfish   Smoothhound shark

Cycloid scales have smooth rear margins, whereas ctenoid scales have comblike margins; placoid scales, found on sharks, are toothlike. Scales generally are layered, overlapping in rows like roof tiles.

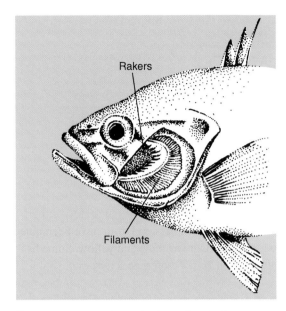

This cutaway view shows the first gill arch of a sunfish. The rakers, which strain the water, are on the left; the filaments, which transfer dissolved oxygen to the blood, are on the right.

constantly have water passing over their gills. To accomplish this, some fish must either move continually or live in water with a strong current.

Although most fish are referred to as cold-blooded creatures, this is not entirely true. Some species are called warm-blooded, yet they cannot sustain a constant body temperature as humans do. Instead, the body temperature of a fish approximates that of its surrounding medium—water. Certain types of fish, such as tuna, by their constant vigorous propulsion through the water, sustain high muscular flexion that creates heat associated with rapid metabolism. Through built-in heat conservation measures, the fish is capable of maintaining a warmer body temperature than the medium that upholds it; for example, a bluefin tuna's fighting qualities are not impaired when it suddenly dives from surface waters where it was hooked down to the colder depths.

Shape

Fish shapes have also evolved to suit the needs of their aquatic life. These body shapes fall into general categories. Some fish are narrow, with bodies that are taller than they are thin, like sunfish, largemouth bass, or angelfish. Some are flat, with bodies that are shorter than they are wide, like flounder. Some are torpedo-shaped, like tuna or mackerel. Some are tubular and snakelike, such as eels.

A fish's shape tends to be related to its habits and habitats. Narrow-bodied fish are extremely agile, and tend to live in reefs or densely weeded ponds where the ability to maneuver between rocks or plants is essential. Flatfish tend to live on the bottom, where their low profiles prevent recognition. Torpedo-shaped fish are built for speed and are found either in open water or in strong currents where less streamlined fish would be swept away. Tubular fish often live in small crevices and areas that are inaccessible to other animals, rather than in wide-open ocean waters.

Color

The amazing variety of colors that fish display clearly demonstrates the importance of color in the fish world. Most fish are colored for purposes of camouflage. When viewed from above, they tend to be dark in order to blend in with the dark bottom of the water. When viewed from below, they look light in order to blend in with the sky (this is called countershading).

Fish have developed a huge variety of colors and markings that allow them to escape detection in their environments. Color is also used for mating purposes. Certain fish have special breeding colors, usually brighter than normal. Many reef fish have brilliant colors year-round, which help to differentiate between the many species that live on the reefs.

Senses

An angler should understand the way a fish's senses work. Knowing what a fish is sensitive to helps an angler approach the fish without scaring it. Although some fish rely more on certain senses than on others, there are statements about senses that apply to all fish.

Fish hear very well. Sound travels five times faster in water than in air, and fish are quite sensitive to loud noises (which is why you should not tap on the glass of a fish tank). Fish can be scared off by the noise from people banging around in a boat, loud talking, and motors. Although fish do not have external ears, they do have internal ones.

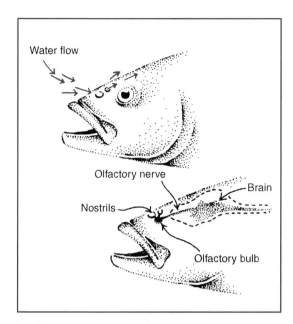

Smell receptors are located in the nostrils, and water (carrying odors) is drawn into sacs that are lined with the organs of smell. Olfactory nerves connect the nostrils and brain.

Set in the bones of the skull, these hear very well. The role of sound in the lives of fish is not entirely understood, but many species are known to be noisy; fish have been recorded grunting, croaking, grinding teeth, and vibrating their muscles.

A fish's sense of smell is often very good, but the importance of this sense varies widely among species and may be subordinate to other senses, especially vision. With olfactory nerves in their nostrils, fish can detect odors in water just as terrestrial animals can detect odors in air. Some fish use their sense of smell to locate food, detect danger, and perhaps also to find their way to spawning areas.

There is evidence that a salmon's keen sense of smell contributes to its ability to return to its birthplace. Certainly a salmon's olfactory sense is incredibly acute: Salmon can detect one part per billion of odorous material in water. They may refuse to use fish ladders if the water contains the smell of human hands or bear paws. Salmon will panic if placed in a swimming pool with one drop of bear-scented water.

With the apparent importance of smell to many fish, removing human scents from fishing tackle is something that anglers should consider, although this practice is disputable and its usefulness varies widely with species. While the practice is considered vital by some anglers, others view it as irrelevant.

Sight varies in importance for fish. Most fish are nearsighted; although they can see well for short distances, their vision gets blurry past three feet or so. Some fish are exceptions to this rule; brown trout, for instance, have excellent vision. An important fact to realize about most fish is that they can see almost 360 degrees; their only blind spot is a small patch directly behind them.

Fish can also see color. In laboratory experiments, largemouth bass and trout have been able to identify red, green, blue, and yellow. Some fish have demonstrated preferences for certain colors, and red has long been considered a foremost attraction, although this is subject to a host of variables as well as disagreements among anglers.

The sense of taste does not seem to be as important to fish as other senses; taste buds are not as well developed, although there are exceptions, especially among bottom-scrounging fish. Some species, like catfish, use taste to find food and utilize this sense much more than other species of fish. Catfish even have taste buds on their barbels, and certain species have them on the underside of their body.

Many fish have an additional sensory organ called the lateral line. Visible along the length of the body, the lateral line is used to detect low-frequency vibrations. It acts like both a hearing and a touch organ, and is used to determine the

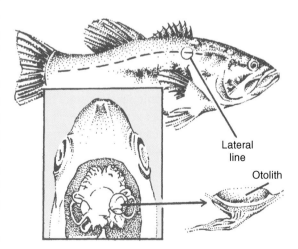

Hearing is accomplished primarily through nerves in the lateral line but also through sound waves detected by the otolith.

directions of currents, the proximity of objects, and even water temperature. The lateral line is sensitive to water vibrations and helps fish escape predators, locate prey, and stay in schools.

Reproduction

Fish reproduce in many different ways. Most lay eggs, but some bear live young; most eggs are fertilized after they are released from the female's body, but some are fertilized inside the body. Since almost all gamefish are egg layers (sharks being the main exception), their reproductive habits are the most important to the angler.

Mating, called spawning in egg-laying fish, usually occurs once a year. Each species has its own spawning habits, which greatly influence its behavior. Some fish do not eat when they are in a spawning mode; others are voracious prior to spawning. Some migrate; some build visible nests, and others have no nests; some move to deep water, and some move to shallow water.

Once fish choose a site for spawning, or the time is right, they begin to mate. Sometimes the mating is an elaborate ritual; sometimes it merely amounts to the female scattering the eggs and the male fertilizing them. After the eggs are fertilized, some fish guard and care for the eggs, and some do not. The eggs hatch fairly quickly, at times in as little as twenty-four hours, although the time is influenced by such factors as water temperature, turbidity, sunlight, salinity, and current.

The young fish just out of the eggs are called fry. Fry are usually so much smaller than their parents that they are not recognizably similar. They live on microorganisms in the water until they are ready for larger food. In certain species, each spawning pair can produce thousands of fry, but only a few grow to adulthood. Most fall victim to predation; fry are eaten by many predators, including other fish and, in some species, their own parents.

Certain types of fish spawn in habitats other than their normal ones. Some fish that live in the ocean spawn in rivers, and some that live in rivers spawn in the sea. Fish that live in the ocean yet spawn in freshwater are called anadromous, the most prominent example being salmon. Fish that live in freshwater and spawn in the sea are called catadromous, most notably eels.

Food and Feeding

Fish have evolved to fill almost every ecological niche. Many are strictly herbivores, eating only plant life. Many are purely plankton eaters. Most are carnivorous (in the sense of eating the flesh of other fish as well as crustaceans, mollusks, and insects) or at least piscivorous (eating fish), and some—like the great white shark and the piranha—are among the most feared predators in the world by humans, although their danger to people is oversensationalized.

Almost all species that are considered gamefish are predators because their eating habits and aggressive behavior lead them to strike bait or lures that essentially mimic some form of natural food. Many predaceous fish eat other fish, but they also eat insects, worms and other invertebrates, and other vertebrates. Some fish will eat almost anything that can fit in their mouths and is alive. Some are scavengers and will consume dead fish or parts of fish. Many fish fill only specific niches and have very specific diets. As a result, it is important for anglers to know the natural food of any particular gamefish.

Growth and Size

Growth in fish is affected by many factors; especially important are heredity, length of growing season, and food supply. Although each species can be expected to reach a predetermined size, the length of time required to reach this size is extremely variable. The growing season is the time during the year when a fish will actively feed and grow. Generally, fish living in northern latitudes and colder waters have a shorter growing season than those living in southern latitudes and warmer waters. If all other growing factors remain the same, the fish with the longer growing season will reach a greater size over a given time period.

Additionally, a fish that has optimum food and space conditions will grow more rapidly than one that must compete more heavily for food and space. This in part explains why fish of the same species in the same latitude and growing seasons, but in different bodies of water, may have different rates of growth.

Obviously fish range widely in size. On the bantam side of the spectrum are tiny Philippine gobies less than half an inch long, the smallest of all animals with backbones. At the behemoth end of the spectrum are giant plankton-eating whale sharks 65 to 70 feet long and weighing as much as 25 tons. Such highly prized game species as bluefin tuna, swordfish, and certain sharks and marlin reach weights of more than 1,000 pounds, with some shark and marlin specimens weighing considerably more. The white sturgeon, one of the largest of freshwater fish, formerly reached weights of well over 1,000 pounds in the Columbia and Fraser rivers.

Fish size is of special interest to anglers, many of whom aspire to match their skills against the larger specimens of various game species. Competitive events often place a premium on large individual catches, and other rewards, both material and intangible, accrue to those who have caught fish deemed to be of large, if not trophy, caliber.

Records for freshwater and saltwater fish caught on rod and reel are maintained by the International Game Fish Association based upon specific standards and on weight. In some cases, fish are known to grow much larger than sport-caught records indicate, but record rod-and-reel catches greatly exceed the average size of most species.

A fish does not have to be gigantic to provide fun, however. In this regard, tackle plays an important role. Anglers, using ultralight tackle in ponds and lakes, find it challenging to catch quarter-pound bluegills, rarely if ever hooking one that approaches a pound in weight, let alone the species top record of 4 pounds 12 ounces. Indeed, line-class record categories were long ago established for each species to recognize the angler's fishing skill by virtue of a notable catch for a particular weight of tackle.

Size is a relative issue both in terms of a fish's fighting ability and in its desirability as a catch. Although most larger fish are more difficult to subdue than smaller ones, that is not always the case. Size is also not necessarily comparable between different species; a 10-pound steelhead, for example, provides far better sport than a 10-pound walleye, and a 10-pound bonefish is much more challenging than a 10-pound barracuda. Growing season and geographic location may be a factor as well. A 10-pound largemouth bass in Florida, where a favorable growing season can allow a bass to grow large fast, is akin to perhaps a 6-pound largemouth bass in Minnesota in terms of age and availability within the bass population, meaning that they are catches of similar accomplishment despite being of different size.

2

Freshwater Fish

The North American freshwater angler is fortunate to have a relative bounty of varied places that support many species of gamefish and the food that sustains them. From bluegills in farm ponds to bass in natural lakes, from trout in streams to salmon in rivers, and from walleyes in the Great Lakes to catfish in inland reservoirs, there is a fish and a location for every interest and ability.

Largemouth Bass, Smallmouth Bass, and Spotted Bass

Largemouth Bass

Micropterus salmoides

The largemouth bass is the biggest and most renowned member of the sunfish clan. As a result of widespread introductions throughout North America, it has become available to more anglers than any other species of fish. Its adoption of varied environments, penchant for aggressive

Largemouth Bass

behavior, and short-lived but action-packed fight, replete with aerial maneuvers and explosive bursts for cover, have helped make it the most popular sportfishing target in North America.

ID. The largemouth bass has an elongate and robust shape and a distinctively large mouth with the end of its maxillary (jaw) falling below or beyond the rear margin of the eye. The dorsal fin has a deep notch separating the spiny and soft rays; and the tail is broad and slightly forked. Although coloration varies greatly, the largemouth bass generally has a light green to light brown hue on the back and upper sides, white lower sides and belly, and a broad stripe of diamond-shaped blotches along the midline of the body. This stripe particularly distinguishes it from its close relative the smallmouth bass, as does the upper jaw, which in the smallmouth does not extend past the eye. The largemouth lacks a tooth patch on the tongue, which helps distinguish it from the spotted bass.

Habitat. Largemouth bass are highly adaptable to many environments and to many places within various types of water. They inhabit creeks,

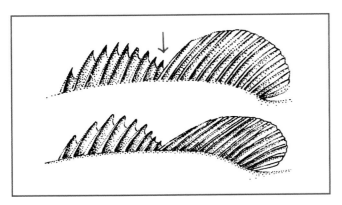

The separation between first and second dorsal fins is less in smallmouth bass (top) than in largemouth bass (bottom), a difference that aids in differentiating these species.

ditches, sloughs, canals, and many little potholes that have the right cover and forage, but they live principally in reservoirs, lakes, ponds, and medium to large rivers. They orient toward cover in those environments and find most of their food in or near some form of concealment, whether it is visible in relatively shallow water or beneath the surface out of sight.

Food. Adult bass predominantly eat other fish, including gizzard shad, threadfin shad, golden shiners, bluegills and other sunfish, small catfish, and many other small species, plus crayfish. They are extremely opportunistic, however, and may consume snakes, frogs, salamanders, mice, and other creatures. They swallow their food whole instead of biting off pieces, which limits the size of the prey they can consume.

Angling. Largemouth bass are suitable for a plethora of fishing techniques. A particular charm of angling for largemouth bass is that bass lures needn't closely imitate specific forage. As a result, there is probably no other freshwater gamefish for which exists such a wide range of lure types, sizes, colors, and actions, nearly all used for casting in and around suitable cover.

The penchant of largemouth bass to strike surface lures, especially when the water is warm, makes them especially dear to anglers who like to cast and retrieve products that will draw a visible strike. Nevertheless, more largemouths are caught on subsurface lures, particularly crankbaits, spinnerbaits, jigs, and various soft lures and worms.

Spring, summer, and fall are popular fishing seasons, with depths, locations, and tactics changing accordingly. Since pinpoint presentations are more important in largemouth bass angling than in many other forms of freshwater fishing, anglers often use boats equipped with an electric motor, as it is important to position the boat in ways conducive to accurate casting and proper presentation. Baitcasting, spinning, spincasting, and flycasting tackle all have merit in appropriate times and places.

Smallmouth Bass

Micropterus dolomieui

The smallmouth bass is the second largest member of the Centrarchidae family of sunfish, coveted for its spunky fighting habits and willingness to take a variety of lures and baits. It is less tolerant of very warm environs and therefore not as widely distributed as its bigger relative, the largemouth bass. The smallmouth is naturally a fish of both clear rivers and lakes, and has been widely introduced to other waters outside its original range. It is occasionally confused with the largemouth where they both occur, and also with the spotted bass and redeye bass.

ID. The smallmouth bass has a robust, slightly laterally compressed and elongate body, a protruding lower jaw, red eyes, and a broad and slightly forked tail. Its two dorsal fins are joined or notched; the front one is spiny and the second has one spine followed by soft rays. Color varies from brown, golden brown, and olive to green on the back, becoming lighter to golden on the sides and white on the belly. The smallmouth is easily distinguished from the largemouth by its clearly connected dorsal fins, the scales on the base portion of the soft-rayed second dorsal fin, and the upper jawbone, which extends only to about the middle of the eye.

Habitat. Smallmouth bass prefer clear, quiet waters with gravel, rubble, or rocky bottoms. They live in midsize, gentle streams that have deep pools and abundant shade, or in fairly deep, clear lakes and reservoirs with rocky shoals. Although they are fairly adaptable, they are seldom found in murky water and avoid swift current. In the typical river, smallmouth bass predominate in the cool middle section where there are large pools between riffles. In stillwaters, smallmouth bass may occupy lakes, reservoirs, or ponds if these waters are large and deep enough to have thermal stratification, and they are usually located deeper than largemouth bass once the surface layer warms in spring or early summer.

Food. These highly carnivorous and predatory fish will eat whatever is available, but they have a clear preference for crayfish and small fish. In lakes, the latter includes small bass, panfish, perch, and assorted fingerling-size minnows. In rivers, it includes minnows, crayfish, hellgrammites, nymph larvae, and leeches.

Angling. In lakes, smallmouths are mainly located around rocky points; craggy, clifflike shores; rocky islands and reefs; and riprap banks, preferring small rocks but also favoring boulders. In flowing water, smallmouth bass concentrate

Northern Smallmouth Bass

around boulders, smaller rocks, gravel, stone, shale, and various obstructions (fallen trees, bridge pilings, and the like) that offer holding and feeding benefits.

Popular natural baits for smallmouth include live crayfish, especially the soft-shelled variety, and nightcrawlers. Crayfish-imitating crankbaits are a popular river and lake lure for smallmouths, and many different surface lures, diving plugs, jigs, spinners, and spinnerbaits have merit, as do assorted flies.

Like largemouths, these fish are popular from spring through fall, using varied techniques and tackle, although light- to medium-duty spinning gear is especially favored, with smaller lures and lighter line necessary in clear waters.

Spotted Bass

Micropterus punctulatus

Often mistaken by anglers for largemouth bass, the spotted bass is less well known than either the largemouth or smallmouth, but this is a spunky and distinguished-looking species that no angler is unhappy about catching, even if the majority are encountered by accident. The general term "spotted bass" really incorporates three recognized subspecies: the northern spotted bass (*M. p. punctulatus*), the Alabama spotted bass (*M. p. henshalli*), and the Wichita spotted bass (*M. p. wichitae*); the last was previously thought to be extinct and is still rarely encountered. Their average and maximum sizes are smaller than those of the largemouth.

ID. Spotted bass have a moderately compressed elongate body with coloration and markings similar to those of the largemouth bass; both have a light green to light brown hue on the back and upper sides, white lower sides and belly, and a broad stripe of diamond-shaped blotches along the midline of the body. The spotted bass has scales on the base portion of the second dorsal fin, its first and second dorsal fin are clearly connected, and its upper jawbone does not extend back to or beyond the rear edge of the eyes. Spotted bass have a distinct patch of teeth on the tongue, which largemouth do not, and there is a large spot on the point of the gill cover.

Habitat. The natural habitat of spotted bass is clear, gravelly, flowing pools and runs of creeks and small to medium rivers. They also tolerate the slower, warmer, and more turbid sections that are unlikely to host smallmouth bass. They are seldom found in natural lakes but have adapted well to deep impoundments, which were created by damming some of their natural rivers and streams. In reservoirs they prefer water temperatures in the mid-70s and are especially suited to deep, clear impoundments. Typical habitat is similar to that of the largemouth bass, although the spotted bass prefers rocky areas and is much more likely to inhabit and suspend in open waters; it may hold in great depths (between 60 and more than 100 feet) in some waters. Rocky bluffs, deep rockpiles, and submerged humps are among its haunts.

Food. Adult spotted bass eat insects, larger crustaceans, minnows, frogs, worms, grubs, and small fish. Crayfish are usually the most important item in the diet, followed by small fish and larval and adult insects.

Angling. Most catches of spotted bass are incidental to attempts for other black bass. Fishing tactics in rivers are similar to those for smallmouth bass, and in impoundments to those for largemouth and smallmouth bass. Spotted bass are likely to be found in groups, so more than one can be caught in specific places. Lures that imitate crayfish, as well as small jigs with grub or other soft plastic bodies, are especially productive. In summer, deep fishing over planted brush piles, especially near a major creek or river channel, can be especially effective.

Butterfly Peacock Bass

Cichla ocellaris

Peacock bass are stronger, harder-fighting, jump more and higher, and are generally meaner than a largemouth bass or most anything else that swims in freshwater. In their native South American waters they also hit surface lures like no other fish, and punish lures, line, and the thumbs of anyone foolish enough to lip-lock the bigger specimens. The butterfly peacock, which does not attain the gargantuan sizes of some of its brethren, was introduced in Hawaii from British Guyana in 1957, and in Florida in 1984 and 1986 by fish from Brazil, Guyana, and Peru; it has also been stocked in Puerto Rico, Panama, Guam, and the Dominican Republic. This superb non-native species has become a popular quarry in south Florida, which is why it is included here.

ID. Butterfly peacock bass possess great variation in color. They are generally yellowish green overall, with three dark, yellow-tinged blotches along the lateral midsection; these blotches intersect with faint bars, which typically fade in fish weighing more than 3 to 4 pounds. The iris of the eye is frequently deep red. A conspicuous hump exists on top of the head in breeding males, and spawning fish have an intensified yellow coloration. They are distinguished by the absence of black markings on the opercula.

Food. In Hawaii, butterfly peacock bass consume threadfin shad, tilapia, bluegills, and mosquitofish. In Florida, they were imported to control exploding tilapia populations in many waters, and undoubtedly consume not only tilapia but assorted other fish as available, including shad and small panfish and especially shiners.

Habitat. Small lakes and hundreds of miles of canals are the places peacock bass call home in South Florida, provided that water temperatures don't drop below 60 degrees, which will kill these fish.

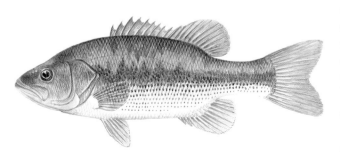

Spotted Bass

Butterfly Peacock Bass

Angling. Butterfly peacocks are caught from the bank and from boats by anglers, with success restricted to daytime hours, as peacocks are inactive at night. Shaded areas, and locations such as points, fallen trees, deep banks with shoreside cover, and the deep ends of canals are prime locations.

Surface plugs, lipless rattling crankbaits, jigs, streamer flies, and live bait are preferred choices. Peacocks like lures that make noise and produce vibration, but in canals and small lakes when the action is slow, live shiners are likely to produce best. Expect the fish to move deeper during midday.

White Bass, White Perch, and Striped Bass

White Bass

Morone chrysops

A member of the temperate bass family, the white bass is a freshwater fish known for its spunky fighting ability and its prolificacy, as well as its merits as an excellent eating fish. White bass usually travel in schools and can provide a lot of action, making them highly desirable among light-tackle enthusiasts and for fishing with family and youths. Generous bag limits and fine-tasting flesh encourage large take-home catches where the fish are abundant.

ID. The white bass has a moderately deep and compressed body that is raised behind the small head and large mouth, deepest between the two dorsal fins. It also has eleven to thirteen rays on the anal fin and one to two patches of teeth at the back of the tongue. Coloration is mostly silvery with a dark grayish green on the back, and anywhere

from four to ten dark horizontal stripes running along the sides. It also has a yellow eye, clear to dusky dorsal and caudal fins, and clear to white pectoral and pelvic fins.

White bass resemble small striped bass in that they possess the same silver sides and black stripes; they are shorter, though, and have a smaller head, deeper body, humped back, and dorsal fins that are closer together. In waters where white perch also exist, these two can be confused; however, white perch lack distinct stripes on the sides of the body.

Habitat. White bass are most abundant in clear, cool lakes, reservoirs, ponds, and pools of small to large rivers. They prefer lakes exceeding 300 acres and with considerable stretches of water at least 10 feet deep.

Food. White bass feed on shad, silversides, crustaceans, yellow perch, sunfish, insects, crayfish, and their own young. Although they stay mostly in deep waters, they usually come to the surface to feed on schools of small shad or other minnows and often make a great commotion that is noted by observant anglers; this normally occurs early or late in the day, or on overcast days.

Angling. Because white bass are a schooling fish, it is common to catch quite a few in one location. This ample action is one of the things that makes these small fish a popular species. Jump fishing action for schools of white bass is often a late-in-the-day or early-morning proposition, especially in late summer and in the fall.

Light tackle is highly suitable for these fish, which are spunky, tugging fighters. Spinning or spincasting rods loaded with 4- to 8-pound line are ideal, although a fly rod can be used at times as well. Lures that correspond to the size and

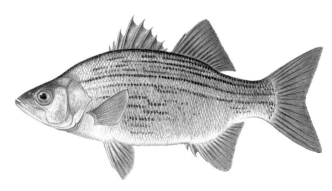

White Bass

likeness of the preferred baitfish are best. This includes small crankbaits, bucktail or marabou jigs, silver jigging spoons, spinners, sinking lures, and tailspinners, as well as small stickbaits and buzzbaits. Some anglers troll for these fish. Jigging, casting, and live baits account for the most success, however.

White Perch

Morone americana

The white perch is not a true perch but a member of the temperate bass family and a relative of white bass and striped bass. It is abundant in some places, rare in others, and underappreciated as table fare. Many anglers catch white perch incidentally while pursuing other species, except in places where they are numerous. In all, there is a small constituency for the white perch, but it is a robust fish that provides fine sport on light spinning and flycasting tackle. White perch taken from cool-water lakes have a firm, white, flaky flesh and are of excellent eating quality.

ID. The white perch has a deep, thin body that slopes up steeply from the eye to the beginning of the dorsal fin and is deepest under the first dorsal fin. Large, older specimens can be nearly humpbacked at that spot. Colors can be olive, gray-green, silvery gray, dark brown, or black on the back, becoming a lighter silvery green on the sides and silvery white on the belly. The pelvic and anal fins are sometimes rosy-colored. White perch are similar in shape to striped bass, and very similar in appearance to white bass, except that they have no stripes.

Habitat. Like its cousin the striped bass, the adaptable white perch is at home in saltwater, brackish water, and freshwater. In marine waters it is primarily found in estuaries and coastal rivers and streams. Some white perch remain resident in brackish bays and estuaries, whereas others roam widely in search of food. The species inhabits scattered freshwater lakes and ponds, but in varied abundance. A prolific fish, they have overpopulated some waters and been deemed a nuisance. In general they tend to stay deep in their home waters, on or close to the bottom.

Food. Perch eat many kinds of small fish, such as smelt, yellow perch, killifish, and other white perch, as well as the young of other species,

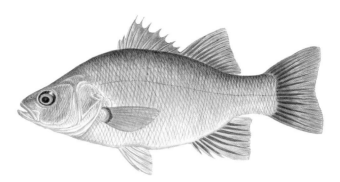

White Perch

particularly those that spawn after them. They also reportedly consume crabs, shrimp, and small alewives and herring.

Angling. In those freshwaters where they are not numerous, white perch are usually caught at random and accidentally. Where they are abundant, they may at times be caught with rapidity. In saltwater and in brackish environs, an angler who locates a white perch has typically come upon a school and may catch a few dozen fish. Tides, current, and water movement may affect their activity in estuaries, but in lakes and ponds the stimulant may more likely be low morning light or nightfall. Generally, you have to search for schools of fish that are not visible to the eye, using sonar in open water, casting in estuary creeks and current-funneling pools, and otherwise prospecting.

Some anglers troll, primarily with small spinners and spinner/bait combinations, but casting with jigs, small jigging spoons, diving plugs, and minnow-shaped plugs is more common, as is drift fishing or slow trolling with worms or minnows under a float. Small spoons and jigs equipped with grub tails or small eel-like plastic tails are effective in the shallow backwaters of estuaries. Getting any of these offerings near the bottom is usually important.

Hybrid Bass and Striped Bass

Morone saxatilis

An anadromous temperate bass native to saltwater, the striped bass has been successfully transplanted to landlocked freshwater environments, some of which contain abundant populations and/or huge specimens. It has also been crossbred with other species to produce very popular hybrid stripers.

Hybrid Striped Bass

Hybrid stripers are the progeny of one pure-strain striped bass parent and one pure-strain white bass parent. When the cross is between the female striper and the male white bass, the result is primarily known as a whiterock bass; in some places it is referred to as a wiper, and in some simply as a hybrid bass or a hybrid striped bass. When the cross is between the male striper and the female white bass, it is called a sunshine bass (primarily in Florida), or simply a hybrid striped bass.

ID. A large fish with a large mouth, the striped bass is more streamlined than its close relative, the white bass. It has a long body and long head, a somewhat laterally compressed body form, protruding lower jaw, a forked tail, and small eyes. These fish are mostly bluish black or dark green above, fading into silver on the sides and white on the belly. On each side of its body, there are seven or eight prominent black horizontal stripes that run along the scale rows and are the distinctive markings of the striped bass; one of the stripes runs along the lateral line, and the rest are equally divided above and below it.

Pure striped bass differ from hybrids in the regularity of their stripes; the hybrid usually has interrupted stripes. The narrow body of the striped bass also distinguishes it from the white bass.

Habitat. Freshwater stripers are commonly found in open-water environs, or in the tailrace below dams. They are seldom found near shore or docks or piers, except when chasing schools of baitfish. In open-water areas they may roam widely following schools of baitfish, particularly shad. In spring, they move up major tributaries, if they exist, during a spawning migration, even though most landlocked striped bass do not successfully spawn.

Food. Freshwater striped bass prefer shad, herring, minnows, amphipods, and mayflies. Feeding

times vary, although many anglers believe that stripers are more active nocturnal feeders and that they can be caught more effectively in low-light conditions and after dark.

Angling. Stripers are predominantly nomads in freshwater, so locating these fish is sometimes a more formidable task than catching them. They are vigorous predators, however, just as in saltwater, and their habitats are usually blessed with abundant forage populations, primarily gizzard and threadfin shad, but also herring in some locations.

Because stripers do a lot of eating, they are a good target for trolling, casting, jigging, and fishing with live baits. Most fishing takes place in open-water areas of large reservoirs, in the deeper waters near the dam, and in the tailwaters below the dam. It is generally important to have some type of sonar to find the places that attract stripers, to locate catchable fish, or to determine the depth at which stripers are gathered so you can place your lures or baits at the right level.

Hybrid stripers, which may be more aggressive than their pure-strain parents, are sometimes caught by chasing schools of surface-feeding fish. Places to locate whiterock and sunshine bass include gravel and sandy bars, points, tailrace runs below dams, spillways, the mouths of rivers and creeks, between submerged or visible islands, along dropoffs, and above humps or levees.

Crappie, Bluegill, and Other Sunfish

The angling community generally lumps the various sunfishes under the heading of "panfish," which is a nontechnical generic term for small freshwater fish that are widely utilized for food as well as sport. Scientifically, however, sunfish are members of the Centrarchidae (meaning nest-building) family.

Centrarchids number some thirty strictly freshwater species of North America and include three generalized subdivisions: black bass, crappie, and true sunfish. All of these are warmwater species with similar or overlapping habitats. They have rough scales and two dorsal fins that are united, the first of which is heavily spined. Their anal fins all have three or more spines, and their tail is

Large crappie are a particularly desirable panfish catch; this one, from a New York pond, struck a small jig.

Other popular species of sunfish are the green, pumpkinseed, redbreast, and redear; the warmouth; and the rock bass.

Sunfish are very adaptable, being tolerant of diverse and warm environments. They have been widely introduced throughout North America, and also to Europe and Africa. In some places they are kept in balance by angling and natural predation, but in others they become overpopulated, resulting in stunting.

The generally shallow nature of true sunfish permits angling by shore-based anglers, making them collectively the number one warm-water pursuit of nonboating anglers. They are characteristically strong, although not flashy, fighters for their size, making them a pleasing catch on light spinning, spincasting, and fly tackle, as well as with reel-less poles.

Black Crappie
Pomoxis nigromaculatus

White Crappie
Pomoxis annularus

Crappie are like the Chinese dog called a shih tzu. Most people don't say the name of that dog in a way that sounds flattering. Ditto for the poor crappie. If its name were pronounced by more folks as if it contained the letter *o* instead of *a*, as in "crop," we would all be better off. No matter how you pronounce the name, both the black crappie and the white crappie are the most distinctive and largest members of the Centrarchidae family of sunfish. Both species are considered excellent food fish and sportfish, and have white, flaky meat that makes for sweet fillets. In many places crappie are plentiful and creel limits are liberal, so it does no harm to keep a batch of these fish for the table.

ID. The black crappie and the white crappie are similar in color—a silvery olive to bronze with dark spots, although on the black crappie the spots are irregularly arranged instead of appearing in seven or eight vertical bands as they do on the white crappie. Both species are laterally compressed and deep-bodied, although the black crappie is somewhat deeper in body, and it has a large mouth that resembles that of a largemouth bass. It also has distinct depressions in its forehead, and

typically broad. Nearly all are nest spawners, with nests built by the males, who also guard the nest and the young briefly. All are carnivorous, and the larger members prey on small fish.

Black bass, which includes largemouth bass, smallmouth bass, and spotted bass, each of which has been covered elsewhere, belong to the genus *Micropterus*; they have more elongated bodies than other centrarchids. Crappie belong to the genus *Pomoxis*; they have a longer anal fin than any of the other centrarchids, generally equal in length at the base to their dorsal fin, and are capable of larger growth than most of the sunfish. There are two species of crappie.

The largest group of centrarchids is the true sunfish. This includes many species that are small and not of much angling interest, although they are of great importance in their respective environments as forage for larger predators and for the foraging they do themselves. However, the larger-growing and more widely distributed sunfish are extremely popular with anglers throughout the United States, and provide countless hours of angling enjoyment. They are widely valued for their excellent white, flaky flesh. Their abundance and high rates of reproduction generally allow for liberal recreational harvest.

The most wide-ranging and best-known true sunfish is the bluegill; it and many other species of sunfish are colloquially known as "bream."

large dorsal and anal fins of almost identical size. The gill cover also comes to a sharp point, instead of ending in an earlike flap.

The best way to differentiate the two species of crappie is by counting the dorsal fin spines, as the black crappie usually has seven or eight, the white crappie six. The breeding male does not change color noticeably, as it does in the white crappie species. The white crappie is the only sunfish with the same number of spines in both the dorsal and anal fins. The breeding male grows darker in color and is often mistaken for the black crappie.

Habitat. Black crappie prefer cooler, deeper, clearer waters with more abundant aquatic vegetation than do white crappie. This includes still backwater lakes, sloughs, creeks, streams, lakes, and ponds. White crappie occur in creek backwaters, slow-flowing streams, sand- and mud-bottomed pools, small to large rivers, and lakes and ponds. They prefer shallower water and can tolerate warmer, more turbid, and slightly alkaline waters. They are usually found near dropoffs, standing timber, brushy cover, or other artificial cover.

Because both species form schools, an angler who comes across one fish is likely to find others nearby. They are especially active in the evening and early morning, and remain active throughout the winter.

Food. Black crappie and white crappie tend to feed early in the morning on zooplankton, crustaceans, insects, fish, insect larvae, young shad, minnows, and small sunfish. Small minnows form a large part of their diet, and they consume the fry of many species of gamefish; in southern reservoirs, gizzard or threadfin shad are major forage, and in northern states, insects are dominant. They continue to feed during the winter and are very active under the ice.

Angling. When you set out in search of crappie, think brush or the nearest thing resembling brush. The reason is simple. Crappie are mostly minnow eaters, and minnows hide around any kind of brush or weeds to avoid being eaten. So crappie go where minnows hide. Other hideouts are fallen trees, bushes, old piers, flooded weeds, or shoals covered with coontail or sphagnum moss, plus wrecked boats, docks, building blocks or brushpiles that have been planted to attract minnows, and undercut banks. When these don't pay off, try drifting with the wind or slow-trolling

Black Crappie

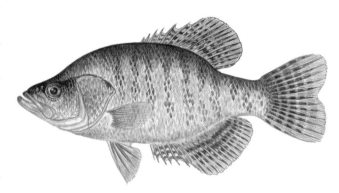

White Crappie

across a lake, plying a minnow at different depths until you cross paths with a school of roving crappie.

Although crappie are caught from time to time on various lures (occasionally on a surface lure or a diving plug), the one artificial that pays off regularly is a small leadhead jig with a soft plastic body resembling a minnow. The trick is to fish this very slow. Jigs weighing from $^1/_{64}$ to $^1/_{16}$ ounce are often better than heavier ones, and obviously this technique requires light line.

Crappie anglers primarily use ultralight spinning or spincasting reels equipped with 4- or 6-pound-test line and 5- to 5½-foot-long rods. Fly rods, telescoping fiberglass rods, and cane poles are popular as well.

Rock Bass

Ambloplites rupestris

Rock bass are caught on many types of baits and lures and put up a decent fight on ultralight tackle. Their meat is white and firm and makes good eating.

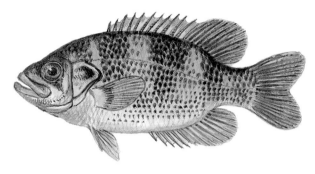

Rock Bass

Because rock bass prefer protected waters, however, they can have a muddy flavor or host numerous parasites.

ID. Looking like a cross between a bluegill and a black bass, the rock bass is less compressed than most sunfish and more similar to a black bass in shape. The back is raised, and the large head is narrow, rounded, and deep. The mouth is also large, especially in comparison to other sunfish; the upper jaw reaches beyond the beginning of the eye but not to the back of the eye. It has two connected dorsal fins, five to six anal fin spines, and large eyes. Coloring is olive brown or bronze on the back and sides, with faint lines of tiny dark marks; the centers of the scales below the lateral line also have dark markings that give the fish a striped appearance. A distinguishing characteristic is the bluish black blotch found on the tip of the gill covers.

Rock bass are frequently confused with the warmouth, which, unlike rock bass, have teeth on their tongue. There are also six spines in front of the anal fin of a rock bass as opposed to three spines in the warmouth.

Habitat. Rock bass prefer small to moderate streams with cool and clear water, abundant shelter, and considerable current. They are plentiful in shallow, weedy lakes and the outer edges of larger lakes, as well as in thousands of smaller lakes and ponds. Rock bass regularly hold over rocky bottoms where there is no silt.

Food. Adult rock bass eat mostly crayfish, as well as minnows, insects, mollusks, and small fish. They can consume relatively large specimens because of their large mouths. Rock bass generally feed on the bottom but may occasionally feed near the surface.

Angling. Rock bass are scrappy fighters, but tire quickly. There is no need to use anything but light or ultralight tackle for these fish. Because they often travel in schools, several or many can be caught from the same location. Sunken logs or tree stumps are prime spots, as are deep-water rocky ledges, quiet, still pools along riverbanks where large rocks are present, deep-water gravel beds where a large weed structure begins, and beneath overhanging willows along a river or lake shoreline.

Many rock bass are caught by anglers using garden worms, nightcrawlers, small crayfish, and small minnows, fishing these near the bottom and using split shot and a float. Small crankbaits, spinners, and spoons may work, as will fly rod poppers or bugs. Light grub or curl-tail jigs and very light spinnerbaits are perhaps even more effective. These should all be retrieved very slowly.

Bluegill

Lepomis macrochirus

At times easily caught by novice and experienced anglers alike, bluegills are among the most popular panfish species in North America. This notoriety is the result of their vast distribution, spunky fight, and excellent taste. Commonly referred to as "bream," bluegills are the most widely distributed sunfish, and so prolific that their populations can grow beyond the carrying capacity of the water.

ID. The bluegill has a significantly compressed oval or roundish body, a small mouth, and a small head. The pectoral fins are pointed. Coloring varies greatly from lake to lake, ranging from olive, dark blue, or bluish purple to dappled yellow and green on the sides with an overall blue cast; some

Bluegill

fish, particularly those found in quarry holes, may actually be clear and colorless. Ordinarily, there are six to eight vertical bars on the sides, and these may or may not be prominent. The gill cover extends to create a wide black flap, faint in color on the young, which is not surrounded by a lighter border as in other sunfish. Dark blue streaks are found on the lower cheeks between the chin and gill cover, and often there is a dark mark at the bottom of the anal fin. The breeding male is more vividly colored, possessing a blue head and back, a bright orange breast and belly, and black pelvic fins.

Habitat. Although mainly lake fish, bluegills inhabit sluggish streams and rivers, vegetated lakes and ponds, swamps, and pools of creeks. They prefer quiet waters and may hold in extremely shallow areas, especially early in the season and during spawning time, although when the surface and shallow water temperature is warm in summer, they may go as deep as 30 or more feet. They occupy the same habitat as their larger relative, the largemouth bass.

Food. A variety of small organisms serve as food for bluegills, including insects, crayfish, fish eggs, small minnows, snails, worms, and sometimes even plant material. The young feed mostly on crustaceans, insects, and worms. Adults will feed at different depths depending on temperature, so they obtain food on the bottom as well as on the surface. Active mostly at dusk and dawn, the larger bluegills move inshore in the morning and evening to feed, staying in deeper water during the day.

Green Sunfish

Lepomis cyanellus

The green sunfish is a widespread and commonly caught member of the Centrarchidae family. It has white, flaky flesh and is a good food fish.

ID. The green sunfish has a slender, thick body, a fairly long snout, and a large mouth with the upper jaw extending beneath the pupil of the eye. It has a larger mouth and a thicker, longer body than most sunfish of the genus *Lepomis*, thus resembling the warmouth and the smallmouth bass. It has short, rounded pectoral fins, connected dorsal fins, and an extended gill cover flap, or "ear lobe." This lobe is black and has a light red, pink, or yellow edge. The body is usually brown

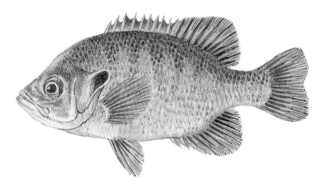

Green Sunfish

to olive or bluish green with a bronze to emerald green sheen, fading to yellow-green on the lower sides and yellow or white on the belly. Adult fish have a large black spot at the rear of the second dorsal and anal fin bases.

Habitat. Green sunfish prefer warm, still pools and backwaters of sluggish streams, as well as ponds and small shallow lakes. Often found near vegetation, they are known to establish territory near the water's edge under brush, rocks, or exposed roots.

Food. Green sunfish prefer dragonfly and mayfly nymphs, caddisfly larvae, midges, freshwater shrimp, and beetles, and will occasionally eat small fish such as mosquitofish.

Longear Sunfish

Lepomis megalotis

Similar in size and general appearance to the pumpkinseed, the longear sunfish is a small, excellent gamefish on light tackle, although in many places it is generally too small to be avidly sought. The white and sweet flesh is excellent to eat.

ID. With a stout body, the longear sunfish is not as compressed as the bluegill or the pumpkinseed. It is one of the most colorful sunfish, particularly the breeding male, which is dark red above and bright orange below, marbled, and spotted with blue. The longear generally has a red eye, orange to red median fins, and a blue-black pelvic fin. There are wavy blue lines on the cheek and opercle, and the long, flexible black ear flap is generally edged with a light blue, white, or orange line. The longear sunfish has a short and rounded pectoral fin, which usually does not

Longear Sunfish

reach past the eye when it is bent forward. It has a fairly large mouth, and the upper jaw extends under the eye pupil.

Habitat. This species inhabits rocky and sandy pools of headwaters, creeks, and small to medium rivers, as well as ponds, bays, lakes, and reservoirs; it is usually found near vegetation and is generally absent from downstream and lowland waters.

Food. Longear sunfish feed primarily on aquatic insects, but also on worms, crayfish, and fish eggs off the bottom.

Pumpkinseed Sunfish

Lepomis gibbosus

The pumpkinseed is one of the most common and brightly colored sunfish. Although small on average, it is especially popular with young anglers because of its willingness to bite on worms, its

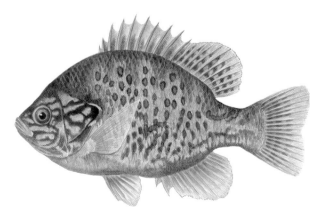

Pumpkinseed Sunfish

wide distribution and abundance, and its close proximity to shore. Its flaky white flesh is also good eating.

ID. A brilliantly colored fish, the adult pumpkinseed is olive green, spotted with blue and orange as well as streaked with gold along the lower sides; there are dusky chainlike bars on the sides of juveniles and adult females. A bright red or orange spot is located on the back edge of the short black ear flap. Many bold dark brown wavy lines or orange spots cover the second dorsal, caudal, and anal fins, and there are wavy blue lines on the cheek. The pumpkinseed sunfish has a long, pointed pectoral fin that usually extends far past the eye when bent forward. It has a small mouth, with the upper jaw not extending under the pupil of the eye. There is a stiff rear edge on the gill cover and short thick rakers on the first gill arch.

Habitat. Pumpkinseeds inhabit quiet and vegetated lakes, ponds, and pools of creeks and small rivers, with a preference for weed patches, docks, logs, and other cover close to shore.

Food. Pumpkinseed sunfish feed on a variety of small foods, including crustaceans, dragonfly and mayfly nymphs, ants, small salamanders, mollusks, midge larvae, snails, water beetles, and small fish.

Redbreast Sunfish

Lepomis auritus

The redbreast sunfish is the most abundant sunfish in Atlantic coastal plain streams. It is a good fighter for its size and excellent to eat.

ID. The body of the redbreast sunfish is deep and compressed but rather elongate for a sunfish. It is olive above, fading to bluish bronze below; in the spawning season, males have bright orange-red bellies while females are pale orange underneath. There are several light blue streaks radiating from the mouth, and the gill rakers are short and stiff. The lobe or flap on the gill cover is usually long and narrow in adult males, actually longer than in the so-called longear sunfish. The two species are easily distinguished because the lobe of the redbreast is blue-black or completely black all the way to the tip and is narrower than the eyes, whereas the lobe of the longear is much wider and is bordered by a thin margin of pale red or yellow around the black. The pectoral fins of both species

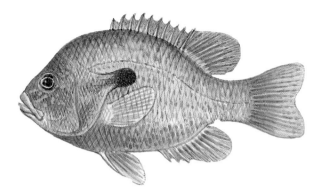

Redbreast Sunfish

are short and roundish in contrast to the longer, pointed pectoral fins of the redear sunfish, and the opercular flaps are softer and more flexible than the rigid flaps of the pumpkinseed.

Habitat. Redbreast sunfish inhabit rocky and sandy pools of creeks and small to medium rivers. They prefer the deeper sections of streams and vegetated lake margins.

Food. Their primary food is aquatic insects, but redbreasts also feed on snails, crayfish, small fish, and occasionally on organic matter from the bottom.

Redear Sunfish

Lepomis microlophus

Commonly known as a shellcracker, the redear sunfish is a popular sportfish because it fights hard on light tackle, reaches a relatively large size for a sunfish, and can be caught in large numbers. It is an excellent fish to eat, with white, flaky meat.

ID. Light golden green above, the redear sunfish is roundish and laterally compressed; adults

have dusky gray spots on the sides, whereas juveniles have bars. It is white to yellow on the belly, with mostly clear fins, and the breeding male is brassy gold with dusky pelvic fins. The redear sunfish has a fairly pointed snout and a small mouth, with blunted molaform teeth that make shell cracking possible. It has connected dorsal fins and long, pointed pectoral fins that extend far beyond the eye when bent forward; the latter distinguish it from both the longear and redbreast sunfish, which have short, roundish pectoral fins. The ear flap is also much shorter than in the other two species and is black, with a bright red or orange spot or a light margin at the edge.

Habitat. Redear sunfish inhabit ponds, swamps, lakes, and vegetated pools of small to medium rivers; they prefer warm, clear, and quiet waters.

Angling for Sunfish

Pound for pound, sunfish are highly respected fighters even though they are diminutive fish. They are most commonly pursued in the spring and early summer while spawning in shallow water and where their round, clustered nests are readily visible along the shoreline of ponds and lakes. Vegetation is a prime place to seek sunfish, especially bluegills and pumpkinseeds, followed by stumps, logs, and fallen trees.

Many anglers pursue sunfish with live worms and floats in relatively shallow water, although the bigger fish are usually found deep. Other baits include crickets, tiny minnows, and mealworms. Small jigs are a fine lure, and small spinners and spinnerbaits can be productive. A slow retrieve is best. Sunfish are popular in winter, too, taken on small jigs, flies, and mealworms.

Light spinning, spincasting, and flycasting outfits are more than adequate for sunfish; in many areas, anglers use long cane poles without reels to dabble baits into selected pockets for various sunfish species. Four- to 8-pound-test line is ample.

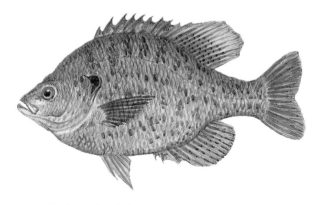

Redear Sunfish

Food. An opportunistic bottom feeder, the redear sunfish forages mostly during the day on aquatic snails, which gives it its common name. These fish also feed on midge larvae, amphipods, mayfly and dragonfly nymphs, clams, fish eggs, and crayfish.

Warmouth

Lepomis gulosus

The warmouth is typically encountered by anglers fishing for other sunfish species. It has white, flaky flesh and is good table fare.

ID. The warmouth has a deep, stout body and is olive brown above and cream to bright yellow below, often with an overall purple luster and a dark brown chainlike mottling on the back and upper sides. Dark red-brown lines extend from the back of the eye. On breeding males, there is a red-orange spot on the yellow edge of the short ear flap, and there are dark brown spots and wavy bands on the fins. The warmouth has a large mouth and a patch of teeth on the tongue, and the upper jaw extends under or past the pupil of the eye. It also has a short, rounded pectoral fin and a stiff rear edge on its gill cover.

Habitat. Warmouth inhabit relatively shallow, vegetated, slow-flowing, mud-bottom creeks, ponds, lakes, swamps, and reservoirs. They are often found around weedbeds, snags, hollow trees, or stumps, and under the banks of streams and ponds.

Food. Because of their large mouths, warmouth have more variety in their diet than some of their sunfish relatives. They feed on invertebrates, small sunfish, darters, mosquitofish, crayfish, snails, freshwater shrimp, dragonflies, and other insects.

Pickerel, Pike, and Muskie

Chain Pickerel

Esox niger

This member of the Esocidae family of pike is a lean, aggressive, sporting battler. Slimy, toothy, camouflaged in green-brown and bearing chain-like markings, the chain pickerel is a smaller but equally fearsome-looking version of its northern pike and muskellunge cousins, and often plentiful where those species are not found or are not particularly abundant.

ID. Long and slender of body, the chain pickerel gets its name from its markings, which appear in a reticulated, or chainlike, pattern of black lines that cover the golden to yellowish or greenish sides. The small, light-colored oval spots on the sides of the northern pike resemble the very large, light oval areas on the chain pickerel but may be distinguished by the dark background behind the pattern on the northern pike; also, the northern pike's spots never appear large in relation to the background, whereas in the chain pickerel the lighter areas are more prevalent.

The chain pickerel has fully scaled cheeks and gill covers. These further distinguish it from the northern pike, which usually has no scales on the bottom half of the gill cover, and from the muskellunge, which usually has no scales on the bottom half of either the gill cover or the cheek. It has only one dorsal fin, which is located very far back on the body near the caudal peduncle. There is a dark vertical bar under the eye, and the snout is shaped like a duck's bill. The lower jaw has a row of four sensory pores on each side, and the mouth is full of needlelike teeth.

Habitat. Chain pickerel inhabit the shallow, vegetated waters of lakes, swamps, streams, ponds, bogs, tidal and nontidal rivers, and backwaters, and the quiet pools of creeks and small to medium rivers, as well as the bays and coves of

Warmouth

Chain Pickerel

larger lakes and reservoirs. Solitary fish, they are occasionally found in low-salinity estuaries. Their primary hangouts are among lily pads and various types of weeds, and they sometimes hold near such objects as stumps, docks, and fallen trees. Invariably, the waters with the best chain pickerel populations are those with abundant vegetation, much of which is found near shore. They move into deeper water during the winter and continue to feed actively.

Food. Capable of eating fish almost as long as they are, chain pickerel feed primarily on other fish, as well as the occasional insect, crayfish, frog, or mouse. Small minnows and fry are among their favorite prey, but they are fond of mid-size fish like yellow perch and other pickerel in the 4- to 6-inch range, and will often eat larger fish. Mainly sight feeders, they lie motionless in patches of vegetation, waiting to snatch small fish, but they can sometimes be lured from a distance to prey that appears vulnerable.

Angling. Not many other sportfish will follow a lure right to the boat with impunity as chain pickerel will. They often make a V-shaped wake in shallow water when dashing out from cover to intercept a lure, and they may hit a lure three, four, or five times in a row while chasing it.

Chain pickerel are primarily attracted to movement and flash. Standard spinners and small spoons are traditionally effective lures, but are prone to hanging up in thick cover. Spinnerbaits, weedless in-line spinners, and weedless spoons are a better option. Worms and jigs are also taken by chain pickerel, but the result is often a line severed by the fish's teeth. Fly fishing is also worthwhile for pickerel, with streamers being especially ravished. Tandem-bladed spinnerbaits with a white or chartreuse skirt are probably the single most popular pickerel lure. Live baits are the top chain pickerel catchers for ice anglers.

Grass Pickerel

Esox americanus vermiculatus

Redfin Pickerel

Esox americanus americanus

The grass pickerel and the redfin pickerel are two nearly identical subspecies of *Esox americanus*, differing only slightly in range. Because they occur

Grass Pickerel

Redfin Pickerel

only in small populations and are of small size, they have little importance as sportfish, although in many waters they are significant predators of more prominent small sportfish. Although the white, sweet flesh of these members of the Esocidae family is bony, it has an excellent flavor.

ID. Slender and cylindrical, grass and redfin pickerel look much like the chain pickerel, with the same fully scaled cheeks and gill covers. They are dark olive to brown or black above, amber to brassy white below, with twenty or more dark green to brown wavy bars along the sides. On the grass pickerel, pale areas between the bars are wider than the bars. The grass pickerel is lighter in color than the redfin pickerel and has a pronounced pale midlateral stripe. The grass pickerel also has yellow green to dusky lower fins and a long narrow snout (although shorter than the chain pickerel's) with a concave profile, whereas the redfin pickerel appropriately has red lower and caudal fins as well as a shorter, broader snout with a convex profile.

Both have large mouths with sharp canine teeth and several sensory pores on the lower jaw. A dark vertical bar extends down from the eye, which is more vertical in the grass pickerel than in the redfin. An easy way to distinguish the redfin from the grass pickerel is to examine the scales on the sides of the redfin, of which there are more notched or heart-shaped ones, specifically six in the area between the pelvic fins. There are up to three on the grass pickerel. Also, the redfin has more than seven of these scales between the dorsal and anal fins, whereas the grass pickerel has four or fewer.

Habitat. Grass and redfin pickerel inhabit quiet or small lakes and swamps, bays and backwaters, and sluggish pools of streams. Both prefer heavy vegetation in clear waters, but the grass pickerel favors waters with neutral to basic acidity, while the redfin inhabits comparatively acidic waters.

Food. Grass and redfin pickerel feed mainly on other fish such as minnows, although they occasionally eat aquatic insects, small crayfish, and frogs.

Angling. Fishing effort is similar to that for chain pickerel.

Northern Pike

Esox lucius

Malevolent-looking and spear-shaped, the northern pike is the namesake member of the Esocidae family of pike. Although disparaged by a few people who catch it while seeking other species of fish, the pike is a worthy angling quarry, one that grows fairly large, fights well, and accommodates anglers frequently enough to be of substantial interest in the areas where it is found.

ID. The northern pike has an elongated body and head. The snout is broad and flat, shaped somewhat like a duck bill. The jaws, roof of the mouth, tongue, and gill rakers are armed with numerous sharp teeth that are constantly being replaced. A single soft-rayed dorsal fin is located far back on the body.

A pike from a clear stream or lake will usually be light green, whereas one from a dark slough or river will be considerably darker. The underparts are whitish or yellowish. The markings on the sides form irregular rows of yellow or gold spots. Pike with a silvery or blue color variation are occasionally encountered and are known as silver pike.

The northern pike can be distinguished from its relatives by three main features. Most noticeably, the greenish or yellowish sides of these fish are covered with lighter-colored kidney-shaped horizontal spots or streaks, whereas all other species have markings that are darker than the background color. The second distinction is the scale pattern on the gill cover and cheek. In the northern

Northern Pike

pike the cheek is fully scaled, but the bottom half of the gill cover is scaleless. In the muskellunge, both the bottom half of the gill cover and the bottom half of the cheek are scaleless. In the pickerel, the gill cover and the cheek are both fully scaled. The third distinctive feature is the number of pores under each side of the lower jaw; there are usually five in the northern pike (rarely three, four, or six on one side), six to nine in the muskellunge (rarely five or ten on one side), and four in smaller pickerel (occasionally three or five on one side only).

Habitat. Although classified as a cool-water species, the northern pike exists in diverse habitats, somewhat like largemouth bass but without a tolerance for extreme warm conditions. It is especially known to inhabit the weedy parts of rivers, ponds, and lakes, but it may be found in deeper, open environs in waters without vegetation, or when the temperature gets too high in warm shallower areas. Warm shallow ponds and cold deep lakes both support pike, but large individuals have a preference for cool water and smaller fish are more likely to be in warm shallow water.

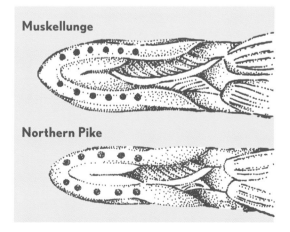

There are six or more pores on each side under the jaw of muskellunge, and five or fewer pores on the northern pike.

Food. Pike are voracious and opportunistic predators. They are solitary, lurking near weeds or other cover to ambush prey. Their diet is composed almost entirely of fish, but it may occasionally include shorebirds, small ducks, muskrats, mice, frogs, and the like. Other pike, plus whitefish, walleye, yellow perch, and suckers, are common food items. Pike feed most actively during the day and are heavily sight-oriented.

Angling. Key locations in lakes include weedy bays, river inlets where weeds are plentiful, shoreline points with beds of cabbage weeds on their open-water sides, reefs with coontail weeds, marshy shorelines, lily pads, and reedy pockets along sandy and rocky shorelines. Many other areas may hold pike, but some form of vegetative structure obviously hosts a significant portion of the pike population. Some pike, especially large ones, inhabit open waters where they forage on schools of baitfish.

Pike lures include the traditional red-and-white spoon, plus a fluorescent orange-bladed spinnerbait or bucktail spinner; an orange-and-yellow-backed minnow-imitation plug; a yellow five-o-diamonds pattern spoon; a black bucktail with a single fluorescent spinner; and various shallow- and deep-diving plugs in gaudy and metallic colors. Good pike lures often tend to be brightly colored and to work with a broad, wide-wobbling action. Lethargic fish may be more inclined to hit large hair- or rubber-bodied jigs, as well as soft plastic jerkbaits, large black streamer flies, and weightless plastic worms.

Muskellunge

Esox masquinongy

The muskellunge is the largest member of the Esocidae family of pike. Although it is bodily pikelike and does occur in some of the same waters, it is vastly different in behavior and abundance (or lack thereof). It is one of the world's foremost gamefish by virtue of its size, strength, and predatory habits, and also due to its contrary nature. Although a devoted coterie of anglers fervently pursues muskellunge, these enthusiasts are a fraction of the total angling populace, most of the rest of whom do not have the opportunity to catch this species or prefer more dependable or abundant species.

Muskellunge

ID. The muskellunge has a long and sleek body. A single soft-rayed dorsal fin is located very far back near the tail. The pelvic fins are located relatively far back on the belly, about halfway between the pectoral fins and the tail, instead of directly under the pectoral fins. The mouth is large, with the maxillae reaching back at least to the middle of the eyes, and it is broad like a duck's bill, but full of teeth.

The coloration and markings on muskellunge are highly variable but usually consist of dark markings on a brownish or green background. There are numerous dark vertical bars that may appear as vermiculations or spots, and sometimes the body has no markings. The variable markings and colorations of muskellunge have led to identity confusion over the years, and although there are no recognized subspecies, there is a sterile hybrid, the tiger muskellunge, which results from the breeding of true muskellunge and northern pike parents.

Habitat. Muskellunge live in medium to large rivers and in lakes of all sizes, although their preferred habitat is cool waters with large and small basins or both deep and shallow areas. They are found in waters no more than 75 acres in size, as well as in enormous reservoirs, natural lakes, and rivers. They rarely venture far from cover and favor shallow, heavily vegetated waters less than 40 feet deep, but they sometimes inhabit deep water that lacks vegetation but offers ample prey.

Food. The muskie is generally a solitary fish that tends to stay in the same area, lurking opportunistically in thick weedbeds and waiting for prey; in some waters it may migrate from deep to shallow environs to feed. Its diet is varied, with a preference for larger rather than smaller fish, as the muskie is well adapted to capturing and swallowing fish of considerable size. Yellow perch, suckers, golden shiners, and walleye are among its favorite foods, but it also consumes smallmouth bass and many other fish.

Angling. Muskellunge are unpredictable and generally harder to catch than any other freshwater species. They generally lurk in or near places where they can lie relatively concealed to ambush forage fish, so anglers must seek places that provide feeding opportunities. The nature of the cover, the depth of water around the cover and nearby, and the presence of current determine the best places. Submerged vegetation, points of land, shoals, bars, submerged islands, and the confluence of currents are among the top areas to focus efforts.

Casting and trolling both have devotees, partially by regulation but mostly by traditional preference. Diving plugs are the primary trolled lures. For casting, large jigs, jerkbaits, a few surface plugs, bucktail spinners, and assorted diving plugs are common lures.

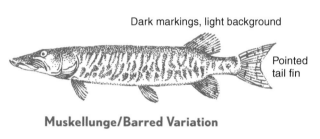

Dark markings, light background

Pointed tail fin

Muskellunge/Barred Variation

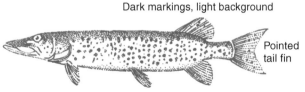

Dark markings, light background

Pointed tail fin

Muskellunge/Spotted Variation

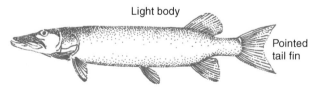

Light body

Pointed tail fin

Muskellunge/Clear Variation

Dark markings, light background

Pointed tail fin

Tiger (Hybrid) Muskellunge

Subtle distinctions differentiate the four variations in muskellunge coloration and marking.

Tiger Muskellunge

Tiger Muskellunge

Esox masquinongy x esox lucius

The tiger muskellunge is a distinctively marked hybrid fish produced when true muskellunge (*E. masquinongy*) and northern pike (*E. lucius*) interbreed. This occurs when the male of either species fertilizes the eggs of the female of the opposite species. This is not a common occurrence in the wild but has happened naturally in waters where both parent species occur, making it an unusual and prized catch.

Deliberate crossbreeding of these species in hatcheries by fisheries managers is now much more common than natural hybridization, and tiger muskies have been stocked in many waters where neither parent occurs naturally. Fish culturists prefer to cross a male northern pike with a female muskellunge because the eggs of the muskie are less adhesive and don't clump as badly in the hatching process.

Populations of introduced tiger muskies are naturally self-limiting because this hybrid is sterile and cannot reproduce itself. Its numbers can therefore be controlled over time. It also grows quickly and is aggressive, making it an excellent catch for anglers.

The tiger muskie has a distinctive look and should not be confused with the true muskellunge. The true muskie may have either bars or spots on the sides or no markings at all, but it is rarely as strikingly beautiful as the tiger muskie, which has dark, wavering tigerlike stripes or bars, many of them broken, set against a lighter background.

As is true with many hybrid fish, the body of the tiger muskie is slightly deeper than that of either comparable-length parent. The cheeks and jaws are usually spotted, with ten to sixteen pores on the underside of the jaws. The tips of the tail are more rounded than in the true muskie, and the fins have distinct spots. In very large specimens, the fins, especially the tail fin, appears to be much larger than for a comparable true muskie.

Habitat, food preferences, and methods of fishing for tiger muskies are similar to those of true muskies.

Yellow Perch

Perch, Sauger, and Walleye

The Percidae family of freshwater fish consists of hundreds of species, some of which are unarguably among the best-tasting freshwater fish available. Most of the species in this family are much too small to be pursued or eaten by humans—including 160 species of darters, which represent 20 percent of all fish in the United States. Fellow family members include yellow perch, sauger, and walleye, which are among the most important sportfish in North America.

All members of the perch family share basic features. The body is typically long and slender, and the two dorsal fins are distinctly separate. The anal fin has one or two spines, and the pelvic fins are located far forward, near the throat. The gill covers end in sharp, spinelike points. The scales are heavy and toothed along their exposed margins.

Yellow Perch

Perca flavescens

The most widely distributed member of the Percidae family, the yellow perch is one of the best loved and most pursued of all freshwater fish, particularly in northerly states and provinces in North America. This is due to its availability over a wide range, the general ease with which it is caught, and its delicious taste. Yellow perch are particularly popular for ice fishing; typically generous bag limits allow anglers to provide a family's worth of meals on a given outing.

ID. Yellow perch are colored a green- to yellow-gold and have six to eight dark, broad vertical bars that extend from the back to below the lateral line, a whitish belly, and orange lower fins during breeding season. Their bodies are oblong and appear humpbacked; this is the result of the deepest part of the body beginning at the first dorsal fin, then tapering slightly to the beginning of the

second dorsal fin. They are distinguished from walleye and sauger by their lack of canine teeth and by a generally deeper body form.

Habitat. Yellow perch are found in a wide variety of warm and cool habitats over a vast range of territory, although they are primarily lake fish. They are occasionally found in ponds and rivers. These fish are most abundant in clear, weedy lakes with a muck, sand, or gravel bottom. Smaller lakes and ponds usually produce smaller fish, although in very fertile lakes with moderate angling pressure, yellow perch can grow large. They inhabit open areas of most lakes and prefer temperatures between the mid-60s and the low 70s.

Food. Adult yellow perch feed on larger zooplankton, insects, young crayfish, snails, aquatic insects, fish eggs, and small fish, including the young of their own species. They are commonly believed to feed in shallows at dawn and dusk, remaining inactive at night, but the conditions under which they feed and under which they can be caught vary widely with their environment and the skill of the angler.

Angling. Yellow perch are not strong fighters, but in cold water and on light spinning or spincasting gear they engage the angler in a feisty battle. Their inclination to avoid turbid and muddy environs and to reside in clean and cool habitat no doubt accounts for their firm white flesh, which has a flavor equal to that of its cousin, the highly touted walleye.

Yellow perch are schooling fish, and anglers land them in open water throughout the season; they are especially popular among ice anglers. They are also caught during their spring spawning runs, in which they ascend tributaries and seek warm shoreline areas in bays and back eddies.

Primarily, yellow perch like cool water and will school deep wherever surface temperatures are warm, although they will move shallower to feed.

The best fishing locations are often the weedbeds in shallow lakes, where it is advisable to fish on or close to the bottom. Yellow perch are caught on a variety of baits and lures, with live worms, live minnows, small minnow-imitating plugs, jigs, spoons, and spinners being among the best attractors. Small jigs with hair or curl-tail grub bodies are especially productive.

Sauger

Sauger

Stizostedion canadense

Saugeye

Stizostedion vitreum x S. canadense

Saugeye

A member of the perch family, the sauger is a smaller, slimmer relative of the walleye, which it closely resembles. It is an important commercial species in some places, especially Canada.

The saugeye is a hybrid fish resulting from the interbreeding of walleye and sauger. It occurs naturally, although infrequently, where the two species mix together. Most populations are produced in hatcheries and are usually stocked in locations where neither parent species has been able to maintain a population. In some literature, it is identified as *Stizostedion vitreum x S. canadense*, which refers to a cross between a female walleye and a male sauger. The meat of saugeye is similar to that of its parents, making it excellent table fare.

ID. The sauger's body is slender and almost cylindrical, and the head is long and cone-shaped. The back and sides are a dull brown or olive gray flecked with yellow and shading to white over the belly. There are three or four dark saddle-shaped blotches on the back and sides. It is easily distinguished from the smooth-cheeked walleye by the presence of rough scales on its cheeks and two or three rows of distinct black spots on the membranes of its spiny dorsal fin, by the absence of a large blotch on the anterior portion of its spinous dorsal fin, and by the absence of a white tip on its tail. The eyes are large and glossy, allowing it to see well at night, and the teeth are large and sharp.

The body of the saugeye is more similar to that of a walleye than to a sauger, although the dorsal fin is sometimes spotted (it is on the sauger but not on the walleye). It also has saddlelike markings on the back and sides, as the sauger does; and the caudal fin has a white border on its lower lobe, like the walleye. Saugeye also have a dark blotch on the membranes of the spiny dorsal fin. The body may have a yellowish cast.

Habitat. Like walleye, sauger and saugeye are schooling species. Habitat preferences tend to large, turbid, shallow lakes and large, silty, slow-flowing rivers. They are more tolerant of muddy water and swifter current than walleye, and prefer water temperatures between 62° and 72°F. Sauger are often found in tailwaters below dams, and along rocky riprap. Eddies near turbulent water are often staging and feeding areas. Gravel bars and points are prominent holding locations in lakes.

Food. These species feed on such small fish as shad, sunfish, and minnows, as well as on crayfish, leeches, and insects. Most feeding occurs over rocky gravel bottoms or along sparsely weeded sandy bottoms.

Angling. Sauger can provide year-round fishing, although they are often deliberately targeted only in specific seasons in certain locales (through the ice in the north, or in winter and spring in the south) and are otherwise caught incidentally. Although locations and fishing methods for sauger and saugeye are similar to those for walleye, these fish tend to live deeper and are also more aggressive when located, usually striking solidly. They also are even more bottom-oriented. Scaled-down presentations, including lighter and smaller lures, are more appropriate.

Walleye

Stizostedion vitreum

The walleye is the largest North American member of the Percidae family and a close relative of the sauger. A popular freshwater sportfish, the walleye is relatively abundant in many waters, grows to large sizes, and known for its delicious, sweet, and fine-textured meat. As a food fish, the walleye has few peers in freshwater, which helps counterbalance its reputation as a sluggish battler when hooked.

ID. The walleye has a slender and cylindrical body with a tapered head. Its first dorsal fin has needle-sharp spiny rays and is separated from the soft-rayed second dorsal fin. The cheeks are sparsely scaled, and the gill covers and teeth are sharp. It has a dark green back, golden yellow sides, and a white belly. The lower lobe of the caudal fin is white, and there is a large black blotch at the rear base of the spinous first dorsal fin.

Perhaps the most prominent feature of the walleye is its large white glossy eyes. The special reflective layer in the retina is called the tapetum lucidum; it gathers light that enters the eye, making it extremely sensitive to bright daylight intensities but also conducive to nocturnal vision. This attribute is also present in the sauger.

Habitat. Walleye are tolerant of a range of environmental situations but seem to do best in the open water of large lakes and reservoirs, as well as the pools of large rivers. They inhabit many smaller bodies of water but are not typically prolific in the most turbid environs. Gravel, rock, and firm sand bottoms are preferred, and they may associate with various weed cover; they will also use sunken trees, standing timber, boulder shoals, and reefs as cover and foraging sites. In large lakes they will orient to open water in schools that coincide with the presence of baitfish, especially alewives but also shad and perch. In the spring, these fish make a spawning run to shallow shoals, inshore areas, or tributary rivers; at other times they move up and down in response to light intensity. They also move daily or seasonally in response to water temperature or food availability.

Food. Walleye primarily consume other fish. Their wide diet includes alewives, smelt, shad, cisco, shiners, sculpin, suckers, minnows, darters, perch, and crayfish, as well as many other items. Some populations feed almost exclusively on emerging larval or adult mayflies for part of the year.

Angling. Walleye are popular because they are often found in concentrations, can be challenging to locate and catch, and are susceptible to varied angling techniques. Although they are theoretically most active in low-light and dark conditions in many environments, they do feed during daylight hours and can be caught during the day.

Walleye abundance relates to baitfish presence and to structure. The activities of the predominant food have a bearing on where walleye are located—suspended in open water, hugging the bottom along sandbars or reefs or points, waiting along weedlines, and so forth. Favored structures include rock reefs, sandbars, gravel bars, points, weeds, rocky or riprap causeways or shorelines, and creek channels. Walleye are particularly known for congregating in or along the edges of submerged vegetation.

Fishing presentations center on jigging, still-fishing or drifting with live baits, trolling with bait rigs, casting crankbaits, and trolling with plugs. Jigs are typically used with leeches, minnows, or worms. Fixed and slip floats are used for live-bait fishing, although sometimes a jig and worm is fished below a float.

Walleye

Black Bullhead

Ameiurus melas

Brown Bullhead

Ameiurus nebulosus

Yellow Bullhead

Ameiurus natalis

Although there are about fifty North American members of the Ictaluridae family of catfish, perhaps the most abundant and best-known members of the *Ictalurus* genus are the brown, black, and yellow bullheads. The most common of these, and the species that has been introduced most widely, is the brown bullhead. In habits and flavor, the three species are scarcely distinguishable.

These fish rank highly as table fare, and anglers overwhelmingly tend to keep them, a practice that within reason is not harmful to most populations of catfish and is encouraged by fisheries managers. Another important reason for their popularity is that they are a fairly willing fish that are generally not too difficult to catch in smaller sizes; they don't require much sophistication in technique, tackle, or presentation methods.

ID. Although the name would imply something else, the "black" bullhead may actually be yellowish green, dark green, olive, brown, or black on the back, bronze or green on the sides, and bright yellow or white on the belly. The entire body possesses a lustrous sheen. Only the young and spawning males are truly black.

The head of the brown bullhead is large for its round and slender body, and the skin is smooth and entirely scaleless. The coloring of the brown bullhead is not always brown, as the name would imply, but may actually range from yellowish brown or chocolate brown to gray or olive with brown or black scattered spots; the belly is yellow or white. The young are jet black and are often mistaken for black bullhead, and adults sport darker pigmentation during the breeding period.

A moderately slim fish, the yellow bullhead has leathery skin without scales. The coloring ranges from yellowish olive to brown or almost black on the back with yellowish olive or brown sides, yellow or white on the belly, and dusky fins. Juveniles are dark brown or jet-black, making them difficult to distinguish from the young of black or brown bullhead.

Distinguishing the black bullhead from brown or yellow bullhead can be done by noting the rear edge of the pectoral fin in the latter two, which have a spine serrated with numerous sharp, thorny protrusions; those found on the spine of the black bullhead's pectoral fin are much less prominent and may be absent altogether. The black bullhead has dark chin barbels that may be black-spotted, whereas the yellow bullhead has lighter ones. Also, the black bullhead has a chubby body that is deeper than the body of both the brown and yellow bullhead. Another distinguishing feature is the squarish tail of the brown and black bullhead, which contrasts with the rounded tail of the yellow bullhead and the distinctly forked tails of the channel catfish, white catfish, and blue catfish.

Habitat. Black bullhead inhabit pools, backwaters, and slow-moving sections of creeks and small to large rivers; they also dwell in impoundments, oxbows, and ponds. They have a preference for muddy water and soft mud bottoms, and are able to tolerate polluted water better than other catfish. They tend to avoid cooler, clearer water.

Brown bullhead inhabit warm and even stagnant waters as well as sluggish runs over muddy bottoms. They occur in farm ponds, pools, creeks, small to large rivers, lakes, and reservoirs. Unlike other bullhead, they are found in large and deep waters, although they are able to withstand low oxygen concentrations and are known to bury themselves in mud to survive such conditions.

Yellow bullhead prefer clear waters, gravel or rock bottoms, sluggish current, and heavy vegetation, in pools, ponds, streams, small to large rivers, and small, shallow lakes. They are more common in smaller, weedier, and shallower bodies of water than brown bullhead and are more tolerant of polluted water and low oxygen levels than most other types of bullhead.

Food. Bullheads are nocturnal scavengers that feed by smell and taste. Adults eat small fish, mollusks, crayfish, worms, aquatic insects, and occasionally bits of aquatic vegetation.

Angling. Bullhead are a frisky but not especially strong fish at the end of a line; they tend to spin when landed and may be problematic to subdue. The spines at the base of the dorsal and pectoral fins can "lock" into an erect position, which evidently helps protect the fish from

Black Bullhead

Brown Bullhead

Yellow Bullhead

predators by making it much harder to swallow. When handling bullhead, anglers must be careful to grasp the fish by positioning the finger behind these fins to avoid being painfully stuck by these sharp protrusions.

Bullhead are not held in great esteem from a sporting standpoint and are primarily pursued for their table virtues. Thus most bullhead that are caught are kept for consumption. This influences angling methods to some degree, as does their primarily bottom-scrounging nature. Most targeted bullhead fishing is done with some form of bait, either by bank- and shore-based anglers or from small boats in backwater environs.

Bullhead are a willing fish for anglers early in the season in northern climes as soon as the ice goes out. The best early-season angling is usually at the mouth of small tributaries to lakes and ponds. If the flow is moderate, bullhead will ascend creeks

and streams and can be quite abundant. In the spring, when the water is warming, bullhead are caught all day long. Later, in the summer or when the water has warmed sufficiently, they become nocturnal and are best caught after dark.

Bullhead and other small catfish are caught by anglers stillfishing with all sorts of baits. Nightcrawlers are the top natural baits for bullhead, used with a float and near-bottom bait rig. Bullhead are susceptible to a variety of other offerings, including many aimed at their larger catfish cousins and possessing scented characteristics. These include rancid cheese, doughballs, liver, fish, chunks of meat or fish, chicken entrails, congealed chicken blood, and an endless array of items that fall under the category of "stinkbait."

For the purposes of sport, most light to medium tackle is suitable, including 5- to 6-foot rods of light to medium action; 6- to 8-pound-test line is the norm.

Blue Catfish, Channel Catfish, Flathead Catfish, and White Catfish

Blue Catfish

Ictalurus furcatus

This is a popular species valued for its flesh as well as its sporting value. The blue catfish is a strong, stubborn fighter that can grow quite large, well over 100 pounds in some locales. It is considered good table fare and is widely pursued by commercial fishermen for the market. Its flesh is white, delicate, and tender, especially in smaller specimens.

ID. Blue catfish are generally blue gray or slate blue and possess no spots or other markings, although they may be almost pale blue or silvery; their flanks taper in color to the belly, which is light gray or white. They have a deeply forked tail, and the anal fin has a straight margin. They resemble channel catfish and when small are most easily confused with that relative. Larger blue cats have a distinct humpbacked appearance, with the hump rising at and in front of the dorsal fin; their head is generally larger than that of a channel cat, and their body is less sleek. They can be distinguished from channel cats by their longer and straight-edged anal fin, which has thirty to thirty-five

Blue Catfish

Channel Catfish

rays. In smaller specimens, a distinguishing characteristic is their lack of black body spots.

Habitat. Blue catfish inhabit rivers, streams, lakes, reservoirs, and ponds but are primarily a fish of big rivers and big lakes and reservoirs. They have been introduced into smaller lakes and ponds but seldom attain large sizes in such places. This species prefers the deep areas of large rivers, swift chutes, and pools with swift currents. Like the channel catfish, they prefer locations with good current over bottoms of rock, gravel, or sand.

Food. Blue catfish evidently eat most anything they can catch; their diet includes assorted fish, crayfish, aquatic insects, and clams. Herring and gizzard shad are mainstays for larger catfish in places where these are abundant. Blue cats primarily feed on or near the bottom, and they are principally nocturnal foragers.

Angling. Blue cats are primarily caught by anglers bottom fishing with live or dead baits and with assorted stinkbaits. They are a strong fish that digs in; in larger sizes they are seldom immediately subdued. For more details, see the box on page 37.

Channel Catfish

Ictalurus punctatus

The most widely distributed of all freshwater catfish, the channel cat is a significant component of recreational angling efforts as well as a mainstay of commercial fishing; its tender, white, and nutritious flesh is highly valued as table fare. It has been stocked widely in lakes and ponds, and provides the backbone of catfish farming. In some states, the sporty channel cat is ranked at or near the top among all species in angling popularity. Channel catfish have the potential to attain large sizes, up to 58 pounds but less gargantuan than other species. Their general willingness to strike baits, their wide distribution, and their high food esteem primarily account for their popularity.

ID. Channel catfish are often recognized at a glance, owing to their deeply forked tails and small irregular spots on the sides. The spots may not be present in all specimens but generally are obvious in smaller individuals. These pigmented spots are most noticeable on younger fish, and obscure on older ones. Blue catfish also have a forked tail, but no spots. Channel cats are more slender than other catfish, perhaps owing to their native riverine existence, and they have a relatively small head. They are distinguished from white and blue catfish by their twenty-four to twenty-nine anal fin rays. Like other catfish, they have heavy, sharp pectoral and dorsal spines, as well as long mouth barbels.

The body of a channel catfish is pale blue to pale olive with a bit of silvery tint, but color variation is subject to location and water conditions. During the spawning season, male channel cats may be entirely black dorsally, and other channel cats may be dark blue with little or no spotting, or uniformly light blue or silvery like the blue catfish or white catfish. Another feature distinguishing them from a blue catfish is the anal fin, which is shorter and more rounded than that of a blue catfish.

Habitat. The channel catfish inhabits rivers, streams, lakes, reservoirs, and ponds. It prefers clear, flowing waters, although it does equally well in lakes and ponds. It also favors clean bottoms of sand, rubble, or gravel in large lakes and rivers. Although it tolerates some amount of current, it is more likely to inhabit warm, quiet, slow-moving areas.

Food. Channel catfish are primarily but not exclusively bottom feeders. They are omnivorous and consume insects, crayfish, clams, snails, crabs, fish eggs, and assorted small fish, including sunfish, darters, shiners, and gizzard shad, plus a variety of plants.

Angling. The vast majority of channel catfish are caught by bottom anglers, but these fish sometimes linger on or near the surface, as well as at mid-depths. They are strong and provide a good fight on light tackle, although the smaller specimens are often overwhelmed by heavy-tackle users. Most anglers use some form of bait, and many find that channel cats prefer live baits over dead ones. For more details, see the box on page 37.

Flathead Catfish

Pylodictus olivaris

A common and large-growing species, the flathead is one of the ugliest members of the freshwater catfish clan. Nevertheless, large specimens are commonly caught, and the fish provides a good struggle on hook and line. It is important both for commercial and recreational uses, and produces good table fare when taken from clean environments.

ID. The flathead catfish is distinctive in appearance and not easily confused with any other species. It has a squared rather than forked tail, with a long body and large flattened head. Medium to large specimens are rather potbellied and have wide heads and beady eyes. The eyes, with their distinctly flat-looking oval shape, accentuate the flatness of the head, and the lower jaw further accentuates this trait by protruding beyond the upper jaw. Compared to that of other catfish species, the anal fin of the flathead is short along its base, possessing fourteen to seventeen fin rays.

Flathead color varies greatly with environment, and sometimes within the same environment, but is generally mottled with varying shades of brown and yellow on the sides, tapering to a lighter or whitish mottling on the belly. As with other catfish, flatheads have heavy, sharp pectoral and dorsal spines, as well as long mouth barbels.

Habitat. This species is primarily found in large bodies of water, especially reservoirs and their tributaries, and big rivers and their tributaries. In rivers, they prefer deep pools where the water is slow, and depressions or holes. They are also commonly found in tailraces below dams. Their chosen habitat often has a hard bottom, sometimes mixed with driftwood or timber. In large reservoirs, they are usually found deep, often in old

Flathead Catfish

riverbeds, at the junction of submerged channels, and near the headwater tributary.

Food. Like its brethren, the flathead is omnivorous and opportunistic, and consumes diverse and available foods. Flathead catfish are primarily but not exclusively bottom feeders, with a diet of insects, crayfish, clams, and assorted small fish, including sunfish, shiners, and shad. Adults consume larger prey, including bullhead, gizzard shad, and carp. Live fish are popular baits for flatheads, more so than other catfish species, as these fish are more reluctant to consume old and smelly bait. Although not exclusively nocturnal, flatheads are more active at night and may spend the day inactive in deep water or under cover. At night they may move to shallower waters and feed at different levels.

Angling. Flatheads are popular and provide a strong and stubborn deep-digging fight. It takes time to subdue larger individuals, which are pursued with heavy tackle, especially because they exist in snag-filled environs. For more details, see the box on page 37.

White Catfish

Ameiurus catus

White catfish are a common and popular fish with a more limited range than other catfish species, and with commercial as well as recreational value. They have been successfully stocked in pay-to-fish ponds and are also cultivated for commercial bulk harvest. Their flesh is white and fine, and they make excellent eating, especially when caught from clean environments.

ID. The white catfish looks somewhat like a cross between a channel cat and a bullhead, owing to its slightly forked tail, broad head, and squat body. Midsize specimens are often thought to be huge bullhead. The white catfish has a moderately forked tail. Its anal fin is rounded along the edge and has nineteen to twenty-three fin rays, fewer than either the blue catfish or channel cat. Without close inspection, it could be confused with other catfish, although it doesn't possess the spots seen on young channel catfish. This fish is olive gray or slate gray on the head, and bluish gray or slate gray on its backs and sides, tapering to a white belly. As with other catfish, the white cat has heavy, sharp pectoral and dorsal spines, as well as long mouth barbels; its chin barbels are white.

Habitat. White catfish inhabit the silty bottom areas of slow-moving streams and rivers, as well as ponds, lakes, and the low-salinity portions of tidal estuaries. They generally avoid the swift

White Catfish

water of large rivers and do not thrive in weedy or muddy shallow ponds.

Food. White catfish have a broad appetite and consume aquatic insects, crayfish, clams, snails, mussels, fish eggs, assorted small fish, and some

Angling for Catfish

Channel catfish probably receive the greatest attention of the North American species, with proportionally less attention given to bullhead and blue catfish, followed by flathead and white catfish. Some aspects of angling for these species are uniform to all of them and some are different. One common but misunderstood element is that catfish are caught only on rotten baits.

On the whole, anglers spend as many hours working these species after dark as they do during daylight hours. Fishing with rod and reel can run a gamut from cane poles for small specimens to heavy-duty levelwind reels and stout saltwater boat rods for big bruisers. Stillfishing and drift fishing are the general methods of catfishing in all of their habitats, whereas casting is generally ineffective.

For the most part, fishing on or close to the bottom with some form of bait is the most reliable way to hook catfish. They will take artificials, but not nearly as well as some anglers might like, and lures are much less effective than baits. Flatheads are fairly susceptible to lures, and crankbaits are most productive. Channel cats are often caught incidentally by anglers who have tipped a jig with a minnow or a lively piece of nightcrawler.

A great deal of catfishing occurs in rivers, the natural habitat of most catfish species. Other popular locations include reservoirs, ponds, small lakes, and the backwaters connected to rivers, so strategies vary according to habitat.

In rivers, look to current cuts, stream mouths, gravel and rock bottoms, deep-cut riverbanks, shallow riffle areas with a hard bottom, river channels, and pools below riffles. Deep holes or pools present good river catfishing opportunities. Channel cats work up into shallow water to feed, and move back into deeper water. Although some

(Continued)

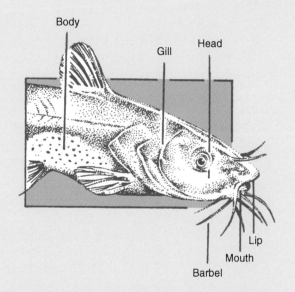

The catfish possesses exceptional external sensory faculties in each of the areas depicted above. The greatest sensitivity is in the barbels and lips.

A 30-pound blue catfish from Lake Moultrie, South Carolina, one of the premier giant-catfish waters in the United States.

Unlike channel cats, flatheads venture only partway out of the deep hole to feed. If hole depth is 20 feet and the upstream area is 12 feet, a flathead may work only into 16 feet of water to feed, whereas a channel cat will work into the shallowest upstream point.

River and stream catfish always feed into the current, so take advantage of their keen sense of smell. Detecting a strike is a key to success, especially with smaller fish and with the particularly adept bait-nibbling channel cat. It's best to position yourself directly upstream of the area to be fished and to cast your offering directly downstream to the target.

In big impoundments there is likely to be good catfishing in the tailrace water below the dam, and in the rivers that feed the reservoir. Current flow may vary with season and the demand for water, and levels and flow can change as water is stored or released, so these factors have an impact on fishing, although methods are generally similar to those already noted.

In big impoundments, places to focus your efforts are varied, but old riverbeds and channels are especially important. In these places, concentrate on the curves, bends, and deepest holes, and especially where two channels come together. Ledges, or any place where the lake bottom drops off to deep water out in the main lake, also produce catfish, as do humps that drop fairly abruptly to deep water, and areas with a soft bottom (such as an old swamp, which has varied bottom contours).

Flats may have catfish earlier in the season when the water is warming, and points are also worth trying but are often sporadic producers. The area near the dam, especially the face of it (if fishing there is permissible—many are cordoned off), and the riprap and boulders along the face can concentrate fish, including spawners.

channel catfish are caught during daylight hours directly from within a hole itself, they are best caught as they move into the shallower areas upstream from the hole. This movement, throughout most of the season, occurs just prior to sundown and lasts for an hour or so after dark.

Flatheads, on the other hand, may refrain from feeding throughout the day and then begin foraging at dark.

aquatic plants. Adults primarily feed on fish and are active at night, although they are less nocturnal than other catfish.

Angling. Where they exist, white catfish are fairly abundant and aggressive, and provide a good fight on light tackle, although the smaller specimens are often overwhelmed by heavy-tackle users. Most people fish with some form of weighted bait. For more details, see the box on page 37.

Common Carp

Cyprinus carpio

One of the largest members of the minnow family and a close relative of the goldfish, the common carp is among the least-favored targets of freshwater anglers in North America. Common carp exist in good supply and in relatively large sizes (compared to most other species), and provide an underutilized resource for anglers, not to mention an ample source of protein. In some circles carp are highly regarded as a food fish and can be prepared in many ways.

ID. The common carp has a deep body form and a heavy appearance. Distinctive features include a short head, rounded snout, single long dorsal fin, forked tail, and relatively large scales. The mouth is toothless and suckerlike, adapted to bottom feeding, and the upper jaw projects slightly past the lower one. The common carp has a single serrated spine at the front of the dorsal and anal fins and two pairs of fleshy barbels on either side of its mouth.

Coloring ranges from gold to olive to brown, with a yellowish coloring on the lower sides and belly and a reddish tint to the lower fins. Each scale on the upper sides of the fish has a concentrated dark spot at its base and a conspicuous dark rim. Juveniles and breeding males are usually a darker green or gray with a dark belly, and females are lighter.

Habitat. Common carp are incredibly hardy and flexible in their habitat preferences. Primarily bottom-dwelling fish, carp like quiet, shallow waters with a soft bottom and dense aquatic vegetation. Although they favor large turbid waters, they also thrive in small rivers and lakes. They can live in low-oxygen environments and can tolerate temperature fluctuations and extremes. In some northern waters where the fish are abundant and such terrain is lacking or offers no food, carp will cruise over shallow, rocky flats and shoals, browsing along the rubble bottom.

Food. Omnivorous feeders, carp have predominantly vegetarian diets but will feed on aquatic insects, snails, crustaceans, annelids, and mollusks. Aquatic plants and filamentous algae are the most popular food groups. They grub sediments from the bottom with their suckerlike mouths, uprooting and destroying vegetation and muddying the water. Carp primarily spend their lives in small groups and are inclined to roam for food.

Angling. Because carp primarily eat aquatic plants, and not other fish, they are less receptive than many other species to the most commonly practiced methods of fishing in North America. Nevertheless, they are strong fish and hearty battlers, capable of stretching a fishing line and testing the skills of most anglers.

Getting a carp to take your offering can be a challenge, as they are not impulsive predators or ambush strikers. For the most part, they are not chasers or stalk-and-attack hunters. They are

A common carp from Lake Oahe, South Dakota.

unlikely to strike most lures, although they occasionally strike a slow-moving jig, and either a weighted or a dry fly.

Spinning, spincasting, flycasting, and baitcasting tackle are all used to land carp, but spinning is probably the most functional method. In North America, carp have been caught on an assortment of bait, primarily doughballs, corn, worms, processed baits, and commercially prepared baits, with and without chumming.

Although they primarily feed on the bottom, carp also feed on or near the surface as well as at midlevels. Fishing for carp is mostly a waiting game, but stealthy anglers can opt to take a more aggressive approach and hunt for them, stalking and casting to visible fish.

Arctic Charr, Dolly Varden, and Bull Trout

Arctic Charr

Salvelinus alpinus

This species is technically among the most widely distributed salmonids, and the most northerly ranging member of the Salmonidae family. There are both anadromous and nonanadromous forms, the latter including blueback trout, Sunapee trout, and Quebec red trout; the anadromous version tends to be larger, and is of more importance to commercial and sport fisheries. The flesh of sea-run charr is deep orange-red and an epicurean delight, although it can spoil quickly. Depending on diet and location, some charr may have lighter-colored or white flesh.

ID. The Arctic charr has light-colored spots on its body, including below the lateral line, and the leading edges of all fins on the lower part of the body are milk white. It is a long and slender fish with a small, pointed head, an adipose fin, an axillary process at the base of each pelvic fin, and a slightly forked tail that almost appears squared. It also has very fine scales and, unlike trout, teeth only in the central forward part of its mouth.

Coloration is highly variable among seagoing and landlocked forms. Generally, the Arctic charr is silvery in nonspawning individuals, with deep green or blue shading on the back and upper sides, and a white belly. Spawning males exhibit brilliant red or reddish orange coloration on the sides, underparts, and lower fins; their backs are muted, sometimes without the blue or green coloration or possibly with orange to olive hues. Spawning males of some populations develop a kype, and some have a humped back. Spawning females are also colorful, although the red is less intense and present only on the flanks and belly; the back remains bluish or greenish. They are often confused with other members of their genus, particularly Dolly Varden.

Habitat. In their ocean life, Arctic charr remain in inshore waters; most do not migrate far. In rivers, they locate in pools and runs. The lakes inhabited by anadromous and landlocked charr are cold year-round, so the fish remain near the surface or in the upper levels and may gather at the mouths of tributaries when food is plentiful.

Food. Insects, mollusks, and small fish constitute the diet of Arctic charr. Ninespine sticklebacks are important forage in some places. The charr often does not eat in winter, when its metabolic rate slows. Rather, it lives on the fat it has accumulated during the summer.

Angling. Some anglers consider sea-run Arctic charr the equal of Atlantic salmon, because both

Arctic Charr (sea-run phase)

Arctic Charr (spawning phase)

are strong battlers that make long runs and thrilling aerial jumps when hooked. The charr are perhaps more prone to furious spinning and head-twisting gyrations.

Sea-run Arctic charr are the main interest of anglers, although landlocked charr are caught in lakes, usually incidental to fishing for lake trout or when they are the only sportfish present. Most of the better fishing for larger charr occurs far north and in a very limited time window, mainly in mid- to late summer. Thus, angling can be a feast-or-famine affair. Charr sometimes are clustered so thickly that a river seems full of these fish, or they can be scarce. These fish are also easily spooked; when a school is alarmed (as can happen when one or more of its members is caught), it will move off, and the spot has to be rested for an hour or two.

River fishing is more dependable than lake fishing, with the charr often holding at the head of a pool. Where current drops over a gravel bar and dumps into a deep pool is a particularly good location. In swift, high water it is necessary to use heavy-bodied spoons, which sink below the surface turbulence; a touch of red or orange on the spoons is helpful. Weighted spinners and some plugs may also do the job, and heavily dressed flies on fast-sinking lines are necessary for fly anglers. Fly fishing is better when the water level is lower; many different wet flies and streamers are appropriate, also with some bright color for appeal, and dry flies may catch fish when there is a hatch (often mosquitoes) in progress.

In lakes, anglers concentrate on inlets, where the river dumps into a lake. Early in the season, charr in lakes can be seen and caught as they wander along the edges of ice floes that are breaking up; a spoon, jig, or streamer fly will take them.

Dolly Varden

Salvelinus malma

Bull Trout

Salvelinus confluentus

The Dolly Varden and bull trout are members of the charr group of the Salmonidae family and close relatives of Arctic charr. They are not as highly rated as most other salmonids, but they do have considerable sporting and food value and have gained more esteem. The flesh of both species is pink and firm and good to eat, and there has been some commercial value for Dolly Varden in parts of its range.

ID. These two charr, as well as the Arctic charr, are difficult to distinguish from external characteristics alone. In general, the Dolly Varden and the bull trout can be distinguished by their size and habitat. The Dolly Varden is usually a coastal species, whereas the larger bull trout inhabits inland waters, namely large, cold rivers and lakes draining high, mountainous areas. Although both can grow large, they seldom do. Dollies are typically smaller and tend to have a more rounded body shape. Bull trout have a larger, flattened head and a more pronounced hook in the lower jaw.

The color of both varies with habitat and locality, but the body is generally olive green, the back being darker than the pale sides; cream to pale yellow spots (slightly smaller than the pupil of the eye) cover the back, while red or orange spots cover the sides; and the pectoral, pelvic, and anal fins have white or cream-colored margins. The male in full fall spawning dress sports a dark olive back, sometimes bordering on black, an orange-red belly, bright red spots, and fluorescent white fin edges, rivaling fall's spectacular colors. Sea-run Dollies are silvery, and the spots can be very faint.

A much greater problem arises in trying to distinguish the Dolly Varden from the Arctic charr. The spots on the Dolly Varden are usually smaller than the pupil of the eye, whereas on the Arctic charr they are larger than the pupil. When returning from the sea, both species are silvery and lack spots. Arctic charr on average have more gill rakers on the first left gill arch (twenty-five to thirty as opposed to twenty-one or twenty-two in the Dolly Varden) and more pyloric caeca (forty to forty-five as opposed to roughly thirty in the Dolly Varden), but fish with intermediate counts are not uncommon in either species.

Habitat. Bull trout and Dolly Varden prefer deep pools of cold rivers, lakes, and reservoirs. Streams with abundant cover (cut banks, root wads, and other woody debris) and clean gravel and cobble beds provide the best habitat. Their favored summer water temperature is generally below 55°F, but they nevertheless tolerate temperatures below 40°F. Spawning during fall usually starts when water temperatures drop to the mid- to low 40s. Cold, clear water is required for successful reproduction.

Food. Bull trout and Dolly Varden are opportunistic feeders, eating aquatic insects, shrimp, snails, leeches, fish eggs, and fish.

Angling. Both species are fairly easy to catch and do not display the leaping tendencies of more

Dolly Varden

Bull Trout

admired salmonids like Arctic charr or steelhead. Anglers cast spoons, spinners, and flies to Dollies and bull trout in river pools. Some troll deep in lakes, as they do for Arctic charr and various salmon.

Brook Trout and Lake Trout

Brook Trout

Salvelinus fontinalis

Technically a member of the charr family, brook trout are a native North American fish and a sensitive one that has been displaced in some habitats as the result of fish stocking or water degradation. In general, they are more eager to come to the hook than brown trout, with whom they cross range and share some common waters. Native brook trout are virtually a delicacy, with bright orange flesh that is best sampled as soon as possible after a specimen has been taken. Commercially raised individuals are important to the restaurant trade.

ID. Brook trout coloration and patterns are so unique that there is seldom any confusion with other species. White pipings on the outer edges of all but the caudal fin identify it as a charr. On the interior of the white leading edges on the fins is a narrow black stripe. Wormlike wavy lines, called vermiculations, appear on the back and head, and look like a series of tiger stripes on the dorsal, adipose, and caudal fins.

Body coloration varies, ranging from a light, metallic blue in fish that enter saltwater (which are called salters) or in fish that leave natal streams and spend part of the year in large, deep, clear lakes (which are called coasters), to dark brown and yellow. In general, back coloration is olive drab or greenish brown, which fades down the sides into a light brown and somewhat yellowish

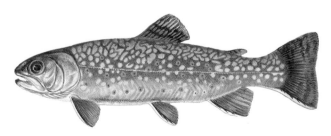

Brook Trout

color below the lateral line. On the abdomen, it merges into a pearly white that during spawning phases is replaced by roseate, then red and orange hues with a black swath along the very bottom. Colors intensify as spawning approaches, but this is more pronounced in males.

Habitat. Brook trout inhabit small trickles, rivulets, creeks, and beaver ponds. They live in larger streams and any lake, from the Great Lakes to little lakes and ponds, to small rivers and big rivers with tumbling falls and rapids. Because of a unique organ (the glomerulus) in their kidney, they are anadromous and can move into riverine estuaries and are at home in brackish streams that feel the surge of tides, in a purely saline bay, or even the oceans themselves.

Food. Brook trout are omnivorous, carnivorous, and piscivorous. Fish from 4 to 8 inches long feed mainly on aquatic and terrestrial insects. Between 8 and 12 inches, they begin feeding on small fish, in addition to aquatic insects. Large trout, particularly in northern waters during summer, are known to eat small mammals (mice, voles, shrews, and lemmings) that find their way into the water.

Angling. Brook trout readily take various lures, flies, and baits and generally provide a showy fight. The larger individuals put up a particularly good one. Their freewheeling appetite and spunky disposition make them susceptible to a variety of tackle types and methods, although fly fishing and spinning are the primary means of catching these fish, essentially by casting, but also by trolling.

Brookies are a terrific species for fly anglers, in part because of their nature but also because many of their habitats suit fly fishing's advantages, especially in rivers and streams. In those waters, brook trout hole up in some nearly impenetrable places, like an undercut bank, beneath a watery tree thicket, in a deep dark hole, and the like, where they wait for meals to come to them rather than chasing after them. When the waterway is narrow with overgrown banks, and the water is fairly shallow, a fly can be roll cast efficiently and quietly.

Spinners, spoons, and small plugs are the primary nonfly hardware used by casters, and a variety of these are effective. Lure sizes are common in the $1/4$ - to $1/8$ -ounce range, seldom larger, and often smaller for low-water situations and shallow streams.

Lake Trout

Salvelinus namaycush

The lake trout is one of the largest members of the Salmonidae family, and not actually a "trout" but a charr. Lakers are generally one of the least accessible freshwater gamefish to most North Americans because of their preference for cold, dark, and mysterious nether depths, or because the greatest numbers exist in far-off or hard-to-access regions of northern Canada. Lake trout flesh has a high fat content and is especially good when smoked.

ID. Lake trout have the same moderately elongated shape as trout and salmon, as well as other charr, although they grow much larger than other charr. Extremely heavy specimens have a distended belly and a less elongated shape. Their tail is moderately forked, more so than other charr, their scales are minute, and they have several rows of strong teeth, which are weak, less numerous, or absent in other charr. Their head is generally large, although fast-growing stocked fish will have small heads in relation to body size, and there is an adipose fin.

The lake trout has white leading edges on all its lower fins and light-colored spots on a dark background. The body is typically grayish to brownish, with white or nearly white spots that extend onto the dorsal, adipose, and caudal fins. Coloration is highly variable. Lighter specimens are often the deep-dwelling fish of light-colored southerly lakes with alewife and smelt forage bases; darker specimens, including some with reddish and orange tones, come from less fertile, tannin-colored shallow northern lakes.

The lake trout has been crossed with the brook trout to produce a hybrid known as a splake. The hybrid's tail is less deeply forked, and its body markings more closely resemble those of the brook trout.

Habitat. Overall, and especially in the southern portions of its range, or where introduced south of its native range, the lake trout is an inhabitant of cool waters of large, deep lakes. In far northern regions it may occur in lakes that are generally shallow and remain cold all season long, as well as in either the shallow or deep portions of lakes that have large expanses of deep water. It is also found in large deep rivers, or in the lower reaches of rivers, especially in the far north, although it may also move into the tributaries of large southerly

Lake Trout

lakes to forage. Lake trout rarely inhabit brackish water.

Food. The diet of lake trout varies with the age and size of the fish, locality, and food available. Food items commonly include zooplankton, insect larvae, small crustaceans, clams, snails, leeches, and various species of fish, including their own kind. Lake trout feed extensively on other fish such as whitefish, grayling, sticklebacks, suckers, and sculpin in the far north, or cisco, smelt, and alewives elsewhere.

Angling. In spring, when lake waters are cold, trout are found near the surface and along the shoreline. As the season progresses, lakers go deeper; in waters where the surface temperatures warm considerably, they eventually reside beneath the thermocline.

Some early cold-water lake trout fishing is done by casting from shore with spoons, spinners, plugs, and flies, especially along rocky shorelines and around tributaries. Most anglers then and throughout the season fish from a boat, occasionally by casting and jigging, but primarily by trolling. In the winter, ice anglers use jigs, live baits, and dead cut baits.

In most large waters, lakers are predominantly caught by anglers trolling slowly with flashy spoons and diving plugs. Jigging for lake trout is possible, as is casting with spoons, spinners, and flies in northerly locales.

Cutthroat Trout, Apache Trout, Gila Trout, and Golden Trout

Cutthroat Trout

Oncorhynchus clarki

The term "cutthroat throat" and its scientific designation *O. clarki*—the species name in honor of

Captain Clark of the Lewis and Clark expedition— is more like a name for a family tree than for a single species of fish. According to some scientific estimates, there are fourteen subspecies, hybrids, and variations, forming what has been called an ichthyological jigsaw puzzle of fish that are endemic to western North America. All of these are members of the Salmonidae family of salmon, trout, whitefish, and grayling.

Of the fourteen species, all but one inhabit only freshwater rivers, lakes, and streams; the exception is the coastal cutthroat trout (*O. clarki clarki*), which has both freshwater and anadromous forms; some fish migrate to sea, whereas others stay in freshwater. The coastal cutthroat is fairly well distributed and available to anglers, and is one of the more prominent cutthroat species, in addition to the West Slope (intermountain) cutthroat (*O. clarki lewisi*), the Yellowstone cutthroat (*O. clarki bouvieri*), and the Lahontan cutthroat (*O. clarki henshawi*). Others species include the Bonneville cutthroat, blackspotted cutthroat, greenback cutthroat, and Rio Grande cutthroat.

Cutthroats are popular with anglers and are generally not as selective as other trout species. They are not as acrobatic as rainbow trout but they are strong fighters. Their flesh, which can range from white to red, has an excellent flavor. They hybridize freely in nature with rainbow trout (which are called cutbows), golden trout, and other close relatives.

ID. This is a highly variable fish in coloration and size. The characteristic that gives the inland cutthroat its name is the yellow, orange, or red streak or slash mark in the skin fold on each side under the lower jaw. The color of the body ranges from cadmium blue and silvery (sea-run) to olive green or yellowish green. There may be red on the sides of the head, the front part of the body, and the belly. In some specimens there may be a narrow pink streak along the sides, but not as broad as in the rainbow trout. The body is covered with black spots, which extend onto the dorsal, adipose, and tail fins. Some are literally covered with spots, whereas in others the spots are sparse and larger, being more numerous on the posterior part of the body. On the tail, the spots radiate evenly outward. The tail of the cutthroat is slightly forked, and all the fins are soft-rayed.

Coastal cutthroat coloration also varies with habitat and life history. Resident fish living in

Cutthroat Trout

bog ponds are typically from 6 to 16 inches long; are golden yellow with dark spots on the body, dorsal, and caudal fin; and have a vivid red slash mark under the jaw. Free-swimming residents in large landlocked lakes can exceed 24 inches. They are uniformly silver with black spots and have rosy gill covers and a faint slash mark. Sea-run cutthroat are smaller, seldom more than 18 inches long. They are bluish silver with dark or olive backs and less conspicuous black spots; the characteristic slash is a faint yellow.

Habitat. Inland cutthroat and resident (nonanadromous) coastal cutthroat live in a wide variety of cold-water habitats, from small headwater tributaries, mountain streams, and bog ponds to large lakes and rivers. During their spawning migration, sea-run cutthroat are usually found in river or stream systems with accessible lakes; otherwise, they stay in saltwater near shore and their natal tributaries. In some watersheds, both anadromous and resident coastal cutthroats occur together.

Food. Inland cutthroats mostly consume insects and small fish. Coastal cutthroats eat various small fish, shrimp, sandworms, and squid.

Angling. Angling techniques vary with the stream, river, pond, or lake environment, and are similar to those used in fishing for other trout. Cutthroats are aggressive fish, and a wide variety of flies, spoons, spinners, and other lures can be effective.

Sea-run coastal cutthroat can be taken in freshwater in the spring, or during the fall when they enter freshwater to overwinter. They are often caught by anglers fishing for steelhead. They stay close to the bottom of deep pools or sloughs, and must be fished close to the bottom. During their migrations, they are caught in their home stream estuaries or bays and salt chucks in the vicinity.

Resident coastal cutthroats can be caught with spinners, spoons, flies, and baits fished deep in pools or along lake shorelines, especially where submerged debris is abundant. Dry or wet flies fished off inlet streams work well. A Muddler Minnow on a fast-sinking line fished along shores with submerged cover is often the best bet. Large trophy-class coastal cutthroat are best caught by trolling hardware or baits off steep shorelines of landlocked lakes.

Apache Trout

Oncorhynchus apache

The Apache trout is Arizona's state fish and was once so abundant that early pioneers caught and salted large numbers of them as a winter meat source. This member of the Salmonidae family is currently considered threatened, although recovery efforts have helped to provide healthy, self-sustaining populations.

ID. The Apache trout is a striking fish, with yellow to golden sides, an adipose fin, and a large dark spot behind the eye. The head, dorsum, sides, and fins have evenly spaced dark spots, and the dorsal, pelvic, and anal fins are white-tipped. The underside of the head is orange to yellowish orange, with a complete lateral line of 112 to 124 scales.

Habitat. Apache trout inhabit clear, cool mountain headwaters of streams and creeks above 7,500 feet and mountain lakes. They are dependent on pool development, shade-giving streamside vegetation, and undercut banks for cover, and are capable of tolerating a range of temperatures.

Food. As with other trout that live in flowing water, Apache trout eat both aquatic and terrestrial insects such as mayflies, caddisflies, and grasshoppers.

Angling. Fishing tactics are similar to those for other stream- and small lake–dwelling trout, as noted in the angling section for golden trout.

Gila Trout

Gila Trout

Oncorhynchus gilae

Along with the Apache trout, the Gila is one of two native trout in Arizona, both severely threatened. Because of interbreeding with rainbow trout and a similarity in appearance to cutthroat trout, it wasn't identified as a separate species until 1950.

ID. A member of the Salmonidae family, the Gila trout is an olive yellow to brassy fish with small irregular black spots across its upper body, head, and dorsal and caudal fins. These markings protect the fish from predators by helping them blend into their environment. There is an indistinct rose stripe along the side, as well as a yellow "cutthroat" mark under the lower jaw and white or yellow tips on the dorsal, anal, and pelvic fins.

Habitat. Growing to 18 inches, the Gila trout was originally found in tributaries of the Verde River in Arizona and still lives in small numbers in the headwaters of the Gila River in New Mexico. It prefers clear, cool mountain creeks above 2,000 meters in elevation and feeds on both aquatic and terrestrial invertebrates.

Angling. Fishing tactics are similar to those for other stream-dwelling trout, as noted in the angling section for golden trout.

Golden Trout

Oncorhynchus aguabonita

California's state fish, the golden trout is classified as two recognizable subspecies, *O. aguabonita aguabonita* of California's South Fork of the Kern River and Golden Trout Creek, and *O. aguabonita gilberti* of the main Kern and Little Kern rivers; an area of warm water where the South Fork joins the Kern apparently serves as a natural barrier separating the two subspecies. This attractive

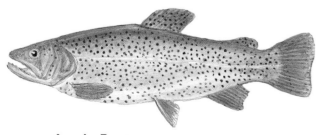

Apache Trout

member of the Salmonidae family is highly desirable to anglers; its pinkish flesh is somewhat oily in comparison to that of other trout, but it is firm, finely textured, and delicious, especially when fresh or smoked.

ID. The golden trout is considered one of the most beautiful of freshwater gamefish because of its striking coloration and markings; it has a bright red to red orange belly and cheeks, with golden lower sides, a red orange lateral streak, and a deep olive green back. The sides have ten parr marks centered on the lateral line, and the golden trout is the only salmonid in which these marks remain prominent throughout life. The tail is a brilliant golden yellow and is covered with large black spots that are also scattered across the back and upper sides as well as on the dorsal fins; the front part of the body may have spots above the lateral line on the back and top of the head, but not always. The lower fins are orange to red with no spots, and the dorsal, ventral, and anal fins often have white tips that are sometimes preceded by a broad black band. The golden trout loses its brilliant colors and becomes steely blue when at lower altitudes than its normal habitat.

Habitat. Golden trout inhabit clear, cool headwaters, creeks, and lakes at elevations above 6,890 feet.

Food. Golden trout feed primarily on small crustaceans and adult and immature insects, especially caddisflies and midges.

Angling. Fishing tactics are similar to those for other trout, and vary according to the environment. These and other trout are often found in some similar locations, such as pockets behind rocks; fishing the so-called pocket water is a standard river fishing ploy, especially in low water and where smaller fish exist. Other such places include the slick water downstream from an eddy

Golden Trout

or pool; dark, swift water just above a falls or rapids drop; the sanctuary beneath a falls; and spring holes.

Flies must be selected according to the type of minnow or aquatic insect prevalent at the time. Small spinners, small spoons, occasionally a light jig, and sometimes minnow-imitation plugs, as well as live worms and salmon eggs where bait-fishing is legal, are prevalent in flowing waters as well as in ponds.

Rainbow Trout and Steelhead

Rainbow Trout

Oncorhynchus mykiss

The rainbow trout is one of the most widely distributed freshwater fish, and occurs in both freshwater resident and anadromous, or sea-run, races. Seagoing rainbows, known as steelhead or steelhead trout, are discussed separately. One landlocked variety of rainbow trout from the interior of British Columbia is called the Kamloops trout, and there are many other variations (as well as hatchery-created hybrids) of rainbows known.

The flesh ranges from bright red in small lake and stream populations to pink or white in large lake and river populations in which the diet is largely piscivorous, and it has an excellent flavor.

ID. Rainbow trout possess the typical elongated and streamlined salmonid form. The back may shade from blue-green to olive. There is a reddish pink band along each side about the midline that may range from faint to radiant. The lower sides are usually silver, fading to pure white beneath.

Small black spots are present over the back above the lateral line, as well as on the upper fins and tail. In some locations, the black spots of adults may extend well below the lateral line and even cover the entire lower side. These spots may cover the entire body or may be more abundant near the tail. The spots characteristically extend onto the dorsal, adipose, and tail fins. Those on the tail radiate outward in an even, orderly pattern. Spots may be present on any of the lower fins. Rainbow trout are positively identified by the eight to twelve rays in the anal fin, a mouth that

Rainbow Trout

does not extend past the back of the eye, and the lack of teeth at the base of the tongue.

The rainbow trout's coloration varies greatly with size, habitat, and spawning periods. Stream dwellers and spawners usually show the darkest and most vivid colors and markings. River or stream residents normally display the most intense pink stripe coloration and heaviest spotting, followed by rainbows from lake and lake-stream systems. By contrast, the steelhead is silvery and may not have a pink stripe along the middle of its sides.

The absence of orange-red slash marks on the underside of the jaw, and the lack of teeth near the base of the tongue, are good keys for distinguishing rainbows from inland or nonanadromous cutthroat trout.

Habitat. Although rainbows do well in large lakes with cool, deep waters, they prefer moderately flowing streams with abundant cover and deep pools. In most streams they are found in stretches of swift-flowing water, at the edge of strong currents, and at the head of rapids or strong riffles. They prefer water temperatures of 55° to 64°F but can tolerate water to 70°F.

Food. Rainbows feed on a variety of food, mainly insects, crustaceans, snails, leeches, and other fish if available. Some studies have shown that they feed less often on the surface than brown trout.

Angling. One of the top freshwater sportfish, the rainbow is tolerant of moderate temperatures, which has allowed it to become available to many anglers around the world.

The beauty, strength, endurance, and spectacular leaps of the rainbow trout and all of its variations and strains have endeared it to anglers in streams, rivers, and lakes. It takes lures, flies, and baits well, leaps often, and fights hard no matter what its size, although larger individuals are especially exciting.

In rivers that also contain salmon runs, rainbow fishing success is typically greatest in the spring and fall before and after the large salmon runs. Angling methods differ depending on whether the fish are found in rivers or lakes, and are similar to fishing for other trout species. Weighted spinners, wobbling spoons, streamer flies, Muddler Minnows, and egg-imitation flies fished near the bottom are especially preferred in river and stream habitats.

Steelhead

Oncorhynchus mykiss

The term "steelhead" refers to the anadromous form of rainbow trout, and the fish known as steelhead bears the same scientific name as rainbow trout. Most scientific evaluations of rainbow trout list the steelhead as a form of rainbow trout. There are no major physical differences between the two, although the nature of their lifestyles results in subtle variances of shape and general appearance and a greater difference in color. Technically, the steelhead is a rainbow trout that migrates to sea as a juvenile and returns to freshwater as an adult to spawn, a process known as anadromy. Pacific salmon do this, too, although steelhead and rainbow trout are positively separated from the various Pacific salmon species by the presence of eight to twelve rays in the anal fin. Unlike Pacific salmon, the steelhead/rainbow trout does not always die following spawning, may spawn more than once, and returns to the sea after each spawning.

No matter what it is called or where it is found, the steelhead is one of the most coveted fish for anglers, both in freshwater lakes and in rivers or streams. It is frequently acrobatic, grows to large and challenging sizes, and is a strong battler. Some anglers consider it the best of all freshwater sportfish, and most would rank it among the top three or five. Its flesh is bright orange or red, and it makes excellent table fare.

ID. Steelhead are generally more slender and streamlined than rainbow trout. As with rainbow trout, the coloration on the back is basically a blue-green shading to olive, with black, regularly spaced spots. These spots also cover both lobes of the tail. The black coloration fades over the lateral line to a silver-white coloration that blends more toward white on the stomach. Steelhead fresh from the ocean or an inland lake are much more silvery than the resident rainbow. On steelhead, the typical colors and spots of the trout appear to be coming from beneath a dominant silvery sheen. This sheen gradually fades when the fish are in rivers, and steelhead become difficult to differentiate from resident rainbow trout as the spawning period approaches.

Steelhead lack the red slash on the underjaw characteristic of cutthroat trout, but they do have white leading edges on the anal, pectoral, and pelvic fins. Spawning steelhead develop a distinct pink to red stripelike coloration that blends along the side, both above and below the lateral line.

Habitat. As anadromous fish, steelhead live a good portion of their lives in saltwater and spawn in freshwater. Steelhead have been successfully transplanted to inland environments, especially the Great Lakes; there they live their entire lives in freshwater, residing in the lake but migrating up tributaries to spawn (which they accomplish more successfully than other introduced trout or salmon). Thus steelhead may exist both in coastal environments and in large inland lake-river systems.

Food. Steelhead in the ocean consume squid, crustaceans, and small fish. In large lakes, they primarily consume pelagic baitfish such as alewives and smelt. When making spawning runs in rivers and streams, they do not feed.

Angling. Steelhead in the ocean are seldom deliberately pursued by anglers; most of those taken are caught incidental to salmon fishing efforts, and are spawning or post-spawning migrants. There is a significant fishery for lake-dwelling steelhead in the Great Lakes, which are caught in a manner similar to salmon and brown trout, primarily by trolling.

Steelhead

Spawning-run steelhead in rivers and streams are eagerly pursued throughout winter and spring by anglers using flies, spinners, spoons, diving plugs, and natural baits, especially salmon or trout roe and crayfish tails. Steelhead like deep, fast-running water, often gathering in deep holes, in fast whitewater areas, and behind rocks and logjams. Angling techniques in general are similar to those for chinook salmon.

Brown Trout and Atlantic Salmon

Brown Trout

Salmo trutta

One of the most adaptable members of the Salmonidae family, the brown trout is a favorite of stream and river anglers. It is the backbone of natural and hatchery-maintained trout fisheries and takes on many forms—river, lake, and sea-run—in diverse environments. Although the brown trout is a true trout, its closest relative and a member of the same genus is the Atlantic salmon. It is a challenge to anglers, a strong fighter occasionally prone to jumping when hooked, and a fish that can be caught using varied tackle and techniques. The flesh of the brown trout is good, although not as esteemed as that of Atlantic salmon.

ID. Brown trout get their common name from the typical olive green, brown, or golden brown hue of their body. The belly is white or yellowish, and dark spots, sometimes encircled by a pale halo, are plentiful on the back and sides. Spotting also can be found on the head and the fins along the back, and rusty red spots also occur on the sides. There is a small adipose fin, sometimes with a reddish hue, ahead of the tail. Sea-run brown trout have a more silvery coloration, and spotting is less visible. Residents of large lake systems have a silvery coloration, dark spots without halos, and no colored spots.

Although both brown trout and Atlantic salmon often occur in the same areas, they can usually be distinguished without laboratory analysis, although lake-dwelling specimens of both are much harder to distinguish. In freshwater as a rule, brown trout are more heavily spotted than Atlantic salmon, and usually a good number of these spots are surrounded by lighter halos. The spots on the Atlantic

Brown Trout

salmon have no halos and usually some take the shape of Xs or Ys, which is not usually the case in the brown trout. The brown trout also has dark spots on the dorsal and adipose fins and vague or no spots on the tail, although nothing like the prominent radiating spots on the tail of the rainbow trout. The Atlantic salmon has no clear spots on any of these fins. Also, the brown trout's tail is squarish or very slightly concave or convex, whereas the Atlantic salmon's tail is slightly forked or indented.

Brown trout sometimes hybridize with brook trout in the wild, and are also manipulated in hatcheries; the pairing of a brown trout female and brook trout male produces a deeply vermiculated fish called a tiger trout.

Habitat. Brown trout prefer cool, clear rivers and lakes with temperatures of 54° to 65°F. They can survive and thrive in 65° to 75°F conditions, which are warmer than most other trout can tolerate, but in streams they do best where the summer temperature is less than 68°F. In streams and rivers, they are wary and elusive fish that look for

cover more than any other salmonid, hiding in undercut banks, stream debris, surface turbulence, rocks, and deep pools. They also take shelter under overhanging vegetation.

Food. Brown trout are carnivores and consume aquatic and terrestrial insects, worms, crustaceans, mollusks, fish, salamanders, and even tadpoles or frogs. In small streams their diet may be largely insects; but in larger flows or where there is plenty of baitfish, it also includes assorted small fish. In large lakes, the primary diet is other fish, especially abundant pelagic schooling species such as alewives; small fish are a primary food for sea trout.

Angling. In flowing water, brown trout tend to lie in slower and warmer waters than brookies and cutthroats, yet they will all inhabit pools and slicks in rapid-flowing waters. Here they primarily feed on various stages of aquatic insects but also on small minnows. They are likely to be found in pockets behind rocks, especially in low water and where smaller fish exist. Other hideouts include the slick water downstream from an eddy or pool; dark, swift water just above a falls or rapids drop; the sanctuary beneath a falls; and spring holes.

Spring and summer insect hatches particularly attract river browns. In the spring these hatches may occur during the day, but later in the season they may be most evident around sundown and last long into the night. Browns will feed on meatier forage in the night as well. Small fish are often preyed upon in a long, shallow gravel flat above a deep pool.

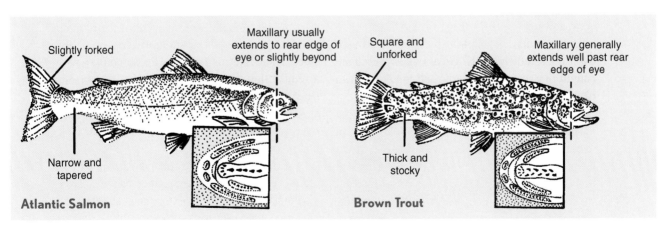

The most obvious differences between adult Atlantic salmon and brown trout are apparent in the head and tail areas. The vomerine teeth, which are inside the upper jaw, are depicted in the insets. On the salmon, these teeth are small and extremely sparse and appear in a straight row on the shaft; on the brown trout, they are well developed and form a zigzag on the shaft.

Fly fishing with assorted types and patterns of flies is productive seasonally, as is using small spinners, small spoons, occasionally a light jig, and sometimes minnow-imitation plugs, as well as live worms.

In lakes, browns move a lot, primarily in search of food. They roam shallow areas early in the season, but as lakes get warmer, they seek preferred temperature zones. An ideal situation in large lakes is to find a place where temperature, forage, and shore structure coincide.

Fishing for trout in lakes is like blind prospecting. To have regular success means covering a lot of water. Trolling, casting from shore or from a float tube, or drifting with baits are all productive angling methods. Trolling is often most popular because anglers can cover a large area in search of active, aggressive fish.

Atlantic Salmon

Salmo salar

The only salmon in the Salmonidae family that occurs in the Atlantic Ocean and its tributaries, the Atlantic salmon has been coveted for its excellent flesh since recorded history. Likewise, anglers since before Izaak Walton's time have known it for its acrobatics when caught, which gave rise to its name *salar*, derived from the Latin word *salio*, meaning "leaper."

The Atlantic salmon has both anadromous and freshwater forms. The former migrate from freshwater streams to the ocean and then return to those streams to spawn, whereas the latter remain in freshwater all their lives. Called landlocked salmon or ouananiche in North America, the freshwater form is the same species as the anadromous Atlantic salmon and shares identical characteristics, except that the freshwater fish is smaller.

As a gamefish, the Atlantic salmon is showy when it leaps out of the water, capable of making strong runs up and down swift-flowing rivers when hooked, and often a challenge to entice. Landlocked fish are known for long runs and superior fighting ability, and are widely sought in lakes and rivers. The reddish orange flesh of both, but especially of the sea-run fish, is excellent to eat and is highly valued.

ID. Compared to the size of its body, a mature Atlantic salmon has a small head. Its body is long and slim, and in adults the caudal or tail fin is nearly square. Individuals that return to spawn prematurely (called grilse) are mostly males and have a slightly forked tail. While in the sea, the Atlantic salmon is dark blue on the top of its head and back; its sides are a shiny silver, and the belly is white. The fins are dark, and there are numerous black marks in the shape of an X or Y on its head and along its body above the lateral line.

When the fish enters freshwater to spawn, it gradually loses its metallic shine and becomes dull brown or yellowish. Many, particularly males, are splotched with red or have large black patches on the body, and may look a lot like the brown trout. At spawning time the males have greatly elongated hooked jaws that meet only at the tips; the fins become thicker, and a heavy coat of slime covers the body. Post-spawn fish appear very dark, leading to the name "black salmon."

The body shape of an Atlantic salmon is generally similar to that of a trout and is distinguished from salmon and trout of the genus *Oncorhynchus* by coloration, size, and location of occurrence, among other characteristics. Landlocked Atlantics look the same as their anadromous counterparts, although spawning fish may be darker.

Habitat. Anadromous Atlantic salmon spend most of their lives in the ocean, ascending coastal rivers to spawn. In coastal rivers, they primarily inhabit deep runs and pools, and seldom favor fast water or riffles.

Although some landlocked salmon may exist in rivers all year, the great majority spend most of their lives in the open water of lakes, ascending tributaries to spawn. In rivers, they inhabit deep runs and pools. In lakes they stay in cooler, deeper levels, where baitfish are abundant.

Food. In the ocean, salmon grow rapidly, feeding on crustaceans and other fish such as smelt, alewives, herring, capelin, mackerel, and cod. Landlocked salmon in lakes eat pelagic freshwater

Atlantic Salmon

fish, primarily smelt and alewives. Neither feeds during its upstream spawning migration.

Angling. Atlantic and landlocked salmon hug the river bottom, resting in pools and deep-water sections. They are not usually caught in the fast-water reaches, although they will frequent the head and tail of pools, as well as slick-water runs. A common tactic is to start fishing above the head of a pool or run, methodically working down through a stretch, casting down and across and letting the fly swing at the end of each cast. Most fish are caught when the fly makes its swing or hangs momentarily in the current at the end of the swing.

Fly fishing is the angling method by law or tradition in most of North America for seagoing Atlantic salmon. Some waters have restrictions on weighted hooks or flies to minimize accidental or deliberate foul hooking of fish.

Wet flies in various colorful patterns and sizes are popular for Atlantic salmon fishing, and the larger flies are generally reserved for fast, high rivers. Dry flies work at times, too, but their success is an anomaly considering the nonfeeding disposition of these fish; the dries used, however, are large flies typically tied with tightly packed deer hair.

The principal method of pursuing landlocked salmon in lakes is trolling. Most activity occurs in the spring, after icemelt and until these fish move deep. Landlocks are likely to be found near tributaries if they attract large spawning runs of smelt, or inshore where schools of smelt or spawning alewives may be located. As the water warms, they move to deeper water and locate in the thermocline, roaming as widely as the size of the lake and water temperature zones will allow.

Pacific Salmon

The term "Pacific salmon" describes certain members of the genus *Oncorhynchus* that are members of the Salmonidae family. That family includes one salmon of Atlantic origin and seven of Pacific origin, five of which occur in North America. These five Pacific salmon—chinook, coho, sockeye, pink, and chum—are anadromous, and some have become accidentally or deliberately landlocked, living and reproducing successfully entirely in freshwater without ever making a journey to saltwater.

Pacific salmon spawn in gravel beds in rivers and streams, and sometimes along a lakeshore. Their progeny have a relatively short freshwater existence and migrate out to the sea, or to large lakes in the case of those living entirely in freshwater. When mature, these five salmon species usually return to the waters of their birth to reproduce, after which they all die.

Virtually all angling attention focuses on chinook and coho salmon, especially in North America. Most sportfishing occurs in rivers and streams when these species are undergoing their spawning migrations, and a fair amount takes place in saltwater, predominantly in bays, estuaries, and inshore waters near the coast. In these waters, anglers target fish that are migrating to their natal tributaries, or those that are gathered nearby awaiting the run. In freshwater lakes, these salmon are pursued in open water as well as in tributaries when they are on the spawning migration.

Chinook Salmon

Oncorhynchus tshawytscha

The chinook salmon is the largest member of the Salmonidae family, and both the largest and least abundant member of the Pacific salmon genus *Oncorhynchus*. It can adapt to an entirely freshwater existence and has done so with such remarkable success in the Great Lakes that it has formed the backbone of an enormous and extremely valuable sportfishery there.

As a gamefish, the chinook is not flashy; it rarely leaps out of the water, but it is bulldog strong and has great staying power. The sea-run chinook is the only Pacific salmon in which the meat can be regularly either red or white, and it has an excellent taste.

ID. The body of the chinook salmon is elongate and somewhat compressed. The head is conical. For most of its life, the chinook's color is bluish to dark gray above, becoming silvery on the sides and belly. There are black spots on the back, upper sides, top of the head, and all the fins, including both the top and bottom halves of the tail fin. Coloration changes during upstream migration; spawning chinook range from red to copper to olive brown to almost black, depending on location and degree of maturation, and they undergo a radical metamorphosis. Males are more deeply colored than females and are distinguished by their "ridgeback" condition and by their hooked nose or upper jaw, known as a kype. One distinguishing feature of the chinook is its black mouth and gums. The smaller but very similar-looking coho salmon has a black mouth but white gums, except in the Great Lakes population, in which the gums may be gray or black.

Habitat. Chinook salmon hatch in freshwater rivers, spend part of their life in the ocean, and then spawn in freshwater. Those chinook that have been transplanted to strictly freshwater environments hatch in tributary rivers and streams, spend part of their life in the open water of the lake, and then return to tributaries to spawn. In flowing water, salmon hug the bottom, resting in pools and deep-water sections. They gather in the tail of a run, ahead of swifter water, and in holes and runs along deep-water banks.

Food. Juvenile chinook in freshwater feed on plankton, then later eat insects. In the ocean, they eat a variety of organisms, including herring, pilchards, sand lance, squid, and crustaceans. Likewise, chinook that live entirely in freshwater feed on plankton and insects as juveniles, and pelagic freshwater baitfish in the lakes. Alewives and smelt are the primary food items.

Angling (for chinook and coho). Because coho and chinook salmon inhabit a variety of environments, anglers practice multiple fishing methods to pursue them. Identifying habitat, structure, and so forth, as one might do for many other fish, is less critical when targeting Pacific salmon than when enticing nonfeeding river fish to strike through careful presentation or locating the right

depth and temperature of open water in which salmon schools will be located.

The coastal fishery for sea-run salmon in Pacific waters primarily occurs in nearshore, tidewater, and estuary environs. The favored angling methods are trolling with spinners and cut herring, trolling with flies (mostly for coho), mooching, some jigging, and some live-bait fishing. The most opportune time to pursue these fish is when they have returned from their sea wandering and are gathering in the vicinity of coastal rivers, waiting for rains to send new water out the rivers and signal the beginning of the "run."

In saltwater, anglers principally troll dead baits or artificial lures. Occasionally they offer live baits or use metal jigs while stillfishing or drifting. Chinook salmon normally stay well beneath the ocean's surface, making a heavy weight or downrigger necessary to maintain a trolled bait at the desired depth. Chinook favor depths between 40 and 250 or more feet, depending on location, temperature, currents, and other factors. Channels, passes, and straits that funnel current are popular sites, particularly along current seams and where a back eddy exists. Steep, rocky shores that are well washed by current and tidal movement are prime spots; here, anglers offer a cut herring, fished very close to the bottom. Fishing in low light, especially at sunset and at dusk, is often more productive than during bright midday light, especially for chinook.

Surface trolling with light tackle for coho salmon is possible when the fish are congregated on or near shoals where food is abundant. Streamer flies are the main offering, trolled fairly fast over kelp beds so that the fly skips over the water.

Coho and chinook in the Great Lakes are widely pursued throughout the season in open water. They are inshore early in the season and ultimately seek out a water temperature of between 48° and 55°F, which occurs at the thermocline. Both gather in schools and traverse great distances as they seek out desirable water conditions and alewives or smelt forage. Various trolling techniques are the primary focus, and among them downrigger fishing is most popular. Some drift fishing and limited jigging are also done.

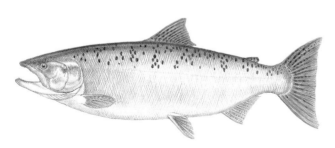

Chinook Salmon (sea-run phase)

Fishing in natal rivers is the predominant method of catching chinook and coho salmon in late summer and fall. Salmon in coastal rivers or lake tributaries do not feed, so imitating a natural food source in appearance or action is unnecessary. Getting the attention of a fish that will aggressively swipe at your offering is the whole game. To do this it is usually vital to make a precise presentation, positioning the bait or lure on the bottom and directly ahead of the fish.

Long rods, medium-heavy lines, and small offerings are the main outfits for coho and chinook fishing in small to medium streams. Eggs, spinners, spoons, flies, and wobbling plugs, often in bright colors, are the main attractions.

Coho Salmon

Oncorhynchus kisutch

The coho salmon is an extremely adaptable fish that occurs in nearly all of the same waters as the larger chinook salmon, but it is a more spectacular fighter and the most acrobatic of the Pacific salmon. Cohos are smaller on average than chinook salmon, and in many places less abundant. But the coho is a much more suitable light-tackle quarry than the chinook, although it is caught with most of the same tackle and methods. Unlike the chinook, it is a streaky, near-surface, and aerial battler rather than a deep and dogged fighter, although it too has great stamina. The coho's flesh is red and of excellent quality.

ID. The body of the coho salmon is elongate and somewhat compressed, and the head is conical. For most of its life (in saltwater or lake as well as newly arrived in a spawning river), this species is a dark metallic blue or blue-green above, becoming silvery on the sides and belly. There are small black spots on the back and on the upper lobe of the caudal fin. Cohos can be distinguished from chinook salmon by the lack of black spots on the lower lobe of the tail, and the white or gray gums at the base of the teeth.

Spawning adults of both sexes have dark backs and heads, and maroon to reddish sides. The males turn dusky green above and on their head, bright red on their sides, and blackish below. The females turn a pinkish red on their sides. The males develop a prominent double-hooked snout,

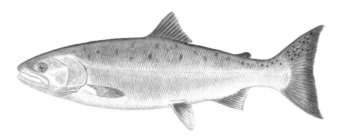

Coho Salmon (Sea-Run Phase)

called a kype, with large teeth, which makes closing the mouth impossible.

Habitat. Ocean, coastal, and freshwater habitats for coho salmon are similar to those of chinook salmon.

Food. Coho food is similar to that of chinook salmon.

Angling. Angling methods and locations are similar to those of chinook salmon. Coho are at times an incidental catch when chinook are the focus; most likely, however, fishing efforts target either or both species. The timing of availability may be different, especially in coastal rivers and in nearshore coastal waters. In addition, coho salmon are likely to remain shallower in open water than chinook. Sometimes coho hold on or close to the surface, which is not a likelihood for chinook. Fishing methods are detailed under the listing for chinook salmon.

Pink Salmon

Oncorhynchus gorbuscha

An important commercial catch, the pink salmon is the smallest North American member of the Pacific salmon group. It has some sportfishing value in Alaskan rivers, less so than coho or chinook salmon, but little elsewhere. The flesh is pinkish, rather than red or white, and is of most value when the fish is still an open-water inhabitant, as it deteriorates rapidly once the fish enters rivers.

ID. The pink salmon is known as the "humpback" or "humpy" because of its distorted, extremely humpbacked appearance, which is caused by the very pronounced laterally flattened hump that develops on the backs of adult males before spawning. This hump appears between the head and the dorsal fin and develops by the time

Pink Salmon (Sea-Run Phase)

the male enters the spawning stream, as does a hooked upper jaw, or kype.

At sea, the pink salmon is silvery in color, with a bright metallic blue above; there are many black, elongated, oval spots on the entire tail fin, and large spots on the back and the adipose fin. When the pink salmon moves to spawning streams, the bright appearance of the male changes to pale red or "pink" on the sides, with brown to olive green blotches; females become olive green above with dusky bars or patches, and pale below.

Habitat. Ocean, coastal, and freshwater habitats for coho salmon are similar to those of chinook and coho salmon. Pink salmon spend eighteen months at sea and then undertake a spawning migration to the river or stream of their birth, although they sometimes use other streams.

Food. At sea, pink salmon feed primarily on plankton, as well as on crustaceans, small fish, and squid. They do not feed during the spawning run.

Angling. In open waters, pink salmon are caught by anglers trolling for other Pacific salmon, although generally smaller lures and flies are necessary to attract this species. They become a deliberate open-water target when either coho or chinook are unavailable. They may be fairly abundant off river mouths for several weeks prior to spawning. In rivers, they are readily caught on small spinners, small spoons, and flies, and on the spinning and fly tackle used for trout.

Sockeye Salmon

Oncorhynchus nerka

The sockeye is like some other members of the Pacific salmon group in having both anadromous and freshwater forms. The former migrate from freshwater streams to the ocean and then return to those streams to spawn, whereas the latter,

called kokanee, remain in freshwater all their lives. Kokanee can be fine gamefish and excellent food fish; sockeye salmon are predominantly prized more for their food value than for sport, however, as the upstream migrants are not aggressive at taking baits or lures.

The flesh of the sockeye is deep red and high in oil content, making it the most commercially valuable of all the Pacific salmon. The meat is especially delicious when smoked, excellent for canning due to the rich orange-red color, and also marketed fresh, dried/salted, and frozen.

ID. The sockeye is the slimmest and most streamlined of Pacific salmon, particularly immature and prespawning fish, which are elongate and somewhat laterally compressed. They are metallic green-blue on the back and top of the head, iridescent silver on the sides, and white or silvery on the belly. Some fine black speckling may occur on the back, but large spots are absent.

Breeding males develop a humped back and elongated, hooked jaws filled with sharp, enlarged teeth. Both sexes turn brilliant to dark red on the back and sides, pale to olive green on the head and upper jaw, and white on the lower jaw. The totally red body distinguishes the sockeye from the otherwise similar chum salmon, and the lack of large, distinct spots distinguishes it from the remaining three Pacific salmon of North America. The number and shape of gill rakers on the first gill arch further distinguish the sockeye from the chum salmon; sockeye salmon have twenty-eight to forty long, slender, rough or serrated closely set rakers on the first arch, whereas chum salmon have nineteen to twenty-six short, stout, smooth rakers.

Kokanee are smaller but otherwise identical to sea-run sockeye in coloration; they undergo the same changes as sockeye when spawning.

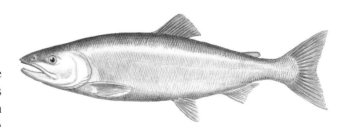

Sockeye Salmon (Sea-Run Phase)

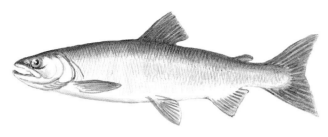

Kokanee Salmon

Habitat. After living at sea for up to four years, sockeye salmon migrate up natal tributaries, most of which have lakes at their source. Kokanee occur almost exclusively in freshwater lakes, migrating to tributaries in the fall to spawn (or to outlet areas or shoreline gravel in waters without suitable spawning streams).

Food. In the ocean, sockeye salmon feed on plankton, crustacean larvae, larval and small adult fish, and occasionally squid. Kokanee feed mainly on plankton but also on insects and bottom organisms.

Angling. Sockeye are strong, and leap out of the water, but are less aggressive than coho or chinook salmon. Small hooks baited with eggs or a piece of worm, small flies, and small spoons or spinners will catch them in rivers; deep presentations that place the offering directly in front of the fish are necessary.

The same items work for river kokanee, and in lakes the best approach is deep trolling, using tactics not unlike those for other trout and salmon species, although with offerings that are on the small side. Some fly fishing opportunities exist when the fish are shallow in early-season cold water, and ice fishing is generally productive, using small ice jigs and small natural baits.

Once the surface water has warmed, kokanee move into deeper, cooler (roughly 50°F) water. They cluster in a small deep band or, in lakes with entirely warm water, on or near the bottom where there are springs or in old channels where it is as cool as possible. Very small spoons, spinners, and occasionally plugs are used, often tipped with a piece of natural bait. Small cowbell attractors are especially popular with many deep trollers. Sometimes a piece of nightcrawler or other bait is fished without a lure, directly behind the attractor.

Chum Salmon

Oncorhynchus keta

The late spawning run of the chum salmon severely affects its popularity as a sportfish. In general, it is caught by anglers fishing for other Pacific salmon. It is an adequate catch on rod and reel, but lacks the stamina and runs of the chinook and the flash of the coho. In Arctic, northwestern, and interior Alaska, this member of the Salmonidae family is an important year-round source of fresh and dried fish for subsistence and personal use, although elsewhere its flesh is not favored. The meat is creamy white or pinkish to yellowish and the lowest of all salmon in fat content.

ID. In the ocean, the slender, somewhat compressed chum salmon is metallic greenish blue on the back, silvery on the sides, and has a fine black speckling on the upper sides and back but no distinct black spots. Spawning males turn dark olive or grayish; blood-red coloring and vertical bars of green and purple reach up the sides, giving the fish its "calico" appearance. It develops the typical hooked snout of Pacific salmon, and the tips of the anal and pelvic fins are often white. The breeding male develops distinctly large front teeth. The color of spawning females is essentially the same as that of males but is less vivid, with a dark horizontal band along the lateral line.

The chum salmon is difficult to distinguish from the sockeye and the coho, which are of similar size, without examining gills or caudal fin scale patterns; the chum salmon has fewer but larger gill rakers than other salmon. The sockeye salmon also lacks the white marks on the fins, and the chum salmon is generally larger than the sockeye.

Habitat. Ocean, coastal, and freshwater habitats for chum salmon are similar to chinook and coho salmon.

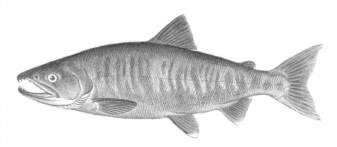

Chum Salmon (spawning phase)

Food. The food of chum salmon is similar to that for chinook and coho salmon.

Angling. Chum salmon are mainly an incidental catch for anglers, both in coastal nearshore saltwaters and in tributaries. They are usually caught using the same methods and lures or bait used for chinook and coho salmon.

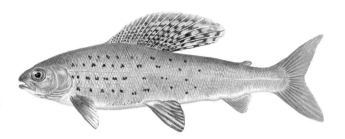

Arctic Grayling

Arctic Grayling and Whitefish

Arctic Grayling

Thymallus arcticus

Grayling belong to the Salmonidae family and are related to trout and whitefish. They are distinctive-looking fish with a sail-like dorsal fin, and a superb sportfish known primarily in the cool- and cold-water northern regions of North America. Their firm, white flesh is good table fare, although it is not on a par with that of the wild trout and charr that inhabit similar ranges.

ID. With their graceful lines, large fin, and dramatic coloration, grayling are striking fish. Most remarkable is their large purple to black dorsal fin, which extends backward and fans out into a trailing lobe, speckled with rows of spots. This fin may look bluish when the fish is in the water. Grayish silver overall, grayling usually have shades or highlights of gold and/or lavender, as well as many dark spots that may be shaped like an X or a V on some fish.

When the Arctic grayling is taken from the water, a resemblance to the whitefish is especially apparent, as the beautiful colors fade to a dull gray. It has a small, narrow mouth with numerous small teeth in both jaws. The Arctic grayling also has a forked caudal fin and relatively large, stiff scales.

Habitat. Grayling prefer the clear, cold, well-oxygenated waters of medium to large rivers and lakes. They are most commonly found in rivers, especially in eddies, and the head of runs and pools; in lakes they prefer river mouths and rocky shorelines. They commonly seek refuge among small rocks on the streambed or lake bottom.

Food. Young grayling initially feed on zooplankton and become mainly insectivorous as adults, although they also eat small fish, fish eggs, and, less often, lemmings and planktonic crustaceans.

Angling. Arctic grayling are routinely found in groups and most commonly observed in flowages while dimpling the water and feeding on surface insects. Dry fly fishing with 5- to 7-weight lines is the preferred method. When not rising freely to insects, grayling may be better pursued with a wet fly or nymph. A floating fly line is best most of the time, but a sink-tip line may be necessary. Grayling can be leader shy, and they pursue flies and often strike at the end of a drift, so attention to detail can be important. Fly size ranges from No. 12 through 18, and the favored offering is skimpy and dark. Exact representations aren't usually critical, but using a black or brown pattern is important.

The grayling is an excellent catch on light or ultralight spinning tackle, too, using 2- through 6-pound-test line. Small spinners and spoons are popular, but the best artificial is a small dark jig. Black or brown marabou or $\frac{1}{16}$- to $\frac{1}{8}$-ounce soft plastic jigs produce especially well in flowing and stillwater.

Although most grayling are caught in the slick water of rivers and streams, and sometimes where it flows quite fast, they are also found in lakes near river inlets, usually along shores studded with small rocks. There, in calm water, they cruise along inhaling surface insects, and are taken on flies, jigs, or spinners.

These are scrappy, feisty fish that jump and fight to the end, but they must be handled gently, as they die quickly when held out of the water or if mishandled. Barbless hooks are especially useful.

Lake Whitefish

Coregonus clupeaformis

The lake whitefish is a larger and more widespread fish than the mountain or the round whitefish, and is more highly regarded among anglers. A member of the Salmonidae family, the lake whitefish is a valuable commercial freshwater fish in Canada, as its flesh is considered superb and its roe is made into an excellent caviar.

ID. A slender, elongated species, the lake whitefish is silvery to white with an olive to pale greenish brown back that is dark brown to midnight blue or black in some inland lake specimens; it also has white fins and a dark-edged tail. The mouth is subterminal and the snout protrudes beyond it, with a double flap of skin between the nostrils. The tail is deeply forked, and an adipose fin is present.

The lake whitefish is occasionally referred to as "humpback" because the head is small in relation to the length of the body, and older specimens may develop a hump behind the head. The body is more laterally compressed than that of the round or mountain whitefish.

Habitat. Lake whitefish are named for their primary habitat of large, deep lakes, but they are also residents of large rivers. They prefer water temperatures of 50° to 55°F and will enter brackish water.

Food. Mainly bottom feeders, adult lake whitefish feed primarily on aquatic insect larvae, mollusks, and amphipods, but also on other small fish and fish eggs, including their own. Young fish feed on plankton.

Angling. Whitefish fight well, occasionally jumping and characteristically making a diving run and shaking near the surface. They are a fine light-tackle fish.

In lakes, whitefish are readily taken when schooled and when rising to flies, but they are often hard to catch otherwise. Although many open-lake anglers catch them accidentally while seeking other game, these fish are successfully pursued through the ice. In rivers, flycasters are routinely successful in landing them; sometimes they are a nuisance rather than a pleasure. They linger in slow pools, beneath waterfalls, and along back-switching bank eddies.

Primarily an insect feeder, whitefish are most likely to be caught on nymphs or dry flies, the latter especially in lakes when these fish rise to the surface in large schools that travel along the shores of a deep-water bay. They rise gently when feeding on floating insects, and often one sees the dorsal fin cutting through the surface momentarily.

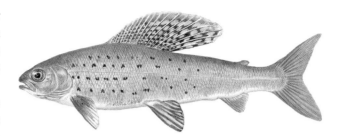

Lake Whitefish

A dry fly presented slightly ahead of the cruising fish will usually be taken. The whitefish has a soft mouth, so a smooth rod-lifting action will set the hook without tearing it away from the fish.

Methods other than fly fishing can be productive, but not reliably so. A whitefish will occasionally strike a spoon or small plug, although a jig is far more likely to be effective. A small dark jig is best; it can be fished plain or tipped with a small insect or grub. Grubs are popular for ice fishing, as are small live or salted minnows and small jigging lures. Chumming is also effective.

Mountain Whitefish

Prosopium williamsoni

Although not as significant a gamefish as the lake whitefish, the mountain whitefish has gained popularity and provides an important winter fishery in certain areas, especially where steelhead are absent. A member of the Salmonidae family, it is a very good table fish, particularly when smoked.

ID. Possessing an adipose fin and an axillary process, the mountain whitefish is long, slender, and nearly cylindrical, although not quite as cylindrical as the round whitefish. It is nevertheless among the species referred to as "round whitefish" and can be distinguished from the lake whitefish, which is more laterally compressed than the mountain whitefish. Silvery overall, it is dark brownish to olive or greenish to blue-gray above, with scales that often have dark borders and ventral and pectoral fins that may have an amber shade in adults. The small mouth is slightly subterminal, and the snout extends clearly beyond it. The caudal fin is forked.

Habitat. Generally inhabiting rivers and fast, clear, or silty areas of larger streams as well as

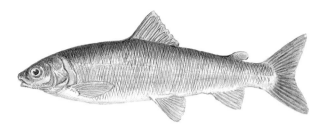

Mountain Whitefish

lakes, mountain whitefish usually occur in stream riffles during the summer and in large pools in the winter. They prefer temperatures of 46° to 52°F and are found in the deep water of some lakes, although in northern lakes they usually hold no deeper than 30 feet.

Food. Mountain whitefish feed primarily on benthic organisms like aquatic insect larvae, mollusks, fish, and fish eggs (including their own), as well as on plankton and surface insects when primary food sources are unavailable.

Angling. Mountain whitefish are underutilized by anglers. Similar to the lake whitefish, they are good fighters and are caught on flies, natural baits, and some artificial lures that they can fit in their small mouths. They bite especially well during the winter months.

Round Whitefish

Prosopium cylindraceum

The round whitefish seldom exceeds 2 pounds and has considerably less commercial value than the lake whitefish, although it is sought to a limited degree by anglers. Its flesh is of good quality.

ID. The round whitefish is mostly silvery and has a dark brown to almost bronze coloring with a greenish tint on the back. It has black-edged scales, particularly on the back. The lower fins are an amber color, becoming slightly more orange

Round Whitefish

during spawning, and the adipose fin is usually brown-spotted.

The round whitefish has a small head and a fairly pointed snout, and a single flap of skin between its nostrils. It also has a forked caudal fin. The round and lake whitefish can be easily distinguished because the round whitefish has a very cylindrical body, whereas the body of the lake whitefish is laterally compressed; the mountain whitefish is almost cylindrical, although slightly more compressed than the round whitefish.

Habitat. Occurring in the shallow areas of lakes and streams, round whitefish may also inhabit rivers with swift current and a stony bottom. They rarely enter brackish water or water more than 150 feet deep.

Food. Round whitefish feed on benthic invertebrates and occasionally on fish and fish eggs.

Angling. Fishing effort is similar to that for lake and mountain whitefish.

American Shad and Hickory Shad

American Shad

Alosa sapidissima

This species is an anadromous member of the Clupeidae family of herring and shad and is highly regarded as a gamefish due to its strong fighting and jumping characteristics. American shad spawning runs provide a popular but seasonal sportfishery on Atlantic and Pacific coasts. The white, flaky flesh of this species is full of bones but makes good table fare if prepared with patience and care; the scientific name *sapidissima* means "most delicious," an appropriate appellation for a fish that supports a considerable commercial fishery and whose roe is considered a delicacy and commands a premium price.

ID. The laterally compressed, fairly deep body of the American shad is silvery white with some green to dark blue along the back, frequently with a metallic shine. The coloring darkens slightly when the fish enters freshwater to spawn. There is a large black spot directly behind the top of the gill cover, followed by several spots that become smaller and less distinct toward the tail;

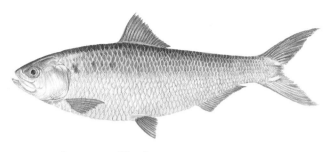

American Shad

sometimes there are up to three rows of these dark spots, one under the other.

The American shad has large, easily shed scales, as well as modified scales called scutes, which form a distinct ridge or cutting edge along the belly. It has a single dorsal fin in the middle of the back, the tail is deeply forked, and there are soft fin rays and long anal fins. Bearing a close resemblance to the hickory shad, the American shad is distinguished by the way its lower jaw fits easily into a deep, V-shaped notch under the upper jaw, whereas the lower jaw of the hickory shad protrudes noticeably beyond the upper jaw.

Habitat. American shad spend most of their lives in the ocean, ascending coastal rivers to spawn. They are found in coastal freshwater rivers only during their spawning migration, and primarily inhabit deep runs and pools.

Food. American shad feed primarily on plankton, swimming with their mouths open and gill covers extended while straining the water; they also eat small crustaceans, insects, fish eggs, algae, and small fish. They cease feeding during upstream spawning migration but resume during their relatively quick downstream post-spawning migration.

Angling. American shad provide drag-screeching runs, broadside-to-the-current fight, and frequent aerial maneuvers. They are as spunky a river fish as is to be found and are especially exciting when caught early in their upstream migration (they are spent after spawning and are therefore less challenging). Their spawning run lasts only six to eight weeks in the spring, and they often move through a river in stages or waves. They are affected by water conditions and are often not present in the same locales on a day-to-day basis.

Anglers often experience the best shad fishing in the evening and early morning. Shad typically remain in river channels, preferring deep water to the swift, riffling shallow sections. The primary place to fish for them is in pools.

Light spinning tackle is standard for shad. Terminal gear largely consists of shad darts (a lead-bodied bucktail jig with a tapered form and slanted nose), streamer flies, small spinners, and tiny spoons. It is usually necessary to maneuver these offerings down to the bottom, a task that is influenced by the depth of water, strength of current, weight of lure, and size of line. Shad do not feed during their spawning runs but apparently strike out of reflexive action; thus they don't go out of their way to chase a lure. The offering has to be placed in front of a fish's nose to be effective.

Hickory Shad

Alosa mediocris

The hickory shad is of significant recreational interest, being a friskier although smaller cousin of the American shad. It is also of commercial value, particularly its roe.

ID. Gray-green on the back and fading to silver on the side, the hickory shad has clear fins with the exception of the dusky dorsal and caudal fins, which are occasionally black-edged. It has a strongly oblique mouth, a lower jaw that projects noticeably beyond its upper jaw, and a cheek that is longer than or about equal to its depth. There is a blue-black spot near the upper edge of the gill cover, followed by a clump of indistinct dusky spots extending below the dorsal fin. There are also teeth on the lower jaw, and eighteen to twenty-three rakers on the lower limb of the first gill arch.

Habitat. The hickory shad is a schooling species that spends most of its life in the ocean; when mature, it returns in early spring through summer to rivers and streams to spawn, inhabiting open water of medium to large rivers. Young shad descend rivers in autumn.

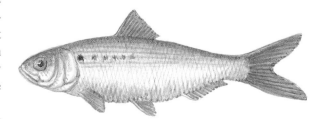

Hickory Shad

Food. At sea, hickory shad feed on small fish, as well as on squid, small crabs, other crustaceans, and fish eggs. In an irony that is common to most anadromous species, they are not pursued or caught by anglers in places where they do feed, but rather when migrating upriver in natal waters when they do not.

Angling. Angling for hickory shad is akin to that for American shad.

White Sturgeon

Acipenser transmontanus

A member of the Acipenseridae family of sturgeon, the white sturgeon is the largest freshwater fish in North America. In some areas, populations have recovered sufficiently since their decline in the early 1900s to support important recreational and commercial fisheries, particularly in California, Washington, Oregon, and Idaho.

ID. White sturgeon have a moderately blunt snout as adults, barbels closer to the snout tip than to the mouth, and no obvious scutes (bony scalelike plates behind the dorsal and anal fins). The fish is gray to pale olive on its upper body and white to pale gray on its ventral side. It has twenty-eight to thirty anal rays, eleven to fourteen scutes on its back, and thirty-eight to forty-eight scutes along the sides.

Habitat. The habitat of white sturgeon is primarily the estuaries and bays of large rivers, and the deep pools of rivers when inland.

Food. Adult white sturgeon are piscivorous and do feed in freshwater. Common forage includes pile worms, ghost shrimp, grass shrimp, squawfish, and carp.

Angling. Sportfishing for white sturgeon is strictly a bottom-working proposition, often with

White Sturgeon

heavy tackle. The tackle must be matched to the water conditions and potential size of fish to be encountered. This includes using heavy-duty lever drag ocean reels with 40- to 80-pound line or more, and a capacity of 200 to 300 yards, in the swift water of upper rivers where huge fish are a possibility.

Sturgeon meander in search of food, using their sensory abilities to locate prey or a scent trail that leads them to food. As a consequence, bait is the ticket to catching fish, and the possibilities are broad. Favorites include assorted fish (carp, squawfish, whitefish, herring, shad, and the like), both whole and cut in halves or chunks, as well as roe or spawn in bags, nightcrawlers, eels, and scented bait concoctions. Sturgeon don't grab and run; look for a slight tap and then wait for the fish to steadily move off with the bait before setting the hook.

Places to fish include deep holes directly below dams and falls, downstream from rapids, along the outside edge of a bend, and in the main channel. They also hold directly downstream from areas where the river bottom shallows up and there is a hard rock area. Stick to the center of the river channel if the river has few or no bends.

In tidal bays, either side of a tide change is good for fishing along dropoffs and by bridge abutments, on points, at bay mouths, and along breakwalls with baits, using a bottom rig with plenty of weight.

Sturgeon look like plodders, but they are strong, fast swimmers when hooked, and the battle can last a long time. They can provide exhilarating moments, sometimes leaping out of the water.

3

Saltwater Fish

Anglers pursue a greater number of saltwater species than they do freshwater, and the saltwater gamefish are perhaps even more diverse, particularly with regard to habitat choices, possible size attainment, and the breadth of areas where they are commonly found. The following are the most important and popularly sought saltwater gamefish found in North American waters.

Flounder

Flounder are part of a broad group of species called flatfish, comprising fish that have developed special features for living on the bottom of the ocean, the most interesting of which is that both eyes are on one side of the head.

Whereas one side of their body appears translucent or milky white, depending on the species, the other is a mottled assembly of muddy browns, reds, whites, and greens, which aids in camouflaging. The simple fins make an even fringe around the body, and a loosely shaped tail seems to have been tacked on.

Flounder have a highly compressed body, their dorsal and anal fins are usually long, the adults do not have a swim bladder, and they can change the color of their skin as well as the intensity of its coloration. This last trait takes advantage of their bottom-dwelling existence, allowing them to match their background or sometimes bury themselves in the sediment and lie in wait for unsuspecting prey.

Like all flatfish, flounder make delicious eating. They have firm, white, delicate flesh that adapts well to a variety of preparation methods.

Gulf Flounder

Paralichthys albigutta

The gulf flounder is a smallish member of the Bothidae family of left-eyed flounder. It is of minor economic significance, and is mixed in commercial and sport catches with summer flounder.

ID. The gulf flounder has the familiar olive brown background of its relatives, the summer and southern flounder, but it has three characteristic ocellated spots forming a triangle on its eye side. One spot is above the lateral line, one below, and one on the line itself, although these spots can become obscure in larger fish. Numerous white spots are scattered over the body and fins, and the caudal fin is in the shape of a wedge, with the tip in the middle. This species has fifty-three to sixty-three anal rays, which is fewer than the sixty-three to seventy-three found on the southern flounder.

Habitat. Gulf flounder inhabit sand, coral rubble, and seagrass areas near shore. They often range into tidal reefs and are occasionally found around nearshore rocky reefs. They commonly favor depths of up to 60 feet.

Food. The gulf flounder feeds on crustaceans and small fish.

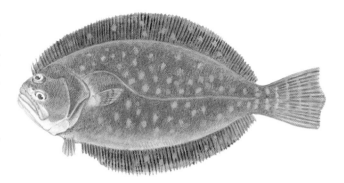

Southern Flounder

Southern Flounder

Paralichthys lethostigma

The southern flounder is a member of the Bothidae family of left-eyed flounder, and is an important commercial catch.

ID. The southern flounder resembles the summer flounder in appearance. Its coloring is light to dark olive brown, and it is marked with diffused dark blotches and spots, instead of distinct ocelli (spots ringed with distinct lighter areas). These spots often disappear in large fish. It can be distinguished from the summer flounder by its fewer gill rakers and the presence of distinct spots. It is also similar to the gulf flounder, which has no distinct ocelli.

Habitat. As an estuarine-dependent bottom fish, the southern flounder commonly inhabits inshore channels, bay mouths, estuaries, and sometimes freshwater. It is tolerant of a wide range of temperatures (50° to 90°F) and is often found in waters where salinities fluctuate from 0 to 20 parts per thousand. No other flounder of the eastern United States is regularly encountered in this type of environment. Anglers regularly catch this fish inshore from bridges and jetties.

Food. Small southern flounder consume shrimp and other small crustaceans, whereas larger flounder eat blue crabs, shrimp, and fish such as anchovies, mullet, menhaden, Atlantic croaker, and pinfish.

Starry Flounder

Platichthys stellatus

The starry flounder is a smaller and less common member of the Pacific coast Pleuronectidae family of right-eyed flounder. It is a popular sportfish

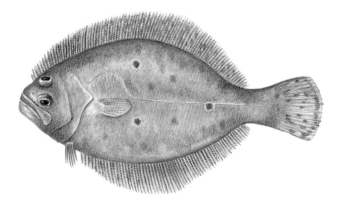

Gulf Flounder

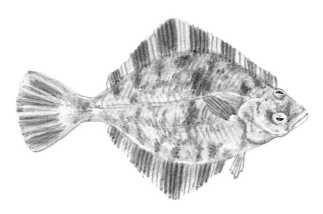

Starry Flounder

because of its willingness to bite and strong fighting qualities. Although the starry flounder has tasty flesh, it is important mainly as a sportfish, possessing only moderate commercial value. Processing is difficult due to its rough skin, and it must be deep-skinned to remove its unappealing dark fat layer.

ID. The starry flounder belongs to the right-eyed family of flatfish, but it can also be left-eyed. Its head is pointed, and it has a small mouth. The anal spine is strong. The caudal fin is square or slightly rounded. Its coloring is olive to dark brown or almost black on the upper side, and creamy white on the blind side. The unpaired fins, its outstanding feature, are white to yellow to orange with black bars. There are patches of rough, shiny, starlike scales scattered over the eyed side of the body, which give rise to its name.

Habitat. It is usually found near shore over mud, sand, or gravel bottoms. Often entering brackish water or freshwater, the starry flounder is most abundant in shallow water but can be found in depths of up to 900 feet.

Food. Adult starry flounder consume a variety of items, including crabs, clams, shrimp, and sand dollars. Large individuals also eat some fish, such as sardines, sanddabs, and surfperch.

Summer Flounder

Paralichthys dentatus

The summer flounder, most commonly called fluke, is a member of the Bothidae family of left-eyed flounder. It is the most northerly and perhaps abundant of the three bothid species, as well as the largest and most prized flatfish caught in the Mid-Atlantic region of the United States. Although

not a powerful fighter, this species provides spirited and often dependable action. The meat is firm, white, and delicately flavored.

ID. The body is wide and somewhat flattened, rimmed by long dorsal and anal fins. Its mouth is large and well equipped with teeth. The eyes are on the left side of the body and close together. The teeth are well developed on the right side of the jaw. Its background coloring is usually gray, brown, or olive, but it adjusts to the environment to keep itself hidden by camouflage. There are also many eyespots that change color. The dorsal fin has eight-five to ninety-four rays; the anal fin has sixty to sixty-three rays. There are only five or six gill rakers on the upper limb of the first arch and eleven to twenty-one on the lower limb.

In addition to their different color patterns, the three species of bothids can be distinguished by the number of gill rakers, anal fin rays, and lateral-line scales they possess. Summer flounder have the most eyespots, gulf flounder have several eyespots, and southern flounder lack conspicuous spots.

Habitat. The summer flounder prefers sandy or muddy bottoms and is common in the summer months in bays, harbors, estuaries, canals, creeks, and along shorelines, as well as in the vicinity of piers and bridges or near patches of eelgrass or other vegetation. It typically prefers relatively shallow waters and depths of up to 100 feet during warmer months, then moves offshore in winter to deeper, cooler water of 150 to 500 feet.

Food. Adults are largely piscivorous and highly predatory, feeding actively in midwater as well as on the bottom. Extremely fast swimmers, they often chase baitfish at the surface, which is not characteristic of most other flatfish. Fluke also

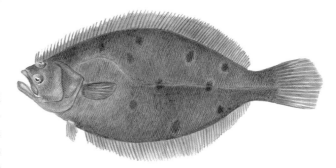

Summer Flounder

bury themselves quickly, using undulating movements of their fins to throw sand or silt on their backs. The eyes remain uncovered and watch carefully for dinner prospects. Fluke are known to eat what is available, including shrimp, crabs, menhaden, anchovies, silversides, sand lance, killifish, weakfish, hake, and other flounder.

Winter Flounder

Pseudopleuronectes americanus

One of the most common and well-known flounder of shallow Atlantic coastal waters, the winter flounder belongs to the Pleuronectidae family. It is a right-eyed flatfish, and gets its name because it retreats to cold, deep water in the summer and

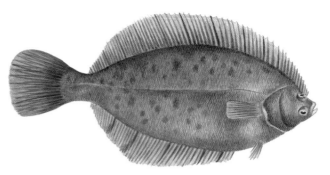

Winter Flounder

reappears in shallower water close to shore in the winter; its relative, the summer flounder, does the opposite. The winter flounder is an important food and commercial species, and a thick, meaty specimen. The meat is firm, white, and delicately flavored.

ID. The body of the winter flounder is oval and flat with a tiny mouth. Color varies from reddish brown to dark brown with small black spots. The underside is whitish and occasionally brown, tinged with blue around the edges. The caudal fin is slightly rounded.

Habitat. Winter flounder are found inshore in estuaries and coastal ocean areas. In the Mid-Atlantic they stay inshore from January through April. Smaller fish occur in shallower water, although larger fish will enter water only a foot deep. They may range anywhere from well up into the high-tide mark to depths of at least 400 feet. Preferring sand-mud bottoms, they are also found over sand, clay, or fine gravel, and on hard bottom offshore.

Food. When on a soft bottom, the winter flounder will lie buried up to its eyes, waiting to attack prey. Due to its small mouth, its diet includes only smaller food like marine worms, small crustaceans, and small shelled animals like clams and snails.

Angling for Flounder

Flounder do not school, so they are found over a wide area; this is conducive to drifting with the tide and/or wind over bay and estuary flats, for example. Also, many species are easily caught in shallow, protected areas that are accessible in small boats.

Unless flounder are known to be in a certain area, it is usually best to drift for them, thereby covering a large area. Likely spots to try include places with rough or irregular bottoms, in or near inlets, and around pilings, wrecks, and jetties. Food is abundant in these locations. If you are fishing in one spot, it helps to jig the line up and down so the bait does not lie motionless on the bottom, as fluke (and other flatfish) are often attracted by movement.

Commonly used baits are minnows, shrimp, and squid; artificial lures that imitate these items are also effective. A sinker of sufficient size must be used so the line stays on the bottom even when there is a strong tidal flow.

Many anglers chum for flounder in order to concentrate them. They will often use a horizontal spreader when fishing two leaders on one line. This lets both baits rest on the bottom where the fish feed.

Other aspects of angling for flounder are discussed in greater detail in the drift fishing and inshore fishing sections of this book.

Atlantic Halibut, California Halibut, and Pacific Halibut

Atlantic Halibut

Hippoglossus hippoglossus

The Atlantic halibut is among the largest bony fish in the world and a member of the Pleuronectidae family of right-eyed flatfish. The Atlantic halibut is a highly prized table fish, with white, tender flesh that has a mild flavor and is often likened to chicken; it has been marketed fresh, dried/salted, smoked, and frozen. It is an excellent fighter, but is a deep-dwelling fish that is primarily caught incidentally by anglers fishing for other deep ocean dwellers.

ID. The body is wide and somewhat flattened, rimmed by long dorsal and anal fins. The lateral line, which has a scale count of about 160, arches strongly above the pectoral fin. The dorsal fin has 98 to 106 rays and the anal fin 73 to 80. The teeth are equally well equipped in both sides of the jaw. Its coloring is usually pearly white and featureless on the blind side. Some specimens, nicknamed "cherry-bellies," have a reddish tint on the blind side.

Habitat. A deep-water species, the Atlantic halibut seldom enters water shallower than about 200 feet and is commonly found to 3,000 feet. It inhabits cold (40° to 50°F) water over sand, gravel, or clay bottoms.

Food. The Atlantic halibut is a voracious feeder, pursuing its prey in the open water. It forages primarily on fish, including cod, ocean perch, herring, skate, mackerel, and other flatfish. It also eats crabs, mussels, lobsters, and clams.

Angling. As noted, there is a minor, concentrated rod-and-reel effort for these fish, owing to their extraordinarily deep-dwelling nature and low population. They are caught in the western Atlantic on banks in 100 to 500 feet of water. Anglers drifting bait rigs or heavy metal jigs on the bottom often catch Atlantic halibut while fishing for such other bottom dwellers as Atlantic cod. Although natural baits may differ, techniques are similar to those used in fishing for Pacific halibut.

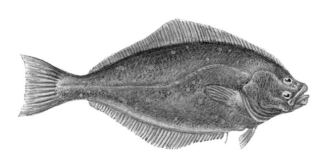

Atlantic Halibut

California Halibut

Paralichthys californicus

The California halibut is a large flatfish and a member of the Bothidae family, or left-eyed flounder. It is the largest and most abundant flatfish within its range, although its maximum size is much smaller than the more northerly Pacific halibut. It is an important commercial quarry and sportfish, one that is often deliberately sought by anglers and valued for its excellent firm white flesh.

ID. The body of the California halibut is oblong and compressed. The head is small and the mouth large. Although a member of the left-eyed flounder family, about 40 percent of California halibut have their eyes on the right side. The color is dark brown to black on the eyed side and white on the blind side. Rare specimens may be either brown or white on both sides or have partial coloration on both sides. The gill rakers are slender and numerous, totaling about twenty-nine on the first arch. Their numerous teeth, very large mouth, and a high arch in the middle of the "top" side above the pectoral fin make them easily distinguishable from other flatfish.

Habitat. Found mostly over sandy bottoms, California halibut appear beyond the surf line and in bays and estuaries. They range from near shore to 600 feet deep but are most commonly caught in 60 to 120 feet of water. They are not known to make extensive migrations.

Food. These halibut feed primarily on anchovies and similar small fish, often well off the bottom and during the day, although they also consume squid, crustaceans, and mollusks. At times they are observed jumping clear out of the water as they make passes at anchovy schools near the surface.

Angling. California halibut are relatively aggressive fish, and offer variety in terms of technique and location. Although drift fishing with bait on sandy flats is almost synonymous with fishing for this species, trolling with lures and bait, fishing in shallow water, and fishing on deep structure are also productive.

Live anchovies are a popular natural bait, and the primary method of fishing these is by drifting along the bottom. Most anglers keep their conventional reel in freespool with a thumb on the line to maintain control, and watch the rod tip, waiting

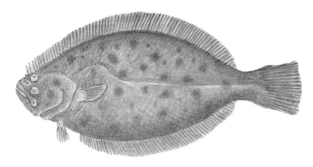

California Halibut

for a sharp tap. When a fish strikes, they yield a lit- tle line, then engage the gears and set the hook.

Although this method catches fish of all sizes, it is often less productive for larger halibut, perhaps because many smaller ones are more aggressive. Some anglers have had more success on larger fish not by drifting but by concentrating on gravel and shale bottoms, wrecks, breakwalls, rockpiles, and other structure. They anchor instead of drift, and use a sliding sinker while bottom fishing with live bait, preferring sardines, queenfish, and squid over anchovies. Leadhead jigs adorned with soft plastic bodies also work, and both bait and jigs are twitched and moved along the bottom.

When the fish are shallow, trolling with mid- to deep-running minnow-style plugs produces halibut; fly fishing also produces fish at this time. Trolling with wire line is favored when the fish are in deeper water with swift current; plastic squid or hoochies on a multiple-lure bottom rig with a heavy (1- to 3-pound) sinker get down to the fish in the 30- to 100-foot depths.

These halibut need to be played with firm, steady pressure, not with aggressive pumping, which sends them on a getaway run.

Pacific Halibut

Hippoglossus stenolepis

The Pacific halibut is the largest flatfish found in Pacific waters, and one of the world's largest bony fish. It is a member of the family Pleuronectidae, or right-eyed flounder. A strong fighter that grows to impressive size, the Pacific halibut has long been a favorite among Pacific Northwest anglers, and its firm white flesh is prized.

ID. The Pacific halibut's coloration varies from olive to dark brown or black with lighter, irregular blotches. More elongate than other flatfish, it has a body about one-third its length. The mouth is large, extending to the lower eye. The small, smooth scales are well buried in the skin, and the lateral line has a pronounced arch above the pectoral fin. The tail is crescent-shaped, longer at the tips than in the middle, which distinguishes it from most other flatfish.

Habitat. Preferring cool water (3° to 8°C), Pacific halibut are most commonly found where the bottom is composed of cobble, gravel, and sand, especially near the edges of underwater plateaus and breaklines. Here they wait for tidal currents to wash food within striking range. Hali- but are strong swimmers, however, and will leave bottom to feed on pelagic fish such as herring and sand lance. They will also inhabit virtually any kind of habitat if crabs, squid, octopus, cod, pollock, sablefish, or other sources of food are abundant.

Angling. Basic halibut fishing techniques apply wherever the fish are found; the key is to get a bait or lure down to them and keep it there long enough for a fish to find it. Most anglers prefer to fish with bait, and large herring are the most popular choice. Squid, octopus, belly skin off halibut or salmon, and whole cod, greenling, or other small bottom fish are also effective baits.

Bait is usually fished on a wire spreader or a sliding-sinker rig, with sinker size ranging from 4 ounces to 4 pounds, depending on depth, current, size of the bait, and line diameter. Halibut use their eyes, nose, and lateral line to locate a meal, so anglers often lift the bait well off the bottom to increase visibility and then drop it quickly to create a thumping vibration.

This same "bottom-banging" strategy also works for anglers using artificials. Favorite lures

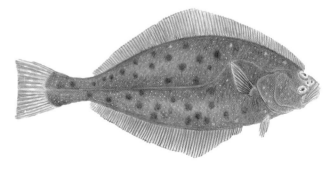

Pacific Halibut

are large, metal slab-type jigs or homemade versions constructed of tubing or small-diameter pipe filled with lead. Both imitate herring and other small fish on which halibut feed. Leadhead jigs also take halibut, especially if adorned with large plastic grub bodies, pork rind, or strips of white belly skin off another halibut.

Croaker, Spot, and White Seabass

Croaker are members of the Sciaenidae family, which includes drum and seatrout. The common name "croaker" is derived from the voluntary deep croaking noise made when the fish raps a muscle against its swim bladder. The sound resonates and is amplified, and the resulting drumming noise can be heard from far away. These bottom-living fish are generally good to excellent table fare, mostly of smaller sizes, and common catches along the Atlantic and Pacific coasts. Profiled in the next several pages are some of the more prominent croaker on both coasts.

Atlantic Species

Atlantic Croaker

Micropogonias undulatus

The Atlantic croaker is one of the most frequently caught estuarine and nearshore marine fish along the eastern coast of the United States. It has lean white meat with a firm texture, often substituted for pompano or mullet in dishes.

ID. The Atlantic croaker has a small, elongated body with a short, high first dorsal fin and a long, low second dorsal fin. There are six to ten tiny barbels on the chin and sixty-four to seventy-two scales along the lateral line, and the preopercular margin has three to five spines. The middle rays of the caudal fins are longer than those above and below, creating a wedgelike appearance. Its coloring is greenish above and white below, with brownish black spots and a silver iridescence covering the body. There are dark wavy lines on the sides. During spawning, the Atlantic croaker takes on a bronze hue (thus the nickname "golden cracker"), and its pelvic fins turn yellow.

It can be distinguished from its cousin, the spot, by its convex tail, which is unlike the spot's concave caudal tail. The Atlantic croaker can also

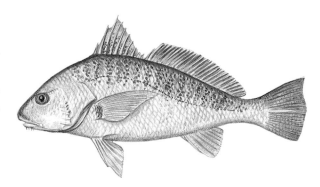

Atlantic Croaker

be distinguished from its relatives by its unique coloring and spotted patterns.

Habitat. Atlantic croaker prefer mud, sand, and shell bottoms; areas around rocks; waters near jetties, piers, and bridges; and the surf. Juveniles inhabit both open and vegetated shallow marsh areas. Adult croaker can occupy a wide range of salinities, from 20 to 75 parts per thousand, and temperatures of 50° to 96°F. Large fish are not found at temperatures below 50°F.

Food. Adults feed on detritus but also consume larger invertebrates and fish. Sensory barbels allow the Atlantic croaker to find food on the bottom.

Angling. Atlantic croaker are caught in large numbers from March through October on such natural baits as shrimp, soft-shelled or shedder crabs, clams, worms, and cut fish, and with artificial lures such as small jigs and weighted bucktails. Light tackle and small hooks are best, and although some fish are caught during the day, angling after dark is often better. Fishing is also often best just before or right after a high tide in channels or deep holes.

Spot

Leiostomus xanthurus

The spot is a small but flavorful fish and an important commercial species. Its migration habits bring it to shore in schools, enabling both recreational anglers and commercial fishermen to catch it in large numbers.

ID. The body of the spot is deep and stout, and the tail is slightly forked. The soft dorsal fin has more than thirty rays, and the anal fin has more than twelve. Its coloring is gray to silver with a gold tint on the sides and twelve to fifteen dark lines

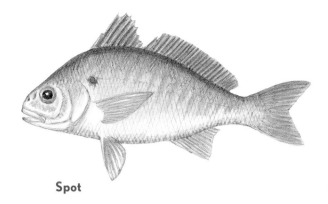

Spot

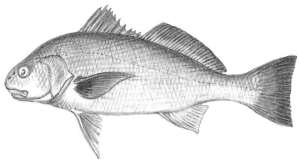

Spotfin Croaker

extending from the dorsal fins to the lateral line. There is a round black spot about the same size as the eye above each pectoral fin. The fins are pale yellow, except the dorsal and caudal fins, which are milky. The spot's color and lack of chin barbels distinguish it from other sciaenids.

Habitat. Spot inhabit estuaries and coastal saltwaters, generally roaming over sandy and muddy bottoms. They may frequent waters as deep as 60 meters but usually remain much shallower.

Food. Spot consume small crustaceans, detritus, worms, and small fish.

Angling. Spot are found over mud and sand bottoms, as well as shell reefs. They are often caught accidentally by anglers pursuing other species, but are best deliberately pursued with light line, small hooks, and pieces of clams and cut fish or worms, presented on the bottom.

Pacific Species

Spotfin Croaker

Roncador stearnsii

The spotfin croaker is a small Pacific coast fish caught by bay, surf, and pier anglers and highly valued as table fare.

ID. The body of the spotfin croaker is elongate but heavy forward. The upper profile of the head is steep and slightly curved, and abruptly rounded at the very blunt snout. The mouth is subterminal, being underneath the head. The color is silvery gray with a bluish luster above and white below. There are dark wavy lines on the sides, and a large black spot at the base of the pectoral fin.

The pectoral fin spot, subterminal mouth, and absence of a fleshy barbel distinguish the spotfin croaker from other California croaker. Large male

spotfins in breeding colors are known as "golden croaker."

Habitat. Spotfins are found along beaches and in bays over bottoms that vary from coarse sand to heavy mud and at depths varying from 4 to 50 or more feet. They prefer depressions and holes near shore.

Food. Spotfin croaker have large pharyngeal teeth that are well suited to crushing clams, which make up a major portion of their diet; crustaceans and worms are also eaten extensively.

Angling. Although some spotfins are caught throughout the year, the better angling period is late summer, after the fish have spawned and returned to the surf line. When a large number of fish have moved into an area, there is generally good activity in the bays, and at piers and beaches. Clams and worms are the main natural baits, fished on bottom rigs; relatively light tackle is best for sporting value.

Yellowfin Croaker

Umbrina roncador

Found along the Pacific coast, the yellowfin croaker is a popular catch for light-tackle surf anglers.

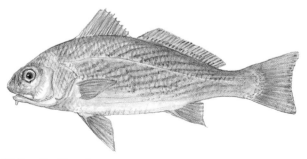

Yellowfin Croaker

ID. The body of the yellowfin croaker is elliptical-elongate; the back is somewhat arched and the head blunt. Its coloring is iridescent blue to gray with brassy reflections on the back diffusing to silvery white below. Dark wavy lines streak the sides. The fins are yellowish except for the dark dorsal fins. The yellowfin croaker has a small barbel on the chin tip and two strong anal spines; the barbel and heavy anal spines distinguish the yellowfin from other California croaker.

Habitat. These fish inhabit shallow parts of bays, channels, harbors, and other nearshore waters over sandy bottoms.

Food. Although the yellowfin croaker primarily consumes small fish and fish fry, it also feeds on small crustaceans, worms, and mollusks.

Angling. These fish are mostly caught in shallow sandy areas by surf anglers. Sand crabs, mussels, clams, cut pieces of fish, and worms are used as bait, preferably on small hooks and light tackle.

California Corbina

Menticirrhus undulatus

Although the California corbina belongs to the Sciaenidae family, it lacks a swim bladder and cannot make the croaking or drumming noises characteristic of the croaker family. This bottom fish is popular with surf and pier anglers, and has excellent table value; it should not be confused with the corvina species that primarily inhabit the Gulf of California.

ID. The body of the California corbina is elongate and slightly compressed, with a flattened belly. Its head is long and the mouth is small, the upper jaw scarcely reaching a point below the front of the eye. The first dorsal fin is short and high, the second long and low. Coloring is uniformly gray with incandescent reflections, and with wavy diagonal lines on the sides. Unlike most other croakers, it does not have a barbel on the lower jaw. California corbina can be distinguished from the yellowfin croaker by the presence of only one weak spine at the front of the anal fin; the yellowfin croaker has two strong spines.

Habitat. Preferring sandy beaches and shallow bays, the California corbina is a bottom fish appearing along the coastal surf zone.

Food. A fussy feeder, the California corbina primarily consumes sand crabs and spits out bits

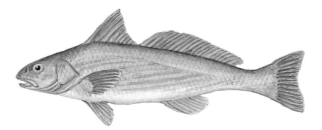

California Corbina

of clam shells and other foreign matter; it also consumes small crustaceans and marine worms. Corbina scoop up mouthfuls of sand and separate the food by sending the sand through their gills. Adults are sometimes seen feeding in the surf, occasionally in water so shallow that their backs are exposed.

Angling. Surf and pier anglers use bottom-fishing rigs to catch corbina on small crabs and worms.

White Seabass

Atractoscion nobilis

A member of the Sciaenidae family, the white seabass is not a true bass or sea bass, and is a fish that has been much sought after commercially and by anglers. Its flesh is white and tender and highly valued, but it spoils quickly without proper care.

ID. The body of the white seabass is elongate and somewhat compressed. There is a characteristic raised ridge along the middle of the belly between the vent and the base of the pelvic fins. The head is pointed and slightly flattened. The mouth is large, with a row of small teeth in the roof and a projecting lower jaw. The first dorsal fin has nine spines and the second two spines and twenty soft rays. The anal fin has two spines and ten soft rays. There are no barbels on the chin. Its coloring is bluish to gray above, with dark speckling, and becomes silver below.

The white seabass can be distinguished from its Atlantic relatives, the weakfish and the spotted seatrout, by its lack of canine teeth. It is most closely related to the California corbina but is the only California croaker to exceed 20 pounds. It is most easily separated from other croaker by the presence of a ridge running the length of the belly.

Habitat. Preferring deep, rocky environments, white seabass usually hold near kelp beds in depths

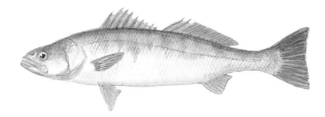

White Seabass

of 12 to 25 fathoms. They are sometimes found in shallow surf or deeper waters. Juveniles inhabit shallow nearshore areas, bays, and estuaries.

Food. White seabass feed on anchovies, pilchards, herring, and other fish, as well as on crustaceans and squid.

Angling. White seabass are fished primarily with live baits in relatively shallow water, but they will also take a fast-trolled spoon, an artificial squid, or a bone jig. Live natural baits appear to be the best offering, but large anchovies and medium-size sardines are also good. At times, large white seabass will strike only large live Pacific mackerel.

Live and dead squid are the primary natural baits in the winter off Southern California, when the squid are abundant and spawning. Fished on a jig or a baited hook with a sliding egg sinker, the squid is freespooled to the bottom, often being pecked by other fish on the way, then worked a few feet off the bottom by repeated lifting and dropping movements.

Black Drum and Red Drum

Black Drum

Pogonias cromis

The black drum is a popular sportfish and a common market fish. It is the largest member of the Sciaenidae family, and appropriately named, as "drum" refers to the loud and distinctive drumming noise that occurs when the fish raps a muscle against the swim bladder. The noise is voluntary and is assumed to be associated with locating and attracting mates, and it can sometimes be heard from a good distance, even by people above the water.

Black drum are bottom feeders. Larger fish are typically caught by anglers who bottom fish in surf and bay areas.

ID. The black drum has a short, deep, and stocky body with a high arched back and a slightly concave tail. The lower jaw sports numerous barbels, or short whiskers. There are large pavement-like teeth in the throat, and the mouth is low. The dorsal fins have eleven spines, twenty to twenty-two dorsal rays, and forty-one to forty-five scales along the lateral line, which runs all the way to the end of the tail. There are fourteen to sixteen gill rakers on the lower limb of the first arch. Its coloring is silvery with a brassy sheen and blackish fins, turning to dark gray after death. Juveniles have four or five broad, dark vertical bars on the body.

The black drum can be distinguished from the red drum by the absence of a dark spot on the tail base, by the lack of dark streaks along the scale row, and by the presence of chin barbels. An unusually large spine in the anal fin and many barbels set the black drum apart from other similar species.

Habitat. An inshore bottom fish, the black drum prefers sandy bottoms in salt- or brackish waters near jetties, breakwaters, bridge and pier pilings, clam and oyster beds, channels, estuaries, bays, high marsh areas, and shorelines. Juveniles are commonly found over muddy bottoms in estuaries. Larger fish often favor shoal areas and channels.

Black drum can survive wide ranges of salinity and temperature. The small fish inhabit brackish and freshwater habitats; the adults usually prefer estuaries in which salinity ranges from 9 to 26 parts per thousand and the temperature ranges from 53° to 91°F.

Food. Young drum feed on small crustaceans and marine annelids. Adult black drum feed on crustaceans and mollusks with a preference for blue

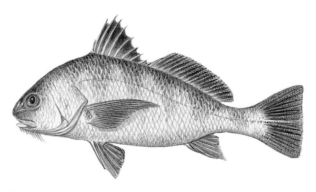

Black Drum

crabs, shedder crabs, shrimp, oysters, and squid. They locate food with their chin barbels and crush and grind shells with their pharyngeal teeth.

Angling. Most larger black drum are caught by standard bottom-fishing methods used in surf fishing and inshore fishing. Bottom rigs with baits, especially clams and peeler crabs, are the predominant offering. This method is often combined with chumming. Shrimp, crabs, squid, and cut fish are also used, and some black drum are also caught on spoons and jigs. Spoons, plugs, and flies can produce in conditions favorable to artificials.

Black drum mouth a bait, so anglers need to wait a few seconds before setting the hook when using natural baits. These fish are strong battlers and require stout tackle.

Red Drum

Sciaenops ocellatus

Commonly known as a channel bass and redfish, the red drum is second only to black drum in size among members of the Sciaenidae family, but probably first in the hearts of anglers. Although it isn't a flashy fighter, it is stubborn and determined, persistent on heading for the bottom. Large red drum are powerful, premier coastal sportfish. Red drum are also excellent food fish. Larger specimens can be coarse and stringy, but smaller fish are quite good. The flesh is white, heavy, and moist, with a fine texture and mild flavor.

ID. The red drum is similar in appearance to the black drum, although its maximum size is smaller and it is more streamlined. The body is elongate with a subterminal mouth and blunt nose. On adults the tail is squared, and on juveniles it is rounded. There are no chin barbels, which also distinguishes it from the black drum. Its coloring is coppery red to bronze on the back, and silver and white on the sides and belly. One black dot (also called an eyespot), or many, are found at the base of the tail.

Habitat. An estuarine-dependent fish that becomes oceanic later in life, the red drum is found in brackish water and saltwater on sand, mud, and grass bottoms of inlets, shallow bays, tidal passes, bayous, and estuaries. The red drum also tolerates freshwater, in which some have been known to dwell permanently. Larger red drum

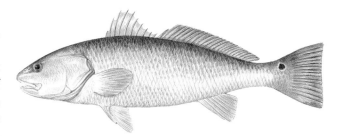

Red Drum

prefer deeper waters of lower estuaries and tidal passes, whereas smaller ones remain in shallow waters near piers and jetties and on grassy flats. They can survive wide ranges of salinity and temperature, and smaller specimens prefer lower salinity levels than do larger ones.

Food. This species uses its senses of sight and touch, and its downturned mouth, to locate forage on the bottom through vacuuming or biting the bottom. In summer and fall, adults feed on crabs, shrimp, and sand dollars. Fish such as menhaden, mullet, pinfish, sea robin, lizardfish, spot, Atlantic croaker, and flounder are the primary foods consumed during winter and spring. In shallow water, red drum are often seen browsing head-down with their tails slightly out of the water.

Angling. Red drum are susceptible to a variety of methods, lures, and baits, in clear as well as turbid waters, and along beaches, at inlets, on grassflats, in marshes, in deep channels, and around shoals. Sight casting with lures or flies, bottom fishing with baits, and surf fishing are popularly enjoyed in various locations. Red drum can be very easy to catch at times, yet spooky and difficult at others.

Sight casting is probably the most favored method, and takes the form of spotting nearshore roving schools along beaches, or stalking shallow-water tailers as they feed. Shallow-water stalking is especially conducive to fly fishing.

When prospecting for larger schools, anglers in boats try to get a high vantage point and cruise along beaches and inlets looking for dark masses of fish just under the surface in water that varies from a few feet to 20 feet deep. Sunny conditions are generally necessary for this, and the clear water of spring makes for the best visibility.

Blind casting along the edges of marshes on an outgoing tide is a standard practice. It is likely to produce generally smaller fish but is excellent for light-tackle and small-boat anglers.

Red drum are more likely to take lures than are black drum, and casting spoons, surface plugs, swimming plugs, spinnerbaits, and jigs with soft shadlike bodies are productive for these fish. Smaller fish in estuaries and flats are suited to many of the same lures that catch largemouth bass in freshwater. Live bait such as crab, shrimp, and finger mullet are also effective.

The bigger red drum of the Atlantic surf are a different story, generally requiring sturdier tackle. Bait is often preferred, with cut mullet, clams, and peeler crabs being especially favored. Red drum frequently mouth a bait before running off with it, so you need to adapt accordingly.

Spotted Seatrout and Weakfish

Spotted Seatrout

Cynoscion nebulosus

The spotted seatrout is a member of the Sciaenidae family of drum and croaker and of the genus *Cynoscion* (weakfish and seatrout), which is named for their tender mouths from which hooks tear easily. Exceptionally valued for commercial and recreational interests, it is intensely pursued throughout its range, especially in the Gulf of Mexico. An excellent table fish, the seatrout has fine and delicately flavored flesh, but it spoils quickly and should be cleaned or stored on ice when possible after being caught.

ID. The spotted seatrout has an elongated body with a fairly regular and even tail fin that has a black margin. Its coloring is dark gray or green on the back, with sky blue tinges shading to silvery and white below; the dorsal fins are gray-green, and many round black spots speckle the back, tail, and dorsal fins. The lower jaw protrudes beyond the upper, which has one or two prominent canine teeth. The first dorsal fin has one spine and twenty-four to twenty-seven soft rays, and the anal fin has two spines and ten or eleven soft rays. There are eight or nine short, stubby gill rakers on the lower limb of the first gill arch. There are no barbels, and the interior of the mouth is orange. The presence of spots on the fins can distinguish the spotted seatrout from other seatrout.

Habitat. An inshore bottom-dwelling species, the spotted seatrout inhabits shallow bays, estuaries, bayous, canals, and Gulf Coast beaches. They prefer nearshore sandy and grassy bottoms, and may even frequent salt marshes and tidal pools with high salinity. They also live around oil rigs, usually within 10 miles of shore. Ideal water temperatures are between 58° and 81°F.

Food. Spotted seatrout feed primarily on shrimp and small fish. When shrimp are scarce, they often consume mullet, menhaden, and silverside. Larger specimens feed more heavily on fish.

Angling. In Florida and on the Gulf Coast, especially in Louisiana and Texas, spotted seatrout are caught throughout the year, although the most productive time is during summer and early fall for overall numbers of fish, and in mid- to late fall and early spring for big fish.

Lures and live baits are both effective. Live shrimp and minnows are the most common live baits, but cut mullet, soft-shelled crabs, worms, and squid are among other effective natural baits. Popular lures include soft worms, bucktail jigs, grubs and jigs with assorted soft tails, surface and shallow-swimming plugs, spoons, and streamer flies. Light tackle is very appropriate for these fish, and many anglers use light baitcasting or light to medium-light spinning tackle. A lesser number employ flycasting gear.

In the Gulf, especially throughout Texas, sight fishing for trout and redfish is extremely popular. Anglers use shallow-water craft to negotiate grassflats—many of which are just inches deep— where they visually locate and then cast to the fish with baits, lures, or flies. In other areas, fishing by wading or casting from boats is common, usually for unseen fish that are moving through an area or are located in feeding or resting places, such as grassbeds and shellfish beds or in deep

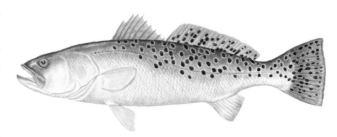

Spotted Seatrout

holes or channels, where blind casting or even trolling can be effective.

Spotted seatrout are caught on a variety of offerings because they feed throughout the water column. Anchoring and casting lures or stillfishing with bait, drifting under the occasional control of an electric motor or pushpole and casting, and trolling slowly through holes and channels are all practiced in appropriate places and conditions. Among lures, however, jigs with soft tails—either curly, grub-shaped, or shrimp-shaped—are especially favored, and these are usually worked slowly via casting.

Weakfish

Cynoscion regalis

The weakfish is also a member of the Sciaenidae family, and its name refers to the tender, easily torn membrane in the fish's mouth, not its fighting ability. It is the gamest of the *Cynoscion* species in North America, striking hard and making one or two strong runs after being hooked. The weakfish is highly sought, although it experiences dramatic fluctuation in stocks. The meat of weakfish is white, tender, and moist and has an excellent flavor. It does not keep well, so it must be stored properly upon capture and prepared for consumption soon afterward.

ID. Weakfish have a slim body not unlike a trout's. The lower jaw projects beyond the upper jaw. There are two large, protruding canine teeth in the upper jaw, and no chin barbels. The first dorsal fin has ten spines, and the second has a single spine and twenty-six to twenty-nine soft rays. The anal fin has two spines and eleven or twelve rays. Coloring is dark olive or greenish to greenish blue on the dorsal surface, and blue, green, purple, and lavender with a golden tinge on the sides. Numerous small black spots speckle the top, sometimes forming wavy diagonal lines. There is sometimes a black margin on the tip of the tongue.

The weakfish is distinguished from the spotted seatrout because its spots do not extend onto the tail or the second dorsal fin, and are not as widely spaced.

Habitat. Preferring sandy and sometimes grassy bottoms, weakfish are usually found in shallow waters along shores and in large bays and estuaries,

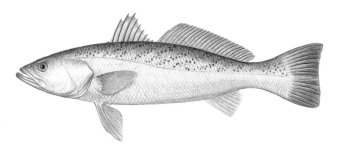

Weakfish

including salt marsh creeks and sometimes into river mouths, although they do not enter freshwater. They can be found in depths of up to 55 fathoms in the winter.

Food. Weakfish feed on crabs, shrimp, other crustaceans, and mollusks. They also consume small fish like herring, menhaden, silversides, killifish, and butterfish, which they catch in midwater levels or near the surface. Because of their varied diet, weakfish forage at different levels and adapt to local food conditions.

Angling. With such a broad diet and feeding range, weakfish are susceptible to an equally wide variety of angling methods, lures, and baits. Drifting or stillfishing with an assortment of live or dead baits is extremely popular. The most common natural baits are shrimp, squid, shedder or peeler crabs, worms, eels, mullet, and other small fish, or pieces of such fish as mackerel or bunker. Chumming is also effective, especially with a grass shrimp mix, ground-up fish, or conglomerations of fish, shrimp, clams, and the like.

Jigging with metal jigs, grubs, or bucktail jigs garnished with a plastic worm body is also a favorite method, again either drifting in a boat or anchored. Bucktail jigs, usually garnished with a soft-action tail or with a strip of squid or other bait, are highly favored lures, as are leadhead jigs with soft bodies. The latter are also often tipped with a piece of squid or shrimp.

Other lures include spoons, tube lures, diamond jigs, and surface and shallow-running plugs. Trolling with plugs and spoons is another technique, although shore fishing, from the surf and by wading, or by casting from piers and jetties, is just as effective. Casting with plugs or streamer flies is usually done when the fish are fairly shallow, as well as in bays and estuary environs.

Weakfish will move into brackish water, and the shallow bay areas of estuaries are a common hangout, particularly in brackish rivers or creeks. In the northerly parts of their range, weakfish are seldom taken deeper than 20 feet in bays or open-water areas.

They will move onto shoals in schools to feed, and concentrate around oyster bars, bridges, and inlet jetties. Anglers should especially focus on structure and edges, including such places as a channel in a shallow bay; a slough, cut, or trough in the surf; the edge of a tide rip, flat, or dropoff; deep holes in a bay; and along a sandbar. In daytime, these fish will usually hold deeper than at night or in low light.

Striped Bass

Morone saxatilis

An excellent sportfish that attains large sizes, the striped bass is a member of the temperate bass family (often erroneously placed with the sea bass family). It has been considered one of the most valuable and popular fish in North America since the early 1600s, originally for its commercial importance and in more recent times for its recreational significance. The striper's pleasant and almost sweet white flesh has made it highly desirable table fare.

ID. A large fish with a large mouth, the striped bass is streamlined and has a long body and long head, a somewhat laterally compressed body form, protruding lower jaw, a forked tail, and small eyes. These fish are mostly bluish black or dark green above, fading into silver on the sides and white on the belly. On each side of its body there are seven or eight prominent black horizontal stripes running along the scale rows that are the distinctive markings of the striped bass; one of the stripes runs along the lateral line, and the rest are equally divided above and below it. Most of the fins are a dusky silver, with the exception of the white pelvic fins.

Habitat. Striped bass inhabit saltwater, freshwater, and brackish water, although they are most abundant in saltwater. They are anadromous and migrate in saltwater along coastal inshore environs and tidal tributaries. They are often found around piers, jetties, surf troughs, rips, flats, and rocks. A common regional name for stripers is rockfish, and indeed their scientific name, *saxatilis*, means "rock dweller," although they do not necessarily spend most of their lives in association with rocks.

Food. An opportunistic predator, the striped bass feeds heavily on small fish, including large quantities of herring, menhaden, flounder, alewives, silversides, eels, and smelt, as well as invertebrates such as worms, squid, and crabs. Feeding times vary, although many anglers believe that stripers are more active nocturnal feeders and that they are more effective at catching them in low-light conditions and after dark.

Angling. Striped bass are caught by all the fishing tactics known to anglers, who can troll live baits, rigged baits, spoons, plugs, tube lures, and just plain hardware. Or they can use spinning, baitcasting, or conventional equipment to cast plugs and spoons, or live, rigged, or cut baits. These fish can be taken from an anchored boat by anglers using casting equipment or conventional equipment to fish on or near the bottom or at different levels in the water column, with or without chum attraction. They can be taken from boats drifting with the tide or pushed by the wind as anglers bounce bucktail jigs off the bottom, drag live eels or bunker near the bottom, or even use chunks of cut baits. Striped bass succumb to the fly rod, on streamers or artificial replicas of real baitfish, in every environment in which they swim.

Those environments are particularly varied in saltwater. Stripers linger off open beaches; in rips where tidal streams flow into bays or open water; off rock jetties or concrete walls; under docks, piers and bridges; or around pilings where baitfish naturally congregate. In other words, where there is something to be eaten, striped bass will at some time be there to feed upon it.

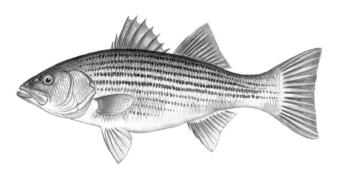

Striped Bass

One of the most enjoyable ways to catch striped bass is from the beach, and surf casting for this fish has developed a devoted following. A highly effective way to fish for striped bass is from a boat, and another dedicated cadre of bass anglers takes bass only by plugging from a drifting boat and casting toward the beach to pull bass from the surf. The deadliest striper method is drifting live eels from a moving boat; the eels are hooked through both jaws and attached to a three-way rig.

Bluefish

Pomatomus saltatrix

Bluefish

The only member of the Pomatomidae family, the bluefish is an extremely voracious and cannibalistic saltwater fish. A fierce opponent, it has gained a reputation among marine anglers as the hardest fighter per pound. These fish put up a long battle, even though they are typically caught in the 5- to 12-pound range. True to their scientific name (*saltatrix* means "leaper"), they will also jump if not caught on very heavy tackle. Schooling bluefish are particularly aggressive. They are an important commercial fish, noted for a strong but delicious flavor; the flesh becomes soft if not eaten fresh and does not keep well if frozen for a long time.

ID. Bluefish have a fairly long, stout, and compressed body, with a flat-sided belly. The mouth is large and has extremely sharp, flattened, and triangular teeth. The first dorsal fin is low and short and consists of six to eight spines, whereas the second is long and has one spine and twenty-three to twenty-eight soft rays; the anal fin has two spines and twenty-five to twenty-seven soft rays. Both the second dorsal fin and the anal fin are covered with small, compact scales. The coloring is greenish or bluish on the back, and silvery on the sides; a distinguishing characteristic is a dark blotch at the base of the pectoral fins. The tail is dusky and deeply forked, and, with the exception of the whitish pelvic fins, most of the fins are dark.

The bluefish is distinguished from the greater amberjack by the spine in the second dorsal fin, the absence of markings on the head, and the lack of a space between the dorsal fins. The absence of finlets easily distinguishes bluefish from mackerel.

Habitat. Favoring temperate to tropical waters, bluefish are known to be sporadic, if not cyclical, in occurrence and location. The young are often found in bays and estuaries. Adults migrate along coastal areas and are caught from the beach by surf anglers, on shoals and rips inshore, or farther offshore.

Food. Insatiable predators, bluefish feed on a wide variety of fish and invertebrates but target schools of menhaden, mackerel, and herring. They may roam in large groups, viciously attacking schools of smaller fish. This feeding frenzy destroys everything in their path, including their own young.

Angling. Bluefish roam widely, at times staying well offshore and at other times venturing up into the surf. They are sometimes caught in marshes, brackish rivers, and estuaries, although these are usually small fish, called snapper.

Birds working a slick are a dead giveaway to bluefish plundering schools of baitfish. Casting, jigging, and trolling on the perimeter of the slick are standard tactics. At other times, however, blues are a little harder to locate; they often favor deep water, tide rips, and unruly water, particularly inshore on a moving tide. Bluefish feed on a wide range of small fish, usually preferring whatever is most available, but they can be selective feeders and will also scrounge the bottom for sandworms and eels.

Bluefish succumb to a host of angling techniques and terminal tackle. This is true for boat and shore anglers alike. Trolling may be the most employed boating technique, using diving plugs, thick-bodied spoons, and surgical tubes; a fast speed is preferred. Drifting and jigging are popular where bluefish are known to linger; metal jigging spoons and bucktails, sometimes tipped with a piece of meat, are preferred offerings. Live baits work better than dead ones, but some anglers chum for blues and successfully drift hooked pieces of cut bait amid the chum.

Casters use a variety of plugs, as well as streamer flies, when the fish are thick. Shore, surf, and pier anglers can stillfish with baits in current, or cast surface or diving plugs and squid-imitation spoons. There should always be movement to the offering, as still lures or baits go untouched. Some anglers, incidentally, "sniff out" bluefish by smell, searching for a fresh-cucumber odor where blues have been plundering baitfish.

Bonefish

Albula vulpes

Although the bonefish was previously thought to be the only member of the Albulidae family, there are now five recognized species. The bonefish is the only significant sportfish among them, however, and is one of the most coveted of all saltwater gamefish. It is a wary, elusive creature, one that usually must be stalked with stealth and that bolts with startling speed when hooked or alarmed. Bonefish have little food value to anglers and virtually all are released, although they are a subsistence food in some locations.

ID. The bonefish has armor plates instead of scales on its conical head and is distinguished from the similar ladyfish by its suckerlike mouth and snout-shaped nose, which are adapted to its feeding habits. It also has a single dorsal fin and a deeply forked tail. The coloring is bright silver on the sides and belly with bronze or greenish blue tints on the back; there may also be yellow or dark coloring on parts of the fin and snout, and sometimes dusky markings on the sides.

Habitat. Occurring in warm coastal areas, bonefish inhabit the shallows of intertidal waters, including around mud and sand flats as well as mangrove lagoons. They are also found in waters up to 30 feet deep and are able to live in oxygen-poor water because they possess a lunglike bladder into which they can inhale air.

Food. Bonefish feed on crabs, shrimp, clams, shellfish, sea worms, sea urchins, and small fish. They prefer feeding during a rising tide, often doing so near mangroves. They root in the sand with their snout for food and are often first detected while feeding with their body tilted in a head-down, tail-up manner, with all or part of the tail fin protruding from the surface. These are referred to as tailing fish. Bonefish also sometimes stir up the bottom when rooting along, which is called mudding; this can be a telltale indicator to the observant angler.

Angling. Although some bonefish are caught accidentally in deep water, the primary habitat explored by anglers is shallow tidal flats and shoals. Bonefish feed on these flats, scouring the bottom. The shallow flats, which range from less than a foot to as much as several feet deep, leave the fish most vulnerable, so bonefish have good reason to be skittish. Boaters prefer to pole silently along in search of fish, staking the boat and fishing from the boat or by foot when bonefish are spotted. Waders walk on hard bottoms and carefully approach feeding fish.

Bonefishing is primarily sight fishing with fly-casting or light spinning tackle, so this species, in effect, is stalked. When bonefish are spotted, the angler maneuvers into position to intercept the fish with a judicious cast. If the terminal tackle lands on top of the fish or a school, the fish will dart away. So the lure, fly, or bait should be cast 6 to 10 feet ahead of feeding or cruising fish.

Small streamers or a weighted fly pattern work best in light browns and yellow; jigs are the primary artificials, in pink, white, and yellow; and shrimp, clams, and conch meat are popular baits. Shrimp is the best natural offering for bonefish. They are particularly attracted to the scent of fresh shrimp, so break off the tail and two of the four fans and thread the shrimp on the hook. A piece of conch or crab will also catch bonefish. Chum slicks are equally effective. Some bonefish anglers anchor or stake their boat and chum with crushed shrimp.

The end of an ebb tide and the beginning of a flood tide are usually best for the sake of spotting shallow fish (bonefish coming in over the flats on a rising tide are not half as wary when the tide starts to fall), but a slack flood tide can produce for anglers who fish waist-deep water by casting blindly with small jigs. Seldom do bonefish feed

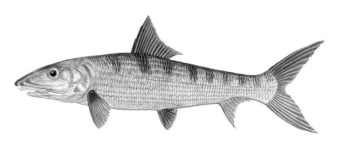

Bonefish

on shallow flats when the water temperature falls much below 70°F; they stay in deeper water then.

Common Snook

Centropomus undecimalis

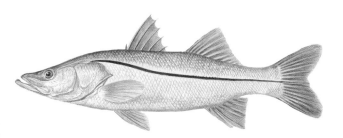

Common Snook

The common snook is the most abundant and wide-ranging of the twelve known species of snook and is highly sought after because of its strength and acrobatics when hooked. It is a member of the Centropomidae family, and was once a favored commercial species in Florida, where it is now strictly a gamefish.

ID. A silvery fish with a yellow green or olive tint, the common snook has a body that is streamlined and slender with a distinct black lateral line running from the top of its gills to the end of its forked tail. It has a sloping forehead, a long, concave snout, and a large mouth with brushlike teeth and a protruding lower jaw. The fins are occasionally bright yellow, although the pelvic fin is usually pale. The common snook has a high, divided dorsal fin and relatively short anal spines that do not reach the base of the tail when pressed against the body.

Habitat. Snook inhabit warm, shallow coastal waters and are able to tolerate both freshwater and saltwater. They are most common along continental shores, preferring fast-moving tides and relying on the shelter of estuaries, lagoons, mangrove areas, and brackish streams, as well as freshwater canals and rivers, usually at depths of less than 65 feet. Occasionally they occur in small groups over grassy flats and shallow patch reefs, and may be found at the mouths of tributaries and along the ocean side of shores near tributaries. Snook cannot tolerate water temperatures below 60°F; in winter, they stay in protected, stable-temperature areas such as those under bridges, in ship channels, turning basins, warm-water outflows near power plants, and the upper reaches of estuaries.

Food. Carnivorous predators that ambush their prey as currents sweep food into their vicinity, snook feed on both freshwater and saltwater fish, shrimp, crabs, and larger crustaceans.

Angling. Commonly caught in brackish water, snook are often found in the far reaches of freshwater rivers, as well as in lagoons and canals, often in the same cover-laden areas inhabited by largemouth bass where these species overlap. Their most common habitat, however, is inshore saltwater areas, particularly along mangrove-lined banks, as well as around such objects as bridges, docks, pilings, oyster bars and sandbars, along dropoffs and island edges, and in deep holes.

Renowned fighters, snook jump, run, dive deep, pull very hard, and are generally tough to land, especially in larger sizes. These fish have a penchant for heavy cover; when hooked, they repeatedly try to reach cover and get free by cutting the line, and they are often successful.

Casting or live-bait fishing are the primary means of pursuing snook. With the latter method, a small bait, such as a mullet, is live-lined by anglers who stillfish or drift. Casters primarily work shallow nearshore areas, often casting into thick mangrove stands and up under the bank.

Although small spoons and flies or poppers are used, the favored snook lures are walking plugs worked rapidly on the surface, or darting shallow-running plugs worked in jerky, erratic motions just under the surface. A moving tide, usually the high ebb, produces well. Some sight fishing is done by anglers drifting and looking for cruising fish on cover-laden flats or shores, but most angling is blind prospecting in likely places. Fly fishing is most prudent when the fish are visible, but it is also practiced in known snook-holding cover where fish aren't visible. Popping bugs and streamer flies are popular terminal items.

Tarpon

Megalops atlanticus

The largest member of the small Elopidae family, the tarpon is one of the world's premier saltwater gamefish. A species of warm tropical waters, it presents the foremost qualities that anglers seek in sportfish: it is very large, very strong, challenging to hook and land, often a target

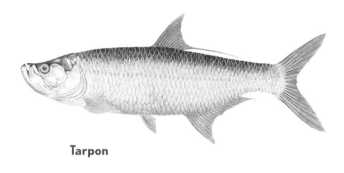

Tarpon

of sight fishing and casting in shallow water, and a spectacular leaper when hooked.

A hardy giant that can survive in a variety of habitats and salinities, the tarpon can even gulp air for extended periods when not enough oxygen is present in the water to sustain it. Despite its popularity among anglers, many aspects of this extremely long-lived fish's life cycle and behavior remain a mystery. This especially includes its migratory habits.

ID. The tarpon's body is compressed and covered with extremely large platelike scales and a deeply forked tail fin. Its back is greenish or bluish, varying in darkness from silvery to almost black. The sides and belly are brilliant silver. Underwater, tarpon appear to shimmer like huge gray ghosts as they swim sedately by. This appearance, along with their impressive size, is likely responsible for their nickname, "silver king." Inland, brackish-water tarpon frequently have a golden or brownish color because of tannic acid.

The huge mouth of the tarpon has a projecting, upturned lower jaw that contains an elongated bony plate. A single, short dorsal fin originates just behind the pelvic fin and consists of twelve to sixteen soft rays (no spines), the last of which is greatly elongated.

Habitat. Tarpon are most abundant in estuaries and coastal waters but also occur in freshwater lakes and rivers, offshore marine waters, and occasionally on coral reefs. Although tarpon do migrate, little is known about the frequency or extent of their travels.

Food. Tarpon often travel in schools and are opportunistic eaters that feed on a variety of fish and crabs.

Angling. The tarpon's powerful leaps, sometimes up to 10 feet out of the water, and bone-jarring bursts of speed test the skill and fortitude of even the most experienced angler.

The better fishing is in spring and fall, but they are caught in all months in some locales. Prominent fishing sites include rivers, bays, lagoons, shallow flats, passes between islands, mangrove-lined banks, and the like. Small tarpon, those up to 20 pounds or so, are usually located in estuaries and river mouths, even considerable distances up freshwater rivers and in sloughs and canals.

Fishing methods include drifting or stillfishing with live mullet, pinfish, crabs, shrimp, or other natural baits, or casting or trolling with spoons, plugs, or other artificial lures and flies. Trolling is generally the least practiced method; casting is generally most favored, as it involves stalking, spotting, and skillful bait or lure presentations. It may not be appropriate, however, when the fish are deep or unaggressive. The best fishing can be at night when tarpon are feeding.

When casting, anglers usually sight-fish for tarpon, staking out a shallow-draft boat near a channel or hole or moving along shallow grassy flats, usually by poling. They wait for tarpon to come within casting range, or try to spot cruising fish and then move to intercept them. A variety of plugs are cast, particularly shallow runners fished in a whip or jerky pull-pause retrieve. Surface plugs are also fished, and flycasters mainly employ large streamers.

Live-bait fishing occurs with anglers drifting or anchored and stillfishing with a float. Mullet, pinfish, crabs, and shrimp are used, usually in deep areas or in channels where the fish cruise through. Some anglers jig in deep-water holes and passes; others slow-troll along the edges of flats near deep water with big spoons, plugs, and feathers.

Great Barracuda and Pacific Barracuda

Great Barracuda

Sphyraena barracuda

A ferocious fighter and an excellent gamefish, the great barracuda is considered potentially dangerous because of its tendency to strike at flashing objects (which it mistakes for fish) and its ability to inflict serious harm, in or out of water, through its prodigious teeth. It is also a dangerous fish to eat because it leads a list of marine fishes that cause ciguatera when eaten, although small fish are apparently not poisonous. Not every barracuda causes ciguatera, but there is no safe or reliable way of recognizing toxic fish.

ID. The great barracuda is long and slender with a large, pointed head, resembling a freshwater pike in body shape. It also has large eyes. The dorsal fins are widely separated, and the first has five spines, whereas the second has ten soft rays. In a large underslung jaw, the great barracuda has large, pointed canine teeth. It also possesses a bluish gray or greenish gray body coloration above the lateral line and a silvery white belly. A few irregular black blotches are usually scattered on the sides of the body, especially toward the tail; it is the only species of barracuda that has these blotches. It grows much larger, in general, than its relative the Pacific barracuda.

Habitat. Young barracuda live in inshore seagrass beds, whereas adults range from inshore channels to the open ocean. They are also found in bays, inlets, lagoons, and the shallows of mangrove islands, as well as around reefs, wrecks, piers, sandy or grassy flats, and coastal rivers where saltwater and freshwater mingle. They prefer shallow areas and appear to move inshore in summer and offshore in fall and winter.

Food. The great barracuda eats whatever is available in its habitat; needlefish, small jacks, and mullet are among the mainstays. They are attracted by shininess or flashes and movement, feeding by sight rather than smell.

Angling. When holding in shallow waters close to shore, barracuda linger around such locales as mangrove edges, bridges, and jetties. When far from shore, they favor reefs, wrecks, oil rigs, coral heads, and the edges of dropoffs.

For a fish with a ferocious reputation, barracuda can actually be shy. They are alert to the presence of anglers and boats, even though they have been known to closely approach divers. They will follow a lure for quite a distance, but they'll scoot off as the lure nears a boat. For this reason, fairly distant casts beyond the fish are recommended. This gives it a chance to follow and strike the lure without being alarmed.

Great Barracuda

Barracuda are best caught on flashy, erratically worked items such as plugs, spoons, and surgical-tube lures. Fly anglers take them on big streamers. Flies and surface plugs, or shallow-running minnow plugs, are sometimes the best offerings, as they do not grab in the grass that is prevalent on so many shallow flats. A quick retrieve is favored, however. Barracuda often follow a lure that is worked at a slow or moderate speed but refuse to strike it, or will ignore a lure that stops altogether, whereas an increase in speed, even if it means working it fast and then faster, can be provocative.

Casters often ply the shallows and flats looking for barracuda, most of which lie motionless, waiting to pounce on unsuspecting prey; they can be difficult to spot when still, despite their length. Light- to medium-action spinning, baitcasting, or flycasting tackle provides the best sport. Many anglers troll for these fish, too, although usually with heavier tackle and while simultaneously pursuing other fish. Their arsenal includes plugs, spoons, trolling feathers, and rigged baits.

Pacific Barracuda

Sphyraena argentea

The Pacific barracuda is the best known of the four types of barracuda found in Pacific waters. It has always been one of California's most prized resources, both commercially and to anglers.

ID. The Pacific barracuda is slim-bodied, has a tapered head, a long thin snout, and large canine teeth in a lower jaw that projects beyond the upper jaw. It also has a forked tail, large eyes, and short, widely separated dorsal fins with five dorsal spines and ten dorsal rays. The anal fins have two spines followed usually by nine rays. Grayish black on the back with a blue tinge, shading to silvery white on the sides and belly, it has a yellowish tail that lacks the black blotches on the sides of the body that are characteristic of other barracuda. Large females have a charcoal black edge on the pelvic

Pacific Barracuda

and anal fins, whereas the male fins are edged in yellow or olive.

Habitat. Pacific barracuda prefer warmer waters. Only caught off California during the spring and summer, they can be found in Mexican waters throughout the year, reflecting a northerly spring migration and a southerly fall migration.

Food. The Pacific barracuda feeds by sight and eats small anchovies, smelt, squid, and other small schooling fish.

Angling. Pacific barracuda are most abundant during the spring and summer, from close to shore to about 7 to 8 miles out. They are caught by anglers trolling or casting with ¼- to 1-ounce feather jigs, strip bait, or live bait.

The primary means of taking Pacific barracuda is with a live bait such as a sardine, queenfish, or anchovy fished at or near the surface. Many anglers simply tie their line directly to a nickel or silver hook and freeline it with or without a small bit of split shot for weight. Be sure to set the hook a few seconds after the strike so the fish doesn't swallow the bait and cut the line.

Larger Pacific barracuda have a greater tendency to attack lures than do smaller specimens, and they also have a tendency to hold in deeper water. Thus a jig is a good lure for larger fish. Jigs can be cast and retrieved in a stop-start fashion, but sometimes it's necessary to fish it deeper and work it vertically.

Cobia and Tripletail

Cobia

Rachycentron canadum

The only member of the Rachycentridae family, and with no known relatives, the cobia is in a class by itself, and a popular food and sportfish for inshore anglers in areas where it is prominent.

ID. The body of a cobia is elongated with a broad, depressed head. The first dorsal fin consists of eight to ten short depressible spines that are not connected by a membrane. Both the second dorsal fin and the anal fin each have one to two spines and twenty to thirty soft rays. The adult cobia is dark brown with a whitish underside and is marked on the sides by silver or bronze lines. A cobia's shape is comparable to that of a shark, with a powerful tail fin and the elevated anterior portion of the second dorsal fin. It can be distinguished from the similar remora by the absence of a suction pad on the head.

Habitat. Adult cobia prefer shallow continental shelf waters, often congregating along reefs and around buoys, pilings, wrecks, anchored boats, and other stationary or floating objects. They are found in a variety of locations over mud, gravel, or sand bottoms, coral reefs and man-made sloughs, and at depths of up to 60 feet.

Food. Cobia feed mostly on crustaceans, particularly shrimp, squid, and crabs, as well as on eels and various small fish found in shallow coastal waters.

Angling. This species has become especially favored and hotly pursued from spring through fall by boaters, in part because it often offers sight-fishing opportunities, making it a species that anglers can cast lures and baits to, and in part because it is fairly predictably found around such structures as bridges, buoys, channel markers, and oil rigs.

Cobia are fairly aggressive a good deal of the time, readily striking plugs, jigs, and flies, and are sometimes caught handily on baits. They are usually not afraid of boats, often approaching and milling around.

The best cobia action occurs when cruising anglers hunt migrating fish. Working from boats, they search for cobia swimming near the surface, sometimes close to the beach but as far as a half mile from it. They use jigs or lures, casting 60 to

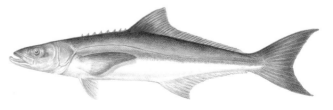

Cobia

80 feet to the brown-backed cobia. Live baits are also cast, although positioning is more of a concern because these baits cannot be cast as accurately over long distances. The same is true for fly fishing, although sometimes live baits are used to draw cobia closer to a boat for fly presentation. These fish move offshore on wrecks and reefs in summer and fall.

Live baits for cobia depend on geographic location and availability, but there's a range of choices. Peeler crabs, spot, and eels are favored in some areas, whereas mullet, pinfish, and grunts are used in others, in addition to pieces of squid. Lures include bucktail jigs, tube lures, and assorted swimming plugs.

Tripletail

Lobotes surinamensis

A member of the Lobotidae family, the tripletail is an excellent food fish with sweet, flaky white meat.

ID. The tripletail is characterized by its rounded dorsal and anal fins, which reach backward along the caudal peduncle, giving the fish the appearance of having a three-lobed, or triple, tail. Its deep, compressed body resembles the shape of the freshwater crappie, and it has a concave profile. The eyes are far forward on the snout, and the edge of the preopercle is strongly serrated.

Compared with other saltwater fish, tripletail probably most resemble grouper but lack teeth on the roof of the mouth. The color is drab, various shades of yellow brown to dark brown, with obscure spots and mottling on the sides.

Habitat. Tripletail occur in coastal waters and enter muddy estuaries, commonly in depths of up to 20 feet. There is some suggestion of a northerly and inshore migration into warm waters in the spring and summer.

Food. Tripletail feed almost exclusively on other fish, such as herring, menhaden, and anchovies, as well as on eels and benthic crustaceans like shrimp, crabs, and squid.

Angling. Anglers usually catch tripletail around wrecks, buoys, and offshore pilings and markers. This species is a strong and determined battler, which light-tackle anglers really enjoy catching, and also one that leaps.

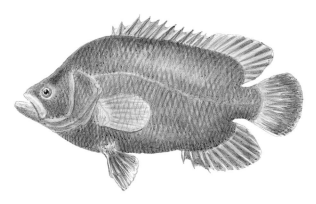

Tripletail

Most tripletail are caught by sight fishing. Anglers observe surface-floating specimens, often near weeds, and pitch bait to them. Shrimp works especially well. Small jigs, tipped with baits or equipped with a soft grub body, and streamer flies, also catch these fish, as do small plugs on occasion. Lures and flies should be worked near the surface, usually with a pausing, twitching motion.

Tripletail usually are best netted rather than gaffed, as they have tough scales. Anglers should use gloves when handling this species, as their gill covers can cause painful cuts.

Sea Bass

Sea bass are members of the Serranidae family of fish, which includes more than four hundred species of widely varying physiques, habitats, and natures. Popular among these are black sea bass, kelp bass, and giant sea bass.

Black Sea Bass

Centropristis striata

Black sea bass are a popular sportfish in the western Atlantic. Their firm white flesh makes excellent eating.

ID. The black sea bass has a relatively stout body three times as long (excluding the tail) as it is deep. It also has a high back, flat-topped head, slightly pointed snout, and a sharp spine near the apex of each gill cover. Both dorsal fins are joined into one continuous fin, and the tail is rounded; the

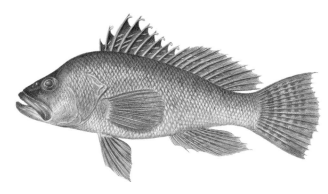

Black Sea Bass

elongated top ray of the tail that sticks out past the rest of the tail, particularly pronounced in larger specimens, is the most distinguishing feature of this fish. Because of the high back, which creates a noticeable rise just behind their heads, some large male black sea bass are called "humpbacks."

Coloration is variable, ranging from black to gray or brownish gray. The dorsal fins are marked by several slanting white spots arranged into lengthwise lines or a more random pattern. There also appear to be thin stripes on the sides, with wide vertical bands overlapping the stripes on some fish, and a large dark spot on the last dorsal spine. The upper and lower edges of the tail are white, as are the outer edges of the dorsal and anal fins. Males differ from this coloration, having a completely bluish black body, except for some white areas on the head and the edges of fins.

Habitat. The black sea bass is a bottom-dwelling species found around wrecks, reefs, piers, jetties, and breakwaters, and over beds of shells, coral, and rock. Small fish are found in shallow and quiet waters near the shore, such as in bays, whereas most larger fish prefer offshore reefs. Black sea bass prefer relatively cool waters, living offshore in winter and moving inshore in spring.

Food. Clams, shrimp, worms, crabs, and small fish constitute the diet of the omnivorous black sea bass.

Angling. When hooked on light tackle, the black sea bass fights hard all the way to the surface. Some are caught by anglers on docks, piers, or the shore, but most are taken by bottom fishing with baits or jigging with 2- to 4-ounce metal jigs from anchored or drifting boats. Fishing over wrecks often produces

large specimens. Preferred baits include fish pieces, shrimp, squid, and assorted crabs, worms, and clams, especially skimmer clams.

Where bigger sea bass are likely, a large piece of clam or squid or a small whole fish might be used, although smaller baits are employed inshore. Sea bass can be nibblers and bait stealers, so it pays to keep an eye on your bait.

Kelp Bass (Calico)

Paralabrax clathratus

One of a large number of sea bass found in the eastern Pacific, the kelp bass is one of the most popular sportfish in Southern California and a mainstay of party boat trips to northern Baja. It is a powerful fighter and an excellent food fish.

ID. A hardy fish with an elongate and compressed shape, the kelp bass has a notch between its spiny and rayed dorsal fins. The longest spines in the first dorsal fin are longer than any of the rays in the second dorsal fin. It is brown to olive green, with pale blotches on the back and lighter coloring on the belly. Kelp bass are easily distinguishable from various sand bass in that their third, fourth, and fifth dorsal spines are about the same length; the third dorsal spine of sand bass is much longer than the fourth and fifth.

Habitat. Kelp bass typically linger in or near kelp beds, over reefs, and around rock jetties and breakwaters or structures in shallow water; larger fish hold in deeper water, to roughly 150 feet.

Food. An omnivorous feeder, kelp bass favor assorted fish and small shrimplike crustaceans when young. Adults consume anchovies, small surfperch, and other small fish.

Angling. Kelp bass are a popular light-tackle fish caught from breakwaters in bays, or around

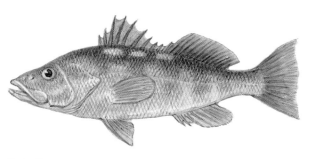

Kelp Bass

kelp beds by anglers trolling, drifting, or stillfishing from anchored boats. Live baits such as anchovies, sardines, queenfish, and mackerel squid are popular, as are a variety of artificial lures, particularly a metal jig and whole squid, as well as streamer flies fished on a sinking shooting-head line. Chumming is often done in combination with baiting and jigging, and larger specimens are often caught at small patches of kelp away from the larger kelp beds.

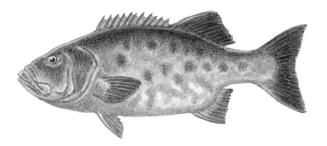

Giant Sea Bass

Giant Sea Bass

Stereolepis gigas

The giant sea bass is not only a formidable fish in size, but is also renowned for its lengthy life span. Mostly an eastern Pacific gamefish, specimens exceeding 500 pounds have been caught.

ID. The body of the giant sea bass is elongate and has dorsal spines that fit into a groove on the back. It is greenish brown or black with black or transparent fins, with the exception of the ventral fins, which appear lighter because of a white membrane between the black spines. There is usually a white patch on the throat and underneath the tail, and the membranes between the rays are also light.

The first dorsal fin is separated from the second by a single notch; the first is extremely low and has eleven spines, whereas the second is higher and has ten soft rays. The presence of more spines on the first dorsal fin than soft rays on the second distinguishes the giant sea bass from similar related species such as the goliath grouper, with which it has been confused in the past.

Habitat. Inhabiting inshore waters, giant sea bass are bottom-dwelling fish, preferring hard, rocky bottoms around kelp beds. The young occur in depths of about 6 to 15 fathoms, whereas larger specimens usually inhabit depths of 15 to 25 fathoms.

Food. The diet of the giant sea bass includes crustaceans and a wide variety of fish. Anchovies and croaker are a prominent food source; mackerel, sheepshead, whitefish, sand bass, and several types of crabs are also favored. Although these bulky fish appear to be slow and cumbersome, they are reputedly capable of outswimming and catching a bonito in a short chase.

Angling. Fishing methods include live- or dead-bait fishing from an anchored or drifting boat with cut baits and large natural baits like mackerel. Fishing is best in the 10- to 25-fathom range in summer, over rocky bottoms and around kelp beds.

Giant sea bass do not instinctively run for cover when they are caught, and they have no teeth to cut the line, so catching them is primarily a matter of having the tackle to match the fish and being able to outlast it. Encountering larger specimens, which often happens while using lighter tackle for calico bass or halibut, requires staying on top of the fish to minimize the chance of the line running into an obstruction, and applying enough constant pumping pressure to pull the fish away from the bottom.

Rockfish and Lingcod

Rockfish

A diverse and important group of marine fish, rockfish are members of the Scorpaenidae family, which includes 310 species generically characterized as scorpionfish. There are roughly sixty-eight species of rockfish in the genus *Sebastes* and two in the genus *Sebastolobus* that are found along the coasts of North America. Nearly all occur in Pacific waters. Both species of *Sebastolobus* and thirty-two species of *Sebastes* occur in Alaska's coastal waters, and at least twelve species range as far north as the Bering Sea.

Rockfish as a group have white, flaky meat with a delicate flavor, as befits deep-dwelling cold-water species. Most rockfish species are important to the commercial fishing industry, which uses otter trawls to catch them, and some are important to anglers. They may also be referred to as rock cod, sea bass, snapper, and ocean perch because

Copper Rockfish

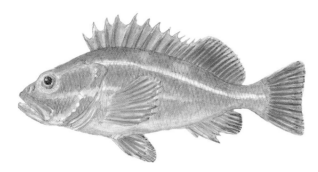

Yelloweye Rockfish

of their resemblance to these species or to the quality of their fillets, but the latter species are not related to rockfish.

Most rockfish are landed in deep water by anglers using bottom-fishing tactics or midwater drifting. These fish are not known for great battles or for large size, although the larger specimens of some species will provide good sport.

Common species encountered in Alaska include the black (*S. melanops*), copper (*S. caurinus*), dusky (*S. ciliatus*), quillback (*S. maliger*), and yelloweye (*S. ruberrimus*).

Common species in Washington include the black, copper, quillback, and yelloweye.

Common species in Oregon include the black, blue (*S. mystinus*), bocaccio (*S. paucispinis*), China (*S. nebulosis*), copper, Pacific Ocean perch (*S. alutus*), and yelloweye.

Common species in California include the black, blue, bocaccio, canary (*S. pinniger*), chilipepper (*S. goodei*), copper, cowcod (*S. levis*), greenspotted (*S. chlorostictus*), olive (*S. serranoides*), starry (*S. constellatus*), vermilion (*S. miniatus*), widow (*S. entomelas*), and yellowtail (*S. flavidus*).

ID. Adult rockfish range in size from 5 to 41 inches, but most species grow to between 20 and 24 inches in length. These fish are characterized by bony plates or spines on the head and body, a large mouth, and pelvic fins attached forward near the pectoral fins. The spines are venomous, and although not extremely toxic they can still cause pain and infection. Some species are brightly colored.

Habitat. Rockfish can generally be separated into those that live in the shallower nearshore waters of the continental shelf and those that live in deeper waters on the edge of the continental shelf. The former comprise species that are always found in rocky bottom areas (called shelf demersal by biologists) and those that spend much of their time up in the water column and off the bottom (shelf pelagic).

Members of some species do not wander far and actually have an extremely strong preference for a specific site. If a fish is captured and relocated elsewhere, it will quickly return to its original home site.

Food. Rockfish feed on a variety of food items. Adult rockfish eat such fish as sand lance, herring, and small rockfish, as well as crustaceans.

Angling. As their name implies, rockfish are found around rocky bottoms—the craggier the better—and at depths of 200 to 700 or more feet. Ledgelike dropoffs, deep rock valleys, and craggy peaks are especially good, as they contain holes and crevices where these fish can hide. In deep-water bottom fishing, it's necessary to use heavy weights or jigs to get to the bottom. Eight to 16 ounces of lead are used depending on the depths. The favored offerings are heavy metal lures, called "jigbars," diamond jigs, and similar heavy lures, often with a plastic grub or piece of squid attached. These are typically bounced off the rocks, but they can be fished up through the water column, as some species are not tight to the bottom.

In shallow water, usually under 100 feet and to maybe only 10 feet, anglers use lighter lures and multibait rigs, although this is usually where smaller rockfish are found. Herring, shrimp, worms, squid, small live fish, and strips or pieces of fish are used for bait. Some rockfish are caught near the surface and are susceptible to cast lures, even flies, although this usually occurs when the water is not rough or murky. The usual bottom rig is made up of three to six hooks above a sinker that is heavy enough to take the line to the bottom on a fairly straight course.

Because of the extreme depths fished, it takes a lot of weight and a lot of line on reels; low-stretch lines are helpful. The bait should be sufficiently firm to stay on the hook while being chewed upon; squid are commonly used for this reason.

Lingcod

Lingcod

Ophiodon elongatus

A Pacific marine species, the lingcod belongs to the family Hexagrammidae. Its name is misleading because it is not a true cod. However, it is an important and highly prized commercial species and sportfish. Its firm white flesh is often deep-fried as the main ingredient in fish and chips, but it may also be prepared in other ways with excellent results.

ID. The lingcod has a large mouth, large pectoral fins, a smooth body, and a long, continuous dorsal fin divided by a notch into spiny and soft parts. Adults have large heads and jaws and long, pointed teeth. Its coloring is usually brown or gray with blotches outlined in orange or blue, but this is closely associated with habitat.

Habitat. Lingcod inhabit colder waters in intertidal zone reefs and kelp beds that have strong tidal currents. They prefer depths from 2 to more than 70 fathoms over rock bottom.

Food. Adults feed on herring, flounder, cod, hake, greenling, rockfish, squid, crustaceans, and small lingcod.

Angling. The aggressive lingcod is as rough and rugged as the jagged, rocky bottom structure it inhabits. When the mood strikes it, the ling may viciously attack any potential meal unfortunate enough to come within striking range, including other lingcod nearly the size of the attacker. Most bottom-fish anglers have stories about lingcod that grabbed hooked fish and hung on, often long enough to be gaffed or netted at the surface. Just as often, though, lingcod will lose interest in feeding, and these apparent fasts may last hours or even days.

Slack tides usually afford the best opportunity to hook lingcod because that's when it's easiest to work a bait or lure straight down to the rocky, snaggy bottoms where this big predator is found; too much current or wind results in a flat line angle and constant hookups on the rocky bottom.

Metal slab jigs that imitate smaller fish work well for ling, as do big leadheads with large plastic grub bodies or pork rind strips. Many bait anglers use herring, and live baits work much better than dead ones. The ultimate lingcod bait is a live greenling, about 10 inches long, fished with a large, single hook through both lips to pin its mouth shut. Live-bait anglers must use a sinker large enough to take the offering down but have to exercise care in keeping it just off bottom, or the bait will dodge into a hole and become snagged before a lingcod finds it.

Cod, Pollock, and Hake

The various cod and hake are all members of the Gadidae family of codfish. All codfish live in cold waters of the Northern Hemisphere, some in the Atlantic and some in the Pacific. Most of the species are harvested commercially, although some have been in serious decline.

All members of the cod family have spineless fins. The pelvic or ventral fins are located far forward, commonly ahead of the pectorals. The body is elongated, and there is a single barbel on

Atlantic Cod

the chin. Most species have two dorsal fins, some have three, others only one.

Cod and other pelagic species in the family produce prodigious numbers of eggs. Cod are mainly bottom dwellers, feeding on small fish, mollusks, crabs, sea worms, and similar creatures.

The Atlantic cod (*Gadus morhua*) occurs off both the European and North American coasts in cool waters and from near the surface to depths of 1,000 feet or more. Smaller fish are generally closer to shore; larger ones remain in deeper water. Cod like cool waters and may sometimes follow cool currents out of their normal range.

Cod

The Atlantic cod has three dorsal fins and two anal fins. The light lateral line against its dark sides is a distinctive feature. The snout is rounded or cone-shaped on top, the upper jaw projecting slightly beyond the lower. The tail is almost squared or is slightly concave. There are two principal color phases, gray and red; in both, the sides are covered with dark dots.

The Pacific cod (*G. macrocephalus*) is found on both sides of the Pacific. Off the North American coast, it occurs from Oregon northward, only occasionally straying southward. The Pacific cod is almost identical to the Atlantic cod, differing only in having slightly more pointed fins. It is somewhat smaller on average.

Haddock

Closely related, and sometimes placed in the genus *Gadus*, is the haddock (*Melanogrammus aeglefinus*), found off both the North American and European coasts in the Atlantic. Haddock, like cod, travel in large schools. Today the catch has declined drastically because of overfishing.

Haddock are bottom feeders, usually found in greatest numbers in water 100 to 500 feet deep. The two most common of the several color variations are grayish green with a dark lateral line and golden brown with a yellow lateral line. Like the cod, the haddock has three dorsal and two anal fins, but it lacks spots on its body. The first rays on the leading dorsal fin are exceptionally long. Just above and behind each pectoral fin is a large dark blotch.

Angling for Cod, Pollock, and Hake

Recreational fishing for cod occurs over rough bottoms and wrecks, generally far offshore, which is the province of long-range party boats. Weights from 10 to 32 ounces are used to get bait down, and heavy jigs of similar heft are also employed. Fresh baitfish is a necessity, with clams and squid preferred.

Because cod are bottom fish, the trick is getting and staying in the right places. The angler must find the weight that will position the rig on the bottom in the given conditions while keeping a little slack in the line. This method enables the angler to detect a strike while the bait is drifting. Jigging does not have to be done right on the bottom, with the jig bouncing off it, but the jig should be fairly close to the bottom.

Pollock

The pollock (*Pollachius virens*) has been the most popular of the cod family with anglers. Averaging 4 to 10 pounds in weight (but with some weighing more than 30 pounds), the pollock is found on both sides of the Atlantic in cool to cold waters, usually close to shore but commonly netted at depths of 400 to 500 feet. The pollock's snout is pointed, the lower jaw projecting beyond the upper; the chin barbel is very small or lacking. The broad caudal fin is forked. Because the back and sides are a greenish brown, another name for the pollock is green cod. There are no spots, however, and the lateral line is white.

Pollock are active feeders, preying mainly on small fish but also taking crabs, mollusks, and other small animals. Anglers catch them principally by trolling, using jigs or spoons, but the smaller fish are known also to take artificial flies along inshore waters. They are strong fighters.

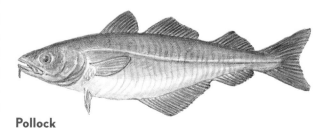

Pollock

Tomcod

The Atlantic tomcod (*Microgadus tomcod*) and its close relative, the Pacific tomcod (*M. proximus*), also have three dorsal and two anal fins, which are rounded, as are the long caudal fins. The pelvic fins extend into long filaments that may be sensory in function. These fish are generally olive brown above and lighter below, the sides heavily blotched with black. Tomcod average less than 12 inches in length, and only occasional individuals weigh more than a pound.

Hake

Hake differ from cod in having the second and third dorsal fins joined to make one large fin that typically is indented or notched where the two are joined. Directly below is an indentation on the anal fin. The lower jaw projects beyond the upper, and the chin barbel is either very small or absent. The caudal fin is shallowly forked. Hake feed on smaller fish and squid. They travel in schools, generally at the edge of the continental shelf or below, down to 2,000 feet.

The common species off the Atlantic coast of North America, from Newfoundland south to the Bahamas, is the silver hake (*Merluccius bilinearis*), which is regionally known as whiting and quite popular. In the Pacific, the only representative is the Pacific hake (*M. productus*).

The white hake (*Urophycis tenuis*), ranging from Newfoundland to North Carolina, is a slender fish that may exceed 3 feet in length and weigh more than 30 pounds. The average is about half this size. As in the hake of the genus *Merluccius*, the second and third dorsal fins are joined. The first ray of the first dorsal is extended into a slim filament, and the caudal fin is rounded. There is a small chin barbel, and the pelvic or ventral fins are reduced to long filaments. The back and sides are reddish, grading into yellowish gray below.

The red hake (*U. chuss*) occurs in the same general range as the white hake. The filament of its first dorsal fin is much longer, and the sides are mottled. The maximum size of the red hake is 8 pounds; the average is about 2 pounds. Several other species in the genus *Urophycis* are all about the size of the red hake or smaller.

Snapper are members of the large Lutjanidae family of fish, which includes more than one hundred species. These fish inhabit tropical or subtropical waters in the Atlantic, Indian, and Pacific oceans. Most are schooling species, although sizes vary widely. Likewise they range by species from shallow nearshore and inshore waters to deeper shelf environs.

They seldom inhabit estuaries and are generally demersal. Some larger-growing species may be confused with grouper; however, they can be readily distinguished from this fish by one or two large canine teeth at the front of the upper jaw. Also, the rear end of the upper jaw slides under the suborbital rim instead of outside it. Snapper have a moderately large mouth and their dorsal fin is continuous or slightly notched.

Many snapper species are important commercial fish and high-quality food fish. Some, particularly reef-dwelling species, are popular with anglers. The more popular species are profiled here.

Cubera Snapper

Lutjanus cyanopterus

The largest of all the snappers, the cubera is a hard-fighting gamefish as well as a fine food fish, although larger specimens may have coarse meat.

ID. The head, body, and fins of the cubera snapper are silver or steely gray to dark brown with an occasional reddish tinge; the body is darker above than below, sometimes with a purplish sheen. Most young fish and some adults have irregular pale bands on the upper body. The cubera snapper

Cubera Snapper

has dark red eyes, thick lips, and a rounded anal fin. It also has connected dorsal fins that consist of ten spines and fourteen rays, and pectoral fins that do not extend as far as the start of the anal fin.

The cubera snapper is often confused with the gray or "mangrove" snapper, although they can be differentiated by the number of gill rakers present on the lower limb of the first branchial arch; there are an average of seven to nine on the gray snapper in contrast to five to seven on the cubera snapper. They can also be distinguished by the tooth patch on the roof of the mouth; the gray snapper has an anchor-shaped patch, whereas the cubera snapper has a triangular one that does not extend back as the anchor-shaped one does. In general, the canine teeth of the cubera snapper are enlarged and noticeable even when the mouth is closed. The cubera can lighten or darken dramatically in color.

Habitat. Adult fish are found offshore over wrecks, reefs, ledges, and rocky bottoms. Cubera snapper are solitary and are usually found in 60 feet of water or deeper.

Food. Cuberas feed primarily on fish, shrimp, and crabs.

Angling. Like grouper and other deep reef fish, the cubera snapper is primarily caught by bottom-fishing methods at the right depth over irregular terrain. They are often caught on wrecks with heavy tackle, using lobsters for bait on bottom rigs and often spotting moving fish on sonar while drifting. Strikes may be rather light, but the fish bulldoze to the wreck or reef quickly and must be outmuscled.

Gray Snapper

Lutjanus griseus

An important commercial fish, the gray snapper is also a good gamefish and an excellent food fish. It is commonly referred to as the mangrove snapper and has white, flaky meat that is easily filleted.

ID. The coloring of the gray snapper is variable, from dark gray or dark brown to gray-green. The belly is grayish, tinged with olive, bronze, or red, sometimes described as reddish or orange spots running in rows on the lower sides. A dark horizontal band occasionally runs

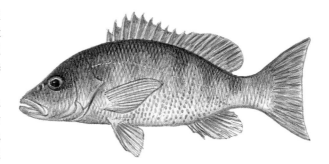

Gray (Mangrove) Snapper

from the lip through the eye, and some fish are said to have dark vertical bars or blotches along the sides. The tail may also have a dark margin, and the anal fin is rounded. There are two conspicuous canine teeth at the front of the upper jaw. The gray snapper can be distinguished from the cubera snapper by the shape of the tooth patch in the mouth, which is triangular in the cubera snapper and anchor-shaped in the gray snapper. In general, the gray snapper resembles other snapper except that it lacks a distinct spot on the sides.

Habitat. Young gray snapper are mostly found inshore over smooth bottom in such places as estuaries, the lower reaches of tidal creeks, mangroves, and seagrass meadows; adult fish generally range offshore over irregular bottom in such places as coral or rocky reefs, rock outcroppings, and shipwrecks, to depths of about 300 feet.

Food. Gray snapper feed primarily at night, leaving reefs late in the day for grassflats, where they consume plankton, small fish, shrimp, and crabs.

Angling. This species is particularly popular in Florida and around the Antilles, where it is caught by hook and line, by beach and boat seines, and in traps. It is primarily caught by bottom-fishing methods at the right depth over irregular terrain. Anglers fish for these and other reef fish from head boats and smaller private boats using manual and electric reels, sturdy boat rods, heavy monofilament line, and two-hook bottom rigs baited with squid and cut fish. In addition to fishing offshore, anglers also catch gray snapper in mangrove- and seagrass-dominated estuaries, using shrimp, clams, bloodworms, and occasionally artificial lures, especially small jigs.

Mutton Snapper

Lutjanus analis

Often marketed as "red snapper," the flesh of the mutton snapper is firm, white, and excellent fare.

ID. The mutton snapper can be striking in appearance, varying from orangish to reddish yellow or reddish brown, or from silver gray to olive green on the back and upper sides. All the fins below the lateral line have a reddish cast, and the larger mutton snapper takes on an overall reddish color, which causes it to be confused with the red snapper. Young fish are often olive-colored and may display dark bars. There is a distinct black spot about the size of the eye on the upper part of the body below the rear dorsal fin near the lateral line, and of all the snapper with this type of dark spot, the mutton snapper is the only one with a V-shaped tooth patch in the roof of the mouth rather than an anchor-shaped one. There are also small blue lines below and near the eye, and the dorsal fin has ten spines and fourteen rays. Adults tend to develop a high back, and all fish have pointed anal fins.

Habitat. Young fish occur over soft bottoms such as seagrass beds, whereas adults are found over hard bottoms around rocky and coral reefs, as well as in bays and estuaries. They drift above the bottom at depths of 5 to 60 feet.

Food. Mutton snapper feed both day and night on shrimp, fish, snails, crabs, and plankton.

Angling. Mutton snapper are strong fighters on light tackle and can be taken on natural baits or small lures fished vertically or slowly trolled near the bottom. They are primarily caught by bottom-fishing methods but are sometimes taken on flats or lured to the surface and caught on a fly.

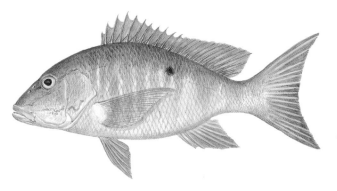

Mutton Snapper

Pacific Cubera Snapper

Pacific Cubera Snapper

Lutjanus novemfasciatus

The Pacific cubera snapper is an excellent food fish and is greatly prized as a sport catch. It closely resembles the cubera snapper in appearance, and displays similar habitat and behavior.

ID. The young Pacific cubera snapper is purplish brown with a light spot in the center of each scale, whereas adults and older fish are almost a deep red. Occasionally a blue streak is evident under the eye, as are roughly nine shaded bars on the flanks. The tail is very slightly forked or lunate (crescent-shaped), the dorsal fin is made up of ten spines and fourteen soft rays, and the anal fin is rounded and has three spines and eight rays. The pectoral fins do not extend to the anal fin or even as far as the vent in adults. The most distinctive feature of the Pacific cubera snapper is four uncommonly large canine teeth, two in the upper jaw and two in the lower, which are somewhat larger than the pupil of the eye. There is also a crescent-shaped tooth patch in the roof of the mouth.

Habitat. Pacific cubera snapper are an inshore species, preferring rocky and coral reefs and caves in shallow waters with depths of 100 feet and possibly deeper. Young fish are found in estuaries near mangroves and the mouths of rivers.

Food. Carnivorous, Pacific cubera snapper prey at night on big invertebrates such as crabs, prawns, and shrimp, as well as fish.

Angling. This species is a strong fighter and a tough sportfish that can be caught on live baits, jigs, spoons, feathers, plugs, or pork rind fished or trolled at up to 5 mph. Where there are plenty of rocky pinnacles, reefs, and islands, anglers can land these fish by casting diving plugs and surface plugs, the latter creating some terrific explosions.

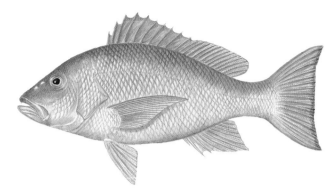

Red Snapper

Red Snapper

Lutjanus campechanus

The red snapper is one of the most valuable snapper for anglers and commercial fishermen; as a result, it has been severely overfished in American waters and is closely protected. It is one of the most highly coveted of all reef fish and usually one of the most expensive fish per pound on the market.

ID. The red snapper is pinkish, scarlet, or brick red on its head and upper body, and silvery whitish below. It has a long triangular snout, a sharply pointed anal fin, and a distinctively red iris. Young fish of under 10 inches in length have a dusky spot below the soft dorsal fin at and above the midline, and the tail sometimes has a dark edge. The red snapper has nine soft rays, forty-seven to forty-nine flank scales, and eight or nine scales between the dorsal fin and the lateral line.

Habitat. Adult fish are usually found over rocky bottom at depths of 60 to 400 feet, whereas young fish inhabit shallow waters over sandy or muddy bottoms.

Food. Red snapper are opportunistic bottom feeders that prey on fish, shrimp, crabs, and worms.

Angling. Anglers use bottom-fishing tactics over reefs, wrecks, oil rigs, and the like, usually fishing with stout tackle and lines in the 50-pound class. Consistently catching red snapper by hook and line is an art. Not only must one know where the best fishing grounds are, but the bait must be presented in a manner that entices the snapper to bite.

Multiple-hook rigs are favored, and selection of baits is critical. Squid heads with long tentacles, whole medium-size fish, and fresh bloody strips of little tunny or greater amberjack catch big red snapper. The fish seem to prefer a still or very slowly moving bait. Fishing from an anchored boat is productive, but when drifting it can be beneficial to freespool the line for a few minutes before slowly retrieving the slack. Gaining line quickly in the first few moments after the strike is critical. A hard strike and feverish winding are necessary.

Although many red snapper are caught right on the bottom, in some situations the larger fish are suspended off the bottom. These may be caught on heavy jigs, often tipped with a strip of bait, or by freelining baits at the proper upper level.

Yellowtail Snapper

Ocyrus chrysurus

The yellowtail snapper is a colorful tropical reef fish, and an excellent sportfish with superb meat.

ID. The yellowtail snapper has a streamlined body that is olive or bluish gray above and silver to white below. It has fine yellowish stripes on the belly. Most striking is the prominent yellow mid-body stripe, which runs from the tip of the snout through the eye to the tail, widening as it extends past the dorsal fins. The tail is bright yellow and deeply forked, and the dorsal fins are mostly yellowish. There is no dark lateral spot, and the eye is red.

Habitat. Inhabiting tropical coastal waters at depths of 10 to 300 feet, yellowtail snapper occur around coral reefs, either alone or in loose schools, and are usually seen well above the bottom.

Food. Yellowtail snapper feed mainly at night on benthic and pelagic animals, including fish, crustaceans, and worms.

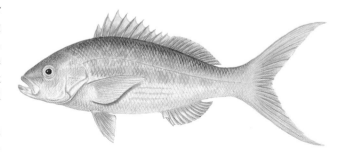

Yellowtail Snapper

Angling. Anglers use cut fish and squid to catch yellowtail inshore by fishing on the bottom from bridges and piers, and they catch them offshore by fishing over reefs from small private boats and party boats. These fish are attracted to chum and can be caught higher in the water column when they come into an established chum slick. They often do not take baits as aggressively as some other snapper or grouper do, however, and many are not hooked due to their small mouth (or too large a hook). They put a good bend in a light to medium-action spinning rod and make an excellent meal.

Grouper

Grouper are members of the Serranidae family of sea bass. Most are nonschooling species that generally congregate in the same area. Dozens of species inhabit all warm seas, preferring rocky shores and deep reefs. Grouper in general are good to eat and are a frequent catch of anglers.

Some species of grouper have the ability to reverse sex later in life, transforming from male to female. Most grow to modest sizes, but a few, such as the Warsaw and goliath grouper, reach gargantuan proportions.

Similar habitat, food, and angling characteristics are noted here, while separate identification information follows.

Habitat. Groupers are often solitary and lie resting camouflaged or within holes. Adults most commonly inhabit rocky bottoms, reefs, rocky ledges or undercuts, caves, and dropoffs. Smaller fish are usually closer to shore and common in or at the margin of seagrass beds. Some may inhabit environs many hundreds of feet deep. Interestingly, the largest of this group, the highly territorial goliath, inhabits inshore waters, and juveniles are common in mangrove areas and estuaries, especially around oyster bars. This species may be found at depths between 10 and 100 feet over rocky bottoms, reefs, ledges, dock and bridge pilings, and wrecks.

Food. Grouper feed on assorted fish, as well as crustaceans, squid, crabs, mollusks, and the like. They hide in holes and crevices and capture prey by ambush or after a short chase, usually swallowing it whole.

Angling. Catching grouper is primarily a bottom-fishing proposition, focusing efforts on irregular bottoms, rocky terrain, and deep reefs. Some slow trolling is done for grouper, including goliaths, but for the most part fishing consists of dropping bait rigs down to the bottom from anchored or drifting boats. Whole or large-cut bait are used, as is live bait. Conch, clams, crabs, and spiny lobsters are used, and especially squid and assorted fish, including mackerel, mullet, grunt, porgy, and snapper.

Heavy tackle is generally employed, especially when fishing really deep water and super-sized specimens are a possibility. Many large groupers will swim back into a deep hole when they are hooked, making them virtually impossible to pull out; so the key is turning a fish right away and muscling it away from its hole. Wire leaders are essential for the likes of Warsaw grouper, while other species, such as hind, require a heavy monofilament leader. Large hooks and heavy sinkers are also necessary.

Black Grouper

Mycteroperca bonaci

ID. Depending on location, the black grouper may be olive, gray, or reddish brown to black. It has black, almost rectangular blotches and brassy spots. It can pale or darken until its markings are hardly noticeable. It has a thin, pale border on its pectoral fins, a wide black edge and a thin white margin on its tail, and sometimes a narrow orangish edge to the pectoral fin; the tips of the tail and the soft dorsal and anal fins are bluish or black. The black grouper has a squared-off tail and a gently rounded gill cover.

Goliath Grouper

Epinephelus itajara

ID. The goliath grouper (once known as jewfish) is yellowish brown to olive green or brown. Dark brown blotches and blackish spots mottle the entire body, including the head and fins; these markings are variable and more prominent on the young. Irregular dark bands run vertically along the sides, although these are usually obscure. The body grows darker with age as the blotches and spots increase and become less noticeable in

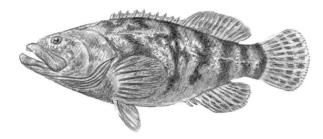

Goliath Grouper

contrast to the body. The first dorsal fin is shorter than, and not separated from, the second.

The goliath grouper is differentiated from the giant sea bass by its dorsal fin soft rays, of which it has fifteen or sixteen; the giant sea bass has only ten. Distinctive features of the goliath also include a very small eye, a rounded tail fin, and large rounded pectoral fins.

Nassau Grouper

Epinephelus striatus

ID. Although its color pattern varies, the Nassau grouper usually has a light background with a wide dark brown stripe running from the tip of the snout through the eye to the start of the dorsal fin, as well as four or five irregular dark bars running vertically along the sides. Two distinctive features are the black dots always present around the eye, and a large black saddle on the caudal peduncle, also always present no matter what color the fish is. The third spine of the dorsal fin is longer than the second, the pelvic fins are shorter than the pectoral fins, and the dorsal fin is notched between the spines. It has the ability to change color from pale to almost black.

Red Grouper

Epinephelus morio

ID. Of varying coloration, the red grouper is usually dark brownish red, especially around the mouth, and may have dark bars and blotches similar to those on the Nassau grouper, as well as a few small whitish blotches scattered in an irregular pattern. It is distinguished from the Nassau grouper by its lack of a saddle spot and its smooth, straight front dorsal fin. On the Nassau grouper the dorsal fin is notched.

The red grouper has a blackish tinge to the soft dorsal, anal, and tail fins; pale bluish margins on the rear dorsal, anal, and tail fins; and small black spots around the eye. The lining of the mouth is scarlet to orange. The second spine of the dorsal fin is longer than the others, the pectoral fins are longer than the pelvic fins, and the tail is distinctively squared off. The red grouper pales or darkens in accordance with its surroundings.

Warsaw Grouper

Epinephelus nigritus

ID. The Warsaw grouper has a gray-brown or dark red-brown body, occasionally irregularly spotted with several small white blotches on the sides and the dorsal fins, although these are indiscernible in death. The young Warsaw has a yellow tail and a dark saddle on the caudal peduncle.

The Warsaw is distinctive as the only grouper with ten dorsal spines, the second of which is much longer than the third. It also has a squared-off tail. In contrast to the goliath grouper, the rays of the first dorsal fin on the Warsaw grouper are much higher and the head is much larger.

Nassau Grouper

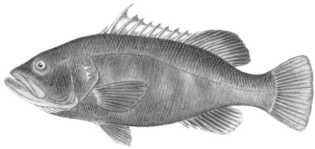

Warsaw Grouper

Yellowfin Grouper

Mycteroperca venenosa

ID. The yellowfin grouper has highly variable coloring, usually with a pale background and horizontal rows of darker rectangular blotches covering the entire fish; the ends of these blotches are rounded, and they can be black, gray, brown, olive green, or red. There are also small dark spots running across the body, which grow smaller toward the belly and usually appear bright red. The outer third of the pectoral fins are bright yellow, whereas the tail has a thin, dark, irregular edge. An overall reddish cast is present in fish from deep water, and the yellowfin grouper has the ability to change color dramatically, or to pale or darken.

Gag

Mycteroperca microlepis

ID. Pale to dark gray or sometimes olive gray, the larger gag is darker than the smaller gag and has blotchy markings on its side and an overall indistinctly marbled appearance. The smaller gag is paler and has many dark brown or charcoal marks along its sides. The pelvic, anal, and caudal fins are blackish with blue or white edges. The gag is distinguished from the black grouper by its deeply notched preopercles.

Red Hind

Epinephelus guttatus

ID. Like all grouper, the red hind has a stout body and a large mouth. It is very similar to the rock hind in appearance, although the red hind is slightly more reddish brown in color with dark red-brown spots above and pure red spots below over a whitish background. It differs from the rock hind in having no spots on the tail or dorsal fin, and no dark splotches on the back or tail. The outer edges of the soft dorsal, caudal, and anal fins are blackish and are sometimes also edged in white. It can pale or darken to blend with its surroundings.

Rock Hind

Epinephelus adscensionis

ID. The rock hind has an overall tan to olive brown cast, with many large reddish to dark dots covering the entire body and fins. Similar in appearance to the red hind, it has one to four distinctive pale or dark splotches along its back, appearing below the middle of the dorsal fin, behind the dorsal fin on the caudal peduncle, and below the spinous and soft parts of the dorsal fin. The tail and anal fins have a broad, whitish outer edge but lack the additional blackish margins found on the dorsal, caudal, and anal fins of the red hind. It can pale or darken dramatically.

Coney

Cephalopholis fulva

ID. Because the coney experiences numerous color phases, it is inadvisable to try to identify this fish by color. These phases range from the common one in which the fish is reddish brown, to a bicolor period in which the upper body is dark and the lower body is pale, to a bright yellow phase. The body is covered with small blue to pale spots, although the spots are uncommon in the bright yellow phase. There are often two black spots present at the tip of the jaw and two more at the base of the tail, as well as a margin of white around the tail and the soft dorsal fin. The tail is rounded, and there are nine spines in the dorsal fin.

Jacks and Pompano

Jacks are among the most important sport and commercial fish and are distributed worldwide in temperate and tropical waters. Some 140 species constitute the Carangidae family of jacks and pompano, which also includes such prominent sportfish as roosterfish, permit, amberjack, and yellowtail. Jacks are almost exclusively saltwater fish, although some species occur rarely in brackish water. They are strong, fast swimmers and virtually all fight like a bulldog when caught on rod and reel, regardless of their size. Some jacks, but not all, are good table fare, although a few species have been associated with ciguatera poisoning.

These fish are distinguished by a widely forked caudal fin and a slender caudal peduncle. The body is generally compressed, although the shape (and color) varies considerably, from very deep to fusiform. Some jacks resemble mackerel and are equally swift, but they lack the distinguishing rows of finlets. Many have extremely small scales, but at the end of the lateral line these are enlarged to form a keel. There are usually two spines in front of the anal fin.

Although young jacks travel in schools, adults of most species are usually solitary or travel in small groups. Some are generally caught in water of moderate depth, others in relatively deep waters, and some are pursued on shallow flats and reefs.

Almaco Jack

Seriola rivoliana

The deep-bodied almaco jack is an excellent and widely distributed sportfish. It is a fine food fish, although it sometimes has tapeworms in the caudal peduncle area, which can be cut away so that the meat can be eaten safely, and it has been associated with ciguatera poisoning in the Caribbean.

ID. The body and fins can be a uniform dark brown, a dark bluish green, or a metallic bronze or gray, with the lower sides and the belly a lighter shade, sometimes with a lavender or brassy cast. A diagonal black band usually extends from the lip through the eye to the upper back at the beginning of the dorsal fin. The front lobes of the dorsal and anal fins are high and elongated and have deeply sickle-shaped outer edges. There are seven spines in the first dorsal fin. The almaco jack is similar in appearance to the greater amberjack but has a deeper, more flattened body and a more pointed head; the greater amberjack has a more elongated body, a lighter band, and a shorter front dorsal fin.

Habitat. A warm-water species, almaco jacks prefer deep, open water and inhabit the outer slopes of reefs, but they rarely swim over reefs or near shore. Almaco jacks often travel alone and occasionally in schools at depths of 50 to 180 feet.

Food. An offshore predator, the almaco jack feeds mainly on fish but also on invertebrates.

Angling. The almaco is caught less frequently than its amberjack cousins, probably because it is a generally deeper and more oceanic species. Almacos are usually caught around buoys, wrecks, or natural reefs, usually incidental to general offshore trolling for various species or fishing for assorted reef dwellers, rather than as a deliberate

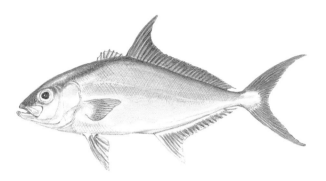

Almaco Jack

target. Trolling with deep-running plugs or bottom fishing with cut baits are both effective.

Bar Jack

Caranx ruber

Small and more like a saltwater panfish, the bar jack is a scrappy species and a good food fish.

ID. The bar jack is silvery with a dark bluish stripe on the back that runs from the beginning of the soft dorsal fin and onto the lower tail fin. Sometimes there is also a pale blue stripe immediately beneath the black stripe that extends forward onto the snout. The bar jack bears a resemblance to the blue runner, an offshore species caught incidentally by anglers and often used as bait in big-game fishing, but has fewer and less prominent large scales along the caudal peduncle than the blue runner. The bar jack has twenty-six to thirty soft rays in the dorsal fin and thirty-one to thirty-five gill rakers on the lower limb of the first arch. When feeding near bottom, it can darken almost to black.

Habitat. Bar jacks are common in clear, shallow, open waters at depths of up to 60 feet, often over coral reefs. Usually traveling in spawning schools, they sometimes mix with goatfish and stingray, although they are occasionally solitary.

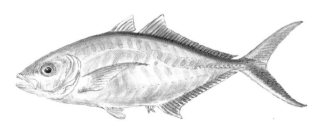

Bar Jack

Food. Opportunistic feeders, bar jacks feed mainly on pelagic and benthic fish, some shrimp, and other invertebrates.

Angling. Bar jacks are usually caught on light spinning outfits and a small jig or small baited hook.

Crevalle Jack

Caranx hippos

Pacific Crevalle Jack

Caranx caninus

These two species are almost identical in appearance and were formerly thought to be Atlantic and Pacific versions of *Caranx hippos*. Both are popular sportfish and are among the toughest of all inshore fish, although they are not highly valued as table fare.

ID. Both the crevalle jack and the Pacific crevalle jack are bluish green to greenish gold on the back and silvery or yellowish on the belly. They are compressed, and the deep body has a high rounded profile as well as a large mouth. The tail and anal fin may be yellowish, and the ends of the dorsal and upper tail are occasionally black. There is a prominent black spot on the gill cover and another black spot at the base of each pectoral fin. Young fish usually have about five broad black bands on the body and one on the head. The soft dorsal and anal fins are almost identical in size, and there are eighteen to twenty-one soft rays in the dorsal fin and sixteen to nineteen gill rakers on the lower limb of the first arch.

The two species are distinguished externally from each other only by the presence of a larger maximum number of scutes, up to forty-two on the Pacific crevalle jack, as opposed to twenty-six to thirty-five on the crevalle jack. The crevalle jack bears a resemblance to the Florida pompano but has a larger mouth. It can be distinguished from the similar horse-eye jack by a small patch of scales on the otherwise bare chest, whereas the chest of the horse-eye jack is completely covered with scales.

Habitat. Both species can tolerate a wide range of salinities and often inhabit coastal areas of brackish water and may ascend rivers, frequenting shore reefs, harbors, and protected bays. Small fish are occasionally found over sandy and muddy

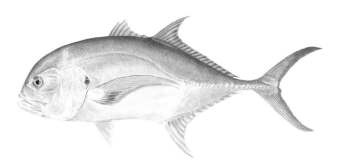

Crevalle Jack

bottoms of very shallow waters, as in estuaries and rivers. They are common in depths of up to 130 feet and often move into cooler, deeper water during the summer.

Food. Voracious predators, these fish feed on shrimp, other invertebrates, and smaller fish. Crevalle jacks will often corner a school of baitfish at the surface and feed in a commotion that can be seen for great distances, or they will chase their prey onto beaches and against seawalls. Fish of both species often grunt or croak when they are caught.

Angling. Tenacious fighters, the crevalle and Pacific crevalle are excellent candidates for light-tackle fishing. The crevalle jack is most often caught by anglers casting and trolling for other species, commonly using artificial as well as natural baits. This superb light-tackle species can be taken by spinning, fly fishing, trolling, or surf casting, and with such live baits as mullet or pinfish. Anglers should retrieve lures and flies at a fast pace without pausing or stopping, as jacks tend to lose interest in anything that doesn't act normally.

Horse-Eye Jack

Caranx latus

A good light-tackle quarry, the horse-eye is not highly esteemed as a food fish, although the quality of its meat can be improved by cutting off the tail and bleeding the fish directly after it is caught. This and other jacks have been implicated in cases of ciguatera poisoning.

ID. The horse-eye jack is silvery, with yellow tail fins and usually dark edges on the dorsal and upper tail fin. There is often a small black spot

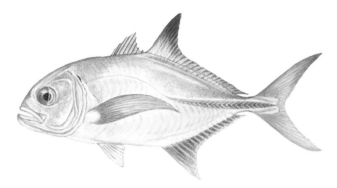

Horse-Eye Jack

at the upper end of the gill cover, and it usually has blackish scutes. The body is compressed, and the entire chest is scaly. There are twenty to twenty-two soft rays in the dorsal fin and fourteen to eighteen gill rakers on the lower limb of the first arch. The horse-eye jack is similar in shape to the crevalle jack, although its forehead is less steep and it is either lacking the dark blotch at the base of the pectoral fins of the crevalle jack or the blotch is more poorly defined. It can also be distinguished by its scales, which the crevalle jack lacks except for a small patch.

Habitat. Horse-eye jacks are most common around islands and offshore, although they can tolerate brackish waters and may ascend rivers. Adults prefer open water and may be found over reefs, whereas young are usually found along sandy shores and over muddy bottoms. Schooling in small to large groups at depths of up to 60 feet, horse-eye jacks may mix with crevalle jacks.

Food. Horse-eye jacks feed on fish, shrimp, crabs, and other invertebrates.

Angling. This is a good light-tackle gamefish that can be taken with live baits such as mullet, pinfish, and other small fish, as well as with plugs, jigs, spoons, flies, and other small artificial lures. They are often encountered in fast-moving schools. Lures should be retrieved at a fast pace without slowing or stopping.

African Pompano

Alectis ciliaris

The African pompano is the largest and most widespread member of the Carangidae family, an excellent light-tackle gamefish, and a superb food fish.

ID. The most striking characteristic of the African pompano is the four to six elongated, threadlike filaments that extend from the front part of the second dorsal and anal fins. These filaments tend to disappear or erode as the fish grows, although in young fish the first two of these may initially be four times as long as the fish. The body shape of the African pompano changes as it grows; starting out short and deep, it becomes more elongated by the time it is 14 inches long, and the forehead becomes steeper and blunter. The body is strongly compressed, and the rear half of the body is triangular. The lateral line arches smoothly but steeply above the pectoral fins and has twenty-four to thirty-eight relatively weak scutes in the straight portion and 120 to 140 scales. Shiny and silvery on the whole, larger fish may be light bluish green on the back; on all fish there may be dark blotches on the operculum on the top part of the caudal peduncle, as well as on the front part of the second dorsal and anal fins.

Habitat. Inhabiting waters up to 300 feet deep, young fish prefer open seas and linger near the surface, whereas adults most often prefer to be near the bottom over rocky reefs and around wrecks. African pompano may form small, somewhat polarized schools, although they are usually solitary in the adult stage.

Food. African pompano feed on sedentary or slow-moving crustaceans, small crabs, and occasionally on small fish.

Angling. An excellent gamefish, African pompano are greatly appreciated for their hard fight, stamina, and beauty. Although they look and fight much like a permit, the similarities are superficial, as these fish are not observed on shallow flats like permit and are mainly caught over wrecks and reefs and in many places incidentally by anglers trolling or baitfishing for grouper, snapper, kingfish, and sailfish. Fish are caught deep on jigs and on baits, and when attracted to the surface by chumming they are caught on cast hooked baits, or plugs or flies.

In addition to wrecks and reefs, these fish are attracted to humps, rockpiles, ledges, and irregular bottom structures that might hold baits.

Large bucktails (1 to 3 ounces are standard), are used to jig deep, and white is the preferred color. Subtle strikes usually follow when the jig falls during the jigging motion, but making a wide-sweeping jigging motion with a tight line is

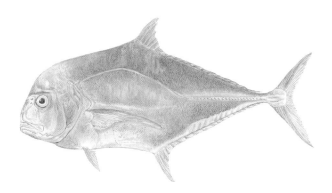

African Pompano

also productive. Slow trolling with deep-fished live baits may also be productive.

Prodigious amounts of live baits are used as chum to attract African pompano to the surface. Anglers offer live pilchards, menhaden, or herring, and often there's action for various other species before African pompano come around. When they do, however, they are caught on live hooked baits, or cast popping plugs, shallow swimming plugs, and streamer flies or fly rod poppers.

Florida Pompano

Trachinotus carolinus

The Florida pompano is an excellent gamefish for its generally smaller size and is an exciting catch on light tackle. It is also considered a gourmet food fish because of its delicately flavored and finely textured meat.

ID. Mostly silvery when alive, the Florida pompano is one of the few fish that is more striking in color after death. It then has greenish gray or dark blue shading on the back, and a golden cast to the belly and fins. Deep- or dark-water fish tend to also have gold on the throat, pelvic, and anal fins; young fish tend to have a yellowish belly, anal fin, and tail.

The Florida pompano has a deep, flattened body; a short, blunt snout with a small mouth; and a deeply forked tail. Unlike most jacks, it has no scutes on the caudal peduncle. The first and spinous dorsal fin is very low and usually hard to see, whereas the second has one spine and twenty-two to twenty-seven soft dorsal rays. The anal fin, which begins slightly farther back on the body than the second dorsal fin, has three spines and twenty to twenty-three soft anal rays.

The Florida pompano is similar in appearance to the permit, although the permit is deeper-bodied and tends to be a much larger fish.

Habitat. Frequenting inshore and nearshore waters, adult Florida pompano occur along sandy beaches, including oyster bars, grassbeds, inlets, and often in the turbid water of brackish bays and estuaries. They usually prefer shallow water but may occur in water as deep as 130 feet. Young fish inhabit sandy, muddy, or open beaches. Florida pompano generally form small to large schools that travel close to the shore and migrate up and down the Atlantic coast.

Food. Florida pompano feed on mollusks, crustaceans, and other invertebrates and small fish.

Angling. Anglers pursue Florida pompano while fishing from bridges, jetties, piers, the surf, and small boats. Fishing on the bottom with natural baits is a successful method, but some anglers cast and troll small artificial lures. Because these fish are sensitive to cold water, late summer and early fall are the best times to catch Florida pompano in their northern range; they are available in Florida waters from late spring through fall in normal years, and year-round during mild winters.

Terminal tackle favored by bait users consists of two or three No. 1 or 1/0 hooks tied on short dropper loops one above the other. Sand fleas, shrimp, clams, and small crabs are good baits. The best fishing conditions are early morning or late afternoon, on an incoming high tide with light to moderate surf and clear water.

Anglers who fish bays, passes, and grassflats from boats are more likely to use small jigs on light spinning tackle. The time-honored pompano jig—a round leadhead equipped with a short

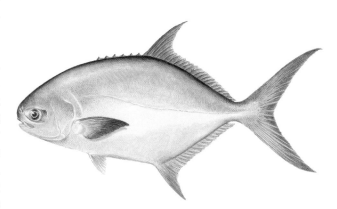

Florida Pompano

bucktail body—is still extremely popular with casters, but also effective are jigs with different head shapes and soft plastic bodies. Occasionally they may be tipped with pieces of shrimp or with sand fleas. Sizes range from ¼ ounce to 1 ounce depending on depth and current.

Jigs can be fished vertically over reefs and on the edges of deep-water flats. Sandbars, passes, clam beds, and other inshore structures, including grassflats, are also targeted, often while the boat drifts and the angler casts ahead. Before and after a flood tide are often better times.

Roosterfish and Permit

Roosterfish

Nematistius pectoralis

The roosterfish is a superb gamefish and a member of the Carangidae family of jacks, so named for the comb of long dorsal fin spines that extend far above the body of the fish.

ID. A striking, iridescent fish, the roosterfish is characterized by seven long, threadlike dorsal fin spines, which are found even on young fish. This comb stands erect when the roosterfish is excited, as when threatened or when aggressively chasing prey, but ordinarily the fin remains lowered in a sheath along the back. There are also two dark, curved stripes on the body and a dark spot at the base of the pectoral fin.

Habitat. Roosterfish inhabit shallow inshore areas, such as sandy shores along beaches, as well as rocky cliffs around islands. They may be

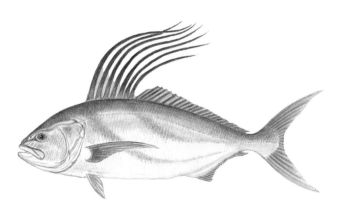

Roosterfish

found in shallow depths near structure or in a few feet of water in the surf, or on the bottom in near-shore environs. They are often solitary, but may be found in schools, and also may be associated with schools of crevalle jack.

Food. Roosterfish are aggressive predators that primarily consume assorted fish.

Angling. This inshore species inhabits moderate depths of water and fights particularly well. It may jump several times after being hooked, dive deeply, and engage in a slugfest. A good-size roosterfish, roughly 20 pounds, will make a startling first run, especially when caught in shallow water.

Roosterfish are frequently found in loose groups and are often spotted under working birds. They are caught by boaters who drift and troll, but also by surf anglers and those who cast from boats. Sandy-bottomed locales are good, as are bays and sections of mild surf. Smaller fish are usually closer to shore.

Trolling with strip baits, live baits, plugs, and feathers is popular; casting and live-bait drifting, particularly when a group of roosterfish is located, can be particularly effective.

The most enjoyable and exciting way to catch roosters, however, is by casting surface lures to the beach from a boat, or casting around rocky islands and pinnacles. The primary lures, especially for larger specimens, are 2- to 3-ounce pencil poppers and surface spoons such as the Robert's Ranger series. Both are cast long distances (helpful with microfilament lines) and rapidly retrieved in a skipping manner over the surface.

When casting to the beach, the tactic is to get the lure working down the back side of the first wave on the beach, skipping it over the trough that is just a foot or two deep and then continuing all the way to the boat. Sometimes roosterfish follow the lure all the way from the surf to the boat and strike nearby, and other times they strike midway along the retrieve. Usually they immediately head back to the surf in a punishing run, and often they are observed as they chase the skipping surface lure, with their dorsal comb erect and sticking out of the water. In some instances, several fish can be observed trying to attack the lure. When a school of fish is located, it is possible to have multiple hookups and truly exciting action.

The tackle for these fish is often quite stout, but medium-action gear with 15- to 20-pound line has merit for smaller specimens, and heavier line where larger fish may be encountered. Fly rods and spinning or heavy baitcasting gear are good choices for casters.

Permit

Trachinotus falcatus

An important gamefish and a particularly prized member of the Carangidae family, the permit is a tough fighter and a handful on light tackle. The permit is also an excellent food fish, although it is much less important commercially than the Florida pompano.

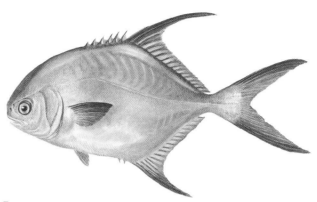

Permit

ID. In overall appearance, the permit is a brilliantly silver fish with dark fins and a dark or iridescent blue to greenish or grayish back. The belly is often yellowish, and sometimes the pelvic fins and the front lobe of the anal fin have an orange tint. Many individuals have a dark, circular black area on the side behind the base of the pectoral fin, and some have a dusky mid-body blotch. The body is laterally compressed, and the fish has a high back profile; young fish appear roundish, adults more oblong. Small permit have teeth on the tongue.

The permit has sixteen to nineteen soft anal rays, and the second dorsal fin has one spine and seventeen to twenty-one soft rays, compared with twenty-two to twenty-seven in the similar Florida pompano. It is further distinguished by its deeper body and a generally larger body size. Also, the second and third ribs in the permit are prominent in fish weighing more than 10 pounds, and these ribs can be felt through the sides of the fish to help in differentiating it from the Florida pompano.

Habitat. Permit inhabit shallow, warm waters in depths of up to 100 feet. Able to adapt to a wide range of salinity, they occur in channels or holes over sandy flats and around reefs, and sometimes over mud bottoms. They are primarily a schooling fish when younger, traveling in schools of ten or more; they tend to become solitary with age. They are sometimes attracted to areas where the bottom is stirred up.

Food. Over sandy bottoms, permit feed mainly on mollusks, and over reefs they feed mostly on crustaceans such as crabs, shrimp, and sea urchins. On shallow flats they feed by rooting in the sand.

Angling. An elusive, coveted, and heralded saltwater fish, permit are renowned for being difficult to approach, difficult to entice to strike, difficult to set a hook in, and difficult to land. As a warm-water fish pursued mostly in South Florida, the Florida Keys, and the Bahamas, permit are unavailable to most North American anglers, and these conditions only enhance their mystique.

Although some anglers favor bait fishing or jigging in intermediate depths over reefs, wrecks, and the like, the vastly preferred practice is to sight-fish for permit while stalking the same shallow flats inhabited by bonefish and casting a jig, fly, or live crab or shrimp. Permit venture onto sandy flats on a rising tide to scour the bottom for food and are often seen cruising or tailing while feeding. They also may locate around channel edges, where a falling tide will wash food off the flats.

On the flats they are skittish, and anglers stalk them carefully in a boat or by wading. Although it is often critical to make a precise presentation, this is made easier and less critical when a school is encountered, as the competitive instinct may prevail. Nonetheless, relatively few fish are hooked, and fewer still landed, in comparison to the number of fish seen, so the importance of stalking and presentation should not be underestimated. Furthermore, the nature of their feeding behavior—rooting down on the bottom—reduces their field of vision, making it important to position the offering where the fish can see it, and then to move it just enough to interest them.

Most permit are caught on live crabs; some respond to live shrimp. Medium-size blue crabs about 2 inches across are best, and many anglers clip the claws off before impaling them on a 2/0 or 3/0 hook. Small jigs produce a fair number of fish. Weighted flies are a more challenging offering, and therefore less effective, but a select few patterns produce consistently.

Amberjack and Yellowtail

Greater Amberjack

Seriola dumerili

The greater amberjack is the largest of the jacks, the most important amberjack to anglers, and, like most of its brethren, a tenacious fighter. It is considered a fair food fish, and a substantial commercial fishery for this species exists in some locales, yet the greater amberjack is high on the list of tropical marine fish suspected of causing ciguatera poisoning, although this problem may be isolated to certain areas, as greater amberjack are regularly consumed without incident in some places.

ID. The greater amberjack is greenish blue to almost purple or brown above the lateral line, and silver below the lateral line. A dark olive brown diagonal stripe extends from the mouth across both eyes to about the first dorsal fin; these are commonly referred to as "fighter stripes" and are prominent in live fish, especially when they are excited. A broad amber stripe runs horizontally along the sides, and disappears after the fish dies. The fins may also have a yellow cast. The greater amberjack has short foredorsal fins, a bluntly pointed head, and no detached finlets.

The greater amberjack bears a resemblance in smaller sizes to the bluefish (as well as other jacks), but it can be distinguished by its more deeply concave tail. Also, it has small teeth in bands instead of the large triangular teeth of the bluefish. The amber stripe sometimes causes anglers to confuse the greater amberjack with the yellowtail, but it can be distinguished by the eleven to sixteen developed gill rakers on the lower limb of the first branchial arch; the yellowtail has twenty-one to twenty-eight gill rakers.

Habitat. Greater amberjack are found mostly in offshore waters and at considerable depths, as well as around offshore reefs, wrecks, buoys, oil rigs, and the like. They can be caught anywhere in the water column, to depths of several hundred feet, but they are mostly associated with near-bottom structure in the 60- to 240-foot range. In some locales, they are caught in inshore waters, even as shallow as under 30 feet.

Food. Greater amberjack feed on fish, crabs, and squid.

Angling. With the exception of tuna, amberjack are as hard-fighting a fish, pound for pound, as any found in saltwater. Those anglers who have engaged in a tug-of-war with a large amberjack know well how their forearm muscles have been strained and how their back and shoulders ache after the duel. Amberjack are especially popular with party and charter boat anglers, as well as those in private boats.

Amberjack are most commonly associated with such intermediate to deep habitats as reefs, rocky outcrops, wrecks, buoys, and other structure. They usually band in small groups, so it is typical to catch an amberjack and have others follow it to the boat. Leaving it hooked or tethered may keep the school around and provide further success.

Amberjack are fast swimmers and voracious predators. Fishing with cut or live baits is very popular, as is vertical jigging with bucktails, jigs with soft plastic bodies, or metal jigging spoons. Lures are sometimes adorned with a strip or chunk of meat. Popular live baits include herring, menhaden, mullet, and especially pinfish and blue runners. In water under 120 feet, some anglers opt for chumming.

Because these fish take a lure or bait very hard, there is seldom a question that a strike has occurred. When fishing in deep water, it is often critical to muscle big amberjack immediately after the fight begins, as they usually head deep for cover and, if they get to it, will cut the line.

On the few occasions when amberjack are encountered near the surface, anglers can cast baits or plugs, spoons, or flies from a boat or from shore. Trollers use deep-diving plugs when

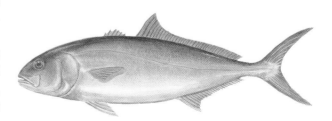

Greater Amberjack

appropriate, and some fish with planers and downriggers.

Yellowtail

Seriola lalandi

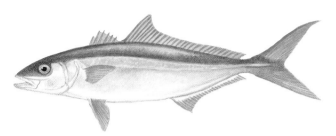

Yellowtail

Members of the Carangidae family and closely related to amberjack, yellowtail are commonly separated by anglers and scientists into three separate species—California yellowtail (*Seriola lalandi dorsalis*), southern yellowtail (*S. lalandi lalandi*), and Asian yellowtail (*S. lalandi aureovittata*)—but it is currently believed that the worldwide yellowtail pool consists of only one species, *S. lalandi*. The three varieties are recognized distinctly, however, because they are isolated from each other and do not appear to interact; there are also size differences with some populations, the southern variety growing larger (especially in New Zealand waters) than the others.

These are fast-swimming, hard-striking, strong-pulling fish that give anglers a great struggle, especially in large sizes, and are a great favorite with shore, boat, and light-tackle big-game anglers. They are a commercially important species and are highly regarded as table fare.

ID. Yellowtail are readily identifiable by their deeply forked, bright yellow caudal fins. Their body coloring graduates from a purple-blue on the back to a silvery white on the belly. The body is elongate and moderately compressed, and a brass-colored stripe runs the length of the body from mouth to tail. There is a small keel on either side of the caudal peduncle.

Habitat. Yellowtail are primarily coastal schooling fish found in inshore waters and out to the continental shelf. In addition to schooling in and around offshore reefs and rocky shores, they frequent deep water around wharves and jetties and man-made structures such as sunken vessels or artificial reefs where baitfish are common. Occasionally they will venture along ocean beaches and into larger estuaries. Large specimens, especially of the southern variety, are encountered in deep water around rocky pinnacles.

Food. Yellowtail will eat whatever is available, but they feed predominantly on small fish, squid, and pelagic crustaceans. They are known to herd baitfish into shallow water off beaches, making themselves vulnerable to the surf angler.

Large specimens will tackle bluefish, salmon, and small tuna.

Angling. Various methods are used to catch yellowtail, including trolling, jigging, casting with lures, rock and surf fishing, and fishing with baits. Tackle ranges from conventional gamefishing outfits in various classes, to roller-tipped boat rods of various configurations, to light and medium gear.

Lures can be large surface poppers, offshore trolling lures, plastic squid, metal spoons, metal jigs, skirted lures, feathered lures, artificial flies, dead fish, and casting plugs, among others. Baits can consist of garfish; pilchards; squid; sauries; strips of mullet, tuna, and bonito; and live fish.

Slow to medium-fast trolling is most effective when close to deep-water rocky shores, along the dropoff from reefs, and over and around underwater pinnacles and wrecks. Jigging requires repetitive lifting and dropping of a heavy metal jig and is very effective when used over offshore reefs; the jig may be hooked with a strip bait or whole squid.

Fly anglers are best served when schools of yellowtail swim close to the surface chasing baitfish. This is also when light-tackle anglers score well by tossing surface poppers. The excitement can be heightened by chumming to keep the fish at the surface, or by tethering a caught yellowtail behind the boat so that its efforts to escape attract the other members of the school and hold them in the vicinity.

Albacore, Bonito, and Little Tunny

Albacore

Thunnus alalunga

A member of the Scombridae family of tuna and mackerel, the albacore is an excellent light-tackle

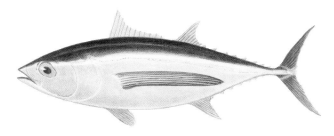

Albacore

gamefish. Its profitability and quality as a commercial fish, and its popularity as a gamefish, make it an especially valuable species. Called "chicken of the sea" because of its white meat, the albacore is commercially harvested in large quantities and called true albacore in some places, not to be confused with the so-called false albacore, which is actually the little tunny.

ID. Albacore have long pectoral fins that reach to a point beyond the anal fin, as well as small finlets on both the back and the belly that extend from the anal fin to the tail. Albacore are colored dark blue, shading to greenish blue near the tail, and silvery white on the belly. A metallic or iridescent cast covers the entire body. The dorsal finlets are yellowish, except for the white trailing edge of the tail, and the anal finlets are silvery or dusky. The deepest part of the body is near the second dorsal fin; in other tuna, it is near the middle of the first dorsal fin.

Extremely long, sickle-shaped black pectoral fins set albacore apart from other family members; pectoral fins of certain other adult tuna may also be moderately long, but they never extend all the way to the anal fin. This distinction is not as marked in young albacore; in some cases, a juvenile albacore may have shorter pectoral fins than a similar-size yellowfin tuna or a bigeye tuna. The albacore can also be distinguished from other tuna by its lack of stripes or spots on the lower flanks and belly, and by the thin white trailing edge on the margin of the tail fin.

Habitat. Albacore favor tropical, subtropical, and temperate waters, commonly in the 60° to 66°F range. These fish seldom come close to shore and prefer deep, wide-open waters.

Food. The albacore diet consists of fish, squid, and crustaceans.

Angling. Anglers avidly pursue albacore wherever these fish occur. Unless warm currents bring

albacore to within a few miles of shore, it is usually necessary to run long distances to find them. They favor those areas where cooler and warmer water meet.

Albacore feed in schools, which sometimes consist of other tuna-family members, and these schools are typically found around floating objects such as sargassum. Although they will feed at middle depths, they ordinarily do so close to the surface.

Locating albacore (and other tuna) is the hardest part of the sport, so anglers invest considerable effort trolling for them. Once a school is found, some anglers stop trolling and immediately begin chumming in an effort to keep the tuna nearby, catching them on live or dead baitfish. Others continue trolling. Charter and private boats, however, usually converge where the albacore are concentrated, so these spots are often a hotbed of activity.

Like all tuna, albacore strike hard and make powerful runs. They are a popular light-tackle quarry (4/0 reels and 20- to 50-pound tackle are standard) and are commonly caught by anglers fishing with mullet, sauries, squid, herring, anchovies, sardines, and other small fish. In some cases, chunking or chumming with dead bait is preferable; in others, light-lining with live bait is more effective. Fly fishing is also possible, usually when a chum slick has been established to attract schools of albacore within casting range.

Some trollers fish with both lures and rigged baitfish, and there's a strong preference for using green trolling lures and natural baits (whole ballyhoo or strips) dressed with green skirts. When albacore action is hot and a school is encountered, multiple hookups can occur on a boat with many trolling rigs set out; this can become a wild adventure, with lines tangling, rods bent double, and everyone onboard involved in a pandemonium rush.

Atlantic Bonito

Sarda sarda

The Atlantic bonito, another Scombridae family member, has a reputation as a tough fighter and a tasty fish, with light-colored meat. This combination makes it highly popular among anglers.

ID. The Atlantic bonito has a completely scaled body (some types of bonito have only a partially scaled body), a noticeably curved lateral line, and

Atlantic Bonito

six to eight finlets on the back and belly between the anal fin and the tail. The caudal peduncle has a lateral keel on either side with two smaller keels above and below the main one. The Atlantic bonito doesn't have a swim bladder or teeth on its tongue. The back is blue or blue-green, fading to silvery on the lower sides and belly; a characteristic feature of the species is the dark lines that extend from the back to just below the lateral line. It has a slimmer body than other tuna, and can be distinguished by a mouth full of teeth and dark lines on its back rather than its belly.

Habitat. Atlantic bonito occur in brackish water and saltwater, particularly in tropical and temperate coastal environs. Schooling and migratory, they often inhabit surface inshore environs.

Food. The Atlantic bonito feeds primarily at or near the surface in schools often 15 to 20 miles offshore, but they are also found close to shore. They prey on small schooling fish, as well as squid, mackerel, menhaden, alewives, anchovies, silversides, and shrimp; they also tend to be cannibalistic.

The Atlantic bonito is an athletic swimmer and a ferocious feeder, occasionally leaping out of the water in pursuit of its quarry. Young bonito develop this killer instinct as soon as they become able to feed. Adults and young alike feed during the day but are especially active at dawn and dusk.

Angling. Bonito are often caught by anglers trolling with baits or lures for larger quarry. When caught on the heavier tackle used for that sport, the fish are understandably overmatched. When caught on light tackle, however, they are a robust battler—diving, surging, running, and generally doing their best to stretch the fishing line. They typically streak away after a smashing strike, making tremendously swift runs, and then head deep, where they may stay until whipped.

Some anglers keep light tackle handy for use while trolling, in case they encounter a school of bonito. They sometimes employ light tackle when drifting and live-bait fishing or when chumming and using live or cut baits. A light- to medium-action spinning rod, 7 to 8 feet long, with 10- to 15-pound line, is about right. Still lighter tackle will ensure more of a battle.

When trolling deliberately for bonito (as well as skipjack and small tuna) a fast boat speed is usually best, as are trolling plugs and feather jigs. The fish are primarily caught near the surface and aren't put off by the wake of a boat or engine noise, so flatline length can be relatively short.

In some places bonito are caught near shore and may be pursued deliberately by casters using various tackle and catching these fish on assorted lures and flies, either from boats or from beach and jetty. Metal jigs, long minnow plugs, and streamer flies that imitate sand eels and spearing are used.

Pacific Bonito

Sarda chiliensis

The Pacific bonito is an important gamefish, often caught from party boats and from shore. It is valued more for sport than for food, as is its cousin the Atlantic bonito, although its flesh is light-colored and tasty.

ID. Similar in size and pigmentation to the Atlantic bonito, the Pacific bonito is distinguished from most other bonito by the lack of teeth on its tongue and the possession of a straight intestine without a fold in the middle. It has seventeen to nineteen spines on its first dorsal fin and is the only tunalike fish on the California coast with slanted dark stripes on its back. Like other bonito, its body is cigar-shaped and somewhat compressed, with a pointed and conical head and a large mouth. It is dark blue above, and its dusky sides become silvery below.

Habitat. Bonito live in surface to middle depths in the open sea and are migratory. Older fish usually range farther from the coast than juveniles.

Pacific Bonito

Bonito may arrive off the coast in the spring as ocean waters warm, but they may not show up at all if oceanic conditions produce colder than normal temperatures.

Food. Pacific bonito prey on smaller pelagic fish as well as on squid and shrimp, generally in surface waters. Anchovies and sardines appear to be their preferred foods.

Angling. Fishing methods for Pacific bonito are similar to those for Atlantic bonito. These include trolling at or near the surface, as well as casting, jigging, or live-bait fishing with small fish, squid, cut or strip baits, or with any of a variety of small artificial lures.

Pacific bonito are excellent fighters, and their hearty appetites make them willing to strike many lures and baits. Once a school is aroused, they will take almost any bait or lure anglers toss their way. Most Pacific bonito are taken by a combination of trolling and live-bait fishing. Anglers locate the schools by using trolling feathers, and live anchovies or squid pieces bait the fish once located. Most fishing for Pacific bonito takes place offshore over a bottom depth of 300 to 600 feet, but it can occur next to kelp beds when the fish are near shore.

Little Tunny

Euthynnus alletteratus

Also a member of the Scombridae family, the little tunny is one of the finest small gamefish available. Frequently misnamed as false albacore and bonito, this species fights so hard on light tackle that anglers are likely to boat dead or near-dead individuals. It has coarse red flesh, however, which does not endear it to many anglers as food, although it does attract some commercial interest.

ID. The little tunny is most easily distinguished from similar species by its markings. It has a

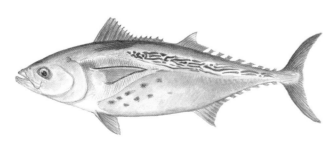

Little Tunny

scattering of dark spots resembling fingerprints between the pectoral and ventral fins that are not present on any related Atlantic species. It also has wavy "wormlike" markings on the back. These are above the lateral line within a well-marked border and never extend farther forward than about the middle of the first dorsal fin. The markings are unlike those of any other Atlantic species. The pectoral and ventral fins are short and broad, and the two dorsal fins are separated at the base by a small space. The body has no scales except on the corselet and along the lateral line, and there is no air bladder. Unlike its close Pacific relative the black skipjack tuna, it has no teeth on the vomer.

Habitat. In North America this species occurs in tropical and warm temperate waters of the Atlantic Ocean. It is not as migratory as other tuna species and is found regularly in inshore waters, as well as offshore, usually in large schools.

Food. Little tunny are common in inshore waters near the surface, where they feed on squid, crustaceans, fish larvae, and large numbers of smaller pelagic fish, especially herring.

Angling. Flocks of diving seabirds often indicate the presence of a school of little tunny. Because this species feeds on small pelagic fish near the surface, any school feeding action tends to attract and excite birds looking for a meal. Fishing methods include trolling or casting from a boat and offering small whole baits, strip baits, or small spoons, plugs, jigs, and feathers.

These fish spread out over the continental shelf and are most abundant within 30 miles of shore during a late-summer to early-fall run along the Mid-Atlantic and southern New England coasts, when they average 5 to 15 pounds. Unlike the other tuna, the little tunny commonly chases baitfish into the surf and can be caught by surf casters retrieving small metal lures and jigs at high speed. Many are also caught by trollers seeking school tuna, and in chum lines intended for bluefish.

Black Skipjack

Euthynnus lineatus

Also a member of the Scombridae family, the black skipjack is commonly caught by anglers, usually while trolling or casting for other pelagic species. Its food value has mixed ratings, although

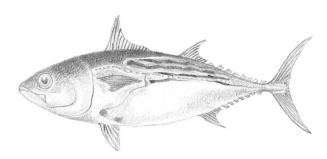

Black Skipjack

it is of some commercial importance. Its flesh is dark red and the taste is strong.

ID. The dorsal fin of the black skipjack has thirteen to fifteen spines and is high anteriorly. This distinguishes it from bonito, which have a relatively long and low first dorsal fin. The anal fin, which has eleven to thirteen rays, is similar to the second dorsal fin in size and shape. The body lacks scales, except on the anterior corselet and along the lateral line. This is the only species of *Euthynnus* with thirty-seven, instead of the usual thirty-nine, vertebrae. Each jaw has twenty to forty small, conical teeth. Bonito have fewer and larger conical teeth. Mackerel have flat, triangular teeth.

The black skipjack is distinguished from similar species by the four or five broad, straight black stripes that run horizontally along the back, and by its dark spots between the pectoral and ventral fins. In live specimens, stripes may be visible on the venter as well as on the back, which has frequently led to confusion with the skipjack tuna. The stripes on the belly rarely persist long after death in the black skipjack, whereas they remain prominent in the skipjack tuna.

Habitat. Like other pelagic and migratory species, the black skipjack occurs in schools near the surface of coastal and offshore waters, sometimes mixing with other scombrids.

Food. Black skipjack feed on small surface fish, squid, and crustaceans.

Angling. These fish can be hooked by trolling or casting small whole baits or strip baits, or small lures such as spoons, plugs, jigs, and feathers. Trolling speeds of up to 8 or 10 mph will catch them. Skipjack are usually caught deliberately for use as whole or cut baits; whole live skipjacks of several pounds are rigged and live-lined in some areas for marlin.

Mackerel

Mackerel are members of the Scombridae family, which includes tuna and numbers some fifty species in fifteen genera. Like tuna, mackerel are mainly schooling fish of the open sea. They provide sport virtually wherever they are found, and they contribute significantly to commercial fisheries due to their table value. All are good fighters as well; larger mackerel can rip line from a reel with tremendous speed, and some even take to the air on occasion.

Like tuna, mackerel are especially streamlined. The body is literally a spindle, with a pointed head and a much-tapered tail. The large caudal fin is lunate (crescent-shaped). Mackerel are much smaller than tuna overall, but they are just as speedy, displaying swift attacking speeds. Some of these fish have slots into which their spinous dorsal fins fit; this adaptation further reduces friction and enhances their speed. The spiny and soft-rayed dorsal fins are separate, and the soft-rayed dorsal fin is matched in size and shape by the anal fin directly beneath it. Following each fin is a series of finlets, the number varying with the species. In all species, the scales are extremely small or lacking.

Most tuna and mackerel are ocean blue or greenish on the back, grading to a silvery shade on the sides and the belly. Some notable exceptions do occur, however. The three most prominent angling species are profiled here.

Atlantic Mackerel

Scomber scombrus

The Atlantic mackerel is a fast-swimming, schooling, pelagic species that garners significant recreational as well as commercial interest. It is known as a feast-or-famine fish; sometimes it is almost completely absent, and at other times it is plentiful in swarming schools. A delicious fish with an

Atlantic Mackerel

abundance of protein, vitamins, and minerals, it has a pleasing oil content. The flesh is firm-textured with a distinctive savory flavor.

ID. Atlantic mackerel have smooth, tapering heads, streamlined bodies, and brilliant coloration. An iridescent greenish blue covers most of the upper body, turning to blue-black on the head and silvery white on the belly. These brilliant colors fade somewhat after capture but still distinguish these fish. The skin is satiny and has small, smooth scales. The tail is forked. Another distinguishing characteristic is the series of twenty-three to thirty-three wavy dark bands on the upper part of the body, extending to a moderately prominent lateral line. There are two fins on the back, one spiny and one soft, followed by a number of small finlets. There are also finlets present on the under surface of the body near the tail.

Habitat. The Atlantic mackerel is pelagic, preferring cool, well-oxygenated open-ocean waters.

Food. The diet of Atlantic mackerel consists of fish eggs and a variety of small fish and fry.

Angling. Finding mackerel is the necessary element in catching them. Anglers typically locate the fish on sonar equipment or by observing slicks on the surface; when this fails, private boats follow charter and party boats (which do a brisk business in mackerel fishing when this species is available), and otherwise look for clusters of boat activity. Most fishing occurs in nearshore environs or in large bays.

A good deal of mackerel fishing is done with a rig that consists of several small tube lures attached at 1-foot intervals to a main leader and weighted with a heavy (3- or 4-ounce) diamond jig. Because mackerel are midwater fish, it's important to present the bait at the right level. Most anglers find this level by dropping their rig to the bottom, then slowly working it back up in increments, pausing and jigging as they do this. Once they catch fish, they return their rig to the same level. When the fish are not too deep, jigs and flies are also effective, and sometimes chum is used to attract and hold the fish near the boat.

King Mackerel

Scomberomorus cavalla

The largest mackerel in the western Atlantic, the king mackerel is a prized gamefish and an important

King Mackerel

commercial species. It has firm meat, and millions of pounds of this fish are landed annually.

ID. The streamlined body of the king mackerel is a dark gray above, growing silver on the sides and below; there are no markings on the body, although the back may have an iridescent blue to olive tint. Most of the fins are pale or dusky, except the first dorsal fin, which is uniformly blue; the front part of this fin is never black, which distinguishes it from the Spanish mackerel.

Other distinguishing features include the sharp drop of the lateral line under the second dorsal fin, as well as a relatively small number (fourteen to sixteen) of spines in the first dorsal fin and a lower gill rake count, which is six to eleven on the first arch. Young king mackerel may be mistaken for Spanish mackerel because of the small round dark to gold spots on the sides, but these fade and disappear with age.

Habitat. King mackerel are primarily an openwater, migratory species, preferring warm waters that seldom fall below 68°F. They often occur around wrecks, buoys, coral reefs, ocean piers, inlets, and other areas where food is abundant. They tend to avoid highly turbid waters. A schooling species, king mackerel migrate extensively and annually in schools of various sizes, although the largest individuals usually remain solitary.

Food. King mackerel feed mainly on fish, as well as on a smaller quantity of shrimp and squid.

Angling. The primary chore in catching kingfish is finding them, and anglers can invest long hours searching. Once located, these aggressive fish can be readily caught in smaller sizes; the biggest specimens are more difficult to come by.

Fishing methods include trolling or drifting either deep or on the surface using strip baits, lures, or small whole baits, as well as casting lures and live baits. Balao, mullet, jacks, herring, pinfish, menhaden (pogies), blue runners, ladyfish, croaker, and Spanish mackerel are among the baits used; the largest baits are preferred for bigger mackerel. Spoons, feathers, jigs, and plugs prove effective under various conditions, as do such combinations as feathers, strip baits, and skirted strip baits. Chumming will attract and hold these fish; at anchor, this method can provide opportunities for fly tackle.

Many anglers land larger fish by trolling with multiple (two or three) bait rigs, rigs of mullet on feathers, spoons, or live fish slowly in the boat's wake. Another effective big kingfish offering is a large plain spoon pulled deep with a planer. Downriggers are used in conjunction with live baits, and live fish may also be run near the surface on kites. Deeper fishing produces large individuals when there are plenty of mackerel, as the large ones are below the crowd.

Many kingfish are caught off inlets and passes, as these areas are important for producing baits, which follow the rising tide in and the falling tide out. Inshore areas with breaks in the bottom depth or with contours are good spots for slow trolling, especially if they hold abundant bait.

Kingfish make a long and powerful run, rest, and then repeat the performance. Now and then a fish will leap from the water. To avoid overpowering the fish and pulling the hook out of its mouth, a rod with a soft tip is helpful.

Spanish Mackerel

Scomberomorus maculatus

The Spanish mackerel is a popular gamefish, especially in inshore waters, and a good food fish that is also of significant commercial interest.

ID. The slender, elongated body of the Spanish mackerel is silvery with a bluish or olive green back. There are sixteen to eighteen spines in the first dorsal fin, fifteen to eighteen soft rays in the second dorsal fin—with eight or nine finlets behind it, and thirteen to fifteen gill rakers on the first arch. The lateral line curves evenly downward to the base of the tail. The Spanish mackerel resembles the king mackerel, but it has bronze or yellow spots without stripes; the king mackerel has neither. The Spanish mackerel lacks scales on the pectoral fins, which further distinguishes it from the king mackerel, which do have scales on them. Also, the front part of the first dorsal fin on the Spanish mackerel is black, whereas it is more blue on the king mackerel, and the second dorsal fin and pectoral fins may be edged in black.

Habitat. Occurring inshore, near shore, and offshore, Spanish mackerel prefer open water but are sometimes found over deep grassbeds and reefs, as well as shallow-water estuaries. They form large, fast-moving schools that migrate great distances along the shore, staying in waters with temperatures above 68°F.

Food. Spanish mackerel feed primarily on small fish, as well as on squid and shrimp; they often force their prey into crowded clumps and practically push the fish out of the water as they feed.

Angling. Casting, live-bait fishing, jigging, and drift fishing are all employed to catch this abundant fish, and a variety of lures—including metal squids, spoons, diamond jigs, and feather lures—are all effective. Bucktail jigs are particularly good, especially when retrieved rapidly with an occasional jerk of the rod tip to impart a darting motion. When fish are plentiful, small jigs may be rigged in multiples behind a single line. Minnows and live shrimp are the best natural baits. Light, 6- to 10-pound spinning tackle provides excellent sport.

After the fish have been located and several hooked, boats make tight circles to stay with the school. Because Spanish mackerel migrate close to land, they are caught from small craft inshore, as well as from larger boats, and by anglers on piers, bridges, and jetties.

Tuna

Tuna are the most prominent members of the Scombridae family, among the most commercially important fish, and among the world's greatest sportfish. Anglers consider them the most powerful

Spanish Mackerel

gamefish of all; the largest members of the bluefin tuna species are the strongest of all fish pursued with rod and reel. They are also among the fastest; schools of these swift swimmers may cruise at 30 miles per hour.

Tuna have an especially streamlined body shape, with a pointed head and a much-tapered tail. The large caudal fin is lunate (crescent-shaped). The spiny and soft-rayed dorsal fins are separate, the soft-rayed dorsal matched in size and shape by the anal fin directly beneath it. Following each fin is a series of finlets, the number varying with the species. In all species, the scales are extremely small or lacking. Like mackerel, most tuna are ocean blue or greenish on the back, grading into silvery on the sides and the belly, but some notable exceptions occur.

Whereas fish are generally cold-blooded, tuna are able to maintain a body temperature up to 18°F above that of the surrounding water. The unique physiology of tuna is such that they must consume great amounts of food to maintain their constant-swimming lifestyle and fuel the rapid growth that is characteristic of these species. Thus tuna are likely to be encountered where massive quantities of schooling baitfish are located and feeding can be accomplished with a minimum expenditure of energy. Yet these eating machines are often no pushovers, as they can also be surprisingly fussy about baits and very line shy.

ID. There is often confusion about tuna species, especially those of small to intermediate size. Some external clues do exist that aid in making a quick identification, which may be necessary to enable the release of specific species and to comply with existing regulations. Most external clues involve fin length.

If the pectoral fin, when held flush to the side of the tuna's body, ends well before the origin of the second dorsal fin, the fish is probably a bluefin tuna. If it extends to or past the origin of the second dorsal fin, it is likely either a bigeye or yellowfin. A tuna with extremely long pectoral fins, extending beyond the origin of the anal fin, is most likely an albacore. A tuna exceeding 40 pounds with extremely long anal and second dorsal fins is most likely a yellowfin.

Habitat. Tuna are found throughout the open waters of most of the world's temperate and tropical seas. They are schooling, pelagic, and seasonally migratory species, many of which make rather extensive migrations. Some species, like skipjack and bigeye tuna, tend to be found deeper, at least during the day, whereas schools of bluefin, yellowfin, and some other tuna are known to occasionally swim at the surface, especially in warm water. Despite their general existence in deep oceanic waters, tuna have been known to come fairly close to shore where there are warm currents.

Food. Although tuna feed on what is locally abundant, there are some commonalities among all of the species. Squid, for example, are a prime food item, as are small mackerel, flyingfish, herring, and sardines. Bonito, mullet, whiting, lanternfish, and crustaceans are among other foods.

Bigeye Tuna

Thunnus obesus

The bigeye is equally revered for sport and for its flesh. The meat of large bigeyes is as favored as that of medium and giant bluefin tuna. Bigeyes are strong fighters and are caught on baits primarily set at depths of 100 feet or more during the night. Anglers irregularly catch them by trolling, even at night around a full moon. Fishing methods include trolling deep with various baits and lures, and live-bait fishing in deep water.

ID. A stocky body and large eyes characterize this species. Generally, there are no special markings on the body, but some specimens may have vertical rows of whitish spots on the venter. The first dorsal fin is deep yellow. The second dorsal fin and the anal fin are blackish brown or yellow and may be edged with black. The finlets are bright yellow with narrow black edges. The tail does not have a white trailing edge like that of the albacore.

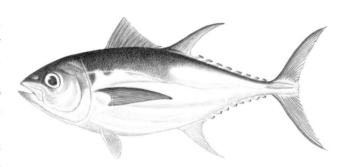

Bigeye Tuna

The pectoral fins may reach to the second dorsal fin. The second dorsal and anal fins never reach back as far as those of large yellowfin tuna. It has a total of twenty-three to thirty-one gill rakers on the first arch. The margin of the liver is striated. The two dorsal fins are close-set, the first having thirteen or fourteen spines and the second fourteen to sixteen rays. The anal fin has eleven to fifteen rays. On either side of the caudal peduncle is a strong lateral keel between two small keels that are located slightly farther back on the tail. The scales are small except on the anterior corselet. The vent is oval or teardrop-shaped, not round as in the albacore.

Bigeye are similar in many respects to yellowfin tuna, but the bigeye's second dorsal and anal fins never grow as long as those of the yellowfin. In the bigeye tuna, the margin of the liver is striated and the right lobe is about the same size as the left lobe; in the yellowfin tuna, the liver is smooth and the right lobe is clearly longer than either the left or the middle lobe.

Blackfin Tuna

Thunnus atlanticus

One of the smaller tuna, the blackfin is primarily a sportfish, with minor commercial interest. Found on or near the surface, it is readily caught on light tackle and is a strong fighter whose flesh is of good quality and flavor. The blackfin can be taken by trolling or casting small lures, flies, or natural baits, as well as strip baits, spoons, feathers, jigs, or plugs. They are also caught by chumming or live-bait fishing from boats at the surface of deep waters 1 to 2 miles offshore.

ID. The pectoral fins of the blackfin tuna reach to somewhere between the twelfth dorsal spine and the origin of the second dorsal fin, but they never extend beyond the second dorsal fin as in the albacore. There are a total of nineteen to twenty-five (usually twenty-one to twenty-three) gill rakers on the first arch (fifteen to nineteen are on the lower limb), which is fewer than in any other species of *Thunnus.*

The finlets are uniformly dark, without a touch of the bright lemon yellow usually present in those of other tuna, and they may have white edges. Light bars alternate with light spots on the lower flanks. The first dorsal fin is dusky, as are the second dorsal and anal fins with a silvery

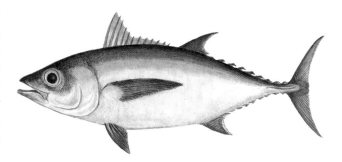

Blackfin Tuna

luster. The back of the fish is bluish black, the sides silvery gray, and the belly milky white. A small swim bladder is present. The ventral surface of the liver is without striations, and the right lobe is longer than the left and center lobes.

Bluefin Tuna

Thunnus thynnus

The bluefin tuna is the largest member of the Scombridae family and one of the largest true bony fish. A pelagic, schooling, highly migratory species, it has enormous commercial value, especially in large sizes. It is of great recreational interest, albeit only to the relative few who have the means and equipment to venture to appropriate offshore environs. High demand for its dark red flesh has made the bluefin tuna the object of intense commercial and recreational fishing efforts and has resulted in a dwindling population of adult fish.

Bluefins are not flashy fighters; however, they are tractor-pull strong and capable of great speeds. Fishing methods include stillfishing or trolling with live or dead baits, and trolling with artificial lures, including spoons, plugs, or feathers.

ID. The bluefin tuna has a fusiform body, compressed and stocky in front. It can be distinguished from almost all other tuna by its rather short pectoral fins, which extend only as far back as the eleventh or twelfth spine in the first dorsal fin. There are twelve to fourteen spines in the first dorsal fin and thirteen to fifteen rays in the second. The anal fin has eleven to fifteen rays. It has the highest gill raker count of any species of *Thunnus*, with thirty-four to forty-three on the first arch. The ventral surface of the liver is striated, and the middle lobe is usually the largest.

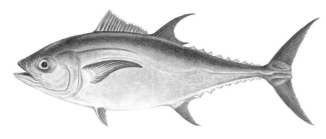

Bluefin Tuna

The back and upper sides are dark blue to black with a gray or green iridescence. The lower sides are silvery, marked with gray spots and bands. The anal fin is dusky and has some yellow. The finlets are yellow and edged with black. The caudal keel is black at the adult stage but semi-transparent when immature.

Skipjack Tuna

Katsuwonus pelamis

One of the smaller tuna, the skipjack is an esteemed light-tackle species and holds great commercial value. It will strike trolled strip baits, feathers, spoons, plugs, or small whole baits. Most are taken by trolling, but some anglers catch them by casting, jigging, or live-bait fishing offshore.

ID. The presence of stripes on the belly and the absence of markings on the back are sufficient to distinguish the skipjack tuna from all similar species. The lower flanks and belly are silvery and have four to six prominent dark longitudinal stripes running from just behind the corselet back toward the tail, ending when they reach the lateral line. Although some other species also have stripes on the belly, they have markings on the back as well, and the latter remain the most prominent after death.

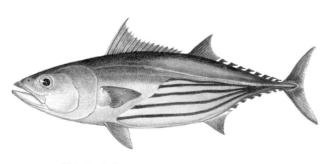

Skipjack Tuna

The top of the fish is a dark purplish blue, and the lower flanks and belly are silvery. The first dorsal fin has fourteen to sixteen spines, and the pectoral and ventral fins are short. The body is scaleless except on the corselet and along the lateral line. This fish has no swim bladder. On each side of the caudal peduncle is a strong lateral keel. There are roughly thirty to forty small conical teeth in each jaw. The teeth are smaller and more numerous than those of bonito and are unlike the triangular, compressed teeth of mackerel.

Yellowfin Tuna

Thunnus albacares

Preferring warm waters, the yellowfin is the most tropical species of tuna. It is highly esteemed both as a sportfish and is an especially important commercial fish; its meat is light in color compared to that of most other tuna, with the exception of the albacore, which has white meat. Yellowfins are a good target for trollers and bait anglers. Trolling with small fish, squid, strip baits, and artificial lures, as well as chumming and live-bait fishing are primary methods. Offshore anglers do especially well with this species by chumming with chunk baits at night.

ID. This is probably the most colorful of all the tuna. The back is blue-black, fading to silver on the lower flanks and belly. A golden yellow or iridescent blue stripe runs from the eye to the tail, though this is not always prominent. All the fins and finlets are golden yellow, although in some very large specimens the elongated dorsal and anal fins may be silver edged with yellow. The finlets have black edges. The belly frequently shows as many as twenty vertical rows of whitish spots. Many large yellowfins become particularly distinguished, as they grow very long second dorsal and anal fins.

Overall, the body shape is streamlined and more slender than that of bluefin or bigeye tuna. The eyes and head are comparatively small. Just as the albacore has characteristically overextended pectoral fins, the yellowfin has overextended second dorsal and anal fins that may reach more than halfway back to the tail base in some large specimens. In smaller specimens under about 60 pounds, and in some very large specimens as well, this may not be an accurate distinguishing factor, as the fins do not appear to be as long in all specimens.

The pectoral fins in adults reach to the origin of the second dorsal fin but never beyond the second dorsal fin to the finlets, as in the albacore. The bigeye tuna and the blackfin tuna may have pectoral fins similar in length to those of the yellowfin. The yellowfin can be distinguished from the blackfin by the black margins on its finlets; blackfin tuna, like albacore, have white margins on the finlets. It can be distinguished from the bigeye tuna by the lack of striations on

Yellowfin Tuna

the ventral surface of the liver. There is no white trailing margin on the tail.

Angling for Tuna

Angling for tuna is fairly similar throughout most of their range, as they are seldom encountered anywhere but in open water. Trolling with rigged baits and lures, and fishing bait from a drifting or anchored boat are the major angling methods. A minor amount of casting is done, usually when fish are attracted close to a boat via chumming.

The vast majority of tuna trolling involves rigged baits or lures being trolled at speeds of 6 to 8 knots or more. It's probably impossible to run away from a tuna that wants to eat at any speed at which that bait or lure can be kept in the water. High-speed trolling is particularly effective, as most species of tuna seem to be attracted by wakes and possibly engine noise. Some lures should always be placed in the whitewater very close to the boat and pinned down to stay there. Feathers and cedar jigs are ideal for that purpose. The wakes created by some boats seem to produce more tuna than others, and theories abound as to the reason for that phenomenon.

Trolling can be "blind" in areas where tuna should be present, or directed to surface-schooling fish. Balao and large squid make good natural trolling baits. Straight-running high-speed offshore trolling lures work well for larger tuna; jethead versions are particularly favored for bigeyes. Lure sizes are scaled down for smaller specimens of large tuna as well as the smaller species, but even the largest tuna sometimes prefer short lures if they're feeding on similar-looking baits. Plugs that can be run at relatively high trolling speeds are also effective.

Chumming is a popular method of attracting tuna in many areas. In some cases it's accomplished with ground-up fish that forms a slick. Tuna seem to be more attracted to meat than scent, however, so chunking with pieces of baitfish tends to be more effective.

The general rule in tuna chunking is to drop over just a few chunks and wait until the current carries them out of sight before repeating the procedure. Baited lines may be worked in the chum line by being dropped back with the chunks and fed out for a couple of hundred feet, after which it will be well below the chunks. Other lines are set at various depths with the aid of sinkers and held in place with floats.

Relatively few tuna are caught on cast lures, but that method is very exciting. Casting usually involves spotting surfacing schools of tuna and getting ahead of them to make a cast. Popping and swimming plugs that can be retrieved at a rapid pace are ideal for this method. When tuna are feeding in chum lines, it's often possible to stir them up with a popping or darting plug.

Various types of jigs can also be worked effectively for tuna. The usual method involves a fast retrieve, but the flutter of a falling jig is often sufficient to attract tuna strikes when the lure is simply moved up and down in long sweeps at a level where the depth recorder indicates the fish are coming through.

More information pertinent to fishing for tuna is found in the section on offshore fishing.

Dolphin, Wahoo, and Sailfish

Common Dolphin

Coryphaena hippurus

Pompano Dolphin

Coryphaena equiselis

Both of these similar species in the Coryphaenidae family are top offshore gamefish and excellent on the table. The common dolphin, which is the larger of the two, is more widely found in the mainland United States, and the pompano dolphin is mostly encountered in Hawaii. Both are hard-fighting species that put on an acrobatic show once hooked, routinely leaping or tail-walking over the surface, darting first in one direction, then another. Both fish are commonly known under the Hawaiian name mahimahi, and sometimes referred to as the "dolphinfish," to distinguish them from the so-called dolphin of the porpoise family, which is an unrelated mammal and not sought by anglers.

ID. The common dolphin's body is slender and streamlined, tapering sharply from head to tail. Large males, called bulls, have high, vertical foreheads, whereas the females' foreheads are rounded. The anal fin has twenty-five to thirty-one soft rays and is long, stretching over half of the length of the body. The dorsal fin has fifty-five to sixty-six soft rays. Its caudal fin is deeply forked, there are no spines in any of the fins, and the mouth has bands of fine teeth.

The common dolphin is so distinctive in body color and shape that it cannot be mistaken for any other fish. Generally, when the fish is alive in the water, it is a rich iridescent blue or blue-green dorsally; gold, bluish gold, or silvery gold on the lower flanks; and silvery white or yellow on the belly. The sides are sprinkled with a mixture of dark and light spots, ranging from black or blue to golden. The dorsal fin is a rich blue, and the anal fin is golden or silvery. The other fins are generally golden yellow, edged with blue. Dark vertical bands sometimes appear when the fish is attacking prey.

To describe the color of dolphin is difficult because the fish undergoes sudden changes in color, which occur in an instant, often when it is excited. When removed from the water, however, the colors fluctuate between blue, green, and yellow; the brilliant colors apparent when in the water fade quickly. After death, the fish usually turns a uniform yellow or silvery gray.

The pompano dolphin is almost identical to the common dolphin in coloring and general shape, although it has greater body depth behind the head than the common dolphin, and a squarish rather than rounded tooth patch on the tongue. There are fewer dorsal rays on the pompano dolphin—forty-eight to fifty-five versus the common dolphin's fifty-five to sixty-five.

Habitat. Common dolphin are a warm-water pelagic fish, occurring in the open ocean and usually found close to the surface, although in waters of great depth. They sometimes inhabit coastal waters and occasionally areas near piers, but in the open ocean they often concentrate around floating objects, especially buoys, driftwood, and seaweed lines or clusters. The young commonly frequent warm nearshore waters in sargassum beds or other flotsam.

Food. Dolphin are extremely fast swimmers and feed aggressively in pairs, small packs, and schools, extensively consuming whatever forage fish are most abundant. Flyingfish and squid are prominent, and small fish and crustaceans around floating sargassum weed are commonly part of their diet, especially among smaller dolphin.

Angling. Dolphin inhabit blue-water environs and, although they roam the unobstructed near-surface waters of the open ocean, are commonly found around objects. Floating debris, buoys, weeds, and even boats can attract and hold these fish, and such objects are searched by anglers specifically looking for dolphin.

Dolphin up to 8 or so pounds, which are called chicken or peanut dolphin, are especially found around floating debris, which offers both

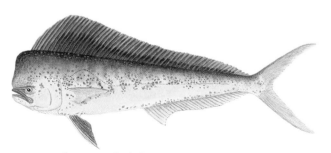

Common Dolphin

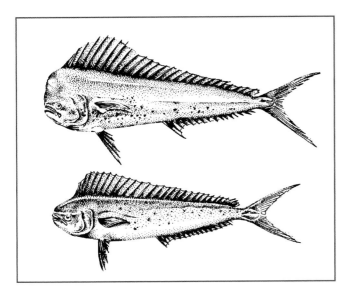

Although both male (top) and female (bottom) common dolphin have a streamlined, tapered body, the male, or bull, is distinguished by a high, vertical forehead.

protection and feeding opportunity. Fish from 8 to 20 pounds or so gather in schools, often segregated by size and/or sex. Larger dolphin often travel in small packs; these fish are more likely to be ocean roamers rather than object ambushers and are harder to deliberately target.

Most dolphin are located by trolling, usually by anglers fishing for other blue-water species, primarily marlin and sailfish. Rigged trolling baits on large hooks are usually used, and flyingfish, squid, mullet, and balao are common offerings. Offshore trolling plugs and feathers are popular as well. A quick trolling speed is optimal.

Trollers often keep spinning and flycasting tackle handy in case they encounter a school of dolphin while trolling. When this happens, they stop and cast to the fish, using surface or diving plugs, bucktail jigs, spoons, and streamer flies. Live baits are also used.

Wahoo

Acanthocybium solandri

The wahoo is a popular gamefish and a close relative of the king mackerel. It is reputedly one of the fastest fish in the sea, attaining speeds of 50 miles per hour and more, and no angler who has hooked a large wahoo and watched it sizzle a

hundred yards of line off the reel in a few seconds will dispute this. The wahoo is good to eat, with sweet, flaky white flesh.

ID. A long, slender, cigar-shaped mackerel with a sharply pointed head and widely forked tail, the wahoo is a brilliant or dark blue color along its back. It has twenty-five to thirty bright or dusky blue vertical bands, or "tiger stripes," that extend down the bright silver to silvery gray sides and sometimes join into pairs below. The stripes are not always prominent or even apparent in large specimens, although they may become more noticeable when the fish is excited. A distinguishing feature is the movable upper jaw, which has forty-five to sixty-four teeth, of which thirty-two to fifty are on the lower jaw; these teeth are large, strong, and laterally compressed. The gill structure resembles that of the marlin more than the tuna or mackerel, and it lacks the characteristic gill rakers of the latter fish. The lateral line is well defined and drops significantly at the middle of the first dorsal fin, extending in a wavy line back to the tail.

Habitat. An oceanic species, wahoo are pelagic and seasonally migratory. They are frequently solitary or form small, loose groupings of two to seven fish rather than large compact schools. They often associate around banks, pinnacles, and even flotsam. They are occasionally found around wrecks and deeper reefs where smaller fish are abundant.

Food. Wahoo feed on such pelagic species as porcupinefish, flyingfish, herring, pilchards, scad, lanternfish, and small mackerel and tuna, as well as on squid.

Angling. This speedy member of the mackerel family is caught in a variety of ways, although trolling is by far the number one activity. A great many fish are caught incidental to other fishing activities, although they can be targeted specifically where abundant.

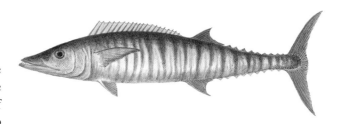

Wahoo

Wahoo are mostly caught in waters that range from 72° to 77°F. They are located over or along structure that causes current to well up and provide good feeding opportunities, as well as along current edges and around floating objects and sargassum. Near-surface trolling at high speeds is a standard ploy for wahoo-seeking anglers, as is deeper trolling via planers, downriggers, and wire line. Because wahoo are seldom found in the concentrations typical of other mackerel and tuna, trolling is a good way to cover a lot of territory. In addition, the fast swimming ability of this species allows for speedy boat travel; wahoo are typically caught at boat speeds of 6 to 10 knots, and a few anglers troll at up to 14 knots.

Trolled offerings include whole rigged Spanish mackerel; mullet, ballyhoo, squid, or other small baits; strip baits and diving plugs; or heavy bullet-head trolling lures and other assorted offshore trolling lures. Live-bait fishing and kite fishing are less practiced but sometimes productive, and on occasion opportunities for casting with plugs, spoons, metal jigs, and flies exist.

Wahoo are most likely to be active early in the day, so anglers who specialize in wahoo like to beat the competition to productive spots and commence fishing at dawn.

Sailfish

Istiophorus platypterus

With its characteristic large dorsal fin and superlative aerial ability, the sailfish is arguably the most striking member of the Istiophoridae family of billfish. Present taxonomy suggests that the Atlantic and Pacific sailfish are the same species. The speedy sailfish is among the most exciting light-tackle big-game fish to catch. Light conventional

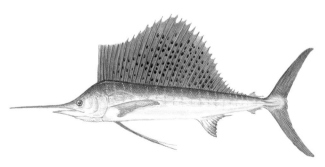

Sailfish

gear, as well as spinning, baitcasting, and fly outfits, are all suitable for pursuing sailfish. The smaller specimens found in the Atlantic are especially good fun and are relatively easy for even inexperienced anglers to enjoy.

ID. The sailfish is dark blue on top, brown blue laterally, and silvery white on the belly; the upper jaw is elongated in the form of a spear. This species's outstanding feature is the long, high first dorsal fin, which has thirty-seven to forty-nine total elements; it is slate or cobalt blue with many black spots. The second dorsal fin is very small, with six to eight rays. The single, prominent lateral line is curved over the pectoral fin and otherwise straight along the median line of the flanks. The bill is longer than that of the spearfish, usually a little more than twice the length of the elongated lower jaw. The vent is just forward of the first anal fin. The sides often have pale, bluish gray vertical bars or rows or spots.

Although sailfish look like similar-size white marlin and blue marlin, they are readily distinguished by their large sail-like dorsal fin.

Habitat. Sailfish are pelagic and migratory in warm tropical and temperate waters, although they may migrate into warm nearshore areas in parts of their range.

Food. Sailfish eat squid, octopus, mackerel, tuna, jacks, herring, ballyhoo, needlefish, flying-fish, mullet, and other small fish. They feed on the surface or at mid-depths.

Angling. Fishing methods for this species are similar to those for other billfish, although lighter tackle is more appropriate. Fishing methods include trolling with strip baits, whole mullet or ballyhoo, plastic offshore trolling lures, and trolling feathers or spoons. Another option is live-bait fishing with or without kites, using jacks, mullet, and other small natural baits. Sailfish are usually caught in depths exceeding 6 fathoms but occasionally also in lesser depths and even from ocean piers where currents and baitfish bring this species near shore. Generally, however, they are pursued in clear blue offshore water and are located on or near the surface.

The spectacular jumping of the sailfish makes it a superb light-tackle quarry, as this leaping and a generally small size prevent it from maintaining long-term stamina. More information is contained in the section on offshore fishing.

Blue Marlin, Striped Marlin, and White Marlin

Blue Marlin

Makaira nigricans

A premier member of the Istiophoridae family of billfish, the blue marlin is one of the foremost big-game species worldwide. It has exceptional size and strength, and is a powerful, aggressive fighter. It runs hard and long, sounds deep, and leaps high into the air in a seemingly inexhaustible display of strength. Because of these characteristics, and because it is more widespread than other marlin, the blue marlin is arguably the most popular and sought-after marlin by anglers. Blue marlin are seldom eaten in North America, and the vast majority caught by anglers are released after capture, with many of those being tagged.

ID. The pectoral fins of blue marlin are never rigid, even after death, and can be folded completely flat against the sides. The dorsal fin is high and pointed (rather than rounded) anteriorly, and its greatest height is less than its greatest body depth. The anal fin is relatively large and also pointed. Juveniles might not share all of these characteristics, but the peculiar lateral line system is usually visible in small specimens. In adults it is rarely visible unless the scales or skin are removed. The vent is just in front of the anal fin, and the upper jaw is elongated in the form of a spear.

The back is cobalt blue and the flanks and belly are silvery white. There may be light blue or lavender vertical stripes on the sides, but these usually fade away soon after death, and they are never as obvious as those of the striped marlin. There are no spots on the fins. Small blue marlin are similar to white marlin, but the blue has a more pointed dorsal fin at the anterior end, more pointed tip on the pectoral and anal fins, and lacks dorsal fin spots.

Habitat. This pelagic, migratory species lives in tropical and warm temperate oceanic waters. These fish are found in the warm blue water of offshore environs, usually over considerable depths and where there are underwater structures (for example, canyons, dropoffs, ridges, seamounts) and currents that attract copious supplies of baitfish. They are usually solitary.

Food. Blue marlin feed on squid and pelagic fish, including assorted tuna and mackerel, as well

Blue Marlin

as dolphin. They feed on almost anything they can catch, and according to availability rather than selectivity. Because they require large quantities of food, they are scarce when and where prey is limited.

Angling. Fishing methods for blue marlin include trolling large whole baits such as bonito, dolphin, mullet, mackerel, bonefish, ballyhoo, flyingfish, and squid, as well as various types of artificial lures and sometimes strip baits. More information is contained in the section on offshore fishing.

Striped Marlin

Tetrapturus audax

Widely distributed in the Pacific Ocean, the striped marlin is the most prevalent marlin in the Istiophoridae family of billfish, the most common Indo-Pacific billfish species, and a prized catch of anglers. It is well-known for its fighting ability and has the reputation of spending more time in the air than in the water when hooked. It is caught fairly close to shore in appropriate waters.

ID. The body of the striped marlin is elongate and compressed, and its upper jaw is extended in the form of a spear. The color is dark or steely blue above and becomes bluish silver and white below a clearly visible and straight lateral line. Numerous iridescent blue spots grace the fins, and pale blue or lavender vertical stripes appear on the sides. These may or may not be prominent, but they are normally more so than on other marlin. The stripes persist after death, which is not always true with other marlin. The most distinguishing characteristic is a high, pointed first dorsal fin, which normally equals or exceeds the greatest body depth. Even in the largest specimens, it is at least equal to 90 percent of the body depth. Like the dorsal fin, the anal and pectoral fins are

Striped Marlin

pointed. They are also flat and movable and can easily be folded flush against the sides, even after death.

Striped marlin have scales, fins on the belly, and a rounded spear, which set them apart from swordfish, which have no scales or ventral fins and a flat bill; and from sailfish, which have an extremely high dorsal fin; and from spearfish.

Habitat. Found in tropical and warm temperate Pacific waters, the striped marlin is pelagic and seasonally migratory, moving toward the equator during the cold season and away during the warm season. The waters around the Baja Peninsula, Mexico, are especially known for striped marlin, which are particularly abundant off Cabo San Lucas.

Food. The striped marlin is highly predatory, feeding extensively on pilchards, anchovies, mackerel, sauries, flyingfish, squid, and whatever is abundant. The spear of the marlin is sometimes used for defense and as an aid in capturing food. When it uses its bill in capturing food, the striped marlin sometimes stuns its prey by slashing sideways with the spear rather than impaling its victim, as some believe.

Angling. Fishing methods for striped marlin include trolling whole fish, strip baits, or lures, and fishing with live baits. Most striped marlin are taken by trolling 8- to 12-inch skirted offshore lures. Blind strikes are the rule, but a fish spotted on the surface can occasionally be tempted to strike if lures are trolled past it, or if live baits are cast to it.

Spotting, stalking, and casting or trolling to surface-located stripers is an exciting possibility, as the fish are often visible in favorable conditions. Surface stripers may be "tailers," which are free-swimming fish with their sickle-like tails exposed; "sleepers," which are inactive fish with their dorsal and tail fins sometimes exposed; "jumpers,"

which are simply unhooked free-jumping fish; and "feeders," which are fish actively feeding along the surface. Different methods may be employed depending on the disposition of the fish. Lobcasting live baits to surface fish works well but requires considerable effort. Once a striped marlin is located, the angler should cast a bait in front of and beyond it, and then reel the bait back toward the fish. Strikes usually result from properly presented live baits, of which Pacific mackerel is the favorite.

These fish are often fickle, and areas where they congregate may change each year. Savvy anglers concentrate on temperature breaks and converging currents in areas with plentiful baitfish and clean blue water.

White Marlin

Tetrapturus albidus

The smallest marlin in the Istiophoridae family, the white marlin is a top-rated light-tackle gamefish and an active leaper. It is the most frequently encountered marlin along the East Coast of the United States, where it is almost exclusively released (often tagged) after capture.

ID. The body of the white marlin is elongate and compressed, and its upper jaw extends in the form of a spear. In overall appearance, the white marlin is generally lighter in color and tends to show more green than other marlin, although it may at times appear to be almost chocolate brown along the back; the flanks are silvery and taper to a white underbelly. Several light blue or lavender vertical bars may show on the flanks, especially when the fish is feeding or leaping. Some specimens have a scattering of black or purple spots on the first dorsal and anal fins.

Its most characteristic feature is the rounded, rather than pointed, tips of the pectoral fins, first dorsal fin, and first anal fin. Some specimens apparently vary from the norm in that the dorsal and pectoral fins may be more pointed; the anal fin is more consistently rounded than the other fins. The first dorsal fin resembles that of the striped marlin in that it is usually as high or higher than the greatest body depth. It differs from that of the striped marlin, or any other marlin, in that both margins are convex. The flat, movable pectoral fins can easily be folded flush against the sides of the body. The lateral line is visible and curved above the pectoral fin but is otherwise straight.

Habitat. Although this pelagic and migratory species usually favors deep blue tropical and warm temperate (exceeding 27°C) waters, it frequently comes in close to shore where waters aren't much deeper than 8 fathoms. It is normally found above the thermocline, and its occurrence varies seasonally. It is usually solitary but sometimes travels in small groups.

Food. White marlin feed on assorted pelagic fish and squid, concentrating on whatever is most abundant at a given time and place; this especially includes sardines and herring. It may use its bill in capturing food, stunning its prey by slashing it sideways and then turning to consume it.

Angling. White marlin can be caught by trolling with small whole or strip baits as well as with small spoons, feathers, or any of a variety of other artificial lures. Live-bait fishing with squid, ballyhoo, mullet, bonefish, mackerel, anchovies, herring, and other fish is also effective in specific situations.

A good deal of successful northwestern Atlantic fishing employs whole rigged small and medium-size ballyhoo. These are usually fished without an accompanying colored skirt and trolled offshore in 100 to 1,000 fathoms over specific underwater contours and where there are surface temperature changes and color breaks, both of which tend to concentrate baitfish. Anglers use outrigger lines and flatlines, as well as teasers, and fast speeds—around 6 knots. Trolled baits taken by whites are dropped back on a three to ten count, to give the fish a chance to get the bait in their mouth before the angler sets the hook.

Due to their size and activity, white marlin make good candidates for fly rodders, provided the fish are numerous and can be teased into casting

White Marlin

range. Anglers fishing for whites often encounter other pelagic species, inviting a chance at larger blue marlin. More information is contained in the section on offshore fishing.

Swordfish

Xiphias gladius

The only member of the Xiphidae family, the swordfish is one of the most highly regarded big-game species in the ocean. Unfortunately, swordfish have been especially coveted in world seafood markets—their meat is excellent—making them the object of large commercial fisheries and resulting in overexploitation virtually worldwide, as well as contributing to a demise in large specimens. Today, primarily fish under 100 pounds—which have likely never had the opportunity to spawn—are encountered, and in some places only rarely, and too few are released alive.

ID. The swordfish has a stout, fairly rounded body and large eyes. The first dorsal fin is tall, nonretractable, and crescent-shaped. The second is widely separated from the first and very small. Both are soft-rayed, having thin, bony rods that extend from the base of the fin and support the fin membrane. The anal fins approximate the shape of the dorsal fins but are noticeably smaller. Ventral fins, on the underside of the fish, are absent. There is a strong longitudinal keel, or ridge, on either side of the caudal peduncle, which leads to a broad, crescent-shaped tail.

Adult swordfish have neither teeth nor scales. The back may be dark brown, bronze, dark metallic purple, grayish blue, or black. The sides may be dark like the back or dusky. The belly and lower sides of the head are dirty white or light brown.

The swordfish snout elongates into a true sword shape. Measuring at least one-third the length of the body, it is long, flat, pointed, and very sharp (especially on smaller fish), and significantly longer and wider than the bill of any other billfish. The lower jaw is much smaller, although just as pointed, ending in a very wide mouth.

Habitat. These are pelagic fish living within the water column rather than on the bottom or in coastal areas. They typically inhabit waters from

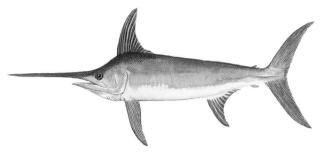

Swordfish

600 to 2,000 feet deep and are believed to prefer waters where the surface temperature is above 58°F, although they can tolerate temperatures as low as 50°F.

Food. Swordfish feed daily, most often at night. They may rise to surface and near-surface waters in search of smaller fish, or prey upon abundant forage at extreme depths. They have been observed moving through schools of fish, thrashing their swords to kill or stun their prey and then quickly turning to consume their catch. Squid is the most popular food item, but many species of midwater and deep-sea pelagic fish, such as menhaden, mackerel, bluefish, silver hake, butterfish, herring, dolphin, and others are part of their diet.

Angling. Swordfish are vigorous, powerful fighters and impressive jumpers. Anglers normally fish for them by trolling and drift fishing.

Swordfish swim alone or in loose aggregations, separated by as much as 10 meters from a neighboring swordfish. They are frequently found basking at the surface, with their dorsal and tail fins protruding from the water, so anglers intent on fishing during daylight will actually scan the water looking for a fish to present a trolled bait to. Swordfish are finicky, however, and are easily frightened by an approaching boat. They rarely strike blindly; typically, the bait must be presented carefully and repeatedly before the swordfish will take it.

Once a swordfish has been spotted, the speed of the boat should not be changed appreciably and the bait should be eased quietly and gently in front of the fish on a long line. Squid is the most popular bait, although Spanish mackerel, eel, mullet, herring, tuna, and live or dead bonito are also used. Casting live bait to surface-finning swords is also practiced.

The odds of catching swordfish are generally better for nighttime anglers. Depths run a wide gamut, from 60 to 80 feet below the surface to 1,200 feet and much more, depending on geographical location, water temperature, and moon phase. Often, baits are staggered at various levels, and light sticks are employed at least 6 feet above the baits to call attention to them, with balloons attached to the line with rubber bands to help indicate pickups.

Sharks

Sharks are a diverse and adaptable group of highly evolved fish, and among the most successful predators in the sea. Following are brief comments about some of the sharks that anglers are most likely to encounter, succeeded by general angling information.

Blacktip Shark

Carcharhinus limbatus

A wide-ranging species, the blacktip often forms large surface schools and is an active hunter in midwater, responsible for very few attacks on humans but dangerous when provoked.

ID. The blacktip is dark bluish gray on the back and whitish below, with a distinctive silvery white stripe on its flank; young fish are generally paler. As the name implies, it is black-tipped on the inside of the pectoral fin, as well as on the dorsal, anal, and lower lobe of the caudal fins in young fish. This shading may be faint, especially on the first dorsal fin, and it fades with growth. The blacktip shark has a long, almost V-shaped snout and serrated, nearly symmetrical teeth.

Blacktip Shark

Blue Shark

Bonnethead Shark

Blue Shark

Prionace glauca

Blue sharks hardly rate as fighters in comparison to makos and threshers, but they are much more abundant and provide fine sport on appropriate tackle in cooler temperate waters. They usually swim slowly, and yet they can be one of the swiftest sharks. Blue sharks are potentially dangerous to humans because they are known for unprovoked attacks, especially during accidents and disasters at sea when injured people are in the water.

ID. A member of the requiem shark family, the blue shark is very slender and streamlined, with a long and pointed snout that is much longer than the width of its mouth. Appropriately, it is a deep, brilliant blue or a dark cobalt to indigo blue above, fading gradually to white below. With up to three rows of functional teeth in each jaw, the larger teeth in the upper jaw are "saber-shaped," or broadly convex on one side and concave on the other; the teeth are serrated along the edges, and those in the lower jaw are narrower.

Bonnethead Shark

Sphyrna tiburo

The bonnethead shark is the smallest member of the hammerhead sharks. Bonnetheads, particularly young fish, are often found over flats, where they can be taken on flies and ultralight tackle.

ID. The bonnethead is particularly distinctive in appearance because it has a smooth, broadly widened head, frequently described as "spade-shaped," with more curve to it than do the heads of any other hammerheads. Also, the front of the head lacks a median groove, which is present in other hammerheads. Gray to grayish brown in color, the bonnethead shark seldom exceeds 3 feet

in length, maturing at about that length to bear six to twelve live young at one time.

Bull Shark

Carcharhinus leucas

A large member of the requiem shark family, the bull shark is common inshore around river mouths and can adapt to life in freshwater. This is the species that is landlocked in Lake Nicaragua in Nicaragua and has gained fame as a man-eater because it has been repeatedly implicated in attacks on humans, particularly in southern African waters. The bull shark can be sluggish and unwilling to strike a fly or crankbait, but it will hit natural baits readily; unlike other sharks that rise to the surface, the bull shark often stays deep and fights hard. Like the hammerhead, it will frequently attack hooked tarpon.

ID. The bull shark gets its name from its bull-like head and is known for its heavy body and short snout, the latter of which appears very broad and rounded from below. Gray to dull brown above and growing pale below, the bull shark has a large first dorsal fin that begins above the midpectoral fin, and the upper lobe of the tail is much larger than the lower.

Bull Shark

Hammerhead Shark

Lemon Shark

Leopard Shark

Hammerhead Shark

Sphyrna species

The most prominent of these species are the great hammerhead (*S. mokarran*), the smooth hammerhead (*S. zygaena*), the scalloped hammerhead (*S. lewini*), and the bonnethead. The great hammerhead is the largest, while the smooth hammerhead is the most widely distributed. These sharks are exceptionally strong and can make fast, long surface and midwater runs when hooked, fighting hard and thrashing about with a great deal of excitement.

ID. Hammerheads are easy to identify, with eyes located at the ends of two thin lobes and the overall structure resembling a hammer. A possible reason for the hammer shape may be that it is ideal for turning and locating odors, making the best use of the electroreceptors present in all sharks, which in turn makes detecting food an easier chore. The front edge of the head of the smooth hammerhead is rounded and unnotched at the center, or smooth, and it inhabits shallow, calm coastal waters of bays and harbors. The scalloped hammerhead is a gray-brown to olive shark; the front edge of its head is rounded and notched, or scalloped. Both smooth and scalloped hammerheads occasionally school in large numbers.

Lemon Shark

Negaprion brevirostris

A requiem family shark, the lemon shark is a good inshore, light-tackle sportfish.

ID. The lemon shark is commonly yellow-brown, although it can also be muddy dark brown or dark gray with olive sides and a paler belly. It has a blunt and broad snout that appears rounded from below. The second dorsal fin is almost equal in size to the large first, and the upper lobe of the tail is much larger than the lower.

Leopard Shark

Triakis semifasciata

The leopard shark is good light-tackle game and very good table fare. It inhabits inshore sand flats and rocky areas. As a smaller, less aggressive species, it is not considered dangerous.

ID. Sometimes called cat shark, the leopard shark is a striking fish, so named for its leopard-like black spots, which run in crossbars across its back and sides over a lighter gray background. The leopard shark has an elongate body and a short, bluntly rounded snout.

Porbeagle Shark

Lamna nasus

An excellent sportfish, the porbeagle is a member of the mackerel shark family, as are the white and mako sharks, and bears a resemblance to both species. The flesh of the porbeagle is of good quality and texture and is said to taste something like swordfish.

ID. The porbeagle has a robust, cobalt blue body with a perfectly conical snout that ends in

Porbeagle Shark

Shortfin Mako Shark

a point. It is easily identified by its teeth, which are smooth and have little cusps on each side of the base. It often has a distinctive white area at the base portion of the first dorsal fin; this fin is farther forward than on mako or white sharks. There is a large, particularly prominent flattened keel on both sides of the caudal peduncle, and beneath that but farther back on the tail is a small secondary keel, which mako and white sharks also lack. Its anal fin is directly aligned with the second dorsal fin.

Sandbar Shark

Carcharhinus plumbeus

The sandbar shark is an inshore fish and a good light-tackle fighter. Sandbars are commonly called browns by anglers along the East Coast of the United States, where they migrate into large bays to spawn.

ID. A relatively heavy-bodied fish, the sandbar shark is dark bluish gray to brownish gray and has a pale or white belly. There is a distinct ridge on the back between the first and second dorsal fins,

and the first fin is large and pointed, starting over the middle of the pectoral fin. Its snout is shorter than the width of its mouth, appearing rounded from below.

Shortfin Mako Shark

Isurus oxyrinchus

The shortfin mako is the most popular of angling sharks and widely distributed. Makos fight hard, have good endurance, and are fast, active, strong swimmers that often jump. Their jumps are spectacular, as they may suddenly appear 20 feet in the air while the line is still pointing at another angle. At the top of their leap, makos typically turn over and reenter the water where they exited. Makos are also very good food fish, a quality that has led to a sharp decline in their abundance. Mako steaks command a good price under their own name, but they used to be a cheap substitute for swordfish steaks, which they resemble in both texture and taste.

ID. The shortfin mako has a streamlined, well-proportioned body that is most striking for a vivid blue-gray or cobalt blue coloring on its back, which changes to a lighter blue on the sides and a snowy white on the belly; this brilliant coloring fades after death to a grayish brown. Other characteristic features are a conical, sharply pointed snout, a large flattened keel on either side of the caudal peduncle, and a lunate (crescent-shaped) tail with lobes of nearly equal size. The large first dorsal fin begins just behind the base of the pectoral fins. The shortfin mako can be easily distinguished from all other sharks by its teeth, which are slender and curved and lack cusps or serrations.

Sandbar Shark

Thresher Shark

Thresher Shark

Alopias species

Threshers are excellent food fish, comparable to mako and swordfish, and they are outstanding fighters. These sharks use their tails to herd baitfish into a mass by slapping or thrashing the water, then stunning or injuring fish before swallowing them. There are four species: the pelagic thresher (*A. pelagicus*), Pacific bigeye thresher (*A. profundis*), Atlantic bigeye thresher (*A. superciliosus*), and longtail thresher (*A. vulpinus*). All are fundamentally pelagic but will occasionally move in close to shore.

ID. The thresher is characterized by its well-muscled tail, the upper lobe of which is usually as long as the rest of the body. Grayish to dark charcoal in color, thresher sharks turn abruptly white on the belly and may be mottled on the lower half of the body. Threshers are further identified by the absence of a keel on the caudal peduncle; by their small, pointed, and broad-based teeth; and by their comparatively smooth skin. Longtail and pelagic threshers have moderate-size eyes, and the first dorsal fin is set almost directly in the middle of the back and far ahead of the beginning of the pelvic fins. The Atlantic and Pacific bigeye threshers have much larger eyes, and the

rear margin of the dorsal fin is located at least as far back as the origin of the pelvic fins.

Tiger Shark

Galeocerdo cuvier

The tiger shark is of interest to anglers because it is commonly encountered in the 300- to 800-pound class, but it is a rather poor fighter. It is one of the largest-growing members of the requiem shark group, and infamously dangerous as a species that will attack and eat humans.

ID. Dark bluish gray to brownish gray above and whitish below, the tiger shark is so called because of its prominent dark brown blotches and bars, or "tiger stripes and leopard spots"; these are especially evident in juveniles and small adults but fade with age. This fish has an extremely blunt snout that appears broadly rounded from below, and a mid-dorsal ridge is present. The tiger shark is also distinguished by its broad and coarsely serrated teeth, which have deep notches and are the same in both jaws. The last two of five gill slits are located above the pectoral fin, and there is a long, prominent keel on either side of the caudal peduncle, as well as a long upper lobe on the tail.

Tope

Galeorhinus galeus

One of the smallest members of the requiem shark family, the tope is a bottom-roaming inhabitant of inshore environs and an active and highly sought species within its extensive range.

ID. The tope has a slender body; a prominent, long, pointed snout; long pectoral fins; and a large and strong tail fin with a large lower lobe.

Tiger Shark

Tope

Angling for Sharks

One of the attractions of fishing for sharks is that almost any tackle will do the job under most circumstances. The vast majority of sharks are caught in open waters, where even large specimens can be handled on relatively light tackle if the angler exercises patience. Light big-game tackle, such as 20- and 30-pound-class outfits, is perfect for most sharks caught offshore. Anglers specifically seeking makos usually opt for 50-pound gear, and 80-pound tackle can be used during tournaments or when tigers, whites, and the largest of makos are sought. Modern stand-up rods, belts, and harnesses can entirely eliminate the need to sit in a chair to fight even the largest of sharks.

Blue sharks are usually pushovers on heavy gear but can be lots of fun on light tackle. This is especially true when they can be chummed to boatside, making it possible to select individuals of suitable size for spinning, baitcasting, or flycasting tackle. That same light tackle is standard for sharks caught on Florida Keys flats, where there is no deep water available. The sporty blacktip, which also jumps, is a favorite of flats anglers who cast lures and flies to them. Blacktips have poor eyesight, so lures must be placed close to these sharks and drawn right in front of their mouths. Lemon sharks also hit lures on the flats, but the largest sharks that wander into that area are primarily tempted with baits.

Terminal tackle for sharks is important. Their teeth make wire leaders a must; 15 feet of No. 12 to 15 single-strand wire is the usual choice for large sharks, so even if they spin in the leader they may not reach the main line. Kinking is also a problem due to a shark's tendency to spin in the leader, but braided wire presents another problem in that very large sharks can chew through it. Some skippers create leaders using very heavy monofilament attached to a large swivel, to which they add several feet of wire at the terminal end.

Sharks of one species or another may be encountered almost anywhere, from rivers and bays out to midocean. Indeed, shore and small-boat anglers catch some of the largest sharks, particularly in warm waters, where some species even enter areas barely deep enough to cover their bodies. Sharks on the Florida Keys or Bahamas flats can be as spooky as bonefish, although it's hard to imagine what they might fear.

The vast majority of sharking occurs in ocean areas, but sharks are scattered over wide areas. Unlike other fish, which tend to swarm over wrecks or dropoffs, most migratory sharks aren't tied to a particular area. Anglers usually select structure (such as a dropoff) at a likely depth to start their drift, but a means of attracting sharks to the boat is important.

By far the most common and productive method of accomplishing that is chumming. Hooked baits are usually distributed from just below the surface down to at least half the water depth. Floats or balloons are used to

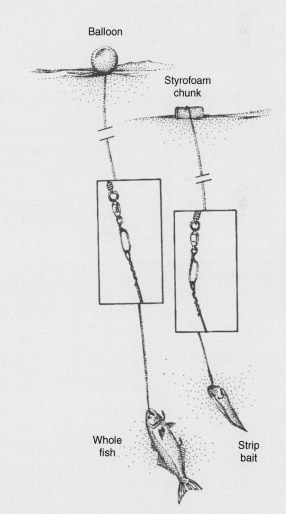

Shark fishing rigs for use offshore and when chumming include a heavy-leader rig with whole bait (left) and a light-leader rig with strip bait (right).

(Continued)

fix baits at the desired depths, and sinkers are normally required to hold the baits down.

Because the vast majority of sharks are now released by anglers, it's best to use just one hook and to strike after allowing only a short run freespool in order not to hook the prey deeply with the reel in. Fillets are preferable to whole baits in that regard, as hooking is easier and quicker.

Some sharks, especially makos and threshers, can be trolled, although unadorned lures don't work well. California anglers add a baitfish to a heavy lure, however, which can be slow-trolled below the surface. These connect with makos regularly.

Some large sharks, such as tigers, tend to fight straight down and are no fun to catch on light tackle. Most sharks will return to the surface even if they do take a dive during the fight. This tendency permits the use of relatively light tackle and makes sharks an ideal target for stand-up fishing. They'll usually tow a small boat after sufficient pressure is applied, and larger boats can follow them if necessary, although the vast majority of sharks can be caught from a dead boat.

White Shark

Carcharodon carcharias

Also known as the great white shark and a popular but rare angling catch, this large member of the mackerel shark group is undoubtedly the most dangerous shark due to its combination of size, strength, ability, and disposition to attack, and because of the many recorded attacks on humans that have taken place. A relatively uncommon deep-water fish, the white shark occasionally enters shallow waters. It often lingers near islands and offshore colonies of seals and sea lions, which are some of its preferred foods; thus it is thought that some attacks on humans occur because the white shark mistakes divers or surfers in wet suits for seals.

ID. The white shark has a stout, heavy body that may be a dull slate blue, grayish brown, or almost black above, turning dirty white below. There are black edges on the pectoral fins, and often a black oval blotch on the body just above or behind the fins. The large head ends in a point at the conical snout, which accounts for the name "white pointer." There is a large, distinct, flattened keel on either side of the caudal peduncle and a greatly reduced second dorsal fin. A distinguishing feature of the white shark is its teeth, which are large and triangular with sharp, serrated cutting edges.

White Shark

PART TWO

Tools

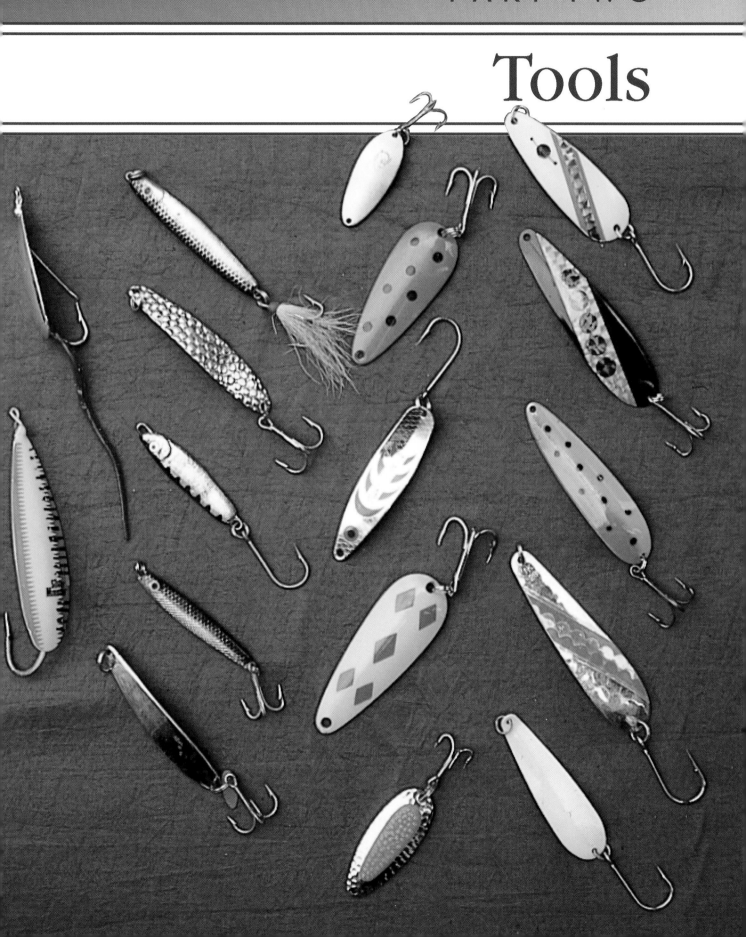

4

Fishing Rods

B y definition a fishing rod is an instrument with a handle, shaft, and reel seat, which connects a reel and line for the purpose of making a controlled presentation of bait, lure, or fly. It is an intrinsic element in all forms of sportfishing, being essential to casting, retrieving, detecting a strike, setting the hook, and playing the fish.

Although some people refer to a fishing rod as a fishing "pole," this is incorrect, since a pole is an implement unaccompanied by a reel or by rod components, and therefore not used in the act of casting. Fishing poles do not have running line; line is directly attached to the tip of the pole.

Effective fishing is in part determined by the use of the proper tackle for the situation; choosing the right rod is an important element of this. However, just as there are many different species of fish, diverse habitats, and methods of angling, so too are there many categories and types of fishing rods, each suited to a particular application. Some fishing rod manufacturers produce scores, if not hundreds, of different rods, covering a gamut from fly, spinning, baitcasting, spincasting, surf, trolling, boat, big-game, flipping, popping, noodle, and downrigger models, to name just some of the possibilities, not to mention specialized subtypes within many categories.

To select a fishing rod, you should have a clear idea of your needs and the general properties of rods.

Obviously, a fly angler can't do justice to fly fishing without the right type of rod, but neither can the same type of spinning rod be used adequately in stream trout fishing as in trolling for trout with downriggers. Even when there is cross-application, some compromise must be made. Different species, special applications, and regional preferences have caused a proliferation of rods for various needs.

Although anglers do stretch the use of some fishing tackle, and although some rods can be used for multiple species and means of fishing, it is generally important to have the right type, length, and style of rod for a particular fishing situation. To make this choice from a potpourri of possibilities it is helpful to understand the categories, functions, materials, features, and components of fishing rods.

Categories/Types

All fishing rods have a handle, shaft, and reel seat. The materials used for each of these features may vary. The shaft is primarily referred to as the blank. This is where the rod guides are attached; the number and type of these vary widely. A very small number of rods do not have a series of external guides; in these, the line runs through the blank within the hollow interior and exits at the tip.

Fishing rods are most commonly of one- or two-piece configuration. Some have three or more pieces; a lesser number, usually for specialty applications, have multiple telescoping sections or a telescoping butt section. Prices range widely, and though many of the specialist and top-quality performance rods are costly, high price is not necessarily indicative of the best quality and may not be synonymous with best value. Many good-quality fishing rods are found at mid-price ranges.

The following text briefly details the most prominent different categories of rods. This information is rather generalized, as there are exceptions and special products in most categories.

Baitcasting. Used with levelwind or baitcasting reels, which sit on top of the rod handle and face the angler, this tackle provides excellent casting accuracy for the skillful user, although achieving top-level proficiency takes practice and experience. Most baitcasting rods are one-piece models, though larger, heavier-duty ones may have a telescoping butt and are generally stiffer than spinning rods. Guides are usually small to medium in size, and handles may be straight or with a pistol grip, both having a trigger hold under the handle.

Spincasting. These rods are similar to those used in baitcasting and are fairly uncomplicated. The guides are mounted atop the rod, and guide rings are generally small. Reels mount a little higher on top of the rod's reel seat, and the handles feature either straight or pistol grip design with a trigger hold under the handle. Spincasting rods usually aren't as stiff as baitcasting rods, having generally lighter action for use with light lines and lures. They are made in one- and two-piece models, mostly of fiberglass, and a few are telescopic.

Spinning. Used with open-faced spinning reels that mount underneath the rod, this tackle is very popular for a wide range of fishing situations and is relatively uncomplicated. Guides have a wide diameter to accommodate the large spirals of line that come off the reel spool when casting. Handles are straight, with fixed or adjustable (ring) reel seats, and both one- and two-piece models are common.

Fly. Unlike other rod types, fly rods are used to cast a very light object via a large-diameter, heavy line. Guides are small, and rod length varies from 5 feet to 12 or 14, although most fly rods used in North America are 7½- to 10-footers. Fly rods are rated for casting a specific weight line; a fly reel usually sits at the bottom of the handle, but some rods have extension butts for leverage in fighting big fish.

Surf. These long rods are used for casting great distances from the beach into the surf and come in both spinning and revolving-spool reel versions. Length varies from 7 to 14 feet, though most are in the 10- to 12-foot range with long handles. They are heavy, in order to cast objects weighing 2 to 4 ounces, and guides are large.

Boat and bay. A lot of different rods fall into this catchall category predominantly devoted to saltwater fishing. These are usually workhorse products with beefy two-handed handles that accommodate conventional reels. They are generally stiff, heavy-action rods, with longer models used in pier fishing and shorter ones in boat work.

Big-game. These rods, meant for subduing the largest creatures of the sea, have the sturdiest construction. Generally short, they feature a roller guide on the top of the tip or throughout the blank, and sport an extra-heavy-duty handle with a gimbal mount butt for insertion into rod holders. These rods are rated according to the class of line (and reel size) they are suited for.

Other rods. Travel or pack rods are found in baitcasting, spinning, or fly versions and are three- or four-piece products (some also have telescoping butt sections). Ice fishing rods are usually very short with a soft tip for use around holes in the ice, mostly necessary for storing and dispensing line. Flipping rods are long (7 to 8 feet), heavy-action rods with telescoping butts that are used for making short casts in close quarters to heavy cover when fishing for largemouth bass. Noodle rods are whippy 12- to 14-foot rods with guides that curve around the rod blank; they are primarily used in stream steelhead and salmon fishing for presentation and fish-fighting advantages, and sometimes in trolling. Downrigger rods are 8- to 9-foot slow-action products that are primarily found in baitcasting versions and take a long, deep bend for use when trolling with downriggers. Some other rods are made for special applications, and many manufacturers make rods designed for particular species of fish or for use with certain lures or baits (crank-bait rods, worm fishing bass rods, mooching rods, and popping rods, for example).

Functions

Rods are often classified by their intended application. Many rods today are subcategorized; for example, a baitcasting rod may be typed or labeled as a bass worming rod or a flipping stick, a big-game rod may be typed as a 30-pound-class offshore trolling rod, and so forth. Type is not completely separable from function, which is the specific task the angler wants the rod to perform.

Angling with a rod entails at least four specific functions: casting, detecting a strike or bite, setting the hook, and fighting/landing the fish. Some of these require opposite properties for optimal performance, which obviously complicates rod design.

Casting

The process of casting consists of a combination of body movements and rod action intended to project terminal tackle. The rod acts as a storage device to deliver smoothly the energy of the angler's arm, wrist, and hand, and it acts as a lever arm to increase tip velocity in the forward casting arc.

A longer rod generally casts farther than a shorter one, subject to the limitations of the individual angler's physical stature. This is because tip velocity is directly proportional to length, although this ignores excessive bend, which tends to shorten the physical length of the rod. A higher launch velocity—the speed at which the lure, at the point of release, leaves the arc of the moving rod tip—results in a longer cast. In rods of equal length, a superior stiffness-to-weight ratio of one rod material over another provides a lighter fishing tool and thereby reduces angler fatigue after hours of repetitive use.

Stiffness-to-weight ratio is an engineering term used to quantify the ability of a material to be used effectively in structures. The higher the ratio, the larger the load that can be borne without excessive weight penalty. An aircraft constructed of solid steel,

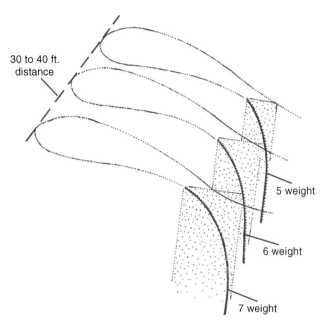

30 to 40 ft. distance

5 weight

6 weight

7 weight

Casting distance and rod action vary with line weight. A 9-foot rod rated for a 6-weight fly line (WF or DT), balances at 35 to 40 feet.

for example, would be very strong, but wouldn't fly. Likewise, a solid steel rod would be strong, but relatively unfishable by modern standards.

Because some rod materials provide a distinct advantage in stiffness-to-weight ratio, they can be incorporated into longer rods to cast the same total weight of lure or bait for which a heavier rod, made of material having a less advantageous stiffness-to-weight ratio, might be considered.

Another factor in the process of casting is energy storage. During a strong cast, the human muscles act in an almost explosive manner. The rod must be designed to smooth this impulse and efficiently cast the terminal rig or lure. Failure to do so results in thrown-off rigs, snapped-off lures, inaccurate casts, and backlashes.

Energy storage is enhanced by loss-free materials in rod construction and by rod taper. Loss-free materials are generally those with long, uninterrupted fibers with strong, mutual bonding. Ideally, a loss-free material acts like a perfect spring and returns all stored energy. Any loose ends to the working fibers, or gaps in the bonds, cause frictional losses, and the angler's energy goes into "heating" the rod rather than casting the lure. This latter case is much like bending a paper clip

back and forth; it does not spring, but instead deforms and noticeably heats up.

In most fishing situations, the ideal taper for casting is very gradual, probably best illustrated by the highly developed field of fly rod design. When flexed, fly rods typically have a gradual bend from tip to butt, so that all portions of the rod assist in the storage and smooth transfer of energy from the angler to the fly line. The fly angler spends a great deal of time casting, often making delicate presentations, so it is appropriate that the fly rod emphasizes properties that are designed for casting.

Detecting a Strike

From the standpoint of rod design, detecting a strike is limited to sensations transmitted by the line through the rod and into the angler's hand. Watching for line movement and noticing telltale ripples on the water are not directly involved with characteristics of the rod.

Here, the requirements for ideal rod design fortunately are aided by the laws of physics, which state that energy transfer occurs equally well in both directions through most structures. An angler imparts energy to a lure when casting, and receives energy in the form of a vibration during a strike. A rod that casts well also exhibits great sensitivity to strikes. Thus rods that smoothly transfer energy from angler to line and lure reciprocally transfer energy well from lure and line to angler. This property is quantified in physics as a mathematical statement called the reciprocity theorem.

There are some fine points to consider, however, because the strike signal can be so miniscule that fishing rod components such as reel seats and reel materials may affect the angler's ability to detect the strike. The rod, then, is not a separate entity, but rather a part of a complete system. In this regard, purposeful design of rod accouterments and reels affects optimal performance in strike detection.

Setting the Hook

This is a rod function that may require a property opposed to those of other rod functions. An analogous example of opposing functions is a catalytic converter on an automobile; the component is not advantageous for engine efficiency, but a necessity to help provide for a cleaner environment. Rod design, too, is a balance of trade-offs.

Ideal rod construction for hooksetting requires great stiffness, so that minimal delay occurs between the strike and the angler's reaction to it. Additionally, such stiffness aids in maximizing the amount of line taken up, which in turn compensates for whatever stretch and slack may be inherent to the line being used. In this circumstance, fast acceleration is desired. Consider the situation of a fish picking up bait and the angler's reaction. In one moment, the hook is motionless; an instant later, it is moving at great speed to become embedded in the fish's jaw.

The bass angler's worm fishing rod is an excellent example of optimal rod design for hooksetting. This type of rod is designed to set the hook hard, fast, and deep. In this type of fishing, failure to set the hook as noted not only translates into a missed catch, but in many instances impacts on verifying whether a detected irregularity in retrieval is the subtle strike of a fish or merely the lure bumping on bottom structure.

Fortunately, the function of setting the hook can be compromised in rod design, in light of special angling techniques and advancements in the design of certain hooks and terminal tackle.

Fighting/Landing Fish

The process of bringing the fish to the angler is also essentially one of energy transfer; this time, that transfer is from the fish to the drag elements in the reel. The construction of the rod is an important factor because it smoothes the pulsing thrusts of the fish's tail and fins, and accommodates changes in the direction and angle of the fish's runs.

In fighting a fish, there are also secondary energy losses in the friction of line bellying through the water, and in fiber bond slippage within the rod structure itself. This latter characteristic is called damping or dampening.

Damping is the process of converting vibrational energy to heat. In an automobile suspension system, for example, the task is accomplished by the shock absorbers. The energy imparted to automobile springs when there is a bump in the road is converted to heat by the shock absorber.

Though desirable in some situations, damping is undesirable in others. A pole vaulter, for example, stores energy in the bending (or loading) of the pole in order to be flung over the crossbar.

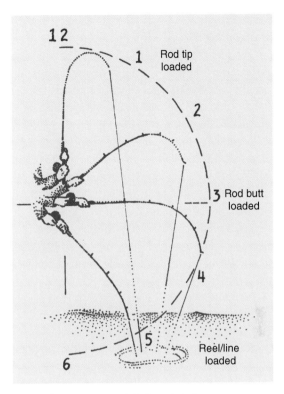

When playing a strong fish directly below your position, power is exerted when the rod is approximately between the 2 and 4 o'clock positions; this is when the rod butt carries the load. When the rod is approximately between the 4 and 6 o'clock positions, the reel and the line carry the load and the rod does little. When the rod is approximately between the 12 o'clock and 2 o'clock positions, the tip carries the load; this can be harmful to the rod and creates a situation in which the angler can do little to influence the fish.

If a shock absorber were placed on the pole, performance would suffer greatly. Likewise, a good casting rod should not be excessively dampened.

When deflected, a properly designed rod returns to equilibrium rather quickly, instead of continuing to vibrate up and down. From a casting point of view, this is an important consideration after the rod has flexed in the forward casting arc.

To some extent, all fishing rods damp; it's a matter of degree. Rod damping helps wear down a fish. Too much of it, however, can cut down casting distance because casting energy is too quickly being dissipated into heat as fiber bond slippage occurs. A well-damped rod is comfortable to use when a fish is on, just as a well-damped automobile is comfortable to ride in, compared with the ride experienced in a stiff-spring pickup truck.

The ideal taper for a rod designed to fight fish is generally abrupt. Abruptly tapered rods are usually called "fast tapers," "magnum actions," or "power rods." They are fashioned through large butt-to-tip diameter-ratio differences.

A good example of this type of rod taper is the classic West Coast albacore or tuna rod. It is characterized by being "tippy," meaning much more flexible at the tip than at the butt. When a fish is hooked, the bend of such a rod may resemble an inverted L shape, with very little deflection near the butt. The location of the bend varies according to the size of the fish and the angler-applied force exerted when pulling on the fish.

For larger fish, the bend of the tippy rod occurs downward toward the grip as well, and the rod can adjust to such a circumstance because of its thicker-walled section near the butt. On the other hand, a small fish causes a bend higher up in the more flexible portion of the rod, at a smaller cross section. A wide range of fish can be accommodated by such a rod. Furthermore, by designing in sufficient butt stiffness, this type of rod will not "bottom out," or tend to exceed its elastic limits, and the angler can exert a great deal of power against the fish. The fishing conditions automatically select that particular portion of the rod cross section best suited to fight the fish.

When such a rod is cast, however, in a like fashion only very particular and limited portions of the rod act elastically to store energy. Therefore, it is a relatively poor casting instrument.

Obviously, ideal rod construction entails a number of compromises. Some of the qualities we seek in rods have similar requirements; others have opposing ones. Thus there must always be a certain amount of give and take in designing a truly fishable rod. In most instances, the particular degree of compromise is intended to give the best possible performance for the type of rod and its function. In other words, good rod design and construction should emphasize those properties most vital to each particular type of fishing.

As noted, fly rods tend to favor casting, but at the risk of bottoming out, or exceeding the elastic limit on a truly strong fish; the exception is big-game saltwater fly rods that are very effective fighting tools but troublesome to cast unless they

are of superior overall design. By contrast, the power rod can quickly exhaust a wide range of fish, but at the risk of tearing the hook out of the baitfish or snapping off a lure on the cast.

Power and Action

The performance and function of rods are commonly described in terms of power and action, which are somewhat nebulous terms that refer to the design of the rods based upon their construction and materials and incorporating all of the issues that have been noted so far.

In a practical sense, power is defined by the amount of pressure it takes to flex the rod; the less pressure it takes, the lighter the rod's power. Designations are made according to an individual rod's ability to efficiently handle a certain range of lure weights and line sizes. These designations are ultralight, light, medium light, medium, medium heavy, heavy, and extra heavy.

The related concept of action denotes where a rod flexes along its blank, which is determined

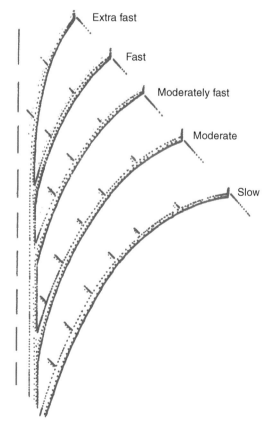

Rod Action

by the taper. A fast-taper rod flexes mostly at or near the tip, a moderate-taper rod flexes through the middle of the rod, and a slow-taper rod flexes through the butt. Specific designations include slow, moderate, moderately fast, fast, and extra fast.

Construction and Materials

Rods are mass-produced by major manufacturers, but only insofar as the blanks are fabricated by large-scale methods. The overall properties of the finished product are extremely dependent on what is done to the blank after manufacture. Thus the number, type, and placement of guides; the wrapping; and the choice and placement of handle material totally affect the end use.

Unlike with reels, rod building can also be a cottage industry, and many small custom rod builders exist; most of them buy blanks from established manufacturers and custom tailor the final product. This tailoring might be done, for example, to make an offshore casting rod suited to the build of a particular angler, or it might be done to wrap a fly rod blank with spinning rod guides to create a special river fishing rod. In addition, individual anglers purchase blanks and component materials to build rods for themselves or family members, either to suit special needs or to have the satisfaction of catching fish on a personally made rod.

A typical rod is manufactured by first cutting what fishing rod manufacturers commonly call "prepreg," a cloth formed of strength fibers pre-impregnated with a bonding resin. From a chemical standpoint the most commonly used resin systems are phenolic, polyester, or epoxy, the latter two being more commonly employed in modern rods.

The prepreg is cut into the proper shape to provide the appropriate thickness of rod wall along the entire blank. In some rods, for instance, the butt section may utilize a wider cut of prepreg or even additional layers for a specific taper.

After it is cut into a shape, the prepreg is wound around a form called a mandrel, which is contoured to define the shape and taper of the finished rod blank. By a number of different processes, pressure and heat are applied to cure the wrapped prepreg and mold it over the mandrel. After the cure cycle, the mandrel is removed from the blank and the rod's exterior is subjected to finishing operations.

To some degree, all rod-building materials are composites. Each rod shaft consists of a strength or stress element, typically a fiber, and a bonding element, typically a resin. The stress element stores and transmits energy by elastic deformation, and the bonding element both fixes the location of the stress element and prevents the failure of one fiber from directly propagating to another.

This latter property is the principal reason why single-material rods are impractical. The failure or development of a defect would easily propagate like a crack in a windshield and the entire structure would fail. Therefore, superior construction techniques entail many small fibers to reduce the risk of breakage.

Another reason for using small fibers in rod construction is that it is far easier to manufacture small fibers without defects than to do so with larger ones. This is because fewer atoms are involved.

As an important aside, a critical element of all rods is the tensile modulus of the fibers used. Modulus is a measure of how effectively a material resists deformation. Tensile means to pull or place under a tension load. A high-tensile-modulus material produces a stiff structure and thus aids in achieving a high stiffness-to-weight ratio.

Bamboo

Bamboo (Tonkin cane) is a natural composite. The stress element consists of tiny fibers that distribute nutrients through the plant, and the bonding element is a material called lignin.

The principal limitations of bamboo are variations in quality and the presence of discontinuities (nodes) within the stalk of the plant. From the manufacturing standpoint, variations in the natural product, even within a single stalk or culm, necessitate an enormous amount of painstaking selection and hand work. It is labor-intensive and very costly to manufacture, which is why the very best split-cane rods are enormously expensive.

The situation with split-cane rods is much like that in a winery. The correct circumstances and precise production control of the grapes lead to a truly outstanding wine; otherwise, the product is merely grape juice. Though capable of giving fine performance under somewhat limited conditions, bamboo is largely a material for the custom rod builder.

Fiberglass

Uniformity of fiberglass filaments was the key to successful early fiberglass fishing rod construction. The manufacturers were not only able to design rods, but be confident that quality would be consistent throughout each production run.

Uniformity also aided in developing mass-production techniques with reduced labor costs, and thereby made it possible to offer excellent fishing rods at attractive prices. Moreover, as fiberglass rod technology matured, the uniformity of the fiberglass materials permitted fine-tuning of manufacturing processes to improve the product.

One example of fine-tuning was the introduction of variations in the chemical composition of the glass melt. Of the types of glass available, E-glass, which is an alkali borosilicate glass, is widely used because of its high resistance to water damage and its high tensile modulus.

A higher-priced, low-alkali, high-aluminum-and-magnesium kind of product called S-glass can be produced with an approximately 30 percent improvement in tensile modulus. S-glass was originally developed for aerospace use but has been largely supplanted in that industry by other materials. It remains in the tackle industry as an intermediate rod material in price and performance between regular fiberglass and graphite.

Graphite

Graphite, called carbon fiber in some parts of the world, has become a generic term. Originally developed for the aerospace industry, it was intended to maximize the strength-to-weight ratio, and the aim was to achieve the highest possible tensile modulus.

The tensile modulus of graphite runs from four to eight times that of fiberglass. Thus a graphite rod intended for the same type of fishing as one made of fiberglass can have thinner walls and be of a more slender configuration. The net result is a significant savings in the weight of the finished rod.

A second property of graphite has both positive and negative aspects. The combination of configuration and bonding properties enhances the alignment of unidirectional graphite fibers in rod construction, so graphite rods can be designed with fibers extending unbroken from tip to butt. This construction style provides smooth energy transfer, which results in excellent casting qualities and more sensitivity than found in a fiberglass rod made from woven cloth. But there is a limitation on the variety of rod tapers that can be designed with unidirectional fibers.

The correct combination of graphite with fiberglass can produce rods with both good sensitivity and a wide variety of tapers. This process requires extremely careful design, however, and the graphite should not only be unidirectionally aligned within the rod, but also uniformly distributed around the rod shaft. Such a composite rod offers both performance and value, for it can be offered at a price between fiberglass and high-content graphite.

It is noteworthy that the major factor in the value or performance of a rod is not the percentage of graphite in it, but rather how that graphite is used.

Boron

Boron is a fiber of great tensile strength. However, the filament (usually a tungsten alloy) is heavy and contributes substantially to the total weight of the fiber. Overall, boron fibers have a significant advantage over graphite in strength-to-weight ratio, but by themselves are not practical in mass-produced rod construction due to weight.

Because of this, boron fibers are usually employed with graphite to form composite rods and thus are subject to the same rigorous design requirements of unidirectional fiber alignment and uniform distribution around the shaft for top performance. High-boron-content tubular rods usually contain less than 15 percent boron fibers by weight, but again, content alone does not constitute an accurate assessment of performance.

Features and Components

A fishing rod is used in conjunction with some type of reel and line and therefore has features and components necessary for various functions. Some are derived from the manufacturing process, such as hoop strength and spine, which we won't discuss here, but other additions are basic to every use and are briefly reviewed next.

Ferrules

The longest practical one-piece rod is about 5 to 6 feet in length. The reason for this limitation is that one-piece rods longer than that will not fit easily into an automobile, and the possibilities for accidental mechanical damage abound.

Therefore, most rods of moderate or more length are produced in several sections. (There are notable exceptions, such as the custom one-piece 11- to 15-foot products used by dedicated surf casters, who regard car-top or bumper roof racks as a necessary part of their sport.) At one time, these sections were produced by cutting the rod blank and joining the sections with a separate metal fitting or ferrule; the additional weight and stiffness, however, degraded the action. Most rods today are joined with integral ferrules that are part of the blank itself.

The merit of integral ferrules is obvious: no discontinuity or significant alteration of the rod action. As an example, backpacking rods for the hiker are produced as five or more sections of about a foot each, yet the assembled rod is very fishable and it requires a diligent search to locate the joints. Even better are the high-end three- or four-piece travel products that result in eminently fishable 6- to 9-foot spinning, baitcasting, and flycasting rods.

The integral ferrule is fabricated in inside and outside forms. The inside ferrule is the lightest and simplest to produce in that the lower section is made a bit larger and the tip section slides into it. The joint is ground with a precision taper, and the

Handle, guides, action, and material are all important elements in using a rod to cast, retrieve, and play a fish.

friction fit is sufficient for a secure grip. Many experienced anglers lubricate this joint (if not already done by the manufacturer) with beeswax, both to increase the grip and to promote smoother assembly. Do not apply the wax excessively or it will trap abrasive dirt particles; always wipe a ferrule before assembly.

Hoop strength at the ferrule is usually increased with a string wrap. The outside ferrule, in turn, is stronger because the thinner tip section is built up at the joint to fit outside the lower section. The tip section is thus as strong as the rear section, which was already strong because of the increasing rod taper toward the butt. The outside ferrule is more expensive to produce because the built-up joint requires the application of separate hoop windings on the rod blank, and each such operation increases costs. When made well, both types of ferrules deliver good service and are very fishable.

Several special products deserve distinct mention. One is telescoping rods in which the ferrules are joined from the inside. Telescoping rods are generally of three or more sections, extending to lengths in excess of 12 feet. The guides are usually of a "slip-on" configuration, always on the rod, and are slid into their correct places as the rod is extended. This process is much simpler in practice than the description.

Another example is blue-water rods for large fish. These conventional rods use the powerful drags of revolving-spool reels to subdue fish that easily outweigh the angler and are many times heavier than the breaking strength of the line. Because the top-side guides generate torque forces on the rod, the blanks are always of one-piece construction to prevent rotation at a ferrule.

In general, however, the ferrule is an essential part of most practical rod designs, and the convenience it provides for transport and storage far outweighs any effect on rod action.

Guides

Nearly all fishing rods have guides; this includes one tip-top guide, which is obviously at the top or casting end of the rod, and a variable number of intermediate guides, which are along the blank between the top and the handle. Of all accouterments, guides are the single most significant factor affecting rod performance beyond the blank itself.

The style, height, number, spacing, and weight are all part of the guide, and therefore important parameters.

Rod guide styles can be termed either "spinning" or "conventional." Although there is some degree of universality, the basic distinction between these is large-ring bottom-mounted guides for spinning rods (as well as fly rods), and small-ring top-mounted guides for conventional rods, which are used with revolving-spool reels (baitcasting, conventional, and big-game).

Guide style incorporates the frame material, which includes welded stainless steel, graphite polymer, brazed wire, and others. However, the fundamental guide parameter is whether it has single or double attachment points to the rod blank, which respectively are called single- or double-foot guides.

Because casting is what spinning tackle does best, the appropriate guides for spinning rods should favor the casting function. Thus a single-foot guide least perturbs the typical light action of a spinning rod, and is the primary choice. The single-foot guide is also suitable for withstanding the forces of the line acting on the guide when subduing a large fish. These forces are directed downward, and the frame of a single-foot guide slung below the rod has sufficient strength to withstand severe tension load on the guide ring.

Double-foot construction is favored for conventional rod guides, especially for models used to subdue strong ocean species. This is because fish fighting is what such tackle does best, and the load of a gamefish on the line applies both a crushing downward force on the guide ring and frame and a simultaneous tendency to torque or twist the rod. This latter phenomenon occurs because the line is located directly above the rod axis and is fundamentally at unstable equilibrium; when torquing begins, the "lever arm" for twisting increases and the condition avalanches.

Such stresses require the rigid configuration of a double-foot frame; the double attachment points of the frame to the rod act in the manner of a triangle, which is the extremely sturdy building block of bridge spans. Light-duty baitcasting rods, such as those used for freshwater bass fishing, have a mixture of guide styles, usually double-foot guides toward the stiffer rear section and single-foot guides toward the slender tip section,

which is often designed to enhance strike detection (as may be necessary when using jigs or plastic worms).

An important function of the guide on all rods is to prevent contact of the line with the rod blank. During a cast, such contact or "line slap" results in shorter casts due to increased friction; when fighting a gamefish, such contact is regarded as an unfavorable and irregular additional force retarding the line.

The height and spacing of guides on the rod are interactive; these parameters are mutually dependent and must be considered simultaneously. In the case of spinning rods, the line leaves the reel in the form of a cone-shaped envelope, defined by the spool diameter at its base and the tiptop at its apex. The theoretically ideal guide ring diameter, height, and spacing precisely lies along the surface of this cone because such a configuration would minimize friction and thereby lead to maximum

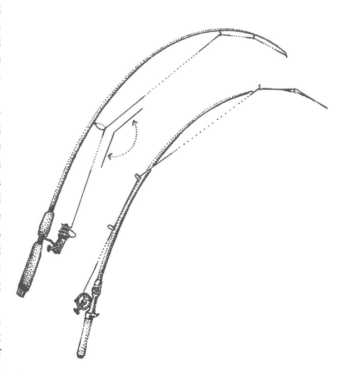

This is a greatly exaggerated depiction of poor guide placement on a spinning rod (top), where guides and line are under the blank, and on a baitcasting rod (bottom), where guides and line are on top of the blank. It helps illustrate that when there is too great an angle (arrows) of line from one guide to the next, excessive strain on the rod and loss of power result.

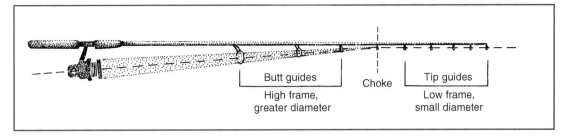

A spinning rod characteristically has the largest guides closest to the butt and the smallest guides closest to the tip. The choke guide is the intersection point where larger spirals of line funnel down when cast.

casting distance. Although there is some disagreement about the location and effects of the lowest or first guide along this cone, most spinning rods are fabricated in a sensible manner and small departures from this ideal cone are not serious.

During retrieval of a large fish, the stress on the line is applied through the guides to the attachment points on the rod. If the number and spacing of the guides is insufficient, the stress is concentrated at these points and the rod will be bent into distinct segments instead of a smooth curve. The final result could be a catastrophic failure.

How many guides are sufficient? The optimum solution requires a compromise because too many guides lead to heavy weight, slow action, and high costs; too few lead to stress concentration and rod failure. A simple test of a spinning rod is to string the rod with monofilament line, and then lift the rod against a load to verify the quality of its design. Note that the common practice of simply wiggling the rod back and forth, or flexing the rod tip against the ceiling, reveals the rod taper but does not generally validate correct guide spacing and number.

In the case of the conventional rod, during a cast the line leaves nearly tangent to the spool so that the guide rings can be relatively small. Because controlling gamefish is what conventional tackle does best, the guide configuration favors the retrieval function. During the fish-fighting process, in the ideal case the guides are required to support the line above the axis of the rod. Compromises are necessary here, too, because increasing guide height reduces the number required but also increases the lever arm and therefore the tendency to torque. The optimum height and spacing depends on the rod action but

is generally regarded as the minimum number that will not permit the line to cross the axis of the rod during maximum bend.

Although some rod designers abhor even slight contact between line and rod surface, the process of the line crossing below the rod axis certainly exacerbates the always present problem of torque. In essence, pulling the line past the rod axis is an unstable state, and the structure responds by torquing, or twisting over. The test for correct design here is the same as for spinning: thread the rod with line and check for contact under load.

Guide Rings

In order to effectively confine the line with minimum disturbance, the ideal guide ring should have low weight, low friction, and high durability. Low weight is particularly important for casting applications where the additional mass of the guide can affect the action of the rod blank.

In the specific case of fly fishing, where superior casting properties for a delicate presentation are of foremost importance, the lightest of all guides, simple helixes of thin wire, are the rule. At the other end of the scale, as in blue-water trolling where weight is unimportant because the rod is supported by a gimbal mount and shoulder harness, the norm is massive roller guides to minimize the friction of heavy lines and to maximize fish-fighting power. Other fishing tackle falls between these extremes. Practical guide ring materials include chrome-plated stainless steel or brass, common and technical ceramics, and various carbide and nitride compounds. These are available, depending on their configuration, in a wide range of weights.

Low friction is attained through good surface polishing, but, as usual, contradictory requirements arise from the property of durability. The wear aspect of durability concerns abrasion of the guide ring by the line; this is usually due to the action of microscopic particles of suspended sediment (quartz) carried by the line. Therefore an ideal guide ring material should be harder than quartz, a requirement identical to that of a precious gemstone.

Common guide ring materials include aluminum oxide (alumina, or in its gemstone form, red ruby or blue sapphire), tungsten carbide (Carboloy), silicon carbide (SiC), titanium nitride (TiN), and zirconium nitride (ZrN). While some of these materials can be formed as a ceramic before firing, all require grinding and polishing, the same as any gemstone. This leads to a contradictory requirement: The desirable hardness property in these materials is the very feature that causes that same material to be stubborn to shape and polish. Silicon carbide guide rings, for example, typically require one week of continuous diamond dust polishing to attain a good surface finish. This manufacturing cost is naturally reflected in the finished product.

Another aspect of durability is "shock resistance," or the ability of a guide ring to withstand a sharp blow. Of the foregoing materials, tungsten carbide is reported to be the most brittle, followed by silicon carbide and aluminum oxide. Titanium and zirconium nitrides can occur in the form of solid technical ceramics, or may be applied as vacuum-deposited coatings on various substrates. The latter materials are routinely used as protective coatings on the turbine blades of jet aircraft; they may sound exotic but are extremely practical and durable. Another application of these coatings is on premium drills and cartridge case dies, where their hardness and low friction properties offer significant benefits. As a result of such applications, these materials are reported to be the most durable of existing guide rings.

The tip-top guide is a type of terminal guide ring, but its service load is substantially more severe due to increased contact and friction where the line has its greatest angular change at the rod tip. As a consequence, many rods are offered at a lower price by mounting a higher-quality material such as Carboloy or silicon carbide for the tip-top ring and using hard chrome or other materials for intermediate guides.

In like manner, the stripping guide of a fly rod contains the major angular change for the line (the tip-top tends to lie parallel to the line due to the combination of line stiffness and soft rod-tip action), thus its "stripper" guide is usually of higher quality than the others, typically the best aluminum oxide or silicon carbide. In general, the rod manufacturer is well aware of the requirements for superior guide service; their choice of materials reflects compromises on cost, quality, and perceived value.

Guide Wrapping

The guide is normally wrapped onto the rod with thread, which both affixes it to the blank and serves in a decorative capacity. The thread can vary in thickness, ranging from approximately the fineness of a hair to the coarseness of 4-pound-test monofilament, and in materials from costly silk to common spun nylon. Generally, the finer thread wraps are most highly regarded because more turns are required per linear inch, which likewise requires a higher level of craftsmanship.

Under load, the guide acts as a point of stress concentration on the rod blank, so the stiffer double-foot guide is often provided with a cushioning underwrap (called "double wrapping") to better distribute the stresses. In fact, for all types of rods, stress concentration at the guide foot is statistically the most frequent cause of failure under load; most rod breakage from a large fish is located at a site of guide attachment. This situation is further exacerbated by the common practice of grinding the end(s) of the guide foot to knife edges to allow smooth thread wrapping.

The transparent coat of epoxy resin is the final step to protect the wrapping thread and, perhaps more important, to firmly affix the guide in place, because any movement could lead to scratches on the rod blank and promote premature failure.

Once the resin has cured, the guide and wrap are an integral part of the rod blank and affect the action. The wrap acts in the manner of an athletic support bandage, adding to the stiffness of the rod, and the weight and stiffness of the guide also affect the action. The completed rod is typically stiffer and slower in action than the unadorned blank as it was originally fabricated. Thus proper rod design must plan for the overall effects of adding guides and wrapping.

Line-through-Blank Rods

Because the use of guides and wrapping necessarily affect the action of the rod blank, the concept of threading fishing line through the center of a rod is as old as the first tubular rod. The absolute simplicity of eliminating not only the guides and wrapping, but torque and stress concentration points, was universally alluring. The nodal segments of early bamboo rods were drilled through, and line was inserted down the axis. The practical problems that arose were those of extreme friction, which impeded the ease of casting and the distance achieved and caused power losses when retrieving lures, bait rigs, and fish. These problems remained with line-through-blank rods until the 1990s, with none commercially available.

The key to solving this dilemma was advanced technology that enabled precise finishing of the *interior* as well as the *exterior* of the rod. These advances include internal polymer finishes and complex internal integrated structures. A limited number of manufacturers produce such products, although models are available for spinning and conventional reel use, and in multipiece configuration for surf and downrigger use.

These cast and retrieve as well as similar rods with external guides; in addition, they offer "perfect" bends without stress concentration, unprecedented lightness (the rod wall can be made thinner

because it does not have to withstand stress concentration due to the guide foot), and torque-free characteristics.

The ability to be torque-free is particular to line-through-blank rods; the fish-fighting ability is effective not only to the front, as with external-guide rods, but acts equally well for strong runs to either side. The tip-top and front section of the rod is axially symmetrical and therefore omnidirectional. Whichever direction the fish runs, the rod responds with equal bending forces. An additional benefit to the omnidirectional tip-top is that it is tangle free.

Grips and Handles

Rod grips and handles serve several functions, including comfort and control for the angler and a seat for mechanically mounting the reel.

The traditional grip material is cork because it is thermally insulating (and therefore warm in cold weather), light in weight, sensitive to vibration transmission, and provides a good grip, even when wet. Drawbacks include somewhat rapid wear because of softness, difficulty in obtaining uniform material, and relative expense in premium grades.

Ground and reconstituted cork, which is the equivalent of particle board, is a compromise material but is generally regarded as physically unattractive. It is used extensively in the form of rubber-bonded tape, which is spiral-wound directly onto the blank for specialty surf rods because of its light weight and durability.

Man-made handle materials include foamed polymers such as Hypalon, typically found in black but available in colors or even "laminated" configurations. These can range from foamed cylinders to molded and shaped offset pistol grips.

The choice of material is largely determined by application: cork for more finesse-like fishing and foamed polymers for rugged applications. The forces that a big-game angler applies to the rod grip would tear many materials right off the blank. On the other hand, a person casting ultralight micro-jigs would likely find the weight of polymer grips oppressive. The former needs Hypalon, the latter premium cork. Both types of grips have shapes that reflect their application; the Hypalon for the big-game angler is often a hand-filling

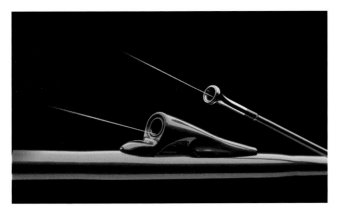

In this Daiwa Saltiga Ballistic Interline rod, fishing line passes through the graphite blank via one entry point, stays inside the blank, and then exits through the tip guide.

triangular cross section to better control torquing; the premium cork for the ultralight caster is bullet-shaped to better encourage the natural pointing tendency of the index finger along the rod axis for pinpoint accuracy.

Reel Seats

The reel of the big-game angler needs not only a physically sturdy reel seat of formed stainless steel or machined high-tensile-strength aluminum, but is often supplemented by a separate accessory clamp (part of the reel) secured around the reel seat by stainless steel bolts. Angled tie rods, shoulder harness, and gimbaled butt are accessories that complete the fishing outfit, all intended to help battle the strongest species.

The reel seat of an ultralight spinning rod, in contrast, can be as simple as a few thin aluminum rings, offering not only light weight but the convenience of positioning the reel anywhere along the handle for best balance. These rings should be secured not by just sliding onto the reel foot, but by rotating them several times to "bite" into the handle.

A more common reel seat is one with a threaded closure, which is regarded as more secure but suffers the drawback of fixed location. Threaded reel seats are offered over a wide range of sizes for various fishing applications. The reel seat materials for these applications are machined aluminum alloys and molded graphite (polymers with strength fibers).

In applications requiring sensitivity, the reel seat is often cut away to allow direct contact of the rod blank and reel seat so that the transmission of the most subtle strike is maximized. The choice of reel seat is determined just as in the case of the handle or grip: it should represent the combination of best comfort and utility that pleases the angler.

Some spinning rods, incidentally, do not possess either a threaded reel seat or adjustable aluminum rings, but have merely unaltered cork handles. These are expressly designed to allow the user to position a spinning reel where it feels most comfortable, using black or colored electrician's tape (preferably 1-inch width) to firmly secure it to the rod. This is preferred by some light jig users, and it is possible for anglers with sliding ring reel seats (which often don't stay put) to remove the rings and use tape to secure the reel to the handle. The main drawback to this is that the reel cannot be easily removed from the handle for storage or changing, and even the tightest manual tape wrapping may not prevent some flex or stretch in the tape at the reel foot when the rod is put under severe stress.

5

Fishing Reels

Fishing reels are basically line management devices that are affixed to some type of rod. Their primary functions are storing, dispensing, and retrieving fishing line.

The storage function relates to the ability of the reel to contain sufficient line to allow continued fishing in the event of a tangle and breakoff, as well as to provide for sustained runs by large fish. The dispenser function is more complex; it ranges from the ideally friction-free event of long-distance casting to the action of a clutch, which allows line to slip outward under tension. The retrieval function likewise ranges from the high-speed recovery necessary to impart lure action to the significant cranking power required to raise a stubborn fish away from its protective bottom structure.

These functions are accomplished via different means, which has resulted in six unique categories of reels. The specific attributes of these will be reviewed categorically later in this section. However, it is first useful to appraise those technical aspects that are common to all fishing reels.

Spool Types

Fishing reels can be divided into two major groupings, depending upon whether the spool revolves or is stationary.

A wide variety of reels, with different features and capabilities, are on the market.

Revolving-Spool Reels

Conventional, or revolving-spool, fishing reels receive their name because the motion of the line is considered conventional; it is pulled from a spool that revolves the same way sewing thread is taken from its spool. Such reels are mechanically straightforward; they are characterized by strong cranking power and the ability to handle heavy lines. Although revolving-spool reels hold the majority of distance casting records, they are relatively difficult to cast and require considerable skill and practice to avoid catastrophic errors.

Revolving-spool reels can be categorized as single- or multiplying-action versions. Single-action reels, which include fly fishing and mooching products, are simply spools with handles that revolve on a shaft. The spool is large because each rotation of the handle must retrieve a reasonable amount of line. However, the large spool severely limits casting distance because the energy to start the spool rotating requires unsuitably massive terminal weights. In the case of fly fishing, the reel is simply a line storage device, and the line is pulled by hand from the reel to facilitate the cast.

Single-action reels are mounted below the axis of the rod so that forward winding retrieves the line. Because of the direct-drive nature of the handle, the mechanical efficiency can be excellent, and the simplicity of the design offers great reliability. The drag function—applying pressure to make it harder for the spool to permit line to flow outward when pulled by a large fish—may be as simple as using the hand to apply friction to the edge of the spool, or may include the use of adjustable mechanical friction washers.

Multiplying-action reels are commonly referred to as multipliers and today are represented by a group of products that are generally termed "conventional" reels. These have comparatively small spools that are driven by a mechanical gear train. The gear train can be disconnected to free the spool, allowing for excellent long-distance casting in lighter-weight products. Spool overrun can occur, however, leading to a vividly descriptive condition of line tangle called a "bird's nest." Avoiding this catastrophe requires considerable skill by the caster.

Because the gear train consists of parallel axes for the shafts, the mechanical forces are simply constrained, frictional losses are minimal, and cranking power is superb. Likewise, the drag system is uncomplicated and extremely effective. In addition, the line is wound directly onto the spool, easing line flexibility requirements and allowing the use of very heavy lines on very small spools. Some models of these reels can be used efficiently with a wide variety of line strengths. Multiplier reels range from freshwater baitcasting reels to big-game reels for offshore fishing applications.

Fixed-Spool Reels

Spinning and spincasting reels are called "fixed-spool" reels as well as "stationary-spool" reels because the line is dispensed from the end of a nonrotating spool. The spool axis is parallel to the rod, and the line is pulled over the spool lip when cast. Such a system does not require energy to rotate a spool, and is not subject to overrun; thus it is extremely simple to cast and relatively tangle-free.

Retrieval is accomplished by winding the line around the fixed spool with a rotating arm. Because this motion requires a 90-degree change of direction, there are mechanical losses even with relatively limp lines. Likewise, the drive gears from handle to rotating arm require a 90-degree change of direction, leading to thrust forces and mechanical losses. Fixed-spool reels thus excel in casting, even for users who are relatively unskilled and unpracticed, but are not as efficient in cranking power as revolving-spool reels.

Two types of fixed- or stationary-spool reels are widely used and very popular, especially in

A revolving-spool baitcasting reel is flanked by two fixed-spool spinning reels.

freshwater fishing. One features a spool that is exposed and always visible to the user, and is commonly called a spinning reel. The other features a covered spool and is commonly called a spincasting reel. The latter has convenient pushbutton casting operation, and a top-mounted hand position identical to that of the (revolving-spool) baitcasting reel. Individual spinning reels can typically be used efficiently with three, or perhaps four, strengths of line; individual spincasting reels can be used with only two or three strengths of line.

The features and use of each of these types of reels is described in greater detail in their specific section.

Body Materials

The manufacture of fishing reels requires a fairly large capital investment in dies, designs, tooling, computer design/manufacturing software, and so forth. The finished product is a mass-produced item, each nearly alike. This is true as well even for limited-production items that are "machined" from barstock, which require an enormous development cost. Fishing reels are not custom-made products that can be created for individual needs and interests, although there is a substantial amount of after-market tinkering that occurs with some, particularly reels that are put to the most demanding big-game fishing uses.

Many manufacturers have stressed the use of metal, or the use of plastic, in their products, but a lot of anglers do not understand why or how this may be relevant.

Metal

The metals used to fabricate fishing reels range from simple die-cast alloys (aluminum and zinc) through machinable, tough aerospace alloys (hardened high-tensile-strength aluminum). The choice is typically determined by engineering requirements and costs. Positive attributes of metal in reels include strength, rigidity, and durability.

For a given-sized part, metals are generally stronger than polymers; this is true even with less expensive alloys. For this reason, the internal gears of reels are almost universally metals, such as brass, stainless steel, aluminum, bronze, or other alloys. Similarly, the metal body of a reel is stronger than its polymer counterpart. In the case of high-end reels, the body is often machined from a solid block or billet of metal, resulting in the strongest possible structure, without regard for cost.

Metals are also stiff, or rigid, by nature and are able to maintain precise alignment between gears, even when subjected to heavy stresses. Frame distortion under load leads to gear misalignment and loss of cranking power. The losses in cranking power are actually delivered as wear to the gear train, and measurably decrease gear life. Being rigid, metals resist this distortion and power loss.

Durability is achieved through the superior wear properties of metals. Many alloys are used not just for the frame but may double as load-bearing surfaces.

The negative attributes of metal reel bodies include weight, corrosion, and lack of shock resistance. Aluminum and its alloys comprise the bulk of metal reel components, offering about a threefold decrease in weight compared to steel, stainless steel, or brass alloys. Titanium, which is extremely light and durable but expensive, is being used more on premium reels, particularly on spool lips and on spinning reel bodies, but as a coating rather than as a base component.

Metal reels generally require surface treatment to inhibit corrosion, particularly in a saltwater environment. This can be done to certain aluminum alloys by an electrochemical coating process called anodizing, which can be both tough and colorful (nearly any color can be permanently dyed into the coating). Many top-end reels with golden or flat black finishes, for instance, use dyed anodized coatings for protection. Some reels even have anodized coatings on internal parts, such as gears. Other alloys are finished with paints, epoxy, or other bases and, depending on quality, can give adequate corrosion protection. In the case of titanium, some manufacturers use a vacuum-deposition process in which titanium molecules are coated over a metal substrate to give the product an ultra-hard scratch-resistant surface.

Plastics/Graphite

Polymer (sometimes called "graphite") reel bodies are injection-molded from a mixture of plastics and strength fibers. The polymers or plastics include ABS, nylons, and similar materials, and the strength fibers are chopped fiberglass, graphite (hence the name "graphite"), or even silicon carbide whiskers. The injection-molding process is well suited to economical mass production. Plastics should not necessarily be confused with "cheap," as in toys; plastics are structural parts of modern firearms, for example, and can withstand enormous loads.

Positive attributes of plastics and graphite in reels include economy of production, light weight, and corrosion resistance. The cost of production and raw materials is extremely economical for these products. The fabrication process is at lower temperatures than with metals, and the die lifetime generally longer; both result in a lower-cost product. Additionally, the weight of such products is about two-thirds that of aluminum alloys, although this number must be modified to include metal parts such as gears, shafts, and screws, which are internal to the reel.

Especially noticeable is that plastics are inherently resistant to corrosion and often do not require any finishing; colored fillers can be added to the polymer before molding. Note also that metallic finishes, often vacuum deposited, can be applied so that the part appears to be made of metal. The durability of the finish is dependent on quality, ranging from the products of the toy industry to those in high-wear applications such as the metal-finish knobs on stereo equipment.

Negative attributes of plastics and graphite in reels include distortion and wear. Distortion results because polymers must retain a degree of flexibility to avoid brittleness, particularly at extremely low temperatures. This is because an overly rigid polymer can fracture through propagation of a crack, much like a piece of glass. The purpose of the strength fibers is to limit crack propagation, so the final mixture must be a compromise of properties. (In the case of metals, brittleness is controlled by grain structure, which is a function of the alloy and heat treatment.) Furthermore, the flexibility of polymer parts should not be regarded as entirely negative; reels made of these materials have wonderful shock resistance and will survive hard falls much better than metal reels. The most important factor in producing a viable polymer-frame fishing reel is careful structural design; done correctly, the product is excellent.

Polymers have many self-lubricating properties but are fundamentally soft and therefore can wear quickly, especially through the abrasive action of sand, dirt, and grit. Again, careful designs that inhibit movement have generally succeeded in eliminating this potential problem. In firearms, for instance, steel inserts are molded into the plastic body to provide bearing surfaces.

For both metal- and polymer-bodied reels, many of the potential problems that can be negative attributes may be avoided through minor maintenance. Generally, the potentially bad aspects of a product are exacerbated through neglect, and the reel is perfectly capable of delivering good service and value whether made of metal or plastics.

Bushings and Ball Bearings

The basic task of bushings and ball bearings is to precisely support a rotating shaft with minimum friction. In revolving- and fixed-spool reels, a rotating shaft supports the handle and gear train, which the angler cranks for retrieve. In revolving-spool reels, the rotating shaft also supports the spool, and in fixed-spool reels it also supports the rotor.

Bushings

A bushing, sometimes called a sleeve bearing, supports the rotating shaft with a smoothly finished hole and a lubricating film. The bushing material can be the same as that of the reel body itself but is typically a distinct material for better wear and lower friction. The physical contact between bushing and shaft is subject to sliding of one surface over the other, so there's a need for smooth mechanical finishing and lubrication.

For relatively low loads, the body material of die-cast reels is a suitable bushing material. The common die-cast metal is Zamak, a zinc/aluminum alloy with good machining characteristics. Its coefficient of friction with a steel shaft (a measure of the amount of friction between the metals) is low, and a lubricating film makes it even lower. The lubricating film is required to keep the surfaces from actually touching, and must not only withstand the pressure of the contact, but retain this property at higher temperatures as well.

Bushing materials that differ from that of the reel body are used for greater loads and include such metals as brass and bronze, as well as fiber-reinforced polymers. These bushings are firmly installed with a press fit, or even adhesives, because inadvertent rotation of the bushing would disastrously wear an oversized hole in the reel body.

Bushing materials are selected to optimize mechanical properties, such as abrasion resistance and low friction. The metals are often sintered from granules (much like a graham cracker pie crust), and the resultant porous structure allows either storage or free passage of lubricants, which extends service life for the bushing. Other alloys contain graphite flakes that "self-lubricate" the bushing. Polymer bushings are strengthened with chopped fibers in the matrix. A well-made bushing

gives extremely smooth rotation for the operation of a fishing reel.

Ball Bearings

The major advantage of ball bearings over bushings is under heavy load conditions. Under low load conditions, the difference between the two systems is virtually indistinguishable, but as the load on the shaft increases, the superior performance of ball bearings becomes increasingly apparent. Ball bearings support their load through a rolling action in contrast to the sliding contact of the bushing. The difference can be compared to moving a rock on wheels versus dragging it along the ground; the heavier the rock, the more apparent the difference between the two methods.

The rolling action of a ball bearing depends on the roundness, precision, and hardness of its components. Lubrication is of secondary importance. High-quality ball bearings have extremely close tolerances or imperceptible "play," and the small ball bearings in fishing reels rotate freely when spun. Many ball bearings are sealed with precision-fitted covers, front and back, to keep contaminants out and lubricants in. In all, the ball bearing is a complex structure, and the many steps required for its manufacture make it expensive. It, and the related roller bearing, are without doubt the best engineering solution to the support of a rotating shaft under load.

Most production fishing reels are designed with both bushings and ball bearings. Because of the difference in cost of the two types of support, the more expensive models contain a larger number of ball bearings, and have a longer projected service life under harder use conditions.

 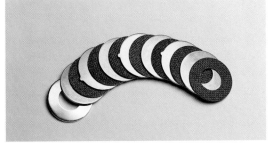

These are stainless steel ball bearings (left) and a series of carbon friction and stainless steel washers, both found on better conventional reels.

Various cost/performance trade-offs give excellent value and satisfy the needs of all levels of anglers.

Cantilever Supports

Although most rotating shafts are supported on both ends, some designs are cantilevered, or supported at one end only. Small flycasting reels are a typical example. The spool is supported on a shaft, which is cantilevered to the sideplate. The handle shaft on some conventional and baitcasting reels is another example.

In these latter cases, the flex allowed by cantilevered designs (also called set plate designs) can seriously affect performance under load because gear teeth engagement becomes compromised, and severe wear can result. The important point is that ball bearings can deliver their full capability only when the total reel design offers rigid support for all of its components. Thus you cannot simply associate increased ball bearing count with increased quality.

Lubrication

The primary purpose of a lubricant in a fishing reel is to reduce wear. Greases are generally used in lubricating bushings, gear teeth, and sliding shafts to prevent direct metal-to-metal contact. The essential property of the grease is that its viscosity is sufficient to resist extrusion from the contacting metal surfaces by the pressure generated by heavy loads. This viscosity should be relatively independent of temperature and unaffected by water.

Suitable greases are sold by fishing reel manufacturers; if they are locally unavailable, white or "lithium-based" general-purpose greases serve well. Flake additives, such as graphite, further enhance performance but can be messy unless carefully applied, and will transfer stains to clothing.

Other flake additives include molybdenum disulfide and Teflon. Flaked molybdenum disulfide is designed for high-temperature automotive disc brake service; it is messy to apply but an excellent lubricant for gears in some large conventional reels. Flaked Teflon is comparatively expensive and is used for some drag washer lubrication. The same chemical inertness that characterizes the nonstick Teflon coating in cookware also yields nonstick drag performance. It is a singular and unusual property, and leads to extremely smooth starting and stick-free drag performance, particularly in reels designed for light lines.

These and other greases, however, should only be applied if the manufacturer recommends it. Some manufacturers have specific grease recommendations, or advise no greasing, so you should follow their instructions.

Light oils are intended for lubrication of ball bearings on the shaft of revolving-spool reels, which must rotate freely for long casts. These ball bearings are designed to operate with a rolling action, and the light oil is intended as much for surface protection as lubrication. Grease or heavy oils inadvertently applied to spool bearings seriously degrade their performance. Such ball bearings should be washed in alcohol or acetone (in proper ventilation) and then lubricated with light oil. The oil also serves the secondary purpose of reducing bearing noise. Such oils can be used for lubricating the shaft ends, and for other light-duty uses such as baitcasting reel clutches and yokes.

If you get oil on your hands while fishing, clean your hands well to avoid the possibility of repelling fish with the odor of the lubricant when you touch lures or natural bait. In some cases, this makes no difference in fishing, but in others it can. Wipe off any lubricant on the exterior surface of a reel with an alcohol-soaked rag, or use a covering scent.

Drag

Drag is basically an adjustable friction clutch that allows line to slip outward from a reel spool when a strong fish cannot be readily hauled in and swims the other way. The drag mechanism on a fishing reel allows line to slip outward by turning or revolving the spool, and it is controlled by the amount of friction applied, primarily by drag washers, to the spool. The amount of friction, or drag tension, is increased or decreased by turning a knob or wheel. How to set drag tension is detailed in chapter 14.

How well the drag operates when it's needed most is a critical fishing-performance issue, and encompasses the following considerations:

- Variation. Does it retain its original setting, or does it stray from that setting? Straying is bad.

- **Maximum drag force.** Can the drag be set so that it doesn't slip at all (lockdown), and should that be necessary? This is useful but not critical to many situations.

- **Range of adjustment.** How many revolutions can you obtain by turning the control mechanism on the reel? Ideally you should be able to get from zero tension to 30 percent of the line's breaking strength with just a short adjustment, then have a lot of adjustment from 30 to 50 percent, and finally ramp up very quickly to full lockdown. The force required to start up the drag is an element of this as well, and it can be hampered by a drag that has been tightened and left to sit for several days, which puts a "set" in the drag washers. For this reason, you should relax the drag tension after every trip.

- **Drag washer size.** Are the drag washers large enough for the most severe tests? The most efficient drag washers are those with a large inside diameter as well as a large outside diameter to best cope with heat dissipation.

Gears

The heart of any reel is the gear set. The moment the handle is turned, the gears engage and the reel begins to recover line, either for the purpose of retrieving a lure or bait or for fighting a fish. The demands placed upon the gears vary with the manner of fishing and the species, and performance is influenced by certain mechanical factors and product properties.

Gear Basics

The gear set in a typical fishing reel consists of the drive gear, pinion gear, oscillation gear(s) or levelwind gear(s), and perhaps a transfer gear. Of these, the most important are the drive and pinion gears, which establish the speed or power found in any reel.

The drive gear is usually directly linked to the reel handle in a spinning reel and indirectly through a drag mechanism in a baitcasting reel or a conventional reel. The purpose of the gear is to set the retrieve of the reel. The pinion gear is normally smaller in diameter than the drive gear and connects to the rotor of the spinning reel or to the spool in revolving-spool reels. The diametric difference between the drive and pinion gears constitutes the basic numerical ratio of any reel.

The number of individual gear teeth machined into each gear is used to calculate the precise ratio.

In almost any simple gear set, one gear material is normally harder than the other. This both directs and controls the action of the two parts throughout their life and actually keeps the gears running smoothly for a longer period. Two hardened gears running together would amplify even the smallest machining imperfection or piece of grit on the gear teeth.

It is common in spinning reels for the pinion gear to be made of brass. This is a hard material, and it allows for the more intricate machining required in this smaller part as well as absorbing the greater anticipated wear in this gear with its fewer teeth. The corresponding drive gear is most often made of aluminum in quality reels, but is sometimes made of easily die-cast zinc, which tends to be somewhat harder than aluminum. In either case, the gear teeth should be machined as precisely as possible to ensure smooth operation and long life.

Baitcasting and conventional reels typically use brass for the drive gear and bronze for the pinion. Here, too, the hardness differential favors the smaller-diameter pinion gear to provide longer life. The gears in these reels are generally smaller than those in spinning reels, and they require a still greater degree of precision and strength. The other gears in any reel will not face anywhere near the stresses and loads encountered by the drive and pinion and therefore do not need to be significantly harder.

Almost all reel gears in better-quality fishing reels are helically milled. This means that each gear tooth is curved, rather than straight, on the gear circumference. Helical milling results in greater strength, thicker cross section, and a high degree of inherent smoothness. The major benefit is that, unlike straight-milled gears where only a single gear tooth is fully engaged at one time, helical gears allow at least partial engagement of several gear teeth at all times, spreading the load and potential wear.

The best way to prolong the life and performance of reel gears is regular maintenance and lubrication. Heavily used reels should be cleaned and properly relubricated on at least an annual basis. A midseason lubricant check, and possibly a small addition, can also be helpful.

Even the best-designed and best-produced gear set can eventually wear out or strip, regardless of regular maintenance or lubrication. Ordinary wear failure results from a weakening of the gear teeth through the removal of material over time. The typical warning of impending failure is that the gears seem to become rougher and "sloppy," with an increase in free play. The final failure results in the gear teeth skipping over one another, particularly in a small area of the handle rotation. Once this occurs, you should replace both the drive and the pinion gears.

Gear Ratio

The basic numerical ratio of the drive and pinion gears in any fishing reel merely establishes the number of revolutions made by the reel spool or rotor per turn of the reel handle. That number is determined by counting the gear teeth on the larger drive gear and dividing that by the tooth count of the smaller pinion gear.

In a gear set consisting of a 60-tooth drive gear and a 12-tooth pinion gear, the ratio would be calculated at 5:1, since the pinion will turn five times for each full rotation of the drive gear. The drive gear is normally linked to the reel handle, and the pinion gear is engaged with the spool or rotor. Thus, in a 5:1-ratio reel, one turn of the handle will cause the spool or rotor to turn five times.

Typical low gear ratios are 3.5:1 or 4:1, and typical high gear ratios are 6:1, although they range both higher and lower. The average or all-around ratio for a spinning reel used in freshwater is 5.2:1. For a baitcasting reel it is 5.1:1; and for a conventional (inshore trolling) reel it is 3.8:1.

This view of helical reel gears helps illustrate the way these objects relate to each other and how numerical ratio is determined by the number of teeth on the respective gears.

These ratios are often referred to in terms of speed; for example, a high-gear-ratio reel is frequently called a high-speed reel, but in fact gear ratio does nothing more than designate the mechanical gear action of the reel, which is not the whole story about the true speed of any reel.

Line Recovery

To determine the useful speed, the mechanical ratio must also be factored by the size of the reel spool, creating a geometric ratio that establishes how much line is wound onto the spool with each turn of the reel handle. The geometric ratio for every reel is determined by spool diameter, which is a key dimension for any reel and sets the circumference of the line level on the spool and the amount of line wound onto the spool with each turn of the reel handle. What the geometric ratio really establishes is a more meaningful number than gear ratio: the *line recovery* ability of an individual reel, or the length of line placed back onto the spool per turn of the handle.

For example, a 4.4:1-gear-ratio reel with a 2-inch-diameter spool will recover 13.8 inches of line per turn of the handle. A 6.2:1-ratio reel with a 1.5-inch-diameter spool will recover less than 11 inches of line per handle turn. Therefore, it is the size of the spool in combination with gear ratio that most affects the recovery of the line. In the aforementioned example, the 6.2:1 reel would be considered a high-speed model based on its numerical gear ratio. But by comparison, the "slower" 4.4:1 reel will move a lure through the water at a faster speed per turn of the reel handle. Of course, if that 6.2:1-gear-ratio reel were equipped with a 2-inch-diameter spool, it would take up almost 19.5 inches of line per handle turn, which is much greater than the 4.4:1 reel.

The point is that you need to know how much line a reel will recover per turn of the handle in order to compare it to another reel; gear ratio alone does not provide enough comparison. Obviously, two reels with identical gear ratios but different spool circumferences will have different recovery rates.

The table on the next page shows a line recovery comparison of spool (line level) diameters by typical numerical gear ratios. These calculations have been simplified by using the maximum line level diameter at all times for the highest resulting linear value, but bear in mind that spools are not normally filled to their maximum possible capacity, and should not be, for practical fishing use. In normal fishing use, the line level will vary as line leaving the spool reduces the working circumference; differences in line thickness can further reduce the line level even when casting identical distances.

The dimensions used in this table are representative of a wide variety of spinning reels marketed for uses from ultralight freshwater through heavy saltwater applications. The same pattern holds for other types of reels, although the range of spool diameters is less broad. A typical baitcasting reel spool will have a diameter between 1.25 and 1.5 inches. Heavier-duty conventional casting and trolling reels can range to spool diameters of over 4 inches.

As shown by the numbers with single asterisks, a quarter-inch of increased spool diameter makes an average-gear-ratio reel (5.1:1) faster than a high-numerical-ratio model. An increase of a half-inch in diameter can make a "slow" numerical-ratio reel (4.4:1) faster than the one that is generally accepted as high-speed, as indicated by those examples with double asterisks.

Thus selecting a reel for a particular technique, lure type, or species of fish involves not only considering numerical ratio, but also line recovery rate to get the best tackle advantage. But there are still other considerations.

Cranking Power

Although the line recovery rate of any reel affects how much line is wound onto the spool, the numerical ratio of a reel indicates the available cranking power of the gear set. This is similar to the operation of an automotive transmission, where the lower ratio of the first and second gears is much more powerful because these gears transmit greater torque to overcome inertia. Once the vehicle is moving, it is easy to step up in gears through second and third to fourth gear or higher. The low-ratio power gears aren't designed for speed, and the high-ratio speed gears aren't designed for power. Try to move a manual transmission car from dead still in fourth gear and see what happens.

In a fishing reel, the ability to winch in a sizable fish—or any object with great resistance—is achieved only through a powerful, low-numerical-ratio gear set. "Pumping" a fish during the fight is recommended with any tackle, but it is almost mandatory with high-ratio reels. You have more ability to crank a fish toward you with a power ratio of 3.5:1 or 4.4:1. These ratios in a reel with a respectable spool diameter deliver a compromise of line recovery and gear power that is hard to beat.

Certain applications or situations demand a conscious choice of gear ratios. When using a highly water-resistant lure, such as a deep-running crankbait with a large lip, the ideal choice would be a low-numerical-ratio reel. A 3.8:1 gear set can comfortably deliver the necessary power to drive this bait down and through the water with minimal wear and tear on the angler. A very high-speed reel can bind under the line load created by this lure's water resistance. Trying to fish high-speed lures with a slow 3.8:1 ratio would wear out most casters before lunchtime. The effort required to turn the handle fast enough to work a truly high-speed lure would be exhausting.

It is more difficult and fatiguing to reel a slow-ratio gear set fast than to reel a high-ratio gear set slowly. A high-ratio reel can easily be used to retrieve slow-technique lures or bait as long as

Line Recovery by Spool Diameter/Gear Ratio

Spool (line level) diameter (in inches)	Numerical gear ratio		
	4.4:1	5.1:1	6.2:1
1.25	5.39	6.25	7.60
1.50	7.77	9.01	10.95
1.75	10.58	12.26	14.91
2.00	13.82	16.01	19.47**
2.25	17.49	20.27	24.65*
2.50	21.59**	25.03*	30.42
2.75	26.13	30.28	36.82
3.00	31.09	36.04	43.82
3.25	36.498	42.30	51.42
3.50	42.33	49.06	59.65
3.75	48.59	56.32	68.47
4.00	55.29	64.08	77.90

*A quarter-inch of increased spool diameter makes an average-gear-ratio reel (5.1:1) faster than a high-numerical-ratio model (6.2:1).
**A half-inch of increased spool diameter makes a low-gear-ratio reel (4.4:1) faster than a high-numerical-ratio model (6.2:1).

they do not create a great deal of water resistance. However, some anglers make the mistake of fishing too fast by virtue of using a high-speed reel when they really need to be fishing more slowly. For instance, when a lure or technique calls for a slow presentation or retrieve, anglers sometimes inadvertently retrieve too fast because of their reel; in such a situation, a low-speed reel would be better if you cannot keep using a high-speed reel slowly.

Some surf anglers will remember that an ideal choice for use with either high- or low-speed retrieve lures was the original Crack 300 spinning reel, an expensive imported reel that had a spool diameter of 3.75 inches and a power ratio of 3.2:1 and was a forerunner for that market until production ceased in the 1980s. It provided anglers with a superb combination of line recovery and gear power, and was one of the most respected surf fishing reels ever made. Its diameter and power ratio had such benefits for surf angling that other manufacturers later developed reels with similar attributes.

The simplest and most powerful reel ratio is 1:1. This is commonly found in almost all flycasting reels, which typically do not have gear sets but are direct drive. They are also typically slow, especially when the level of line is low, such as when a fish has stripped the fly line off the reel and gone down to the much thinner-diameter backing.

The more modern designs of saltwater flycasting reels achieve greater line recovery speed by increasing spool diameter. They are employing the geometry factor to achieve a line recovery advantage. The capacity of the reel, however, does not necessarily increase. This is because the central arbor area of the spool is also increased in diameter. This large arbor helps minimize line set, and it reduces the amount of backing required to properly fill the spool. One such 10-weight reel needs 27 percent fewer turns of the handle to retrieve a 90-foot line than a standard-design reel. It recovers more line and puts less wear on the angler, and is still a powerful 1:1 reel, but it may not have the total capacity (fly line and backing) that some fishing circumstances warrant.

True big-game fishing reels start out with fairly powerful ratios (3.1:1 to 3.5:1) and large-diameter spools. These reels are expected and designed to deal with big, powerful fish. The large spool diameter

An angler uses a large-capacity conventional reel without a levelwind mechanism while bottom fishing in the Gulf of Mexico off the Texas coast.

allows for sufficient line capacity in a variety of line tests and for acceptable line recovery.

Fishing for big-game species requires power to control their movements and bring them to the boat as quickly as possible. Large-diameter spools on big-game reels can rapidly recover line when a speedy fish charges the boat or even when clearing lines from the trolling pattern upon hookup. The 3.1:1 ratio is, of course, mechanically powerful. Anglers can quickly wind significant amounts of line onto the spool and have the ability to winch in line against a large fish.

Two-Speed Reels

Sometimes even a powerful 3.1:1 gear ratio isn't enough to control big-game species. Controlling these fish can often require a reel with two separate gear ratios. In the case of the modern two-speed big-game reels, the ratio shifts from the typical 3.1:1 to the still lower and more powerful 1.3:1. The very largest two-speed big-game reels intended for use in fighting giant fish can offer ratios such as 4:1 and 1.7:1 or 4.5:1 and 2:1. In these cases, the reel delivers both the speed necessary to catch up to a charging gamefish and the power to exert control over its movements.

These reels change gear sets in different ways. Some demand that the angler physically relocate the reel handle to switch gears. Simpler designs require the push of a button to shift in one direction and the turn of a knob or movement of a lever to return to the original ratio. All of these operations have to be fast and easy to permit up- and downshifting in the heat of battling a large, powerful fish. And obviously the gear sets have to be strong, precise, and durable to withstand the stresses applied.

Attempts at producing multiple-speed spinning reels have not been successful, although a few manufacturers have applied a good deal of time and effort to the project. Two-speed baitcasting reels have been introduced, and these unique tools provide both a higher-speed ratio and a true power ratio in a single reel suited for most freshwater and some inshore saltwater applications. Some of these products even offer an automatic shifting design that downshifts as the load on the line increases (as upon hookup). When the load decreases, such as when a fish turns toward the angler, the reel automatically upshifts to permit rapid recovery of line with the higher-ratio gears and to catch up to the movements of the fish. This reel also allows the angler to adjust the amount of force needed to cause the gears to shift up or down. It's a very versatile item and ideal if the amount of tackle available to you is limited.

Retrieval Considerations

Some of the important fishing considerations relative to the subject of gear ratio and line recovery have already been noted, but it's worth recapping these to emphasize some of the advantages and disadvantages of different ratios and line recoveries.

Although recent trends favor high-ratio or so-called high-speed reels, and many people equate speed with fishing value, it is important to recognize that line recovery is the real issue, not speed. Reels with a technically low gear ratio, but a high line recovery rate, are actually better in situations where large fish are encountered, powerful fish are played, and where hard-pulling lures are cranked. These reels simply have more power, are less likely to bind, are less likely to get stripped gears (assuming the gears are of strong material to start with), and require less effort to land tough fish.

One of the main reasons why high-speed reels are popular in freshwater is because most of the fish caught in freshwater are small on average (bass and walleye, in particular) or do not put up a long tackle-testing struggle. Anglers like the high-speed retrieves because, among other reasons, they feel that they can quickly catch up to fish that run toward them (as many bass do). This is only true when the spool diameter is large enough to permit a lot of line recovery with each turn of the handle, and if the fish is not so large as to be difficult to handle.

People who fish jigs and worms in freshwater are likely to be good candidates for a reel with a high gear ratio, since it lets them pick up a lot of slack with each turn of the handle. But fishing a large spinnerbait and especially a deep-diving plug will be wrist-punishing unless the reel has cranking power for the drive, meaning that a low-speed reel is preferable there.

For many anglers who cast and retrieve lures, especially those using baitcasting tackle, a reel with 5.1:1 retrieve ratio is a good all-around choice for most fishing, especially if the line recovery is adequate.

Baitcasting Reels

Baitcasting tackle is very popular in North America, primarily used in freshwater fishing yet suitable for a range of light saltwater applications. It is characterized by a reel with a spool that revolves when retrieving and dispensing line, and by a levelwind guide that lays retrieved line evenly on the reel spool. The style and method of reel operation is similar to that of conventional tackle, which generally lacks a levelwind mechanism, although both baitcasting rod and reel are light to medium-light multipurpose fishing equipment, whereas conventional tackle is heftier.

Despite what its name suggests, baitcasting tackle is not exclusively, or even primarily, relegated to use with natural bait; it is most prominent for use in casting lures, but sometimes in fishing with bait and in trolling. Baitcasting tackle can provide very accurate lure placement for casters, and is compatible with diverse fishing methods.

Baitcasting reels predate spinning and spincasting reels. They were once notorious for being difficult to learn to use without incurring a backlash, or spool overrun, in which a bird's nest of line had to be painstakingly untangled. Modern reels

The components of a Daiwa baitcasting reel and their interrelationship are evident in this composite image.

have greatly reduced this problem. Compared to spinning and spincasting reels, they have the advantages of accurate lure placement in casting, superior cranking power, and better control over strong-fighting fish.

Many baitcasting reels have a lot of features, some of them specialized for particular fishing activities, since most are used for cast-and-retrieve angling and are commonly employed with heavier lures and weights than spinning or spincasting reels. Larger models are not comfortable for continuous casting, however. Some baitcasting reels are used with very light lines and lures, and some heavy-duty, large-capacity models are used in very demanding situations.

Gears, cast control, and drag are the most critical components of baitcasting reels. The cast control and gears are especially important because they significantly affect casting and retrieving functions.

Casting Features

With all baitcasting reels, controlling the flow of line off the spool is important to proper use. A baitcasting reel is placed in freespool by depressing the line release clutch. On most reels the clutch is situated on the front of the reel to permit quick, one-handed operation. This may be a contoured bar (called a thumb bar) over the spool that bridges the sidewalls, or a switch that is recessed into the sidewall and permits the thumb to slide onto the

spool. On older reels, the clutch is a button that is located away from the spool.

When you put the reel in freespool you must apply thumb pressure to the spool to prevent line from paying out prematurely. Place your thumb on the spool so the spool can't turn; this is done when the reel has a thumb bar or recessed switch, because the thumb of the casting hand immediately contacts the spool as it depresses this clutch. In reels with a clutch button, you need to use two hands, keeping the thumb of the noncasting hand on the spool while you press the button with your other hand.

There are three means of controlling the spool when line is flowing off the reel: manual, mechanical, and magnetic.

Manual spool braking is done by applying thumb pressure to the moving spool. This is learned through trial and error and perfected with experience; it requires the application of different degrees of thumb pressure for the weights on the line, distances being cast, and types of rods and reels being used. Although you can learn to use a baitcasting reel without applying thumb pressure, you cannot fish without some manual control all the time and with all reels.

Mechanical spool braking is done by applying pressure to the moving spool with centrifugal brakes (also called weights). Reels with centrifugal brakes have blocks that have to be engaged to effect spool braking. These blocks exist on one side of the reel, usually the left. They are accessed on some reels by removing the entire sideplate or on others by unlocking a quick-release bayonet cover. Some reels feature an external adjustment via a sideplate dial, which is by far the easiest method of adjusting centrifugal pressure.

Centrifugal brakes are used in conjunction with the spool tension knob. This device is a knurled knob or bearing cap on the sideplate where the handle is located; it is adjusted by hand. Tightening this puts tension on the spindle of the spool, but it is not purely a spool braking device, as it is primarily intended to control excessive end play, or sideways movement, of the spool.

Spool tension must be adjusted according to the weight of the object being cast; if you switch frequently to lures of different weights, you should reset the tension. To set tension when the reel is on the rod with line attached to a lure, hold

Removing the sideplate of this Zebco Quantum baitcasting reel allows spool changing and reveals the spool control magnets.

the rod out and dangle a lure from the tip, place your thumb on the spool, and put the reel into freespool. Decrease thumb pressure and allow the lure to fall. Adjust the spool tension knob so the lure slowly descends to the ground when thumb pressure is relaxed. The spool should stop revolving at the instant the lure hits the ground. For continued long-distance casting, decrease spool tension and put the centrifugal brake blocks in the off position.

Magnetic spool braking is a completely different system, and common on the majority of reels. This system employs a magnetic field to place variable degrees of force on the spool. A series of small disclike magnets are located in the interior of the sideplate opposite the handle. When an exterior magnetic control knob is turned it changes the distance of the magnets from the metal spool; when the magnets are closer more force is applied and when they are farther less force is applied. Lower settings enable longer casts; higher settings help prevent backlash under adverse conditions, such as when casting into the wind.

While these systems are touted as eliminating backlash, they're not foolproof, and if magnetic spool braking reels aren't used correctly they will still backlash. However, they are excellent for those who are learning to cast with this equipment when the proper settings are selected.

Beginners should use a higher-tension setting when they start; this will cut down on the distance achieved at first, but it is better to do this than to

be frustrated by backlashes. With a little practice you can ease off on the tension and keep learning until you become comfortable with less tension. Some magnetic spool control systems are very sophisticated, and have the ability to alter magnetic force according to the speed of the spool during the cast.

To set a magnetic spool reel up for casting, begin by adjusting the spool tension knob as previously detailed, starting with the magnetic control at the lowest setting. Once the mechanical tension knob is adjusted, turn the magnetic setting from zero to an appropriate level, make a few medium-intensity casts, and adjust the magnetic control up or down as necessary before you start serious casting.

Slight thumb pressure on the spool is advisable when starting with low magnetic control, but you can apply less pressure than you would if using only mechanical braking. Complete beginners should set the magnets at maximum level until they're proficient at releasing the lure and applying thumb pressure.

Many baitcasting reels have a selectable switch that automatically engages the pinion. This is known as the flipping switch because it is primarily used in this method of bass fishing, which requires specialized short-distance casts. It can also be employed, however, by anglers who use bait and need to let a fish run when it takes the bait offering.

With this switch on, the reel is out of gear only when the thumb is kept on the freespool bar. When you release thumb pressure, the reel is instantly in gear. The advantage is that you don't have to turn the handle to put the reel in gear. Because the reel is already in gear when a fish takes or when the line tightens, no time is wasted setting the hook.

Retrieving Features

Most baitcasting reels are right-hand retrieve models and are not convertible. Although right- and left-handed anglers have been using this system for many decades, it favors the minority of people who are left-handed. There are a few reels with left-handed retrieve, but these are not nearly as prevalent in the marketplace as right-retrieve reels.

It is theoretically beneficial for people who are right-handed to reel with their left hand and

Most baitcasting outfits, especially low-profile models as depicted here, are held during a retrieve by palming the reel, with the fingers wrapped around the trigger grip underneath the rod handle.

for lefties to reel with their right hand, so that the dominant hand is the one that holds the rod and is used to play the fish or direct the retrieve. This is especially significant when frequent casting is involved. Since the dominant hand is used to cast the rod, there is no need to take further action after casting to start using the reel; the other hand is immediately placed on the reel handle grip and it turns the handle. This lack of time delay is important in some fishing situations.

Most anglers both cast and retrieve with their right hand, meaning that they have to switch the rod and reel from right to left hand at some point. Most good casters become adept at making this transfer while the lure is in flight, taking their right thumb off the spool just as the lure touches the water and then quickly grabbing the reel handle and cranking before the lure has a chance to get deep. This takes fine timing.

If you're new to baitcasting and right-handed, consider getting a left-retrieve reel, since you don't have old habits to break. If you're already accustomed to casting a spinning outfit with your right hand and reeling with the left, this is the same principle. Many new right-handed baitcasters have found it worthwhile to start out with a left-retrieve reel and continue with it (left-handed anglers can simply use the many standard right-retrieve reels).

Line is wound directly onto the spool of a baitcasting reel, but it is not necessary to manually level or disperse that line across the spool.

All baitcasting reels have a mechanism known as a levelwind that automatically disperses line evenly across the spool. The levelwind may be gear-driven by the spool or by the main gear; it turns whenever the spool revolves and is located in a carriage that spans both sides of the reel.

Most winding lays line on the spool evenly in side-by-side wraps, but some reels use a cross-wrapping wind. The cross wrap helps with some lines, especially slick thin-diameter microfilaments, which have a tendency to dig deep into side-by-side wraps when subjected to severe tension.

In regard to gears, baitcasting reels generally have stronger and more efficient gears than exist in a stationary or fixed-spool reel because the gear set operates on a parallel axis. The drive gear is linked to the reel handle and the pinion gear connects to the spool. This system provides the multiplying gear ratio for ample line retrieval rates with a small spool and still delivers substantial cranking power. It also allows for the use of heavy lines.

When using baitcasting reels, some methods of fishing cause high-stress cranking. This requires a rigid gear support system so that under great duress there is no flex to affect the inner workings of the reel. The use of heavy line, and cranking large fish in extreme conditions, can put tremendous stress on all components, and both the material and construction of the frame and shaft supports are what keep the gears aligned properly and able to last long.

Gear ratios are generally categorized as high (fast) or low (slow), but this is relative to the type of reel and application. Low gear ratios are about 3.8:1 and high gear ratios are from 6:1 to 7:2. With baitcasting reels, a high gear ratio is preferable for cast-and-retrieve fishing of lures that do not pull hard, but a low gear ratio is preferable for hard-pulling lures. What is gained in retrieve speed is lost in cranking power.

The length of the handle also affects cranking power, so the distance from the center of the gear stud to which the handle is attached to the handle knob is a key element in retrieval. A long handle equals power, and a short handle equals speed, but you can't get power and speed simultaneously.

All baitcasting reels have dual-grip handles, which provide a counterbalancing effect and easy grabbing of the handle without having to look at it. A baitcasting reel grip, or knob, is mainly grasped with the fingertips and operated by wrist motion, and is not affected by the presence of a second handle knob. The size of the grips and the handle is often a problem for many people who have long fingers and large hands. The smaller baitcasting reels seem designed for small hands and are not comfortable in a large hand when used for a considerable period of time.

Most better baitcasting reels now have continuous anti-reverse, a feature that restricts backward movement of the handle. This feature is especially relevant to cast-and-retrieve applications and to some styles of baitfishing, primarily because it is relative to how the reel operates when the forward-turning motion is stopped. Ideally a reel used for casting should engage instantly and firmly. A continuous anti-reverse feature keeps the handle and drive gear from moving even the slightest bit backward.

Drag

On baitcasting reels the drag is located on the main gear and is usually a multi-element system with washers that are keyed together to increase the working surface area. Different materials are used in the friction washers. Drag tension is increased or decreased by turning a drag star (radial-arm star wheel), which is located under the handle on the sideplate. The drag star threads onto the gear stud or drive gear, which is connected to the handle, so it rotates concurrently with the handle without affecting the setting. The drag tension is set to the desirable level at the beginning of each day's fishing and relaxed at the end of the day.

The range of drag tension adjustment is somewhat more limited on baitcasting reels than spinning reels, although it looks like more because of the star wheel knob. With these products, it is often the case that a smooth drag and the ability to fully lock down the reel (so the spool cannot turn backward) are not compatible, although better baitcasting reels do have good drag systems with a wide range of adjustment.

Ergonomic Features

The shape and weight of baitcasting reels is especially important because of the amount of casting done with these products. Baitcasting reels were once entirely round in design, but they are now ergonomic, with low-profile and teardrop designs very common in addition to round models. Teardrop reels are especially favored by anglers who tend to palm the reel, so a smooth sideplate that cups neatly into the palm of the rod-holding hand is quite popular.

Although weight is a major concern of manufacturers, this is (or should be) subordinate to strength and durability. The majority of baitcasting reels weigh between 9 and 12 ounces. Some are between 7 and 9 ounces and mini versions with plastic bodies may weigh less, while large-spool versions may weigh up to 21 ounces. Light weight can make a difference after many hours of use, but so can comfortable styling.

Conventional Reels

Conventional reels are larger than baitcasting reels. They have a star-spoked wheel drag, are likely to be used with heavier lures and weights, and may or may not have a line-leveling mechanism. Some models may be cast, but many are used for bottom fishing and trolling. In saltwater, they are extremely popular for diverse usage; in freshwater, they are mainly used for the most demanding applications. Conventional reels differ from lever drag reels, which are essentially a big-game fishing tool with a different method of achieving freespool and applying drag tension (using cam rather than threaded adjustment).

Most conventional reels are more elementary in design and features than contemporary baitcasting or spinning reels, primarily because they are used for more demanding fish and in more punishing circumstances. Unlike contemporary baitcasting reels, which are primarily used for cast-and-retrieve angling activities (with lures rather than with natural bait), modern conventional reels are less frequently cast.

Many conventional reels are never used for casting, but exclusively for trolling lures or bait and for fishing at various depths with sinking lures or bait, both of which call for paying line off the reel rather than casting. A widening interest in varied methods of fishing, coupled with a need for greater line capacity than even the largest baitcasting reels can provide, has resulted, however, in demands to use some modern conventional reels for casting either lures or natural bait. This requires some models to have features appropriate

Assorted conventional reels and rods are displayed at a sport show.

to the demands of frequent casting and retrieving. Thus some conventional reels are used for casting as well as other types of fishing, despite their comparatively large size and greater weight.

One of the most distinguishing differences between a conventional reel and a baitcasting reel is that the latter have a level line-winding mechanism and the majority of the former do not. Thus when using most conventional reels the angler must manually direct the placement of line on the spool to produce an even line lay.

Manually leveling line on a spool is the biggest drawback to using conventional tackle, and often a problem for inexperienced anglers or those who are unfamiliar with this action. When line is not wound evenly, it bunches and impedes retrieval or dispensing, and contributes to binding of line wraps. Manual line leveling can seem even more burdensome when combined with the fact that conventional reels, which sit on top of the rod facing the angler, are heavy and, for some people, awkward to hold.

Being heavy is a double-edged sword, however. The weight is a result of the size necessary for adequate line capacity, which ranges from about 275 yards in smaller models to over 1,000 yards in the largest, and a result of the sturdy components necessary for the frame, spool, and gears, which is what makes these reels capable of handling tough fishing.

Line capacity, gears, and drag are the most critical components of conventional reels. One of the problem areas with conventional reels in the past was a drag that became erratic when heavy pressure was intense and sustained or as a result of long-term compression of friction washers during storage. Modern conventional reels have improved, particularly the drag systems, which have become smoother due to modern friction materials, and which better resist compression and the effect of heat.

Unlike baitcasting products, conventional reels are basically classified by the strength of line they're designed for and the capacity they hold. Some have long been characterized by a "0" (or aught) designation that was created many years ago, and which has gradually faded from common parlance. However, some conventional reels for saltwater use have been labeled from 1/0 to 14/0 sizes, the latter meant for 130-pound-test line. The most popular sizes have been the 2/0, 4/0, and 6/0 models, which are respectively meant for 20-, 30- and 50-pound line.

Many contemporary reels are designated by manufacturers according to a product series name, accompanied by some combination of model numbers and letters. These may or may not have an obvious connection to the intended line strength or line capacity.

With a few exceptions, the majority of conventional reels today are only set up for right-handed retrieve and are not convertible. Some conventional reels are made in left-retrieve versions. The left/right retrieve situation with these products is akin to that for baitcasting, and it mostly favors people who are right-handed.

Operation

A conventional reel has a lever that activates or deactivates the gears, in essence taking the reel into or out of freespool. With the reel on top of the rod handle and facing toward the angler, place your rod-holding-hand thumb on the spool to keep the line in check, and move the gear lever backward with your free hand. This disengages the gears and puts the reel in freespool.

To retrieve line, engage the gears by moving the lever forward, and turn the spool by rotating the handle, which winds line onto the reel. When winding line onto the spool, you generally must level the line manually for even line distribution. (Unevenly wound line bunches up, which may prevent retrieval and dispensing, and may cause binding in the spool.) This is done by using your thumb to direct the line across the spool as it is retrieved; some lighter-duty conventional reels have a levelwind mechanism that automatically distributes the line back and forth across the spool. Having to manually level line on a spool is the biggest drawback to using a non-levelwind conventional reel.

Spool Control

When the gears are disengaged and line is dispensed from the reel, a spool overrun can occur if the revolving spool turns faster than the line is carried off that spool. Applying light pressure to the spool is necessary to prevent this. When thumb pressure is relaxed, line flows off the spool and out through the rod guides, carried by the weight of the object at the terminal end of the line. Conventional reels feature a click ratchet that is used to signal that line is being taken off the reel; it may be employed when a reel is left unattended.

As with baitcasting reels, mechanical, magnetic, or manual methods are used to control line when it flows off the reel.

The majority of conventional reel users primarily or solely employ thumb pressure to brake the spool. Applying thumb pressure for the purpose of casting with a conventional reel is an action learned through trial and error and perfected with experience; it requires the application of different degrees of braking tension for the weights on the line, distances being cast, and types of rods and reels being used.

This effort is somewhat aided by properly adjusting the screw tension mechanism found on most conventional reels. This device is sometimes the knurled knob or bearing cap on the nonhandle sideplate (usually on the left sideplate, but it may be on the right sideplate), which is adjusted by hand. In some reels it may be a slot that is adjusted with a screwdriver or coin. Tightening this device does put tension on the spindle of the spool, but its real purpose is to control excessive end play, or sideways movement, of the spool.

On conventional reels, a small piece of rubber or a dished spring lies on the sideplate fronting against a brass or bronze wear plate. As the adjustment knob is tightened, the wear plate rubs against the stainless steel spindle. Tightening is usually a clockwise motion, and this should be adjusted

so that there is barely any perceptible sideways motion of the spool.

To see how much play there is, take both thumbs and put them on either side of the spool and press back and forth to see if you can move it. Adjust it to a tight but not totally immovable tolerance. Do not fully tighten the spool tension adjustment mechanism; this can damage or cause premature wearing (and failure) of the right and left side bearings. The rubber should provide some cushion for a better range of adjustment, and in the event that something wears out, it will preferably be the wear plate and not the spindle.

In reels that are not employed for casting, the tension control mechanism is seldom used after any sideways spool movement has been eliminated. Most people don't use this adjustment much. Experienced anglers who cast often with a conventional reel will tighten or loosen the adjustment knob, employing this level of control in conjunction with an educated thumb. People who are unfamiliar with casting a revolving spool need a tighter adjustment for some assistance with spool braking, however, or they will be picking backlashes out with every cast. This tension should gradually be lightened as they become more proficient with thumb control.

Magnetic spool braking systems, which employ a magnetic field to place variable degrees of resistance on the spool, are less common on conventional reels than on baitcasting reels, because conventional reel use is more prevalent in saltwater fishing, where component corrosion is always an issue. However, there are newer premium conventional reels intended for saltwater casting that sport sophisticated digitally controlled electromagnetic brakes and are engineered to resist corrosion. These have multistep adjustment knobs to coordinate spool tension to various conditions (weight of the object being cast, desired distance, wind, and so on). Magnetic spool braking is described in more detail in the baitcasting reels section earlier in this chapter.

Some conventional reels have a mechanical means of controlling spool braking via centrifugal brakes. Those with it have blocks that must be engaged to effect spool braking. These are usually found on the left side of the reel, accessed by removing the left sideplate. Underneath the click ratchet and next to the spool flange is a cross pin with a centrifugal brake block on either side. To be employed, these brake blocks must be moved out toward the flange and snapped into a notch. In this position they rub against the flange and, due to centrifugal pressure, exert the greatest force at lightest speeds, and slow down the spool to help avoid a backlash.

This system is common on baitcasting reels but less common for conventional reels, although models with this feature are used for specific saltwater casting applications, especially in long-range party boat and kingfish angling, and some bluefish and tuna angling.

Gears

Conventional reels usually have efficient heavy-duty gears. The drive gear is linked to the reel handle and the pinion gear connects to the spool. Most better conventional reels have a stainless steel pinion gear and a bronze main gear. In a few reels both are stainless steel. Some conventional reels, especially those with a higher gear ratio, have helical gears, which allow at least partial engagement of several gear teeth at all times, spreading the load and potential wear. This is mainly an issue where the gear teeth are small, as is found on higher-ratio models, and there is less surface to make contact. Obviously the high-stress cranking that is experienced with conventional reels requires a rigid support system, so that under great duress there is no flex to affect the inner workings of the reel.

As with other reels, gear ratios in conventional reels are generally categorized as high (fast) or low (slow); however, the size of the spool may be such that a low-gear-ratio reel actually recovers more line per full turn of the handle than a high-ratio reel with a smaller spool. What is high for many conventional reels is low for nearly all baitcasting reels, at least according to just numerical ratio.

Typical low gear ratios for conventional reels are 2:1 to 3:1, and typical high gear ratios are 3.5:1 to 5:1. A high gear ratio is preferred for cast-and-retrieve fishing; a low gear ratio is preferred for deep bottom fishing. What is gained in retrieve speed is lost in cranking power, which is the ability to handle a heavy load. The lowest-gear-ratio reels have the greatest cranking power and the highest-gear-ratio reels have the least cranking power.

Drag

Conventional reels all have an adjustable drag mechanism, activated by turning a star wheel on the drive gear. Drag tension should be set to the desired level at the beginning of each day's fishing and relaxed when fishing is concluded. On most conventional reels, this drag system is usually a multi-element system with washers that are keyed together. Washers are alternately stainless steel and some type of friction material.

The material of friction washers is critical to drag performance, with the ideal being smooth, nonhesitating drag operation, with the drag starting immediately when needed, maintaining constant tension as line flows continuously off the reel, and keeping the same level of tension as it is periodically called upon during the time it takes to play and land a strong fish. Performance is affected by the range of adjustment designed in the reel, and by the number and material of the friction washers.

Most conventional reels today use woven carbon fiber friction washers, which show no appreciable wear after extensive or rugged use, and have excellent range. This material is also especially good when applying maximum tension to the drag washers, or deliberately locking down the drag tension as far as it will go. Some friction washers (including asbestos and Teflon) can't be locked down enough when fighting big fish, and still slip even when the drag star is turned as tightly as possible.

In most conventional reels, and especially better-quality models, carbon fiber friction washers are used with stainless steel washers, generally

These are low-speed (left) and high-speed gear sets from different conventional reels; both feature a stainless steel pinion gear and bronze alloy main gear.

varying from seven to thirteen elements, the greater number being used on bigger reels. More friction washers increases the total drag surface area.

Most conventional reels have good to excellent drag performance. These reels do have a drag-related drawback, however, with respect to striking and fighting large, powerful fish (also true for baitcasting reels). This drawback is that drag tension is not easily or readily adjustable to known levels.

Turning the star wheel adjusts the drag tension, which is usually set to a predetermined level before fishing. If that wheel is deliberately or accidentally turned later, especially while playing a fish, drag tension is changed and may be too little or too great for the circumstances. Once the tension is changed, it cannot be recalibrated with absolute certainty while playing a fish.

It may also be desirable to deliberately increase or decrease drag tension while playing a fish (usually a very large and powerful one for the tackle), but doing so means making an adjustment to an uncertain level of tension, and being unable to return to the original preset level if necessary later on, as well as possibly exceeding the limits of the tackle. This drawback is primarily related to big-game fishing, which is why lever drag big-game reels evolved.

Handles/Grips

Nearly all conventional reels have a single handle grip, or knob, which you hold on to in order to turn the handle. This is contrary to baitcasting reels, where nearly all handles have dual grips. However, because conventional reels are large, the handles and the grips are large. Small and medium reels have a soft nonslip handle grip with a large and comfortable surface area. Many reels, particularly larger models, have barrel- or torpedo-shaped grips, which tend to be grasped by the whole hand rather than just the thumb and index finger.

Some conventional-reel handles are equipped with two center holes so you can change the distance from the crankshaft connection to the handle knob and thus affect power and speed to best suit the physical build of the angler. Some sport a counterbalanced handle, which is used in applications where there is a lot of fast retrieving.

Using a fairly substantial conventional reel and rod equipped with wire line, a fisherman plays his catch with the butt of the rod in a seat gimbal.

Big-Game (Lever Drag) Reels

Used exclusively in saltwater fishing, big-game reels are extremely durable heavy-duty revolving-spool products. They are similar to conventional reels in many respects, but greatly different in that they feature a lever drag. Big-game reels (which are also called lever drag reels), and appropriate rods, are mainly associated with offshore blue-water trolling or baitfishing for billfish, tuna, and sharks; however, smaller models are used for some reef and inshore fishing, and some may also be used for limited casting activities. Able to endure extreme pressures, big-game reels help subdue tough fish quicker than would be possible with other equipment, largely due to the gears and the type of drag.

This tackle has evolved a lot in recent decades, with the advent of smaller reels, improved drag materials, reels with greater line capacity, new rod designs, and microfilament lines. However, because lever drag reels are susceptible to extreme stresses and fishing conditions, construction and materials must be of the highest caliber.

One-piece frames are standard and more resistant to torque and twist, providing superior strength

Big-game reels, such as this group, are premium products in price, features, and performance.

and precision alignment of the spool and other components. These frames, which also help dissipate heat, are usually made from the highest grade of extruded marine alloy aluminum, although some are made of graphite.

The spools are aluminum, and may be extruded, machined, or forged, and sideplates are usually machined aluminum. The finish is anodized, an aesthetic and corrosion-inhibiting feature that doesn't affect performance. Other materials, incidentally, include aircraft-quality stainless steel ball bearings.

Big game reels are classified by the strength of line that they are designed for and the capacity they hold. Unlike conventional reels, which use a "0" (or aught) designation from decades ago, big-game reels conform to well-established line classifications from 12- through 130-pound strengths, with corresponding capacity and drag system capability. These classifications are usually specified as being IGFA class, which means that they conform to established parameters of line breaking strength for world record consideration.

Line is wound directly onto the spool of lever drag reels, but they do not have a mechanism for leveling or dispersing that line across the spool (called a levelwind). This leveling must be done manually. The hand that holds the rod (usually the left) must be situated in such a way that the thumb can be used to direct the line back and forth onto the spool as it is retrieved.

This means holding the rod at the foregrip ahead of the reel, and extending the thumb to the right

to catch the line with both sides of the tip of the thumb, moving it to the left and right to disperse the line. (An alternate method when using a harness is to run and direct the line between the fingers while the rod hand is held over the reel.) This leveling has to be done whenever the handle of the reel is turned and line is recovered onto the spool.

The largest big-game reels, the 80- and 130-pound class versions, are used for the biggest game, such as monster billfish and tuna. The 30- and 50-pound reels have been more popular for wide-ranging offshore applications, but greater interest in light-tackle and stand-up fishing has increased the popularity of 12-, 16-, and 20-pound reels. Line capacity is great for all of these products. The 80- and 130-pound-class reels will hold about 1,000 yards of conventional nylon monofilament line; lighter models hold between 500 and 900 yards of line, but this varies with wide-spool versions and according to the diameter of the line used.

Spool Control

As with other revolving-spool reels, controlling the flow of line off the spool is an important element of usage. Technically, there is no such thing as freespool on a lever drag reel, although the term is universally used and is a carryover from other types of revolving-spool reels, where the gears are disengaged to achieve freespool. In lever drag reels, the gears are always engaged, and the drag mechanism drives the spool. To achieve freespool—in this case meaning a state where there is no tension on the spool and line can flow off without resistance—disengage the drag by moving the adjustment lever fully backward. This disengages the clutch parts while leaving the gears intact. Moving the drag lever forward applies tension to the spool and allows a return to a known, preset level.

Before putting the reel into freespool, you must apply finger pressure to the spool to prevent line from paying out prematurely or haphazardly. Without this pressure, and assuming that a lure or weighted bait was tied to the end of the line, the weight of either object would cause the spool to turn the moment the reel was placed into the freespool position, which could cause an instant backlash on the spool.

It is therefore necessary to place the thumb of the rod-holding hand on the spool so the spool can't turn, and then move the drag lever fully backward. Now the line can be released by easing the tension. Thumb pressure is lessened on the spool to pay line out at a controlled rate; the objective is to let a sufficient amount of line out for the fishing circumstances at a rate that doesn't cause the spool to turn so fast that it causes a backlash. This is important because a revolving spool can gather speed quickly and an uncontrolled spool can lead to a serious backlash in seconds. The backlash not only impedes immediate fishing effort because of the time required to undo it, but can also cause damage to the line.

Drag

The lever drag on big-game reels is a great improvement over the star drags that exist in baitcasting and conventional reels, which are also revolving-spool products. The latter reels can only be preset to one drag tension setting, which cannot be reliably changed to precise levels during use.

Most anglers cannot make accurate on-the-fly adjustments to the preset tension of a star drag reel, which is a problem when fishing for the toughest species, when using light lines, and in circumstances where a lot of line is taken from the reel.

The drag on big game reels can be fine-tuned, and they feature a device to limit drag-setting range. In these reels, the drag adjustment mechanism is separate from the reel handle and doesn't turn with the handle as the star wheel on a conventional reel does. This, plus the fact that the position of the drag lever is constantly visible, means less chance of inadvertently changing drag tension, and always being certain of the level of tension applied. Big-game reels also have several tension settings that permit preset tension at one level for setting the hook and at another level for applying maximum pressure on a stubborn fish.

The lever of a big-game reel applies various amounts of drag tension on the spool; the greater the tension the more force it takes to pull line from the spool. Completely releasing tension allows the spool to turn most freely (freespool). In use, the reel sits atop the rod and faces toward the angler; the thumb of the rod-holding hand is placed on the spool to keep the line in check, and the free hand is used to move the drag lever backward to minimum tension, which places the reel in freespool.

When thumb pressure is relaxed, line flows off the spool and out through the rod guides, carried by the weight of the object at the terminal end of the line. Big-game reels feature a click ratchet, also called a warning click, that is used to indicate that line is being taken off the reel, and this may be employed when a reel is not held or left unattended. To retrieve line, the drag lever is moved forward to apply some degree of tension on the spool, and the spool is turned by rotating the handle, which winds line onto the reel.

The adjustable drag mechanism is activated by moving a lever located on the same sideplate as the handle. Unlike other reels, this equipment has dual drag settings, usually referred to as strike and full, which are preset to the desirable level at the beginning of each day's fishing and relaxed when the day is concluded.

Whereas other revolving-spool reels have multiple friction washers and multiple metal washers, big-game reels have either single-plate or multi-plate clutches. Many have just one friction washer, so there is low inertia startup, but the size and material of that washer is critical. The drag in any reel should ideally operate smoothly, without hesitation. In other words, it will start immediately when needed and maintain a constant rate of tension as line flows continuously off, as well as keep the same level of tension during the time it takes to play and land a strong fish. The less variation in the performance of the drag, the better.

This friction washer is called upon to slip freely and also create a high amount of pressure. Thus you're looking for two opposite attributes. Most modern big-game reels have a woven carbon fiber friction washer, referred to by some as graphite, which does an excellent job of addressing these demands.

Some large big-game reels have a preset drag lock that is tamper-proof and meant to keep the preset drag adjustment from being accidentally altered. Pressing a button overrides the lock; this is mainly an advantage to charter captains who don't want anglers to accidentally turn the drag adjustment button and lose a prized fish.

No big-game reels possess level line-winding mechanisms. You must manually direct the placement of line on the spool to produce an even line lay. This can be a problem, since these reels, which sit on top of the rod, are heavy and, for some people, awkward to hold. Unevenly wound line bunches and may prevent either retrieval or dispensing, as well as contribute to binding of line wraps.

Like other revolving-spool reels, the spool of a big-game reel revolves as line pays out, and also when line is retrieved by turning the handle. When the reel is placed in freespool and line is dispensed from the reel, a backlash can occur if the revolving spool turns faster than the line is carried off that spool. Applying light pressure to the spool prevents this.

Unfortunately for left-handed anglers, big-game reels are manufactured in only a right-handed-cranking version and cannot be converted by the angler as a spinning reel can, although some may be converted to or even originated in left retrieve by custom shop operators. This is because applications with big-game reels are very demanding, the outfits are generally heavy, and most people are right-handed, meaning that it is normal to want to use the dominant hand for the hard cranking work that is often an element of big-game reel use.

Since these reels are used for landing big fish, it is common to attach them to a harness, which relieves the rod-holding arm. If a person is right-handed, all of the heavy-duty cranking of the reel is done with the stronger hand, which in theory is better for anyone who is right-handed, although not as desirable for a lefty.

The increased use of low-diameter high-strength microfilament lines on big-game reels caused changes to angler use and to manufacturing processes. The ability to put much more thin-diameter line on a reel led to many anglers dropping down to smaller reels (for the weight advantage), which were rated for a lighter class of conventional mono line, but also ratcheting up the drag tension to conform to the higher strength of line used. That, in turn, put more stress on reel components, in particular drag washers. So manufacturers had to respond by beefing up the components of smaller reels, in particular the drag components.

Gears

Big-game reels have heavy-duty gears. A large main gear engages a smaller pinion gear. The drive gear is linked to the reel handle and the pinion gear to the spool. The best reels have stainless steel main and pinion gears. Due to high-stress cranking with big-game reels, they typically have a rigid support

system so that under great duress there is no flex to affect the inner workings of the reel. Using heavy line, and cranking large fish in extreme conditions, can put tremendous stress on all components; thus both the material and construction of the frame and shaft supports are what keep the gears precisely located and deliver a long life.

The gear ratio of most big-game reels is fairly low, and what is high for many big-game reels would be low for other revolving-spool reels, if comparing just numerical ratio. Low gear ratios for big-game reels range from 1.2:1 to 1.8:1 and high gear ratios range from 2.2:1 to 4.5:1.

In the past, most reels with lever drag were single-speed, having one fixed gear ratio. Today, nearly half have dual-speed operation, which means that they can alternately operate at two gear ratios, one high and the other low. Shifting from one gear to the other is simple, generally by pressing a button on the handle.

Two-speed operation allows you to shift from high ratio, which would be used for most purposes, to low ratio for the extra cranking power necessary for demanding situations. Low is used for power, and high is used for speed. If you must clear lines quickly, for example, you can best do this in high gear; there's little resistance and you can crank away quickly. Being able to instantly shift from

The two-speed gear components of a big-game reel are evident in this composite image; quick one-step gear shifting is possible with such a reel.

high to low speed provides benefits for various situations, including outmuscling a big fish that has sounded directly below you, or pulling a large fish away from its craggy bottom hole.

In principle, less line is recovered per turn of the handle in low gear, so you theoretically spend more time when using this gear. However, when using low gear it is easier to get a strong fish's head, turn it, and be in control. If you were using a high gear ratio to battle a stubborn fish, it might actually take more time, since it will be harder to turn the handle, and thus you'll actually have to work harder with the fish.

The greater power of the low-speed mode, used in combination with high-speed (gaining line quickly, for example, when a fish runs toward you), can reduce fighting time overall, which is clearly helpful for releasing fish in good health, as well as diminishing angler fatigue, which can otherwise lead to mistakes and prolonged battles.

High and low are relative terms when discussing gear ratio, and categorization is relative to the size and diameter of the reel. A 2.2:1 gear ratio might actually be a "high" gear ratio on a large line capacity big-game reel (like a 130-pound-class model), and would provide a lot of line recovery compared to a smaller-diameter reel that had a numerically greater gear ratio. This generally low numerical gear ratio also provides a lot of cranking power. Reels that can easily handle a heavy load are said to have a lot of cranking power. A longer handle, which many big-game reels possess, also helps with this.

Other Features

Lever drag reels all have clamps to secure the reel to the rod, lugs for attachment to a fighting harness, and, on some versions, a brace for additional support. The harness lugs are situated on the top of the reel because when fighting a large fish, the angler is likely to wear a shoulder or kidney harness, which is attached to these lugs. Forward and rear braces on the largest models are used to provide torsional stability on rods.

Some large lever drag reels have a preset drag lock that is tamper proof and meant to keep the preset drag adjustment from being accidentally altered. You must purposely press a button to override the lock; this is mainly an advantage to charter captains out for big marlin and tuna, who

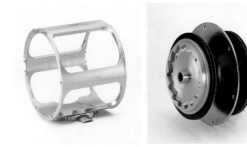

The one-piece frame (left) and lever drag system shown here are from a Penn International big-game reel.

don't want an itchy-fingered client to accidentally turn the drag adjustment button and thereby cause the loss of a prized fish.

Flycasting Reels

Unlike all other reels, fly reels do not play a role in dispensing line; this is because line is stripped off the spool of fly reels to help deliver a weightless fly to the fish. Unlike all other reels except spinning models, fly reels are always situated under the rod and below the handle grip, a placement that counterbalances the weight of the rod, feels natural, and reduces arm fatigue.

Used in freshwater and saltwater, fly reels range from light small-profile models matched with the lightest line weights in freshwater to large-profile saltwater heavyweights with a lot of line capacity and drags that help pressure the strongest fish. Size is important in terms of capacity to handle large fish, and for matching up with the rod and line being used. Lighter lines used for smaller fish don't need large reels, but heavier lines, which have a larger diameter and are likely to be used for stronger and bigger fish, obviously require a large reel.

With the exception of the smallest reels that accommodate the lightest line weights, the non-fishing end of fly line is attached to backing, which is a line that helps fill up the spool and stands in reserve to aid in playing large fish. Without backing it would take more turns of the handle to retrieve line onto the spool, and the line would be stored in small coils, which is harder to stretch out and may inhibit casting by having the line flap

Flycasting reels are basically simple line storage devices, although some have more advanced drag control features.

against the guides when cast. Backing promotes line storage in large coils, which are more easily straightened for easier use.

Backing also provides a reserve for those instances when a large fish takes a fly and heads to the next county. In most freshwater fishing and some saltwater fishing, the angler seldom gets to the backing on the reel when playing a fish, but when you need it, you'd better have it.

The size of the reel spool in conjunction with the length of the fly line determines how much backing is suitable; in turn, the size of fish that might be encountered and its fighting abilities determine how large a reel and overall capacity (fly line plus backing) is appropriate. Braided Dacron and braided or fused microfilament line, which have very low stretch, are the best products for backing because they wind on easily with less chance of binding than nylon monofilament line.

A fly reel has no casting or line-dispensing function. It holds line, which is pulled out by

hand to become available for the actual casting exercise; it retrieves line for storage but not for the act of manipulating a fly; and it provides a variable degree of drag to pressure a strong fish when it pulls line from the reel.

Action

Manufacturers and anglers often refer to fly reels as trout reels, salmon reels, saltwater reels, and so on, which reflects more on line capacity and features than actual use. Fly reels are best identified as being single-action, multiplying-action, or automatic; these categorizations are all related to line recovery.

A single-action model features a spool inside a frame with the handle built on the spool. Each turn of the handle causes one turn of the spool, so there's a 1:1 ratio in line retrieval. This is also referred to as direct drive, and comprises about 90 percent of fly reels; most of these are fairly lightweight models. For many fish sought with flycasting tackle, single-action reels have plenty of line and backing capacity. The single-action reel has few moving parts and minimal features, so it is simple and reliable.

It is easy to change line quickly on a single-action reel by carrying an extra spool filled with different line. This is most common for freshwater anglers and lets you adapt with one reel to fish throughout the water column. However, in heavier products used for big fish, a second reel might be better than an extra spool; if something goes wrong with the primary reel, having an extra spool won't help.

It is worth noting that the evolution of all revolving-spool reels began with a single-action reel to suit the purposes of line storage and retrieval. By the mid-nineteenth century in Europe, a revolving-spool reel called a centrepin was widely used for varied fishing activities, although it had an inert and relatively wide spool and two-handled cranking. This was the forerunner of the fly reel, and in appearance then it was not unlike the earliest models of baitcasting reels. Still in specialized use today in Europe for coarse fishing with floats, centrepins are also known as float reels, commonly have a 3- to 4-inch overall diameter, and feature a simple flanged spool on a single axle. They are highly valued in coarse fishing because of the sensitivity that is afforded by their smooth, free-spinning spool.

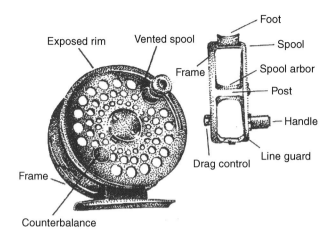

Exposed rim Vented spool Foot Spool Frame Spool arbor Post Handle Line guard Drag control Frame Counterbalance

Single-Action Fly Reel Parts

A so-called mooching reel, used for deep slow-trolling with cut bait, is also a single-action product, albeit larger to accommodate greater lengths of heavier line. The differences between these products and single-action fly reels are mainly size, weight, handles, and application.

A multiplying-action fly reel is similar in design to a single-action reel, except that its gearing causes one revolution of the handle to turn the spool more than one time, which is how spinning, spincasting, and baitcasting reels operate. The spool of a multiplying-action fly reel with a 2:1 ratio revolves two full times for each full revolution of the handle. Multiplying-action fly reels are more expensive than comparable single-action reels, and are used where rapid recovery of fairly long lengths of line is important to keep up with a fast-moving fish; some steelhead, salmon, and big-game saltwater anglers favor a multiplying-action fly reel.

An automatic fly reel automatically winds in line when a trigger is depressed, which releases tension in a prewound spring. That tension is built up when line is stripped off the reel. Automatic fly reels are fairly heavy, have limited line capacity, and do not have an extra spool option. They are not used in saltwater, and are mainly preferred for close-quarters freshwater fishing where quick pickup of loose line is desirable. Used mainly for panfish and small trout, an automatic fly reel is also a viable flycasting tackle option for someone who only has the use of one hand or limited use of both hands.

Frames and Spools

The key elements of a fly reel are smooth operation, durability, and, in the case of reels used for strong fish, good drag performance.

All fly reels have a foot that is attached to the frame or housing and holds the reel in the rod handle. Most better frames are made from highly anodized machined aluminum. Some frames may be of open or full design, and vented or solid. A full frame provides structural strength for reels made of less expensive materials and requires that line from the spool be directed through the frame before it can be run through the rod guides.

Open frames make line changing and rigging easier, and in better reels that are machined from strong materials they don't sacrifice strength. A vented frame is perforated with holes of varying sizes and shapes, and is preferred for stylistic as well as practical reasons; spools may be vented as well. These holes also reduce weight slightly, although few people can tell the difference of an ounce or two in loaded reels.

Fly reel spools are generally deep and narrow. Newer designs incorporate a large arbor for greater line retrieval per turn of the handle without sacrificing capacity. Large-arbor spools recover significantly more line than conventional arbor spools, and cause less fly line memory (coiling). Many spools also have an exposed or overlapping rim flange, known as a palming rim; this allows you to apply judicious tension on the spool with your fingertips or palm when a fish is taking line, or, more importantly, when pumping a large fish during a battle.

One-piece machined spools are found on better reels, and top models also have a counterbalanced design and turn easily on ball bearings. Balancing prevents spool wobbling, which occurs on unbalanced reels when a strong fish takes line and makes the spool spin at a furious pace, since the handle is on one side of the spool and there is nothing on the other.

Drag

Most fly reels have a simple drag system that is accessed by depressing a spring-loaded switch on the face of the spool to remove the spool. Underneath is a simple brake or click drag that has one or two pawls engaging a gear. The simplest reels should have a drag that allows for enough adjustment so that when line is pulled off the reel quickly it doesn't cause a line overrun and tangling. These pawls cause an audible clicking sound that differs when line is being dispensed or retrieved.

A lot of fly reels have a compression drag system that utilizes one or more washers (also called discs) to press against the spool. Turning an external drag adjustment knob puts tension on a friction washer, which applies pressure to the spool to slow it down. There may or may not be a metal drag washer in the system, which presses upon the friction washer. Cork is the primary material used for the friction washer, although a few big-game models use carbon fiber. Some fly reel drags have metal and friction washers in an adjustable caliper-type system that uses friction washers like dual braking pads to apply pressure to the spool. Some reels use O-rings in a caliper-like system instead of disclike friction washers.

In all cases the rings or washers that are made of friction material compress with pressure, and in hard use there's a lot of heat built up within the drag system. As with all other types of reels, the better drags are those that operate smoothly over a wide range of adjustments with good braking systems.

Other Features

Some fly reels have an anti-reverse feature; when line is pulled from the reel, the spool turns but the handle does not. Another feature of some reels is readily convertible right- or left-hand retrieve. Fly reels by tradition are commonly set to retrieve right-handed, and many older reels were only designed for this operation (similar to conventional and baitcasting reels). But this seems more suited to left-handed anglers, as they can hold the rod in their dominant hand and retrieve with their subordinate hand. Thus some right-handed anglers prefer left-hand cranking and right-handed rod holding, and convertibility (with some internal reconfiguring) is important to them, especially if they'll tangle with large fish that require a lot of pumping and reeling.

Handle knobs also play into this. The handle knob is built on the edge of the spool, and it comes in many lengths and styles. Some anglers prefer a handle knob that is fairly short and round to keep loose line coils from wrapping on it when a fish takes and streaks off with line. Others like a large knob that is easy to grab and hold, especially when fighting big fish and when your fingers are wet or cold. A handle should be easy to release (when a fish streaks off), and many anglers prefer not to have one with an indentation so that they can let go of it in a heartbeat when they have to. Comfort is especially important in larger reels used for big fish, since a lot of winding is likely to be done; thin and/or short handles are generally not favored for this use, even though they're less likely to catch loose fly line.

Although many fly reels are suitable for the average range of fishing conditions that anglers encounter, some stand out from others under stress, abuse, frequent use, and the most demanding situations. That is when the value of better-quality items becomes apparent. One indication of better quality is a finely machined and finished frame and spool. An anodized finish, or other corrosion-resistant finish, is common to the better reels and any that are to be used in saltwater, and top reels are made of aluminum and stainless steel. Other quality matters include a smooth drag system and easy drag startup, a good range of drag adjustment, and a strong and smooth handle knob.

These all add up to durability and top performance for demanding fishing. However, many fly reels are used in routine fishing for generally small or medium-size fish, and do not require the best drag features or the top materials. Most fly reels are used in freshwater and many times the angler does not get into the backing on the reel.

Spincasting Reels

The spincasting reel is the youngest of all reel types, having been invented in 1947, with the first production models introduced by Zebco two years later. It is the easiest of all fishing reels to learn to use, and is suited to a variety of light- to medium-duty angling applications. It is durable, adequate for the majority of freshwater angling activities, and relatively inexpensive.

Some people erroneously believe that spincasting tackle is only meant for panfish and catfish angling, or for fishing with bait and a float. Usage really depends on a person's abilities and preferences, and on the grade of equipment. That said, few spincasting reels are used in saltwater because most spincasting reel components are enclosed, which makes cleaning the reel with freshwater a challenging task, and because of low line capacity and reduced cranking power.

Spincasting reels are characterized by a stationary spool covered by a front cover with a hole or opening through which line passes. Line is wound on the spool under the cover or hood, and a button is used to release the line. This design is very different from other reels, and is one that inherently lacks cranking power.

Also known as spincast reels and closed-face reels, these products are distinguished from spinning reels by that front cover, as well as the fact that spinning reels always sit underneath the rod seat, while spincasting reels usually sit atop the rod seat. Some hybrid spincasting reels sit underneath the rod handle, but they still have a covered stationary spool and otherwise basically function like a conventional spincasting reel.

Another significant difference between spinning and spincasting reels is the ability to change line. Although changing line on a spincasting reel is not actually difficult, it is less easy with this reel than with spinning products, which have easier access to the spool. On spincasting reels, the spool is shrouded by a spinner head and both are underneath a front cover. To get to the spool you have to remove the cover and raise the spinner head (which might also be referred to as an internal rotor).

This is one reason why all spincasting reels come from the manufacturer prespooled with an appropriate strength and length of line. Another reason is that performance is greatly affected by line limpness and diameter. The spincasting reel is the least tolerant of all reel types in this regard and can fail to function with improper line. Yet another reason for prespooling, and one that plays to the greatest strength of spincasting reels in the marketplace, is that it makes them more appealing to the less experienced angler. Virtually no other reels come from the factory prespooled with line.

Spincasting reels range from ultralight models that weigh a few ounces and are used with 4-pound line, to heavy freshwater and light saltwater models that weigh between 15 and 17 ounces

Current-model spincasting reels on display in a store rack in Santee, South Carolina.

and are used with 20- to 25-pound line. They work best when the terminal gear (lure or hook plus sinker) weighs between ¼ and ¾ ounce.

The spincasting reel usually has a pushbutton (under-rod-mounted models have a trigger) that controls the release of line, a stationary spool around which line is wound by a spinner head with a line pickup pin, and a round or cone-shaped cover with an opening for line to pass through. It also has an adjustable drag that is controlled mostly by a thumb wheel or star wheel, and either a single- or dual-grip handle.

Convertible retrieve is not generally an element of spincasting reels because of the dominance of on-center gears, which by their nature prohibit convertibility. Therefore, the majority of spincasting reels are set up for right-handed cranking. However, some models have off-center gears and can have convertible right or left retrieves. These are always higher-end products and include models that sport line-release triggers and sit under the rod handle.

A primary constraint to spincasting reels is relatively low line capacity. They hold less than 150 yards of 25-pound line; most, in fact, hold far less line of much lighter strength. By contrast, most baitcasting and spinning reels have much greater line capacities.

The spool of a spincasting reel, which is enclosed by the front cover, makes the reel easier to use but also creates a misperception that the line cannot be easily feathered on the cast to control accuracy. Furthermore, because the line on the spool is not in constant view of the angler, several line-related functional problems can unknowingly develop. Too much line, too little line, tangled line, frayed line, or twisted line are difficult to detect with spincasting reels.

Operation

The operation of a spincasting reel essentially starts with depressing the pushbutton, a component that is usually touched with the thumb and frequently called the thumb button. This releases the line and allows it to come off the spool. As long as the pushbutton is fully depressed, it acts as a brake and keeps the line in place. When tension on the button is released, the line flows unimpeded off the spool, through the opening in the cover, and out the line guides of the rod. A pushbutton should be easy to activate, with little force necessary, and virtually all of them are.

When the pushbutton is pressed, it also causes a line pickup pin to drop out of the way. The pickup pin winds line onto the spool. As long as the pin is extended in the retrieve position, it holds line in place and you can't cast or let line out (except when the drag functions). Thus pressing the pushbutton causes the pickup pin to drop out of the way, moves the spinner head forward, and sandwiches the line between the spinner head and the inside cover, so that in the casting motion the lure doesn't drop to the ground.

When you release the pushbutton, the spinner head drops back, allowing line to flow freely off

This internal view of a spincasting reel reveals the connection from handle to gear shaft, as well as this product's brass worm gears.

the spool. Naturally, this works the same when you are simply releasing line rather than casting, as might be done when lowering bait or a jig; you just press the pushbutton and let go of it to let line flow from the reel. At this point, and until you turn the handle, line is free to flow off the spool, and the reel is said to be in freespool.

Casting Distance/Accuracy

Generally, a large-diameter spool is good for distance casting, but spincasting reels have more areas that come in contact with the line during casting than spinning or baitcasting reels. These contact areas impart friction to the line, thus reducing potential casting distance.

Line flows freely off the end of a spinning reel, only hitting the front flange of the spool before reaching the first line guide (stripper guide) on the rod. In contrast, line on a spincasting reel comes in contact with similar components, plus the inside surface of the front cover and the edges of the protective front cover line guide as it exits the reel. This friction reduces casting distance and cranking power. Thus casting distance is generally greater on spinning reels than spincasting reels. However, for the average angler spincasting and spinning reels both inherently have the capability to cast longer distances than baitcasting reels—compliments of a stationary spool versus a revolving one.

Some anglers think that spincasting tackle is not very good for making accurate casts, but this is often a function of poor casting technique, mismatched tackle, or both. Some exhibition casters are remarkably accurate with conventional spincasting tackle, more so than they would be with other equipment, simply because they've mastered all of the elements of the spincasting game and have properly matched gear. And some of the best European match tournament anglers use specialized spincasting reels because of the ease with which the reel can be controlled.

The typical angler, however, uses spincasting tackle primarily in situations where accuracy and distance are not critical, and where the species of fish sought are usually small. This tends to reinforce the perception that accuracy is not an attribute of this equipment.

As with any type of tackle, accuracy is really a function of practice and using the right technique.

The spincasting reel has the capability of being quite accurate; if you use your forefinger to contact the line as it exits the front cover, you are in almost constant contact with the line. Because the line is making a loop as it exits the front cover, in theory, the angler may not be in constant contact with the line as would be possible when using a baitcasting reel. In addition, hand position on most spincasting reels is the same as on baitcasting reels, making the transition from using spincasting tackle to baitcasting tackle easier.

Gears

The gearing system on spincasting reels is similar to that on spinning reels. Both transfer crank handle rotational forces through a 90-degree bend to the reel's mechanism that wraps line on the spool. This is accomplished through a gear system capable of converting motion between two 90-degree shafts. In comparison, revolving-spool reels transfer motion from the crank handle directly to the spool through two parallel shafts.

Of the different categories of fishing equipment, spincasting reels display the most inherent limitations in gearing efficiency, and many anglers feel that it is more difficult to retrieve identical weights with a spincasting reel than with a spinning or baitcasting reel. In essence, this is what accounts for limited cranking power.

Incidentally, many spincasting reels have a low gear ratio, ranging from 2.5:1 to about 4:1. Some of the models intended for use with artificial lures have a higher gear ratio. However, spool diameters are typically larger.

Drag

The drag mechanism on better spincasting reels has improved markedly in recent years. The lowest-priced spincasting reels do not have sophisticated drags, but most other models have reasonably good ones, and a few are excellent in this respect.

There are several different types of drag systems used in spincasting reels. The simplest uses a drag wheel and features a spring arm that puts pressure on the edge of the spool. It is reasonably effective for modest fishing applications.

The most common system has a threaded shaft that rotates by means of the drag wheel (or occasionally drag star), which puts pressure on a clutch plate located between the spool and the body of the reel. This system has the ability to produce extremely smooth drags at low tension settings.

Both of these rely on the spinner head remaining stationary and the spool rotating to release line from the spool. An advantage of this is that line exits the spool in a fixed location. Because line is not traveling around the spool, as it would do if the spinner head rotated, a loop, such as the one generated in the casting mode, is not produced. The absence of this loop contributes to reduced drag variation, which means smooth drag performance.

A disadvantage of a stationary spinner head and rotating spool is that if the reel handle is rotated while the drag is slipping, the line becomes twisted, which can cause tangling problems if not remedied. For this reason, many spincasting reels have a spool clicker built into the reel. When the spool turns backward to release line, a clicking sound indicates that the drag is functioning. This is an audible reminder not to rotate the handle until the drag stops slipping.

Unfortunately, many people inadvertently put twist in their line by continuing to reel when the line is slipping via the drag. This is especially likely to be done by inexperienced anglers.

A unique type of drag system found in some spincasting reels functions with a slipping gear instead of a slipping spool. It has the advantage of producing less twist in the line, regardless of the level of expertise of the angler. In this system, the spinner head rotates backward, unwrapping line from the spool much like back-reeling. This is accomplished by a floating drive gear and is controlled with a drag star. A disadvantage to this system, however, is uneven drag performance. As the spinner head unwraps line from the spool, a loop is formed. This loop results in drag variations much higher than that found in other spincasting reel drag systems.

Other Features

Some spincasting reels have a depth-locating feature that is meant to allow an angler to repeatedly let out the same amount of line, usually in order to lower a bait or lure to the same depth. This is often used in panfishing, especially for crappies, and may be known as a crappie locator or crappie finder.

Usually this feature is activated by a lever on top of the reel. The lever is attached to a pin, which is pushed forward by the lever and lies across the spool. When you start retrieving, the recovered line goes over the pin. When you release the line, it goes out until it reaches the pin and then stops; line cannot be pulled from under the bottom of the pin with ordinary tension (although in some models the depth-locating selector switch automatically releases when there is heavy pressure, as might be applied suddenly by a large fish). Now you have a preselected depth to fish or the amount of line to set out.

A few spincasting reels have an audible clicking mechanism, which may be known as a strike detector or bait clicker, to alert you to activity when the reel is in the cast or freespool mode. This can be important when a rod is left unattended or out of reach, usually when fishing with bait and when the reel is in freespool (anti-reverse off). If this feature is activated, it produces an audible clicking sound when a fish strikes and the line starts running.

Better-quality spincasting reels have continuous anti-reverse or infinite anti-reverse, a feature that keeps the drive gear from moving backward when the forward motion of the handle stops. Ideally, the reel should engage instantly and firmly; this aids hooksetting and prevents a loop of slack line from developing on the spool during some retrieval motions, which could eventually impair casting. Older models of reels and some lesser-quality current models have considerable play in the handle and rotor when the reel stops, and the handle may actually turn backward slightly before engaging.

These two diminutive Shakespeare spincasting reels exemplify a trigger-release model (left), which mounts under the rod, and a pushbutton-release model (right), which mounts atop the rod.

Spinning Reels

It is fair to say that the importation of spinning reels to North America after World War II greatly helped stimulate sportfishing interest. These products were called fixed-spool reels at first, and, together with the near-simultaneous emergence of fiberglass rods and nylon monofilament line, they made angling easier for thousands of people who had previously not been very involved with this activity.

Despite their name, spinning reels have a spool that does not spin or revolve, but is fixed in place. Because the spool does not move during a cast, there is no chance of a backlash forming. During the retrieve, line is wound, or spun, around the spool, giving rise to the name of this equipment. When spincasting reels, which also have a stationary spool, evolved, spinning reels were called open-faced reels because they did not have a cover over the spool like spincasting reels did.

No matter what the terminology, spinning reels are very popular and widely used. They are fairly easy to cast with, relatively backlash-free, and well suited for fishing with light or small terminal tackle, especially in casting.

Spinning tackle has a greater following in freshwater fishing than in saltwater fishing because of differences in conditions, techniques, and size of fish, yet technical advances have resulted in a wide range of equipment that is suitable for applications ranging from ultralight panfishing to offshore fishing for sailfish and white marlin. Reels range from small-profile ultralight models designed for use with 2-pound-test line to large-profile saltwater heavyweights for use with up to 30-pound line. Appropriate models can be used in casting, trolling, and fishing with bait, making this truly versatile equipment.

One factor that contributes greatly to the popularity of spinning tackle is that the reels are mounted underneath the rod handle, a position that is only shared by fly reels. This feels comfortable and balanced to many people, especially inexperienced anglers, and it reduces arm fatigue from constant casting. That spinning reels are convertible to either right- or left-hand retrieve assures that the rod is held in the dominant hand, which is often not the case for those using other tackle.

Spinning reels have undergone many changes over the years, perhaps the most significant being

There are many spinning reels with various features available.

in drag and casting features, as well as in line twist reduction aspects. Spinning (and spincasting) reels have long been products that were conducive to producing line twist through angler misuse or the activation of the reels themselves. Twisted line hampers casting and general fishing effectiveness and may result in damaged line, so it is a problem to be avoided and corrected. Therefore, reducing or eliminating twist, from whatever source, has been a major focus of spinning reel manufacturers, and continues to be a work in progress, notwithstanding advertising claims to the contrary.

Operation

Virtually all spinning reels feature a bail. Because the bail holds line in place, it must be opened to cast or to allow line to flow off the reel without casting. There are manual and automatic bail opening systems, the latter utilizing a trigger for one-handed line pickup and bail opening, the former requiring two hands but found on the vast majority of spinning reels.

In use, with the reel under the rod handle and facing away from the angler, the bail is opened and the line is held, usually by the index finger of the hand that holds the rod handle, to prevent the line from coming freely off the spool until released by the finger. When the finger is removed, released line flows off the spool and out through the rod guides, carried by the weight of the object at the terminal end of the line.

To retrieve line, the gears are engaged by rotating the handle. As the line roller, which is connected to the rotor, rotates around the spool, line is wrapped on the spool. The spool's axial motion causes it to move toward the front of the reel and then toward the back. This motion, coupled with the rotor motion, causes line to wrap onto the spool in an equal layer instead of piling up in one place.

Spool Design and Line Twist

A key factor affecting casting efficiency is the design and material of the front spool flange (lip), and the ratio of the front spool flange diameter to the spool hub diameter. The flange obviously has to help retain or catch line when tension is momentarily relaxed, but it cannot impede the flow of line off the inner spool when a cast is made. When line is low on the spool, it is more likely to contact that flange, which increases friction and reduces distance, so the problem becomes amplified.

Spinning reels that have a big, broad radius on the lip certainly hold the line against the spool as you cast, but they also funnel the line down into a small cone pattern, which constricts the line coming off the spool. A very sharp radius on the edge of the spool tends to explode the line off the spool. It will actually make the line blow off as it heads toward the first rod guide. Some manufacturers say that the sharp edge can provide 10 to 15 percent additional distance.

The material of the front spool flange also has some influence on casting distance or casting ease, and this boils down to friction. Aluminum and stainless steel spools produce less line friction and are preferable for top performance. Spools made of synthetic materials, including graphite, composites, or different plastics, are usually found on lower-priced reels. These materials are used primarily for economic reasons. Such spools are easily made, but the material has a relatively high coefficient of friction in relation to nylon monofilament line, so it causes a noticeable loss in casting distance. A lot of manufacturers upgrade synthetic material spools by putting a metal rim, mainly aluminum, stainless steel, or titanium, over the flange.

The size of the spool is an element of casting, especially with regard to the width relative to the depth of the spool. Many spinning reels now have relatively large width-to-depth-ratio spools. In a very narrow spool line will pull from deeper in the spool and make a sharper angle as it comes off. On a wider spool, more of the line remains closer

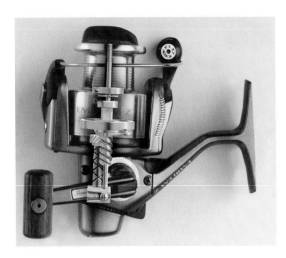

This composite image reveals the gears and some internal components of a Daiwa spinning reel.

to the top of the spool flanges. When casting, the line doesn't make as dramatic an angle as it passes over the spool flange as it does on a narrower spool. This is the premise behind so-called long-cast or long-stroke reels. Overall spool diameter has an influence on casting distance also.

Spinning reels have always suffered from a tendency to produce line twist. Twisted line hampers casting and general fishing effectiveness and may result in damaged line, so it's a problem to be avoided and corrected. Reducing or eliminating twist is an ongoing focus of spinning reel manufacturers.

Although improper use of fishing equipment is the major cause of line twist (especially reeling at the same time that outgoing line is causing the drag to slip), the normal operation of a spinning reel may promote line twisting. Twist can occur if the line turns over on itself while moving from the bail to the spool.

Most line rollers turn as the line comes in. The size and shape of the line roller are factors that affect twisting. Better reels have a larger diameter, sharp roller slopes, and grooves to help prevent twist. These keep the line in one spot on the roller and prevent it from moving around, plus eliminate slack line movement. These components by themselves do not prevent twist but they do help keep the line in such a position that it does not spin over.

Gears

The gears of a stationary-spool reel are generally less efficient than those of a revolving-spool reel because they are offset (the drive gear shaft is at a right angle to the pinion gear shaft) rather than being directly in-line. While this has some cranking-power drawbacks, the crankshaft of a spinning reel running through the whole reel is what allows for convertible right- or left-retrieve, which is not possible with existing revolving-spool reels.

A wide range of gear ratios exist in spinning reels. Many are in the high, 6:1 to 7:1, category. Many spinning reel users prefer a high ratio, but fail to take into account the actual line recovery of the reel, which is the amount of line recovered per turn of the handle. That is determined by spool diameter. If two reels have the same gear ratio but one has a larger spool diameter, that one will recover significantly more line per turn of the handle. Furthermore, a lower gear ratio usually means more cranking power.

Drag

The drag mechanism on spinning reels used to be fair to poor but has improved markedly since this gear started to be used for more challenging fishing. Low-end spinning reels have unsophisticated drags, most medium- and higher-quality models have reasonably good drags, and many of the higher-priced ones have very good drag systems.

Spinning reels have predominantly front- or rear-mounted drag systems. Many experienced anglers prefer front drag because of smoother performance. Both systems feature one or more discs or washers that direct adjustable tension on the spool shaft by turning an adjustment knob.

A third type of spinning reel drag, though not in wide use and not currently offered by manufacturers, is the center drag, where the drag control mechanism is located on the middle of the reel atop the lower housing of the spool. Although this placement theoretically means that the drag control mechanism is easy to adjust when line pays off the reel, it is more significant for providing a large friction washer surface area that dissipates heat efficiently and provides a smooth, lockup-resistant drag.

On a front-mounted drag the adjustment knob is at the very top of the spool. On some of these reels, there is a pop-off button in the middle of the knob, which is pressed to free the spool from the shaft, allowing the drag adjustment to be unaltered when the spool is removed.

On a rear-mounted drag the adjustment knob is at the bottom of the reel. The spool on this reel is simply removed by pressing a pop-off button at the top of the spool, regardless of the drag tension setting. Such easy spool removal is an advantage to rear-mounted drag reels, although spool removal is not a frequent necessity for many anglers.

Rear-drag reels are somewhat easier to adjust during the act of fishing because they keep hands away from the line. Adjusting drag tension on a front-mounted drag while playing a fish means that your hand may get in the way of the line. On a reel with top-mounted drag, the line extending from the bail roller, which is usually under a lot of tension, is often in the way when a quick adjustment is necessary. This is generally viewed as a disadvantage to top-mounted drags, although for many anglers it is seldom necessary to increase or decrease drag tension during the act of fighting a fish, and, in fact it should not be adjusted if it has been set properly.

With any of these systems, drag smoothness, or ability to perform without erratic motion over a wide range of adjustment, is especially critical. This is controlled by the materials, the way they are assembled, and the size of the washers.

The design and placement of front- and center-mounted drags allows for the use of larger washers, which is one reason why they perform well. A rear drag can be every bit as smooth but has difficulty maintaining that smoothness at higher line tension settings unless it uses the same size drag washers as the front and center drags. When large washers are used in a rear-drag reel the body starts getting bigger, which to some people is less aesthetically attractive. Since the trend in most reels has been to smaller overall size, rear drags have had correspondingly sized washers. Front and center drags, however, allow for small overall body size but larger washers, which means that they perform better than rear drags if the drag material allows.

The primary material in modern high-end spinning reels, most of which have very smooth drags, is Teflon or a proprietary synthetic composite that is a mix of fiberglass, graphite, and Teflon; in spinning reels these materials do a reasonable job of satisfying two opposite demands: starting up quickly and smoothly, and maintaining even performance. Since heat dissipation is one of the most important elements of a properly functioning drag, metal washers, which dissipate heat well, are used in

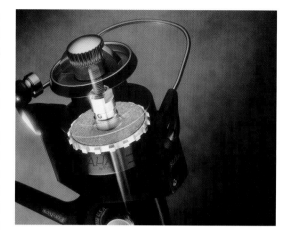

This exposed view of a Fin-Nor Ahab spinning reel reveals a very large drag disc in a front-drag system that allows two-way access to the drag; the spool can be rotated counterclockwise and removed without affecting the preset drag setting.

conjunction with friction washers made from other materials, which provide the smooth slip surface.

In most mid-priced spinning reels the drag system is generally of fairly good quality, while in most high-priced models it is good to excellent. Since the majority of spinning reels are used for light and medium-light applications in freshwater, for the majority of users the drags are actually overbuilt.

With the exception of fishing for steelhead, salmon, stripers, and big trout, freshwater anglers generally don't require exceptional drag performance. Saltwater anglers often need, and really test, the performance of a spinning reel drag. Thus drag performance and drag components are mainly significant to people who will catch fish that will put some pressure on a reel. Sometimes, of course, you never know when a fish will come along that will do just that.

A few spinning reels have combined drag systems in which there are both front and rear drags, the front drag being the primary one for fish fighting and the rear drag being a means of releasing tension on the line while the bail is closed. The rear drag is small and has a very light setting, so that if a fish takes live bait, for example, it can move off under minimal resistance. When ready, the angler engages the main system and uses it to play the fish. Generally there is a lever to engage or disengage the main drag; in some systems the main gear is engaged automatically when the handle is turned. This is primarily an advantage in fishing with bait.

Other Features

Most of the better spinning reels feature a continuous, or infinite, anti-reverse function, which is very helpful. This feature assures that the reel engages instantly and firmly because the drive gear doesn't move even the slightest bit backward. This helps avoid slack line and errant loops from forming on the spool, and it aids solid hooksets.

Nearly all spinning reels have a single-knob handle, and some have a counterbalanced handle. Handles on spinning reels are made from engineering-grade plastic resins, zinc, and aluminum die-cast alloys. The knobs vary in material, although most anglers prefer a soft material that is easy to grip, especially when wet, and that may be contoured for comfort. On higher-end reels, a soft rubber is often used on the knobs rather than hard plastic, and they are more flat and paddle-shaped than round. If the handle and the knobs are not large and comfortable enough for the user, they will be fatiguing and perhaps counterproductive.

Other factors that determine comfortable use include fit in the hands, easy access to features, and overall weight.

Spinning reels sit under the rod handle; the stem of the reel has a foot that is seated in the handle so the outfit is held by wrapping your fingers around the reel foot, with the stem lying between the fingers. Most people place the stem between their middle and third finger. A minority place it between their third finger and little finger. In each case, it is held close to the base of the fingers, and this contact with the stem, as well as the separation between the fingers and the weight that sits there, may be uncomfortable, especially if the reel is held continuously for long periods.

Obviously this part of the reel needs to be as comfortable to hold as possible. The thickness and width of stems vary on reels, and preferences among anglers do as well. A thin stem is generally viewed as being more comfortable, as is a perpendicular stem in the area where it is held, but to some people a wider stem, which puts more surface area between the fingers, provides greater support than one that is thinner and narrower. Some reel stems have been padded for cushioning or contoured to relieve pressure points. The design of the stem becomes more important as the weight and the amount of continuous use increase.

Another factor, especially for cold-weather anglers, is how the stem feels when the reel is cold and handled with bare hands. Metal is colder than composite materials, so the latter feels better in cold weather and a padded area may offer some warmth. A bit of electrician's tape or some type of padded tape wrapped tightly and evenly around the handle stem can help ward off the cold contact, as can using lightweight gloves.

An especially important ergonomic issue is that the distance from the foot to the spool or bail roller has to be such that the line or bail trigger can be readily grabbed with your index finger. For people with small hands, including children, this may be a problem, especially with larger reels. People who have large hands or thick fingers often have a problem with lighter spinning reels, which seem to have a clearance between the foot and bail assembly or trigger that was designed for small or thinner fingers. Thus when they press the bail trigger, it pinches against their fingers, or when they turn the handle, the bail assembly smacks their knuckles.

This may not only occur to people with large hands or thick fingers, but to others with normal-size hands who hold the reel between their third and little fingers, primarily when using bail triggers. That type of hold, while it is comfortable to those who prefer it, places two fingers above the stem, so that when the trigger is pressed by the forefinger, there is less room for it to lever back, meaning that it pinches against the middle finger and may not open.

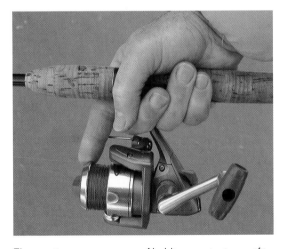

The most common means of holding a spinning outfit is by wrapping the middle fingers around the reel foot and stem, as shown; use the tip of the index finger to stop line at the end of a cast.

6

Line

Line is the essential element of tackle that delivers a lure or bait from a rod to the water. Modern fishing lines possess attributes conducive to the various techniques employed in sportfishing and are engineered to provide specific performance features. Made from different materials in varying strengths, diameters, and colors, fishing line is produced in labeled breaking strengths ranging from 1 to 200 pounds. Nylon monofilament accounts for the bulk of fishing lines sold; there is also significant use of braided microfilament, fused microfilament, and fluorocarbon lines. All of these are unweighted lines. More specialized and heavier products such as weighted and wire lines, as well as fly line, are used less often. Leaders, which are made from different types of line, are a special configuration for particular uses.

Nylon, Fluorocarbon, and Microfilament Lines

Commonly referred to as "mono," nylon monofilament is a single-strand product made from nylon, copolymers, or nylon alloys; various brands of nylon monofilament line possess the same derivatives, but the way they are processed and extruded, and the way their molecules are compounded, determine the different characteristics and properties.

Fluorocarbon, which is a monofilament nylon alloy, is unique among single-strand nylon lines because of its density, which makes it sink, its low refractive index (the degree to which light is bent while passing through), which makes it harder to see in the water, and the fact that it is impervious to ultraviolet light, which makes it very durable.

Braided lines consist of intertwined strands of Dacron, gel-spun polyethylene fiber, or aramid fiber; braiding of the latter two synthetic fibers has produced ultra-thin, super-strong, and very sensitive lines. Fused lines are created by fusing the same synthetic fibers as are used in braided lines, producing a cheaper single-strand-like line. Both braided and fused microfilament lines are simply referred to as microfilaments, because of the super-thin strands of their core materials.

The fishing performance of nylon, fluorocarbon, and microfilament lines is based upon the properties engineered into them. To some extent, a good line is one with a proper balance of characteristics, primarily being strong, relatively thin, and durable. However, manufacturers can manipulate properties to improve certain performance features, which has resulted in a wider, and arguably more confusing, variety of products than ever. Here's a review of some of the most important line characteristics.

Breaking Strength

There are two breaking strength designations: "test" and "class." Class lines are predominantly used by saltwater big-game tournament anglers, by anglers specifically interested in establishing line-class world records, and by fastidious anglers who want to know exactly what their line strength is. Class lines are guaranteed to break at or under the labeled metric strength in a wet condition; that's why you always know what the actual breaking strength is. Class lines are more expensive than test lines and are primarily differentiated from them in the wet breaking strength feature; other properties should be similar to those of test lines.

Any line that is not labeled as class line is test line, which means perhaps 95 percent of all line sold, even if the word "test" is not used on the label. Despite the labeled strength there is no guarantee as to the amount of force required to break the line in either a wet or dry condition. The labeled strength may not reflect the actual force required to break the line in a wet condition. Since

Fishing line is an angler's most critical connection, and it sometimes undergoes a lot of stress.

there are no guarantees with test lines, they may break at, under, or over the labeled strength. An overwhelming number break above the labeled strength, some just a little above, some very far above.

Because there is a great deal of difference in the actual breaking strength of various test lines, and since people only know what the label tells them, many anglers fish with line that is much stronger than they think. Many are also misled into believing that some lines are stronger than others because they physically feel that way.

It is meaningless to take a piece of nylon monofilament, wrap it around your hand, tug on it, and proclaim it has great strength. This is dry strength, and it is irrelevant for most nylon lines, which absorb water and have a 10 to 15 percent lower strength in a wet condition than in a dry condition. An exception is fluorocarbon, which does not absorb water and therefore maintains the same strength characteristics whether wet or dry. The same is essentially true of microfilament line.

To determine the actual fishing strength of most line, you have to soak it in water for a while, then test it. This is what the IGFA does when certifying records, which have to be submitted with actual samples of the line used. Since few anglers have the machinery to calibrate exact breaking strengths, they are usually in the dark as to the actual strength of a line, although some independent analyses (with widely varying results) have been published, and line manufacturers will provide this information if you ask.

Diameter

It used to be that the breaking strength of a line was directly related to its diameter. The greater the breaking strength, the larger the diameter. While that is still true with some products, nylon monofilament line manufacturers now produce ultra-thin lines that have most of the same performance characteristics of conventional mono, yet are markedly thinner. Similarly, microfilament lines are exceptional in regard to thin diameter. Therefore, the diameter of a line is no longer necessarily a corollary to its breaking strength.

The diameter of a line, however, does influence the amount of it that will fit on a spool and is therefore available for fighting strong fish. This is of special concern to light-tackle anglers who need plenty of line on a reel. It is also a factor in achieving distance when casting and in getting lures to work effectively; thinner line has less drag and can be cast farther, and it allows lures to dive or sink deeper or faster. Because thin-diameter lines are less visible to fish, they help draw more strikes, especially in clear water.

To compare products, you have to know the diameter as well as the actual breaking strength. Many manufacturers provide diameter information on the label of their line spools. As a general rule, solid, round single-strand nylon monofilament provides a uniform diameter through a spool, but microfilaments are a bit less consistent.

Abrasion Resistance

Abrasion resistance is important in fishing line, but tough to evaluate under real or simulated fishing conditions. Some lines are more abrasion-resistant due to greater diameter, the composition of the line, or an applied coating. Determining differences among brands is subjective, and you can only make this judgment through use.

Some lines, particularly premium nylon monofilaments and fluorocarbon, have excellent abrasion resistance. Some are just barely adequate. Dacron has very poor abrasion resistance, which is why it is barely used any longer; microfilament lines are less abrasion-resistant than good nylon monofilament and fluorocarbon lines, which is why anglers use monofilament or fluorocarbon leaders with microfilaments in some situations.

No castable line completely withstands abrasion, but some do so better than others. The key

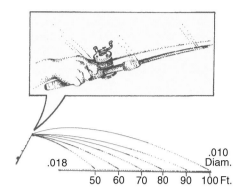

There is a clear relationship between casting distance and line diameter when using the same weight lure.

is to find a line that resists abrasion adequately while still possessing other properties important for fishing performance.

Stretch

The average amount of stretch in nylon monofilaments was once around 30 percent in a wet state but now has been reduced in better products from 10 to 25 percent. Nylon monofilament line has slightly more stretch in a wet state than in a dry one. Lines with high stretch are great for casting, but terrible for hooksetting and playing fish because they have too much elasticity.

Lines that have low stretch increase your ability to detect strikes, aid hooksetting, provide more control in playing a fish, increase sensitivity to feel what a lure or bait is doing, and theoretically help catch more fish. These have been the most important attributes of microfilaments, which have virtually no stretch, and fluorocarbon, which has little.

While you would think that it would be best to fish with a line that had virtually no stretch, such as the different microfilaments, many anglers have difficulty with these products precisely because they have no stretch and are unforgiving. Anglers set the hook too hard or pull too intensely on a hooked fish and yank the hook out of the fish. Because of low stretch, anglers have to use these products differently than nylon monofilament, and make adjustments (such as decreasing the reel drag and using a more limber rod).

Flexibility

A limp, or very flexible, line is advantageous for distance casting, in part because the line comes off the reel spool easily in smaller coils and straightens out quickly. It can be managed on a reel more easily than a stiff line, but lacks sensitivity. Stiff lines tend to spring off the spool in large coils, which flap against the rod guides, decrease distance, and increase the likelihood of developing a tangle.

The flexibility of a line is hard to judge by sight, although in some instances one can feel that a line is very stiff or very limp. Braided lines are limper than nylon monofilaments, which vary a great deal in flexibility. Nylon monofilament line forms a memory when placed in a set position (such as being spooled) for an extended period of time. Nylon lines with less memory are considered limp and are more castable than stiff lines, a factor that is important in light-line angling. Nylon lines with a lot of memory are considered stiff, which contributes to spooling and twist problems and makes casting more difficult.

Castability is also affected by water absorption in lines that absorb water; wet lines usually cast better than dry lines. It is also affected by line diameter; the greater the diameter, the harder it is to cast. With nylon monofilament, the stiffer the line, the less stretch it has but the more difficult it is to cast. Thus, there's a dramatic tradeoff between castability and stretch in nylon monofilament. It's a good idea to wet nylon monofilament line (place the spool in the water) before you start using it on a given day, to help the molecules relax.

Braided and fused microfilaments are different in this respect. They have low stretch, good limpness, and high castability, wet or dry.

Visibility

The visibility of a fishing line has no effect on its basic performance and generally has nothing to do with the other properties. Yet it can be a very important factor in certain fishing situations, especially when fishing in clear water, for finicky or especially wary fish, and when using small lures and hooks. This is the primary reason why clear fluorocarbon line has become popular; as previously noted, the low refractive index of fluorocarbon makes it less visible in the water than other types of line.

Fishing line is available in many colors and shades as well as in fluorescent versions. As fluorocarbon demonstrates, how a line looks above the water is less of a factor than how it looks on or in the water where it is used. However, fluorocarbon, which is also more dense than mono and therefore sinks, is not appropriate for all fishing situations. Furthermore, there is a correlation between line diameter and visibility in all lines, with visibility increasing as diameter increases.

While it would seem that low-visibility lines should always be used, there is merit to using higher-visibility line, at least as the main line connected to a less visible leader. High-visibility line, particularly fluorescent line, is of great value to anglers whose eyesight isn't as keen as it used to be. It is also useful to anglers who bottom bounce, troll long lines on the surface, fish with jigs or plastic worms, and otherwise have reason to watch their lines for an indication of a strike. Sometimes, high visibility above the surface outweighs high visibility beneath the surface because the angler fishes more effectively by virtue of being able to see the line better.

Fly, Wire, and Weighted Lines

Fly, wire, and weighted lines are distinctly different in principal usage than most other lines. Weighted and wire lines are trolled rather than cast. Fly line is cast but it is used to carry nearly weightless objects; other lines that are cast are virtually weightless and carried by the weight of the object being cast.

Fly Line

Castability is the first and most critical performance characteristic of a fly line, which is a relatively thick product with a core and a coating. The core is a braided synthetic that determines tensile strength and stretch, and influences stiffness. The coating is mainly polyvinyl chloride; it provides most of the weight needed to load the fly rod for casting, and some of the line's flexibility, plus color, shape, and density.

Individual fly lines are designed to be stronger than the heaviest tippet that the product will be used with, so their breaking strength ranges from approximately 20 pounds (lightweight freshwater lines) to over 40 pounds (heavy saltwater lines).

There are floating, sinking, and floating/sinking lines. A floating (F) line is for surface or near-surface fishing. It is the easiest fly line to cast, to

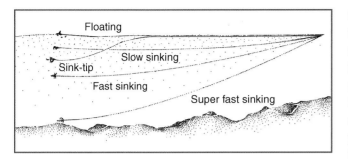

Fly Line Types

pick up off the water, and to fish, which is especially important for someone new to this activity. A sinking (S) line is used only for fishing below the surface. Sinking lines are also known as full-sink lines and are classified according to the speed at which they sink. Floating/sinking (F/S) lines possess a floating body and a sinking tip section and are commonly called sink-tip or sinking-tip lines. The length of the sinking tip varies, usually from 10 to 30 feet; like full-sinking lines, they vary in sink rate.

The four main line shapes are level, double, weight forward, and shooting. A level (L) line is the same weight and diameter throughout, and essentially has no taper to it; it is difficult to cast and control in the water. A double taper (DT) line has the same taper at both ends and a section of level line in the middle, and is used primarily in short- to medium-range casting. A weight-forward (WF) line is tapered only at the fishing end; it is designed to fish well at short, medium, and long distances, and is especially useful for casting large flies, bugs, and poppers. A shooting (ST) line, which is also known as a shooting head (SH), is a 30-foot length of tapered fly line, similar to the head of a weight-forward line; it is difficult to cast and mainly used in big-water fishing and for long casting.

Fly lines are commonly about 85 to 90 feet long; they may vary in overall length from 75 to 100 feet or more, with the exception of short shooting heads. The portion devoted to the head and the running line varies, but it is the grain weight of the first 30 feet that determines its classification, according to a standard system in which lines are measured in weights from 60 to over 800 grains and translated into line weight or size, which is interrelated with the rods that are designed to properly cast such a class of line.

Line weights range from 1 to 15 in designation, the higher numbers being heavier and more difficult for the average person to cast. Line weights from 3 to 8 cover most freshwater needs, and from 7 to 12 most saltwater needs. The heaviest lines are used for casting huge flies with muscle rods and handling big-game pelagic species, while the lightest lines are used on ultralight rods for minute flies and small-fish angling. Sizes 5 through 8 are most popular, with 5 or 6 the most common because of their versatility in freshwater trout fishing.

Wire Line

Used exclusively for trolling, wire lines are primarily constructed of single or multiple strands of stainless steel or Monel, a corrosion-resistant alloy that is more expensive than stainless steel, more pliant, and less prone to kinking. Multiple-strand wire is easier to handle but poses difficulties when burrs develop; it sinks less readily than single-strand wire, and is used less.

There is very little stretch to wire line and it is very resistant to abrasion. This makes hookups a little surer and there's less chance of breaking it during a fight with a fish than if you were using other types of line, provided that it doesn't have a kink.

Found in various strengths, but primarily used in 30- and 40-pound test, wire line is a little more difficult to work with than other types of line, and does require some precautions. It must be wound on a reel spool under tension or it will spring off and create a terrible tangle. Tangling is possible whenever tension is removed, so when trolling it's imperative that wire be let out carefully and under controlled tension, usually keeping a thumb on the spool as the line is paid out.

Weighted Line

Weighted lines are uncastable core-heavy products that sink and are used for deep trolling. Lead core is the foremost type of weighted line, but similar products have a flexible nontoxic lead substitute.

These lines feature a pliable, dense core that is covered by braided nylon or Dacron. Available from 15- to 60-pound test, weighted lines have the density to sink on their own without the addition of external objects, although their bulky diameter offsets some of the sinking ability at trolling speed, usually meaning that to get very deep, great lengths of line have to be trolled or the boat moved very slowly.

Weighted lines are much easier to use than wire. They rarely have kinking or jamming problems, and can easily be wound on a reel and set out. They are color-coded to help determine how much is out, although this won't necessarily tell you how deep the trolled lure is.

Weighted lines are available in coated and uncoated versions, the former using some type of plastic. Coating may help abrasion, but generally these lines are not very abrasion-resistant. They have less stretch than some similar-strength nylon monofilaments, but they do stretch. They will corrode in saltwater, and have to be taken off the reel spool and rinsed, in part explaining why wire line is universally preferred in saltwater.

Leaders and Tippets

A leader is a length of nylon monofilament, fluorocarbon, or wire line that is attached to the end of a fishing line. It is intended either to have low visibility so that it does not appear to be connected to a lure, hook, or fly, or to protect the main line from cutting or breaking. No leader material is able to do both of these perfectly and simultaneously, although fluorocarbon comes closest to achieving both.

Leaders vary in length; the terminal end is connected directly to a lure, fly, hook, snap, or swivel, and the butt is connected directly to the fishing line. Sometimes a leader is used from a swivel to a weight, baited hook, diving planer, or bottom rig.

A leader may be lighter or heavier in strength than the main fishing line, depending upon its application, and level or tapered in both diameter and strength. Always used in fly fishing, it is electively used for other types of casting, as well as when trolling and baitfishing, and while using all types of tackle.

Leaders are used more commonly in saltwater angling, owing to the greater number of nasty fish encountered in the marine environment and some of the different techniques employed; some type of leader, for example, is virtually always used in offshore big-game fishing and shark fishing. Leaders are most likely to be used for fish with sharp teeth, scales, or gill covers; for fish that are very big and powerful; for fish that are hard to land or unhook and release near the boat; and for species that live in places where line-damaging obstructions are frequently encountered.

Tapered Fly Leaders

In fly fishing, nylon monofilament leaders of varying lengths (up to 9 feet) are a necessity. This is because the fly line is too thick to be attached directly to the fly—its size would alarm fish if it were. The leader, when tapered down, is important for turning over and quietly presenting a fly as well as getting it to float or sink naturally.

Fly leaders are nearly all tapered from a heavy butt end (which is usually 20- to 30-pound test) through the midsection to a light end, with or without a tippet. However, in some situations, a short length of level, or untapered, leader can be used; this is most common when using sinking lines and leaders under 6 feet long, and when angling for fish that are not highly selective or leader-shy.

Fly leaders are available in premanufactured knotless tapered versions, or they can be constructed by the angler in knotted compound tapered sections that successively taper down in strength and diameter. Lengths and strengths of fly leader vary with fish and conditions.

Tippets

A tippet is the terminal section of a fly fishing leader that is tied to the fly. Generally made of nylon monofilament like the leader, it may be heavier and stiffer than the remainder of the leader, in which case it is called a shock tippet, or lighter and softer, which is necessary for most fly fishing presentations.

A tippet is a standard and especially important component of a tapered leader. It may be the final link in a personally constructed knotted compound tapered leader, or a section that is added to a commercially manufactured knotless tapered leader. For most freshwater fishing, and especially when angling for trout, a tippet is the lightest and thinnest-diameter portion of a fly fishing leader, and thus the weakest link in the chain from fly line to fly, as well as the section most easily cut or broken.

In some circumstances it is necessary to protect the end of the leader from being cut by the teeth, jaws, or gill covers of a fish. This is when a shock tippet, which is a short length of heavy monofilament or wire, is added to the end of the fly fishing leader. The breaking strength and

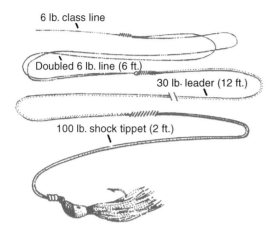

6 lb. class line

Doubled 6 lb. line (6 ft.)

30 lb· leader (12 ft.)

100 lb. shock tippet (2 ft.)

Using double line and line-to-line knots, you can create a heavy shock tippet for a light line. This example depicts lengths that conform to record-keeping rules.

diameter of the shock tippet exceed the breaking strength of the rest of the leader, sometimes by a great deal.

Level Mono Leaders

In non-fly-fishing applications, level leaders may be used with any type of tackle and with a variety of techniques. A level leader has one unknotted line section of the same strength and diameter throughout. When casting with other types of equipment, there is no benefit to a tapered leader for presentation, since the weight of the object being cast carries the line.

Whether a leader is necessary or desirable at all depends on the situation and the species. Consistent fishing in areas where the terminal end of the main fishing line is likely to be abraded might call for a heavy nylon monofilament leader, provided that doing so doesn't alert the fish. Fish with sharp teeth and sharp gill plates might need a heavy (shock) leader. Fishing in ultraclear shallow water and for wary species might require a fluorocarbon leader. Shorter lengths, which keep the line-to-leader knot off the reel spool, are preferred for casting situations, but greater lengths are used in fishing with heavy tackle and large species.

Using at least a heavier leader (or a double line, or both) definitely aids catching large fish on light and ultralight lines. Anytime there is a lot of stress on the terminal end of light line (especially when landing fish), a leader or a double length of line should be a consideration.

Wire Leaders

The purpose of a wire leader is to prevent the terminal line from being cut. It is generally used in circumstances where other materials are apt to fail, such as when the teeth, bill, or other portions of a fish will slice or abrade the line. There are essentially preformed and self-made wire leaders; all are level in diameter, and they come in bright or dark brown versions, with the latter preferred by most anglers (the brighter wire is more noticeable and subject to being struck by fish).

Pre-manufactured wire leaders from 6 to 36 inches long are mainly used in freshwater lure casting and trolling, primarily for toothy species. They are also used for some saltwater casting and inshore trolling activities, but not for heavy-duty big-game or offshore work, or when fishing with bait. Some anglers make their own, using lengths and materials of their choice.

For offshore trolling and big-game activities, it's necessary to use a long leader made from single- or multistrand wire, which may or may not be coated with nylon. Coils of such wire are available from under 20-pound strength up to at least 250-pound strength in some varieties, and over 300 pounds in others, and in ample lengths for making numerous leaders.

Single-strand wire, also known as piano wire, is made of stainless steel and is comparatively cheap. It is nearly bulletproof when it comes to resisting cutting by a fish, but it is highly prone to kinking. Multistrand wire, referred to as cable, is more supple and does not kink as readily, but it has a thicker diameter, creates more drag, and is subject to weakening when thin individual strands are nicked or cut. Most offshore and big-game anglers make their own. Length depends on the application, but for offshore trolling and shark fishing, wire leaders are commonly from 12 to 18 feet long but can be longer, although such lengths require that someone grab the wire and pull a caught fish close enough to be landed or unhooked.

Shorter lengths are more common for most applications, with inshore and bottom-fishing lengths being from a few feet long up to 10 feet. It is desirable in some situations to use lighter-strength wire, which has a smaller diameter, to enhance bait or lure presentation and minimize detection.

7

Lures and Flies

Most anglers classify objects used to catch fish as being either natural bait or lures. Thus a simple twenty-first-century definition of a lure is any nonnatural object with a hook that is used to catch fish. These objects are made from a variety of materials, primarily wood, metal, lead, and hard and soft plastic, but also including feathers, fur, yarn, and combinations of materials.

Lures catch fish because of their appearance and the manner in which they are deployed, which are interrelated factors. Even though some lures don't specifically imitate or suggest food through their physical appearance, they imitate or suggest food in the way that they're used. Thus, in one sense or another, all lures represent some form of food, either mimicking it closely, as is true of artificial flies or minnow-style plugs, or suggesting it broadly, as is true of jigs, spinners, and spoons.

Even though lures represent food, they are not only or always struck by fish that are feeding. Fish strike lures for many reasons. Hunger is a prime motivation. Instinctive reflex, aggravation, competition, and protection are others. Fish refuse to strike lures at times for many reasons, too. Predatory fish, which are of major sportfishing interest, spend varied portions of their time feeding; some species, especially many in saltwater, are necessarily eating machines and constantly forage, whereas others, especially many in freshwater, feed less frequently and are often more selective.

All lures are somehow meant to imitate natural food; here, a 5-inch-long alewife is contrasted with wooden (top) and plastic minnow-imitating plugs.

The range of food consumed by these predators is extremely wide and varies with the species, environment, and season. Some fish are more likely to strike lures, and some of those are more likely to strike certain types of lures fished in a particular manner. Thus the way in which many lures are used is an important component of success. Since there is great variety in lure types, as well as a tremendous array to select from within each type, the following text is a summary review of each primary category.

Flies

In a generic sense, a fly is a type of extremely lightweight lure, also known as an artificial fly (to distinguish it from a natural fly, which is rarely used by anglers), that is cast with a fly line and fly rod. Some flies are more imitative in appearance of natural insects than any other lure. Other flies are highly imitative of baitfish, crustaceans, and various small, natural, noninsect foods. Still others are more suggestive than imitative, meant as attractors rather than deceivers.

An extremely wide array of flies is employed in fly fishing for diverse species in all areas of freshwater and saltwater. Flies range from less than $^1/_8$ inch long up to 10 inches long. Unlike many other lures, they are entirely handmade, being tied on a single or double hook (seldom the latter) from a variety of natural and synthetic materials. They can generally be categorized as floating or sinking flies, and specifically typed as dry flies, wet flies, nymphs, streamers, and bugs.

Floating flies are made with buoyant materials and sit on the surface of the water. They include dry flies and bugs and imitate a host of foods, including natural insects, frogs, mice or lemmings, snakes, and other creatures. Like natural insects, dry flies are generally allowed to drift on the surface subject to whatever natural current or wind exists, but, to avoid drag, the presentation may require in-air or on-water line mending. Bugs include hard- or solid-bodied poppers and hair-bodied bugs; both are large and usually look nothing like other artificial flies or natural insects.

Sinking flies are fished below the surface and are made with materials that absorb water or are more dense than water. They include wet flies, nymphs, and streamers, and also imitate many foods. Wet flies represent subsurface forms of aquatic insects or, to a lesser extent, drowned terrestrial insects or small fish; they may be imitative or suggestive and generally drift in the water subject to whatever natural current exists. Nymphs are usually smaller and represent the larval stage of aquatic insects, as well as some noninsect foods; many are more suggestive than imitative, and also drift naturally. Streamers represent baitfish as well as leeches, worms, eels, and so on; they are generally tied on long-shanked hooks, are fairly colorful, and may or may not closely mimic specific prey. Sinking flies are more productive overall because gamefish feed most often below the surface.

With the exception of bugs, the basic and standard fly has these components: a hook, which includes a point that may or may not be barbed, an eye that may be straight or turned up or down, and a shank that may be straight, curved, keeled, or humped; a head; a body, which is the main section along the shank of the hook and that may have ribs; and a tail. It may also have wings, hackle, a thorax, and sometimes legs.

The particular appearance of a fly—in essence the parts that make up its likeness, the way they are incorporated onto the fly hook, and the colors—not only characterize it by type, but also constitute a pattern, and make a given fly distinguishable from others.

There are literally thousands, perhaps tens of thousands, of patterns. This can be confusing and intimidating, and it is impossible for even the most astute fly angler to recognize all of them.

That many fly anglers tie flies (comparatively few users of nonfly lures make their own lures) contributes in large part to this proliferation of patterns. A beginning fly angler is best advised to seek counsel at a local fly tackle shop for the recommended fly patterns and sizes for a specific area at a given time.

The myriad of fly patterns is not unlike the existence of many specific nonfly lures for freshwater and saltwater fishing, and specifically for such species as bass, walleye, stripers, and so on. Like those products, certain flies have crossover application. Small trout flies are equally effective on panfish, for example, and many saltwater streamers are also effective on northern pike and lake trout.

The huge proliferation of patterns, some of which are barely distinguishable from one another, would seem to suggest that a fly angler, especially one seeking trout in streams, needs hundreds of different patterns to be able to use the right fly that will catch fish at a given time. It is true that many fish, stream trout in particular, can at times be very selective about feeding and about what artificial flies they will take because of its resemblance to their currently preferred food; this makes matching the hatch, whether there is in fact a hatch or merely just a predominance of a certain food item, advantageous if not essential.

However, it is also true that fish take flies that merely suggest food rather than duplicate it, and there are many patterns that are close enough to food duplications to be effective. In truth, even the best flies that imitate specific insects are not clones of those insects. And in any case, the best fly cannot be effective if it is not properly presented and/or retrieved. Therefore, the best course of action is to focus on the type of fly that most closely represents the food that fish are feeding on, and to fish it properly.

Lures

Spinners

Spinners are metal lures that sport one or more blades that revolve around a central shaft and spin when retrieved. To fish they evidently represent the suggestion of something to eat, since they don't exactly imitate food. Available in a variety of models and sizes, their flashy movement and appearance has made them effective and very popular, especially in freshwater fishing.

Most spinners are used for casting, but some are trolled. They are relatively uncomplicated to use, and in most sizes hook fish fairly readily. The blade is central to the effectiveness of the spinner, not only because of its visual appearance when moving, but because it generates a good deal of vibration, which can be detected by fish in murky water where visibility is limited. The blade vibrates differently from one style to another.

There are essentially two types of lures in this category: in-line spinners and weight-forward spinners.

> **In-line.** In-line spinners feature a freely rotating blade (or blades), mounted on a single straight (in-line) shaft. Behind the blades are beads or bodies of lead or metal, which provide the lure's basic weight and make it castable. Skirts of feather, hair, or plastic tubing, may be added to the hook to increase the spinner's appeal, but many hooks are unadorned.
>
> These lures are available in weights from $\frac{1}{32}$ ounce to several ounces; with single, double, and treble hooks; with blade lengths from

A fly box with western–U.S. shad flies.

½ inch to several inches; and with assorted types of tail material. Squirrel and bucktail hair are traditionally favorite hook garnishes, but soft plastic bodies are increasingly used on single-hooked spinners, and some feature rubber or plastic minnow bodies.

A majority of spinners are equipped with a treble hook, but some have single hooks, and a few feature an interchangeable hook. The ¹⁄₁₆-, ⅜-, and ¼-ounce sizes are best for bass fishing; the smaller sizes are used in panfishing; and the biggest models are fished for large pike, muskies, and possibly striped bass.

The blade design controls the action and the angle of blade revolution. Blades that are attached to the shaft via a clevis are mainly of Colorado, Indiana, French, or willowleaf shape, although there are variations on these and some nonconformist styles as well. The willowleaf, which is the narrowest blade, has less water resistance, so it rotates closest to the shaft and thus spins faster. The Colorado is the broadest blade and has the most water resistance, so it rotates farthest from the shaft and spins slowest. The others are in between these two.

Another style, the so-called sonic blade, is somewhat like a broad willowleaf; it is concave at one end and convex at the other, mounts directly on the shaft (which runs through the lure), and has a narrow rotation to make it work well in fast current. In a properly designed spinner, the blade spins even at a slow retrieval speed, so water conditions and current flow, if present, help determine which style to use.

The actual spinner blade is available in many colors, but the blade's color is not nearly as important as its visibility under fishing conditions. A good reflective quality is desired. Spinners also give some vibration when retrieved, which is important to the fish and probably accounts for the success of spinners when used at night and under very poor water clarity conditions.

It is always necessary to use a swivel or snap-swivel with these lures to counter the tendency of the rotating blade to turn the lure over repeatedly and cause line twist. A few spinners are very good at resisting line twist, and bending the upper shaft may help avoid it, but line twist is such a serious problem with spinners that you should not take a chance in going without a good quality swivel or snap-swivel.

Weight-forward. Weight-forward spinners are long-shanked lures with a lead weight molded to the shaft ahead of a spinner blade, which in turn is ahead of a single hook. The hook is primarily supplied bare and impaled with a live worm. Some have a single or treble hook that is dressed with hair, fur, or a soft plastic body such as a grub.

These spinners are used for slow trolling, drifting, and casting in freshwater, and are mainly popular for smallmouth bass and walleye fishing on northern lakes, especially when garnished with a live worm and drifted across rocky reefs. Simpler versions, which feature a long-shanked hook and a single rotating blade with beads along the shaft, have long been known as June Bug spinners.

Weight-forward spinners come in small to intermediate sizes and with a variety of weight and blade shapes. The positioning of the weight on the lure causes it to sink headfirst, meaning that, unlike in-line spinners, the blade can spin on the descent and possibly catch fish. Narrow weight shapes allow a weight-forward spinner to sink quickly, and are good for fishing in current

Assorted spinners, from top to bottom, include small versions for trout and panfish, midsize versions for bass and walleye, and bucktail spinners for larger fish, including pike and muskies.

and deep water. Wider weights have more water resistance, and are preferred for shallow-water use. The head is usually preceded by a long wire shaft (sometimes removable), to foil bite-offs from sharp-toothed fish, and the twist-free nature of the lure allows usage without a swivel or snap-swivel.

Spoons

Spoons are various sinking, wobbling lures primarily made of hard metal and used for casting, trolling, and jigging. They are unlike other lure forms in that the bladelike metal body wobbles but doesn't spin, is not attached to a center shaft, and generally suggests an injured or fleeing baitfish through a range of retrieval speeds.

Spoons will likely catch nearly any species of fish, although they are more preferable for some species than for others, predominantly employed in freshwater, and most useful in clear water due to their visual appeal. Trout, salmon, and charr species are the primary targets, but northern pike, largemouth bass, smallmouth bass, striped bass, and walleye are also susceptible to specific types of spoons. Smaller predators are generally not good targets for these active lures, except for the smaller jigging versions.

Most spoons are generally slender, with a slight curvature that provides swimming action when retrieved and a flashy appearance. There are two basic yet vastly different categories.

Casting and trolling. Casting and trolling spoons include a wide array of lures, some of which are used strictly for trolling, some strictly for casting, and some for both. Those used strictly for casting can be subdivided into weedless and non-weedless models, the former having some type of hook-guard to minimize snagging on objects.

The design of the metal body and the overall weight govern what can and cannot be cast, as well as the overall action and working speed. In a general sense, these can be separated into thin- or thick-bodied lures.

An assortment of thick-bodied spoons are used in both casting and trolling. These range from tiny $1/32$-ounce versions used for panfish and trout to objects 9 inches long weighing several ounces and used for large lake trout and saltwater striped bass. Wafer-thin spoons,

which are too light and too air-resistant to be cast, are used in trolling, where a weighted line, a sinker, a downrigger, or some other device is employed to get the lure down to the desired fishing depth.

No matter what the application, casting and trolling spoons are made of hard metal, usually brass or steel, and have a curved body (one side is concave). This curvature causes the lure to drag and wobble as it moves through the water. Generally, the longer the lure, the wider and slower the wobbling action; the shorter the lure, the narrower and quicker the action. Likewise, the more pronounced the curvature, the more resistance the lure has and the more accentuated its action; spoons with little curvature have less water resistance and a narrower and less pronounced action.

Virtually all spoons feature one hook on their back end. Trebles are more common than singles, especially on lightweight spoons. Most hooks are attached via a split ring to the back of the lure, but a few (especially weedless versions) have single hooks that are integral to the metal body.

Spoons always have a hole at their front end for attachment to the fishing line. Line should never be tied directly to this hole but instead to a snap or a snap-swivel; the latter will minimize or prevent line twist.

Jigging. Jigging spoons are thick-bodied lures made of hard metal or lead that lack a curved profile. Though somewhat spoonlike in appearance, they don't have a distinctive wobble when retrieved, which makes them suitable for vertical jigging. Their action is essentially that of darting upward and fluttering backward.

Most jigging spoons, especially those used in freshwater, have a flat, compressed, two-sided body, but others, especially large versions used in saltwater, have a three- or four-sided profile tapering at either end; the so-called diamond jig of saltwater prominence has four sides and is wide at the middle and tapered to a point at either end.

Jigging spoons used in freshwater vary in shape and size; they are commonly used in ¼- to ½-ounce sizes for black bass, white bass, and stripers, and mainly employed for vertical jigging in situations where fish may be schooled or

Spoon types, from top to bottom, include weedless, jigging, casting, and trolling versions.

suspended. However, smaller models are used to catch panfish and for ice fishing, and larger models (up to 2 ounces) are occasionally used for striped bass and deep bottom fishing for lake trout.

Many versions are long, narrow, and tapered, but others are wide and squat (called slabs or slab spoons). The former usually have a plain or hammered plated finish while the latter are painted, generally in white, yellow, silver, or gold. In saltwater, jigging spoons are usually larger and commonly fished up to several ounces in inshore waters, though versions up to 16 ounces (more of a lead lure with a hook than a spoon) are used on appropriately heavy tackle for the greatest depths. These are often referred to as metal jigs, rather than jigging spoons, but the effect is the same.

Jigging spoons have an integral line-tie ring or hole at the head, and some are equipped with a split ring. Nearly all have a treble hook attached to the rear via a split ring. The trebles are likely to get hung up a good deal, but their weight helps unsnag them fairly easily if you have a direct line of pull overhead. Fishing line should be tied directly to the lure or to a split ring; avoid using a snap or snap-swivel, which increase hook fouling.

Plugs

A plug is a relatively buoyant wooden or molded hard plastic lure with built-in swimming action, although due to diverse materials with different properties and a plethora of lure designs, there are many plugs that do not exactly fit this umbrella description. Most plugs float, but some sink and others combine floating and sinking characteristics. Most imitate or suggest some type of fish, although they may also imitate or suggest many other types of aquatic food. Though the vast majority are constructed from wood or hard plastic, many are fashioned from other materials, such as soft plastic or urethane foam, or a combination of materials.

Plugs exist in all sizes, shapes, colors, and performance functions, in straight as well as jointed versions. There is some type of plug for virtually every freshwater gamefish of importance to anglers (although it is usually out of character for carp, sturgeon, whitefish, and catfish to strike a plug). There are also plugs that will catch many species of saltwater fish, although the usage of plugs in freshwater far outweighs that in saltwater.

Plugs come in three categories: floating/diving, sinking, and surface. The first two are primarily fished under the water's surface, at various depths, with sinking plugs much less prominent than floating/diving plugs, which exist in countless forms. Surface plugs are detailed separately in this chapter under Surface Lures.

Floating/diving plugs sit on the surface of the water at rest and dive to various depths when retrieved or trolled. The extent to which they do so usually depends primarily upon the size and shape of their lip, and the location of the line-tie on the nose or lip of the plug; the lip and overall body shape determine the inherent swimming action.

Perhaps most popular among floating/diving plugs are minnow- or baitfish-shaped versions with small lips, which are designed to be fished very shallow, and which may double as surface lures. Other floating/diving plugs of intermediate size are more bulbous or elongated (referred to as crankbaits by many freshwater anglers). These are strictly meant for below-surface retrieving or trolling duties. Some of these models have small round weights, or BBs, inside that allow them to

Assorted diving plugs fill the drawers of a tackle box.

rattle when being retrieved and thus have a greater noisemaking value. Their running depth may vary from 1 to 25 feet, and accordingly, they are classified as shallow, medium, or deep divers.

An exception to these basic types is a popular trolling plug for salmon in the Great Lakes and West Coast waters known as a cut-plug lure that weaves wildly and is predominantly used in conjunction with a downrigger. This is a floating/diving lure, but one that attains very little depth on its own.

Sinking plugs are simply plugs that do not float but are weighted to sink when they enter the water and will sink as far as the angler allows. These are often allowed to sink to a specific depth by counting roughly a foot of depth per second of descent (or whatever rate equals one second), and then are retrieved. These are primarily used in freshwater bass fishing and are also referred to as sonic vibrators. There are metal, plastic, and wood-bodied models.

Some of these, as well as some floating/diving plugs, are specially balanced to have a neutral buoyancy, so they will not sink or float upward once they have achieved a running depth. This makes them appear to maintain a certain depth and be retrieved in a swim-stop motion like a natural baitfish. Pure sinking plugs are greatly outnumbered by floating/diving models, and are primarily fished in a similar manner once they are allowed to sink to the desired depth.

Regardless of whether they float at rest or sink, plugs that swim under the surface can be

typecast as shallow, intermediate, or deep divers. Though most are between 2½ and 5 inches long, their bodies range from under 1 inch to over 10 inches long. Weights are typically from ¼ to ½ ounce, but some weigh several ounces and a few are under ¹/₈ ounce. Longer and heavier versions are typically used in saltwater and for certain large freshwater species.

Nearly all of these plugs are equipped with treble rather than single hooks, although some are equipped with single hooks by the manufacturer or can be changed by the user. The number of hooks varies, generally depending on the length and swimming action of the lure. Smaller models normally have two treble hooks; others have either two or three, usually the latter.

Most plugs are one-piece lures, but some have segmented bodies; the latter are called jointed plugs, which are more expensive to produce but have an appealing action. The most notable aspect of jointed lures is that they wiggle and shimmy wildly because they move with two or three segments rather than as a straight, one-piece body.

All swimming and diving plugs must run true to be effective. They must run straight on the retrieve, not lie on their side or run off at an angle. Some lures do this fresh out of the box, and some don't. If not, they must be modified, or tuned, to make them run true; this is discussed in the basic skills section.

Surface Lures

Also known as topwater lures, surface lures are almost exclusively fished by casting and retrieving, and many require proper manipulation to be effective. They appeal to highly aggressive fish and to species that attack from hiding places or gang up on prey, but not to bottom-dwelling species, true deep-water denizens, and fish that don't hunt near the surface in packs.

Because surface fishing requires aggressive fish behavior, it is more of a warm-water phenomenon than a cold-water one, which also restricts its suitability in many places (summertime for most species, especially in temperate climates). For some species—freshwater bass, for example—surface lures are more effective in shallow water and places with cover than in open deep-water environs. But that depends on the nature of the fish. Some saltwater species may be taken on the surface miles from the nearest shore, when they happen to be feeding on baitfish that have been pushed to the surface.

Anglers find using surface lures highly appealing, since there is the added benefit of watching a fish strike. The keys to successful surface fishing include knowing when and when not to use them; knowing what type to use and how; knowing where to use them; knowing when to switch to other techniques; and being able to put those lures in the position where they will be most productive.

Any lure worked on the surface or fished both on the surface as well as within the first 1 to 3 feet of the surface is part of this category; in a broad sense, dry flies and fly fishing bugs and poppers are also surface lures, but are discussed under flies. Types of surface lures include popping and wobbling plugs, floating/diving plugs and darters, propellered lures, stickbaits, and specialty surface lures.

Specialty surface lures include a number of soft and hard plastic lures that swim through and over heavy cover in fishing for freshwater bass; most imitate frogs or mice (the latter often called "rats"). Soft lures usually have one hook, sometimes a double hook, which rides up, and the lures are buoyant enough to keep the body of the lure atop the surface cover. Many use a silicone skirt or single or double curly tail for some extra action.

Nearly all poppers and chuggers have a concave, scooped-out mouth, and are both noisemakers and attractors; the actual popping or forward chugging motion is made by jerking the rod up or back, not by reeling line in, to achieve the proper movement. Poppers and chuggers come in small sizes for light-tackle casting in freshwater to long heavy versions used in surf casting. Many are short and squat, some are long and slender, and the rear treble hook on many is dressed with bucktail or synthetic material for extra pizzazz.

Wobbling surface plugs are strictly a freshwater lure, mostly used in bass fishing, and less numerous than poppers. Wobblers are characterized by their to-and-fro undulating action, resulting in large part from a wide, spoonlike metal lip or metal side "wings" that rock the lure from side to side.

Floating/diving plugs are generally minnow-shaped and have a small lip that helps bring the lure a short distance beneath the surface when cast and retrieved. They are most effective when worked in a deliberately erratic fashion to imitate a crippled

Surface lures by row, from top to bottom: propellered plugs, soft weedless frogs, walking plugs, and popping plugs.

baitfish. Most are plastic, but some are made of wood, which produces differences in buoyancy.

Propellered surface plugs catch pickerel, pike, inland stripers, and some saltwater fish, but are mostly associated with largemouth and smallmouth bass. These are wooden- or plastic-bodied plugs, generally cigar- or torpedo-shaped, with propellerlike blades both fore and aft, or just aft.

Buzzbaits are also primarily a bass lure. They have either in-line or overhead configuration. The overhead version features an overhead arm with a blade and a lower arm with a lead head and single skirted hook, while the in-line version features a weedless spoon or a bucktail or rubber skirt behind the blade. The revolving "buzz" blade itself is of unique design, vaguely resembling an airplane propeller, with cupped ends that give the lure a clicking, *chop-chop-chop* sound. Unlike a propellered surface plug, a well-designed buzzbait is reasonably weed-free and can be fished effectively in all but dense concentrations of matted vegetation.

Stickbaits are tail-weighted cigar- or torpedo-shaped lures similar to propellered plugs or surface/diving plugs but without a lip or propeller, and which have a pronounced walking or wide-swimming action. When retrieved they dart, splash, and seem to be lurching in and out of the water. Many versions of these lures are called walking plugs. Using a snap or a loop knot with a stickbait is especially important; it allows the line to go back and forth quickly and unimpeded.

Soft Lures

This is a catchall term for a lure or body component of a lure that is made of a soft substance, as opposed to a lure made of metal, wood, or hard plastic. Also called soft baits (as in artificial bait), these are primarily fashioned from soft plastic, but some are produced from soft processed natural food or a combination of both, and a few products are rubber.

Soft lures are not a category of lure per se; they are mostly found as artificial worms, as various body shapes for leadhead jigs, and as trailers or add-ons for a variety of other lures. Some plugs and surface lures have soft bodies as well.

Most soft lures exactly or closely represent some type of natural food. The list is headed by various kinds of worms and small baitfish, and includes eels, leeches, salamanders (often called lizards), frogs, crayfish, hellgrammites, and mice. These are used in freshwater and saltwater; in the latter, most soft lures are used as jig bodies.

Soft lures have a feel that is unmatched by hard lures; in many cases, this means that they may be held by a striking fish for a moment or two longer than a hard lure. Since the strike and rejection of some lures happens in an instant, this extra holding ability can make a difference in catching fish. The use of scents with some soft bodies might have an added measure of appeal to certain fish. They also have the advantage of being relatively inexpensive and easily replaced. Some bodies—especially the fish-shaped products known as swimbaits—also have a swimming action that is not only different but better than that of most hard lures, and often can be fished effectively at a slower pace than hard lures.

Worms. Often called plastic worms, soft worms are artificial wormlike bodies molded from supple synthetic material. Most are made of soft plastic and commonly called plastic worms, but they may be made from other substances as well as imitate other food, such as a leech, snake, eel, or salamander. Soft worms are perhaps the most productive artificial lures for largemouth bass, but they do catch other species and are frequently used as components of other lures.

These lures are fairly substantial in size, have a realistic feel and action, and move naturally through cover, especially when fished along the bottom. They must be properly manipulated to be effective; how the angler gives these lures action, detects strikes, and reacts reflexively to strikes are major factors in their success.

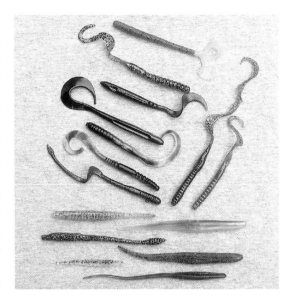

In this assortment of soft worms, the horizontal group includes various jerk worms.

Soft worms may float or sink, and come in all types of tail designs in a whole spectrum of colors and color combinations or patterns. They're made in small, medium, large, and huge sizes. Some are scented, some are oiled, some come prerigged. The most important features, in descending order, are softness, buoyancy, size, body and tail shape, color, and scent.

Rigging methods also vary with soft worms. The weedless Texas rig, in which the hook point is buried in the worm, is favored where there is cover. The (usually) exposed-hook Carolina rig is favored in nonobstructed areas and in deep water. Other rigging options exist as well.

Jerkbaits. A variation on the standard soft worm is a specially balanced model called a jerkbait or jerk worm, which has no built-in swimming action and is fished fairly shallow beneath the surface in a twitching motion. The great majority are used in freshwater for largemouth bass, but some are suitable for saltwater casting in estuaries and shallow flats for striped bass, redfish, and seatrout.

These lures are not as supple as conventional soft worms and are usually fished just under the surface in a pull-pause, slow-jerking type of retrieve, which is different from the way most other soft lures are worked.

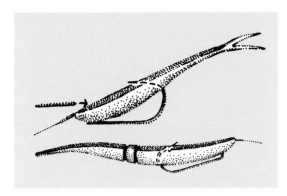

Shown are two common types of soft jerkbaits. Note that in rigging, the point of the hook is pushed through the soft lure, then retracted to just under the surface. Some models are weighted for balance or depth, often with a slender lead weight (top).

Soft jerkbaits are usually rigged without a conventional sinker. They may be fished unweighted for shallow use or may be fished with a thin-diameter 1-inch-length lead stick or nail segment inserted into the head for deeper use, longer casts, and less erratic action. The hook should be deployed in a semi–Texas rig manner, with the point slightly protruding through the wider top (or back) of the bait for better hookups. Hook point placement, and style of hook shank, varies with different baits.

Spinnerbaits

These lures feature one, two, or more spinner blades on an overhead shaft, combined with a lower shaft that has a lead weight and hook covered by a skirt. Primarily cast, spinnerbaits are generally retrieved steadily so that the blades and upper arm run vertically above the bottom part of the lure.

Spinnerbaits are popular bass fishing lures, especially for shallow-water angling, but can be used in deeper water and for a few other freshwater species. They are relatively easy to fish, and fairly weed- and tangle-free when retrieved around cover and obstructions. Although their appearance is unlike natural forage, their flash and vibration draw strikes.

Spinnerbaits are available in a wide range of sizes, from micro to maxi models. The lightest ones, in $1/16$- to $3/16$-ounce sizes, are used with light line and light spinning tackle, primarily for bluegills and crappie, but also for smaller specimens of largemouth and smallmouth bass, plus

white bass. Small spinnerbaits usually feature a single blade on the overhead shaft and a soft grub-shaped body rather than a multi-tentacled skirt. For the most part, these are fished in shallow areas and near the surface.

The weight of a spinnerbait is in large part determined by the size of the head on the lower shaft. This is essentially a lead jig head, and is usually tapered to facilitate swimming. On small spinnerbaits, that head may be rounded, like a ball-head jig, but for most bass models it is shaped more like a cone or bullet. Some heads may be turned up slightly to resist diving and enhance upward or shallow movement, especially on a fast retrieve.

Spinnerbaits principally feature Colorado, Indiana, and willowleaf design blades, or hybrid versions of these basic styles. The Colorado is between round and pear-shaped and is generally believed to produce the most vibration, although this is a function of how much it is cupped. The more cupping there is to the blade, the greater the vibration. The common size is No. 4, which is roughly the size of a quarter, but the range is from No. 2 to the magnum No. 8. Colorado blades are often found on single-blade spinnerbaits. They are good for slow retrieves, murky water, and dark conditions. A small Colorado may precede a larger willowleaf blade on a tandem spinnerbait.

Indiana blades are teardrop-shaped and produce good vibration, too, though they spin faster, and work well on tandem blade lures. They too are used in combination with other blade types, either in front of a willowleaf or behind a Colorado. Willowleaf blades, shaped as the name implies and coming to a sharply tapered tail point, were less commonly used in the past but are now extremely popular. These long blades are mainly used on a tandem rig with a big No. 4 or 5 willowleaf, usually in silver or copper, behind a smaller Indiana blade; however, willowleaf blades can be used in tandem or as a single, and are preferred in the magnum sizes (up to No. 8) for big fish. The willowleaf doesn't offer as much vibration as other types of blades, but it revolves freely and produces a lot of flash. It is an attention getter, especially when hammered or fluted or spiced with light-bouncing colors.

The style or combination of blades to use may be a reflection of where and how you fish. Tandem

Spinnerbaits come in a variety of configurations, with differing blades, lead heads, and body colors.

angled designs), as does the color of the head and body. Various metals may be used for the head, although lead is by far the most common and its use is partly why many people refer to this type of lure as a leadhead. Head size primarily determines weight, which is normally between $1/8$ ounce and 2 ounces but can be several ounces more or down to $1/64$ ounce.

A jig is one type of lure that cuts across species, since some type or size of jig has near-universal appeal to the widest possible range of gamefish. Its other virtues include the fact that it is aerodynamic and casts very well, it sinks quickly so it gets down in the water column fairly fast, and it can be effective in cold and warm water alike. Nevertheless, at rest jigs don't closely resemble fish, insects, or other aquatic forage, so success with them is directly proportional to the angler's ability to impart action to them, effect a proper retrieval, and detect strikes.

The generic categories of jigs, based upon their dressing, are jig and pork/eel combinations, which are popularly used in freshwater bass fishing, and jigs with hair, synthetic, or soft plastic bodies, which are available in all sizes and used widely in both freshwater and saltwater. Both types are fished differently and have distinct characteristics and applications.

Pork rind has been used for years as a jig garnish, starting with strips and continuing with shaped chunks. These combinations have proven versatile and especially effective for largemouth and smallmouth bass. Pork strips are made of pork rind that has been stripped of fat. Chunks have a layer of fat on them, giving them bulk and weight in addition to different action.

Conventional jigs come in various head styles, featuring bucktail or synthetic hair bodies, or soft plastic bodies. Jigs with a bucktail dressing are commonly called bucktails or bucktail jigs, and are popular in large sizes, especially in saltwater, because they have good bulking characteristics and display movement well.

Soft plastic bodies are more abundant and can be attached to the hook of a jig for use as is or in combination with a hair or synthetic body. They come in many styles. Some are in the form of hellgrammite, crayfish, or shad imitations; others are spider-legged or shaped like a tube or grub. Many are simply long and

spinnerbaits are generally meant for speedy retrieval. A twin willowleaf combination is the best for pure quick retrieving, and a willowleaf-Colorado combination is for more intermediate retrieval. To get a slow retrieve, especially in shallow water, you need a blade that grabs a lot of water and spins well. This might be a Colorado combination, or more likely a single Colorado blade, perhaps of large size.

Although some anglers use tandem blades for deep fishing, their effectiveness there is primarily when being retrieved rather than when falling, because the blades usually get tangled on the drop and don't rotate. Try spinnerbaits that produce more vibration when the water is turbid or when it is cold, and spinnerbaits that produce more flash when the water is clear or when it is warm.

Jigs

Jigs are artificial lures with a metal head molded to a single hook. The hook shank is never fished plain and may be dressed with fur, feathers, pork rind, rubber, soft plastic, or other synthetic materials, and occasionally with live or dead natural bait. In some cases these materials are permanent; in others they're removable and easily replaceable.

The shape of the head varies widely (primarily variations of oval, ball, bullet, pancake, and

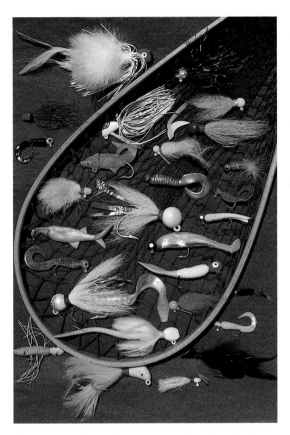

Jigs are manufactured in a variety of weights, bodies, and colors.

curly, somewhat like a worm, snake, eel, leech, and so on.

Grubs and tubes are probably the top soft plastic body forms for jigs used in freshwater fishing; in saltwater these and longer eel-like bodies are equally popular. Grub bodies are solid and either flat-tailed or curl-tailed; they are threaded onto the hook from the head and have a tight, well-defined action if rigged properly. Tube jigs are hollow with many squidlike legs in lieu of a tail; a tube jig head is worked through the body from back to front with only the line-tie hook exposed; the jig has an erratic action when fished on a drop-and-fall.

The weight of the jig itself is the most important aspect in fishing it. Choice should be dependent upon the depth of the water and its clarity, plus wind conditions, the strength of the line used, and the type of jig.

A few lures are a cross between a spoon and a leadhead jig, and are mainly used for vertical jigging, though they are sometimes fished in a standard cast-and-retrieve manner. A few of these

are primarily thin metal bodies, called blade baits by some anglers; they may be vertically jigged or fished on a cast-settle-jig-settle-jig manner for white bass, smallmouth bass, largemouth bass, and panfish. Likewise, some lures, called tailspinners, have a rounded lead body and a spinning blade on the tail; they are fished similarly to the thin-bodied baits.

As a group, these lures are sometimes called jump baits, meaning that they are primarily used in quick-casting to schools of surface-feeding white bass, largemouth bass, and striped bass, although the same can be said for various spinners, casting spoons, and vertical jigging spoons.

There are also some balanced jigging lures, made of metal and used for vertical fishing in a different manner than jigging spoons. The lead bodies of these lie horizontally instead of vertically in the water when fished, and have their line tie on top just behind the head. These are used in open-water deep jigging as well as in ice fishing.

Saltwater Trolling Lures

In saltwater fishing there are many lures used for trolling that have no casting or jigging application because they're too large, too hard-pulling, or too cumbersome for anything but trolling. These special items are used for roaming vast areas of water, and in some cases with the heavier tackle that is often demanded for really big fish.

Saltwater trolling lures include offshore lures, feathers and trolling jigs, teasers, and tubes, many distinctive items but some closely related to the others or fished in conjunction with one another.

Offshore lures. Also called blue-water lures, big-game lures, and trolling lures, offshore lures are specialized items meant strictly for such offshore game as billfish, tuna, wahoo, and dolphin, usually at speeds that no other lure is capable of handling and under a range of sea conditions.

Offshore lures are fished either on the surface or under but fairly close to the surface. Unlike rigged natural dead baits used in trolling, they are readily available and require one-time rigging.

A distinguishing characteristic of offshore lures is their ability and effectiveness—some would call it necessity—to be trolled at high speeds. High speeds in offshore fishing go way beyond the higher speeds that are used in most other forms of trolling, being on average in the 8 to 10 knots range, but on the low end starting at 5 knots and on the high end going into the upper teens (with some reports of offshore trolling lures catching fish up to 24 knots).

Surface runners create a silvery trail of bubbles, produce a lot of surface commotion, and especially appeal to fish that strike from the side, like marlin. Underwater runners generally swim in a straight or near-straight manner, not far under the surface, and especially appeal to fish that strike from beneath, such as tuna or wahoo.

Offshore lures mainly consist of a weighted head and a synthetic tail or skirt; the face of the head has one of the following shapes: cone, slanted, flat, and concave. Most heads are made of durable hard plastic and the skirts from soft plastic or vinyl; some have soft heads.

Cone-shaped faces are also called bullet faces and swimmers, and they have a narrow point to provide minimal water resistance. These run underwater and are usually weighted; they primarily run straight, but some versions swim from side to side. Slanted or angled faces provide a moderate amount of water resistance, less than flat models but more than cone-shaped faces. These lures track straight when trolled fast, and create quite a commotion in the water, moving up and down as well as diving.

A flat-faced lure provides a lot of water resistance and a big bubble trail but without

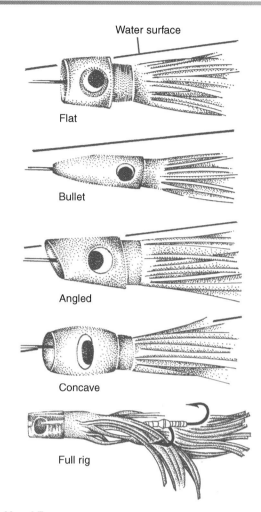

Head Types

the motion of other lures. This style of surface lure handles a wide range of speeds, although it can fly out of the water in rough seas. Concave-faced lures, also called chuggers, track well and are designed for rough water; the cupped or dished face digs into the water so that it doesn't fly out. It pulls the water so well that it is also useful in calm or light sea conditions.

Feathers and trolling jigs. These are weighted trolling lures that can be fished hookless as single teasers or part of a daisy chain, or they can be run with hooks as lures unto themselves. The heads are either metal or plastic covering lead, and the skirts are made of colorful feathers.

Trolling feathers are perhaps the single most popular offshore trolling lure, and are fished for dolphin, various small tuna, wahoo, and other species that may rise from the depths to feed just below the surface.

Assorted offshore trolling lures.

Feathers consist of a head, often weighted, in front of a binding over feathers as a skirt, all holed to allow the leader to pass through to rigged hooks, which nestle within the trailing end of the feathers. Other lures are similar to feathers, sporting soft plastic bodies and streamerlike skirts, and are fished in a similar manner.

Trolling jigs are lures with cone-, bullet-, or torpedo-head shapes, usually dressed with feather skirts or hooks, some of which have little or no practical value for vertical or deep jigging. They include cedar jigs and leadheads, and their single hook, which is part of the body or attached to it, may be adorned with a strip of pork rind or leathery fish flesh.

Both feathers and trolling jigs are smaller on average than other trolling lures, but move over and through the water easily. They may also be effective at slower speeds when an angler works them occasionally with a quick, jerking rod action.

Teasers. Teasers are hookless lurelike devices designed to be trolled and create commotion in the water to attract gamefish to rigged baits or lures that follow the teaser. These are mainly offshore fishing devices used for pelagic species, particularly billfish and to a lesser extent tuna.

There are many kinds of teasers, and they're made from assorted materials and in varied shapes. The most common are hard or soft conventional single teasers, trolling birds, and daisy chains.

Single teasers have large molded bodies of hard or soft plastic or hardened foam; they dive and dart, occasionally rising to the surface to grab air and smoke a churning bubble trail in their wake. They may be nothing more than giant Kona head lures, or chuggers with broad faces, or they may be fancy affairs with air-grabbing holes drilled in their faces or flashing mirrors glued to their flanks.

Many experienced trollers favor soft teasers because the fish seem to hold on to them longer and are more likely to return to them because they feel like natural bait. While the objective is not to catch fish on these hookless teasers, the fact that they are soft is more likely to cause a fish that strikes one to return to take a hooked lure that is following in the spread.

Trolling birds are bird- or airplane-shaped trolling teasers. These specialized teasers are designed to be dragged hookless behind the boat, or rigged in-line on the fishing line itself, and placed one leader length in front of the lure. They come in sizes from 4½ to 13 inches long and attract attention by creating a unique surface-splashing action.

A daisy chain is a combination of natural or artificial teasers rigged together in-line and trolled separately or on a fishing line. Artificial daisy chains mainly consist of a string of lures, birds, or soft plastic baits (usually squid but sometimes other body types). These are primarily dragged hookless behind the boat on a heavy cord like a standard single teaser.

Tubes. Tubes are long, slender, hollow trolling lures made with rubber or plastic tubing. They have a lead head, which may or may not have eyes, and two hooks that are attached to a wire leader that runs through the tubing; one hook is placed midway along the tube body and the other is at the tail. Trolling tube lures range from 5 to 18 inches long, imitate eels or long sandworms, and are top lures for striped bass, bluefish, and barracuda.

8

Natural Bait, Hooks, and Terminal Tackle

W hile rods, reels, line, lures, and flies get a dispropor-
tionate share of attention from anglers, natural bait,
hooks (which are used with bait as well as lures)
and terminal tackle such as sinkers, snaps, split rings,
and swivels are also critical fishing tools.

Natural Bait

In the most strict, narrow, and accurate sense as used by anglers, the
term "bait" refers to any natural or processed food that is used to catch
fish; this is distinguished from a lure, which, through popular usage, has
come to mean any man-made object that represents or imitates food.

Generally, food that is normally eaten by a particular fish is preferred
by anglers as hooked bait for that fish, primarily impaled on a single
hook, sometimes on a treble hook, and in some cases fished as part of a

multicomponent bottom rig. Natural bait is used popularly in both freshwater and saltwater and includes a wide array of items that are used whole live, whole dead, in pieces, or chunked/ground for chum. These include, but are not limited to, alewives, anchovies, ballyhoo, bunker (mossbunker or menhaden), butterfish, chubs, clams, corn, crabs, crayfish, crickets, eel, eggs, frogs, grubs, grasshoppers, hellgrammites, herring, killifish, leeches, mackerel, maggots, minnows, mullet, mussels, pilchards, pinfish, porgy, salamanders (waterdog), sand eels, sardines, sculpin, seaworms, shad, shiners, shrimp, silversides, smelt, spearing, squid, suckers, sunfish, waxworms, whiting, and assorted earthworms.

Some miscellaneous freshwater natural baits include caddis larvae for stream trout; mayflies for trout, crappies, and so on; bluegills for striped bass (where legal); grass shrimp for panfish; perch eyes for tipping on a jig when ice fishing for yellow perch; cisco, whitefish, and other large species fished alive for northern pike; and chunks or strips of fish meat, for tipping on a jig, especially for lake trout, or behind a spoon for pickerel or pike, or in some instances, dead-bait bottom fishing for assorted species (pike, lake trout, catfish, sturgeon).

Most live baits are hooked through the head or lips (tail for crayfish) for casting and freelining,

but through the midsection for stillfishing with or without a float. A float is a lightweight surface-floating device attached to the fishing line for indicating a subsurface bite or strike by a fish. It is often called a bobber, which is rounded plastic, and sometimes a cork, although the better modern floats are primarily made of balsa.

Bait must be presented properly to be effective. This includes the physical appearance as well as the movement or, in some cases, lack of movement. Natural bait is generally fished in a more passive manner than lures, because the target fish have time to watch it, smell it, and perhaps touch it before striking. If it moves in a swift or unnatural manner, it may cause alarm, although a natural bait that appears to be struggling, as many do when hooked, can in itself be attractive to a predator because it appears more vulnerable and easier to capture.

There are some exceptions to this slow-fishing mantra, however, such as when live bait is trolled below the surface or when rigged dead bait is pulled over the surface for pelagic species, although these tactics are still designed to represent natural prey actions. Another exception is when a live natural bait is hooked on a jig and fished more actively than it would be if fished alone.

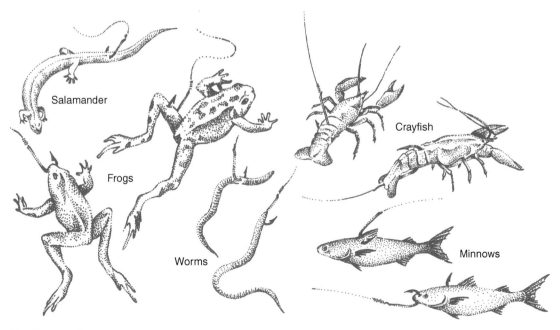

Freshwater Live Baits

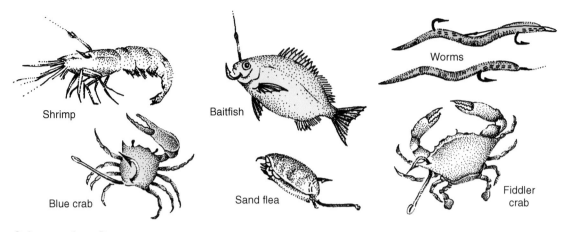

Shrimp

Baitfish

Worms

Blue crab

Sand flea

Fiddler crab

Saltwater Live Baits

Where live bait is used, liveliness is vital. Many fish aren't interested in inactive or dead bait, so it's important to keep your bait as fresh and vigorous as possible. Change live bait whenever the current offering seems to be losing its vitality, and make sure that it acts naturally. A crayfish that rolls instead of crawls, for example, or a minnow that doesn't swim energetically, lessens the chance of success.

Hooks

A fishhook is truly an indispensable piece of sportfishing equipment. In sportfishing use, hooks are stand-alone equipment used with various types of natural or processed bait; they are attached as is or with dressing to an extremely diverse range of hard and soft artificial lures; they are dressed with various materials to become artificial flies; and they are used in molds for the construction of lead and hard-metal lures. Today there is an astounding array of hooks in production—many quite similar and many vastly different—and the number of patterns and sizes is impressive and confusing. The array of hooks is due to fishing methods, the differing mouths of fish, and the lures and bait used to attract them.

The majority of fishhooks are made from high-carbon steel; a good number are made from stainless steel, and some are made from alloys. The physical parts of a hook include the eye, shank, bend, point, gap, and throat. The point may have a barb, and the eye may actually be flattened solid instead of having an eyelike opening.

There are three commonly accepted hook types, described according to the number of points. These are characterized as single, double, or treble hooks.

Single hooks are the most common hook and the overwhelming favorite for fishing with most types of bait; they are used on all but a tiny percentage of artificial flies and are attached to many types of lures. Double hooks are by far the least common type; they are mainly used in tying artificial flies, but some are employed in baitfishing, and some are fastened to weedless lures. Treble hooks are very popular on a wide range of lures, which are prerigged by lure manufacturers; they are almost never used in fly tying and are only occasionally fished with bait.

Patterns

The name by which a style of hook is known is called a pattern. This is a function of its bend, which is the curved section between the point

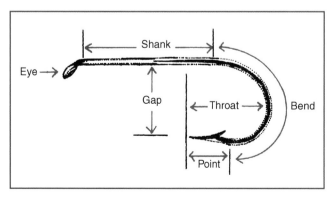

Eye

Shank

Gap

Throat

Bend

Point

Hook Features

and the shank. The bend has a lot to do with the strength of the hook. Ideally a hook should resist bending up to a stage where it would almost break, preferably bending instead of breaking.

Resistance to direct-pull pressure is influenced by hook style and size, is substantially aided by forging, and is related to the bite and gap. The gap is the distance between the tip of the point and the shank. The distance from the peak of the bend to the gap is known as the bite or throat. Most hooks have a deep or relatively deep bite and a fairly wide gap, both of which keep hooked fish more secure than a shallow bite or narrow gap.

Most hooks avoid having a sharp angle to the bend and are formed such that the initial stage of the bend is gradual and the final stage is pronounced. This design is actually less easily bent than a symmetrically round one.

Popular patterns and attributes include:

Sproat	Straight point; popular with flies and lures.
Kirby	Offset point helps prevent hook from slipping out; good for baitfishing.
O'Shaughnessy	Outward bend to the tip of the point; heavy wire; many applications.
Aberdeen	Light wire, round bend good for use with minnows; will bend before breaking.
Carlisle	Stronger than Aberdeen; used with bait; long shank prevents fish from swallowing the hook.
Siwash	Heavy wire; extra-long point offers good retention; used for big, active fish.
Salmon egg	Short shank; concealed by small bait.
Claw or beak	Point is offset and curved inward to aid penetration; used often with bait.
Limerick	Long shank, wide bend provides extra hooking space.
Circle	Inward-curved hook point; excellent for catch-and-release; hooks fish in corner of mouth.

There are many more patterns, of course, and many with very specialized applications. Freshwater bass anglers, for example, have such an affinity for fishing with soft lures, especially worms, that there is a whole genre of wide-gap worm and stickbait hooks, as well as models with various humps and bends to the shanks.

One of the more specialized hooks is a circle hook, which has become very popular in saltwater baitfishing, especially for tuna, but now is also found on fly hooks and used in a wide array of saltwater and freshwater applications. The circle hook has a wide bend and long inward point that at first glance makes you wonder how it could ever stick a fish, but not only does it avoid stomach and throat penetration and stick the fish in the corner of the mouth, it also doesn't need a hard hookset (a solid pull is preferred), so a greater number of fish are hooked and landed. Moreover, there is an exceptional conservation benefit to using circle hooks and being able to release fish unharmed.

Size

No matter what the pattern, hooks are all designated according to size, which in principle is the

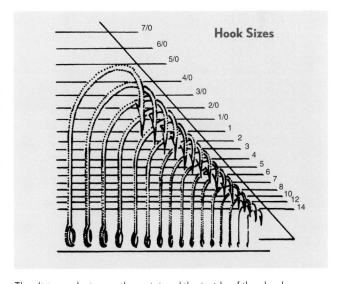

The distance between the point and the inside of the shank, known as the gap, determines hook size. Large hooks (1/0 to 7/0) increase in size as the number increases. Small hooks (1 to 14 and beyond) decrease in size as the number increases, and come in many smaller sizes than are depicted here. This illustration is based on a standard, popular American bait hook, the rolled-point, forged Eagle Claw No. 084. Hook sizes appear here slightly smaller than actual scale.

width of the gap. This is just a relative designation, however, instead of an absolute one. Gap width may differ between families of hooks, and there is no consistency between manufacturers in sizing.

Sizes are specified in whole numbers at the smaller end of the spectrum and as "aught" fractions as they get larger. The smallest hooks, depending on manufacturer, are No. 32, 30, or 28; the largest hooks range from 14/0 up to 19/0.

Gauge

Although not reflected in size designations, the diameter of the wire used to make the hook has a bearing on its performance and its proper use. This diameter is reached in manufacturing by taking steel wire rods and reducing them to the wire gauge that is necessary for a particular pattern.

There are fine, medium, and heavy wire gauges corresponding to relative diameter. Heavy wire is used in making hooks for the strongest applications and for situations where it is beneficial for a hook to sink fast (large wet flies, for example, or big-game baitfishing); fine wire is used in making hooks for light-line fishing, angling with small and delicate bait, and in slow-sinking or floating uses; and medium wire is used for general-purpose hooks.

Finish

In the manufacturing process, different finishes are applied to hooks to provide either cosmetic value or corrosion resistance. Some carbon steel hooks are given color varnishes or lacquers; these are mainly blue, black, bronze, green, and red, but fluorescent and luminescent colors are also applied. Tin, cadmium, nickel, black nickel, gold, and chrome/zinc platings are applied to other carbon steel hooks. Most stainless steel hooks receive no finishing after being polished.

Obviously the ability of hooks to withstand corrosion varies, particularly in saltwater, and is an important aspect of selection. No finish is completely rustproof. As a material, carbon steel is significantly less resistant to corrosion than stainless steel or cadmium-tin and chrome-zinc.

Terminal Tackle

Terminal tackle is a broad term for the individual and collective equipment used at the end of a fishing line. The major and most widely employed components of this are sinkers, snaps, split rings, and swivels.

Sinkers. Metal fishing weights used to sink a lure or bait, sinkers come in many different shapes and sizes, and have diverse applications. They are employed in freshwater and saltwater and primarily used for fishing with lightweight objects, especially natural bait.

Sinkers are made from a number of metals. They were once virtually all made of lead, and most sinkers in North America still are; however, an increasing number are being made from other materials due to toxicity concerns, and because prohibitions exist for the use or sale of lead sinkers of certain sizes in some places. This has led to the development of nontoxic small sinkers made of brass, steel, tin, and tungsten.

In an overall sense, there are fixed and free-sliding sinkers. Fixed versions attach directly to a fishing line or leader (dropper line) by being pinched, twisted, or tied; they move whenever the bait or lure moves and when a fish takes the bait or lure. Free-sliding, or slip, sinkers ride along the line; they are used almost exclusively with bait and allow the line to move when a fish takes the bait without moving the sinker, which provides less resistance than a fixed sinker and may be preferable for shy or light-biting fish.

Obviously, heavier sinkers are needed the deeper you fish, the greater the wind pushes you

Sinkers

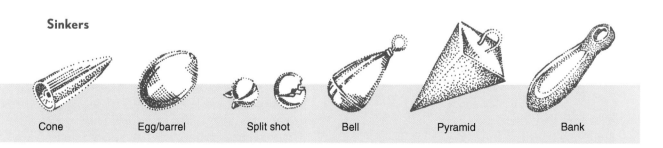

Cone   Egg/barrel   Split shot   Bell   Pyramid   Bank

while drifting, the faster you troll, or the faster the current. A golden rule for using sinkers is to use the lightest sinker that you can get away with and still fish in the necessary manner or place.

In addition to weight, sinker shape has an effect on casting, sink rate, and ability to hold bottom. Bulky sinkers are least castable and offer most air resistance; bottom-heavy sinkers offer the most accuracy because they don't roll over in the air. Streamlined and compact sinkers have the best sink rate, which is of special interest in current and partially explains why split shot is so popular in rivers and streams. Split shot is good for resisting snagging in current, because it rolls over rocky bottoms. In stillwater or where there is a soft bottom with light current, a sinker with a rounded bottom is adequate, but where there is heavier current or surf action, an angled sinker that digs into the bottom is necessary.

Snaps. Snaps are metal connectors that are knotted to the fishing line and attached to the wire line-tie loop of a lure or to a split ring that is fixed to that loop. They are used to enhance the action of some spoons and floating/diving plugs, and make it easy to change lures quickly without having to retie knots.

Though convenient, snaps lead to problems and should only be used if really necessary. Poor-quality snaps, or light snaps used with too heavy tackle, are the main causes of problems. Though you should generally use the size of snap that complements the lure and line diameter, strength is a function of size and thickness of the metal. It is misguided economy to use thin metal snaps—especially the common two-piece safety snaps that are cheap and popularly used in freshwater—so avoid these or replace them on lures or rigs that come equipped with them.

Strength and ease of use are also functions of the locking design. The safety snap model, which has a sharp bend and doesn't really lock (the tag end sits in a guarded channel), is one of the poorest snaps but cheap and commonly used. A similar two-piece snap is the interlock (or lock snap) model, which is only slightly better because the tag end rests in a guarded channel and tucks around the edge for more holding power. Both of these are subject to failure after repeated opening and closing.

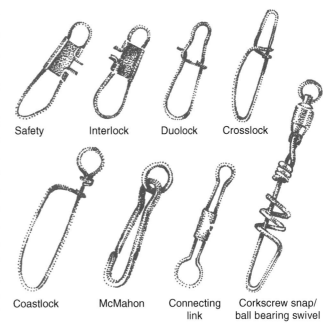

Safety   Interlock   Duolock   Crosslock

Coastlock   McMahon   Connecting link   Corkscrew snap/ ball bearing swivel

Snaps

One-piece all-wire snaps in which the tempered wire wraps around itself are better than the previous items. The common duolock model has a double-end opening that allows attachment to two items with closed eye rings; this is a good, moderately priced, easy-to-use connector. This snap is used by many freshwater anglers when tied to spoons and plugs, and is favored because of its rounded bend.

Another popular and strong model is the crosslock, which has double ends that meet on the same plane and abut each other; the bend is less rounded, however, so it does not maximize action for some lures. Other types that are especially popular in saltwater include the coastlock snap, which has a single-opening end that is especially strong and common on many big-game swivels; the tournament snap, which is similar to but stronger than the coastlock; the heavy-duty corkscrew snap; and the McMahon snap, a dual-grip model.

As for color or finish, some anglers prefer flat black, others silver and gold. Silver and gold colors sometimes help attract fish, which is viewed positively by many freshwater anglers and negatively by most saltwater anglers. Fish attracted to the snap may strike ahead of the lure instead of at the body of the lure where the hooks are; in bigger and toothier saltwater species, this may result in cutoffs.

Split rings. A split ring is a small steel ring with two spiral turns. Similar to a key ring but smaller, split rings are primarily used to connect the closed eye of hooks to a closed wire loop on a lure and to serve as a line-tie connector to certain lures. In the latter capacity, split rings are used with many spoons, being connected to the line-tie hole at the head of the lure, and with most floating/diving plugs, being connected to the wire loop at the head or on the lip. Split rings are used in place of open rings, where a gap in the ends can allow a hook eye to slip out, and in place of solid rings, which prohibit easy hook changing.

Anglers often add split rings to some lures that don't have them in the line-tie area to improve their action; this is best for lures that don't incur twist and for which the line can be directly knotted to the split ring. Split rings are also changed when lure hooks are changed or if the ring spirals spread apart under pressure. To give added action to a lure or to move the hook a little farther away, you can add one or two split rings between the hook eye and the body wire loop.

When split ring spirals are out of alignment, the ring has lost its strength and should be replaced; you're likely to lose the lure to a strong fish or a snag unless you change the ring.

Split rings are available in a range of sizes and should be used in a size that complements the lure and hook. However, a split ring can be the weakest link in the angler-to-fish scenario. If the rated breaking strength of a split ring is 12 pounds, for example, and you're using 20-pound line, it's possible that you could open up the spirals of the ring, and lose the lure and/or fish, when maximum pressure is applied. It is unlikely that you will know the breaking strength of most split rings when they are preattached to a lure or when buying them in bulk, but you can test them with a heavy-duty spring scale.

Swivels and snap-swivels. A swivel is a freely turning metal connector meant to prevent twist in fishing line that would otherwise be caused by the action of a lure, bait, or sinker. Swivels are used by themselves in connecting two lines or a line

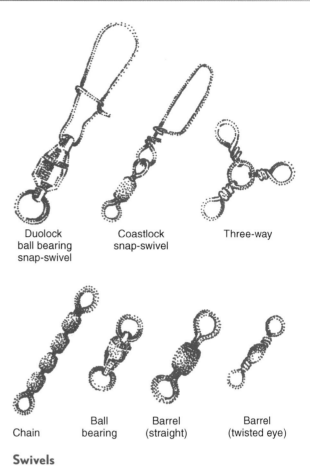

Duolock ball bearing snap-swivel

Coastlock snap-swivel

Three-way

Chain

Ball bearing

Barrel (straight)

Barrel (twisted eye)

Swivels

and one or more leaders, or used in conjunction with a snap, in which case the combined entity is known as a snap-swivel. Swivels without a snap are not attached directly to a hook.

Swivels can cause problems by breaking or by failing to actually swivel, and should only be used if really necessary. Poor-quality swivels, or light swivels used with too heavy tackle, are the main causes of problems. They can be the weakest link in the angler-to-fish scenario due to their strength. If the rated breaking strength of a swivel is less than the fishing line, it's possible that you could break the swivel and lose the lure and/or fish when maximum pressure is applied. Most swivels are relatively strong, so this is less likely to be a problem with them than with snaps or split rings.

Swivels used without a snap are slide bearing or ball bearing. Most slide-bearing swivels are of the two-way barrel, the chain, or the three-way dropper variety. The bearing surface of these types of swivels—the strand and curved barrel or ring body—slide against each other and, when subjected to linear tension and torque, become deformed and bind, thereby negating their effectiveness.

Barrel swivels that have a twisted and single-strand head are the cheapest and poorest style available, and often unreliable. A little better in performance, because they're less prone to binding, are barrel swivels that have a straight and double-strand head; these are sometimes called crane swivels. Both of these styles are made of brass, and are used singly or as part of a snap-swivel. Three-way swivels are made of brass and feature three twisted and single-strand rings equally spaced on a central ring. These are used to separate bait or lure from sinker via separate leaders. They are even more subject to binding than similar-quality barrel swivels and rarely swivel well.

A chain swivel is a series of barrel-like swivels with an eye at each end; the better ones are made of stainless steel, are less prone to binding than barrel swivels, and are mainly used in conjunction with trolling sinkers. A dropper-line arrangement exists with some models that have a second chain attached to the middle of them, forming a T-shaped setup.

Although brass barrel swivels are the most commonly used swivels, especially among freshwater anglers, they are not nearly as functional as ball bearing swivels, which are much more expensive but greatly superior in operation and reliability. The rings of the best-quality ball bearing swivels rotate freely due to highly polished stainless steel ball bearings and tapered design. These may be solid rings or split rings.

A snap-swivel is strictly intended for attaching an artificial lure directly to a line, or leader to an artificial lure. It is only used with some spoons, and with spinners (especially when trolling or when retrieving these lures in current), and is unnecessary with other lures. Snap-swivels are distinct from snaps in function, even though they may be used together. Swivels used with a snap are always barrel-shaped, with closed-eye rings at both ends; snaps may be of various design.

The same issues that apply to swivels and to snaps apply to the combined product. Preventing twist is their primary purpose, with a secondary one of providing a convenient means of quick attachment and detachment. Lures that do not need both of these (which is the majority of them) should not be fished with a snap-swivel. It is one more piece of equipment that can cause a problem, and may be the weakest part of the terminal tackle. Moreover, it can inhibit the action of some lures.

It's best to tie your line directly to a lure whenever you can, and to change knots when putting new lures on. However, some situations demand the use of snap-swivels, and these should be of the highest quality in terms of strength and durability in both the snap and the swivel.

As with other terminal tackle, it is best to use the smallest size of swivel or snap-swivel that is compatible with the size of lure, strength of line, and type of fishing to be done.

9

Accessories

There are likely thousands of accessories available in catalogs and on the store shelves of major sporting goods suppliers. Some of these accessories—such as electric motors, sonar, and downriggers—are viewed as virtually indispensable tools by their users. A diverse group of the most significant accessories is described here.

General Accessories

Lure and Tackle Storage

There are a host of versatile ways to store lures and terminal tackle. The type of storage to use largely depends on the amount and size of objects that you need to store. Many people who do a lot of angling and/or who fish for various species keep several boxes or storage systems, often organized by lure types or tackle by species. For all but a relatively few anglers, the one common denominator in tackle storage is portability.

Traditional portable storage systems evolved from wooden to metal to rigid plastic boxlike containers with pivoting, compartmented trays. They are known as tackle boxes. Most tackle boxes now have movable compartment dividers that allow you to fashion the number and size of storage compartments to suit your needs.

The realm of items in which to hold tackle has vastly expanded from large boxes to a potpourri of storage systems, many suited to specialized

This display represents some of the box, tray, and satchel possibilities for lure storage.

applications, and with an accent on individual traylike plastic utility boxes of varying size stored within soft-sided carriers or satchels. Plastic utility boxes are easy to care for and come in a great range of designs; they fit into a variety of soft-sided, and sometimes waterproof, carrying bags.

A few small metal boxes, particularly small, pocket-size aluminum models used to store flies, are still in use, and even some wooden ones. Leather, suede, nylon, and cloth tackle satchels or wallets are also available, as well as flexible, foldable tackle systems made of dense sailcloth with compartments covered by vinyl.

Wading anglers who are mobile need something that can be worn instead of toted. Enter the fishing vest, a multipocketed and compartmented tackle storage system that is worn over shirt or jacket and predominantly used by flycasters and river and stream anglers. Full-length versions are standard, but shorter models are used by deep-water waders and float-tube anglers. Both have many pockets, some designed especially to hold specific items, and are intended for the storage of many small items; they even include a pouch in the back for small fish.

For waders, alternatives to vests are rigid chest boxes, soft chest packs, and soft fanny packs, which may not hold as much but are the utmost in light portability.

Pliers

Pliers are nearly indispensable tools for a host of applications in fishing and boating. A wide variety of pliers is used for such common and important purposes as cutting fishing line, heavy leaders, and wire; unhooking fish; pulling on knots; pinching lead weights or sinkers; crimping connector sleeves; and tightening bolts. Most pliers come with sheaths that are worn on a belt so they are immediately handy; sheaths should keep pliers snug but be open for fast access.

For the most part, the tool needs of freshwater anglers are different from those of saltwater anglers; the former predominantly use light nylon monofilament lines, and the latter are likely to cut heavier material, crimp hard objects, and grasp and unhook large and thick hooks. Freshwater anglers generally are well served with standard needle nose pliers, for example, which are very popular for unhooking fish and used in conjunction with nail clippers for cutting line and trimming fishing knots. Pliers with side cutters are also useful, and multipurpose utility pliers—those with knife blades, screwdriver blades, awl, and so on—are also favored by many people for general use, although they are generally not as well suited for heavy-duty uses, especially in saltwater applications, as specialty pliers.

From a fishing perspective, the major concerns with pliers are durability, ability to stay sharp, performance at cutting fishing line and wire, and ability to crimp objects such as sleeves and sinkers. Pliers with side-cutting blades are generally preferred for wire and most monofilaments except the lighter strengths; models with spring-loaded jaws, which keep them open when at rest, are favored by many users. Anglers who regularly make up wire or nylon monofilament leaders and fishing rigs must have a top-quality pair of crimping pliers to do the proper job because crimping the retaining sleeves, not simply crushing them, is essential.

Temperature Gauge

One of the most important aids for anglers is a temperature gauge. For many types of fishing, including shallow spring angling in freshwater, deep-water fishing, big-lake trolling for salmon and trout, and offshore fishing for pelagic saltwater species, the ability to find preferred temperatures is a big help in catching fish.

You can use a stand-alone surface temperature gauge on a boat, with the sensor mounted on the transom, or you can use a handheld pool thermometer, or a combination temp/sonar or temp/speed electronic instrument. Many sonar devices have optional temperature and speed sensors, and the unit displays these measurements whenever the sonar is on. These devices read only surface temperature, but they are particularly valuable in the spring and fall when water temperature is changing on a daily basis.

Small clip-on thermometers or pool thermometers are available for waders, tubers, shore anglers, and small-boat anglers who wish to check the surface water temperature. To check temperature at greater depths, tie a pool thermometer to a snap, lower it to a specific depth on fishing line, leave it for a few minutes, then reel it up quickly. Or tie it to a downrigger weight and lower it with the weight to a known depth, let it stay for a few minutes, then raise it quickly.

For some deep-water trolling, it is helpful to constantly check deep-water temperature. This can be done using electronic equipment featuring remote-operating probes that are attached to a downrigger weight.

Scale

A scale for weighing fish is one of the most popular accessories for anglers. Handheld scales are of the spring variety, and they have exterior incremental markings to show weight or depict weight on some type of readout. They are notoriously variable and, with few exceptions, are best for getting a "ballpark" estimate of the weight of a fish. Some, however, are surprisingly accurate—enough to be used for record purposes if certifiable.

If absolute weight is a concern for any reason, it's a good idea to verify the ability of a given scale by checking it against a known weight, so you'll know if it's off the mark and by how much. A fish that may be a world record must be weighed on a certified scale, however.

Landing Devices

Landing net. Used for capturing individual hooked fish, a landing net is a mesh bag mounted on a wooden or metal frame with a handle. This is an important and regularly used accessory for freshwater anglers, from stream trout waders to big-water boaters, but a less

A good net is an important accessory for landing fish, like this coho salmon caught near Tofino, British Columbia.

frequently used accessory for saltwater anglers, mostly for smaller fish in bays and shallows.

Stream nets for trout have a short handle and small hoop diameter for use with small fish, while boat nets have longer handles and larger hoops. The farther one has to reach, the longer the handle needed; however, the heavier the fish you may catch, the sturdier the handle necessary. A few nets incorporate a scale into the handle in order to weigh a fish that has been netted.

For small-boat fishing, a net that is at least 4 feet long from net rim to handle butt, with a wide rim and a deep net bag, is a popular choice. For very big fish in big water and boats with a high freeboard, a 6-foot handle is better. Most nets feature aluminum handles and frames. Mesh bags are rubber, polyethylene, nylon, or cotton, although cotton tends to rot. All nets should be rinsed after use to increase their longevity.

Cradle. This device is used to land long fish that are intended for release, and which supports the full body of the fish in a horizontal position. The most popular version features two long narrow wood boards that are connected by ¼-inch soft mesh netting that is closed at the ends and which droops into the water to envelop a fish as if it were slipped into a purse. The cradle is kept in the water while the fish is unhooked and then released. Another version for shorter fish is smaller, with open ends and an open-grip handle. Cradles are best used from boats with a low freeboard.

Creel. A basket, bag, or pouch for holding a mobile angler's fish, a creel is primarily used by bank or wading stream trout anglers, the latter of whom carry it around the back via a strap. Pouches to retain fish are also incorporated into many fishing vests or can be added to them.

Cast net. A cast net is a circular net with fringe weights that is thrown for collecting live baitfish. Shad, herring, and mullet are among the most common targets, and they are usually netted in shallow waters, although some netting takes place in the ocean in deep water, where large schools of baitfish are attracted to the surface with chum and then netted. In use, when a cast net is thrown, the full net opens as it hits the surface of the water, the weights carry it down quickly, the bottom of the net closes around fish, and the net is retrieved via a long connecting polypropylene line.

Cast nets come in different mesh sizes, different diameters, different weights, and with different strengths of mesh. They are commercially made and custom made, the latter preferred by people who gather bait professionally and by guides or charter boat captains who routinely use a cast net. Heavier weights and larger diameters are needed for deeper-water use.

The smallest cast nets have a 6-foot diameter and ½-inch mesh, and weigh 10 pounds. They should be stored in a tall bucket when not in use, preferably one with large holes to allow drying and prevent rotting, and kept out of the sun; rinse the net in freshwater after use, and when it hasn't been used for a while, soften it in warm water with fabric softener.

Waders and Wading Footwear

Waders. Anglers who fish from the bank, who wade, or who get in and out of boats during the course of fishing often need to cover that portion of the body that will be in the water. Such a covering is generically called waders, which are chest- or hip-high products with connected or separate boots that keep anglers dry and sometimes warm, and also help provide good footing.

The ideal wader should be totally waterproof, warm in cold water yet cool in hot weather, durable or long-lived, lightweight, supple and stretchable, tear- and puncture-proof, not bulky, and not damp inside when worn. Many of the better modern waders are extremely functional products, and there are waders to suit nearly all angling situations; some anglers have two or three pairs for different conditions.

There are two general types of waders: chest and hip. Chest waders are worn in water that is too deep for the use of hip waders and for extra water and weather protection in cold weather. A bit heavy and bulky, they provide warmth but make for more difficult distance walking or climbing. A modified version, referred to as a waist-high wader because it extends only to the waist, is made for anglers who get in and out of boats frequently.

Hip waders are short and more like boots, and used for wading in relatively shallow water. It is easier to get in and out of a boat or vehicle in them, and they are easiest to take off or put on. They are also cool to wear in warm weather and, if fitted properly, good for long-distance walking on land.

Both basic wader types can be further categorized by the nature of their bottom, or foot section. Those with integral boots are known as boot foot models. Boot foot waders are generally popular with anglers who do a moderate amount of wading and are found on virtually all rubber chest and hip waders and on many neoprene chest waders. They are easier to take off or put on than stocking foot waders, and are warmer in the coldest water. They generally are not as comfortable as, and are heavier than, stocking foot waders with wading shoes. The ankle portion of the boot provides support as good as that of a wading shoe. The ridge where the stiffer boot area joins the upper wader material can be a source of leaks, as well as of chafing to the angler who has to walk considerable distances.

Those waders that require separate boots are called stocking foot models, or sometimes pants. The actual wader itself is a separate component from the boot, and features an integral stocking-style foot section worn inside a pair of

Neoprene waders, such as the chest-high model worn by this steelhead angler, are invaluable for cold-weather fishing.

wading boots or shoes; these may be chest- or hip-high products, mostly the former. Stocking foot waders fit the lower body closer, which can mean less drag in the water and easier climbing; the wading shoes worn with them often provide better ankle and foot support and traction; the soft ankle and calf section of the wader provides for more comfortable walking over distances. They take more time to get on or off, there is a greater chance of grit working into the boot, and they are not as warm in extreme cold-water wading.

Soles. Traditional hard rubber-bottomed soles with luglike gripping tread are best suited to traversing soft bottoms and gravel. Soft felt soles and similar woven polypropylene soles are a vast improvement for boulders and slick rocks, though not a help on wet shore grass or icy banks; felt wears out, however, and has to be replaced or at least reglued from time to time.

An option to smooth felt is a flat compressible soft rubber sole that is akin to rock climbing shoe soles. This grips as well as or better than felt on slippery stream bottoms and better on other surfaces, and is far more durable.

Metal gripping cleats, or creepers, which are either permanent attachments or strap-ons of various shapes, provide the most stable walking on boulders and slick rocks, but are cumbersome to walk in and not welcomed in some situations. Metal cleats are absolutely essential for jetty fishing, where rocks are moss-covered and extremely slippery. They are also vital where wading anglers have to engage ice along rocky banks.

Wading boots/shoes. Wading boots (worn with stocking foot waders), which are often called wading shoes, should always be a consideration for fishing that requires wading in large, turbulent, or fast waters. They provide hiking boot–like support for walking on unstable ground, and superior protection from falls and below-ankle collisions. It is much easier to walk longer distances in wading boots than in boot foot waders or booties, and they come in a varied selection of soles, making it possible to choose the best sole for the best application.

Wading boots are fairly heavy and rugged; most are of high quality and truly bootlike, made from leather or synthetic materials, with the latter preferred because they don't absorb water and become heavier, nor are they subject to rotting and cracking.

There are various grades of wading boots. Choose one based upon the degree of wading difficulty that you will most likely encounter. An angler who has one pair of stocking foot waders and fishes easy wading streams most of the time can get a lightweight boot for everyday fishing, and also have a more solid and heavier boot for occasional fishing on swifter rivers and where there is more slippery and rugged bottom terrain. Obviously, outer sole considerations apply to wading boots, as previously discussed.

When wading wet in warm waters, including beaches, flats, and streams, special booty-style wading shoes provide a tight ankle fit to keep gravel and sediment out, and offer overall foot protection. Many are made of neoprene, are calf-high in design, and have sturdy rubber composition bottoms.

Wet-wading shoes with hard, ridged soles are good for varying applications, while those with felt bottoms are best for stream usage. Some have a zippered entry, which can be annoying when fine grit lodges in the zipper teeth. Most also have a heel bump that helps secure swim fins, which are used when fishing from float tubes. Dark-colored booties work fine for continuous wading, but not for saltwater flats fishing where you may spend a lot of time in a boat, subject to the sun heating the dark boots.

Boating Accessories

Charts and Maps

Technically, a map details land features and a chart details water features. Topographic maps depict land features in great detail but do not provide sub-surface details about water. They may help some freshwater anglers locate places worthy of fishing (ponds or river backwaters, for example) but are of no value from a hydrographic standpoint.

Navigational charts, on the other hand, and underwater contour maps depicting hydrographic details, provide little information about land areas but significant detail regarding depth, obstructions, and navigational aids.

Every angler who fishes a large or unfamiliar body of water should have a good chart of that place and use it in conjunction with sonar and perhaps GPS. Charts that show underwater contours and hydrographic features can help you navigate without getting lost or possibly running into obstructions, and can help you find areas that may provide good fishing. Maps that are studied at home, prior to on-the-water fishing, often allow anglers to devise a plan and avoid haphazard fishing, which is especially useful when time is limited.

Electric Motors

An electric motor is one of the most important and useful items that any boating angler can have. Called a trolling motor by most of the angling fraternity, it allows you to maneuver and position your boat in the proper angle for casting and to make the type of presentation that is required for the fishing circumstances, all as quietly and carefully as possible. An electric motor can be used in trolling but is primarily for positioning while casting.

Electric motors are predominantly used by freshwater anglers; saltwater usage is less widespread, although modern saltwater motors are specifically designed for the harsh marine environment, having stainless steel and corrosion-resistant parts, tighter seals, improved torque, remote-control operation, and more power.

Saltwater operation is generally more demanding than freshwater, partly because a lot of power is needed to combat currents and wind, and partly because saltwater casters may have to do a bit of moving to keep up with quickly moving and widely roaming fish.

On most fiberglass and on many aluminum boats in freshwater, the electric motor is mounted permanently on the bow, with the bracket support installed on the bow port to put a little weight on that side and counterbalance the console and driver weight on the starboard side. On small craft such as rowboats and jonboats, electric motors can be mounted on the front or back.

Boats move with greater ease when pulled rather than pushed, so many anglers prefer bow mounting; plus, with bow mounting, they can see where they're headed and know when to avoid objects. Bow mounting is preferred for casting to cover and working along specific edges.

Permanent bow-mount electrics are used on conventional bass boats and large craft and can be operated manually or remotely, depending upon the unit. Most remote units are operated via a foot-control pedal on the bow deck; some have merely a long electric cord, and some are totally remote-controlled, operated by a wireless touch pad or by voice command. The latter eliminate the hindrance of wires and cable, and have become increasingly popular.

Manual models do not have a foot-control pedal or cable running to the motor and are steered by turning a fixed handle or a handle extension device. They are mostly operated by hand but may

Maneuvering for precise casting is an important component of bass fishing; these anglers are fishing on Table Rock Lake, Missouri.

be maneuvered with your foot or knee, although you have to be properly balanced to do this. At least one model has articulated steering, which is a great benefit as it allows you to turn the motor 180 degrees while only moving the handle a short distance.

One important feature in bow-mount motors is a breakaway bracket; this device allows the shaft of the motor to slip back should the motor collide with an immovable object. Another important consideration for bow-mount models is the length of the shaft. Big boats and boats that will be used in rough water conditions require a long-shaft motor so that the propeller will grab properly.

Pushpole

Made of wood, aluminum, fiberglass, or graphite, a pushpole is used to propel a boat quietly, or to temporarily stake (anchor) it in shallow water. Almost any open boat under 20 feet long can be propelled by a single pushpole. Though many people associate fishing use of a pushpole with saltwater flats angling, any small boat can be poled in a situation where the water is shallow and it is desirable to quietly move along. Pushpoles are used to propel a canoe upstream against a current, glide a skiff across a bonefish flat, or muscle a bass boat through heavy weeds.

The advantage offered by a pushpole is accomplishing movement with less noise than the quietest electric motor, with no batteries to become depleted or moving parts to wear out. The disadvantage is that a person who poles cannot fish while in the act of poling.

The diameter of a pushpole is generally from 1¼ to 1½ inches, with the smaller diameter being better for smaller hands. The main section of the pole may be one piece or multiple pieces (some are three-piece units). Graphite pushpoles are most expensive, but they tend to be lighter, which is important because even the lightest poles feel heavy by the end of a day of poling. They are also stiffer, which helps when you have to pole fast.

Ends may be round and blunt, tapered to a point, or fitted with a triangular or forked foot. Usually one end has a point and the other a foot or fork, so the pole can be reversed depending on the bottom material. The pointed end is used for burying in a soft bottom—to hold the boat in position for a while or to stake out—and for

A guide uses a pushpole to quietly stalk the flats.

poling over hard bottom. It features a silent and relatively splashless entry and exit from the water. The larger foot end is used for poling over soft bottom or mud. Feet shapes include a Y, triangle, or hybrid of the other two.

Rod Holder

A rod holder is a device that a fishing rod is inserted into when not being used, or when being used but not held by hand. Rod holders come in many forms; adjustability, ease of rod removal, sturdiness and stability, and placement options are the key factors in selecting and using these accessories.

Some rod holders are primarily used for stowing rods out of the way when not in use. There are various ways to do this, depending on the design of the boat. Open boats, center consoles, and cuddy cabin craft often sport through-the-gunwale or flush-mounted holders that store rods upright. This isn't practical for many small boats, though, and horizontal mounting is preferable for some. The decks of many small boats are often cluttered with rods; here, a snap-in floor holder can be used to secure rods and prevent them from bouncing freely.

Holders used to contain rods that are being still-fished or trolled are mounted on or in the gunwale and transom, as well as on a guardrail, handrail, trolling board, or downrigger. In-gunwale models, and those bolted to downriggers, are in a fixed position. Other rod holders should be adjustable to different positions and angles, and should be able to support a long-handled rod, a rod with a trigger grip, a spinning rod, and a heavy-duty rod with crosshair-style gimbal footing.

A rod holder should allow quick removal of the rod. Some designs cause anglers to fight with the holder to remove a rod when a fish is on the line and exert a lot of torque on the handle, which is buried in the holder.

Rod Belt and Harness

A rod belt is a device with a receptacle for holding the butt of a fishing rod and used for playing large fish while protecting the angler's lower abdomen, kidney, and groin. The primary purpose of a rod belt, which may also be called a fishing belt or a fighting belt, is to relieve the pressure that an unprotected rod butt can exert on the body while fighting a fish, especially one that takes a lengthy time to subdue.

A rod belt is commonly used in saltwater, sometimes in conjunction with a fighting harness, and occasionally in freshwater for the likes of sturgeon. It may be used with any type of tackle, but is most often associated with stand-up fishing and the use of conventional and big-game tackle.

There are rod belts to suit light-, medium-, and heavy-tackle fishing. Most are made from highly durable synthetic materials, and some designs offer fish-playing benefit as well as personal protection. They are usually belted behind the back, and in front feature a wide reinforced area with a molded open cup, a gimbaled cup, or an angled cup entry to facilitate rod butt placement.

The more experienced the angler and the more strenuous the fight, the more it is likely that an angler will prefer having a gimbal rest, which locks a gimbal-butt rod in position and allows it to pivot easily when the rod is raised and lowered. A rod that does not have a gimbal butt should be used with an open-receptacle belt.

A good rod belt greatly helps anglers fight strong fish.

Heavy-tackle belts are large and bulky, and meant for positioning the rod butt receptacle across the thighs. These are used with 50- to 130-pound tackle and usually in conjunction with a fighting harness, which is worn around the shoulders and upper back to provide back support, arm relief, and reel security.

A fighting harness is worn like a vest, may be padded, and is usually made from nylon, canvas, or nylon webbing. In use, a harness-wearing angler with rod butt in the belt gimbal leans back against the pull of the fish, making the knees, rather than waist or back, the pivot point.

Sea Anchor

A sea anchor, also known as a drogue, is a light but large megaphone- or parachute-shaped bag used to slow down a drifting or trolling boat.

The need for using a sea anchor arises when a boat is moving so fast that a lure or bait cannot be presented properly, or spends almost no time in the strike zone. It is also important on windy days when you have to fish a particular place where the fish are very finicky about presentation, or are tightly grouped.

Sea anchors open up like a huge funnel or rounded bag when pulled through the water. Their wide-mouth opening can be restricted to lessen

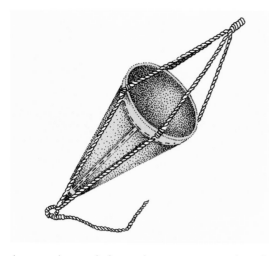

A sea anchor works by catching water in its wide end and funneling it through a narrow end, which slows momentum.

drag according to conditions, so that a lesser amount of water passes through the narrow end.

Many anglers attach sea anchors to the gunwales amidship, especially for drifting in open water and in situations where two or three anglers are casting downwind. They can also be tied to the bow if conditions warrant.

For forward trolling, a sea anchor can be tied to the bow, with just enough rope to reach midship; tie a tail rope to the funnel end so that when you need to retrieve the bag, you can pull on the tail to collapse it. For slow backtrolling with the wind you can tie a sea anchor to the bow so that it extends in front of the boat facing the bow, and then, if necessary, supplement control with a transom-mounted electric motor or outboard motor.

Sea anchors must be tied to sturdy cleats or to bow eye bolts. These devices exert a lot of pull, so be wary of tying them to a handrail or guardrail or around rod holders.

Deep Anchors

Deep anchors are heavy objects, usually of lead or metal, that are fastened to a chain and/or line and set on the lake, river, or ocean bottom to keep a boat in position.

Of the great variety of anchor types, a relatively small number are used by anglers. Some modern and newly designed anchors are hybrids, and some are slight variations of the standard designs. The weight and/or the design of the anchor usually determine its holding power, but a heavy anchor is not essential for holding a big boat; bottom conditions, sea conditions, anchor design, how the anchor was set, the amount of line let out, and other factors all play a role.

Small-boat owners have used cement blocks, cement- or sand-filled cans and jugs, sash weights, pieces of iron, truck tire chains, and other makeshift and economical dead weights as anchors. Most of these are suitable only for small to medium-size boats, generally under 20 feet in length, and in fairly calm water. They may not hold sufficiently in heavy waves or in current and typically have little ability to grab the bottom and dig in, although they may hold if they snag behind a big object, such as a rock.

Many river anglers use an improvised anchor, especially chain, which functions primarily as a weight to slow their downstream movement. This is particularly helpful in sections of water with riffles, rapids, or shoals. Chains are noisy and may spook fish in some waters; an option is an industrial-strength jug, filled with sand or mud, that bounces along quietly like a piece of wood. Here's a brief review of other common anchor types:

- Mushroom. This anchor has a 360-degree cupped lip and an upside-down mushroom appearance. It is more popular among small-boat owners in freshwater, and is mainly useful under ideal conditions, especially where there is a soft bottom. A mushroom anchor is not adequate in fast-moving water and cannot hold a heavy boat well, especially in a marl or hard bottom, unless that bottom has plenty of large rocks.

- Danforth. The Danforth is made of steel or aluminum and features two long, flat, and pointed flukes that dig into the bottom as upward pressure is applied on the anchor line. It is especially effective in mud, sand, and clay and may actually bury itself if left long enough, as line pressure forces the flukes deeper. On rocky terrain the flukes may skip over the bottom instead of digging in, and the flukes tend to pick up debris when they're retrieved.

- Navy. This design combines movable flukes with a lot of weight. It is made of lead, sometimes coated with vinyl, and features bulb and pivoting weight design. Navy anchors hold

Anchor Types

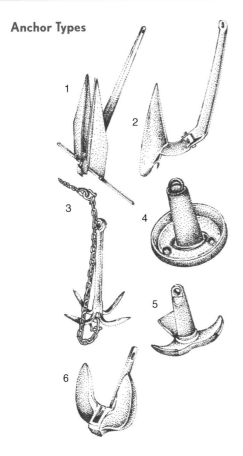

Common anchor types include: Danforth or fluke (1), plow (2), grapnel (3), mushroom (4), river (5), and Navy (6).

especially well in soft bottoms and are fairly popular, especially in freshwater, but they have a poor holding-power-to-weight ratio. They are manufactured in 5- to 20-pound sizes, the larger of which do not hold as well as much lighter Danforths.

- **Plow.** This device sports a broadhead-like blade and a design that rights the anchor and causes the blade to furrow into the bottom, eventually burying itself if the bottom is soft enough. It has application over diverse bottoms and is especially good in sand and moderate grass. Some versions have a shank that pivots, which reduces the tendency of the anchor to pull out when there's a sharp change in the angle of pull.
- **Grapnel.** This is a metal gang-hook anchor that sports four to six upward-sweeping claws. It has no value on soft bottoms but is excellent on rocky bottoms, as the claws readily catch onto

objects. Grapnels are of moderate weight and are manufactured in small versions that serve backup duty or are used to scour the bottom for dropped equipment.
- **River.** This lead anchor is usually vinyl-coated, with three wide, cupped blades. It has no benefit in soft bottoms but is meant to hold in rocky bottoms and varying current conditions.

Electronics

Sonar

"Depthfinder," "depth sounder," and "fishfinder" are common terms for sportfishing sonar. Whatever term you use, this electronic equipment is the boat angler's underwater eyes, and in some circumstances is viewed as virtually indispensable. With it, the angler can find concentrations of migratory, suspended, schooling, and nomadic fish, and locate submerged habitat that may be attractive to particular species. Thus an angler can become accurately acquainted with the beneath-the-surface environment of any body of water in significantly less time. Additionally, sportfishing sonar allows for better navigation, although it is not actually a navigational device.

The most common sportfishing sonars in general use feature a liquid crystal display (LCD). These depict fish, objects, and bottom information in a scrolling videolike manner via a grid of dots called pixels. The number of pixels in each vertical column on a screen determines its ability to display detail, while the number of pixels in each horizontal row determines how long information stays on the screen before it scrolls off the edge. The greater the number of vertical pixels, the better the resolution or screen detail. The deeper the water and the more screen detail, the more vertical pixels you need for better images. The same is true for power; for deep water you need greater wattage.

Many LCDs have large screens and a split-screen zoom feature. This allows you to split the screen and show the normal image of everything in the water from surface to bottom on one side and a magnified portion of the water column on the other side. The zoom feature usually can be adjusted in size and magnification on better units, or will do so automatically. Some LCDs also have a three-dimensional viewing feature;

however, many users may find this confusing and difficult to relate to for fishing applications. Three-dimensional viewing is offered as an option on some sonar, subordinate to conventional chart-style display.

Transducers and Cone Angles

Sonar is essentially made up of a display unit and a transducer, which are connected by coaxial cable. The display unit indicates the information that the transducer has provided by issuing signals through the water.

In general, there are high and low operating frequencies for sportfishing sonar. Low frequency is meant for very deep water (beyond 300 feet) while high frequency is meant for shallower use. Some sonar features dual-frequency operation with corresponding transducers.

Transducers dispense pulses in a three-dimensional cone-shaped wave. Cone angles range from narrow to extremely wide and their diameter influences how much detail will be seen. High-frequency transducers come in "wide" and "narrow" cone angle versions. As a rule of thumb, you can quickly find the diameter of a transducer's coverage at any depth by dividing that depth by 7 for a narrow cone or by 3 for a wide cone.

A narrow cone angle has about a 2-foot diameter at a depth of 15 feet and about a 4-foot diameter at a depth of 30 feet. A wide cone angle has a 5-foot diameter in 15 feet of water and a 10-foot diameter in 30 feet. Most low-frequency transducers have a cone angle of about 45 degrees, which covers a diameter about equal to the depth. Its diameter is about 15 feet at a depth of 15 feet and about 30 feet at a depth of 30 feet.

The narrowest cone angles are most useful in extremely deep water, such as 150 feet or more. The widest cones enable you to see a lot more of what's beneath you, are especially useful for downrigger trolling and fishing directly below the boat, and work best at slow boat speeds. The only draw-back to a wide cone angle is that in deeper water it takes in so much information that you may trick yourself into thinking that fish it details are directly below the boat when they may be well off to the side.

In addition to looking down, some units look to the side, either via a rotating transducer or a fixed-mount, side-viewing transducer. The advantages of side viewing are obvious: finding fish that are not below the boat, looking along a bank for fish to cast to, scanning through a river pool to see if it holds fish, and so on.

Getting good readings from sonar is important to interpretation. Unfortunately, improper transducer installation leads to many problems and can hamper fishing efforts; it is the most common cause of poor sonar performance.

Whether the transducer is mounted inside or outside the hull, it must be placed in a position that receives a smooth flow of water at all speeds. If it doesn't have a smooth flow of water, interference from turbulence can cause poor sonar readings or intermittent readings when the boat is under power. If you don't want to make the installation yourself, take the sonar and transducer to a boat dealer who has experience in rigging fishing boats.

Portable and Fixed Mounts

Sonar is available in portable as well as permanent-mount versions. Portable models work on almost any boat but are primarily used on small craft. The transducer is generally attached to a bracket and clamped to the gunwale or transom, or to a suction cup placed on the transom.

A fixed bow-mounted sonar is particularly helpful for freshwater anglers who spend much of their angling time in the bow, casting and running the electric motor to maneuver along likely fishing areas. Ideally, the transducer for this unit should be located on the bottom of the bow-mounted electric motor to give readings directly below the front of the boat.

A fixed console-mounted sonar is used by many boaters, sometimes as their only type of sonar, sometimes in conjunction with a bow-mounted unit. When it's the only sonar aboard, an accessory swivel bracket can let it be turned as necessary to be seen from anywhere in the boat. The transducer for console-mounted sonar (as well as for sonar located near the stern on a tiller-steered boat) is located on the transom or, in a few cases, mounted in the sump or integrated into the hull during construction.

Usage

Most people want to simply turn the device on and let it run, as if it were television. Thus many people simply run their units in automatic mode and never get into the finer points of operation. Take the time to read every page of your manual. The place to do this is out on the water (but not while fishing), so that you can go through the operations step by step, gain confidence in the unit, and actually see the machine do what it's supposed to do.

Most anglers use sonar, especially LCDs, in the automatic mode. Modern units work well in this state, and automatically adjust sensitivity, bottom settings, and other features as necessary so that you don't have to do too much. On the other hand, older sonar often works better in the manual mode, where you control the sensitivity and range settings to get much finer detail. When most older units are used in manual mode, however, the bottom setting does not change automatically, and it is a nuisance to have to do this whenever you move into deeper or shallower water.

When you do control settings yourself, pay careful attention to the sensitivity and suppression. The sensitivity control, which used to be called gain, is akin to the volume control on a radio. Many inexperienced sonar users keep this turned down too low, either because they are experiencing electrical interference or because they think

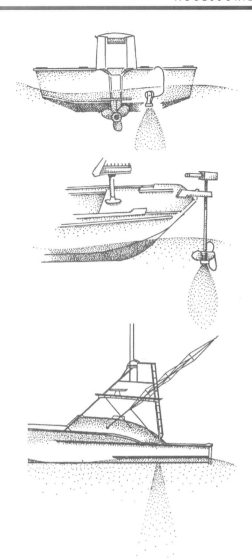

Depending on boat and fishing needs, sonar transducers are located on the transom (top), beneath an electric motor (middle), or in the sump (bottom).

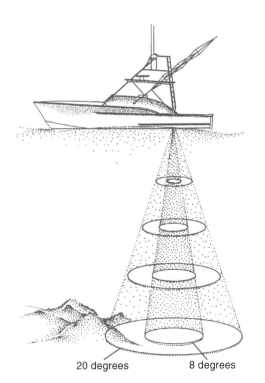

20 degrees   8 degrees

The diameter of the transducer cone angle affects coverage area.

a low setting is adequate. When the sensitivity is too low, sonar may fail to register key bait, fish, or bottom readings. Modern units run on automatic don't usually have this problem. On older units, more detail can be observed from higher sensitivity settings.

If you turn sensitivity too high, you might clutter the screen with a lot of nonfish debris. The best marriage is a high enough sensitivity to get a solid bottom reading with a distinguished bottom differentiation, some surface clutter (minute "scatter" near the surface), and a lot of detail in between. A good rule of thumb is to turn sensitivity up until you see random dots of interference on the screen, then turn it down until they disappear.

If it's possible to adjust the scroll rate of your screen, crank that up too, especially when you're on the move or when trolling. A slow speed compresses readings horizontally, which may hide important details. When you know what to expect, are continuously going over the same ground, or are interested only in depth, a slow speed might be adequate.

GPS

Global Positioning System (GPS) units are navigational devices that use satellites orbiting Earth to locate position. GPS features extremely quick fixes and easy use; you simply turn the receiver on and start navigating. It can be used twenty-four hours a day, in any weather, wherever there is an open view of the sky.

GPS receivers are available as handheld portables, as stand-alone bracket-mounted or in-dash models, and as "black boxes" combined with sonar devices. Sportfishing boaters use GPS to get to and from selected locations and to determine the exact location of important fishing grounds. In addition, they use GPS as an aid to actual fishing activities, especially when angling in wide-open waters for nomadic schools of fish or pelagic species or when fishing specific bottom structures. Many models today store a tremendous amount of information inside (which can also be updated), not only pertaining to such matters as the location of aids to navigation, as would be found on charts, but also with regard to the location of marinas, boat ramps, and even facilities on land.

Some boating anglers use handheld, or portable, GPS products while fishing. These are especially useful for anglers using canoes, inflatables, rental boats, and other craft without electrical systems, or when temporarily fishing from someone else's boat. They are also perfect for hike-in fishing on remote waters. Although they are a good compromise for anglers who use GPS for a variety of outdoor activities that require portability, they aren't the best choice for a permanent mounting in your boat. It can be more difficult to see their smaller screens and press their smaller keys while bouncing across the water than when using a full-sized, permanently mounted model.

Photographed in operation on the Chesapeake Bay, this combined GPS and color sonar device shows many striped bass (in red) from 20 to 30 feet deep.

Permanent mount units, which have larger, easier-to-see displays, are favored for boat installations. While some are available as stand-alone units, used on large boats with plenty of console space, many are available in combination with sonar units. With these, you can view either sonar or GPS readings on the whole screen, or split the screen to show sonar info on one side and GPS info on the other.

The navigational value of GPS is obvious. The additional value to anglers is in pinpointing places to fish, schools of fish, or significant underwater structures, and being able to return to them unerringly. In some instances there is great value to pinpointing the specific part of an area to fish such as the riprap near a submerged wreck.

The locations saved in GPS receivers are called waypoints. Once a waypoint has been saved, an angler can return to it at any time. Saving is most commonly done by pressing a button while the unit is located at the waypoint's position; the position can also be saved by entering its latitude and longitude coordinates through the keypad. These coordinates are important because with the lat/lon coordinates you can find a place that you have never been to; the coordinates can be given to you, or you can take them off a good navigational chart.

It's a good idea to record waypoint information in a logbook as a backup, in case the unit is lost, stolen, or breaks down. You can reenter the waypoints manually after fixing or replacing your unit or acquiring another. Integrating with a personal computer will allow you to store appropriate information as well as plan trips.

Trolling

Speed Gauge

Maintaining a consistent boat speed can be critical to trolling success. Conventional console-mounted boat speedometers measure water pressure picked up by a tube mounted on the transom or built into an engine's lower unit. They don't generally work below 5 to 10 mph and are useless for trolling.

Therefore, anglers who troll use various other instruments, referred to as speed gauges, speed sensors, or speed indicators, to accomplish this. These include electronic instruments fitted with a paddlewheel, which is secured to the boat transom flush to the hull; GPS navigational devices; and non-electronic drag-weight gauges, which measure speed relative to markings on a plate. Additionally, there are devices, attached to downrigger weights, that measure via paddlewheel the speed of the lure at the depth of a downrigger weight. This is sometimes different than surface speed.

The most accurate speed gauge is a GPS unit, which measures distance traveled over time. If you've used an automobile navigator you know how reliable this system is at determining speed. Most larger sportfishing boats are equipped with some type of GPS unit, often in combination with a sonar device, and when trolling, the speed is always known and displayed.

Attractors/Rigs

Cowbells. Used mainly for deep lake trout trolling, cowbells are a form of attractor featuring multiple in-line blades and used in trolling to simulate a group of baitfish. They feature a series of lightweight spoonlike willow-leaf, Colorado, or Indiana blades from 1½ to 5 inches long spaced at intervals over a short to medium length of braided-wire line. Some feature a rudder at the head, to which the fishing line is attached, and all sport a swivel to prevent line twist. A short leader (6 to 24 inches) and lure is attached to the end of the rig.

Usually a spoon or streamer fly is attached to cowbells, but sometimes a shallow-swimming plug or strip of bait is used. Blades are predominantly silver, but can be painted or taped with colors. A few anglers use cowbells while downrigger fishing, but traditionally they are

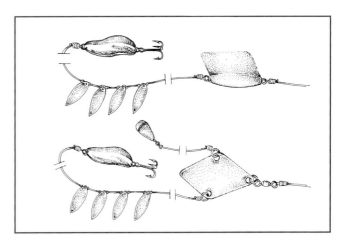

Two versions of cowbell rigs, both with a rudder and a series of spinning blades, are depicted here, each followed by a spoon.

fished on wire or lead-core line, or on lines weighted with a heavy sinker.

Dodgers and flashers. These attractors are used exclusively in trolling and primarily in freshwater to get the attention of deep fish, especially trout and salmon species. Both are thin metal objects, oblong and rounded at the ends, usually 2 to 3 inches wide and 5 to 10 inches long. Dodgers sway from side to side and do not rotate unless they are being run too fast; flashers rotate but don't sway. Both have swivels at each end, come in various sizes and colors, and can be altered in appearance with the application of prism tape. Dodgers are more widely trolled than flashers.

Plugs, spoons, flies, and imitation squid are fished behind dodgers and flashers. Flies and squid are the most popular trailing lures, particularly for steelhead and coho salmon, and are run 12 to 18 inches behind the attractor. Plugs (primarily cut plugs) and spoons are run 18 to 30 inches back. There is no need to use long leads; short leads make netting fish easier.

These attractors don't have any built-in weight, so they are usually fished behind a downrigger, but they also are used in conjunction with diving planers and heavy sinkers. The distance from the planer or sinker to the attractor is 2 to 6 feet; a short lead improves its action. When attractors are trolled with a

Typical dodger (top) and flasher (bottom) trolling rigs.

downrigger, it's important to have a moderately tight tension setting on the line release because attractors pull fairly hard and may pull the line out of a lightly set release.

Umbrella rig. The umbrella rig is a heavy wire multilure saltwater trolling rig primarily used with tube lures and most effective when schooling bait such as sand eels are present. However, almost any lure that doesn't create excessive drag (such as small spoons or soft plastic swimbaits) can be hung on umbrellas.

In a standard setup, an umbrella rig has four teaser tubes, one each midway on the wire arm, and four hooked tubes, one each on a leader tied to the end of each arm. A larger lure, such as a longer unweighted tube or a plug, is often fished from the middle of these rigs on a long leader to create the impression of a predator chasing a school of baitfish. There are other variations, of course, and rigs of different size with different-size lures.

Because of their overall size and the drag they exert, umbrella rigs are almost invariably trolled on wire line for striped bass and bluefish, although they also attract bonito, weakfish, and even little tunny.

Release

A release is a device that serves both to secure fishing line to some towing mechanism (downrigger cable, planer board tow line, or outrigger) and to free it from that mechanism when a fish strikes or when the angler wishes to change lures. Most releases have adjustable tension settings to allow for changes in pressure exerted by the object being towed. Most of the time, a release is used in trolling, but it can also be used for live- or cut-bait fishing.

In downrigger fishing, releases can be attached to the weight, to the downrigger cable at the weight, and to the cable at any location above the weight. In planer board fishing, releases can be attached to the board and to the tow line at any location ahead of the board. When using outriggers, a release (also called a clip) is used on a short length of line attached to the outrigger, and generally placed midway up on the outrigger.

With all releases, the fishing line is clamped into it under variable pressure. Some feature a trigger that can be set to open under greater or lesser tension. Others feature spring-loaded jaws capped with rubber pads; how far into the pads you set the fishing line determines the tension. A release used on a downrigger cable should be small and streamlined to avoid causing drag. A release used on a sideplaner should be able to slide freely down the tow line.

Planer Boards

Planer boards are devices that aid flatline trolling substantially and increase the versatility of trolling presentations. They can be used for many species, but are primarily used in freshwater for trout, salmon, and walleye. They increase presentation capabilities by allowing lures to pass near fish that may be spooked by your boat or that are in areas where you can't, or don't want to, take your boat.

There are two versions of planer boards, sideplaners and in-line planers. A sideplaner is a plastic or wooden surface board that works something like a downrigger on the surface. A nonfishing line or cable tethers the board to the boat and allows it to run at varied distances off to the side (there are port and starboard models that sport two or three runners). One or more fishing lines, using almost any type of tackle, attaches to the planer or tow line via a release; you fight a fish unencumbered when it strikes your lure and the release frees the fishing line.

There are commercially made sideplaner boards and retrieval devices, but many people make their own. Most sideplaners are about 30 inches long with double runners, but some homemade models are longer, up to 4 feet for some charter boat captains who deal with rough water.

An in-line planer is smaller but similar to a sideplaner and attaches directly to your fishing line. A lure is set out the desired distance; then the fishing line is run through a snap at the rear of the board and also into a release clip at the towing point. The in-line planer is set out at whatever

Trolling tools include a planer-board retriever, large planer boards, and small in-line planers.

the boat make it dive. When a fish strikes, the back-pulling tension trips a release that causes the diver to flatten and offer minimal water resistance as the fish is played. Diving planers are an alternative to using downriggers, wire or lead-core lines, or weighted lines to troll deep. Also, their size, color, and swimming motion can serve as an attractor to some species.

There are two versions: nondirectional, which only run straight down, and directional, which can be run straight down as well as down and off to the left or the right of a straight path. Directional divers are more versatile and more popular.

Because directional divers can take lures down and to the side of a boat, many anglers use them in conjunction with downrigger-set lines. Some fish in the path of the boat are spooked by downrigger weights and move down or away from them. Directional diving planers direct lures off to the side of other presentations. They help to cover more deep territory, and as a result offer further presentation opportunities to shores, piers, and the like.

Downrigger

A downrigger is a device that is used primarily for trolling and offers controlled depth presentation of a lure, bait, or fly. Downriggers take the burden of getting a lure to a specific depth away from the fishing line and put it on an accessory product, meaning that they can be used with light and ultralight tackle that tests angling skills and provides extra enjoyment.

The components of a downrigger include a spool, cranking handle with clutch, boom, cable, and pulley. A heavy lead weight attaches to the end of the downrigger cable, and a line-release mechanism is located on or near the weight or at any other place along the cable.

A lure attached to your fishing line is placed in the water and set at whatever distance you want it to run behind your boat. The fishing line is placed in the release attached to the downrigger cable. The downrigger weight is then lowered to the depth you want to fish. When a fish strikes the lure, the fishing line pops out of the release and the fish is played on your fishing line, unencumbered by a heavy weight or strong cable.

Downriggers are made in manual and electric models, the latter being preferred by busy veteran trollers.

distance off the side of the boat you desire. When a fish strikes, the line pulls out of the release and the board slides down the line. The board can be rigged to stop ahead of the hooked fish by using a barrel swivel, bead, and leader. It can also be rigged to fall completely away from the fishing line, but then it will have to be retrieved from the water. Because of heavy towing strains, a stout rod and fairly strong line are necessary for in-line planer fishing.

How far you set out the boards depends on how close to shore you want to be, how far apart you want to spread your lures, how much room you have to fish, and how much boat traffic there is; 80 to 100 feet out is standard when boat traffic is moderate. Sideplaners can be run out as much as 200 feet if you have a high anchor point in your boat for the tow line. In-line boards are run 30 to 100 feet out.

Diving Planer

A diving planer is a trolling accessory that attaches to fishing line a few feet ahead of a lure and dives deeply. No weights are used with this device; the design of the planer and the forward motion of

An angler attaches fishing line to a release on the downrigger weight.

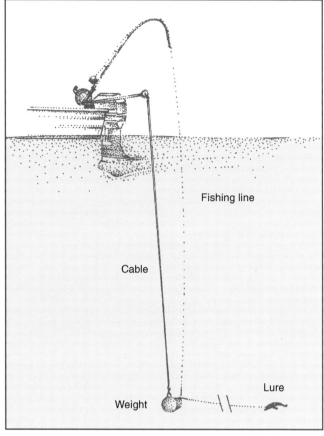

The general concept of fishing with a downrigger is very simple. Fishing line is attached via a release clip (not shown) to a weight, which in turn is attached to a heavy cable. When a fish takes the lure on the fishing line, the clip releases the line.

The length of the boom, or arm, which carries the cable from the spool to a pulley, can vary from 1 to 8 feet, depending on the boom's location on the boat and the need to spread out weights over the greatest possible horizontal range of water. As the vertical distance from gunwale to water surface increases, the length of the downrigger arm increases.

Downriggers use a line counter to measure the length of cable that comes off the spool. Cable is 150- to 200-pound-strength braided steel; the depth on the line counter will conform exactly to the length of cable let out.

The size of lead weight used varies, with 10- to 12-pound weights the norm. Such heavy weights are needed to keep the cable directly below the boat, or as close to it as possible, for precise depth determination. In relatively shallow water, in places where there is no current, and when you are trolling slowly, you can use a 7- or 8-pound weight.

Weights are often referred to as cannonballs because the earliest models, and many current ones, are shaped like a round ball. A round ball with a stabilizing fin on the back is the most popular shape, although there are various configurations. Weights shaped like a fish or a torpedo are fairly popular; a favorite with some anglers is a "pancake" weight with a slender head and a broad fin.

Manufacturer-supplied weights are available in white, black, chartreuse, green, orange, and red. Fish are often attracted to the trolled downrigger weight, possibly because of the color but most likely because of the vibration.

Rod holders are critical to downrigging, and some downriggers come with integral holders or can be fitted with them as accessories. A line-release mechanism is also critical to the downrigging system. The release must free the fishing line when a fish strikes or when the angler chooses to detach the line in order to retrieve it.

Line releases can be attached to the weight, to the downrigger cable at the weight, and to the cable at any location above the weight. Easily adjustable tension settings are important in line releases, and getting the right tension is critical for catching fish.

Slider Rig

A slider rig is a lure that is affixed to a short leader and run down a fishing line while trolling. Also known as a "cheater," it's a means of fishing more than one lure on a single line attached to a downrigger.

To rig it, tie a snap-swivel to one end of a 3-foot length of line and attach a lure, preferably a spoon, to the snap-swivel. Tie a snap to the other end of the leader, then clip it to the line that is already connected to a downrigger release below the boat. With the boat moving forward, carefully toss the lure into the water behind the main fishing line and watch to make sure it isn't fouled. The slider rig will drift out of sight and ultimately stop well above the downrigger weight at a point where the main line is bowed most sharply in the water.

When a fish strikes the slider lure, it pulls back on the main fishing line and pops the release to which that line is attached. The rig slides down the main fishing line and stops at the snap or lure there (use a bead to keep the upper snap from marring the lower snap, knot, or line-tie area). The exact depth of the slider rig will be unknown, but you'll have two lures on one line and one downrigger.

Outriggers

Indispensable tools for offshore trolling, outriggers consist of long aluminum poles mounted on the top or sides of offshore sportfishing boats.

Outriggers are designed so that they can be raised or lowered. They are kept in the raised position when running and not trolling. They are fished in the lowered position, with some type of cord running in a loop to the outrigger's tip. This lanyard contains a release clip, to which the fishing line is attached. The clip is then run up the outrigger pole so that the fishing line leaves the rod tip, goes up to where the release clip is situated on the outrigger line, and then back to the bait behind the boat.

Outriggers are used for several purposes, depending on the kind of fishing being done and the bait or lures being trolled. The most common use is when trolling either bait or offshore lures for pelagic species. Here, using an outrigger causes the bait or lure to be pulled from an elevated point, making it skip across the surface.

Outriggers vary in length according to the size of boat, and allow for a greater horizontal spread of lures or bait, permitting increased spacing of these objects and sometimes less likelihood of tangling trolled lines. When fishing rigged natural bait in big-game trolling, using an outrigger creates an automatic dropback when a fish strikes the bait, since the line instantly releases from the clip and goes momentarily slack. This gives the fish a moment to mouth the bait and results in a better hookup.

PART THREE

Basic Skills

10

Knot Tying

A strong knot is essential in connecting the fishing line to your hook or lure. The ideal knot is one that retains the full breaking strength of the line as if it never had a knot in it. If you use a knot that regularly achieves only 75 percent of the strength of your line in maximum stress situations, the knot will break before the line. However, if you tie a knot that achieves 100 percent of the breaking strength of the line, the line will usually break before the knot.

Here are some pointers for effective knot tying:

1 Learn to tie a knot at home and practice with several different strengths (diameters) so that you can do it uniformly time after time with confidence.

2 Be neat. Keeps wraps and other steps uniform so that when you draw a knot closed, it is neat and precise. Make sure that wraps don't cross over one another.

3 Don't twist a line that is meant to be wrapped. Knots that create a jam do not form as well if the line is twisted instead of wrapped over itself.

4 Snug knots up tightly with even, steady pressure. Don't pop the knot to tighten it. With heavy line, you may need to use pliers to pull on the tag end.

5 Moisten the knot and area of line around it as an aid to drawing it up smoothly.

6 Don't nick the line or knot with clippers or pliers when you cut off the protruding tag end. Clip the knot as close as you can; a properly tied knot won't slip.

7 Check every knot after it is finished by looking at it and by hand-pulling on it in both directions. If a knot breaks repeatedly when you tighten it, check your hook eye or lure connection for rough spots that are cutting the line. If it continues to break, the line may be defective and may need replacement.

8 Use plenty of line to complete tying steps without difficulty and to avoid malformed knots.

9 Wet stiff nylon line so that it absorbs water and relaxes, which makes it easier to knot.

10 Keep doubled lines as parallel as possible and avoid twisting them as the knot is being tied.

11 Test your knots occasionally with a scale to see if they're delivering top performance.

If you experience strength or holding problems with an otherwise reputable knot, there are several possible causes. You may be weakening the line by drawing the knot down too roughly or by failing to moisten it first. Another cause may be the type of line; the same knot will not perform as well when tied on some lines as on others. Super-thin lines, for example, are more problematic than conventional-diameter lines. Try making more wraps or more turns around the hook eye than you might otherwise. When all else fails, try a different knot for the line you're using.

Just because a knot is easy to tie—and some are much easier than others—does not make it the best choice in every circumstance. Some knots are very bulky and would not be useful on a small hook or wouldn't easily pass through rod guides when you are casting or—more importantly—when a big fish is pulling the leader or backing off a reel and through a bunch of rod guides at phenomenal speed. By knowing a number of knots, you can adapt to changing circumstances.

Fishing knots are primarily categorized as terminal connections and line-to-line connections, but some knots are used to create double-line leaders. Terminal knots are used to tie a line directly to a lure or hook. Line-to-line knots join two lines of similar or dissimilar diameter, including fishing line to a leader or tippet. In this chapter, knots are discussed in order of their significance and usefulness.

Terminal Knots

Improved Clinch Knot

This is probably the most popular terminal connection, especially in freshwater and with nylon monofilament line. It is best used for lines under 20-pound test. Tied properly, this knot has a strength of 90 to 100 percent; poorly tied, it may yield only 75 to 85 percent, which is insufficient, especially for a light line. It is not a good knot to use on lines with a slick finish or on microfilaments.

To tie, pass the line through the eye of the hook and then make five turns around the standing part of the line. Thread the end through the loop ahead of the eye, and bring it back through the newly created large loop. Moisten the knot with saliva, and check that the coils are spiraled properly and not overlapping one another. Pull firmly to tighten. Test the knot with moderate tension, and clip off the loose end.

Depending on the type and diameter of line being used, six spirals may be best for line through 12-pound test and five spirals for 14- to 17-pound test. For 20-pound test and over, make four spirals and use a pair of pliers to pull on the loose end and snug up the knot.

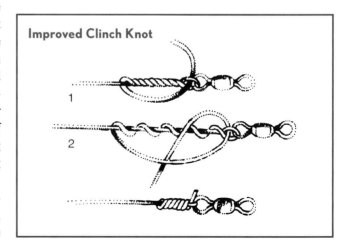

Improved Clinch Knot

1

2

If you experience slippage, try running the line through the hook eye twice before completing the other steps. This is a Double Loop Improved Clinch Knot. A variation on this is the Double Loop Clinch Knot, sometimes called a Trilene Knot, which also features two turns around the hook eye but the tag end comes back through both turns and then is snipped off.

Palomar Knot

Many people feel that this knot is easier to tie than the Improved Clinch and more consistent. Since it is easy to tie, fewer anglers experience difficulty with its use. Tied properly, it yields a strength of 90 to 100 percent. Some anglers use it mainly for tying leader tippets to flies, since it results in a smaller-profile knot than the Improved Clinch. It is an especially valuable knot when used with braided and fused microfilament lines, provided that two or three turns are made around the eye.

To tie the Palomar Knot, double about 6 inches of line and pass the loop through the eye of the hook. Tie an overhand knot in the doubled line, and pass the loop over the entire hook. Moisten the knot, pull on both ends, tighten, and clip the tag end.

The Palomar can be problematic used with large, multihooked plugs, where a longer loop must be created to allow the big lure to pass through it. Take care not to twist the doubled sections of line.

Uni Knot

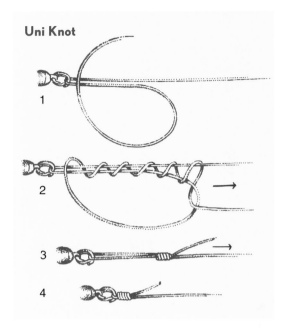

Uni Knot

This knot is a very versatile creation applicable to most fishing situations. The Uni Knot is actually a do-it-all system and can also be used in line-to-line connections. It can give 90 to 100 percent strength as a terminal tackle connector. When doubled, it can be used with braided and fused microfilament lines.

To tie the Uni Knot as a terminal connector, pass at least 6 inches of line through the eye of the hook and make a circle with the tag end. Bring the tag end around the double length and through the circle six times, moistening and then pulling snugly after the last turn.

Palomar Knot

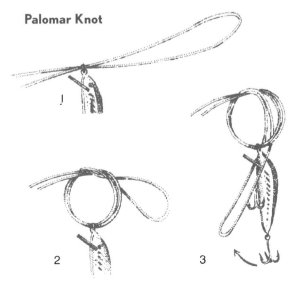

Nonslip Loop Knot

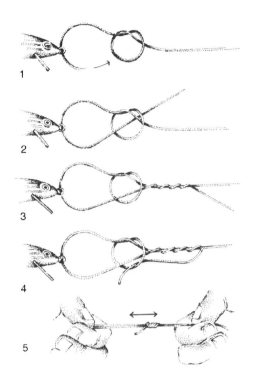

Nonslip Loop Knot

Loop knots are useful terminal connections when you want to get more action out of a lure and you prefer not to use a snap. They are also helpful with some jigs and weighted flies, allowing them to appear more natural on the fall, swim, or drift. Anglers have devised a number of loop knots, and many work fairly well, although some slip under extreme pressure and few hold a high percentage of line strength.

The Nonslip Loop Knot is primarily used with nylon monofilament, is not as difficult to tie as it seems, and has very good strength. To tie it, make an overhand knot in the line, leaving about 6 inches at the tag end. Pass the tag end through the hook eye and then back through the overhand knot the same way that it came out. The size of the overhand knot determines the size of the loop; for most situations, keep it small.

Hold the overhand knot softly with one hand, and pull on the tag end of the line to bring the overhand knot down toward the eye. Wrap the tag end around the standing line (seven times for nylon line under 10 pounds, five wraps for 10- to 14-pound line, four wraps for 15- to 40-pound line, three wraps for 50- to 60-pound line, and two wraps for heavier line). Bring the tag end back through the loop of the overhand knot the same way that it exited. Moisten, pull on the tag end to form the final knot, and then pull from both ends to snug up completely.

Offshore Swivel Knot

This knot is a very strong connection for use with a doubled line leader, primarily employed in saltwater and by big-game anglers. It is mainly tied on a swivel or a snap but can be tied to a hook or an eyelet, and it will continue to hold if one of the two lines is cut.

To tie the Offshore Swivel Knot, bring the loop end of the doubled line through the eye of the swivel and make one twist in the loop beyond the swivel eye. Bring the end of the loop back against the standing double line, and hold the two together with one hand. With your other hand, slide the swivel to the opposite end of the loop and rotate the swivel through the center of both loops six times. Hold the double line tightly, and release the end of the loop while pulling on the swivel. Grip the swivel with pliers, and pull on both the swivel and the standing double line with even pressure. Push the loops toward the swivel as necessary.

Offshore Swivel Knot

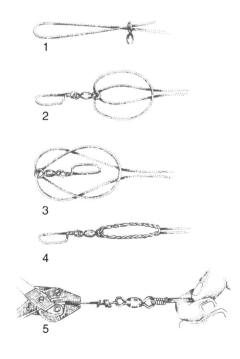

Conventional Snell Knot

A Snell Knot is applied only to hooks with a turned-up or turned-down eye and has the advantage of a direct pull for increased hooksetting efficiency. It is used in fishing with bait and is an especially popular knot with salmon and steelhead anglers, which is why it is sometimes called a Salmon Hook Knot.

To form the Conventional Snell Knot, bring at least 6 inches of the tag end of the line through the hook eye, lay it along the shank, and form a loop. Pinch both sections to the shank with one hand, and with the other hand wrap the looped line tightly and closely without overlays toward the eye. After making ten wraps, snug down the knot. Slide the snell toward the eye if it is not going to be used to hold bait and to the midshank if it is to be looped to hold bait (primarily it is used to hold an egg or spawn sack to the shank). Pull the line with equal pressure in opposite directions, and trim the tag end.

Conventional Snell Knot

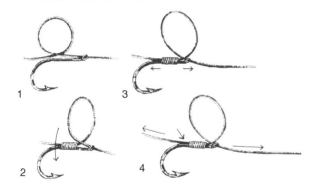

Unless you have taken pliers to the tag end of the snell and pulled it extremely tight, you can usually move this knot along the shank of a bait hook. If you move it to the middle, hold the shank of the hook in one hand and with the other hand push the standing line in through the eye until a loop forms. The loop can now be tightened around bait, especially a cluster of salmon eggs or a spawn sack, and these can be readily replaced.

Uni Snell

For many people the Uni Snell is an easier method of snelling a hook and, once mastered, is quicker to tie than the Conventional Snell Knot.

To tie the Uni Snell, pass 6 inches of line through the hook eye, pinch the line against the

Uni Snell

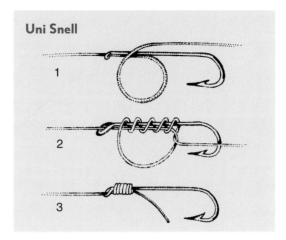

shank, and form a circle. Make five to seven turns (fewer for stronger line) through the loop and around the standing line and hook shank. (Locate the knot on the midshank if it is to be looped to hold bait or close to the eye if it will not hold bait.) Snug the knot tightly by pulling in both directions, and trim the tag end. See the previous instructions for making a bait-holding loop.

Double Turle Knot

Popular with fly anglers, this knot is easy to tie, has moderate strength, permits a direct pull through a turned-up or turned-down eye, and may help a dry fly sit better on the water.

To tie the Double Turle Knot, pass the tippet end of the leader through the turned-up or turned-down hook eye, going from the eye toward the point. Make a loop, wrap the tag end around twice, and snug up. Open the loop and slip the fly through; then place the loop around the neck of the fly just behind the eye. Pull on the standing line until the knot is tight against the neck.

Double Turle Knot

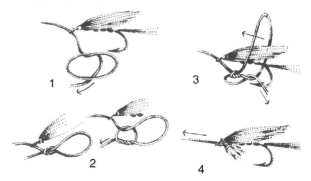

Improved Figure-Eight Knot

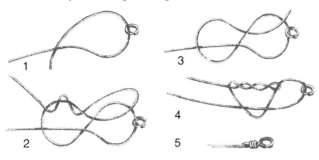

Improved Figure-Eight Knot

Sometimes referred to as the Orvis Knot, the Improved Figure-Eight Knot is useful with nylon monofilament line and leaders, and is easy to form.

To tie the Improved Figure-Eight Knot, pass the tag end of the line through the hook eye and bring it back toward the standing end. Pass the tag end under the standing end, up and over it, and through the loop in front of the hook eye. Wrap the tag end twice through the loop farthest from the hook eye, and pull on both the hook and standing line to snug the knot.

Haywire Twist

A method of forming a loop in single-strand wire or Monel wire, the Haywire Twist is primarily used to prevent wraps from coming loose under severe pressure.

To form the Haywire Twist, start by making a loop and crossing the strands (1). Hold the loop tightly with one hand or pliers, and with your free hand press down at point A (the upper strand) with the forefinger and up at point B (the lower strand) with the thumb; then twist the tag end around the main stem. Check to see that the twist looks as

Haywire Twist

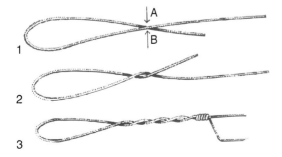

illustrated in step 2, and make four more twists in the same manner. Then wrap (not twist) the tag end of the wire as snugly as possible several times around the main strand (90 degrees to the main stem) to keep the entire rig from unwrapping (3). Bend the end of the tag wire to form a crank handle (3); holding the loop tightly in one hand, crank the tag wire in a circle in the same direction as the wrap and parallel to the main strand until the wire neatly parts where the last wrap was made. A neat cut is necessary because this wire is likely to be handled, but it is not accomplished by cutting, since cutters cannot sever the wire close enough to avoid a sharp end.

Line-to-Line Knots

Line-to-Line Uni

This knot is excellent for joining two lines and is perhaps the easiest line-to-line connection to make. Quicker and easier to tie than the time-honored Blood Knot, the Line-to-Line Uni is equally reliable. It is best for joining lines of similar diameter, especially in strengths up to

Line-to-Line Uni

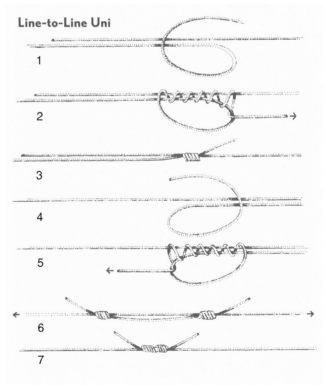

20 pounds, but can also work on those of different but not hugely disparate diameter by decreasing the number of wraps on the stronger line. It can also be used to join nylon monofilament and microfilament or braided lines.

To join two light lines of fairly similar diameter, overlap each at least 6 inches. Hold these in the middle of the overlap with your left hand, and make a circle with the line extended to the right. Bring the tag end around the double length six times, pulling snugly after the last turn. Repeat the process in reverse direction on the other side. Moisten the lines and knots, and pull the two sections away from each other to draw up the knot; then pull the lines firmly and clip both loose ends. Use five wraps for 10- to 17-pound line, four wraps for heavier line.

To tie the Line-to-Line Uni with lines of different diameter, use the appropriate number of wraps for each line. For example, when joining 12-pound to 20-pound, as might be done for a short leader, make five turns in the lighter line and four turns in the heavier line. With heavier lines, you may need to use pliers to pull on the tag ends and snug up. For lines of different material or vastly different diameter, consider doubling the lighter or more slippery line; in other words, when joining 6-pound line to 20-pound line, make a Uni Knot with a double length of 6-pound line, tying it to a single length of 20-pound. You do not need a double-line knot to do this because adding another knot to the equation is not an advantage. Simply fold the lighter line back over itself, and make the same wraps with two strands as you would with one.

Albright Knot

This knot is excellent for joining two lines of unequal diameter but is moderately difficult to tie. It is useful for connecting nylon monofilaments to each other or to microfilament or wire, for making shock leaders, for connecting fly line to braided backing, and for tying a Bimini Twist in the end of the lighter casting line.

To tie the Albright Knot, make a loop in the tag end of the heavier line (or fly line) and hold the loop between the thumb and forefinger of your left hand. Pass 8 to 10 inches of lighter line (or fly-line backing) through the loop from the top, and pinch it tightly against the two loop strands. With your right hand, wrap the lighter line back

Albright Knot

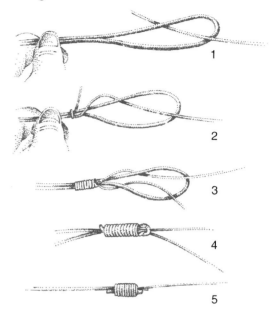

over itself and the loop strands. Make ten to twelve tight wraps, starting next to your fingers and working toward the loop end. Pass the tag end of the lighter line through the loop from the bottom, and exit out the top; both strands of the lighter line should be on the same side of the loop. With the left hand still holding the knot, move the knot gently toward the loop and then pull on both the standing and the tag ends of the light line. Pull tightly on the standing and tag ends of all lines, and trim tag ends.

Surgeon's Knot

This is a good knot for tying a leader with lines of different diameter and is popular with fly anglers for connecting a tippet and leader, especially when using a shock tippet. This is a very simple knot to tie, and especially valued in cold weather.

Surgeon's Knot

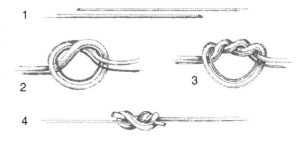

To tie the Surgeon's Knot, bring the tippet and leader lines parallel to each other and overlap about 6 inches. Make a loose overhand knot, bringing the tippet completely through the loop. Bring both lines through the loop a second time, keeping the strands together. Hold both lines at both ends, and pull the knot tight. Trim closely because this knot is slightly bulky and any protrusion could catch in the rod guides.

Surgeon's Loop

A common and easy-to-tie knot, a Surgeon's Loop is used to put a loop in the end of a line for connecting other lines. It is primarily used in fly fishing for loop-to-loop leaders but is slightly bulky and can snare the rod guides.

To tie the Surgeon's Loop, double the end of a line and make an overhand knot at the point where the line is doubled. Leave the loop open and pass the end of the double line through it a second time. Hold the single standing line and adjust the loop size; pull on the loop to tighten it, and clip the excess.

Surgeon's Loop

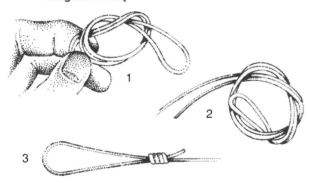

Blood Knot

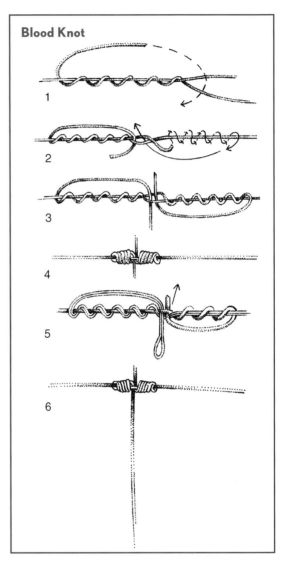

Blood Knot

The Blood Knot is a strong knot if tied properly, and it has long been a popular connection for two nylon monofilament lines, although some anglers prefer the simpler Uni Knot for tying one line to another. However, the Blood Knot has a low profile if properly formed and if the tag ends are trimmed close, and it runs through rod guides nicely. Some anglers consider the Blood Knot an easy knot to tie, but the plethora of tools invented over the years to aid in tying it seems to disprove this statement. It isn't really difficult to tie, and regular users can

tie it virtually blindfolded, but some attention to detail is required when learning it.

The Blood Knot is primarily used by fly anglers for connecting different lengths of line when making their own multipiece tapered leader, and it is best when tied with lines of the same or generally similar diameter. For tying to dissimilar diameters (such as 30-pound line connected to 12-pound line to make a shock leader), double the tag end of the smaller-diameter line and wrap it around the thicker-diameter line by using the same general instructions that follow but making just three wraps in the thicker-diameter line. This variation is called an Improved Blood Knot.

To tie the basic Blood Knot, cross two lines and wrap one five times around the other, bringing the tag end back and between the strands. Pinch this section to keep it from unraveling. Wrap the second line over the first five times in the opposite direction, bringing the tag end of the second line back and into the center loop in the opposite direction of the other tag end. Slowly pull on both of the joined lines to draw the wraps together; then tighten firmly and trim.

A modification of the knot is the Extension Blood Knot, which provides a short length of trailer line for a dropper fly. It is tied in the same manner as an ordinary Blood Knot, except that a longer length of line is used on one section and drawn completely through the middle loop. Leave between 8 and 12 inches of this line extending from the knot; too little will not be enough to tie a fly to it, and too much will encourage tangling. This extension should be used whenever you plan to fish a dropper fly; it provides the best and strongest connection to the main line (or leader).

Common Nail or Tube Knot

Known primarily as a Nail Knot, but also a Tube Knot, this knot is meant for joining lines of dissimilar diameter. It has long been a preferred method of connecting the butt end of a leader to a fly line, as well as reel backing to a fly line. It is formed with the use of a smooth instrument like a nail, small tube, piece of straw, straightened paper clip, or sewing needle. The Tube or Nail Knot is a nicely compressed knot that moves through rod guides well and does not pull out. Although experienced anglers can tie this knot fairly readily, many people who have infrequent occasion to join lines find it troublesome and time-consuming, usually having to make a couple of attempts before they get it right. That an accessory like a nail or tube is needed (but often unavailable on the water) is also a drawback.

To tie a Tube Knot using a tube (a short piece of rigid plastic from the tube of a ballpoint pen is great), lay the tube, the butt end of the leader, and the tip end of the fly line alongside each other with the fly line headed left and the leader headed right. Pinch all three in the middle with your left thumb and index finger, and allow 8 to 10 inches of leader overlap. With your right hand, wrap the leader snugly five or six times around the fly line, leader, and tube. Working from right to left, line the wraps up against each other and pinch the entire assemblage in with the left fingers. Pass

Nail/Tube Knot

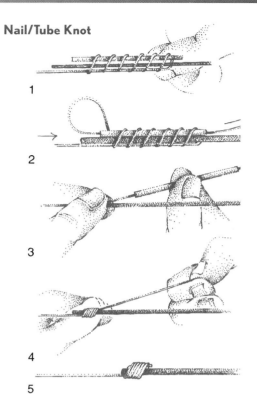

1

2

3

4

5

the butt end of the leader through the tube from left to right. Pull both ends of the leader tight and remove the tube. Tighten both ends of the leader again, and simultaneously pull on the leader and fly line tightly before clipping off the ends.

To tie a Nail Knot, place a nail between the two lines and follow the same instructions as for a tube, with the following exceptions: Make the wraps less snug, and run the tag end of the leader down alongside the nail. Using a small-diameter tube is actually easier.

Double Nail Knot

The Nail or Tube Knot has a number of variations. One of these is a Double Nail Knot in which two nail knots are tied in opposite directions; it can be used to tie similar-diameter lines together, although the Line-to-Line Uni is far easier to tie and just as useful if you are simply putting more line on a reel. The Double Nail Knot is used with heavy monofilament leaders by some fly anglers because of its lesser bulk; it is used by some big-game anglers for connecting a shock leader to a double line, in part because it can be easily wound through guides and onto a reel.

To tie the Double Nail Knot, overlap both lines with an ample length, form the first knot, remove

Double Nail Knot

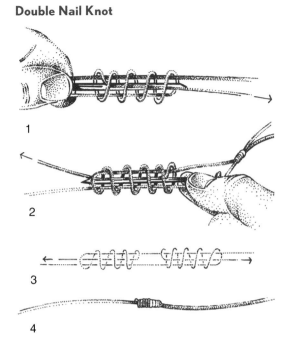

1

2

3

4

the nail, and gently draw the knot together without tightening; then form the second knot in the opposite direction, remove the nail, and pull this knot snug. Finally pull both together and tighten firmly.

Speed Nail Knot

The Speed Nail Knot, also called an Instant Nail Knot or Fast Nail Knot, is an interesting version of the Common Nail Knot. More like a snell, this knot originated with steelhead anglers who used it for snelling bait hooks. It looks much more

difficult to tie than it is and with a bit of practice can be whipped up in mere seconds.

To tie the Speed Nail Knot to a fly line, use a nail or something smooth and rigid. Hold the nail parallel to the fly line with the end facing right and extending no farther than the edge of the nail. Take whatever length of leader you want to make, cross the ends, and place the crossed portion against the nail and fly line; pinch all three in your left thumb and first joint of your index finger. Keep the tag end of the leader a short distance from the nail, in effect creating a very large loop that dangles below. Take the upper right side of the loop in your right hand, and wrap only that portion of the loop around the tag end of the leader, the fly line, and nail five or six times, using the tip of your index finger to keep the wraps in place. With the wraps secure in your left hand, let go of the loop with your right hand and grab the tag end of the leader, pulling until the loop dissolves and the knot snugs. Gently slide the nail out, and pull on both ends of the leader to tighten, then on the leader and fly line. Clip the excess.

With practice you can tie this knot in under twenty seconds, and without the use of a nail.

Double-Line Knots

A double line is in essence a leader, though one made from the actual fishing line by virtue of a Bimini Twist or Spider Hitch Knot. If properly tied, these knots, especially the Bimini Twist, hold the full 100 percent breaking strength of a line and knot,

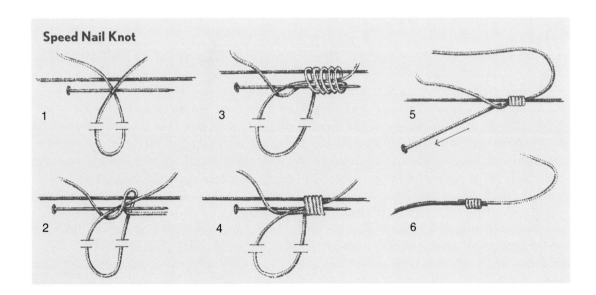

Speed Nail Knot

1

2

3

4

5

6

offer more resistance to abrasion, and offer added breaking protection in the event (which is relatively unlikely) that one of the two strands breaks.

Bimini Twist

The Bimini Twist has such an intimidating reputation that many anglers have avoided learning to tie it. It is a knot primarily associated with saltwater fishing, especially the use of heavy leaders and big-game angling; however, its usefulness extends much further than that, especially for making a double-line leader in light-tackle fishing, where a lot of stress might be applied to the last section of the line. This knot is difficult at first to tie, but you can accomplish it in under a minute once you've got it mastered.

To tie the Bimini Twist, follow these steps, which are keyed to the illustration:

1 Measure a little more than twice the footage you'll want for the double-line leader. (First-time tiers should use shorter lengths.) Bring the end back to the standing line and hold together. Rotate the end of the loop twenty times, putting twists in it.

2 Spread the loop to force the twists together about 10 inches below the tag end. Step both feet through the loop, and bring it up around your knees so that you will be able to place pressure on the column of twists by spreading your knees apart.

3 Grasp the tag ends firmly, and force the twists as tightly together as possible by spreading your knees. Hold the standing line in your left hand, which is just slightly off a vertical position, and keep the line taut. With your right hand, move the other end to a position at a right angle to the twists, keeping it taut as well. Keeping tension on the loop with your knees, gradually ease the tension of the tag end in your right hand so that the tag-end line will roll tightly over the column of twists, beginning just below the uppermost twist.

Bimini Twist

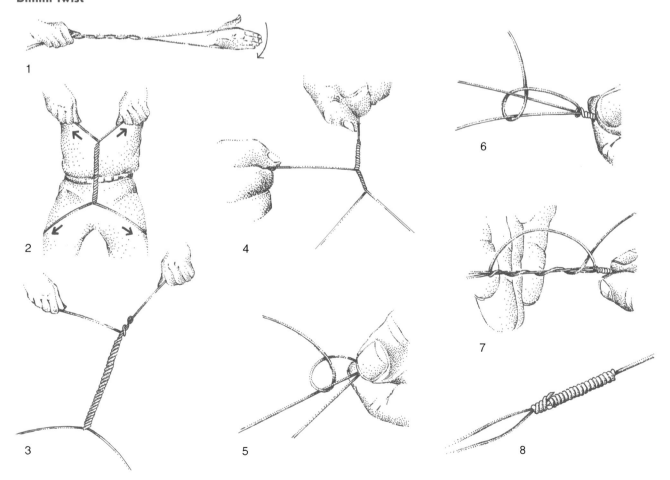

4 Spread your legs apart slowly to maintain pressure on the loop. Steer the tag end into a tight spiral coil as it continues to roll over the twisted line. Keeping a balance of constant tension without slack is critical to this process.

5 When the spiral of the tag end has rolled over the column of twists, continue keeping knee pressure on the loop and move your left hand down to grasp the knot. Place a finger in the crotch of the line where the loop joins to prevent slippage of the last turn; take a half-hitch with the tag end around the nearest leg of the loop, and pull up tight.

6 With a half-hitch holding knot, release knee pressure but keep the loop stretched out. Using the remaining tag end, take a half-hitch around both legs of the loop but do not pull tight.

7 Make three more turns with the tag end around both legs of the loop, winding inside the bend of the line formed by the loose half-hitch and toward the main knot. Pull the tag end slowly, forcing the three loops to gather in a spiral.

8 When the loops are pulled up nearly against the main knot, moisten and tighten to lock in place. Trim the end.

These directions apply to tying double-line leaders of 5 feet or less. For longer double-line sections, two people may be required to hold the line and make initial twists. Or the line could be looped around a firm object, like a cleat, and the twisting done at the tag end. It is also possible to use a Bimini Twist to tie short lengths of double line by placing the loop over one knee that has been tucked underneath your thigh.

Spider Hitch

The Spider Hitch is a very good alternative to the Bimini Twist that is much easier to tie, especially with cold hands. This knot is very useful in lighter-strength line, particularly as a leader in freshwater fishing.

Spider Hitch

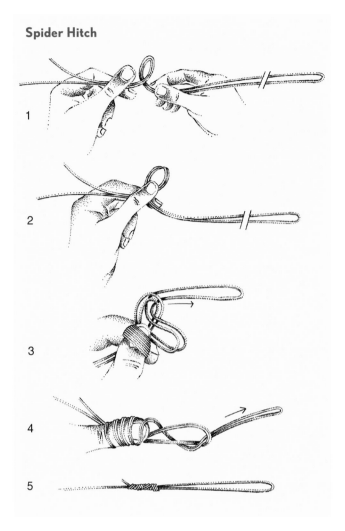

To tie the Spider Hitch, make a loop of whatever length of line you want to use as a leader, and hold the ends between thumb and index finger at the first joint of the thumb. Make a small loop in the line, tuck it between the fingers, and extend it directly in front of the thumb. Wrap the doubled line around the thumb and small loop five times, working toward the tip of the thumb. Then pass the doubled line through the small loop, making the five wraps unwind off the thumb and using a steady draw. Pull firmly on all ends to snug the knot.

11

Hook Sharpening

Even though modern hooks, especially smaller and finer-diameter wire hooks, are factory sharpened to better levels today than ever before, hooks quickly lose sharpness through use, especially from impacts. Sharpening new and previously used hooks smoothes out the rough spots and facilitates getting the point and barb deep enough in the fish to keep it on your line.

The best way to sharpen bigger, hardened thick-bodied hooks, including those of cadmium and stainless steel, and hooks that are forged (flattened around the bend on both sides) is with a file. The file cuts only on the forward stroke. Start by sharpening the barb and the inside cutting edges that lead toward the point, as shown in the accompanying illustration. Use the same angle as the factory-made cutting edge. Do both sides, then move the file forward and do the same thing to the immediate point area, filing repeatedly toward the point on both sides. Put a mini cutting edge on the very tip of the point opposite the barb to facilitate penetration.

For smaller hooks, use a medium-grit honing stone with a channel in it. If a file is all you have, use it to the best of your ability. The key

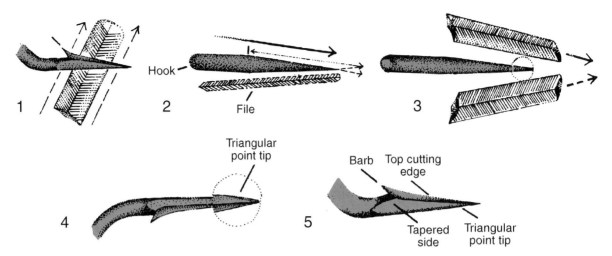

When using a file to sharpen a hook, effect a triangulated cutting area by filing across the inside or top cutting edge, including the barb (1), and by filing along both sides of the hook point (2). With this accomplished, focus on filing the extreme point area (3), creating a mini-triangulated point tip (4). The result is a well-sharpened barb, top, sides, and point tip (5).

to sharpening is not the shape of the sharpening device or its cost, but that it is abrasive and you use it to put a triangulated shape on the hook. Honing stones (generally in the form of a stick) should be sized to the hook being sharpened.

Sharpening stones can be run forward and backward and should be used in the same manner as a file, first grinding on the inside of the point and then on the left and right sides and the very tip. If you use the channel in a sharpening stone, rotate the hook so that all parts of the point are affected. Hold the stone and hook firmly to avoid pricking or hooking yourself with the point, and make smooth, deliberate motions.

To test for sharpness, take a hook, rest the point on your thumbnail, and lightly drag the point across the nail. If the hook is sharp enough, it will catch on the nail; if not, it will slide across.

Avoid oversharpening. If the tapered wedge of the point becomes too short through excessive sharpening, it may not penetrate as well. If it is ground too thin, it may be susceptible to bending or breaking.

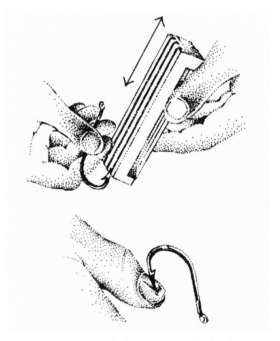

When using a channeled stone, move the hook point back and forth in a channel, changing the angle; then turn the stone crosswise and run it across the barb and sides. The point is sharp enough when it digs into your thumbnail when you drag it across the nail.

12

Putting Line on a Reel

Many problems associated with line actually begin at the first step of line use: putting new line on a reel spool.

Filling Non-Flycasting Reels

How you put line on and how much of it you put on are keys to minimizing twist and enhancing casting. This is especially critical with spinning and spincasting reels.

The best performance of a line and reel is achieved when the reel has been spooled properly. This means filling it almost to the edge, within $1/8$ to $3/16$ inch. If you overfill a spinning reel, line will fall off loosely when slack is given, causing a snarl to develop; several loops of line will pile up and jam in the spool or in a rod guide. Also, line can become pinched in the side flanges of the spool of an overfilled baitcasting or levelwind reel.

A properly filled reel allows you to achieve good distance in your casts, particularly with light lures. An underfilled reel hampers your casting range, since more coils of line (causing more friction) must come off the spool. After a period of time, through cutting frayed line, tying knots, and experiencing breakoffs, the level of line on the reel will become too low. In addition to hampering casting in some fishing situations, too little line might cost you a big fish if you hook one that takes all the remaining line off the reel. Additionally, drag pressure increases as line on the reel arbor decreases, creating a sometimes difficult situation for the angler when fighting a strong, surging fish.

You can put twist in the line by improperly spooling it, which happens often to inexperienced anglers. Unlike microfilaments, nylon monofilament has a memory factor, and it returns to its "memoried" state after being used. Line thus develops a set in the position in which it has been placed for a long time, such as the plastic spool on which it is wound for packaging.

On a consumer spool, not only has the line taken a set, but it actually is slightly coiled already, which is an inherent part of the manufacturer's spooling process. The manufacturer has huge bulk spools of line from which the smaller retail spools are filled. Line that comes off the extreme periphery of a full bulk spool has less coiling than the line that comes off the core of the bulk spool.

You and a friend could conceivably possess the same brand of line in the same strength, and one would be noticeably more coiled than the other. The reason is probably that they came from different locations on the bulk spool, or that they were produced at different times (when one batch of line was more coiled than the other). In any event, the longer that line stays on the retail spool, the more its coils conform to the diameter of the spool. Coiling is less pronounced in top-grade lines and lines that come off large-diameter bulk or service spools.

On baitcasting reels, which are aptly called levelwind reels, line is fairly free of the twisting problems caused by spooling. This is because the line is wound straight onto the reel arbor in a direct, level, overlapping manner. The spooling suggestions that follow can also be applied to baitcasting reels.

Open-faced spinning reels and spincasting (closed-face) reels pose many problems in line spooling for beginning anglers. The reason is that these systems actually put a slight twist in the line as it rotates off the bail arm and onto the arbor. If the line is of poor quality or if it already has a fair degree of manufacturer-instilled coiling and the angler improperly spools it onto a spinning reel, the result can be twisting, curling, coiling line—endless trouble unless it is run out behind the boat and rewound.

The first secret to successful spooling, particularly with nylon monofilament, is watching how the line comes off both sides of the manufacturer's spool. Take line off the side with the least apparent coiling. Then apply moderate pressure on the line before it reaches the reel.

Follow this technique for proper spooling: Place the supply spool on the floor or any flat surface. The line should balloon or spiral off the spool as you pull it up. After you've threaded line through your rod guides and attached it to your reel, hold the rod tip 3 to 4 feet above the supply spool. Make fifteen to twenty turns on the reel handle and stop. Now check for line twist by reducing tension on the line.

Lower the rod tip so that it is a foot from the supply spool, and check to see whether the slack line twists or coils. If it does, turn the supply spool upside down. This will eliminate most of the twist as you wind the rest of the line onto the reel. If the other side has more of a coiled or twisted nature, go back to the first side and take line off while it is face up. The trick here is to take line from the side that has the least amount of coiling. In effect, this method counterspools the line on your spinning reel and cancels the curling tendencies that would otherwise exist.

Although manufacturers have recommended placing a pencil or other object inside a spool to let it run freely while you put on line, this is not as good a method as the one previously described. Although the pencil method may suffice for direct spooling of levelwind reels, it seems to compound the spooling problem on spinning and spincasting reels.

Keeping moderate tension on the line with one hand as you reel with the other is important when filling a reel. Do this by holding the line between your thumb and forefinger with your free hand. A loosely wound reel results from not applying spooling tension and causes loops of line to develop on the reel spool. Excessive tension, however, may bind up the line and allow more line to be spooled than necessary—a fact that you will discover later after the used line starts to bunch

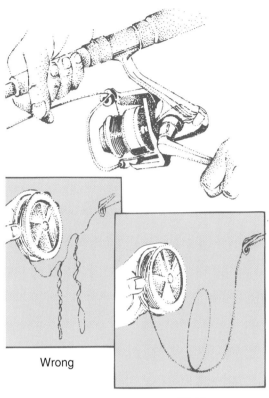

Wrong

Right

Always apply a moderate amount of tension while putting line on a reel (top), and be sure to take line off a filler spool from the side that produces the least coiling.

spooled onto the reel, these types of line need more tension than a comparable nylon monofilament.

Filling Flycasting Reels

A fly reel has to be filled appropriately with backing, then fly line and leader (in that order), and should be filled so that the business end of the fly line is just below the full spool level. Filling it properly helps reduce coiling and lessens the memory of the fly line on the spool.

Technically the process is attaching one end of the backing to the spool of the reel, filling an appropriate amount on the reel, attaching it to the fly line, and then winding the full fly line onto the reel. The sticking point in this is getting the right amount of backing so that the reel is neither underfilled nor overfilled.

Since backing lines vary in diameter, it's hard to do the most logical thing and measure out the manufacturer's suggested backing length and then put it on the reel. You can estimate what seems right, but this often goes awry. The most precise way to fill the reel for the first time is to do it backward, working in an open field or on a large lawn.

Wrap the business end of the fly line around the spool arbor gently so that it gets a bite, and then reel it fully onto the reel, leveling it carefully as you fill it up. Then attach the backing firmly to the exposed end of fly line (use a Uni Knot) and wind the backing on, leveling it until the reel reaches a nearly full level. Cut the backing from the filler spool. Tie the backing to a solid object, and walk off with the reel, allowing the entire line to lie stretched out on the ground. When all the line is off the reel, walk back to where the line is tied and connect the end of the line to the reel arbor. Wind all of the backing and then the fly line onto the reel, leveling it as it fills. Attach a leader to the fly line, and you're ready to rig the rod.

up as you begin to spool it naturally by reeling. So you have to find the right medium.

For some strengths and types of line and some types of fishing tackle, it is important to spool line very tightly onto the reel. Large conventional reels and big-game reels, for example, require that line be wound tightly on them so that the pressure of fishing or of fighting a large fish does not cause wraps of line to become buried into a loosely packed spool. A similar issue holds for using braided or fused microfilament lines; when

13

Casting

The act of delivering a bait, lure, or fly to a fish is an intrinsic element of every type of angling. Good presentation begins with such obvious skills as accurate casting, using a bit of stealth, minimizing noise, and not coming right up on, over, or through areas to be fished. However, effective presentations are greatly aided by getting within proper casting range to make accurate casts and appropriate retrievals.

In many cases, the first cast to a prospective fish lie is the most important one, so getting yourself in the best possible position is especially important. Also important is making repetitive presentations to certain places, and varying the angle of presentation.

Casting, which is the act of throwing an object that is connected to a fishing rod via line, is a fundamental element of many angling activities. The objective is to present a lure or bait at some distance away from the caster's position, and to place it where it will be attractive to the species sought. In many instances, anglers cast to specific habitats, or targets, where fish may be present, or to roaming fish that must be intercepted; in such cases, accuracy—and possibly distance—are vitally important.

Two diametrically opposed principles govern casting. One requires the use of a weighted line to cast a nearly weightless object. This is the principle involved in fly fishing; a fly line carries a fly or flylike object that is virtually weightless although not necessarily small or wind-resistant. This specifically focused activity is detailed separately.

More than 90 percent of all sportfishing activity does not involve fly fishing. In all other forms of fishing, a light or virtually weightless line is used to cast a weighted object—a lure, baited hook, or practice casting plug. The weight of the object cast varies, but it is the terminal weight that carries the line forward or backward. This form of casting is particularly employed with spincasting, spinning, and baitcasting tackle, and is a uniform activity, except when very long rods and very heavy objects are employed, as in surf casting. Surf casting is described separately.

Practice

Accurate casting is a function of experience. For most anglers, especially those who are new to fishing or to using a particular type of tackle, achieving proficiency, and especially accuracy, is derived from practice. Beginners should not wait until they go fishing to learn to cast but should practice before they get near the water by casting at targets in a yard or park.

The best targets to start with are brightly colored plastic hoops or children's wading pools. Set a pair of these out at 25 and 30 feet. Don't try to throw a foot farther until you can hit these targets consistently. Forget about distance and concentrate on accuracy.

Physical strength has little to do with good casting. What does count is developing timing and coordination through practice. If you concentrate on accuracy until you're hitting those targets eight times out of ten, then greater distance will come as a fringe benefit.

Practicing in the yard must be done with hookless objects known as casting weights or casting plugs. These are available in several sizes and in round or flat-sided versions. Flat versions are preferable to round for yard casting. On a hard surface the flat-sided weight is retrieved without much line twist. That's not true of the round type, which roll and spin and can cause twisted line.

Weight size varies with the tackle used. Once you've gotten some confidence by practicing at the learning distances, try using more targets and setting them at varied ranges. In actual fishing, you will be making one cast to an object that is 20 feet away, then to one that is 50 feet away, and then to another that is 35 feet away, perhaps from the same shore or boat position, with each cast separated by only a few seconds. You must be accurate at all distances at any given time, so position the targets at varied ranges.

Make the targets more challenging as you progress. Try plates, cups, tires, and the like. Once you've developed some confidence with one weight, switch to lighter and heavier weights. Not every lure cast will be the same weight nor, for that matter, as aerodynamic as a practice plug.

Spincasting

The spincasting reel is enormously popular because of its ease of use. No better reel exists for the child or adult who wants to enjoy fishing without working too hard at learning how to cast. Although it is fairly easy to cast a country mile with a spincasting reel, it is unfortunately the most difficult reel with which to learn accuracy unless you know the right technique. The problem centers on the pushbutton line-release device.

To operate a spincasting reel, you must depress the pushbutton and hold it in until you're ready for the casting plug to fly out. Many people unfortunately think they must press that button in again to stop the plug; even some manufacturers' manuals recommend this practice. As you'll discover the first time you try it, if you depress the pushbutton while the casting plug is airborne, the plug stops with a jerk and lurches back several feet. But if you don't stop the plug somehow, it flies too far and winds up in the brush or nearest tree, and if you've put much power into the cast while fishing, when you clamp down on the pushbutton again, the lure (and hooks) may come hurtling back at you.

To avoid this and thereby cast accurately, use the forefinger on your noncasting hand (the left forefinger for most people) to control the line.

Casting with a spincasting reel is essentially accomplished by pressing the pushbutton with your thumb (or the trigger with your forefinger) and holding it throughout the backcast, then releasing it at the optimum point of rod flex during the forward motion of the cast. When the button is released, line flows off the spool, through the opening in the reel cover, and out through the guides, carried by the weight of the object at the terminal end of the line.

Before making a cast, set the drag to the proper amount of tension and adjust the position of the plug at the rod tip. The plug (or lure or bait) should hang a few inches below the rod tip. You can get it to this position by reeling in the line until the lure is a few inches from the tip guide; if the reel is right at the tip, then pull a few inches of line off the reel drag, which will cause the lure to hang a few inches below the tip.

If you're right-handed, place the rod and reel in the palm of your left hand so that the handle of the reel is up and facing you. Extend the left forefinger to trap the line against the opening of the spool. Depress the pushbutton with your right thumb and point the rod tip at your intended target. Lift the rod back toward you swiftly, using your wrist and forearm (not the whole arm), and allowing the weight of the plug to flex the rod. In a continuous and unhesitating motion, and still using the wrist and forearm, bring the rod forward in an accelerated motion. Release the line and the pushbutton at the same instant during the forward stroke to cast the plug toward the target. While the casting plug is in the air, the line should flow across the tip of your left forefinger. To put the plug right where you want it, increase upward pressure with

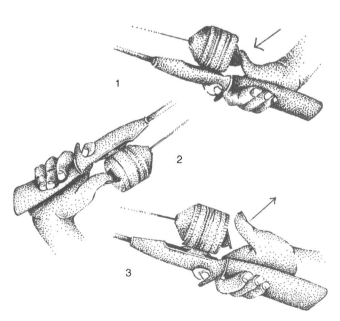

Casting with a spincasting reel begins by pressing the pushbutton with your thumb (1) and holding it throughout the backcast (2); release the pushbutton at the optimum point of rod flex in the forward motion of the cast (3).

the left forefinger. With a bit of practice you will learn at what exact point in the forward stroke to release the line and the pushbutton, which is a major element in attaining the proper trajectory for accurate placement. Casting is the same for left-handed anglers, although hand positions are reversed.

Although these instructions belabor the act of casting, it is really a simple technique that almost anybody can master quickly. You'll quickly learn to feather the line with your left forefinger so that the plug drops right where you want it. Although spincasting does involve the use of both hands, your right hand still executes the casting stroke. The only function of the left hand is to get your left forefinger out where it needs to be to control the line. (Again, this text assumes a right-handed angler.)

For maximum accuracy, get the rod and reel out in front of your body with both hands and make the rod follow an imaginary line from your nose to the target. The most important single phase of the spincasting technique is to have the line flowing over your forefinger while the plug is in the air.

Spinning

Unlike spincasting, spinning tackle is available for nearly all angling applications. Nevertheless, most casting with this equipment involves tackle on the lighter end of the spectrum, and tossing objects that weigh less than half an ounce.

As with all casting equipment, accuracy with spinning tackle requires that you stay in touch with your line while the practice weight is in the air. Spinning reel users usually do this by dropping the right forefinger to feather the line as it comes off the spool, which is moderately but not superbly effective, even in the hands of experts. There are other techniques you can utilize, and they will be described shortly.

Accuracy and distance are affected by the level of line on a spinning reel spool, so you must be attentive to this. Overfilling a spinning reel is a common mistake, and it contributes to loops and errant coils that lead to tangles and hinder casting. Having too little line is better than too much when you are spinning, although you reach a point where too little line can impede achieving distance.

The basic method of casting with spinning equipment involves the following steps: Begin with the reel under the handle and facing away from you. Adjust the drag to the proper tension level. Hang the casting weight (or lure or bait when fishing) from 3 to 6 inches below the tip of the rod, and turn the handle to bring the bail roller close to the reel stem. If the weight is not in this position, reel it up to the tip and strip line off the reel by pulling on the line above the reel. Pull just enough line off the spool that the weight is the right distance below the rod tip, while at the same time bringing the bail roller close to the reel stem and extended index finger. The bail roller must be properly positioned to allow the finger to easily grab the line and to touch the lip of the spool.

To open the bail manually, grab the line at the roller with the tip of your forefinger and flip up the bail with your other hand. To open the bail automatically, depending on the reel, either extend your forefinger over the roller and grab both the line and the trigger, or simply grab the trigger.

Keep tension on the line with your finger; the tension will be released at the optimum point of rod flex in the forward motion of the cast. When this tension is released, line flows off the spool and out through the guides, carried by the weight of the object at the terminal end of the line.

To execute the cast, the reel should face away from you and you should be looking at the back of your hand. Point the rod tip at and slightly above your intended target. When you are learning, and whenever you're striving for accuracy, get the rod and reel out in front of your body and make the rod follow an imaginary line from your nose to the target. Bring the rod back sharply, using your wrist and forearm (not the whole arm) and allowing the weight of the lure to flex the rod. In a continuous and unhesitating motion, and still using the wrist and forearm, bring the rod forward in an accelerated motion, releasing the line with your forefinger during the forward stroke when the rod tip is pointing above the target.

The degree of flex in the rod will depend on the rod design and material; pure graphite rods require only a short hammering type of stroke, whereas more parabolic composite or fiberglass rods require a back-and-forth motion. With a bit of practice, you'll learn what adjustment to make for the rod action as well as for different lure weights, and you'll learn at exactly what point in the forward stroke to release the line, which is a

major element in attaining the proper trajectory for accurate placement. If the lure goes too high in the air, the line was released prematurely; if the lure lands a short distance in front of you, the line was released too late.

The released line can be moderately controlled during a cast by allowing it to brush against an extended index finger from the rod-holding hand; the finger should be held near the spool lip. This is called feathering and is the most common method of controlling line that is cast from a spinning reel, although it is only moderately effective at achieving accuracy.

Better accuracy can be obtained by allowing the outgoing line to brush against the forefinger of the noncasting hand, although the open bail wire may make this difficult. To do this, the front of the reel has to be in the palm of the other (usually left) hand; extend the left forefinger out and press it against the lip of the reel's spool, keeping it there during the casting motions. When the cast is made and the weight released, keep the left hand

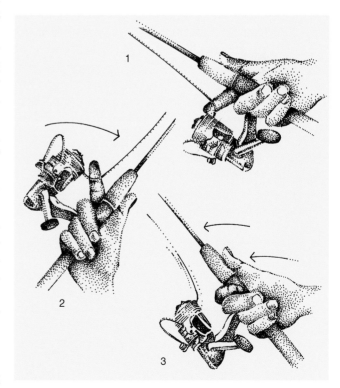

To cast most spinning reels, open the bail and use the tip of the forefinger to grip the line (1); then bring the rod back (2). As the rod comes forward, release the line (3) when the rod tip is pointing above the target.

in place and control the line by applying slight pressure on it with the left forefinger. This method puts your left forefinger on top of your line as it peels off the spool during the cast.

On some reels, the location of the open bail arm makes this two-handed method of line control a little difficult, but it can nevertheless be done. An improvement is removing the bail arm.

In lieu of feathering the line in either of these manners, many spinning reel users simply stop the cast altogether either by pressing the extended index finger against the spool, by closing the bail, or waiting for the end of forward momentum when the lure or weight reaches its target. Abruptly pressing a finger against the spool and closing the bail may cause the plug to stop abruptly and even lurch back toward you; allowing the lure to stop when it loses its own momentum is suitable only for open-water situations and cannot be used when obstructions are present or when pinpoint accuracy is necessary. These acts are not conducive to pinpoint casting, although they may be acceptable in situations where exact placement of a lure or bait isn't required.

Many people find it more comfortable and more secure to use two hands on the rod; this way they are able to attain greater distance and/or straight-line casts. Two-handed casts are made by placing the secondary hand on the lower part of the rod handle and using both forearms and wrists to execute the proper motions; the secondary hand can be released from the rod while the casting weight is airborne, and moved up to the reel if desired. Many anglers use two hands for nearly all casting with spinning rods; when using large tackle and heavy lures, it is virtually mandatory.

Lowering your casting weight, lure, or bait a short distance below the rod tip is a necessary component of casting, but exactly how far is variable. You can put it too far or not far enough. This depends to some extent on the rod you're using as well as the weight of the object being cast. When using spinning gear, leave a longer drop from rod tip to practice plug than you would with a baitcasting outfit; timing on the cast seems to work out better if you do. Usually, the lighter the object you're casting, the longer drop you'll want between it and the rod tip. Practice will determine what works best for you. Try letting out different amounts of line between your rod tip and the plug. When you find out what you like best, stick with it.

Spinning tackle is relatively easy to cast; with it you can cast light lures a significant distance.

An alternative to releasing the line with your forefinger after you've opened the bail is simply to drop the forefinger straight down to trap the line against the side of the reel's spool. When you cast, release finger pressure; then use the same forefinger to feather the line while the plug is in the air.

Line loops that form on reel spools often occur because of slack line that is momentarily present after a cast. To minimize slack line, don't crank the handle right away after a cast. Instead, reach out and manually close the bail arm with your left hand; then grab the line ahead of the bail roller with your left hand and pull off a few inches. Raise your rod tip at the same time. If you discipline yourself to do this after each cast, you'll eliminate a lot of problems; however, this technique is obviously not applicable in situations where you must begin retrieving the instant your lure hits the water.

Baitcasting

Baitcasting tackle shines at providing accuracy, particularly where anglers need pinpoint lure placement, yet it gets rapped for being difficult to learn, being prone to spool overruns that produce horrible line snarls known as backlashes, and not being useful for casting lightweight objects since its foremost use is in casting objects that weigh upward of $\frac{3}{8}$ ounce.

It is true that a person who has never used a baitcasting reel cannot pick one up and become an accurate or effective caster in a few minutes. However, if the rod and reel are of good quality and set up properly, and if a new user follows proper instructions and is willing to practice, he or she will soon be reasonably accomplished. Furthermore, that angler will be on the path to great proficiency as well as successful fishing with a form of tackle that is often preferable to spinning or spincasting.

Baitcasting reels are noted for accuracy because they feature revolving spools that can be controlled constantly by the user's thumb. They are considered problematic because learning to apply appropriate thumb pressure to the spool in order to control it takes practice, and failure to control the spool produces an annoying overrun. To simplify casting, reel manufacturers have developed braking devices that apply tension to spools to prevent, or at least minimize, overruns, although not all reels have them and not everyone is benefited by them. Users must learn to cast without the aid of these devices so that they will be able to use any type of baitcasting reel under any circumstance.

Practicing with baitcasting tackle is as important, or more so, than with other gear. When practicing with baitcasting equipment in a yard or park, use a heavier weight than you would with other gear; a ⅝-ounce weight is best for new users and helps achieve a feel for the game. You can practice with lighter weights after you've achieved a comfortable level of proficiency.

Assuming that you are right-handed, the basic cast starts with holding the outfit in your right hand with your thumb on the spool. The drag should be adjusted for angling conditions, and the casting weight should be adjusted to the proper position at the rod tip. The weight (or lure or bait when fishing) should hang a few inches below the rod tip. You can get it to this position by reeling in the line until the lure is a few inches from the tip guide; if the reel is right at the tip, then pull a few inches of line off the reel drag, which will cause the lure to hang a few inches below the tip. With the weight in position, depress the freespool button or bar with your thumb and then rest it on the spool to secure the line.

To cast, take a relaxed stance with your rod and reel out in front of your body. Rotate your wrist to the left so your knuckles and the reel handle are up. This unlocks the wrist joint. The

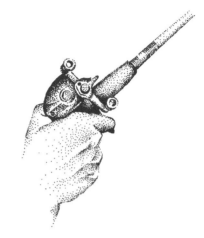

This is the common way to hold baitcasting tackle; turn your wrist so that reel handles face upward when casting.

wrist does almost all of the work in a well-executed cast. When the wrist is turned so that the knuckles face up, the joint has greater flexibility and can work the rod so that the tip comes up far enough to provide the necessary casting power. Wrist action along with a slight upward movement of the right forearm is all the effort needed to cast properly.

To make the casting weight go where you want, draw an imaginary line from your nose to the target. Make your rod move back and forth along this line as you cast. The entire casting stroke should be executed out in front of your body; do not let the rod tip come way back over your shoulder. If you keep your rod and reel out in front of your body as you cast, and your rod moves back and forth along this imaginary line, there's no way you can be off to the right or left of your target. You'll be off in depth in the beginning, but not to the left or right, and depth perception will improve with practice.

Casting in this manner keeps you from making the mistake of letting the rod tip come way back over the right shoulder. If you do that, your arm will be doing the work of the rod, and you won't be able to make the rod travel along that imaginary nose-to-target line that is helpful for achieving accuracy. Keeping the rod in front of your body forces it to work for you.

With practice you'll develop and hone timing and coordination. As you become more skilled, you'll find that you never completely remove

A baitcasting tackle user shows good form by keeping his rod directly in front of him to help direct and follow a lure toward its target.

your thumb from the reel except at the instant you let the practice weight fly out. You lift the thumb so that the spool can start, but you maintain contact to keep the line flowing smoothly and to slow the spool and drop the lure neatly into the target. This constant contact with the line as it pays out is what enables the expert caster to obtain pinpoint accuracy and, in some situations, a soft landing.

Many people find it more comfortable and more secure to use two hands on the rod, and are able to attain greater distance and/or straight-line casts. Two-handed casts are made by placing the secondary hand on the lower part of the rod handle and using both forearms and wrists to execute the proper motions. This is easiest to accomplish on rods with a long, straight handle. Some anglers use two hands for almost all their baitcasting; when you're using big outfits and heavy lures, two hands are virtually mandatory.

Preventing an overrun by screwing down every tension control device on your baitcasting reel is indeed possible, but it is not a good idea, even for beginners. Timing, coordination, and a trained thumb are developed through practice. Don't

depend only on mechanical features to eliminate your backlashes.

This doesn't mean that you shouldn't use these controls at all as you learn. Read what the manufacturer has to say about tension controls in the manual supplied with the reel. But no matter what the best of these reels promises, realize that you will lose casting efficiency when you rely entirely on those controls.

Most reel manufacturers suggest setting your controls so that a casting weight drops slowly when you take your thumb off the spool, and the spool stops turning as soon as the casting weight hits the ground. This technique is all right for starters, but strive to train your thumb so you can depend on it to control the spool.

Types of Casts

The basic casting information provided here for spincasting, spinning, and baitcasting tackle applies to all types of casts. The example used is the most common and straightforward situation, known as the overhead cast or the straight-ahead cast because the rod tip is raised vertically and

Types of Casts

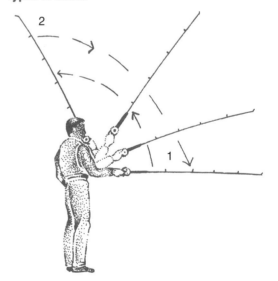

Shown is the basic overhead casting motion for spincasting, spinning, and baitcasting tackle. Note that the process starts with the rod aimed at the target and that the backcast (1) extends no further back than an imaginary 1 o'clock position before the forward cast (2) begins.

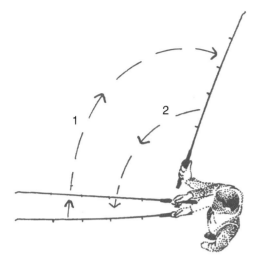

The dynamics of the sidearm cast for spincasting, spinning, and baitcasting tackle are the same as those for the overhead cast. The process starts with the rod aimed at the target, and the backcast (1) extends slightly past a perpendicular position before the forward cast (2) begins.

the line is projected directly in front of the caster, whose eyes pick up the flight of the line and the cast object immediately. There are many situations, however, when it is not possible, or beneficial, to cast in this manner, either because of the nature of the cover in which some species are found or because of the necessity for accurate lure placement. Such situations give rise to a side cast, underhand cast, lob cast, and flip cast, which will be discussed shortly, and to specialized procedures such as flipping and pitching.

To recap the overhead cast, the wrist and forearm do all the work, using the top section of the rod for thrust. The cast begins with the rod low and pointed at the target. The rod is brought up crisply to a point slightly beyond vertical position, where flex in the rod tip will carry it back; then, without hesitation, the forward motion is started sharply, the lure being released halfway between the rod's vertical and horizontal positions. The entire casting action is a smooth, flowing motion; you are doing more than just hauling back and heaving.

The side cast, or sidearm cast, uses essentially the same motion as the overhead cast, except that it features horizontal movement. It begins with the rod low and pointed slightly outward. The wrist and forearm are used to flex the top section of the rod back and then forward, releasing the line

just before the rod tip is pointed at its target, and following through with the forward motion after line release in order to bring the rod in front of you.

Getting the timing down, especially the proper moment to release the line, is a little more difficult and requires some practice, as does achieving accuracy, and accuracy is affected by the fact that the line, lure, and rod are not immediately aligned with the caster's eye and the lure is not as quickly picked up as it heads toward its target, although it does have a much lower trajectory than the overhead cast.

You can modify the conventional side cast into a side lob cast by starting with the rod tip pointed low toward the water and raising the tip on the forward motion; this action raises the trajectory but produces a soft landing, which is good for shallow water. The same thing can be achieved by reaching across your body and sending the lure out with a backhand motion.

The conventional side cast is advantageous when overhead cover (like an overhanging tree limb) has to be avoided, or when there is a lot of wind; keeping the line and lure low to the water minimizes drifting off course and is a good way to deal with a blow. This cast is not very effective when distance has to be achieved, and it can be dangerous if performed next to another angler in a

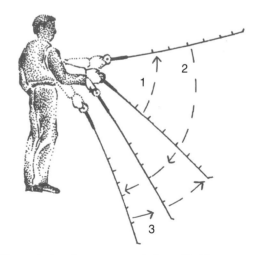

The underhand cast starts with the rod held waist-high, angled halfway between vertical and horizontal positions. From this attitude the rod must be flexed up (1), then down (2), then up (3) again to gain momentum for the lure through the flex of the rod; on the second upward flex, the line is released.

small boat, so you must be mindful of the position of your companions at all times.

To make an underhand cast, hold the rod waist-high, angled halfway between vertical and horizontal and pointed at the target. The rod must be flexed up, then down, then up again to gain momentum for the lure through the flex of the rod; on the second upward flex, the line is released.

This cast has very little arm movement but plenty of wrist action and can be useful when other casting motions are severely restricted. Many rods, however, are too stiff to permit this kind of casting.

The flip cast is another cast used in special situations. Employed in tight quarters or for short ranges, it is a cross between the sidearm and underhand casts (different from flipping). It starts with the rod horizontal to your side, but you bring it backward only a short distance and then make a loop with the tip so that the tip springs around in a 270-degree arc and flips the lure straight out and low. This cast is used for short-distance (under 20 feet) work in areas where you can't bring your rod up or back for a conventional cast. It is a very efficient and very accurate cast when mastered but is almost impossible to accomplish while sitting down in a boat.

Another cast is the bow-and-arrow cast, which is a short-distance cast used with a limber rod in tight quarters. In this cast, you hold a lure by its rear hook in one hand and simultaneously release the hook and line from a freespooled reel. This cast is rarely used in actual angling situations, since many rods, especially graphite baitcasters, are not limber enough for it, and a flip cast will do just as well. Obviously you have to be careful about holding the hooks if you try this cast.

Casting Distance Issues

Although surf anglers and people fishing in special situations have always had to make long casts, in recent times emphasis on achieving distance has increased. Thanks to thinner line diameters, improved reel and rod design, and even more aerodynamic lures, casting a great distance with all forms of casting tackle except fly gear is easier to accomplish than ever, although long casts are not always necessary or desirable.

With some species of freshwater fish, and in some types of water, seldom do anglers need to cast great distances. The clarity of the water is

This angler gains casting leverage by using his left hand on the butt of the rod to propel a large lure a long way from the beach.

one criterion for distance. Generally, fish in clear water are spookier than those in turbid water. The more difficult it is to see the lure as you drop it in the water, the murkier the water is; this is an indication that you can probably get fairly close to your quarry.

A prime benefit of getting close is simply the ease with which you can achieve accuracy. This is especially true when fishing in heavy cover. The effect of wind is also minimized at shorter distances; when using baitcasting gear, a shorter distance means that the chance of a backlash is lessened.

One of the drawbacks to long-distance casting with any type of tackle is the loss of fish; at long distances, more fish that strike lures and get hooked are lost before being landed than those that are hooked at shorter ranges. This is because anglers are more effective at setting the hook at short and midrange distances than at long distances.

Using a line with little or no stretch may help increase hooksetting efficiency at longer distances, as will using ultrasharp hooks. Most long-distance fish are lost because the hook slipped out or was thrown when the fish jumped. Rather than casting long distances as a matter of habit, you might try making a stealthier approach.

Flycasting Technique

Casting with fly rod and fly line has the aura of being difficult, but it needn't be. It does require an adroit combination of coordinated wrist and forearm movement, but brute strength isn't necessary, nor is a lot of wrist action or quick, whippy rod movements. Flycasting is different from other types of casting because the line is cast instead of the lure and because two hands are used in the process, one for rod control and the other for line control. There are two primary casts: the overhead and the roll, with the former predominating. Hauling is a maneuver used in overhead casting to accelerate the line.

Overhead Cast

The overhead cast is the basic cast in fly fishing. It has both forward and backward movements, with a brief pause in between, and starts with picking line up from the water. A good backcast is dependent on picking the line up off the water properly and is important for presenting the fly ahead of you, so all of the elements of this cast are interrelated.

This is the basic overhead flycasting process, assuming that you are facing right and casting to the right: Beginning with the fly line and leader fully extended straight out in front of you and the rod in an approximate 3 o'clock position (if viewed from the right side), raise the rod decisively to the 12 o'clock position and flick your wrist sharply, allowing the rod to go no farther than an 11 o'clock position. This action brings the fly line and leader off the water and sends it in the air behind you. Pause for an instant to let the line straighten out, and, just as it does, bring the rod forward to the 1 o'clock position. A tight

loop should unfurl. As the line straightens and the fly reaches its destination, follow through by lowering the rod tip. The forward casting movement is akin to hammering a nail into the wall, and the right timing is needed to load the rod properly for optimum forward impetus. Realize that the clock positions mentioned are guidelines for casting, but not absolutes, and that the quality of the rod and length of line cast have a bearing on exact positions and variances in timing.

Since this cast starts with the action of raising the rod, which picks up the line in front of you and starts it into the air, it is important to get the initial element right. This is best done with a somewhat slow and deliberate motion rather than a quick, snapping one. Using your left hand to pull down on the fly line, which is known as a single haul, helps.

Unlike casting with other types of tackle, most flycasting is not a series of one-shot casts. It is often necessary to move the fly line and fly through the air in a series of continuous motions to get out the right amount of line to place the fly correctly. This is called false casting, and it means making two, three, or sometimes four backward and forward casting motions without allowing line or fly to touch the water before laying down the line and fly. This is also used to dry surface flies out so that they float better.

The overhead cast is used for all distances, although as the distance to be cast increases, many anglers tend to push at the end of the forward cast, or wait too long for line to unfurl on the backcast. Shooting tapers and weight-forward lines help

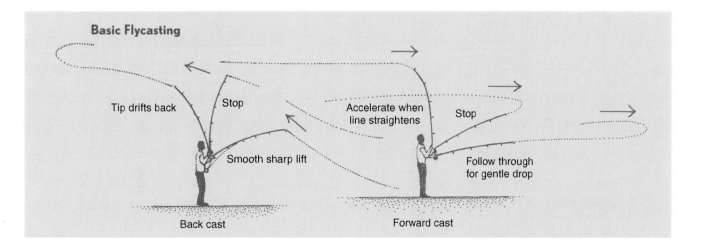

Basic Flycasting

Tip drifts back Stop Accelerate when line straightens Stop

Smooth sharp lift Follow through for gentle drop

Back cast Forward cast

achieve distance, as does employing coils of line in one hand for quick release or using the single- or double-haul technique.

Beginning flycasters should practice on a closely cropped lawn with targets and then move to practicing on the water, instead of trying to learn while actually fishing. Beginners, and anglers having casting trouble, should make short-distance casts and watch the line unfurl behind them to get the timing between the end of the backward motion and the beginning of the forward motion right, and to see if they are managing to get tight loops in the unfurling line. If you hear a snapping or cracking sound when casting, the forward cast was started too soon; this rarely happens when you start the backcast because the line is in front of you and you can see it readily. Watch behind you to help develop timing and rhythm.

Getting in-air line loops under control is important to good casting and also for dealing with certain situations. The size or width of the loop is determined by the length of the casting stroke and the movement of the rod tip. If the tip of the rod moves in a wide arc due to a long powerful stroke,

the line will have a wide, or deep, loop, and the line will fall on the water with a lot of slack in it. This may be desirable in some situations, such as when you need to have a long natural drift in flowing water. A short stroke produces a tight, or narrow, loop, which has less air resistance and thus is better for distance and accurate fly placement. Generally, a tight loop is preferable for fishing, and it is especially desirable when casting into the wind.

It is important to keep your arm movements to a minimum, relying on wrist and forearm action when casting; do not lift your elbow up high or raise your arm so that the rod hand winds up over your head. If your arm moves a lot, casting will suffer. Try to perfect a motion that is more akin to hammering a nail than to tossing a ball.

Hauling

Hauling is a means of accelerating the line to load the rod and is used to help pick the line off the water for the backcast or to shoot out a greater length of it in the forward cast. Doing either one of these alone is a single haul, and doing both in the same casting sequence is known as a double haul.

Double Haul Casting

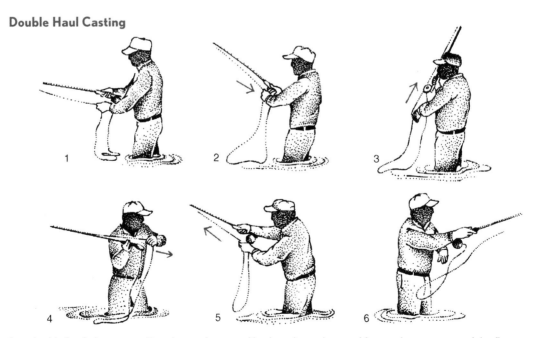

In a double haul, the non-rod hand provides speed both to the pickup and forward momentum of the fly line. On the backcast, use this hand to grip the line (1), then briskly pull the line as you raise the rod (2). The line hand drifts back up toward the reel (3) as it yields some line and as the line straightens on the backcast. On the forward cast, the line hand, now closer to the reel, briefly comes forward with the rod and then briskly pulls the line (4), which speeds up the outflow (5). Release the line from your noncasting hand and allow extra fly line to shoot out the rod guides (6) to gain distance.

In a double-haul cast, the angler uses the non-rod hand to give some speed to both the pickup and the forward momentum of the fly line. It is a technique that takes practice to master because the motions have to be blended properly together.

Assuming that you cast with the right hand and hold fly line in your left, you would accomplish this as follows: Hold the line firmly in your left hand ahead of and close to the reel; at the same instant that you raise the rod to lift line off the water for an overhead cast, pull sharply on the line in your left hand, bringing it down toward your left hip. As the line rises into the air on the backcast, raise your left hand and release some of the line to extend the backward length of the fly line in the air; as the line straightens out behind you, grab the line near the reel with your left hand and, at the same time as your right hand begins to power the rod forward, pull sharply down on the line in your left hand. As the rod comes forward, release the line in your hand to shoot it through the guides and extend the casting distance.

To get greater amounts of line out, which is called shooting the line, you can strip 10 to 12 feet of it off the reel onto the ground (beware of line-catching obstructions) and send it "shooting" through the rod guides by properly hauling it. This is preferable to using a series of tiring false casts to extend the length of line being cast.

Inexperienced flycasters should not attempt hauling until they have mastered a fluid basic overhead casting motion with tight loops. Start with the single haul, especially for lifting line off the water, and begin with modest amounts of line to master the motion.

Roll Cast

The roll cast is a very practical cast for making fly presentations at a distance of 40 to 50 feet and also as a means of laying out line to pick it up for a standard overhead cast. It is often used as a standard means of manipulating a line and presenting a fly when there is no room behind you to make a backcast for overhead casting. A roll cast has no backcasting motion per se, and the line is not lifted off the water into the air as in an overhead cast.

To roll cast: Raise the rod tip up steadily but not too quickly until it is just past a vertical position (generally when the rod gets past your ear)

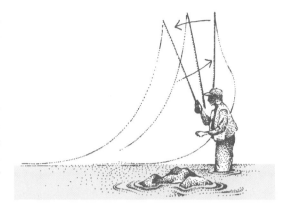

The critical elements of roll casting are smoothly bringing the rod tip up to just past a vertical position, keeping the fly line to the far side of the rod, and punching the rod sharply forward.

and at a point where there is a curved bow of line extending from the rod tip behind you; then bring the rod sharply forward and downward in a nail-hammering motion. The last action brings the line rolling toward you with leader and fly following, then rolls it over and lays it all out straightaway. When you bring up the rod to execute this cast, cant it slightly outward; the line coming from the rod tip must be to the outside of the tip, not between the tip and your body.

You can also use the roll cast to straighten out line that is crumpled in front of you, or otherwise lying awkwardly, and lift it smoothly off the water. Make a relaxed roll cast to get the line straight ahead of you, and then immediately lift it off the water to execute an overhead cast.

Roll casting is easiest with floating and slow-sinking lines and with sink-tip lines that are not too deep. A distance of 20 to 30 feet is easiest to roll cast.

Specialty Casts

The fly line, leader, and fly can be manipulated during or after the cast. Manipulation during the cast is called an in-air mend; after the cast, it is an on-water mend. The technique of mending fly line is used in flowing water to aid the natural drift of a fly, and is something not done with other types of fishing line or tackle.

The same motion that is used for overhead flycasting can be adapted to sidearm casting with a bit of practice. In close quarters and wind, the best way to get a fly to a target is to turn your body directly away from the target, cast in the opposite direction, and use what would ordinarily be the backcast to lay the fly down.

Problems and Solutions

Casting problems essentially result from bad habits and poor technique, which underscores the importance of learning fundamentals. Some of the common difficulties experienced by flycasters are briefly noted here, along with ways to deal with them.

A wind knot is an overhand knot that is usually found in the leader and most often results from overacceleration of the rod; a smooth stroke helps eliminate this and also prevents the fly from hitting the rod or hooking the line.

Hitting the water on the backcast is a result of a low backcast, caused by overextending the backward casting stroke, which drives the line down, or is the result of slow line speed; the solution is to cast with a stiff wrist, stop the backcast in a high position, and keep the rod tip from drifting back.

Piling up line, leader, and fly at the end of the cast is caused by a wide loop, which results from an overextended casting arc; shorten the casting stroke, and stop the rod abruptly to get a tighter loop and extended line.

Slapping the water with the fly, leader, and fly line is caused by lowering the rod tip at the end of the forward casting motion; keep a short stroke, and aim the cast higher so that the line and fly settle gently.

Failure to get even a short amount of line out and moving fluidly is often the first problem a beginning caster has and is due to mismatched tackle, letting line slip out during the casting stroke, or waving the rod through a wide instead of narrow arc. Using properly matched tackle and keeping a firm grip on the line will solve this issue. Proper technique requires using only your wrist and forearm to move the rod in a narrow path to create tight loops, which will allow the line to cast smoothly.

Surf Casting

Propelling heavy objects a considerable distance to get away from the beach or a jetty is the critical issue in surf casting, and long rods are mandatory. A 7- to 10-foot rod will work well up to 150 feet. An 11- to 13-foot rod will cast as far as anyone

A North Carolina surf angler prepares to launch a heavily weighted bait.

needs to go if it is well matched to the angler. There's no need for anything longer.

Although thick-bodied metal lures and weighted surface plugs, which are often used in surf fishing, produce long casts, they may not always produce fish. Sometimes only a big hunk of cut bait will catch a fish. The problem with casting a heavy sinker and a big hunk of bait is trying to move two different objects in the same direction at the same time. The sinker sits at the very end of the line and by itself would be easy to cast. Add a second weight that has completely different aerodynamic properties and is dangling from a leader offset from the main line, and you encounter a problem.

When trying to get a lure or bait into distant water, you do not need to start running from the base of the dunes to just short of the water's edge before making a cast. Forward body speed is not carried over to the cast. Stay in one spot and concentrate on making a good casting motion, using the rod to maximize leverage.

As a safety matter, always look behind you before making a cast to make sure that no fellow anglers, children, bathers, or pets are behind you. If you are casting in big waves or on a jetty, wait for the proper moment to cast rather than risking that you may fall or take a plunge.

To begin the most basic cast, start with the bait and sinker lying on the beach behind you. While facing the ocean, point the tip of the rod directly at the rig, take out all line slack, and then bring the rod tip up sharply over your head, stopping at an imaginary 10 o'clock position as you release the line. Many beginners have a problem releasing the line at the proper time. Practice will overcome this problem.

Small rigs with one or two hooks are much easier to cast. Some rigs have a release system that holds the hook tight to the line but lets it swing free when the rig hits the water. This produces an aerodynamic packet that should go farther toward the horizon.

For extreme distances, try the pendulum cast, a technique that requires swinging a single weight around, behind, and over your head to load the rod with the maximum amount of energy. With this technique, surf casters may top 600 feet using outfits capable of bringing in a fish. To practice this cast, you'll need a very long practice field with plenty of room on all sides because a breakoff will often travel to the right or left of the caster.

A modified version of the pendulum cast will do the job in most fishing situations. Hold the rod over your shoulder, and let the rig swing just above the ground. Push the rod back until the rig swings straight out, loading the rod. Come around in a sidearm fashion, and release the line when you feel maximum load.

Conventional reels permit longer casts than spinning reels because their revolving spools actually push the line off the reel, and there is less coiling and friction from the departing line. If left uncontrolled, the line will overrun the spool and create a backlash. Expert casters control the line with light thumb pressure on the spool; most people rely on counterweights or magnets to do this job, in some cases with a moderate amount of thumb pressure. These cast-control mechanisms cut down on maximum casting distance, however, especially when dealing with such forces and distances as are required for surf fishing.

Flipping

Flipping is a fairly simple, controlled short-casting technique used in close quarters for presenting a moderately heavy jig or plastic worm in a short, quiet, accurate manner to cover that cannot be properly worked by a lure cast from a long distance away. It is a premier close-to-cover fishing technique almost exclusively used by bass

anglers standing up in a boat. The basic principle of flipping, however, can be useful when fishing for other species and when wading, fishing from shore, or fishing from a float tube. It is best when there is thick cover, when the water is turbid, and when a jig or weighted worm is used, but it can be employed at times with other lures and in other circumstances.

The tackle required is a long rod, heavy line, and a jig or worm. The rod should be between 7 and 8 feet long, with a long, straight handle. It must be stout and preferably one-piece, with an upper section that telescopes down into the handle for easy transportation and storage. Most flipping is done with baitcasting tackle, but some anglers prefer spinning gear. The same rod features, however, are applicable. Flipping takes a toll on arm muscles if done for a long period of time; because of this, a graphite rod, weighing considerably less than fiberglass, is desirable.

The reel used on a flipping rod can be the same that you use for other bass fishing applications, but it is best if the reel has a narrow spool (line capacity is not a factor) and is light. It should also have

This thick fallen cover on Missouri's Truman Lake could not be fished properly by casting from afar.

a clear sideplate (no knobs sticking out on which to catch line). A reel that allows one-handed operation is preferable. A so-called flipping feature, which allows the line to be stripped out without having to disengage and reengage the freespool, makes a difference in convenience when flipping, since you often have to strip off more line but don't have to take time to crank the handle to engage the gears. The rod and reel are complemented by heavy-strength low-stretch line.

The goal is to make a pinpoint bait presentation to a particular object within 10 to 20 feet of the boat and to do so in a quiet, splash-free manner. Seldom are you able to flip while sitting down;

To flip, let out about 7 to 9 feet of line from rod tip to lure; strip line off the reel and hold it in your left hand (1). Point the rod tip up and out, and swing the jig forward (2). The bait will come back toward you; when it reaches the top of its pendulum-like swing, direct it toward the target (3). Lower the rod tip, and let line flow through your free hand; extend your rod arm if necessary to reach the target, and keep the line in your hand (4).

this is a technique that requires stand-up work. To begin flipping, let out about 7 to 8 feet of line from rod tip to lure; the rule of thumb is to let out an amount about equal to the length of the rod. Strip line off the reel until your free hand and rod hand are fully extended away from each other; this will give you 5 to 7 feet of line in your free hand. If you have a 7½-foot rod, you're now able to reach a target about 20 feet away.

To flip your bait out, hold the flipping rod at about a 45-degree angle and pull on the line with your left hand to get the bait moving backward. Now drop the rod tip, and start bringing it up to move the lure forward. Practice so you can speed the lure forward to its target with just a slight flexing of your wrist. Let the extra line you're holding in your left hand slide out through the rod guides. Move your left hand forward as the line flows out. Do it right, and the practice plug should go out in a low trajectory and land accurately and softly on its intended target. Extend your rod arm if necessary to reach the target, although you're too far away if you have to do this.

Do not hold on to the line in your hand once it reaches the target. As a flip cast is completed, let your left hand move forward as the extra line you've been holding in it slides out through the guides. It's natural and easy to make this movement. You should wind up with your left hand up close to the rod and just in front of the reel. At that point, position your thumb and the forefinger of the left hand on top of the rod. The other three fingers of the left hand should go under the rod. Make sure the line coming from the reel runs under your thumb and over the forefinger of your left hand. Having the line in this position lets your thumb and forefinger feel every little bump as the lure you're using works through cover. Having your left hand out there also permits you to grip the rod in two hands at the strike, making for a stronger, more solid hookset. Then you may play the fish in the conventional manner, with one hand on the reel handle and the other on the rod handle, and work it out of the cover.

When you retrieve the lure to move it to another spot, lower the rod tip and point it toward the lure; grab the line between the reel and the first guide with your free hand and strip it back while lifting up on your rod. Swing the lure out and back, and send it forward again to the next object.

When the lure is in the water, you may jig it up and down or crawl it along after it has fallen freely to the bottom. Climb it up, over, and through all of the cover. Closely watch the line for the slightest movement, and be attentive to the softest strike. Don't keep it in any one place long, and try to nudge it through cover instead of ripping it.

Pitching

Pitching is a technique for casting under obstructions by using a low-trajectory approach to the targeted area. It is a cast that does not develop a lot of rod-tip speed and isn't used for great distances, yet one that provides accuracy and soft presentations for lures dispatched to hard-to-reach places.

Rods that are best for pitching are often 6½ feet long and designed for lines ranging from 8 to 17 pounds. This is a versatile tool that can be used for many other activities. It should be matched with a good-quality baitcasting reel, preferably one with a flipping feature for versatility, since you might get a strike as soon as your lure enters the water, in which case it's good to have a reel that engages the moment you release pressure on the freespool device.

The pitch cast is made with either a two-handed, low-trajectory cast or with a one-handed pendulum motion. Both work well but serve slightly different purposes. Practice is the key to learning either one.

To execute the pendulum cast with a practice casting weight, let out line so that the weight hangs down to just above your reel. Put the reel into freespool, and keep your thumb on the spool. Raise the rod tip to swing the lure forward, and then permit it to swing back toward your body. Swing it forward again, and release thumb pressure on the reel's spool as the lure comes forward. If your timing is right, the lure will fly out in low, level flight to its intended target. When practicing on land, the weight should stay down close to the ground so that in actual fishing the lure stays close to the surface of the water. The key to making this cast properly is getting enough movement in the practice weight to pull line off the spool as you release thumb pressure.

Be sure to use a ⅝-ounce weight in practice sessions. This weight may be heavier than the lure you'll use for fishing, but the beginning

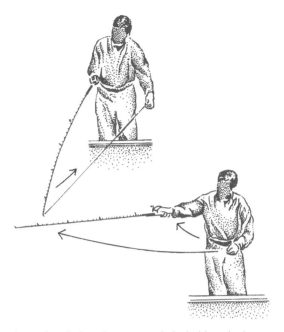

A two-handed pitch cast is made by holding the lure (be wary of hooks) in your left hand and pulling on the line to bring your rod tip down so that it has a slight bend (top). Bring the rod up as you let go of the weight, and take your thumb off the reel spool (bottom) to send the lure toward its target on a low trajectory.

objective is to learn how to execute the cast and polish your timing, and such a weight makes it much easier to do this.

An educated thumb and a low spool tension setting on the reel are critical. You won't be able to develop the power in pitching that you get with a conventional cast, so you need to set your reel so that the spool operates fast and easy. Having the tension set lightly means you have to control things with your thumb. The only way to do that is through practice.

The pendulum method for pitching is best when using fairly heavy lures and where most of the targets are close. Most pitching is done with a jig and pork frog or perhaps a jig and grub combination. The pendulum method works best with a leadhead jig weighing ⅜ ounce and up.

Like the pendulum cast, the two-handed pitch technique permits you to keep a lure down so that it can be made under an overhanging obstruction. The main advantage is greater distance without sacrificing accuracy or soft presentation.

To make a two-handed pitch cast, put the reel into freespool and let out enough line that the practice weight drops down even with your reel. Hold the practice weight in your left hand, and pull on the line to bring your rod tip down until it has a slight bend. Bring the rod up as you let go of the weight, and take your thumb off the reel spool at the same time. If you do it right, the lure will speed away to its target with a low trajectory.

Make sure you don't overload the rod on the two-handed pitch. If you pull the tip of your rod down hard to get more distance, the reel will start with a quick jerk that even an experienced thumb can't control; you don't have to pull hard on the line to bring the rod tip down. It is essential that your pitching rod have a fast enough tip to send the lure to its target with just one smooth movement.

Practice lifting your rod arm at the exact instant you release the casting weight. This is the key to good pitching. If your timing is just right, the practice weight or lure will shoot out easily and give you adequate distance.

In both pitching methods, keep the lure down close to the surface of the water. This is accomplished by having the proper timing when you release the lure with your left hand. If you release the lure too late, it will go right up. If this happens, learn to let go of it sooner. If you're right-handed, hold the lure in your left hand and bring it back so that your hand is alongside and slightly to the rear of your left leg. Try releasing the lure (or practice weight) when your hand is about even with your left leg. If you do it right, this should bring the lure down where you want it.

14

Setting Drag Tension

The drag mechanism on a fishing reel is an adjustable friction clutch that allows line to slip outward from a reel spool when a strong fish cannot be readily hauled in and swims the other way. Without drag, the line may break, the hook may straighten or rip out, or other bad events may occur. The drag essentially allows an angler to wear down and land a fish whose overall weight and strength outmatch the breaking strength of the line. It's an important function of a fishing reel, especially when light line is being used, when large and strong fish are being played, and when fish make strong and sudden surges while being landed.

Drag tension is controlled by the amount of friction applied, primarily by drag washers, to the spool. This amount of friction is increased or decreased by turning a knob or wheel.

Drag tension ideally should be set before fishing and should not be adjusted during a fight—unless it has been improperly set to start with—because most anglers can't tell by a quick feel whether too little or too much tension has been applied, and the wrong decision is likely to hinder efforts to land a fish.

Most people set the drag via the "feels good" method—pull a little line off the reel, fiddle with the drag adjustment, and pull a little more until it feels "about right." The most precise way to set drag tension is to use a calibrated scale and measure the tension. The drag should be adjusted to the point where it slips at between 30 and 50 percent of the wet breaking strength of the line. That would be 3 to 5 pounds of tension for a 10-pound line. Most people are better off in the 30 to 35 percent range.

There are two methods to measure drag tension, both using a line that is run through the rod guides and tied to a calibrated scale (a good spring scale will do). One way is to hold the rod parallel to the ground and pointed directly at the scale, pulling on the scale so that there is no tension on the rod; adjust drag tension until it takes 30 percent of the line's breaking strength to make the drag slip. This is the least amount of pressure you can apply when fighting a fish, assuming that when a big fish steams off you point the rod directly at it until it stops running and then raise the rod up again to fight it.

In the other method, hold the rod at a 45- to 60-degree angle as if you were fighting a fish, and use the scale to pull on the line so that tension is applied to the rod as it would be in many fishing situations. Adjust drag tension until it takes 30 percent of the line's breaking strength to make the drag slip. In either case, you can apply judicious supplemental tension by placing your palm or fingers on the spool.

Once you have set drag tension in either manner, you'll readily appreciate the difficulty of getting a precise setting by the "feels good" method

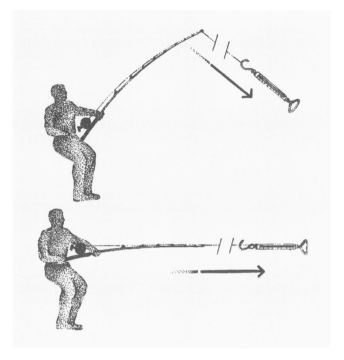

The most accurate way to measure reel drag tension is with a scale and by pulling line off a fully loaded rod from a greater distance than is shown in this compressed depiction. Measuring with the rod at a high angle (top) produces greater drag resistance due to friction from rod guides. Pointing a rod directly at a fish or at the scale (bottom) results in line being pulled straight off the reel, producing the least amount of drag tension.

and, more important, the inadvisability of changing tension in the midst of battle. If you unintentionally up the ante to 70 percent of breaking strength, for example, you're flirting with disaster. If you don't think so, just set the tension at 50, 65, or 80 percent, walk off about 30 feet, and try pulling on the line attached to a scale.

15

Finding Fish

Successful fishing is the result of many activities, the foremost of which is finding gamefish and their prey. The act of finding fish involves a combination of elements, including visual observation, intensive searching, an understanding of the habits of fish and their preferred habitat (which varies from species to species), and the personal savvy and good judgment to realize how these elements relate to one another and how they can be taken advantage of.

Fish are not found everywhere in a given body of water; they inhabit specific places, primarily for food, cover, and temperature reasons. The extent to which they inhabit specific places or prefer certain habitat varies with the species and may be influenced by seasons, spawning, water conditions, and other factors. Many variables influence the location of fish and where they are found at any given time.

Environmental Factors

Weather

Obviously anglers are affected by weather every time they go fishing. The extent to which fish are affected by the weather has been a source of uncertainty and speculation for ages. Some elements of weather are known to have certain general effects on fish, but there is no clear scientific proof, nor is there solid evidence that all fish are affected in the same way. Freshwater species, for example, are more adversely impacted by exceptional weather events than saltwater fish, and deep dwellers seem less affected by most weather than residents of shallow environs.

Certainly some elements of weather are most significant because they impair fishing techniques or angler effectiveness. And some types of weather affect the personal comfort of anglers more than they do the fish, since the majority of fishing is done when conditions are most suitable to humans. Yet fishing is a four-season sport, and the entire gamut of weather possibilities can come into play for different anglers in different geographical areas.

The presence or absence of sunlight is a basic element of weather. Clear skies and bright sun are indicative of a high-pressure system, and are often accompanied by a strong wind. Cloudy conditions can cause light-sensitive fish to be more active, especially in shallow freshwater. In freshwater fishing this is generally viewed favorably; in most saltwater fishing it is not as significant. Cloudy cover makes it harder to see shallow saltwater fish that are caught by sight-fishing methods, so good

light with low wind is preferred. In freshwater, strong overhead light from the sun is often poor for shallow-water fishing activities.

Rain or fog is similar in effect to clouds. Light and warm rains are often more conducive to fish activity than heavy or cold rains, although warm heavy rains in the spring in freshwater do a lot to move feeding and spawning activities along.

Wind, or the absence of it, is often the most influential factor in fishing activities. This is discussed separately in this section.

A cold front is less favorable than a warm front and may be very unfavorable for some fish (shallow-water residents in particular). In North America, most cold fronts arrive from the northwest, and most warm fronts arrive from the south and southwest. Severe storms are usually poor for most fishing, because they cause great changes in the environment. It often takes a few days to a week or more to improve fishing after some severe storms. Periods of stable weather tend to produce good fishing, and a continual series of unstable weather and cold fronts, accompanied by high winds, tends to sustain poor or at least subpar fishing.

Wind

Wind is one of the most significant natural elements that affect sportfishing. No matter which direction it comes from, wind is one of nature's phenomena that can be a blessing or a curse to anglers, although usually more of the latter.

Anglers often face the dilemma of whether to get out of a strong wind or fight it. If the wind is a precursor to a front, changing several days' worth of stable weather, it may signal the beginning of fish activity that you don't want to miss because that period before a new frontal system is often a good angling time.

In some places, you have no such choice. In winding or island-studded bodies of water, you often do. However, even though getting in the lee may allow you to fish comfortably, you may not be very successful there or you may have to pursue a species of fish that you were not already after. However, the wind-whipped shore may be, and often is, a good place to be fishing.

Small fish and baitfish can be greatly disturbed by hard-driving winds, becoming disoriented or finding it very difficult to move, sometimes even being pinned against wind-driven shores. Wind

An angler fishing miles offshore from Islamorada in the Florida Keys rides out a midday squall.

Wind is more of a problem for anglers than for fish, and it can stimulate fish activity. These lake trout anglers are encountering strong wind on the cold waters of Kasmere Lake in Manitoba.

pushes minute organisms into the windward shore; the organisms attract small fish and in turn larger fish. Oxygen is enhanced on windward shores because of the continued wave-beating. Fish may be facing out toward deep water here, and a controlled drift or troll is a good idea.

Fishing along those shores, or around the sides of wind-driven islands or shoals, can also be a good move. Baitfish may try to move out to deeper water to escape the turbulence, and predators sense this and move from deeper water to shallow to capture their prey. Casting into the shallows and retrieving outward may be the ticket, provided you can hold boat position. Keeping position is often hard, however, and sometimes impossible.

There will be times when you can't make any headway into the wind or are constantly being blown about, and fishing becomes a hardship. You can't make the right presentation or retrieval, and you can't detect strikes properly. Dedicated anglers learn to deal with it.

Trolling is one activity that can be done quite well in the wind if your boat is suitable, but you have to be mindful of several factors in order to make an effective trolling presentation. Probably the most important of these is the effect of the wind on speed.

A boat moving with a motor at a constant engine speed of 500 rpm, for example, will go much faster with the wind than when headed into the wind. Often, fish are caught only when the boat

is headed in one direction; this is because the lures being used aren't traveling at a suitable speed in the opposite direction (and don't have the proper action). Traveling into the wind at a moderate speed may bring lures deeper or shallower, depending on the lure, so depth attainment, rather than speed, can be the main factor. The worst thing you can do is troll blindly in one direction, then turn around and head blindly in the other direction, not knowing much about either the real speed or the depth at which your lures are working.

Maintaining a course is another matter that trolling anglers don't anticipate as a problem, but which is affected by wind speed and direction. To counter the tendency of a quartering wind to push a boat forward and away, for example, you must get the boat slightly sideways to the wind. This can be a difficult position to steadily maintain.

Because it helps maintain boat position even in wind, backtrolling is popular with walleye anglers. By using some type of sonar unit, a backtroller can maintain position along specific depths, nearly hover over selected spots, and maneuver the boat to use whatever wind direction is present to position the boat in such a way that a following bait is kept in the proper place and worked very slowly.

Casting is an altogether different story than trolling. Depending on what you are tossing to the fish, the act of casting is itself difficult in a brisk wind; accuracy and distance are often sacrificed. With lures you may have to cast farther upwind, or cast low and sidearm, be more accurate, or use a heavier lure. You may have to cast only with, or quartering into, the wind instead of directly into it. With flies, you may have to position yourself much closer to your target than you would otherwise, since you may be unable to get the necessary distance.

High winds impact just about every form of cast-and-retrieve angling, primarily because boat control and lure presentation are made much more difficult the greater the velocity of the wind. Wind particularly affects jig and plastic worm fishing, which are games of feel and depth attainment. With a bow in your line, you don't have the sensitivity you need, and often your lure spends far too little time in the places it should be.

Anchoring is one way to deal with the wind for casting, but few anglers who are accustomed to positioning with an electric motor and casting to cover a good deal of water are satisfied with repeated anchoring and reanchoring. Electric motors are certainly very helpful for fishing in the wind and maintaining position, provided the motor is powerful enough to move your particular boat and the battery has enough juice. An electric motor's energy reserves are depleted more quickly in brisk wind because you run the motor more often and at higher speeds. With a bow-mounted electric motor, it may be necessary to have a long shaft to keep the motor in the water as the bow lurches up and down.

Water Temperature

Water temperature is an important element of all aquatic habitats and is relevant to the habits and habitat of baitfish and predators. Most species have preferred comfort zones as well as upper, lower, or upper and lower temperature thresholds. Spawning is related to water temperature for many fish, and the hatching of eggs and the success of fry is usually dependent on suitable water temperatures.

In addition, feeding is related to temperature, especially for fish that live in a temperate zone, where seasons are well defined. These species eat more during warm months than during cold months, and their metabolism slows down greatly during winter.

Temperature is one of the many factors that anglers should consider when seeking gamefish in both freshwater and saltwater. Some offshore big-game anglers rely on ocean surface temperature data provided by satellites to guide them to billfish and tuna hotspots. Big-lake anglers in early spring use surface temperature gauges to find pockets of warm, nearshore water that are likely to hold trout.

Big-river anglers know that the upper region near the headwaters is colder and more conducive to trout, whereas the middle region is often more temperate and conducive to bass and walleye. Panfish that make nests in spring along the shores of lakes and ponds do so because the water temperature has reached a certain level and their eggs and milt are almost ready to be discharged.

The warming and cooling of water bodies, and especially the influence of tributaries in the spring (which bring warm water to cold lakes), are important factors in the presence of many fish species.

Throughout the season, both surface and deep temperatures influence where to fish. Water stratification sends cold- and cool-water fish to deeper freshwater locales in the summer. Thus, when you fish open-water areas, you must know the preferred temperature of the species you seek, attempt to find out the depth at which this temperature is found, and try to relate this to prominent areas that would attract your quarry (such as long sloping underwater points, submerged creek channels, sharp dropoffs, and so forth).

The thermocline is usually a fairly narrow band of water, but it is found where temperature drops off sharply, often averaging a drop of .5° to 1°F degree every foot. Sometimes the thermocline spans only 10 feet and is 15 to 20 feet below the surface; usually the spread is greater and begins deeper. To locate the thermocline, lower a thermometer on a rope or fishing line, checking it every 5 feet or so. Give the thermometer enough time at checked depths to register the proper reading.

Most lakes that stratify have a good deal of deep water. Shallow lakes don't stratify, since they become uniformly warm with too little variation from top to bottom. Fewer southern lakes stratify than northern ones; many lakes display the same patterns from year to year.

In lakes with clearly defined thermoclines, you can identify it on a good sonar instrument. Try to fish in and around the thermocline because it will have the best combination of food, oxygen, and temperature. But keep in mind the temperature preferences of the fish you seek, since the actual temperature of the thermocline will vary by locale and the fish may be just above or below it.

A thermocline usually lasts until the fall, or when there is a trend toward cool air temperatures. When the surface water cools off enough, a body of water mixes and the thermocline dissipates. This is often referred to as the "fall turnover."

Big waters are slow to warm up in the spring and slow to cool off in the fall. This means that small bodies of water may be better to fish in the earliest part of the season—until the larger waters warm up—and that big waters may sustain good fishing for a longer period of time in the fall.

Water Clarity

In both freshwater and saltwater, water clarity, or transparency, ranges widely. What people consider clear or murky is varied and very subjective. Nevertheless, water is most likely to be turbid in large rivers and in lakes and ponds, where runoff, tributaries, erosion, plankton blooms, and various factors influence the transparency of water.

Water clarity is a factor in angling, both in the sense of where to locate some species as well as how to fish for them. However, the clarity of freshwater varies markedly from one lake to another and even varies in a particular lake through the course of the fishing season.

Clear water is generally more productive than muddy water for sight-feeding fish and for most aquatic life; muddy water is best suited to species that feed primarily through sense of feel or smell. If clear water is classified (as it is by some biologists) as having visibility over 30 inches, this water may be many times more productive for certain species, such as bass and bluegills, for example, than water with only 5 to 6 inches of visibility.

Naturally the clarity of any water is important to the color of lures that are fished, and this is also intertwined with issues pertaining to depth and the intensity of the light.

Currents

Currents are a factor in the presence of fish and in fishing efforts. Defined as horizontal movements of water, currents are an everyday part of fishing for virtually all saltwater anglers, for freshwater anglers who fish in rivers or streams, and for some freshwater anglers who fish in large lakes with major sources of inflow and outflow.

The most visually obvious influence of current is in rivers and streams, whose character and aquatic life are molded by the velocity of water, from trickling runoff in the headwaters to the silted and expansive delta. The types, sizes, and even shapes of fish and aquatic life vary greatly from small, shallow, fast waters in the hills to wider, deeper, and slower waters downstream, possibly even affected by tides in the most downstream reaches. Within the different sections, there are variations in current; narrow, constricted areas cause a swifter flow than wider and deeper areas. Nevertheless, currents flow slower near the banks than in the center of the river, except along the outside bank by a sharp bend.

Currents may exist in large lakes and impoundments but are usually less visually obvious. In some impoundments, when there is high and regular demand for water, usually in summer for power generation, the drawdown of water creates a current that astute anglers can observe around points, around bridge and roadway supports, and along some shores. Since it is intermittent, it is less likely to be a major influence on the composition of aquatic life, although it may influence the behavior, especially feeding, of some species, particularly striped bass.

Continual current, which may exist at subsurface levels in some of the Great Lakes, is unlikely to affect fish behavior, but it can affect the behavior of lures and influence fishing patterns when strong, although many anglers are unaware of its existence.

The world is well acquainted with surface ocean currents, which are vastly different natural elements than currents in freshwater, and affect the annual and seasonal availability of many gamefish species. The oceans also have subsurface currents, although these are generally very slow and the result of deep-water circulation. This is a vertical movement that is the result of cold water from the polar regions sinking.

Another vertical movement of ocean water is an upwelling, which occurs when deep current meets the shelving bottom or submerged banks. A persistent blow of wind can also bring about a form of upwelling by pushing surface waters outward and turning colder deep waters toward the surface. These factors influence the entire food chain, often causing predatory species to be

Fishing for stripers and many other species is often good at Thimble Shoals Channel, shown here between portions of Virginia's Chesapeake Bay Bridge Tunnel. Strong tidal current and the presence of tunnel and bridge piling structures make this a fish magnet throughout summer and fall.

more numerous when such currents attract and/or concentrate prey species.

Tidal currents exist in all the oceans and are mostly observed in coastal areas as water flows into and out of bays, increasing and decreasing in speed; dangerous, turbulent currents may form where rivers meet the sea and several currents mix. Tidal currents also exist in offshore waters, usually observed with little change in speed, but slowly and steadily changing direction. Lastly, local currents may also occur due to wave action along the shore or beach, creating undertows as water rushes back into the sea from the beach. Such currents provide foraging opportunities for various predatory species, thereby making them places to focus fishing effort.

Tides

Tidal ranges vary widely around the world. Where the coastline provides open access to the sea or to large bodies of water (such as rivers), the tidal range may be less than a foot. In the Gulf of Mexico along the Texas coast, the tidal range is 1 to 2 feet. Where an irregular coastline forms an inlet, the tidal range can be as much as 40 feet, as occurs in the Bay of Fundy in Nova Scotia.

Since tides are predictable, tide charts or tables for specific areas are published, and tide times for other nearby areas can be calculated by adding or subtracting correction factors. These tables provide daily high and low tide information, as well as the time at which the tide is going out or coming in. The incoming portion of a high tide is commonly known as a rising tide or a flood tide; the outgoing portion is known as the falling tide or ebb tide. The tide is said to be slack when tidal current velocity is near zero.

There is often a clear relationship between tidal activity and fish feeding activity. Tidal effects and influences are most obvious in estuaries and along the coastline by the shore and surf, rather than in the open ocean, except for tidal rips; they are especially obvious in rivers and marshes.

In a salt marsh, large fish enter the marsh with the incoming and high tide in search of small fish, crabs, or other food, and they depart when the tide gets to a certain ebb point. The incoming tide can present more food, and the outgoing tide can flush food out with it, making the activity of gamefish and their location most likely at these stages of the tide.

Redfish, like this nice specimen from a tidal marsh on the Cooper River in South Carolina, are most likely to be caught when the tide is moving.

A change in tide movement, no matter whether it is to or from high or low tide, is generally a preferred time to fish; slack tides are often unproductive. Many anglers find that the hour or so of flood tide before high slack, and the hour or so of ebb tide after it, tend to generate the most fish activity, with best results during the latter.

Visual Observation

One way to find gamefish is to visually locate them or to look for signs that indicate their presence. Most people prefer this, although it is not often possible to do for a variety of reasons.

General Observation

Many anglers don't notice the little things that sometimes make a big difference in sportfishing. They don't see fish swirl after a lure. They don't see that quick moment when a fish spooks a bunch of bait and gives its presence away. They don't notice characteristics of the water that attract fish or stimulate activity.

Often this inattention is a matter of not being observant or of not knowing what some signs may mean. Observation is an important factor in fishing success. To some extent, on-the-water angling observation is a function of frequent fishing, but it is also a function of being in the right frame of mind and applying yourself to finding fish and thinking about what you're doing. This is especially so when the action is not fast and easy.

Some anglers are simply not observant enough of natural signs because they rely too much on various electronic devices, forgetting that there are other aspects to fishing success besides the information gleaned from instrumentation.

Watching the water, for example, is very important in many ways, and helpful when pursuing many species of fish. Watching the water includes watching for reefs, rips, near-surface vegetation, current flows, shade, and water color.

The clarity of the water can be important to fish movement and/or location as well as to lure selection. If the water always looks the same to you in all places, you may not be looking closely enough at it.

Some species of fish are more likely to be found in clear water (or the clearest possible) or are more prone to strike lures in clear water (because they can locate them better), and it would behoove you to look for such. The places where clear and turbid water mix—runoffs, creek mouths, tidal influxes, wind-affected edges, and so on—and the immediate environs around them are sometimes the best locales to fish.

In certain instances, where dirty water, such as from a creek, enters a clearer body of water, the dirty water is carrying nutrients or small forage that attracts bait, and the bait in turn attracts predators. Another good place to put a lure is where there are a lot of baitfish (or perhaps a place to not put a lure if there are none). When fishing for some species of fish at certain times of the year, especially in unfamiliar waters, it can be disconcerting if there is little or no sign of bait. That doesn't mean you won't catch fish; however, when you see bait flitting on or near the surface or in the shallows, that is often a sign directing you to the kinds of places to fish.

When the water is calm, you can spot bait or baitfish movement without much trouble by being attentive. When the water is roiled by wind and waves, it is much more difficult to make visual observations.

When bait are schooled and being pushed aggressively by predators, it's quite easy to spot the action. Other times, just one fish is pursuing a single prey or a few fish, and the action is less obvious and perhaps more likely to be missed.

Probably every angler has noticed a fish swirling and creating a commotion when it captured or chased some type of prey in open water or in the shallows. Occasionally, casting to this activity results in a strike and hookup, although a gamefish may not even be responsible for the commotion. People confuse the splash of a jumping mullet, for example, with feeding gamefish activity.

Nevertheless, fish that are stalking shallow water, that spook bait, or that capture some prey item on or near the surface usually give away their presence and often are aggressive fish susceptible to capture at that moment. If you look for the signs of the presence of such fish, you'll probably be disappointed; but if you keep your eyes open and—just as important—listen while fishing, you'll become aware of gamefish movement. This is especially true when casting and when fishing for most warmwater species of freshwater fish.

It is also true when fishing in coldwater streams. Both Atlantic and Pacific salmon, for example, will roll occasionally on or near the surface, sometimes in a very subtle manner. If you are unfamiliar with the water that you're fishing, this movement, though unrelated to feeding activity, will give you an indication of a fish lie and will point you toward an appropriate place to direct your efforts. Noticing a fish that jumps or rolls is obvious to many anglers, but not to all, especially when there is merely a rise on the surface that can be confused with the swirl of current.

Noticing bait that is in an agitated state can also help anglers, who describe this phenomenon as "nervous water," which is quite accurate although hard to convey. Nervous water is a surface patch, usually just a few yards across, where there is some slight rippling on the surface, distinctly different from that caused by current or light breezes. It happens when a pod of small baitfish is balled up and flitting about, neither feeding nor fleeing, but disturbed—usually because something is lurking nearby that means to maraud them shortly. If you see this action, work the area hard, keeping a lure handy that might imitate a small fish that is injured or struggling.

One of the easiest and best ways to enjoy more success through being observant is to watch your lures when you retrieve them, especially as they near the boat. Some fish are prone to swirl after shallow-running or surface lures and create a sizable boil in the water after they miss the lure in an apparent attempt to stun it. Anglers who aren't watching closely don't see those occasions when a fish strikes and misses the lure, and they cast elsewhere, though they might have been able to catch that particular fish or at least note its location for a later visit.

Stalking Shallow Fish

On some occasions, you're able to see fish in shallow water that are not actually in the process of chasing bait but are foraging below the surface, or merely taking a feeding or resting position. Spotting such fish is certainly helpful for making the best presentation in the proper locale. Obviously some species of fish actively feed in shallow water, and they are primarily caught in those environs by stalking and sight-casting to them, often by intercepting them. This is the basis of most flats fishing.

The most common fish that are stalked by sight fishing in shallow water include tarpon, permit, bonefish, and redfish in saltwater, as well as other species, like sharks, cobia, and mutton snapper. In freshwater, various trout and Atlantic salmon are objects of stalking, as are certain members of the sunfish family—largemouth bass, smallmouth bass, and bluegills—especially in springtime when they are spawning. Other stalked freshwater fish include northern pike and, very rarely, lake trout in far northern areas when they are feeding in the shallows.

When trying to spot shallow-water fish, look not at the surface but below the surface and at the bottom. Look for something that stands out as being different, whose movement contrasts with the bottom locale enough for you to detect it. Don't stare at one spot for long, especially when you're searching for fish, and try to bring your peripheral vision into play. When you see the wake of a moving fish, realize that the forward edge of the wake is behind the fish and take this into account when making a cast that is intended to intercept it.

Sometimes it's important to be able to see fish before you cast to them because you have to be able to approach them without alarming them. Other times, it's important to see certain objects that might be harboring fish. Polarized sunglasses are a big help here; those with wraparound side-view protection are best. A cap with a wide bill and dark underside is also a good aid. For difficult

viewing, even with a cap or sunglasses, put your hands around the corners of your glasses and cup them to reduce side glare.

If you're fishing with someone who sees a fish that you do not, use the clock system (the bow of the boat is 12 o'clock and the stern is 6 o'clock) to figure out the specific location of the fish by having your companion give you specific directions; if your companion says a fish is at 2 o'clock and about 60 feet away, you know where to be looking. These directions can be accompanied by rod pointing to help narrow down the positioning; you can point to the spot where you think the fish is, and your companion can tell you to point more to the left or right to zero in on it.

Remember that visibility is improved from high vantage points. Wading anglers (and those sitting in a kayak or canoe) rarely can see into the water the way someone fishing from a boat can. However, in freshwater, especially on salmon rivers, anglers will walk high banks to get a viewing vantage, and some have been known to climb trees; watching from bridges is also common.

A person sitting in a boat cannot see as well as someone standing, and a person standing in the well of a boat has inferior vision compared with someone standing on a deck. The best vision comes from standing on platforms or towers. The boats of most flats guides have transom platforms from which they pole, and these offer good visibility.

Wading the flats to cast to wary species is a game of spotting and stalking; this angler is fishing for seatrout in Shell Key Preserve near St. Petersburg.

Some flats boats have mini-towers over a center console; these are even better for visibility but are less conducive to flycasting, though fine for those using other types of tackle.

Following the Birds

Birds are a good indicator of fish in saltwater, although less so in freshwater. In freshwater environments, anglers are likely to see such fish-eating birds as herons, kingfishers, loons, mergansers, and cormorants, as well as seagulls. Herons are shorebirds usually found where there are many small fish in shallow water. Mergansers and most other diving ducks are seldom of much assistance to anglers, although actively feeding loons and cormorants may indicate the nearby presence of baitfish schools. Seagulls are seldom of much fish-locating value in freshwater, except when they are actively following schools of surface-feeding striped bass in impoundments.

The situation in saltwater is quite different, however, because there are more birds and more surface food to attract birds. In the marine environment, noticing birds, learning to recognize them, and following them can help find gamefish. Knowing which ones to follow and when is a skill that comes from experience.

When to follow them is usually dependent on whether they are searching, actively feeding, or flying by. When birds are searching, their flight path is straight, graceful, and relaxed. Once they spot a food source, they speed up; their turns become sharp, and eventually they begin swooping down to the water. An increased level of excitement is obvious from loud chattering, which is meant to attract other birds. Take notice if birds seem afraid to sit on the surface. If so, bluefish are probably present, and the birds have good reason to fear having their feet bitten off. Pelicans, though, will actually dive into the water and feast on smaller bluefish.

The number of birds that you see is not necessarily an indication of the number of fish below them, although it can be. A single large billfish might push up a large ball of bait and attract many birds, yet only a few birds may be observed at a site where there is a school of other gamefish.

Not all birds are reliable fish indicators; examples in saltwater include cormorants and albatrosses. Birds that are often good include terns, frigates, shearwaters, and seagulls.

Coastal anglers watch for birds, such as these working the surf near Morehead City, North Carolina, to indicate the presence of feeding gamefish.

Located within a few miles of shore, terns are great indicators of baitfish; offshore, they often provide a clue that schools of baitfish are being worked over just beneath the surface. If the flock is moving quickly, the baitfish are likely being run by schools of king mackerel, tuna, or bonito. In inshore waters, they can be indicators of mackerel, bluefish, tarpon, snook, and kingfish.

The most reliable offshore fishfinders are frigate birds, also called man-o'-war birds. High-flying frigates help anglers find big blue-water gamefish by shadowing their movements from above. They'll follow large, solitary predator fish in anticipation of diving quickly to the surface to grab fleeing baitfish.

Shearwaters will swim underwater to catch bait, at times feeding so heavily that they struggle to fly. Offshore, look for them on top of kelp paddies. They are often associated with tuna, and their movements are a clue to the direction in which these fish are headed.

Inshore, seagulls can be terrific indicators of fish activity along the beach, especially for mackerel, bluefish, tarpon, snook, and kingfish. They lift scraps and wounded baitfish off the surface, which could be an indication of feeding gamefish in the area. Offshore, seagulls are less reliable due to their tendency to get excited about picking at floating garbage.

Reading Water and Habitats

Most of the time when fishing in either freshwater or saltwater, you don't readily locate fish by visually observing the fish, and have to search for them without actually spotting them. To a large extent, that means knowing what lies below the surface, studying the water and the surroundings, and knowing the habits and appropriate habitats of the species you seek.

You have to evaluate the place that you're fishing, observing water conditions to determine where fish may be and how to present lures or bait to them. This skill is referred to as "reading water" and can be practiced in all types of environments, especially in freshwater. It is sometimes easier in rivers than in stillwaters (ponds, lakes, reservoirs) because many elements are more obvious.

In current, for example, any sizable obstruction (boulder, bridge footing, pier, and so on) creates a slack pocket where fish can lie without exerting much effort and watch for food; these are readily located. Stillwaters especially pose problems for many anglers, particularly in places that they do not know well, and for the obvious reason that the surface usually gives no indication of what is below.

Lakes, ponds, impoundments, bays, oceans, and other bodies of water are all quite different, so the type and the size of a body of water play a role in what you do and how you do it. The species available and/or desired is another consideration; obviously the more you know about fish behavior and habitat, the better. Gamefish are usually found in certain places for specific reasons, and the better you understand the relationship between their depth, cover, temperature, food needs, and other requirements, the better you are able to put the pieces of the underwater puzzle together.

The pieces of that puzzle can be filled in by making preparations before you get on the water. You can get a head start (especially on unfamiliar water) by simply talking to those who know something about it. Visit local tackle shops (several if possible), and talk to the people there as you purchase bait, license, lures, and so on. Talk to people at the launching ramp and marina. Ask specific questions and be observant. Look at the products being sold in the stores to see what the most popular lures and colors are.

Obtaining and studying charts and maps, particularly those with underwater contours and with depth and channel markings, can be a key factor. At the very least, they will familiarize you with the general layout of the place and its characteristics, but they also may detail some very specific structures (such as rock reefs, rips, shoals, flats, old roadbeds and culverts, sunken weeds, and so on) that may be important to fish. Such maps are not available for all waters, unfortunately, or the ones that are available may not be as detailed as you'd like. Even the best maps often fail to pinpoint certain underwater features that attract gamefish. Such features might include a nearshore trough that is created by wave action, or a slight pinnacle, mound, or hump that rises high enough off the lake or ocean floor to attract baitfish and thus predators, but not enough to be highlighted on a map. So don't let maps be the last word.

Observing Features

In freshwater environments, much can be learned simply by observing the shoreline and surrounding topographical features. If the shore is sandy or rocky, the bottom of the body of water nearby will likely be similar. When the land declines steeply down to the water level, the lake there will drop off sharply into deep water, but where the shore slopes gradually, the lake near shore will likewise. This is particularly true in man-made bodies of water and at times of high water.

Points are an important landform in fishing. Many points extend underwater well out into a lake before dropping off abruptly into deep water. This feature can attract both migratory and nonmigratory species of fish and can be worth exploring, although by looking strictly at the water's surface you seldom have a clue that anything unusual is below and near the point.

Perhaps more obvious are such features as rock walls, fenceposts, and roadbeds, which are typically found in bodies of water that have been artificially made or enlarged, and which extend from shore into the water and provide cover for some species of fish.

Even more obvious, of course, is vegetation, stumps, timber, docks, and the like, which provide cover and attract bait and smaller prey fish. Some species of fish are especially attracted to various forms of cover, and you should look for emerged and submerged cover, especially if it is near deep water, because it may hold the type of fish you seek. By judiciously fishing these objects (and in the case of vegetation, seeking the pockets and edges within), you can enhance your opportunities for success.

Using Sonar

For anglers, the question of where to fish—presumably in a place where the quarry is or will be—can become a big issue when the fishing location is new or unfamiliar, or simply when the body of water is big and diverse. Boating anglers have come to rely on increasingly sophisticated electronic equipment, particularly sonar, not only for navigational assistance but for learning about the depths, contours, and features below, as well as for locating gamefish and baitfish. Sonar, in fact, has become almost indispensable to many ardent anglers.

Interpreting what you see on sonar is the million-dollar question. What signals are fish, what kind of fish they are, how big they are, what kind of bottom is below—these are the foremost puzzles.

Bottom characteristics are not as easy to distinguish as some anglers would like, perhaps in part due to the deficiencies of some units or perhaps because of the settings employed. In general, a hard bottom returns a strong signal, and a soft bottom a weaker one.

On liquid crystal display sonar, a hard bottom is seen as a dense, thick band. If the grayline feature is engaged, a hard bottom is shown as a thin black line with a wide gray band beneath. The harder the bottom, the wider the gray band. A soft or muddy bottom returns a weaker signal, and is displayed as a thinner, less dense band. With grayline on, it will appear as a dark band with little or no gray area beneath it. A rocky bottom produces a hard, thick signal with a ragged band.

This is different with color video sonar, however, because different colors are used to indicate different echo strengths. Thus on a color video sonar a hard bottom appears as a wide band in the color reserved for the strongest echoes (red in some units), a mud bottom appears as a narrow band in a "weaker" color, and a sand bottom will be somewhere in between. On monochrome video sonars, the harder the bottom or the stronger an echo from suspended objects, the wider (top-to-bottom) and brighter the mark on the screen.

Fish signals often appear as arches on better units unless the fish are very small, the scroll speed is very slow, or the boat is moving very fast.

This is because a fish is first picked up on the outer edge of the cone where it is farthest from the transducer; then, as the fish passes directly underneath the transducer, it gets closer so its reading curves upward.

Because the sound is strongest in the center of the cone, the arch also gets thicker from top to bottom in the middle. The fish then gets farther away again as it passes through the opposite outer edge of the cone, causing its screen reading to curve downward again. A partial arch or diagonal line means that a fish was moving either into or out of the cone when you passed by. A fish that swims along under the boat prints as a solid horizontal line until it swims out of the cone. A school of bait shows up as a big pod, which may be vertical or horizontal depending on the school's orientation. Not all units depict fish in arches, however, and fish will not always appear as arches on any unit.

It is very difficult to tell the specific size of fish detected with sonar because this varies according to the species, the speed of the boat, the scroll speed, the sensitivity setting, and even where the fish is within the transducer's cone. If you catch a fish out of a school that you've just marked, you may have some idea how fish size compares to signal size, but if any of these factors change as you continue fishing, it's a new ballgame. Determining size of fish is somewhat possible but determining species is not, although educated guesses based on extensive experience and knowledge of

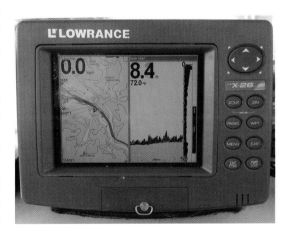

This image of a combination GPS-sonar unit, taken on Lake Marion, South Carolina, shows shallow bottom terrain and surface temperature on the right, and a hydrographic chart and navigational view of the immediate area on the left.

individual species behavior and certain environments can be accurate.

To get the most out of your sonar you need to use it correctly, and it pays to spend time learning this. With older sonar it is a good idea to choose the manual mode over the automatic mode; this allows you to fine-tune settings in order to get a clearer idea of bottom features. Newer models, however, are much more sophisticated than those of the past, and work extremely well in the automatic mode, filtering out clutter and providing the proper sensitivity and resolution without your having to play with major settings.

Working Edges

When trying to find fish by observing habitats it helps to think in terms of edges. Like most animals, fish are attracted to some type of edge, whether one of structure or temperature. Think about the type of edge—for example, a long sloping underwater point, a reef or shoal, or even a rocky versus sandy bottom—that may appeal to your target species for reasons of comfort, security, or feeding.

A prominent edge lair might be a shoal or reef. Underwater mounds or islands, sandbars, and gravel bars are similar. These locations may be rocky or boulder-strewn, or they may be sandy with moderate weed growth, but they attract small baitfish, which in turn attract predators. Often there is deep water on one side.

In big lakes and river systems, tributaries play a critical role in gamefish behavior and therefore fishing success. The area where a tributary intersects a lake is an edge that attracts bait and major gamefish. Water that is a few degrees warmer than the main lake temperature flows into the lake and mixes with it, encouraging fish activity. A distinct mudline, the result of stained or muddy spring runoff, is often created around tributary mouths. On some waters, this mudline attracts gamefish because there is usually a thermal break here as well, with the inner edge being warmer and the mudline itself being attractive to bait and prey species.

The deep-water/shallow-water interface near islands can be similarly thought of as an edge, as can a sharply sloping shoreline. These are places to which bait migrates naturally, and logically they present feeding opportunities.

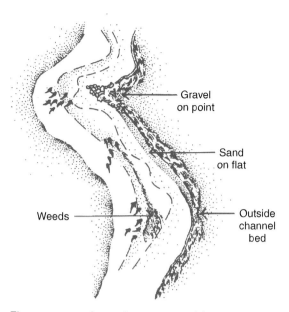

This compressed view depicts some of the common characteristics of a river.

Back eddies, tidal rips, and current edges are more good spots. In rivers, the place where a secondary tributary meets a major flow is also a promising intersection, especially in summer when the secondary tributary may be dumping cooler and more oxygenated water into the main flow.

Knowing which types of edges appeal to which species of fish makes a difference when fishing in current. For example, the inside bend of major tributaries is often a hotspot to troll or cast for stripers in the spring. Stripers like a point where water rushes by, so they hold on the inside bend of a channel and use this spot to ambush whatever comes around.

Walleye are known for locating along an edge, particularly along a deep-water breakline. Walleye commonly move shallower in the evening to the fringes of a bar or a rock or gravel point that breaks sharply to deep water. One successful fishing tactic here is to use plugs that dive to 8 or 10 feet and troll from deep water to the point; then go along one side and work along the edge.

Some fish are known for congregating in or along the edges of vegetation. Weeds attract small baitfish and larger fish in the food chain, and they also offer protective cover. Working submerged weedlines, where the weeds end and the bottom begins to drop off to deeper water, is not only possible, but an especially effective fishing method.

Many fish use the edges of vegetative cover or other structures to hide and to ambush prey. They lurk in or by places where food is abundant and where they can lie relatively concealed to pounce on appropriate-size forage. These feeding stations are ambush points, and are best if they are close to deep water, dropoffs, shelves, ledges, creekbeds, channels, and the like.

Whether you angle for species that prefer the confines of cover or the vastness of open water, be aware of the subtle borders and margins of these habitats and seek and fish those places.

Flowing Water

Much of the preceding information also applies to flowing water, especially large rivers. The reading of water is most obviously practiced by anglers who fish in smaller rivers and creeks, where some boating is done, but most fishing is by wading or angling from the bank. Current in rivers and creeks is a premier influence on where and how fish are situated, both for resting and for feeding purposes. Fish face flowing water, so lures must generally come downcurrent toward them in a natural manner.

In flowing water, the deeper places are the ones that often hold fish and are sought by anglers. Slow-moving water is a sign of depth. Water is deepest where the current comes against the bank; years of this action have gouged the bank and bottom, resulting in deeper water. Shallow water is found on the inside of a bend. In many places the bank is much steeper on the outside of a bend than on the inside, and this is another clue to the location of the deeper and shallower portions. This information is important not only for angling but also for navigating a boat or wading safely.

Riffles, which are shallow areas with choppy water, are common in many streams and rivers. The area above and below them is usually more likely than the riffle itself to hold fish, either resident fish or those that are temporarily resting before migrating upstream. Small fish and other aquatic life are often disturbed, disoriented, or overwhelmed when they get into a riffle, and become easy prey at the end of the riffle where it empties into a pool.

If there is a boulder or series of large rocks or other protection in a riffle, the object may have a deep pocket behind it that is out of the current and is conducive to capturing food that comes by or is washed into the pocket; in such an instance, gamefish (like trout or smallmouth bass) might reside in that specific location in a riffle.

When current strikes an object, it may cause less turbulence in front of or behind that object. Fish may locate here because they don't have to work as hard to resist the flow and also because it may be a good place to find food. Boulders are the most common objects in currents, but small islands or shoals also exist; in high water, stumps and fallen trees are objects that can attract fish.

16

Retrieving

An intrinsic element of angling, retrieving is the act of manually manipulating lures or flies that have been cast or lowered into the water to impart fish-imitating or fish-attracting action to them. Fly retrieval is detailed in chapter 23, while trolling with lures, which is the corollary to retrieving, is detailed in chapter 27.

The keys to successful retrieval of most lures are depth control, action, and speed, all of which vary in importance depending on the situation and the lure. Achieving the proper depth is perhaps the most important factor, since you can't hope to catch fish without getting your offering to the fish's level. With many lures, the ability to achieve a certain depth is a function of the design of the lure and the way in which it is used. Action is also a function of the design, but only to the extent to which the lure is properly fished; achieving the proper action is a necessity for the lure to have maximum attractiveness. Speed is often the most ignored factor in retrieval and is influenced by the diameter of line being used, type of lure, current, and the retrieve ratio of the reel.

Retrieving Surface Lures

As a category, surface lures are the most presumptuous of all lure types because they must draw fish to a place where they spend the least amount of their time. Thus surface lures appeal to highly aggressive fish and to species that attack from hiding places or gang up on prey and "corner" them at the surface, but not to bottom-dwelling species, true deep-water denizens, and fish that don't hunt near the surface in packs.

Because surface fishing requires aggressive fish behavior, it is more of a warmwater phenomenon than a coldwater one, which also restricts its suitability in many places. For some species—freshwater bass, for example—surface lures are more effective in shallow water and locations with cover than in open deep-water environs. Yet some saltwater species may be taken on the surface miles from the nearest shore, when they happen to be feeding on baitfish that have been pushed to the surface.

Basically, any lure that is worked on the surface or is fished both on the surface or within the first 1 to 3 feet of the surface is part of this category. There are basically four types of surface lures: popping and wobbling plugs, floating/diving plugs and darters, propellered lures, and walking plugs. There is also, in the broadest sense, the dry fly, which is detailed separately in chapter 23 because it is vastly different in principle and application from other lures, as is the fly rod popper or bug.

Poppers and Wobblers

With poppers, the actual popping or forward-chugging motion is made by twitching the rod up or back, not by reeling line in, to achieve the proper movement. In most instances it's best to keep the rod low and pointed toward the lure; this helps avoid slack to work the lure well and puts the rod in the best possible position to react to a strike. For long-distance casting, however, it's often necessary to keep the rod tip up to help work the lure properly, especially when there is much wave action; when a strike occurs, drop the rod tip while reeling up slack and quickly set the hook.

Popping plugs should be worked with varying degrees of emphasis. Seldom is it worthwhile to jerk hard to create a loud commotion. Usually when the surface is calm, you need only to effect a mild popping noise; a loud noise under this condition is alarming. When the surface is disturbed by a mild chop, make a slightly noisier retrieve.

If it appears that fish are feeding actively, you can shorten the time between retrieval strokes, but in nonfrenzied situations it's usually best to maintain pauses of several seconds' duration. A good tactic is to let a popper lie motionless awhile after splash-down, then reel up all slack line and gently jiggle the rod just enough to impart the slightest sign of life to the lure. In situations where there is plenty of bait or where there is surface-feeding commotion, however, work the popper with a quicker motion. Don't use a popper continuously unless you're having exceptionally good success.

Poppers work best near cover and in water that is not too deep. Early and late in the day (particularly in the summer), night, and cloudy days are the best fishing times for this lure.

Wobbling plugs are used in much the same manner as poppers. They are more effective for largemouth bass, but can produce some dandy smallmouths at night, and are probably more effective in the dark than at dusk, daylight, or dawn.

The common retrieval method for wobblers is a straight, continuous motion. At times, a worthwhile technique is to make the lure stop and go, or to give it a pull-pause motion, particularly as it swims next to an object like a stump or dock support. As long as there is some cover present or the water is not excessively deep under the boat, it's wise to work these lures all the way back to you; they may be struck at any point along the retrieve, especially at night.

Keep your rod tip low and resist the urge to reel too fast. Wobblers don't have as good an action when retrieved quickly as they do when worked slowly. Moreover, a fast retrieve is more conducive to missed strikes. Try a stop-and-go retrieval cadence if the fish keep missing it.

Resist the urge to set the hook the instant a fish slashes at the lure, and momentarily wait to feel the fish take your plug before setting the hook sharply. If the fish misses altogether, try stopping the lure in its tracks and twitching it a little, then moving it a few inches and stopping it. Repeat this before resuming the retrieve.

Floating/Diving Lures

Probably the most universally applied method of surface or near-surface fishing involves the use of plastic or wooden floating/diving plugs that are generally minnow-shaped, which cause them to be generically called minnow plugs by some anglers. They have a small lip that brings the lure beneath the surface at a maximum of about 3 feet on a conventional cast-and-retrieve.

These lures are most effectively worked in a deliberately erratic fashion to imitate a crippled baitfish. To get the most out of this lure, it has to be fished convincingly. Start a retrieve by reeling in all slack line, and keep the rod pointed low in case a fish strikes a well-cast surface lure shortly after it hits the water or has been retrieved a few feet.

The objective with a floater/diver is to make it gyrate enticingly in a stationary position. Keep the rod tip pointed low toward the water and use your wrist to move the rod. Jiggle the rod tip in a controlled, not frantic, fashion. Then jerk the lure back toward you a few inches. Then gyrate it some more, all the time reeling in an appropriate amount of line to keep the slack to a minimum.

Another way to use this lure type is on a straight retrieve, allowing it to run a foot or two beneath the surface. This is more like using it as a crankbait, and sometimes fish strike it this way. But a better technique, especially when fish won't hit this plug on top of the water, is to make it run just below the surface in a series of short jerk-pause movements, running it forward half a foot with each motion. This retrieve is more in the style of darters, those plugs that float but have no significant surface action and are used solely just below the surface. Some plugs that are fished this way, incidentally, are called "jerkbaits" by bass anglers, and some manufacturers use the words "jerking" or "ripping" in labeling such lures that they make for stop-and-go retrieves.

In freshwater, any type of relatively shallow cover can be a target for this lure. An especially good place to use a floating/diving plug is over submerged grass that comes to within a few feet of the surface. In less covered locations, it can be quite effective as well, including spots such as long, shallow points, the backs of bays, and rocky shorelines.

Propellered Lures

The basic retrieval technique for propellered surface plugs is similar to the surface retrieve of floating/ diving minnow plugs. It constitutes an erratic jiggling-jerking-pausing motion that represents a struggling or crippled baitfish. Keep the rod down, utilize the rod tip to effectively impart action, and make your wrist do the rod-manipulating work.

You can retrieve a propellered plug either quickly or slowly. The slow retrieve is good when prospecting for unseen fish, using a deliberate, convincing action. The propellers make a loud churning noise with some bubbly effect, and this may aid in attracting the attention of bass in the vicinity. A rapid, ripping retrieve is warranted for schooling largemouth bass, and the noise thereby created seems to imitate the slashing surface-breaking feeding activity common to this situation.

Another type of propellered surface lure is a buzzbait, which does not float but is used solely on top of the water and almost entirely for largemouth bass, although it does catch some other species. Summer and early fall are consistently productive buzzbait times, usually in the first few hours of the morning, in late evening, and at night.

The best place to retrieve a buzzbait is over and around thick vegetation. It is also highly effective around brush, in timber, and around any fallen wood that might conceal a bass. The closer you can work a buzzbait to such shallow cover, the better. Retrieval technique is very straightforward, since you have to reel at a speed sufficient to keep this lure churning up the surface.

When bass strike a buzzer, they usually crush it. There are times, however, when they either miss (this happens a lot at night) or strike short. A lot of short strikers can be caught by placing a trailer hook on the bend of the lure's main hook.

Walking Plugs

The wooden or plastic plugs in this category are similar in size and conformation to propellered plugs, except that they don't have propellers or a lip. They're retrieved much like and are fished in the same areas as propellered plugs and to a lesser extent floating/diving lures. However, they have a more pronounced walking or wide-swimming action than other surface plugs, which can be seductive when done in a slow and deliberate or fast and frantic manner.

These lures are effective for largemouth, smallmouth, and spotted bass, and also productive at times in angling for stripers, muskies, pike, pickerel, peacock bass, seatrout, redfish, snook, tarpon, and an assortment of other saltwater fish.

Walking plugs require an artful retrieval technique that causes the lure to step from side to side. This sidestepping technique is called "walking the dog." To effect this, begin with the rod tip pointed down. It's helpful to stand or be seated high, to have most of your line on the water to help create

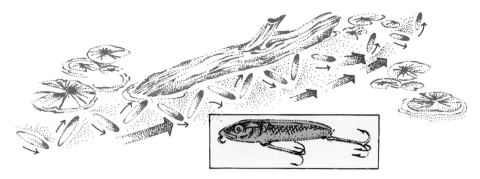

Walking the Dog

drag, and to tie the fishing line to the lure with a rounded snap or a loop knot.

To walk the dog, you need to make rhythmic short jerks with the rod tip while simultaneously advancing the reel handle a quarter turn or so with each jerk to take up line. Done slowly, the lure's travel path widens; done quickly, it narrows. The line should lie slightly slack in the water to avoid pulling the lure ahead. The right cadence allows the lure to swim from side to side, but a taut line jerks it ahead. A skilled retriever can slow-fish a walking plug so that it almost stays in place, nodding from left to right, an action that can be highly seductive to otherwise uninterested fish.

"Half-stepping" is an advanced technique for working a walking plug very close to logs, bushes, docks, and so on. Here the plug swims repeatedly to one side instead of from left to right. To do this, you must first get into proper casting position by aligning your line with the object being fished. Walk the lure up to the object so that the plug faces it. Barely nudge the rod tip so that the head of the plug turns away. Now jerk the rod tip; the plug heads inward toward the bush. Nudge again; jerk again. The lure continues to swim toward the bush and actually works around it as if using it for protection.

Walking plugs can be productive in all cover situations where you'd expect to find fish that ambush their prey. You can work specific objects or fish blindly. Vary retrieval speeds. A moderate retrieve is often best, though there are times when the best approach is to work the lure slowly and seductively, or with a very quick, constant retrieval speed (this is when there is very active fish feeding).

A lot of fish strike or boil after a walking plug and miss it. Many of these fish can be enticed to strike again if you can control your reflexes. When fish strike such a lure, the overanxious angler often rears back to set the hook and jerks the lure away from the fish. Try to restrain yourself until the fish has clearly taken the lure. If the fish misses the plug and you don't jerk it away but keep it walking, there's a good chance it will strike again. If you jerk the lure far away from the fish, you probably won't get a second hit.

Specialty Surface Lures

A few surface lures do not quite fit into the standard categories previously mentioned. The soft plastic frog or mouse is one such, as are other styles of soft and hard plastic lures that are meant to swim through and over heavy cover in fishing for freshwater bass.

A frog-patterned popper is eyed by a large-mouth bass.

These lures are strictly for fishing in and over thick vegetation. Some can be retrieved steadily, while others, like frogs, must be fished extremely slowly and deliberately. When a fish hits, delay hooksetting momentarily until you actually feel the fish with the lure. This is less of a problem with soft lures than others because of their consistency, which makes it feel more natural to the fish and results in the bass holding it a bit longer than it might otherwise. When you do set the hook, it must be done hard.

Retrieving Crankbaits

Most floating/diving plugs—generically referred to by freshwater anglers as crankbaits—are relatively easy to use, and have excellent fish-hooking capabilities. Depending upon lip size, all crankbaits can be classified as shallow, intermediate, or deep divers, and the size to use depends on the depth you need to reach.

It is generally a good idea to retrieve crankbaits faster in warm water and clear water, and slower in cold water and muddy water. Bottom scratching is usually critical, so you should try to keep your plug rooting along the bottom, over objects, and along impediments. Keeping the rod tip down during the retrieve assists in hooksetting and also allows the lure to run deeper. If the rod tip is close to the water, you'll gain an extra foot or two of depth.

Many crankbaits are exceedingly buoyant, a feature that adds a different dimension to their retrieval compared to other lures. If you stop the retrieve, such plugs bob toward the surface. You can take advantage of this feature. A pull-pause action is easily accomplished by retrieving in the standard fashion and stopping momentarily, then repeating the procedure. In its most exaggerated form, this can be extended to stopping the retrieve long enough for the lure to float to the surface, and then resuming the retrieve. When fishing for cover-oriented species, try making the lure hesitate by objects that might hold gamefish.

A few crankbaits have little buoyancy or are neutral in buoyancy. These lures remain stationary in the water when stopped. A few others sink very slowly when stopped. Such suspension has a lot of validity in fishing plugs, especially smaller crankbaits, which essentially represent small baitfish. Baitfish rarely rise or sink significantly in their natural environment. When they stop, they stay at the same level, using their fins as stabilizers and relying on their internal organs to maintain their level. Making a lure stop and suspend at its running level has the most usefulness when fishing over some type of cover.

Certain places are particularly well worked with crankbaits. In freshwater this includes rock walls and roadways, underwater islands, and other irregular features that the lures can reach. Sunken or exposed bridge abutments are worth working and so is flooded timber; in all cases fish to, from, over, and around these objects, and don't be concerned about bumping the lures against them.

You must know how deep any diving plug runs to be effective with it. Diving abilities depend

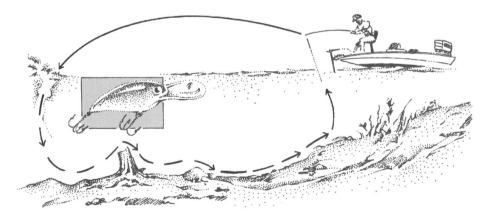

Although most plugs, especially diving versions, are fished along the shoreline, it can be worthwhile to cast deeper-running versions (inset) away from shore. A bottom-scouring stop-and-go retrieve is often best.

on the lure's lip, the diameter of your line, and the speed of retrieve. The larger the surface area of the lip, the thinner the diameter of the line, and the slower the retrieve, the deeper a crankbait will dive. Use the information supplied by the manufacturer with its product as a guideline, but learn for yourself how deep your lures run.

There are, incidentally, lipless plugs that are not used as deep divers so much as swimming plugs. Many of these sink; some float. They are primarily used in bass fishing (sometimes for northern pike and redfish) and are excellent for catching schooling fish, for casting over submerged vegetation, and even for deep running using a countdown method to get sinking models near the bottom. In cooler water, these are often fished in a stop-and-go manner, retrieving a few feet and then pausing momentarily before retrieving again.

Retrieving Sinking Lures

Sinking lures are retrieved differently than floating lures, although there are some weighted wooden and plastic plugs that are used in a manner similar to floating/diving plugs. The former includes weighted minnow-shaped shallow-running plugs, or weighted crankbaits; these sink when they enter the water and when a normal retrieve is stopped, and they have the capability of being fished deeper than their more buoyant counterparts.

Counting Down

It is often important to know what depth you're fishing when using lures that sink. You can determine this in many cases by counting each second that it sinks. The sink rate of a lure varies with its weight, material, and shape, so not every lure has an identical sink rate.

To determine relative depth, start counting every second once the lure enters the water until it strikes bottom and the line goes limp. If you counted to ten, then the next time you let out the lure you know that counting to five puts that lure halfway in the water column, and counting to nine brings it just above the bottom.

By measuring the line, you can be more precise and determine the sink rate. If it took a count of ten to put the lure on the bottom in 20 feet of water (measured from the surface), the lure falls at a rate of 2 feet per second under existing conditions;

therefore, to fish it precisely at 16 feet, count to eight before engaging the reel and retrieving (or jigging).

By knowing the sink rate, you can cast a sinking plug, for example, a long distance away, count it down to a certain level, and then begin retrieving to keep the lure at a specific level. A jig can be fished at a certain level vertically by counting it down from the instant it enters the water by the boat; jig it upward and then count it down to a different level. By repeating this action, you can fish through the water column at known levels, and return to levels where strikes have been received.

Spoons

The most important factor in using spoons is achieving the right retrieve or speed to get the proper action. Some spoons swim lazily and sink too deep when worked slowly; or they swim too rapidly and rise too high when worked fast. You should always swim a spoon near you and observe it to determine the best speed for using it.

When casting in current, you normally cast up and across stream or directly across stream, reel in slack line, keep the rod tip angled up, and allow the spoon to drift downstream with the current (sometimes reeling it very lightly), then lower the rod tip and reel it in with a slow, steady retrieve, a jerk-reel motion, or a combination of both. You can also fish it directly downstream for a sustained period, keeping the rod tip high and allowing the movement of the water to activate the lure; this is best with a spoon of thin or intermediate thickness.

When casting in lakes, let the lure sink after it enters the water, perhaps counting it down to a certain level (you have to predetermine sink rate) to reach the desired depth before beginning the retrieve. A straightforward retrieve sometimes does the job, especially if fish are numerous and aggressive, or a periodic stop-and-go retrieve may be better. It usually pays to put a twitch or jerk into a straight retrieve occasionally to stimulate a strike.

In-Line Spinners

With every spinner it is important to retrieve it at the right speed to get the blade working properly. If a spinner is fished too slowly, the blade may not spin or may spin erratically, but if it is retrieved too quickly, the blade cannot catch the water, and it will fall flat against the lure's body, keeping the blade from rotating and probably causing the whole lure to spin, which will not catch fish.

In moving water, you generally don't fish a spinner directly downstream, but cast it upstream at a quartering angle. The lure is tumbled by the swift water and also reeled forward at the same time, or it is fished like a spoon with rod tip held high and the lure retrieved just slowly enough to let the blade turn while the spinner swings downstream.

Fish a spinner as slowly as you can under the circumstances. With a sensitive rod you should be able to feel the blade revolve. Depth of retrieve can be altered by raising or lowering the rod, or changing retrieval speed. Hanging the spinner directly downstream in the current before completing the retrieve can be effective, as long as the current has enough force to turn the blade freely.

Spinners can get snagged easily, especially in current. In streams, it's important to get the lure working the moment it hits the water. Hesitation often means hung spinners, particularly when casting across a fast flow. Matching the size and weight to the water is also important.

In lakes and ponds, small and intermediate-size spinners are mostly fished fairly close to the surface or relatively shallow and on a straight retrieve. In deeper water, they are worked by counting the lure down to a specific level (you must predetermine the sink rate) and retrieving slowly.

Because lighter spinners don't have the weight or lure action to stay at one level, they angle upward on the retrieve; a long cast, an unimpeded

Casting for muskies at daybreak on Pennsylvania's Allegheny River, this angler keeps his rod tip down to aid lure retrieval and hooksetting.

freefall to deeper levels (keep an open bail on a spinning reel), and a low-angled rod help lengthen the time that the lure is in the right zone. Although a steady retrieve is often productive, it pays to vary a straight retrieve occasionally by hesitating the lure, twitching it quickly, and otherwise briefly altering its movement, which may cause a following fish to pounce.

It is usually necessary to use a snap-swivel with these lures to counter the tendency of the rotating blade to turn the lure over repeatedly and cause line twist. Twist can also be caused by debris on the lure, especially on the clevis. This or anything else that causes the blade not to spin freely deserves attention.

Weight-Forward Spinners

Principally used in freshwater fishing, weight-forward spinners are most commonly trolled, but they can be cast. Unlike in-line spinners, weight-forward spinners stay at a deep level when retrieved slowly. They should be counted down to the proper level when fished high in the water column, and allowed to reach bottom when it's necessary to crawl deep.

To start the retrieve, snap the rod tip up to help get the blade turning. These lures catch fish on both a routine uninterrupted retrieve and when the lure is hesitated and jerked occasionally during a normal retrieve. However, they are prone to fouling when cast. To minimize this, bring the rod tip back gently and lob the lure forward instead of making a standard rod-loading cast; also, pull the rod tip in as the lure hits the water to turn it toward you and straighten it out. Avoid using a snap-swivel or snap to further decrease fouling.

Spinnerbaits

Spinnerbaits are primarily fished on a standard cast-and-retrieve, usually in shallow or intermediate depths, but they can also be retrieved in deep water, although the methods in each case are quite different.

Freshwater bass are by far the most common catch on spinnerbaits, and the most common technique is to retrieve them steadily from within a few inches to several feet beneath the surface. If the water is clear enough, you can see and watch the lure coming through the water on the retrieve.

It is not only beneficial but highly enjoyable to watch a spinnerbait when it is being retrieved this shallow. Nearly every time, if you can see the lure, you will see the fish strike it. You can also see if a bass misses the lure, hits short, or is merely taking a close look. Sometimes these fish can be caught with another cast of that spinnerbait in the same area, or with an alternative lure that works more slowly.

It is important to begin retrieving a spinnerbait the moment it hits the water when working the shallows. Sometimes, bass are holding by objects at a level deeper than your lure is being retrieved and will not come up for it, even though you're fishing in what is generally considered shallow water. If you're fishing a spinnerbait close to the surface with poor results, try letting it sink out of sight to a depth of between 4 and 8 feet, and retrieve it steadily at that depth. Occasionally you'll have to fish a spinnerbait out of sight right along the bottom like this, in intermediate or greater depths.

An effective method for working weedbeds and weedlines is to crawl a spinnerbait slowly over the top of grass that is submerged a few feet. For grassbeds with definable weedlines, however, it may be better to cast parallel to the edge or bring the lure over the top and let it flutter down the edge. For lily pads, it's best to work the channel-like openings, but don't be afraid to throw into thick clusters and far back into pockets, then ease it over the pads and drop it in another pocket.

Perhaps the most reliable pattern for spinnerbait fishing, especially in the spring, is working the wood. This includes stumps, logs, and stick-ups. Make sure your spinnerbait is close to these objects; in fact, bump them with the lure at times. The momentary fluttering of the bait's blades and the object contact seem to produce strikes. Stickup trees, bushes, and floating logjams also are productive for spinnerbait users. In these locales, you should get your bait as far back in them as possible before commencing the retrieve. Boat docks and boathouses, too, fit in this category.

Deep fishing with spinnerbaits is something that relatively few anglers try but which has merit for fishing along sharply sloping shorelines, dropoffs, rocky ledges, and among deep timber, whether on a lift-and-drop motion, in a series of short hops, or on a straight retrieve at a deeper than normal level.

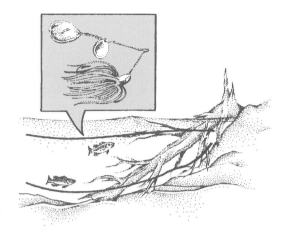

When cast into cover along the bank, a spinnerbait can be retrieved shallow at a moderate pace (upper dark line) through the top layer of water, or more slowly and deeper (lower dark line) through the lower layer.

Where there is submerged cover in deeper water—points, open-water humps, stumpy flats or ridges near deep water, ledges, and assorted vegetation—you can make a long cast and either let the lure fall to the bottom or count it down to the proper level before beginning the retrieve. Watch the line for indications of a strike as the lure is falling, and after it reaches the desired level start a steady retrieve. If you crank the reel handle too fast, the lure will rise and lift away from the bottom of the desired zone, so be sure to reel slowly to keep the spinnerbait in the right place.

Jerkbaits

Jerkbaits are usually fished suspended or just under the surface in a pull-pause, slow-jerking type of retrieve. These lures look like a wounded darting fish when jerked or paused, because they descend slowly like a dying fish.

Like conventional plastic worms, soft jerkbaits are rigged with a single hook embedded inside, which makes them reasonably snag-resistant and capable of being fished amid heavy cover, especially vegetation. They may be fished unweighted for shallow use or internally weighted for deeper use, longer casts, and less erratic action.

Some jerkbaits dart well from side to side, and others have more of a slightly canted darting-rolling action. You should experiment a bit with hook size and placement to achieve the desired effect, and be attentive to proper rerigging after a fish has been caught.

When retrieving a jerkbait, keep your rod tip down and pointed at the water. When the lure is a long distance away, it may be advantageous to retrieve it with the rod tip held at a raised rod.

Soft Worms

Learning to detect a strike or to differentiate a strike from contact with underwater objects is the most difficult aspect of soft worm fishing. There is no shortcut to learning this. An ability to detect strikes and learn the "feel" of a worm comes through experience. The more you fish with a worm, the quicker you'll develop this feel.

One key to detecting strikes is closely watching your line. In the most radical instances, an eager bass may pick up a worm and immediately run with it, in which case the line noticeably moves away. Sometimes you'll see the line move like this before you feel the strike. Usually, however, there is a barely perceptible flickering of the line, particularly the section nearest the water.

To retrieve a soft worm that has been rigged with a slip sinker, begin with the rod butt and your arms close to your body, with the rod held perpendicular to you and parallel to the water. Raise the rod from this position (we'll call it 9 o'clock) upward, extending it between a 45- and 60-degree angle, which would mean moving it from 9:00 to 10:30 or 11:00. As you raise the rod, the worm is lifted up off the bottom and swims forward, falling to a new position. Make this motion slowly, so the worm does not hop too far off the bottom and swims slowly. When your rod reaches that upward position, drop it back to its original position while at the same time retrieving slack line. Keep your motions slow. When you encounter some resistance, as would happen when crawling it over a log or through a bush, first gently try to work the worm along; if this fails, try to hop the worm along with short flicks of the rod tip.

Sometimes the slip sinker gets hung up under rocks, and if you jiggle your line, the sinker falls back and becomes free. Other times, the sinker will fall over a limb and slide down the line, while the worm stays back behind that limb. This makes detection and retrieval difficult and can be solved by pegging the slip sinker with a toothpick and breaking it off, thus preventing the sinker from sliding up the line. The sinker remains directly in front of the worm.

Pegging is useful for fishing brushy areas, lily pads, hyacinths, moss, and grass as well as amid stumps and trees, and it makes retrieval and strike detection easier. It goes against the theory of having a freely sliding slip sinker so a fish can pick up the lure and run off with it without detecting the weight, but this is minimized by a quick hooksetting reaction, a sensitive rod, and a sensitive line to detect strikes more readily.

Set the hook as soon as you can after detecting a strike. Lower the rod tip and extend it out and point it toward the fish. This momentarily gives the bass slack line. Quickly reel up the slack and as the line draws tight, set the hook. Continue to reel in line to counteract the effect of stretch and to ensure that no slack is present. The whole maneuver is accomplished in an instant and appears to be one fluid motion. Removing slack line is critical, because your hook must penetrate not only the balled-up worm, but the cartilaginous mouth of the fish as well.

It is difficult to fish a worm properly in wind. It may be necessary to anchor your boat in such a way that you can fish directly upwind or downwind of that spot and gain a better feel of the retrieved worm. At other times you may elect to drift and fish, using an electric motor to either slow the drift speed or keep a desired position.

Occasionally, you may find it beneficial to swim an unweighted worm slowly just off the bottom. This works best in lily pads, in moderately thin grassy areas, and similar spots.

Retrieving Jigs

One thing that a jig is not is a throw-it-out-and-reel-it-back-in kind of lure, one that can catch fish in spite of the abilities of the person using it. An angler has to put some work into making a jig catch fish and into being able to detect strikes. There is a knack to jigging. Good jig users have a feel for what is happening to their lure and they have a razor-sharp ability to detect and respond to strikes.

The key to jigging success is establishing contact with your lure, getting and keeping it where the fish are, and using the right rod to feel a strike. The greatest concerns are often how deep you need to fish a particular jig and how effective you are at doing that. Jigs excel at being on or close to the bottom, which is where the majority of jig-caught fish are found. They also are productive for covering the area between the bottom and upper levels via vertical presentations.

Two conditions that make strike detection more difficult when jigging are fishing under windy conditions, when it is difficult to maintain depth and control, and fishing in and around weeds or other obstructions. Developing a keen feel, especially in weeds, takes patience and practice, and a sensitive well-tapered rod with a fast tip.

Many strikes on jigs and jigging spoons occur when the lure is falling after you've completed the jigging motion. Therefore, it's good to tight-line a jig backward without so much tension that it falls unnaturally and stiffly. Slightly lower your rod tip as the jig falls; when you feel something take the jig, set the hook quickly, keeping the rod tip high and reeling rapidly at the same time.

Covering Bottom

When fishing on or close to the bottom, many anglers do not have success because they fail to reach and keep their jigs on the bottom. The simplest way to get a jig to reach the bottom is to open the bail of your spinning reel or depress the free-spool mechanism on a baitcasting, spincasting, or conventional reel; let the lure fall freely until the line goes slack on the surface of the water and no more comes off the spool. If the water is calm and the boat still, you can readily detect when you're on the bottom. If it is somewhat windy or if current is present, you have to watch the departing line carefully to detect the telltale slack and to differentiate between line that is leaving the spool because the lure has not reached bottom and line that is being pulled off by a drifting lure or boat.

The lighter (and thinner) the line and the heavier the lure, the easier it is to reach the bottom. The stronger the line, the greater its diameter will usually be and the more resistance it will offer in the water. A quarter-ounce jig will fall more quickly on 8-pound line than it will on 14-pound line, if the same type of line is used.

A typical scenario for jigging the bottom is to let the jig fall freely until the line goes slack. Reel up slack and lift the jig off the bottom. Once you're on the bottom, you need to maintain contact with it. Assuming that you cast your jig some distance away, let it settle to the bottom, and are now retrieving it toward yourself, you should keep it working in short hops over the bottom as long as the terrain and length of paid-out line enable you to do so.

If you are in a boat and drifting, the jig will eventually start sweeping upward and away from you and the bottom as you drift, unless it is very heavy; so you need to pay out more line occasionally until the angle of your line has changed significantly and then reel in and drop the jig back down again.

Choosing the right weight of lure to use is critical to most types of jigging. The ideal is to have a lure that gets to the bottom and stays there under normal conditions but that is not too large to intimidate the fish. Most anglers who fail to reach bottom don't use the right retrieval technique or don't compensate for wind or current; in addition, they may use too light a jig for getting down to the bottom under the conditions they face.

Sometimes you need to swim a jig by pumping it slowly and reeling, never actually letting it hop along the bottom. Other times you may need to slowly drag it. When fishing a moderately sloping shoreline or point, for example, you should slowly pull the lure a little bit off the bottom, let it settle down while keeping in contact with it, take up the slack, and repeat this. When working a ledge or a sharply sloping shoreline, slowly pull the lure over the structure until it begins to fall, let it settle, and then repeat. Don't hop the jig up quickly here, because it will fall out and away from the bottom and likely miss a good deal of the important terrain.

With some jigs, such as grubs, a good technique is to make them jump quickly off the bottom rather than make short hops. You can also swim a jig on the edges of cover by reeling it slowly across the bottom and giving it occasional darting movements by manipulating your rod tip.

Vertical Jigging

Jigging vertically is useful when fishing through the ice in freshwater, angling on the bottom in deep water, and angling for suspended fish in open water. Here, both leadhead jigs and metal or lead spoons are used and you needn't maintain bottom contact. Sometimes you'll need to get to a particular depth and regularly jig at that spot.

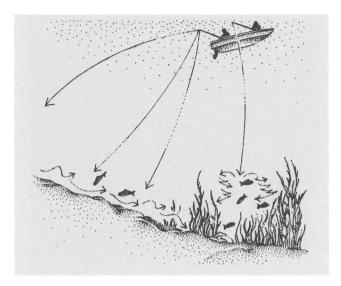

Depending on circumstances, anglers can fish by casting toward shore and jigging a lure back along bottom, or by vertically fishing a jig or jigging spoon on or just slightly above bottom or objects.

If you know what depth to fish, you can let the desired length of line out and commence jigging, never reeling in any line and paying out line only if you begin to drift. Here's one way to know how much line you're letting out: Reel the jig up to the rod tip, stick the rod tip on the surface, let go of the jig, and raise your rod tip to eye level; then stop the fall of the jig and lower the rod tip back to the surface. If eye level is 6 feet above the surface, your jig will now be 6 feet deep. Repeat this. Now you've let out 12 feet of line. Continue until the desired length is out. With a levelwind reel having a freely revolving line guide, you can measure the amount of line that is let out with each side-to-side movement of the line guide; multiply this amount by the number of times the guide travels back and forth. If you use a reel that doesn't have such a guide, you can strip line off the spool in 1-foot (or 18-inch) increments until the desired length is out. Another method is to count down the lure's descent.

For some vertical jigging, you may need to let your lure fall to the bottom and then jig it up toward the surface a foot or two at a time. Bring the lure off the bottom, and reel in the slack; then jig it there three or four times before retrieving another few feet of line and jigging the lure again. Repeat this until the lure is near the surface. The only problem here is that you don't usually know exactly how deep a fish is when you do catch one, and you can't just strip out the appropriate length of line and be at the proper level.

17

Hooksetting

Some angling situations and techniques cause a fish to hook itself when it strikes a bait or lure; all you have to do is keep tension on the line to keep the hook point from slipping free. One example of this is using circle hooks. Most of the time, however, and nearly always when casting and retrieving lures, an angler must react to a strike by setting the hook. This is harder on some fish than on others, and there are many variables that influence the outcome.

Effective hooksetting requires proper technique and has little to do with physical stature or with brute strength. It depends on timing and hook point penetration. Raising up the rod with steady pressure after you detect a strike is not how you should set the hook.

There are two recognized and effective techniques in hooksetting, one with a no-slack approach and the other with a slight, controlled amount of slack.

With a no-slack hookset, you lean toward the fish, reel up slack until the line is taut, and then punch the hook home. This is accomplished in the blink of an eye, and it is crucial that you reel up slack only until the line is taut but not pulling on the fish. If you tighten the line so much that the fish feels tension, it may quickly expel your offering; this is especially true with bait and with soft-bodied lures. This technique takes timing, which is acquired through experience.

With a controlled slack-line set, the line is not reeled taut to the fish, but nearly so; and the hook is punched home quickly to provide shock penetration. The theory is that you get better hook point penetration from a snappy shock force than from a tight-line pull.

Many times a fish strikes without warning; the angler feels tension immediately and reacts by bringing the rod back sharply. Sometimes that is all it takes, but occasionally the hook never becomes firmly embedded in the fish, and experience with certain lures or species may indicate that a second or third hookset is warranted.

A principal reason why many anglers are ineffective at hooksetting is not their inability to respond quickly and generate rod-tip speed, but the way they use their bodies and contort themselves while doing so. Hooksetting is not a whole-body maneuver, but an exercise of wrists and arms.

Prepare for a strike by keeping your rod tip down so you're in the best position to respond quickly. If there is little or no slack in the line, you can make a forceful sweep up or back when you set the hook and then be in immediate control of the fish to begin playing it. When working certain lures, however, you need to keep the rod tip up to work the lure properly and to readily detect a strike. Compensate for a high rod position by bowing the rod slightly toward the fish while reeling up slack; this action enables you to get a full backward sweep and be in the proper position for the beginning of the fight.

Where possible, you should be reeling and striking all in one swift motion, bringing your rod back and up sharply while holding the reel handle and reeling the instant you feel the fish. The position of the rod is important. The butt is jammed into the stomach or mid-chest area, and the full arc and power of the rod is brought into play, without having your hands or arms jerk wildly over your head.

In order to countermand stretch in nylon lines, you must reel hard and fast the moment you set the hook. Because of line stretch, an angler is more effective at setting the hook at short and midrange distances than at long distances. Thus you can generate more force and be more efficient at setting the hook at short distances than at long distances.

One way to deliver better than average hooksetting force is to strike with both hands on the rod, one on the handle around the reel and one on the foregrip. Most anglers set the hook with one hand on the rod handle and the other on the reel handle. Usually this is adequate. Certain circumstances, however, may necessitate using two hands to reef the

Proper hooksetting begins with the rod low and pointed toward the fish (top) and concludes with the rod butt held chest high (bottom), where power is delivered and control is maintained.

hooks home. Occasionally it is desirable to set the hook two or three times in rapid succession.

Most of the time when fly fishing, especially when using light-wire hooks on small flies and thin tippets, you only need to snap the tip up and keep the line taut to set the hook, although the bonier the mouth of the fish, the larger the hook needed, and the heavier the tippet or shock leader, the more forceful you need to be.

Whether you set the hook or not when trolling depends on the situation and the fish. When the quarry is large and hard-mouthed, you should still set the hook after pulling it out of a rod holder. When using very light line or angling for soft-mouthed fish, you usually don't set it because you run the risk of pulling the lure out of the fish.

In big-game fishing and offshore trolling, heavy-duty reels are adjusted with greater drag tension for setting the hook (called a strike drag), and drag tension is relaxed to a lighter preset tension once the fish is on. The heavier drag allows a lot more force to be applied when the hook is set, and counters the effect of stretch.

18

Playing and Landing Fish

W hen it comes to playing a fish, which is also commonly referred to as fighting it, the degree of work that is involved obviously varies from a second or two for the smallest species jerked out of shallow water, to many hours of muscle-aching, perspiration-inducing, and tackle-straining exertion for offshore leviathans. There is not much out of the ordinary involved in the playing of small or less powerful species, but those that strain fishing equipment—and that includes small but very strong fish caught on light tackle—require more than just holding the rod and winding the reel handle to catch.

Playing Fish

There are certain techniques for manipulating the rod that help land fish without adversely affecting the tackle, and which help apply maximum pressure to a fish throughout the entire period of playing, keep the fish away from obstacles that might cut the line or tear out the hook, and land the fish as quickly as possible.

Landing a fish quickly is important for several reasons in addition to simply wanting to catch the fish. For some species of fish and in some circumstances, it is critical immediately after hooking them, or later during the fight, to use pressure and angle position to keep the fish away from any objects—reef, piling, vegetation, the bottom of the boat, and so on.

In addition, a prolonged period of fish playing may result in losing the fish because the hook has worn a large hole in its mouth and then pulled out. Furthermore, in some saltwater environs, long battles attract large predators, primarily sharks, that will attack and kill a hooked fish.

Also, and sometimes most important, prolonged fish playing can exhaust a fish to the point that it cannot recover its strength and be released alive and well, whether you are releasing it by law or by choice.

Methods

Fish-playing activities generally take place in a short period of time, and the action is often fast. Your reactions must be swift and instinctive, and your tackle, particularly line and reel drag, must be capable and of good quality. Many fish are lost as a result of the way in which the angler plays the fish, usually by allowing the fish to do things that it could be prevented from doing. Within the capabilities of your tackle, take the fight to the fish; don't sit back and be casual. Confidence in playing fish well and hard is derived from experience and also from knowing what your tackle can do.

Line breakage is often the reason for losing large fish, and much of this boils down to inferior-quality line, line that is damaged, or bad knots. Another reason for losing fish is an improper reel drag setting. When the drag is set too tightly, line

In this sequence of a guide and angler landing a 9-pound bass in a Mexican lake, note how the angler strains to direct the active fish toward the netter and into the outstretched net; he keeps a tight line even as the fish nearly escapes while the guide is trying to get both hands on the handle.

won't freely come off the spool under the surges of a strong fish; this is a problem because tension increases as the diameter of the spool decreases and as the amount of line in the water increases.

Playing a fish begins with hooking it well and staying with its antics from the moment that the hooks gets stuck in its mouth. The position of the rod is very important. Right from the start, the rod butt should be jammed into the stomach or mid-chest area, and the full arc and power of the rod should be utilized. You cannot play and land a fish well if your rod is held up over your head or extended out and away from your body. These are not power or control positions. You do have to keep the tip up, however, throughout a normal fight and constantly maintain pressure on the fish. Slack line must always be avoided.

In a boat, you generally don't need to move once a fish is on the hook; but if the fish is a very large one, you will need to move to one corner of the stern so that the captain has a clear view of the line and the action in case it's necessary to move the boat quickly. If you are wading in a lake or river and hook a good fish, you should immediately and carefully step backward until you're in ankle-deep water or on the bank, where you can move quickly if necessary.

"Pumping" is a technique that is used for playing all but the smallest fish, and it is critical when fighting a large or strong fish and/or when using light line. It is employed whenever a fish is deep and often when a fish is up and some distance away, not budging or swimming to one side or the other. To pump, keep the rod butt in the stomach, lower the rod tip and reel in line simultaneously, and then pressure the fish as you bring the rod back up. Once the rod is up, lower it and reel. Continue doing this. Some fish and some tackle require constant short pumping motions, often called short stroking; this is more common when using stand-up tackle for tuna and billfish. To best really tough bruisers, the pumping must continue unabated because on some fish, like tuna, if you stop to rest, the fish does too, and it can regain strength and prolong the battle when it rests.

Often when a fish is fairly close to you, it is still energetic. Continue to keep the rod tip high or fully taut when held to the side. This is a time to be directing the fish. If you're in a boat and the fish streaks toward it (perhaps to swim under it),

Keeping the rod too high is not an effective way to control a strong fish when it is very close to the boat. To keep it clear of the boat and motors, reel down, dip the tip of the rod in the water if necessary, and steer the line clear of objects.

you could be put at a disadvantage, particularly when using light tackle. You must reel as fast as possible to keep out slack. If the fish gets under the boat, stick the rod tip well into the water to keep the line away from objects.

You should anticipate that a fish will rush the boat and should be prepared to head it around the stern or bow. Sometimes a companion can manipulate the boat to help swing the stern or bow away from a fish. If possible, go toward the bow or stern to better follow or control the fish. Walk around the whole boat if you have to. Don't hang back in a tug-of-war with a large, strong fish; use finesse rather than muscle.

When a fish swims around your boat, keep the rod up and apply pressure to force its head up and to steer it clear of the outboard or electric motor and the propellers.

At times you need to change the angle of pull on a strong and stubborn fish, perhaps to help steer it in a particular direction or make it fight a little differently. Accomplish this by applying side pressure. Bring the rod down and hold it parallel to the water while turning your body partially or entirely sideways to the fish. Fight the fish as you would if the rod were perpendicular to the water. Switch sides as necessary when the fish moves far enough in any direction.

With very large fish that get near the boat but are still energetic, or with big fish that stay very deep below the boat and can't be budged, you

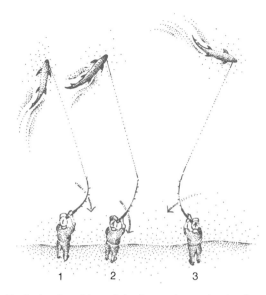

To deal with stubborn fish, change the angle of pull. When a fish is running straight away, change the rod from an overhead to a side position (1) and continue with this method until the fish changes attitude (2). To dissuade it from streaking to the side, switch rod position and apply pressure from the opposite direction (3).

when the fish jumps by bowing the rod toward it so that the jumper cannot use taut line as leverage for pulling free of the hook. Sometimes you can stop a fish from jumping by putting your rod tip in the water and keeping a tight line, which changes the angle of pull and may stop a fish from clearing the surface.

A momentary slack line also may prevent a fish from jumping, although slack is an invitation for the hook to fall out. The only good reason to prevent a fish from jumping—and jumping is one of the thrills that anglers live for—is that you know the fish is poorly hooked and you fear a jump will cause the fish to throw the hook.

Eventually the fish is next to you and may be ready for landing. If it still has a last burst of energy, however, this will be a crucial moment. Because of the short distance between you and the fish, there will be a lot of stress on your tackle. You must act swiftly when the fish makes its last bolt for freedom.

As it surges away, don't pressure it. Let it go. Point the rod at the fish at the critical moment so

may have to quickly move the boat a fair distance away, letting line peel off the drag. This changes the angle of pull on the fish and usually helps bring it up from the depths.

Using a boat to play a very big fish is a standard practice in large bodies of water. Under some circumstances, it may be questionable from an ethical standpoint, though not from a practical one. Chasing a fish is sometimes necessary to prevent the reel from being despooled, or to avoid obstacles, or to help a struggling and inexperienced angler. Many big fish in offshore waters are caught as much by the boat-handling and boat-maneuvering actions of the captain as by the angler's efforts.

In current, a big fish that gets downriver and through rapids where an angler is unable to follow may return upriver if the angler releases line from the reel and allows slack line to drift below the fish. The line below the fish acts as a pulling force from downstream (instead of ahead) and may cause the fish to head upstream again. If this strategy does not work, you have to get below it or break it off.

With some species of jumping fish (Atlantic salmon and tarpon, for example), and when using flycasting tackle, you need to slacken the tension

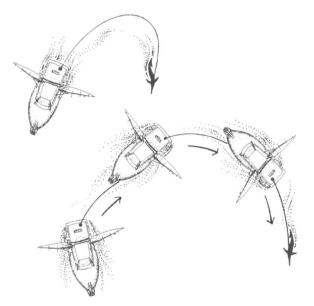

In this exaggerated view of a big-game fishing scene, hundreds of yards of line separate the angler and a turning fish, forming a belly in the line (top) that causes a great amount of drag tension, which in turn can lead to line breakage. When this belly forms, the boat needs to move in the direction of the line (bottom), not directly toward the fish, to remove the belly; this action also lets the angler quickly regain line on the reel and puts the line in a straight position with the fish.

that there is no rod pressure, just pressure from the drag on the reel. A large fish will peel line off the drag, which if set properly (and not sticking) will keep tension on the fish within the tolerance of the line's strength and provide the least amount of pressure possible. As the surge tapers, lift up the rod and work the fish.

Landing Fish

Landing is the act of taking a fish into possession once it has been played close to the angler. This is accomplished in a number of ways, the most common being hand-holding, netting, or gaffing. The circumstances, species, size of fish, type of terminal tackle used, strength of line or leader, and other considerations affect the decision to use one method or another. An especially important factor is whether the fish will be kept or released.

Many fish are lost at or close to the boat because of the actions of the angler or the person attempting to land the fish. Sometimes, even when everything is done right, a fish manages to get free just when it is almost landed; this usually happens when the hook pulls out even though the angler has kept a tight line. However, in most cases, when fish are lost at or near the boat, either just prior to being landed or while in the act of landing, the cause is a mistake or series of mistakes.

Perhaps the greatest mistake is reeling a fish right up to the tip of the rod when a fish is at boatside. It's better to leave a few feet of line between the rod tip and the fish so that you can direct the fish or lift/swing it onboard. A common mistake is applying too much pressure on an active fish that is near the boat; finesse, not muscle, is the solution. To properly land fish, especially large, strong, and active specimens, the key is to employ common sense, anticipation, and finesse.

Before you attempt to land a fish the decision has to be made whether you will keep it or not. If the answer is not, then consider not landing it at all but unhooking it in the water to minimize injury to the fish. You can do this by holding the line with one hand or gripping the fish around the lower jaw with a jaw-gripping tool and using a pair of pliers, a hook gripper, or a hook puller to get the hook out; then let the fish go immediately. In this manner, the fish is never or minimally touched and is least likely to be injured.

However, whenever a fish is on the surface or its head is removed from the water, there is the danger that it will flip, spin, thrash, lunge, or take other action to escape, and this may result in injury to you or the fish or result in a fish that escapes. You have to be very careful when you lift a fish to unhook it, and you should remember that when landing a fish, by whatever means, you should leave the head of the fish in the water to minimize problems (although when you net a fish, it's best to get the head up to the surface). Many fish react instinctively when their heads are lifted and the buoyancy of being supported by water is gone; they'll use their tails to take some type of action. If you keep its head in the water, a fish may be less inclined to do this; and if you can grab it by the tail, its main source of power is gone and it usually can't take action.

Hand-Landing

When you grab or hold a fish with your hands, you may potentially harm yourself or the fish, so do it carefully. If a fish is going to be released, handling should be reduced to a minimum to avoid harming the fish. If the fish will be kept, then it doesn't have to be handled as carefully, the major concern then being to avoid personal injury. The sharp fin rays, gill covers, and teeth of some fish, as well as the barbels and pectoral spines on others, can easily cause a cut or stab wound that is likely to be sore for a while and may become infected.

In addition, the landing of fish that are still green, or fresh, or that are very powerful has the potential for causing more serious bodily harm, as well as for damage to equipment. Being careful is mandatory whenever you are handling a fish, especially one that is hooked.

There are several locations on a fish that should be avoided if you are going to release them but that make good holding spots if you are keeping them. The foremost location is under the lower edge of the gill; this is a secure, but deadly, place to grasp a fish. A specimen that is tired and on its side may be grabbed under the lower gill cover for landing, and this location usually keeps your hands away from the hooks in a fish's mouth.

Many fish can also be grasped one-handed under the upper gill cover by the back; place the thumb under the upper edge of the gill cover and place the tip of the middle finger under the edge

The largemouth bass is one species that can be easily grabbed by the lower lip, but be careful to avoid hooks.

of the opposite gill cover. Another secure but fatal grasping spot for small and medium-size fish is by the upper edge of the eye sockets.

Grabbing by the jaw is a possibility with some fish; the characteristics of their mouths, lack of teeth on the jaws, and size make them quite easy to grasp in this manner. Such species as largemouth bass, panfish, and small stripers can be landed by grasping the lower lip, provided the fish is well tired before the attempt is made.

Simply insert the thumb inside the lower jaw and pinch the jaw against the bent forefinger, which is outside and pressing against the lower jaw. If you'll be landing a lot of fish, you can wear a leather thumb guard to keep from raking your thumb and the skin in the crease between thumb and forefinger. This method of grasping immobilizes the fish and is good for unhooking as well as landing, and has no adverse effect on releasing a fish. It may, however, be hard to accomplish when the mouth opening is covered with one or two treble hooks from the lure.

Larger and stronger fish that lack teeth on the jaws can also be held by the jaw in reverse fashion. For such fish, keep the thumb outside and below the jaw, and put the other four fingers inside the jaw—preferably you are wearing a wet glove when you do this. Gloves, especially versions with a sure-grip surface, aid in grasping and holding the fish. Wet cotton gloves are best for fish that will be released.

Most fish cannot be held by hand in the mouth, usually because of teeth. One way to hand-land

and hand-hold species by the mouth is with a jaw-gripping tool. These clamp over the lower jaw to secure the fish and don't require touching the jaws by hand; these tools don't harm the fish, although many models work best on smaller fish.

Some small fish can be gently lifted with a hand placed under the belly. This may be a good alternative when a fish has been caught on a lure with multiple hooks; however, it is really a technique for small fish. Some fish can be calmed by turning them over and holding them upside down; this is more useful for a fish that will be unhooked and released.

A lot of fish, especially small to medium-size specimens in freshwater, and smaller specimens in saltwater, are hand-grasped behind the mouth and the head in the "neck" or nape area. Holding too tightly here can damage internal organs if the fish is to be released, but bigger fish, with more meat in this area, can be held firmly without problem. Fish with prickly spiny rays may be a problem to land this way; instead, run your hand from head to tail with thumb on top and other fingers on the belly. Depress the dorsal fins with the thumb; now you can safely hold the fish around the middle of the body.

Catfish must be held properly to avoid a puncture from their sharp pectoral fins. The best way to do this is to grab behind, and at the base of, the pectoral fins in order to keep them pointed sideways.

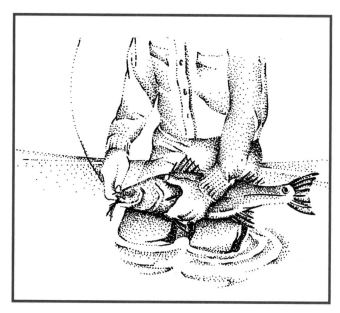

Wading anglers may need to pin a large, strong, or frisky fish to their wet legs, as shown, to land and unhook the fish.

Lifting and Swinging

An easy way to boat small fish that are well hooked is simply to lift them aboard with your rod and line. This method is practical only for small to medium-size fish caught on sturdy tackle. Landing is best accomplished by working the fish to the surface and leading it toward the boat; when the head clears the surface near the boat, continue the momentum and lift the fish up, swinging it in. Small fish that are swung into a boat then have to be grabbed by hand, and obviously they may wind up flopping on the floor. Such treatment is not conducive to proper handling and release but is all right for fish that are to be kept.

Billing

The long bills of sailfish and small marlin provide a good handle for landing, or at least for holding while the fish is unhooked. That bill is used as a weapon when the fish chases prey, and it can become a weapon used against you if you're not careful. To avoid this, try to grab the bill with both hands when it's just below the surface. On small boats, billfish are usually landed on the starboard side so that the operator can see what is happening, but on larger boats they may be landed on either side or at the stern.

In any case, grab the bill with both hands, with your thumbs facing each other but slightly apart. Be prepared to push away from the bill and head if the fish suddenly lunges up, and be ready to hold on if the fish thrashes moderately.

Tailing

The tails of some fish are rigid enough to permit you to grab them by placing your hand over the caudal peduncle just ahead of the tail fin. You can grab a jack or a tuna this way, and you can grab large salmon and pike by the tail. Smaller fish usually can't be grabbed by the tail, and the tails of many bigger fish are not rigid enough. You can't grab a big largemouth bass securely enough by the tail, nor can you grab most trout (except really large ones) this way. But for some fish, the tail provides a good handle for landing, and it is far enough from teeth or hooks to be an attractive gripping point.

When you do grab a fish by the tail, you can do it either by hand for fish that will be released, or with a tailer for fish that will be kept. A tailer, also called a tail rope or loop, is a nooselike device that slips over the fish and cinches down on the caudal peduncle (the stem just forward of the tail fin). A tailer is best for fish with a stiff rather than flexible caudal peduncle.

Netting

Avoid netting if you plan to release the fish or if it has been caught on a multihooked lure. Fish that have been hooked with a multihooked lure and then netted may be easily damaged. The decision to release a fish has to be made before the fish is in the net. Cotton mesh nets are softer and don't seem to hurt the fish as much, but hooks are harder to get out, and the cotton nets are not as widely available as nylon or rubber nets.

Fish that are netted usually can be released alive if they have not been handled excessively and have not spent too much time out of water. One way to facilitate the release of netted fish is to keep the net in the water while unhooking the fish. Those who wade can do this quite easily. Once the hook has been removed, the net can be turned over and the fish gently jiggled out.

Proper netting technique is as much a matter of knowing what not to do as it is knowing what to do. Under most circumstances, you shouldn't put the net in the water and wait for the fish to come close. Nor should you wave the net overhead where a fish might see it. Keep the net solidly in hand and at the ready, either motionless or out of sight, until a fish is almost within reach.

Don't attempt to net a fish unless it is within reach, and don't try to net it if it is going away from you or appears to be able to go away from you. Ideally, the fish should be heading toward you so that it must continue moving forward, or so that you can move the net in front of it if it turns. As a rule, don't try to net a fish unless its head is on the surface or is just breaking to the surface, which is when it has little mobility.

Don't try to net a fish from behind. And try not to touch the fish with the rim of the net until it is well inside. Touching fish, particularly if they are still lively, often initiates wild behavior.

Snagging a multihooked lure on the net webbing is a major problem when anglers try to net a fish that is in a poor position or when the fish doesn't come squarely into the middle of the net. Snagging like this is one of the surest ways to lose fish, particularly those that are heavy and cannot be readily hoisted into the boat or scooped up in the now tangled net.

The angler can help the netter by making an effort to get the fish's head up so that it is near or on the surface and not deep in the water. When the fish comes up and is being worked toward the net, you should back up, put more pressure on the fish to gain line, raise the rod high to keep the fish's head up, and tell the netter that the time is right, attempting to lead the fish closer as the netter goes into action.

Be prepared for miscues. When a strong fish, and especially a green one, is brought to the net, try to back off a bit on the reel drag, or perhaps open the bail of the reel or put it into freespool, keeping a finger on the line to maintain tension. If the fish flops out, runs through the net, or charges away, there may be a lot of pressure on your tackle, so anticipate this possibility and let the fish go in the manner noted previously. When it stops, reengage the reel and work the fish back.

Netting a fish by yourself is often a tricky chore, made more difficult by the influence of current, wind, and tide. Bringing a fish to net or boat as quickly as possible may not be feasible when you are alone and have a large specimen, and often you must play the fish out thoroughly before you can slip the net under it. Try to get the fish to within several feet of the tip of the rod; then raise the rod high over and behind your head while you reach for the fish with net extended in your other hand. Keep the line taut, and don't let your rod hand come down to create slack.

Netting efforts are sometimes more arduous in fast-moving waters because fish are usually below you, and it is hard to get big fish back upcurrent and positioned for proper netting. Another problem is that when you don't gain on fish in current, they rest momentarily and recoup enough strength to prolong the battle or give that last extra kick just when you think you have them. For this reason, those who are netting a big fish for someone else in swift water should usually be a reasonable distance downriver, in a position to land a tired fish as it wallows near the bank, still resisting the angler but unable to swim off with vigor.

If netting the fish isn't feasible because the net is too small you always have the option of landing it by hand or beaching it. In either case, the

The angler has to keep the head of a big, strong fish up and guide it toward the net, and the netter shouldn't stab at or chase the fish.

fish must be thoroughly whipped and under your control before you do so.

Perhaps the best method of netting a fish that will be released is to use a type of net called a cradle, or release cradle. This is not a net in the traditional handle-and-dipping sense, but it has similarities and is a benign way of landing and subduing a large or long fish that will be unhooked and released.

The most popular release cradles have two long narrow wood boards or metal tubes connected by ¼-inch soft-mesh knotless netting that is closed at the ends; the netting droops into the water to envelop the fish. The cradle is laid alongside a boat, and the netting droops into a trough below. The angler leads a captured fish alongside the boat and over the netting, and the net is folded up like a purse to enclose the fish, which remains full-length and in the water. Perhaps most important, the cradle supports the full body of the fish in a horizontal position.

Another version, usually homemade and intended for shorter fish, is smaller, with open ends and open-grip handle. In both cases, the fish stays relaxed in the net while the hook is removed and can be released without having to be handled.

Moreover, you can rig up the cradle for weighing, keeping the fish in the cradle and providing excellent horizontal support for it. A cradle is difficult to use when fishing by yourself; in that case, it is better to avoid a cradle or net altogether and try to unhook the fish while it is in the water.

Gaffing

Gaffing is a landing option primarily used in saltwater and, with one exception, is not recommended for fish that are to be released. That exception is when a fish is gaffed in the mouth through the lower jaw.

You gaff a fish by getting the point of the gaff in the water beneath the fish and then strike upward sharply. Being too excited or careless can cause problems. When gaffers flail wildly, they often miss the fish, strike it in a spot that makes control and lifting difficult, or, worse, strike and break the angler's line. Poking the fish with the gaff instead of ramming it home is likely to make the fish surge enough to break free.

When you plan to keep the fish, the location where you gaff it is not critical and you can stick the gaff in the upper back muscle of the midsection. This may damage some meat, but it is a good secure spot. The ideal location for saving meat is in the upper back behind the head. Gaffing a fish in the belly may cause the fish to react violently and either shake free, pry the gaff out of your hand, or break the gaff. It also contributes to a heavily bleeding fish that makes a mess in the boat.

In these photos, a big dolphin is skillfully gaffed and brought aboard a large sportfishing boat. Note how the mate uses one leg to brace himself as he extends far out (1), sticks the gaff hook into the fish and instantly grabs it with two hands as the fish starts to thrash (2), begins to lift up as the fish is under control (3), and then swiftly lifts the fish over the high gunwale (4).

Gaff the fish with a firm, sure motion and follow through with the upward motion by lifting the fish out of the water if it is small enough to lift; otherwise, a second gaff (or tail rope) or two people hauling will be necessary to get the fish in.

To gaff a fish when a boat is moving and the fish is swimming or is being towed alongside the boat, reach across the back with the hook down

A hand gaff can be used on some fish that will be released, especially those having large mouths (left); the best place to gaff small and intermediate-size fish that will be kept is in the upper back, as shown (right).

and pointed at the side of the fish facing away from you. When the handle is close to the back of the fish, sharply drive the point all the way to the bend and keep the gaff coming to you.

The technical procedure is the same when gaffing from a boat that is at anchor or drifting, the difference being that your target is moving and you have to plan the strike well. Try to plant the gaff hook when the fish has just turned and is facing away from the boat rather than when it is headed toward the boat; if you miss, the fish will probably steam away from you rather than go underneath.

Flying gaffs and bridge gaffs are used in big-game and bridge fishing, respectively. The procedure is similar, although a bridge gaff is used more like a snagging tool and is less precise.

Fish to be released can be gaffed in the lower jaw with a hand gaff, preferably by driving the point through the inside of the mouth and out the lower jaw (rather than coming from outside to inside). This is done when the fish is thoroughly played out.

Obviously, the point of the gaff must be razor sharp to do the most effective job. The point should be covered when the gaff is not in use.

19

Measuring and Weighing Fish

Anglers who intend to keep their catch must know how to take proper length measurements of individual fish. Acceptable measurement methods vary according to species and local regulations. Weighing fish is generally optional, yet formulas exist for estimating the weight of fish you've released if you've taken some basic measurements before returning the fish to the water.

Measuring

Fish are measured in various ways and for a variety of reasons. The simplest kind of measurement and the most common reason for doing so is because the angler wants to keep the fish; such fish need to be measured for length to comply with existing laws pertaining to that species. Many species of fish, especially those in freshwater, cannot be kept by anglers unless they meet certain length requirements.

It is critical that anglers know how to measure a fish that they will keep. Measuring is done differently in some places, and it may vary with the species, especially with fish that have forked tails. Many regulations brochures define how to determine length and illustrate it graphically.

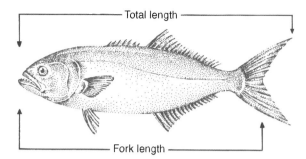

Fish are measured according to either total length or fork length.

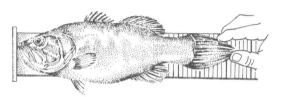

Total length is the distance from the tip of the snout to the end of the tail, as measured with the fish laid flat, the mouth closed, and the tail slightly compressed.

Some are rather vague, simply saying that minimum length is determined from the tip of the snout to the tip of the tail. Some can be confusing when they also refer to total length.

To measure any fish, you should lay it down, preferably on a clean, wet surface, and take the length measurement in a straight line starting at the snout with the mouth closed. For smaller fish it is helpful to have a ruler with the beginning edge at a right angle so that the snout of the fish can be pressed against it.

Total length is commonly obtained, especially in freshwater, by measuring to the end of the compressed tail. Some regulations refer to a pinched tail, others compressed, but the idea is to bring together the upper and lower portion of the tail fin, called the lobes, and measure to the longest point. This is also referred to as total length and is how freshwater fish, and saltwater fish without forked tails, are measured.

To determine fork length, measure the straight-line distance from the tip of the snout to the center of the tail fin. This method is used for saltwater species with a forked tail. Often fish with a rigid forked tail will suffer damage to their tails during transportation from fishing grounds. If they

were measured on a total-length basis back at the dock, they may no longer be legal, even though they were legal when initially caught. Measuring these fish by fork length removes that problem and standardizes measurements to make it easier for anglers.

Weighing

Many types of spring and digital scales are available and can be carried with anglers. The accuracy of these varies widely, not to mention that they are often used when a boat is unsteady and moving with wind or waves—a condition that tends to allow the fish to surge on the scale. Some spring scales, however, are so accurate that they can be calibrated well enough to pass official weight-inspection tests and may actually be certified for use in record keeping.

For record establishment, it is mandatory to weigh a fish on a scale that has been recently certified for accuracy. Most weighings of fish are performed on scales at stores (grocery, meat, and produce scales), at fishing lodges or camps, at marinas, and at fishing clubs. For conscientious anglers who catch fish that are large but not record-class, even ordinary pocket or tackle box scales should be checked periodically against known weights so that their degree of accuracy can be determined.

Estimating Weight

Weighing on the water may be impractical or harmful to big fish, because they may be out of the water for a long time and held in a position that doesn't support their internal organs well (being hung by the mouth). Weighing fish that will be released is specifically not recommended by some fisheries agencies, and as a practical matter it is good to minimize handling of any fish that is to be released.

Large fish that are not weighed before being released, however, are often subject to speculation regarding the actual live weight. For many years, anglers and fisheries biologists have worked on ways for people to reasonably determine weight based upon length and/or on length and girth measurements. No single table or formula applies to all species, owing to the vast differences in body shapes among fish. And no method has been totally perfect time after time, but there are ways to come close enough to knowing the live-released weight for most fish.

Tables and Formulas

The best way to get a quick, on-the-spot idea of a fish's weight without having to do multiplication and division is to refer to a table. Some companies and regulatory agencies provide weight-estimation tables for popular and common species; these are generally correlated only to total length (no girth) and based upon the average weight for fish of that length in that jurisdiction or region.

Formulas have long been developed in freshwater and saltwater for using length and girth to estimate the weight of a fish, and these have evolved to take body shape into account so that different formulas apply to different popular fish species. The following formulas are generally accepted freshwater standards:

Walleye	Length^3/2,700 (length $\times$ length $\times$ length divided by 2,700)
Pike	Length^3/3,500
Sunfish	Length^3/1,200
Bass	Length^2 $\times$ girth/1,600
Trout	Length $\times$ girth^2/800

The formula for pike is not accurate when applied to large, heavy muskies (it makes them far too large), although some people use length $\times$ girth^2 $\div$ 800 for these fish (which is also above the actual weight by a small amount). Very heavy specimens of any species are often tough to fit into these formulas because their bellies tend to become distended, and fish of equal lengths can have much different thickness.

Formulas and tables are based on averages using standard-size fish up to large-size fish, but seldom extraordinary sizes of fish (because there are so few of them). So these formulas are guidelines, not absolutes. The difference between an estimated 39-pound fish and an estimated 42-pound fish is really minor in the overall scheme of things unless a record is involved, which likely means killing the fish anyway; and the main purpose is releasing the fish unharmed.

Likewise, in saltwater, determining the weight of virtually all released billfish species is mostly an estimate. The same is now true for tarpon, since very few tarpon are actually killed and weighed and many people fishing for them have little experience in weighing tarpon of any size, let alone of all sizes. Eyeball estimates are usually well off the mark, generally being higher than the fish actually weighs.

The old formula of length $\times$ girth^2 $\div$ 800 is still used by some people for billfish and other saltwater species, but this is as much off the mark as it is close; some people add 10 percent to this figure for a fat specimen. Other anglers divide by 900 for species that are very long and thin-bodied, like wahoo, king mackerel, and barracuda.

20

Caring for and Storing the Catch

Eating the fish that you or friends and family catch and prepare is nearly as satisfying as catching a fish on a lure of your own making. In a world where most of the flesh from living creatures comes to us in sanitized pressure-wrapped packaging, having been killed and prepared by others, catching, cleaning, and eating your own fish is a direct reminder of the connection with these creatures and the dependence that human beings have always had upon them. Of course, fish have a high nutritional value and, if properly cared for, are delicious when prepared in many different ways.

The foundation for enjoying good-tasting fish is the treatment it receives after it is caught, the care that is given to transporting it from where it is caught to where it will be stored or consumed, and the storage it receives between cleaning and preparing for consumption.

It does no good to properly care for a fish until you get it home but then store it improperly for later consumption. On the other hand, if you've let a fish become stale in the hours after catching it, it will not improve in flavor no matter how well you later wrap and store it.

After the Catch

Before you go fishing, give some thought to whether you want to keep any of the catch and then to how you will store and transport it to maintain maximum freshness. The worst thing you can do is pay no attention to fish you've just caught. Leaving fish exposed to air and sun for a long time is undesirable, as is leaving fish undressed overnight. Unaerated livewells, livewells filled with warm water, and stringers that are overcrowded or trolled or hung in warm surface water do not enhance the edibility of fish.

Ideally you should clean or dress fish immediately after they've been caught and then put them on ice. If this isn't possible, clean and dress the fish as soon as possible afterward. If you've planned ahead, you have a cooler or ice chest and ice to keep the fish cool.

Air and water temperatures are partial keys to good fish care. The warmer the air and temperature, the harder it is to keep fish alive and/or fresh until you are ready to clean and store them, and the sooner you need to begin preparations. Do whatever you can to keep fish protected from heat and warmth. At the very least, that may mean putting them in the shade, stopping fishing after a reasonable length of time to clean them, covering them with a wet cloth, or taking care to keep them alive in a protected, cool environment.

Keeping her crappie alive in the water in a wire basket has helped ensure that this angler will have fine eating.

Containing Fish Alive

Many boats are equipped with a livewell, which can be used for keeping small- to medium-size fish alive. Livewells work better for some species than for others. A good livewell will not only aerate the water and provide plenty of oxygen, but also circulate the water to keep the temperature down and bring in fresh outside water.

If you have a livewell and can keep the water temperature down, this is a desirable way to store fish until you can get to the dock (or home in the case of trailered boats) and clean them. If fish die while they are in the livewell, remove them and place them on ice. Many livewells are not large, so watch out for overcrowding, particularly with large specimens.

Anglers without livewells, which include those who fish from shore or from small boats, need some other method of retaining fish. One way to keep fish alive without a livewell is to use a wire

Start out with plenty of ice to help keep your catch in great shape.

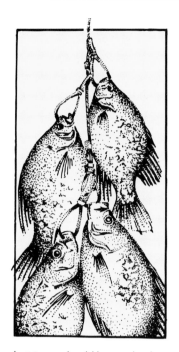

A stringer should be used only to retain fish that will be kept for consumption; the clip-on style, depicted here, is best for small fish and prevents overcrowding.

or net mesh basket. This collapsible basket is commonly used for panfish and is hung over the side of the boat in the water. Fish need to have enough room to move around in the basket, so it can't handle larger fish and great numbers. Be sure to pull the basket out of the water when moving, and don't keep the fish out of the water long when you do move.

A stringer or rope is a common way to contain whole fish until you can bring them home or to the landing site, but it is a poor method of retention. The fish inevitably become stressed and bruised while on a stringer, and they often die slowly. Nevertheless, using a stringer is better than just laying fish on the floor of the boat, exposed to sun and dirt.

If you must string fish, make sure they are allowed to breathe so they stay alive. Contain the fish through their lower jaw instead of the gills. Try to keep the stringer in the shade yet away from gasoline in the water or any other substance that might affect the flavor of the fish. Take the stringer out of the water when the boat is under way at full speed, and avoid leaving it out of the water for a long time.

Killing

There is merit to killing some fish immediately, even if you have the option of keeping them alive. On the other hand, some fish are better if kept alive. Fish that die slowly, struggling and bruising themselves in the process, won't taste as good as they might if they were simply dispatched with a couple of quick blows to the top of the head and stored temporarily in an appropriate environment.

If ice is available, the best option is to kill the fish after you've caught it, field dress it quickly, and then put it on ice. However, cleaning a fish

on the water may not be legal in some places. In this situation, you can still dispatch the fish and ice it down, and then clean it later at a fish-cleaning station or at home. Killing a fish immediately after catching it and then cleaning it, even if legal, is not always practical. If that is the case, stop to take care of the catch as soon as you can later.

Killing a fish soon after capture seems reasonable from a humane standpoint, the purpose being to prevent death through a slow and presumably painful process. Although many anglers simply toss still-lively fish into a cooler and cover them with ice, many others dispatch fish by inserting a pick or knife blade into the back of the head from the top, rap them on the head with a small club, or, in the case of some small species, snap their heads to sever the spinal cord.

Storing with and without Ice

Storing fish that you've just caught on ice is always best. But what if you don't have ice immediately available? Avoid placing whole dead fish in a plastic bag; without air circulation, fish or fillets placed in a nonporous bag and kept outside will deteriorate quickly. On the other hand, if you fillet the fish immediately, place the rinsed fillets in a bag (sealable is okay now) and put the bag on ice as soon as you can. If you have a paper towel or napkins, place the rinsed fillets on the paper towels and then put both towel and fish in the bag so that the towel can absorb moisture. Try to keep the fillets or the fish from soaking.

If you have a creel, layer it with moss or grass or ferns. Creels are adequate for short-term storage (a few hours) of small fish and are preferable to canvas bags or other nonporous retainers.

If no conventional containers are available, you can improvise. A burlap bag, a mesh fruit or potato sack, wet newspapers or towels, or other objects that would allow fish to cool and allow air to circulate can be employed. Rinse or clean them first. Keep the wrapping moist and shaded.

When ice will not be available for a while, use table salt and a burlap or similar-type bag. When you catch a fish, eviscerate it and wash it. Rub about one tablespoon of salt for each pound of fish into the cavity, and then lightly salt the skin. Put the fish and enough wet seaweed to surround it into the bag. Keep the bag in the shade or bury it in moist sand. If you are at a suitable place, like

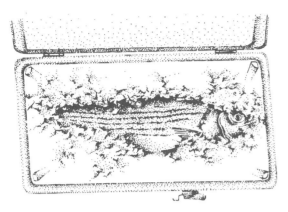

The best method of keeping fish in top condition is to put them on crushed ice in a cooler.

the beach while surf fishing, and no container is available, bury the fish in moist sand near the waterline. To avoid losing your fish, mark the location carefully and watch the tide.

If you're not keeping fish alive, dispatch them right away and place them in an ice-packed food or beverage cooler for later cleaning. Separate the fish from food and beverages by placing the latter in bags. You can leave undressed fish on ice all day and clean them at the end of the day without sacrificing freshness or taste. Plan for this by obtaining ice before going fishing. For short-term storage, cube ice is better than block ice because you can cover fish fully with it, touching all parts. The best, however, is crushed, chipped, or shaved ice.

When anglers talk about icing down fish, they often say they are putting fish "on ice." What is really best, though, is putting fish *in the ice*. To quickly cool the entire fish, including the core, use a cooler to surround the fish with ice cubes or crushed or flaked ice. If the fish have been eviscerated, store them in the ice with the belly facing down so that meltwater does not accumulate in the cavity.

Periodically drain the water; dead fish are stored better on ice than in water, even if that water is ice cold. This is because the flesh becomes soft in water, and once softened it is very unappealing.

Wintertime—Care on the Ice

How you care for fish caught through the ice in winter is different. Most anglers, because the air is cold and the lake frozen, simply drop their fish on the ice or snow and leave them there until it's time to go home. Naturally the fish freeze. If the fish are transported inside a heated vehicle, they warm up on the way home. Or they warm up later at home when it's time to clean them. If they are going to be consumed immediately or within a few days, this thawing may be fine, but it may not be fine if the fish (or fillets) are to be refrozen for longer-term storage. And in any event, the rapid change in temperature advances spoilage, so you would be wise to avoid premature thawing, especially since fish caught from cold winter waters have such firm and delicious meat. Although fish should not be frozen more than once, fish that have been frozen and then thawed and smoked can be frozen again.

One way to keep fish caught on open ice is to make an icewater tub in the area you're fishing. Chip out an area of ice that is large enough (maybe 2 by 3 feet) to hold a reasonable number of fish, poke a small hole in the bottom with a spud, and let the tub fill with water. Then put freshly caught fish in the tub, where they will remain alive until it's time to go home. Make sure the fish can't escape through the bottom. To avoid this problem, you can locate the tub near your fishing hole and chip a narrow channel from the fishing hole to the tub to import water. A tub works well when the temperature is relatively mild, but when the temperature is less than 20°F and/or the wind is blowing, the tub may freeze up.

An alternative is to bring a cooler with you, fill it with cold water, and put your fish in that, although the lack of aeration will cause the fish to expire after a while. You could always put your catch directly in the cooler with some shaved ice collected from around your fishing holes. If there is snow on the ice, you might be able to use that for insulation around a bucket, and place the fish in the bucket with a cover over the top.

Bleeding and Eviscerating

To ensure the quality of fresh fish, the commercial fishing industry bleeds and eviscerates (guts) many species. These practices enhance the appearance, shelf life, and overall quality of some commercially important fish. Although the beneficial effects of bleeding are still undocumented for many species, it is reasonable to assume that anglers can also use this technique to maximize the quality of the fish they catch. You will have to decide whether this practice makes a difference. Some anglers bleed their fish all the time, some never do, and some bleed only certain species (like bluefish and tuna).

Removing the blood from fish does, however, retard deterioration. Fish that have been bled also tend to have lighter-colored fillets with fewer bruises, blood spots, and other defects. Before bleeding a fish, you may want to stun it to make the fish easier to handle. If you do not kill it, more blood will flow out if the heart keeps pumping.

To bleed a fish, make a tail and/or throat cut. Make a tail cut about an inch from the caudal or tail fin, across the caudal peduncle. Slice across the tail until the knife touches bone. To ensure maximum bleeding in some species, such as dogfish, cut the tail completely off just behind the anal fins. However, the tail portion of the fillet may spoil faster when the entire tail is removed unless the fish is kept clean and iced down quickly. On some species, cutting the tail may not produce significant or quick bleeding, but it will serve to keep a lively fish from flapping, since the muscles and tendons connected to the tail will be severed.

The throat cut minimizes the risk of bacterial contamination to the edible part of the fish. Make a single cut, severing the main artery that runs from the gills to the heart. Do this by slicing through the flesh just behind the gill cover. Make sure the cut is ahead of the heart, which must be undamaged if it is to continue pumping blood.

The fish should be bled for 10 to 20 minutes. Bleeding is more effective if you immerse the fish in clean water or seawater after making the cut. The water you use should be as clean and as cold as possible. Use a bucket, cooler, or tub, and change the water in the bleeding container frequently. If containers are not available, hang the bleeding fish over the side of the boat in a mesh bag. If this method is not practical, the fish can be bled without a container. Pour water over it from time to time to remove the blood before it coagulates.

Eviscerate a fish as soon as possible after it has been bled or after you catch it. Keep the entrails intact if possible when eviscerating. The stomach and intestines contain enzymes and bacteria that can contaminate the edible part of the fish and accelerate spoilage, so try not to puncture them. Bile from the gallbladder will also taint any part of the fish it touches, and it is very difficult to wash

away. Rinse the cavity to remove blood, slime, and bits of viscera, and rinse the exterior as well.

Keep your work area clean and avoid contaminating other fish with eviscerated matter. Wash your work area and knives after each eviscerating operation. Finally, do not allow your fish to become tainted by coming into contact with oily or dirty areas of a boat, workstation, or dock.

After Cleaning

Once you've cleaned the fish (see chapter 21), they must be stored properly, most likely in a refrigerator or freezer. If you're traveling and many days from reaching home, this storage may be a cooler. Obviously your catch will at times exceed what can be consumed in one sitting; then you will want to store the extra fish for later consumption, perhaps when the season is past. The length of time that you plan on storing the fish determines the type of storage.

Cold Storage

How long fish will stay fresh in cold (unfrozen) storage once they've been cleaned will depend not only on storage temperature but on the fish and how you've treated them. Some delicate species, like stream and river trout, do not lend themselves to many days of cold storing, even under the best of conditions. Bluefish, with their strong flavor and oily texture, do not keep well for more than a day after cleaning. Lean fish, however, may keep well for several days. And some fish can be kept for up to a week if they are ultrachilled.

It is possible to keep fish that are whole but eviscerated in good condition for up to five days if they are kept on crushed ice that is drained regularly and in a container that is seldom opened.

If a vacuum-sealing machine is available, vacuum seal smaller fish, steaks, and fillets, then store the bag in the coldest part of the refrigerator where it will be unaffected by repeated opening of the door, or on ice in a cooler. Vacuum sealing is the best method of short-term unfrozen storage but it may not be available if you are afield or away from home.

The colder the storage temperature, the longer you can hold fish. Thirty-four degrees is better than 50°F. If fish are kept in an iced cooler for a long period, the ice should be checked every few hours, and the drain should be opened every time that the cooler is checked to release any liquid. Avoid opening the cooler any more often or longer than necessary.

If you have to hold whole fish in a cooler for a long time, they can be ultrachilled by using a 20:1 mixture of crushed ice (chipped ice will work if you can't find crushed ice) and coarse salt. Spread half of the mixture on the bottom of the cooler. Place the fish, enveloped securely in a plastic wrap, on the mixture and then cover with the other half. This should bring the temperature down below 32°F, making it cooler than a refrigerator but not as cold as a freezer.

If you plan to store dressed fish, steaks, or fillets in the refrigerator for several days, temperature control is critical. Because many home refrigerators operate at 40°F or higher, fish can spoil fairly rapidly. It's good to pack dressed fish on ice in the refrigerator. Seal fillets or steaks in plastic bags or containers and then cover them with ice in trays or pans. Empty meltwater regularly and add ice as necessary. Fillets take up less room in the refrigerator or freezer and cool more quickly.

For fish that will be consumed immediately, rinse thoroughly in cold water and pat dry with paper towels. Put a double layer of paper towel on the bottom of a plate or tray, place small fish, fillets, or chunks of fish on the towel, and then cover tightly; plastic wrap is the first covering choice, aluminum foil second. Make sure the wrapping is tight and holds. Uncovered fish can dehydrate quickly and lose flavor even if you're going to cook them in a few hours. For large pieces of fish or whole fish, rinse and pat dry, wrap tightly in plastic wrap, and wrap tightly in freezer paper. Take the fish out of the wrapping only when you are ready to prepare it for consumption; don't leave it lying out on the kitchen counter for a long period of time.

Frozen Storage

Freezing only protects the quality of the fish at the time it was frozen. Airtight packaging and proper temperatures are critical to achieving this protection, however.

Although freezing prevents the growth of microorganisms, it only slows down the enzymatic and chemical reactions that cause flavor, color, and texture deterioration. As the temperature is lowered, these reactions occur more slowly; thus, frozen foods, including fish, should be stored at the lowest possible temperatures, and preferably in the coldest part of a freezer. Rapid freezing at the outset is very important for good long-term storage. Home freezers are primarily designed for storage, not for rapid freezing. A home freezer can properly freeze 1 to 2 pounds per cubic foot in 24 hours.

Don't overload the freezer. Fish will freeze faster if uncrowded, so don't bunch together pieces or whole fish or pans of fish when you first place them in the freezer. For the fastest freeze, place packages in direct contact with the freezer floor or walls until they are frozen. If the packages take more than 5 to 6 hours to freeze, they are too large. Store packages at a temperature of 0°F or colder, where the temperature doesn't fluctuate. The farther away from the freezer door, the more stable the temperature.

Properly packaged fish can be kept for a long time, although how long varies with the type of fish and the method of freezing. Although it is generally advised that frozen fish can be kept for up to one year, this is merely a guideline for shelf life in a freezer rather than an indication of whether the fish will still be appetizing after such a long period. It is probably a very generous advisement, except for frozen smoked fish, which can last more than a year, and even longer if vacuum-sealed.

If your freezer allows for really low temperature, you may be able to freeze fish longer than someone whose freezer temperature is barely below 32°F. Thus if you have a separate freezer it is better to store fish in that than in the freezer compartment of your refrigerator, which is subject to frequent opening and closing.

Large fish typically last a little longer than small fish, and whole fish last a little longer than steaks or fillets because they retain more moisture. Oily fish are best thawed and consumed within one to two months after initial freezing, and lean fish in three to six months. These are general guidelines, however; you can keep some fish, especially lean species, for longer periods, especially if they are vacuum-sealed.

Regardless of these time frames, it's wise to eat fish as soon as possible. By labeling and dating packages, you can consume stored fish on a rotational calendar basis, using the older fish first.

Many of the undesirable flavor and color changes in fish are caused by oxidation of the unsaturated fats, oils, and color pigments. This is a chemical reaction that cannot be stopped once started. Oily fish, like salmon and bluefish, are highly susceptible to oxidation. However, airtight packaging, especially if it is accomplished on a freshly caught fish, can help prevent oxidation, more so for some fish than for others.

Another benefit of airtight packaging is the prevention of water evaporation from the flesh of fish during freezing. When water evaporates from food, it causes the food to become dry and tough; this effect is called freezer burn. Freezer burn promotes oxidation and is always accompanied by substandard flavor, color, and odor. By packaging and freezing properly, you can entirely eliminate freezer burn.

Without doubt the best way to freeze fish, either short- or long-term, is by vacuum sealing them in appropriate plastic storage bags. When done properly, this removes all air from the bag, minimizing the effects of oxidation and the likelihood of freezer burn. It is possible to store fish frozen in a vacuum-sealed bag much longer than when it is frozen by other means. An additional benefit is that fish frozen in this manner take up the least possible amount of freezer space. Vacuum sealing works especially well for fillets and steaks, and for smaller whole dressed fish.

A larger whole fish that is drawn or dressed, and that is too large for vacuum sealing, is more difficult to wrap and to protect from oxidation. It should be dipped in water, placed temporarily in an unsealed plastic bag, and frozen as is. Once the fish is frozen, take it out of the bag and dip it in cold water, then put it back in the bag and return it to the freezer. You might repeat this a few times to form a thick glaze over the entire fish, and check it every few weeks to reglaze.

When freezing fish, be sure to pack them in large enough quantities for a single meal, whether for yourself or your family and friends. Fish that are frozen separately will defrost more quickly than those frozen together. Also, label each package by writing on the outside with an indelible marker, crayon, or grease marker. Label the package with the date, type of fish, and number of servings or pieces.

How you thaw fish is important to their quality as table fare. The poorest choice is using hot water; never thaw fish in warm or hot water. Also poor is thawing the fish at room temperature, which hastens surface spoilage. The best option is to thaw fish gradually over an extended period. If you plan a day or two ahead of time, you can thaw a meal of frozen fish somewhat gradually in the refrigerator. A 24-hour period should be enough for smaller fish, pieces, and fillets that are separated; large fish can take longer.

Most people do not plan this far ahead and like to speed up the process. Some accelerate the thawing process with smaller fish and steaks or fillets via a microwave oven; microwaves have excellent thawing capability for most foods but require careful attention where fish are concerned. Whole fish, or pieces of fish, do not have uniform thickness, so a thinner section will defrost faster and may actually cook a little when thawed quickly in a microwave. If this happens, which it can easily, you would defeat all of your previous efforts to ensure a good-tasting fish.

Vacuum-sealed fish are especially easy to thaw, even on short notice, by placing the sealed bag in a large bowl of cool water. Empty and refill the bowl periodically. If you're really in a hurry you can carefully give the process a boost by lightly microwaving the bag before you place it in the water bowl. Open the bag after the fish have thawed and pat the fish dry with paper towels prior to cooking.

Shrimp, gravlax salmon fillet, and yellowfin tuna steak in vacuum-sealed storage bags.

Storing for Transportation

Sometimes you must transport fish a considerable distance or for a long period of time before you can permanently store them. Examples of this situation would be while driving, boating, or flying back from a distant location. Refer to the earlier discussion of cold storage methods for information on keeping fish in good condition during transportation. Ultrachilling, or superchilling, as described, is one method. Get a large supply of crushed ice; if that is not available, get cubed ice. You'll need a lot of ice, especially if the weather is warm. If dry ice is available, and your cooler is large enough, place the dry ice in the cooler surrounded by crushed or cubed ice. If you can't get dry ice but can get regular ice in block form, put the block ice in a cooler surrounded by crushed or cubed ice with the fish mixed in.

For long-term transportation, place fish on crushed ice in a cooler and open the vent to let water escape, so that the fish doesn't lie in the water. Add more ice as necessary.

Don't let the fish lie in melted water. Keep a cooler drain open if weather and conditions permit, or periodically open the drain and let out accumulated water. This is not possible in a cooler transported by air carrier, since the cooler is out of your control for a long time; so proper packing is essential. If the cooler is transported in a vehicle, position it so that it is accessible and can be drained.

If you're transporting fish by air as checked baggage, be advised that some carriers may not allow the shipment of a container with dry ice or may require notification that it contains dry ice. A noncrushable heavy-duty cooler is the best container for shipping; the lid should be completely secured with duct tape. Write the word "perishable" on the tape in several spots.

At some remote camps and lodges, your fish can be frozen and then packed and shipped. The fish are usually shipped in a well-packed cardboard box. Unfortunately, the cardboard box isn't as good as a cooler. If the shipment is delayed in transit, the frozen contents could begin thawing and you may have to prepare and consume the fish at once upon reaching your final destination. If the fish haven't been frozen but have been packed in ice well, then a delayed trip may not adversely affect them as long as the ice holds up.

If the ice does not hold up, the fish may spoil. How far you have to travel, whether an overnight stay is involved, and how much faith you have in the air carrier are factors in deciding whether or not to freeze.

If you are a traveling a long distance you may have an overnight stay between leaving the fishing site and flying home. If this is the case, you'll need to make freezer storage arrangements. If the outfitter or expediter doesn't make arrangements for you (they usually do), you'll have to fend for yourself. The situation may be difficult if you arrive late and leave early and haven't planned for this in advance. Many people no longer bring back fish from distant locations because of the hassle, the extra baggage charge, the possibility of spoilage, and the preference for catch-and-release, so storage arrangements may not be a concern.

When you do transport fish, you must follow appropriate laws. These may require you to leave on the skin, or a patch of skin, for identification purposes; to keep the fish whole after evisceration (to determine legal size); to apply a tag to it until it reaches its permanent storage; to identify the contents on the outside; or to follow some other procedures established by state and provincial authorities.

21

Cleaning and Dressing Fish

Preparing a fish for the table or for storage is usually referred to as cleaning or dressing. For many people, even those who love to eat fish, the job of cleaning them is a distasteful or repulsive one because of the sight, smell, and feel of the dead fish and its body parts. This problem can be overcome if you have fresh air, running water, and a clean workstation to minimize exposure to the objectionable elements.

If you like to eat fish, keep in mind that cleaning them is the price you pay for having good table fare; so you might as well learn to clean the fish properly, safely, and as enjoyably as possible. Think about how good the fish are going to taste later on.

A dislike for the cleaning process, or pure ineptitude, can result in unattractive table fare or, worse, the wastage of potentially fine food. If you can't learn to clean fish properly, then you probably shouldn't keep them in the first place. Learning to clean fish simply takes a knowledge of what to do (either by watching someone else or following written instructions), the right tools, and a willingness to practice and be patient. Patience is necessary because cleaning fish can be exasperating when you're learning, and it helps to go slowly, despite the fact that the natural inclination is to hurry and get it over with.

A mate fillets striped bass onboard a charter boat in the Chesapeake Bay. The carcasses go into the bucket to prove at dockside that the fish were of legal size.

First Steps

Although the terms used in this book are generally understood by anglers, supermarkets and fish markets may use slightly different terms, so here are some definitions:

A whole fish is unprocessed and exactly as it comes from the water, complete with head, scales, skin, and entrails. Another common term is "in the round."

A drawn fish has only its entrails removed. It may need to be descaled or filleted, or to have the head cut off, and so on.

A dressed fish has been descaled and eviscerated, with the head, tail, and fins removed. "Whole dressed" means that the head and tail are left on.

Steaks are bone-in crosscuts from a large drawn fish. Fillets are boneless strips from the flanks of a whole fish.

Knives

If you've tried to clean fish and found it difficult, you're probably using the wrong knife or a dull knife or you're unfamiliar with using a knife. A dull knife defeats nearly all fish-cleaning efforts, whereas a sharp knife keeps you from hacking away at a fish and losing meat or making it unattractive.

The perfect knife for all fish-cleaning tasks does not exist. A thin 6-inch blade is universally popular, especially for filleting most freshwater fish. A longer blade, in the 9-inch range, is necessary for larger fish, particularly many saltwater species.

A small knife with a 3- to 4-inch blade is fine for dressing most small panfish and trout. You do not have to spend a fortune on knives for cleaning fish, but you should have the right one for the job.

Although a 6-inch blade does work when you're eviscerating (gutting) small fish, you don't have enough control over it unless you're especially careful; you have more control over a shorter blade. With the shorter blade, it's less likely that you'll poke the blade too deeply into the stomach or cut too far through the belly. A pocketknife with a narrow and pointed blade is adequate for the simple act of field dressing; it's portable and easily accessible.

For filleting, you need a blade that is slightly flexible and thin and that tapers to a sharp point at the tip. Many good filleting models sweep up slightly at the tip as well. The length is a function of the size of the fish.

For steaking, you need a broad heavy-duty blade to cut through the backbone. A large inflexible knife with a less tapered point, or a cleaver if you have one, makes a neat, instant steak.

A knife sharpener is a necessary fish-cleaning accessory. The more fish you do at one sitting and the tougher their skin, bones, and scales, the quicker the knife seems to lose an edge. A knife that is hard to sharpen quickly will be a hindrance when you're filleting a number of fish. Blades made of soft steel sharpen quickly, although they may lose their edge a little faster than hard steel knives. A thin knife with a tapered rather than a beveled edge will cut best, so try to hold the blade at a low angle when you sharpen it.

Electric knives are popular with some anglers, especially those whose grasp and dexterity isn't as firm as it used to be. These knives are particularly useful when filleting or cleaning a lot of fish, and many public fish-cleaning stations provide electrical outlets for them.

Location

If you're going to clean the fish on the water or on the shore, make sure that it's legal to do so and find out the extent to which it is legal (for example, you may be able to eviscerate the fish but not fillet it, or you may have to leave the skin intact).

In some places (and with certain species) you may be able to clean fish on your boat, perhaps while headed back to port if it's not a rough ride, or just before you finish fishing for the day. Many boaters improvise a removable fish-cleaning work board that fits over the gunwale or sits in a rod holder. Such a board should have back and side stops to keep fish and tools from sliding off, and should be large enough for the usual size of fish. Cleanup on the boat is easy, provided you have a washdown hose or at least a bucket and scrub brush.

Many marinas, launching sites, camps, and other public places have fish-cleaning stations or houses (in warm areas a screened site helps keep the bees and flies away). Some have waist-high aluminum tables with backstops for the cleaning chores; these are good for cleanup and don't absorb refuse, but they can be very slippery and tough on knife blades. Others have a wooden or poly table, which is less slippery and easier on knives but not as clean for the fastidious angler. If you can put your own clean board down on an aluminum fish-cleaning table, you should be in good shape.

Most public facilities have a water supply at the fish-cleaning station for rinsing fish, as well as electrical outlets. Some have a central pit for

Using electric knives, guides prepare seatrout at a fish-cleaning station in Lafitte, Louisiana, where there is proper disposal of entrails.

disposal of offal, and others grind the remains for appropriate disposal (disposal is a big benefit because it's one less thing you have to do at home). If you can use these facilities, you should do so; after cleaning your fish at a public facility, be sure to store them properly and keep them iced before heading home.

If a public fish-cleaning facility isn't available to you, it's best to do the cleaning outside, especially if you'll be scraping the scales off the fish. Dry scales may fly all over the place, and they can be a nuisance indoors, not to mention an obstruction in the kitchen drain. If you have to scale fish inside, then wet the fish thoroughly to moisten the scales and remove them under running cold water. This will minimize scale dispersion, but it will clog the sink strainer.

When cleaning outside, make sure you cover the surface of the work area; cleanup will be a lot easier. You can put a clean board over the location, covering it with multiple sheets of newspaper; the paper is also good for small fish that are cleaned indoors on a countertop. Newspaper grabs the fish well and helps hold it in place, as well as soaks up moisture. When you're working on newspapers, periodically bundle up the soiled paper and fish remains and put them in the garbage. This gives you a clean surface to work on and avoids a large pile of repulsive refuse at the end. Keep the cleaned fish off the newspaper to avoid picking up ink or sticking to the paper.

If you have no source of running water, fill a deep bowl or clean bucket with cold or cool water for rinsing the fish. Two such bowls are better, because one can be used for rinsing and the other for a final clean-water bath. In the ideal scenario, you have a helper who rinses the fish thoroughly after you clean them and then places them on paper towels.

If you're working solo, you can put the fish aside after you clean them and rinse them afterward, but waste matter, especially blood, will harden and be much more difficult to rinse off even a short time later, especially if it's on the flesh instead of the skin. If you're doing all this fun work alone, you have two choices: You can stop and rinse each fish after you've cleaned it, which many people don't want to do because their hands are constantly getting dirty and then wet, or you can place the fish in a bowl of water (ice cold is best) and rinse them all at once after you're finished. Putting chunks of fish and fillets in water for long periods is not desirable, especially if the water is not super cold.

A final reminder: Wherever people congregate for fish cleaning, flies and bees seem to follow. Watch out for bees that may have congregated in the garbage container where fish carcasses are disposed.

Methods

How you clean a fish depends on the size of the fish and what will be done with the end product. Small fish, for example, are seldom stuffed and baked but are often pan-fried. Very large fish are hard to cook evenly throughout, so steaking them, or the thickest parts of the body, is a good idea. Scaled fish that will be presented whole need to be eviscerated and the scales removed. Fish that will be filleted do not need to be eviscerated, and so on.

Be careful when handling knives, especially when you're cleaning fish in cold weather and when your hands are cold. Gloves made of a high-tech material that resists knife piercing and slicing are available; they also give you a good grip on the fish and protect your hands from spiny fins, sharp gill covers or gill edges, and teeth. If you'll be doing a lot of fish cleaning, you should consider using a pair of gloves.

Holding fish properly and working at a moderate and careful pace will prevent mishaps. Finally, be careful if others are helping you with fish cleaning or with cleanup; they should not reach into the work area when the fish cleaner is cutting.

Field Dressing

The cleaning of small fish, such as stream trout and panfish, is referred to as field dressing. In field dressing, freshly caught fish are killed soon after their capture, eviscerated, and the bodies spread in well-ventilated wicker creels lined with grass to facilitate cooling. Field dressing requires the removal of the entrails, gills, and kidney. It is sometimes also referred to as gutting, although gutting usually refers to larger fish and basically implies the removal of just the intestines.

Field Dressing Small Trout and Salmon, Head Intact
Small trout and salmon are the simplest fish to field dress. They don't have to be scaled, and

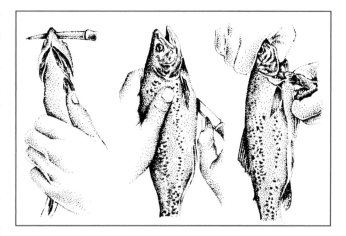

To eviscerate a small whole trout with head intact, slice the lower jaw away from the gill membrane (left); insert the knife blade into the anal vent and slice up to the gills without puncturing the intestine (middle); then push your thumb into the throat and pull down to remove the gills and entrails (right). Clean the body cavity thoroughly. This process can be done in the field with a small sharp knife.

once eviscerated and cleaned, they are ready for cooking. After you have learned to field dress a fish and have practiced a few times, the process takes only 30 seconds.

To field dress a small trout or salmon, begin behind the lower jaw by sticking the tip of your knife through the tissue that connects the lower jaw to the gills and slitting this tablike section free. This is actually the tongue that is being freed. Then insert the point of the knife into the vent (the anal opening); slit through the skin and up the center of the fish's belly in a straight line to the gills, stopping before you get to the V-shaped spot behind the jaw.

Try not to puncture the intestines as you make the slit. Put the knife down and hold the fish by the head with one hand. With the other hand, grab the tongue and pull down on it toward the tail; this will free the gills and the entrails. Remove the kidney, which is the bloodline along the backbone, with your fingers or a knife or spoon; then rinse the cavity with cold water and dry it with a paper towel or napkin.

Field Dressing Small Trout and Salmon, Head Removed
This procedure is one to follow when you don't want to leave the head on the fish (and are not restricted by laws). Begin the process by inserting

the point of the knife into the vent (the anal opening) and then slitting through the skin and up the center of the fish's belly in a straight line to the gills, stopping before you get to the V-shaped spot behind the jaw. Try not to puncture the intestines as you make the slit. Place the fish belly down and make a cut behind the head down through the backbone until it is severed, stopping after severing it and without cutting the head entirely free. Put the knife down, hold the body in one hand, and with the other hand grasp the head and pull it away from the body. This will remove the entrails and the head. Cut off the tail if you wish; then remove the kidney by the backbone, rinse, and pat dry.

Field Dressing Other Fish

Most small to medium fish can be field dressed by following the previous directions, with some minor changes. Species like bluegills or perch, for example, must be scaled first. Do not field dress and then attempt to scale the fish. Also, be aware that the belly skin of some fish is tougher than others and requires more careful slitting. The belly skin of a trout is soft and easy to cut with a sharp knife; that of a yellow perch is tougher. Field dressing some fish (including perch) requires the additional step of cutting away the gill connections in order to remove the entrails and gills in one motion. To do this, pull up on the gill covering and slice under the gill to free it from the body; do this for each gill; then slit the tongue and the belly, and remove everything in one pull.

Of course, for any fish you can simply cut off the head, slit the belly from the anal opening on up, and then grab the entrails and remove them. The disadvantages of this method are that it is usually messier than the other methods, requires more scraping and pulling to remove the contents of the cavity, and some of the innards contact the flesh (an action you should try to avoid). After cleaning a fish this way, make sure you rinse it immediately and thoroughly.

Pan Dressing

Small fish that are unsuitable for filleting or that are to be cooked whole by various methods can be prepared in a manner called pan dressing. The standard and most common method leaves the skin and ribs intact, but a more involved method allows

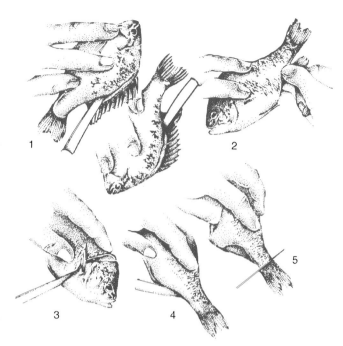

To pan dress a small whole panfish with skin and ribs intact, cut the top of the fish along both sides of the dorsal fin (1) and remove the fin; cut along both sides of the anal fin and remove it (2); cut off the head at an acute angle (3) and remove it; slice along the belly to the anal vent (4); as an option, cut off the tail (5). Clean the body cavity thoroughly.

for their removal. Both methods remove the head, entrails, and fin bones. Small fish should be pan dressed with a narrow knife having a short blade and a pointed edge, as opposed to a standard fillet knife having a longer, flexible blade.

Pan Dressing, Skin and Ribs Intact

Start by laying a scaled fish on one side and slicing along the dorsal fin on both sides. Then pull out the fin. Do the same thing for the anal fin. Do not cut these fins flat because you'll leave bones in the meat.

Cut off the head as close to the gill cover as possible, angling the knife over the top of the head to maximize the amount of meat. Slit the belly and remove the entrails; cut off the tail if desired and then rinse quickly in ice-cold water and pat dry.

Pan Dressing, Skin and Ribs Removed

Start by laying a fish with scales intact belly down on a cutting board. Make a cut over the top of the head and close to the gills, and continue cutting down through the backbone without completely severing the head. Slice the skin along each side of the dorsal fin from the head to the tail, making the slice as shallow as possible. Grasp the dorsal fin between your thumb and the fat part of the knife blade and pull it free; this will remove the dorsal fin bones. Turn the fish around and slice along both sides of the anal fin; pull the fin free to remove the anal fin bones. Now make a shallow slice from where the anal fin was to the tail. Turn the fish over again, and position the knife blade under the upper fold of skin near the back; pinching that fold between the knife blade and your thumb, peel the skin halfway down the body. Repeat on the opposite side. Then grab the partially skinned carcass in your left hand and the head and skin in your right hand, and pull both apart; this will liberate the head, skin, and entrails in one piece. Finally, hold the skinned carcass

belly up, and slice off the rib cage by cutting from behind the first rib down to and then along the backbone. Rinse quickly in ice-cold water and pat dry.

This method produces a fish with only the backbone, which easily parts from the meat after cooking. It also saves more meat than filleting.

Scaling

Removing the scales on a fish is referred to as scaling. You do not need to remove the scales on a fish if it will be filleted with the skin removed or if it is from a species that has no scales (bullhead) or extremely small scales (small trout). Species that have large, loose scales and that will not be skinned should be scaled before field dressing. If you do not do this, and even if you have no intention of eating the skin, loose scales will almost

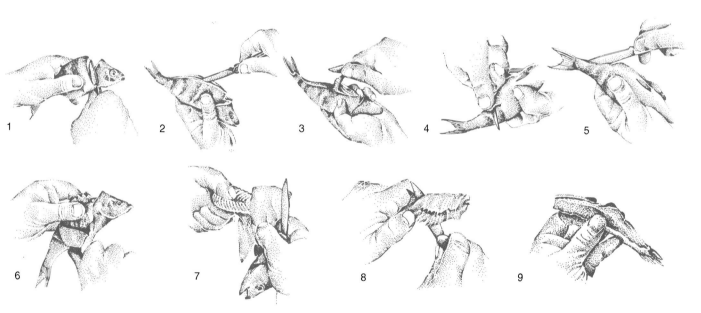

To efficiently dress a small whole perch in a manner that produces a skinless fish with maximum meat, cut down through the backbone without severing the head (1); cut the skin along each side of the dorsal fin (2); pinch the forward end of the fin between thumb and knife blade and pull it toward the tail, removing it and attached bones (3); turn the fish over, cut under the anal fin until the blade meets the supporting fin bone, pinch the anal fin between thumb and blade, and then twist away the bone and fin (4); slice the belly skin between the anal fin and tail (5); turn the fish over, grip a corner of upper back skin between thumb and blade, peel back the skin along the flank, and repeat for the other side (6); holding the partially skinned body in one hand, grab the head and skin in the other hand and pull them toward the tail in order to remove these items plus entrails in one piece (7); hold skinned fish as shown, bring knife blade up from belly behind the rib cage to the backbone, and then slice forward to separate the rib cage from the backbone (8). The final result (9) is a skinned, beheaded, eviscerated fish with just backbone.

certainly find their way into the food, which is unpleasant and shows carelessness.

Scaling can be performed on fish that have been eviscerated, but this is more difficult and could lead to tearing of the meat and an incomplete job. Scaling, therefore, is best accomplished on a whole fish, in the round, that can be scraped and pulled freely while still intact.

Scale removal can be accomplished with various devices. A knife blade is commonly used and is effective, provided you're careful and can handle the knife skillfully enough to avoid slicing into the skin. Using a knife for scaling will dull the blade, however. Many anglers like to use scaling tools, usually called scalers, which have serrated edges; others prefer a thin-metal spoon for scaling small surface areas. The spoon can also be handy for scraping the bloodline out of the cavity.

Always scale against the grain, moving from the tail of the fish toward the head. Working against the grain can be a messy process, sending scales everywhere, but you can minimize the mess by wetting the surface of the fish before scaling, or scaling under the running water of a faucet. If you have a hose with a high-pressure nozzle and you're working outside on fish that have been kept wet, you can scale them quickly by holding them about 6 inches from the high-pressure water stream; it's effective, but it sends scales flying. The hosing method works better for loose-scaled species like bluegills and crappie than for tight-scaled species like yellow perch or walleye. In general, the longer a fish has been left dry and out of water, the harder the scaling process. If you have to scale in a kitchen, you can immerse the fish in a sink of cold water and ice, pin the fish against the bottom of the sink, and scale it. The scales stay in the water and should be caught in the strainer when the sink is drained.

Filleting

Generally the quickest method of cleaning fish is to fillet them. Filleting means cutting the sides of a fish lengthwise parallel to and free from the backbone, accompanied by removal of the rib cage. A fillet is typically a boneless piece of fish, and it may or may not have the skin removed. When correctly done, filleting causes little loss of meat, is accomplished easily with the proper

instrument, and, most important, removes all the ribcage bones that anguish many reluctant fish eaters. The word "fillet," incidentally, is properly pronounced "fill-lay," not "fill-it."

Basic Filleting, Version 1

Place the fish on one side, and make an angled cut behind the pectoral fin down to the backbone, being careful not to sever the backbone. Reverse the direction of the blade so that it is facing the tail and lying flat on the backbone, and slice back toward the tail along the backbone. A smooth cut, rather than a stop-and-go sawing motion, is best. If the fish has been scaled, cut through the skin at the tail.

If the skin is to be removed in the filleting process, do not cut through the tail but slice to the end without severing, and flop the meat backward.

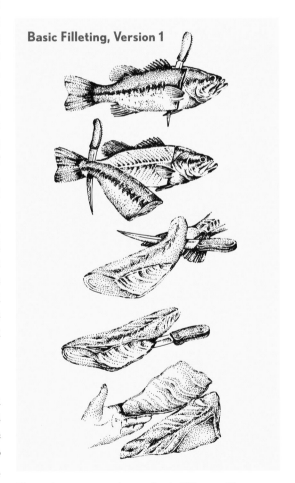

Basic Filleting, Version 1

This is the most popular method of filleting. The same process is followed for both sides; slicing the rib cage away from the fillet is the final step.

If the fish has a thin skin that is easy to slice through, make sure you leave plenty of it attached to the caudal peduncle so that it grabs there and makes the skinning process easier. Angle your knife through the meat to the skin; then slice along the skin, separating the meat while exerting pressure on the skin with your free hand. If you accidentally cut through the tail, freeing the fillet from the carcass, you will find that removing the skin is a little more difficult. In this case, press the thumbnail of your free hand on the tail of the fillet (or use a fork), and cut between the skin and meat with your knife hand. You can use a sawing motion here and aid the effort by pulling on the tail of the fillet in the opposite direction of the cut.

Now, with either scaled or skinned fillet, cut behind the rib cage, slicing the whole section away. Use the same procedure for the other side of the fish. Rinse fillets quickly in cold water and pat dry. This filleting technique can be used on many fish, except those with additional Y-shaped bones.

Basic Filleting, Version 2

Place the fish on one side, and make an angled cut behind the pectoral fin down to the backbone, being careful not to sever the backbone. Slice the skin along the backbone from the head toward the tail, running the knife along the top of the rib cage but not cutting through it. Push the knife through the flesh at a point opposite the anal vent, and continue cutting, running the knife along the backbone until the blade slices the flesh away at the tail. A smooth cut, rather than a stop-and-go sawing motion, is best.

Lift the top of the fillet up to expose the rib cage; with smooth, measured strokes, flesh the meat away from the ribs, skimming the bones to procure as much meat as possible. Slice the fillet away from the carcass at the stomach. Turn the fish over and repeat on the opposite side, concluding with two boneless fillets with skin attached. If you have previously descaled the fish, the job is complete except for rinsing and patting dry. If not, you can remove the skin by pressing a fork or the thumbnail of your free hand on the tail of the fillet; cut between the skin and the meat with your knife hand. You can use a sawing motion here and aid the effort by pulling on the tail of the fillet in the opposite direction of the cut.

Basic Filleting, Version 2

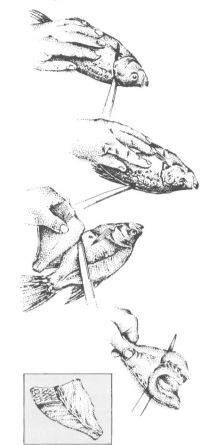

This is a good method of filleting; it requires a sharp knife and produces the maximum meat. The same process is followed for both sides. Leaving a patch of skin on a fillet (inset) may be necessary for legal identification purposes.

The second version is generally used less often than the first, but it has some benefits. It does not dull the knife as quickly since there is no cutting through rib bones. It produces slightly more meat than the first version, and it is better for use on larger fish. Large fish would be those for which the blade of the knife was not long enough to reach the top of the back and the bottom of the belly.

For really large fish and those with thick bones, you may need a bigger, sturdier knife. It's easy to lose meat on large fish when filleting if you don't do the job right. A heavy-duty blade will easily cut through the rib cage so that you don't have to hack at the fish; this is a big consideration if you're using the first filleting version. If you don't have a larger knife, you can still fillet with a smaller one by using version two and slicing in small sections while folding back the side of the fish to allow deeper penetration and continued slicing. To cut off the skin with a smaller knife, cut the skinned fillet in half lengthwise and then take off the skin as previously described.

If you make a mistake when filleting, try to correct the error rather than continuing with the mistake. The biggest problem when filleting, especially when the fish are small and you're using a sharp knife, is inadvertently cutting through the backbone. If this happens, withdraw the knife and come back at another angle until you strike the backbone; then lay the blade flat and make the stroke along the backbone. Another common mistake is cutting through the skin when you're trying to remove the skin from the fillet. If this happens, go to the head of the fillet, angle the blade through the flesh to the skin, and then start skinning from that direction.

Butterfly Filleting

If you keep the skin attached to the sides of the fish while filleting and leave them joined at the belly, you can achieve a double fillet. This has some panache from a presentation standpoint. This method is used for smoking or planking fish, as well as for baking when stuffed. The skin helps hold in the juices for baking.

To butterfly a fish, first scale it if the species or your presentation demands it (planked fish do not need to be scaled since the meat is flaked away), and then cut off the head. With the belly away from you and the tail to the left, run the knife along the backbone, slicing through the rib bones and continuing through the tail, taking care not to cut through the skin at the belly. Turn the fish over and around so the tail is to the right and the belly is away from you; this time work from the tail toward the ribs, slicing the meat through the tail and then close to the backbone, continuing through the ribs and again taking care not to cut through the skin at the belly. Remove the entrails and backbone, and lay the double fillet skin-side down and open. Trim away whatever remains of the rib bones; then rinse in cold water and pat dry.

Butterfly Filleting

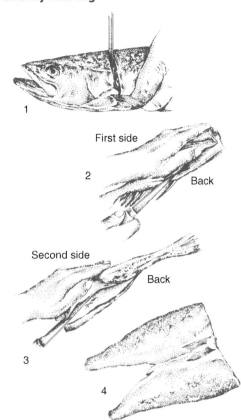

To create a butterfly fillet, first cut off the head (1); with the tail to the left and the belly up, slice along the backbone, cutting through the rib bones and continuing through the tail without cutting through the belly skin (2). Turn the fish over so that the tail is to the right and the belly is up, and cut from the tail toward the ribs (3), slicing the meat through the tail and then close to the backbone, continuing through the ribs, again not cutting through the belly skin. Remove entrails and backbone, and trim away whatever remains of the rib bones (not shown), creating a double fillet (4).

Filleting to Remove Extra Bones

Some fish have more than the usual number of bones, and these cannot be removed through standard one-cut filleting. Such species include pike, pickerel, and muskellunge, all of which have additional intermuscular, or floating, Y-shaped bones. To deal with this, you can fillet the fish as previously described in version 1 and remove the skin. The Y bones are located on the fleshy back portion of the fillet above the ribs and run lengthwise to a point equal with the ventral opening. Locate the lower edge of the Y bones just above

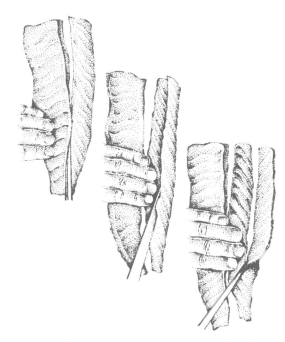

To remove Y-shaped bones from a skinless fillet of pike, pickerel, and muskellunge, locate these bones just above the midsection of the fillet and cut through the flesh beneath them all the way to the tail (top). Run the knife blade along the upper edge of the Y bones (middle), scraping gently against the bones and slicing down and away to the tail (bottom). Discard the middle piece, leaving two boneless segments.

the midsection of the fillet, and cut through the flesh beneath them all the way to the tail. Then guide the knife blade along the upper edge of the Y bones, scraping gently against the bones and slicing down and away to the tail. The upper and lower portions will be free of bones and can be rinsed in cold water and patted dry.

Some meat is obviously lost in this process, but a safer and more enjoyable fillet results. If you use the bony fillet for fish stock, and use a fine strainer, the bony strip does not have to be wasted. An alternative is to leave the strip of Y bones in the fillet, cut the skinless fillet into chunks, and run the chunks through a food grinder with fine blades, after which you can create patties or a fish loaf.

Filleting Flatfish

Flatfish such as flounder are among the most popular of inshore saltwater species. Although they have a different body shape from most other fish, they are not difficult to clean, especially if you use a sharp knife with a long, slightly flexible blade.

To fillet a flounder, slice the meat across the body just behind the head and down to the backbone; then slice the length of the fish from head to tail, scraping the blade along the backbone. Continue this cut down to the other side of the fish, lifting the fillet up as necessary and slicing the entire fillet free. Lay the fillet skin down, and remove the skin by pressing a fork or the thumbnail of your free hand on the tail of the fillet; cut between the skin and the meat with your knife

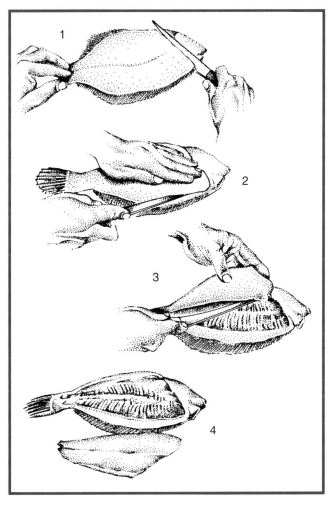

To fillet a flatfish, cut across the body just behind the head and down to the backbone (1) and then slice the length of the fish from head to tail, scraping the blade along the backbone (2). Continue this cut down to the other side of the fish, lifting up the fillet as necessary (3) and slicing the entire fillet free (4). Remove skin if desired.

hand. You can use a sawing motion here and aid the effort by pulling on the tail of the fillet in the opposite direction of the cut.

Steaking

Steaking fish for frying or broiling is a good way to handle large specimens. To steak a fish, scale and eviscerate it first; then make a slice on both sides of the fins and pull them free. If the fish is firm or partly frozen, and you have a good cleaver, cut off the head and tail and make the steaks from ¾ to 1 inch thick, starting from the head and working toward the tail. You may find it easier to leave on the head and steak the fish from the tail toward the head, grasping the fish by the head. Trim the belly fat and any obvious bones from the steak; then rinse each steak quickly in cold water and pat dry. When you get to the tail section where no more steaks are available, fillet it.

A fillet knife won't do an adequate job of steaking fish. Steaks should be neatly cut, not ragged and hacked. Use a butcher's knife or a cleaver for steaking. Don't use a serrated knife or one that is likely to grind the backbone; fine pieces of ground backbone may get in or on the steaks. Fish that are very cold or partially frozen steak better than those that are soft and fleshy, so if your knife isn't super sharp or you're making do with a less rugged blade, it might be good to chill or partly freeze the fish before steaking.

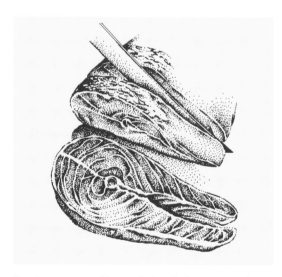

Steaks are created from a beheaded, eviscerated carcass by making equal-thickness cuts across the body and through the backbone.

Skinning

Most fish skinning takes place during the filleting process, with the skin being separated from the flesh as a next-to-last step. However, some people like to have a whole fish without the skin and certain fish—like dolphin, for example—do not yield their skin very well when their sides have been cut away from the whole body. If you think that the skin may leave an objectionable flavor in the flesh, remove it; removing the skin also helps spices or sauces penetrate the flesh better.

If the fish is slimy (some freshwater species have more abundant and more offensive-smelling mucus than others), the skin should be removed.

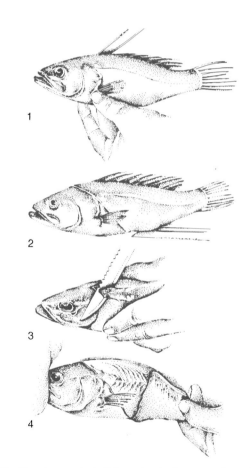

To skin a large whole fish, make shallow cuts along the back and past the dorsal fin from just behind the head to just ahead of the tail (1). Then cut diagonally across the body, meeting with the forward end of the dorsal cut (2), and cut along the belly from the end of the diagonal cut past the anal fin to the tail. At the intersected cuts behind the head, pry up a small strip of skin with the knife (3); grab this strip with your fingers or a pair of pliers, and peel back the skin (4).

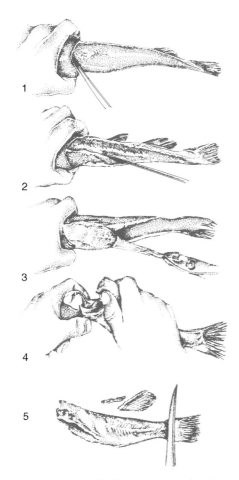

To skin and eviscerate bullheads and small catfish, hold them carefully at the head with your fingers pinning the sharp pectoral fins; make a shallow cut of the skin around the entire head of the fish (1) and also along the backbone from the dorsal fin to the adipose fin (2). With pliers, grab the skin at the back and pull it to the tail (3); repeat on the other side. Holding the fish as shown, bend the head down to break the backbone (4), and then pull the head away from the fish toward the tail, removing skin and entrails in the process. Cut off the tail (5) and rinse the fish.

Wiping with a cloth doesn't seem to remove slime unless you have a lot of clean cloths available. You can try placing the fish in a solution of one part vinegar and three parts water to help remove the mucus. You can also rub the fish with generous amounts of salt and then rinse with cold water.

Small fish can be skinned by following the procedure described earlier for pan dressing, with skin and ribs removed. Large whole fish can be skinned by making three shallow cuts: along the back and past the dorsal fin from just behind the head to just ahead of the tail; diagonally across the body, meeting with the forward end of the dorsal cut; and along the belly from the end of the diagonal cut past the anal fin to the tail. At the cut corner behind the head, pry up a small strip of skin with the knife; then grab this with your fingers or a pair of pliers and peel the skin back. Repeat this on the other side, and finish the fish by any method you choose.

If you have already eviscerated a fish but want to keep it whole without the skin, then cut the skin around the tail and head (behind the pectoral fins) and along the back. Pry up a small strip of skin at the tail, grip this with pliers, and peel back the skin while holding the tail firmly.

Bullheads and small catfish pose cleaning problems for many anglers, yet these fish can be dressed easily with proper treatment. They have a tough skin that is thin and slippery, and it cannot be removed like other fish. To skin and eviscerate bullheads and small catfish, make a thin slice on the top of the fish from behind the adipose fin up to the dorsal fin, and continue with a vertical cut from the dorsal fin down to the backbone. Put the knife aside, grab the head with one hand and the body with the other, and bend the head down to break the backbone. Hold the body portion firmly, with your finger over the broken backbone, and pull the head away from the fish toward the tail, removing skin and entrails in the process. Cut off the tail and rinse the fish.

With larger catfish, it's best to slice the perimeters of the skin. Hold the head firmly. Slice completely around the fish behind the pectoral fin. Slice along the top of the fish and around both sides of the adipose fin; then slice along the belly and around both sides of the pectoral fin. Use a pair of snub-nose pliers to grasp the skin near the pectoral fin, and pull back firmly toward the tail to remove it. Repeat on the other side. Sever the head and tail and remove the entrails. You can now fillet the fish, keep it as is, or steak it.

Trimming for Health and Taste Reasons

Some fish contain a dark lateral line that has a different flavor than the rest of the meat. If you fillet these fish and remove the skin, you can slice away this dark flesh.

Many fisheries agencies advocate trimming away the fatty parts from fish, as well as removing the skin, to reduce the intake of certain environmental contaminants. We are not talking about the taste or the flavor of fish flesh here. This is about the hidden and tasteless elements with such foreboding names as mirex, PCBs, dioxin, and chlordane. These contaminants have a long residual life in the aquatic environment and work their way through the food chain into the flesh of prey and predator fish.

A high percentage of contaminants is found in the fatty portion of fish, so the best policy is to trim away the fatty area of the back, belly, and lateral line. A study that evaluated untrimmed brown trout fillets versus trimmed fillets found that trimming resulted in an average reduction of 62 percent in fat content and 45 percent in contaminants.

Researchers note that cooking trimmed fillets in a way that allows the remaining fat to drain out and away from the flesh will further reduce levels of contaminants. Some studies suggest that baking or broiling on a rack will result in further

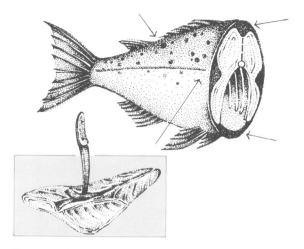

To remove fatty flesh that may contain contaminants, trim the flesh from the back and belly and also along the lateral lines (inset); then remove the skin.

reduction in fats and the contaminants stored in them, although the exact percentage varies.

Depending on where you fish and what you keep for consumption, you can lessen potential health risks simply by carefully cleaning your catch.

PART FOUR

Techniques

22

Light-Tackle Fishing

There is no established standard for what constitutes light tackle, since the species, size of average catch, angling circumstances, and other factors all vary on a case-by-case basis in both freshwater and saltwater fishing. Furthermore, some tackle that would be considered heavy in freshwater is considered light in certain saltwater situations.

Although most people directly associate light tackle with the breaking strength of the line, this is not an absolute criterion. Generally, the use of any gear that calls upon above-average efforts to hook, play, and land a fish is light. If even greater effort or more extreme skill is needed to do these things, it is ultralight.

The hallmarks of using lighter than average fishing equipment are a good bow in the rod, a lot of stress on the line, a good scrap by small fish and a real battle for larger ones, and the need to take extra steps to keep a moderate-size fish from getting free. They also include taking more than a few seconds to land even a small fish, and using skills and finesse more often than brawn.

Since ultralight fishing is just an extension of using light tackle, and in some cases may be nearly the same thing, it will be considered the same for purposes of reviewing the basic aspects of light-tackle fishing.

Pros and Cons

In addition to the obvious elements of fun and challenge, there are practical advantages to using light gear, the foremost of which is producing more strikes. Using a fine-diameter line and a smaller lure induces more strikes, especially when angling in very clear water and when fish are spooky, heavily pressured, or in a negative mode. Also, a light line can make strikes easier to detect and can help increase casting distance.

On the downside, you'll probably lose a few more fish and definitely more lures and hooks with light tackle than with heavier gear. That's because light line gets frayed and weakened more easily, mistakes are magnified, and hangups on the bottom are harder to free. Also, since you generally can't use large, heavy lures, casting and hooksetting may pose problems.

These are minor issues, however. Light tackle under the right circumstances is very appropriate for freshwater and saltwater, and more people should gear up for fish of average size than for extreme size. However, some circumstances are inappropriate for light tackle, so you have to be practical.

You can catch big fish on light tackle, as well as more fish of average size, if you know what you're doing. The seriousness and the effect of making mistakes when using ultralight gear is greatly magnified. The margin of error is slim, and there's no gimme even if you use perfect knots, have good reel drag, and skillfully battle fish. Therefore, it takes a more complete angler, with well-rounded skills, to be consistently effective.

Necessary Components

No matter how you define light tackle or what you fish for, the elements of using it are the same. Rods used for light-tackle fishing tend to be a bit limber in order to provide more of a cushion for the lightness of the line. They can be short for small fish, but a longer rod is a distinct advantage for landing big specimens. Long rods (7 to 9 feet is the norm but 10- to 14-footers are used by some anglers) give you more leverage to pressure a fish, putting less

strain on your arms and wrists, and they're very helpful when a hooked fish is near the boat and you need to steer around obstacles.

An important aspect of light-tackle use is having fresh line in top condition. Light line must be checked periodically for nicks and abrasions, and replaced more often if severely stressed. Only the best knots, tied consistently perfect, will do for light tackle, since more is demanded of these critical connections.

Hooksetting can be more difficult with light line if you're timid, but you must be able to set the hook with authority no matter what tackle you use, and this requires confidence in the condition of your line and the ability of your knots, and especially having the sharpest hooks. Maintaining ultrasharp hooks also helps minimize losing fish.

Another aid to successful fishing with light tackle is using a doubled length of line or a heavier leader, both to ensure greater strength in the knot and to help minimize the effects of abrasion. The doubled line or heavier leader also makes dealing with strong fish on light tackle easier at the boat, which is where a lot of good fish are lost.

Depending on the species and the circumstances, you may want to double the last 3 to 5 feet of light line used on casting tackle with a Bimini Twist or Spider Hitch knot, keeping it just short enough that the knot doesn't reach the spool of the reel. You should have no trouble casting these knots through the rod guides if you make them correctly, especially with smaller lines.

When angling for big fish with light line on a spinning outfit, it can be worthwhile to first make a 3- to 4-foot section of doubled line and then add a 2- to 3-foot heavier leader to it using a Uni Knot. This setup really helps avoid abrasion and overcome near-the-boat stress. For some toothy species, add a short wire leader to the heavier monofilament leader or to the doubled line.

Another key component of light-line fishing is having a smooth-operating drag and using it properly. Do not set the drag too loose, which impedes hooksetting (the drag slips) and puts too little pressure on a fish; and don't set it too tight, which might cause the line to snap under the extreme pressure of a surging fish. Knowing your limits, based on the line strength, the effectiveness of your knots, and the type of tackle that you're using, will determine how you play a fish caught on light tackle.

Playing and Landing Fish

Under ideal conditions of little boat traffic or few anglers nearby, you can play a strong fish in open water without too much difficulty because the line has nothing to snag on. The deck can be cleared and the boat maneuvered to your advantage. If the drag is set properly, the fish can take plenty of line and do its stuff. But if there are obstructions beneath the surface, or if you hook a big fish unexpectedly in a place having plenty of snags, then you have to be very aggressive and take the fight to the fish as quickly and as well as you can.

The essential elements of playing and landing fish are covered in chapter 18. Remember that if you use good equipment, including a quality line with a knot that retains full strength and a rod with backbone, you can pressure a fish very well with light tackle.

With light tackle it's important to pressure a fish from the very beginning and to periodically change the angle of tension from vertical to horizontal (left and right), which directs the fish

Using a light spinning outfit, an angler plays a brook trout on a pond in the Adirondacks of New York.

away from obstructions and keeps it disoriented. When the fish swims off, let the drag do the work; otherwise, try to gain line at every chance. If the drag slips when you pump, use some extra tension. Place your thumb on a baitcasting spool, palm on a spinning reel spool, and fingertips on the inside of a fly reel spool to add moderate extra tension when you're reeling down.

23

Fly Fishing

One of the oldest forms of angling, fly fishing is most commonly associated with casting lightweight objects via a heavy line, which distinguishes it from all other forms of angling in which weighted objects carry lightweight line. There are exceptions to this, because not all lightweight objects are actually cast with flycasting tackle (they may be trolled or dapped, for example), and some of the objects used are bulky if not weighty (such as saltwater streamers). Today an extremely wide array of lightweight natural food imitations are employed in fly fishing for diverse species in all areas of freshwater and saltwater.

In general terms, more fly fishing is done in freshwater than in saltwater, although the bounds of saltwater fly fishing have been greatly expanded. Most fly fishing in freshwater is done for trout in streams, but fly fishing for panfish, largemouth and smallmouth bass, northern pike, salmon in streams, and some trout in stillwaters has devotees. Other freshwater species can be caught on flycasting tackle, but many of them, for various reasons, are seldom pursued with this equipment.

In saltwater, most fly fishing occurs in inshore environs and tidal rivers and estuaries for striped bass, bonefish, tarpon, bluefish, redfish, seatrout, snook, and mackerel, plus some other species. Pelagic fish, especially sailfish and smaller marlin, are caught with specialized techniques in offshore environs. With all of these fish, except for trout in streams and Atlantic salmon, fly fishing as a method constitutes a minority of fishing effort overall.

Principle

An artificial fly may imitate various types of food, from an insect to a crustacean to baitfish, in appearance as well as in the way it is fished. In some instances, it does this better than other objects that also represent natural food. The fly is carried to its destination by the casting of heavy line that is connected to a leader, which in turn is attached to the fly.

To the uninitiated angler, the mechanics of casting an artificial fly and a large weighty fly line appear difficult. In fact, many aspects of fly fishing can seem complicated if you read one of the many advanced books that are devoted to fly fishing and if you review the thousands of fly patterns and involved esoterica of the activity. In truth, casting an artificial fly is no more and no less complicated than other types of fishing, all of which can be taken to extreme levels of involvement by those who desire.

The casting hurdle, however, is a large one to overcome, because if you can't get your offering to the fish, you're completely lost. While it is not simple to learn flycasting, it is not exceedingly difficult either. Flycasting invokes a different principle than casting with spinning, spincasting, or baitcasting tackle, and is a little more involved. This is why fly fishing schools spend a lot of time on casting instruction.

Pros and Cons

Besides the casting difference, some things are possible in fly fishing that aren't when using other fishing tackle. Precise placement of small flies, for example, is not possible with other tackle choices without the use of casting aids. Likewise, when using flies it's possible to precisely match many food items, especially insects, that some fish eat; this ability can be essential when they are exclusively consuming specific insects. Natural movements and actions of insects are also easily imitated through proper manipulation of the tackle.

Furthermore, the ease and quickness of making repeat presentations, especially when using a floating line, is often a benefit that is unmatched with

Fly line intersects with a rainbow as an angler fishes for Atlantic salmon on the Miramichi River in New Brunswick.

other tackle, not to mention that the art of flycasting in itself can be an enjoyable activity. In addition, fly fishing offers a complete package of natural imitation and selectivity, which makes many practitioners more observant in the outdoors.

On the downside, although there are quick, deep-sinking fly lines, fly fishing is often an inefficient method of angling for fish in deep water, especially in large bodies of water and in really turbulent flows. This applies to fish that cruise deep midlevel water as well as those that reside on the bottom. The difficulty is not that you can't get deep enough but that you need time to do so, and also more time to retrieve the line.

Also, casting in open environs, such as flats and big rivers, when the wind is blowing hard, is a problem for many anglers, and it hampers their effectiveness; other types of tackle handle this common situation better for the average angler. Likewise, achieving significant distance is difficult with flycasting tackle for all but the most proficient casters, although distance is not a necessity in many angling situations.

General Techniques

Fishing techniques with flies depend on the type of fly and the environment in which it is fished. Since flies are delivered with a heavy line, the type of line used is also essential to presentation methods.

Dry Flies

Like natural insects, dry flies are generally allowed to drift on the surface subject to whatever natural current or wind influences exist, but to avoid drag the presentation may require in-air or on-water line mending. Less often, some deliberate movement of a dry fly by the angler may be appropriate. This would occur if the natural insect being imitated moved about, such as an adult depositing eggs, which is well imitated by dapping. As a means of attracting fish, gliding or skating a dry fly is a technique used for Atlantic salmon and occasionally trout, often with a long-hackled fly referred to as a skater.

In flowing water, dry flies are primarily fished by casting upstream and allowing the fly to float downstream in a natural manner. The line should not be cast directly over the fish, or over the area to be worked with a fly, in order to avoid spooking the fish; the best manner of presentation is to cast up- and across-stream, floating the fly down. Seldom are dry flies fished by casting directly downstream, because this limits the length of the drift owing to the line that can be dispatched and is almost certain to create drag.

Watch the fly as it floats on the surface so that you know when a fish takes it and you can react quickly. When a fish rises to a dry fly, it may do so in a violent and splashy manner, which is obvious and exciting, or in a nearly imperceptible dimpling manner, which can be missed if you're not paying attention. In either case, however, do not react with a violent hookset; this is likely to pull the fly away from the fish or to break it off if the fish has already hooked itself. Simply react with a moderate flick of the wrist to raise the tip of the rod, keeping the line pinched to the handle with your finger.

When dry flies lose their floating ability, some air drying by repetitive false casting, if conditions permit, may temporarily restore floating characteristics, but more likely the fly will need a dressing to help it repel water. If the fly has absorbed a lot of moisture, press it with a cloth to remove the moisture and clean it; then apply some form of dressing to it.

Wet Flies

Wet flies are unaffected by wind or surface current, but obviously they move with subsurface current; the connecting leader and fly line are affected by current on and below the surface, which may cause drag and unnaturally move or restrain what should be a free-drifting fly. Like natural insects, wet flies are generally allowed to drift in the water subject to whatever natural current exists, but to avoid drag the presentation may require line mending.

In flowing water, wet flies are primarily used by an angler who is above the fish's position, with the angler casting across-stream or across and downstream and allowing the fly to drift downstream. In this manner the line, leader, and angler approach a fish from above. They may be retrieved across the flow as well as drifted naturally, and are often employed in tandem, with a second fly as a dropper or with several wet flies (usually close to the surface). Depending on the circumstances, especially water depth, a wet fly may be fished with a floating line (fly just under the surface), a sink-tip line (fly at mid-depths), or a full-sinking line (fly at greater depths).

In ponds or lakes, a wet fly is generally used with a sink-tip or full-sink line and is fished with a stripping retrieve of the fly line, the speed of which varies according to whatever the fly is supposed to imitate. Wet flies that are attractors are generally fished at a quick pace.

The strike of a fish on a wet fly is typically felt rather than seen. The reaction of the angler should be to quickly pull on the fly line in the line-gathering hand, removing any slack, then pinch the line to the handle with the rod-holding hand and flick the wrist upward to raise the rod tip.

Nymphs

All types of fly lines are used to fish nymphs, and choice depends on type of nymph, current flow, depth, and length of drift. Small nymphs, for example, are often fished on a floating line in small shallow waters, using a tiny split shot a short distance ahead of the fly to get it down quickly for what is usually a short drift. As a rule, floating and slow-sinking lines are used in all shallow waters, sink-tip lines in intermediate depths in streams, and full-sinking lines with a fast sink rate in all deep waters.

In moving waters, a nymph is cast upstream or up- and across-stream with a floating line, with the fly sinking and drifting down with the current for a relatively short drift, or it is cast slightly up- and across-stream with a sink-tip or full-sink fly line to maintain contact with the nymph either when drifting it downstream or when swimming it. A strike indicator is often used on the leader to help show leader movement when a fly has been taken by a fish in moving water, so the angler can react quickly to a strike.

Often, and especially in small streams, nymph-fishing anglers hold the rod tip high to help maintain a desirable fly drift and keep more of the fly line off the water to minimize drag. In ponds or lakes, a nymph is generally used with a sink-tip or full-sink line, allowed to sink to a desired level, and fished with a generally slow stripping retrieve of the fly line.

Streamers

Streamers are fished on all line types in a manner that is similar to some aspects of wet fly and nymph fishing; choice is dependent on the type of water and depth to be fished, the circumstances, and so on. Sink-tip lines are especially useful for streamers that are fished at moderate depths; full-sink lines are used for deep-water work; and floating lines are used for shallow fishing, where flies are weighted enough to get them beneath the surface a short distance.

There are many types of streamers, and size and silhouette are important to success depending on what you are fishing for. These flies are only occasionally fished on a dead, natural drift (and usually when cast directly upstream in a river), and they have to be manipulated with the fly line and/or rod tip, usually by stripping in fly line to swim the fly. Retrieval speed varies with the behavior of individual species; some require a slow pull-pause movement, whereas for others, including many saltwater fish, the streamer cannot be stripped too fast.

In current, a streamer is normally cast across the current and fished downstream in a retrieval combination of drifting and twitching until it reaches the full downstream extension of line, and then it is strip-retrieved back to the angler. It is sideways to the current when moving downstream, which may suggest an imperiled fish or other food; when it darts upstream, it may simulate the action of mobile prey. In open-water situations, a streamer is dispatched a full casting

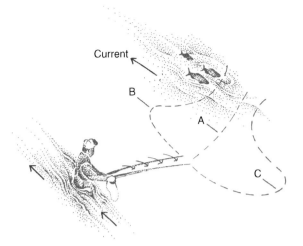

When a fly line is laid across current (A), a strong midstream flow will catch the belly (B) and place unnatural drag on the fly. This can be countered by mending line that is already on the water. After making the initial cast (A), use your rod to pick up the belly of the line and drop it upstream (C), which permits a drag-free float of the fly that lasts long enough for it to drift naturally to the fish.

distance away or near a breaking fish, allowed to sink to the desired level, and then erratically strip-retrieved.

Surface Bugs and Poppers

Cork and hair bugs are fished on the surface probably 90 percent of the time with a floating fly line, although a sink-tip line may be employed with some diving and swimming bugs to help pull them briefly under the surface during retrieval.

The way bugs and poppers sit in the water, as well as the contoured design of their head or face, governs the action and degree of commotion that they make. Small versions, usually worked slowly, are preferred for panfish; larger ones, fished at various speeds, are intended for largemouth and smallmouth bass, northern pike, striped bass, and other saltwater fish.

Mending

Mending is an important and basic line-manipulating skill used by fly anglers to effect a proper presentation and/or drift of a fly without drag. Drag is the influence of current on a fly that inhibits it from drifting in a free manner as if it were a natural insect.

A drag-free drift is highly desirable and often necessary for all, or as much as possible, of the presentation, and certainly for the period when the fly is in the likely zone where a fish lies. In some situations a drag-free drift is possible for only a few seconds before the current grabs the line and pulls the fly downstream too fast.

To avoid or minimize drag on the fly, an angler must maneuver the line in such a manner that the fly floats unhindered with the current. It is usually the effect of converging current, or of currents that operate at different speeds, that causes the fly line to flow either faster or slower than the fly and pull on it, either dragging it across the surface if it's a dry fly, or up- or across-current if it's a nymph.

There are various methods of mending the fly line to prevent or postpone the current from dragging the fly. This mending is accomplished by throwing additional slack into the line; most often slack is thrown into the belly of the line when the line is already on the surface, but it may also be accomplished in other ways and in a variety of situations, some of which are described here.

On-Water Mends

A standard mend on a cast made quartering upstream is performed the moment the fly and line are on the water; the angler lifts the rod quickly and flips the belly and forward part of the line upstream. This is best done with some slack line hanging between the reel and the stripping guide on the rod. If the cast is long, the forward part of the line may be mended several times to lengthen the drift. This tactic can also be employed to lift the line a few inches above the surface to get it over an object, like a rock, in the current. The objective is not to move the fly from the path of its normal drift, but to extend the length of a natural drift.

A series of roll casts or tip rolls of the slack line is another way of mending a small amount of line, and is especially useful when you're already well into a drift and need to extend it but cannot with an upstream mend, which would in itself pull on the floating fly. Stripping some slack off the reel and feeding it out will also give the drift a little more mileage.

A variation on this technique would be throwing a mend downstream when you're casting across slow-moving water and placing your fly in swifter current. Flipping the line downstream

allows the fly to float naturally and faster and then meet up with the pace of the line.

In-Air Mends

Mending can also be accomplished by manipulating the fly line and leader in the air at the end of the forward cast but before the line contacts the water. This is done in several ways that throw slack into the line, resulting in the term "slack line casts."

One way to do this is to drop the rod tip from a vertical position to one side and then return it to the vertical position while the forward cast is in progress and before it lands. In essence, this action forms a curve in the line and is thus called a curve cast; it can be accomplished upstream or downstream.

Another version, sometimes called a reach cast, is done by reaching upstream with the rod while the line is in the air and then laying the line on the water. In a similar fashion, slightly overpowering

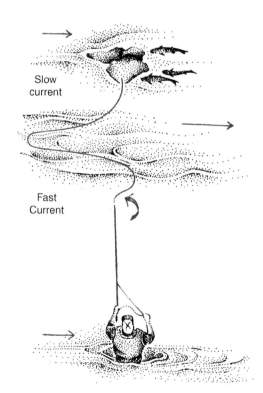

When making a presentation across a fast, narrow flow of water, you can avoid instantaneous drag on a fly by making an upstream curve cast. Here, as the forward cast nears completion, the angler throws an upstream in-air curve in the line, which deposits most of the belly into the fast current, allowing the fly to float for a short distance drag-free in the slower current.

the cast and stopping the line so that the fly stops in midair and bounces a bit backward, then letting the line fall to the surface, creates a series of curves in the line on the water. This is called an S-cast, or S-curve.

In all of these maneuvers, further mending can be accomplished without creating drag by sending slack out in a tip roll, which is an abbreviated roll cast. A version of this for short drifts in quick water, or pocket water, is called a pile cast. It is accomplished by casting high above the target spot, stopping the cast abruptly, and dumping the line on the water. This action piles up the line closer to the fly and allows a short drag-free float.

Dapping

The oldest form of fly fishing, dapping can be very tantalizing to fish, especially trout. The term was coined by Izaak Walton for dancing a dry fly on the surface of the water with leader and line held out of the water.

In general, dapping can be done with any rod to which a light monofilament line is tied and attached at the terminal end to a dry fly; this includes a cane pole, standard-length fly rod, or extra-long fly rod or pole. The shorter the rod or pole, the closer the fly must be fished to the angler, and the less likely a fish is to strike.

In a small, brush-lined creek, where making casts is very difficult, an angler can use a conventional fly rod, kneel behind or beside a streamside bush, extend the rod over the water, and dap the fly over the surface as if it were a natural insect depositing eggs in the water or struggling to stay out of the water.

Dapping is most practical, however, in open areas with the use of long poles. Irish and Scottish anglers dap for trout from boats, using poles that are 14 feet long or longer. In England, dapping poles range from 20 to 30 feet long. The long pole not only provides outward reach in open areas but also allows for a good length of line from the pole to fly. The long line is able to catch any breeze and move the fly around in a manner that cannot be replicated with conventional casting and recasting; the surface of the water remains undisturbed, except when a fish fiercely strikes the fly. When a strike occurs, the angler pauses for a moment to let the fish turn away with the fly and then lifts up the rod to set the hook.

British anglers use a length of silk floss (untwisted silk thread) above a fine tippet to catch the breeze, with a shorter length for breezier conditions and a longer length for calmer conditions. Heavily hackled flies are good for getting the attention of fish. The technique works on small waters in either a strong or a light breeze, but it can be frustrating in places where shoreside cover or trees tend to snag an errant fly or line. In a boat, an angler can avoid shoreside snags and can dap while at anchor or while drifting.

24

Float Fishing

Presenting a hooked bait naturally is an important concept in all types of fishing, especially when using floats. Many species of fish, particularly those that live in stillwater environments, inhale their food most of the time. Thus when they suck in a bait that is attached to a float, they are acutely aware that something is wrong if the bait doesn't move readily when they inhale it. As a result, anglers have to use methods and equipment that will not alarm even the wariest fish.

A major factor in making a guileful presentation is the float. In places where fish are not very astute or when fishing for aggressive species, a float that has a lot of buoyancy, such as the common round bobber, may be used with success often enough to overlook its deficiencies. However, such buoyancy acts as a drag on hooked bait and is a dead giveaway to light-biting fish. So it's better to fish with a float that is designed to avoid alerting fish and is still sensitive enough to alert the angler to a bite.

Correct float selection requires knowing the depth of the water to be fished. In a boat, depth is readily determined by using sonar; without sonar, and for shore fishing, it is necessary to use some type of weight attached to the line to determine the depth. Determining depth in this manner is known as plumbing. This can also be used to determine the composition of the bottom (mud, gravel, weeds, and so on), the location of stumps or other snags, and changes in depth so that the angler can create a mental picture of the area and visualize where the fish might be.

A major factor in float usage is balancing the float properly. This balancing is also known as shotting, since small split shot or a jig, or a combination of both, is added in just the right amount and placed so that only a minimum amount of the float tip is above the surface and visible to the angler, depending on the circumstances. It is always best to have the least possible weight to get the float in a balanced position.

When casting modern floats, always lob the float upward slowly and smoothly. Never snatch it or cast it quickly, which causes tangles. When a float starts to lose momentum, feather the line as it comes off the spool; this pulls the float back so that the baited hook passes over the float before it hits the water.

Float Fishing with a Pole

Float fishing with a pole on stillwater and slow-flowing water is the oldest and simplest way to fish, and is ideal for children or beginners of any age. With proper balancing only a fraction of the float sits above the surface. This is vital because it gives the float almost neutral buoyancy and means that the most discriminating fish, or even a tiny specimen, can suck the bait into its mouth and simultaneously pull the float under, signaling the angler to set the hook. The golden rule is to always use the smallest float possible for the conditions and carefully balance it with shot.

Poles

There are actually two styles of poles: one-piece or telescopic versions that are 9 to 20 feet long, and multipiece (or take-apart) poles that are 18 to 60 feet long. These are both useful in any type or speed of water, but since they do not have a reel, the distance from the angler and the depth of water that can be fished are limited to the length of the pole.

Longer poles allow anglers to reach out to distant locations (such as a weedbed) from a bank or boat and carefully lower a float and bait into small pockets that would be impossible to cast into (or to cast into delicately) with a rod and reel. The length of the line from the tip of the pole to the hook should always be shorter than the pole; use 12 feet of line, for example, for a 14-foot pole, and 18 feet of line for a 20-foot pole.

The main tackle component in pole fishing for the average angler is a 10- to 14-foot-long pole, which may be as simple and inexpensive as a cane pole; fiberglass or graphite poles, however, though more expensive, are superior for anglers who are serious about catching more and bigger panfish.

Floats

For pole fishing in shallow water from 6 inches to 4 feet deep, mini-floats from 1 inch to 2½ inches long are perfect and are not likely to scare fish because of their smaller shape and lesser splash.

For pole fishing in water from 4 to 18 feet deep, a simple crow or porcupine quill float, or a balsa-bodied float on a thin dowel stem (called a shy bite by some and about 7 inches long in several sizes), is extremely sensitive and deadly for all panfish, catfish, and small carp. Because these floats have longer stems, they are more stable in the wind. Even the wariest old crappie, perch, or bluegill can easily suck these floats under when they are balanced to sit just ½ inch or less above the surface.

Both of these styles are attached to the line and held in place by two silicone sleeves (which are first slipped onto the line before it is tied to the hook), one at each end, which allows the angler to

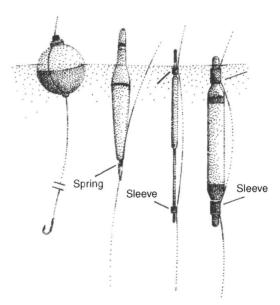

Pole Floats

Shown are common floats used with poles. The two versions on the left typify highly buoyant floats that are not sensitive enough to depict light bites and the action of small fish; the two floats on the right, if balanced with the proper amount of weight, are very sensitive and able to indicate lift bites and the immediate bite of even small fish.

Floats for Flowing Water

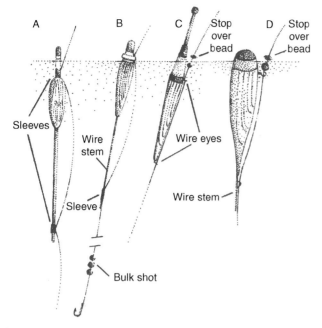

A   B   C   Stop over bead   D   Stop over bead

Sleeves

Wire stem

Wire eyes

Sleeve

Wire stem

Bulk shot

Shown are common balsa floats used in flowing water. The two on the left are fixed in place with silicone sleeves, with one being used in medium-speed flows (A) and the other in faster flows because of greater buoyancy (B). The two on the right are slip floats (C and D), in which line passes through wire arms, with a stop knot used for positioning.

interchange floats if the conditions or the location change. Each time the float is changed, however, it has to be balanced either by adding or subtracting split shot. These floats are especially deadly for crappie fishing with small minnows.

Since these floats are attached to the line and held in place by silicone tubes at each end of the float, only the length of the pole limits the depths that can be fished.

Multipiece Pole Use

Multipiece, or take-apart, poles are used by professional tournament anglers in major match fishing events, and exist in lengths from 18 to over 60 feet long. These poles allow the angler to fish any depth of water, from as shallow as 8 inches to the length of the pole minus 24 inches from pole tip to float. For example, to catch crappie 2 feet deep and 30 feet away from your position under a dock or trees, simply place the float rig precisely where you want it. With just 6 inches of line between the float and pole, you can place or push the float into tight places.

To land fish, draw in the pole behind you until the section where the pole is joined (about 5 or 6 feet) is reached and then take the sections apart to land the fish. After rebaiting, the pole is put together again and the float rig is placed anew.

These are very expensive graphite poles, however, and not necessary in normal angling situations; only when there are lots of anglers and spectators do these poles become important. There is also an entire range of pole floats that are specially designed for use with the long take-apart poles; these too are very expensive and much more fragile than other floats, and are not necessary unless competing in bank-fishing events where the presence of competitors and spectators makes the fish much more difficult to catch.

Float Fishing with Rod and Reel

The techniques and float designs for float fishing with a rod and reel on stillwater and flowing water are completely opposite to each other.

Flowing Water

In flowing water with a rod and reel, it's necessary to fish a controlled float that is connected to the fishing line on the top and bottom of either a fixed or slip float. When fishing a float in flowing water, the angler must be stationary in order to find the correct float speed that catches fish at that moment; this means anchoring when fishing from a boat. The reason is that stream flows vary from top to bottom and, even though floats are used on the surface, the baits are fished on or near the bottom.

On a straight section of a trout stream that is 4 feet deep, for example, the flow just off the bottom will be approximately 20 to 25 percent slower than the surface speed. On a river that is over 20 feet deep, there will be very little current near the bottom, even if the surface speed is swift. These variations mandate that a float be controlled with the rod tip and that the angler be stationary.

Even if you know the exact speed just off bottom, the fish may want the hookbait faster or slower. These factors can and do change daily.

The type of float used varies with the flow speed. Among fixed floats shown in the accompanying illustration, the classic bulblike Avon style (A), for example, is used for medium flows, whereas a more buoyant float (B) is needed for fast and more turbulent water, where bait must be dragged along the bottom without being pulled under easily. These and other fixed floats stay on the line at a preselected position, usually being held in place by silicone sleeves at both the top and the bottom of the float.

There are two eyes on all flowing-water slip floats—on the top and the bottom of the float. These floats slide on the line, with depth setting controlled by attaching a stop to the line. Smaller-bodied versions (C) are good all-around floats for any species when using small- to medium-size bait; larger and more buoyant versions (D) are good for big bait and big fish. A float stop and a bead must be used for both of these.

The simplest and often the best weight placement for balancing in flowing water is a bulk pattern. Place all the shot together a few inches in front of the hook if you want the bait to be just above, or just on, the bottom; or place the shot 18 inches from the hook if the bait is to be dragged along the bottom. In smooth-flowing water, shot can be spread out evenly from float to hook. There are many other ways to place shot, these being the most basic.

Stillwater

An important element of fishing a float with a rod and reel in stillwater is to cast a relatively long distance (in some places close to the far bank) with floats that are attached only at their bottom, then push the rod tip as deeply under the water as possible, and wind in quickly. This sinks the line and prevents the wind from affecting the float. If anglers will do this, they can master float fishing in windy and wavy conditions.

The floats that have been developed for fishing with rod and reel in stillwater are called wagglers; they are used for fishing at any distance and at any depth, and may be used as slip or fixed versions. They are attached to the line only at the bottom, and because of their aerodynamic shape (bulbous at the bottom and long-stemmed at the top) they cast very well, infinitely better than any round type of float.

When such floats are correctly balanced in the water, their shape is hydrodynamic, meaning that they slide through the water (with less drag than a round-shaped float) when a fish bites. When using these floats, you can catch fish as your bait falls through the water—fishing on the drop—and see bites if the fish moves up in the water as it takes the bait.

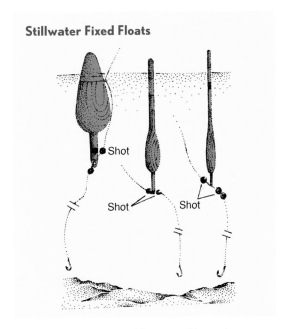

Stillwater Fixed Floats

Shot

Shot   Shot

Shown are common fixed floats used for making distant casts when fishing in lakes and ponds. Although not drawn to scale here, they depict how split shot is used to fix various floats at given positions. The length of line below the float determines the level of the baited hook.

Generally the float settles in the water after the hookbait has fully dropped into position; when a fish takes the hookbait, the float lifts up in the water, indicating a strike. This is known as a lift bite. The angler sets the hook upon observing this, and since the float folds over when the hook is set (because the float is attached at the bottom only), the angler gets a better hookset. Always strike sideways with the tip near the surface, and after the fish is felt, lift the rod back up to normal playing position.

There are small and low-profiled balsa-bodied wagglers for casting to shallow water along the bank or up to 30 yards away, with larger models for windy conditions or longer casts. Deep fishing or very windy conditions require long peacock quills, some with and without a balsa body, to present the hookbait correctly. Some of these models are up to 13 inches long.

As a general guide for balancing, fixed wagglers should have at least 60 percent of the total lead shot positioned to lock the float in place, with the rest of it being drop shot (lower and closer to the hook or jig head). For slip wagglers, start with a bulk pattern, and for a rest shot place two smaller shot 4 feet from the bulk shot, which helps minimize tangles.

25

Chumming

Chumming is an effective technique for attracting, holding, and concentrating fish in which various foods, called chum, are put into the water to draw fish. Chum may include live baitfish; whole dead baitfish; chunks of fish; a ground-up hashlike or souplike mixture of fish; various aquatic organisms (including mollusks and crustaceans), worms, or sundry other foods; bread; grains; and processed foods.

In saltwater, the items used for chum are usually endemic to the area, such as anchovies, herring, menhaden, or other forage fish, and are ordinarily favored by the species sought. However, chum is not necessarily limited to the food on which fish normally feed. Bread is often an effective chum for some fish, as is whole kernel corn, neither of which exists in the normal food chain.

Chumming is most often done from a fixed position, such as an anchored boat, but chum may also be utilized in nearshore areas by a bank-, beach-, or pier-bound angler, and may be used while drifting in a boat. It is not employed when trolling but may be used to attract fish into casting range for both lure and bait presentations, although most chumming is coincidental with the offering of hooked bait.

Nearly every saltwater fish, and many freshwater species, respond to some type of chum. However, chum is most practical for pelagic, or roaming, species, and for bottom-feeding fish. It is also more practical for fish that rely on their sense of smell and taste more than vision, especially in freshwater.

Dispersing chum in the water and then placing a hooked bait among it seems, at first glance, an easy technique and one that would guarantee successful angling, but this is not necessarily the case. There is an art to chumming, as well as to fishing in places where chum has been established. You must plan and work at it to be successful.

Although chumming isn't always essential for a good day's catch, sometimes it does make the difference between success and failure. Moreover, although chumming is generally employed in conjunction with fishing a hooked bait, it can also be used along with lure or fly fishing. Saltwater fly anglers, for example, often chum on flats and in offshore waters to draw fish close enough to cast a fly to them.

Knowing where to anchor, whether to anchor or drift, how frequently to dispense the chum, when to add weight to your line to take the bait deeper, when to use a float to keep it at the right level, as well as other issues, is important to success and often comes from experience. Since so much of angling is finding and attracting fish, chumming is a technique that deserves consideration by every serious angler.

Saltwater Chumming

Chumming is an important element of catching fish in saltwater, yet this technique varies from area to area and for each species sought. There are literally scores of variations, and the following sampling is representative of the most popular. Chumming in saltwater should be in every angler's arsenal of options; keep in mind that although most saltwater chumming takes place from boats, it may also be practiced from jetties, beaches, bridges, piers, and bulkheads.

Because saltwater is affected by tides and current (plus wind), chum is dispersed according to the movement of water. It may be dispensed by hand or from some type of container that is lowered into the water, or via a combination of both approaches, plus some innovative spot methods (like sand balls mixed with chum, which disperse as they lower). Putting chum into some type of dispenser is common.

Devices used to contain various types of chum include a pot, bucket, mesh bag, wire basket, plastic crate, and an assortment of similar commercial

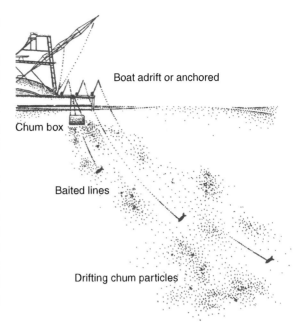

Boat adrift or anchored

Chum box

Baited lines

Drifting chum particles

This is a typical ocean chumming scene; chum particles drift with the current, and hooked bait is allowed to drift at different levels amid the chum.

or homemade devices. The overall size of these, and the size of holes or mesh, will vary with the bait used. There are also commercially available chum logs. Most objects are hung from a transom cleat and lie in the surface of the water aft of the boat. Some chum baskets or cages may be lowered to various depths, or near to the bottom, with a heavy weight. Long-distance placement of chum is made via quick-release arrangements.

In chumming, the tide or current moves the pieces or particles away from the place where they are dispensed, and they form an underwater trail called a chum line. A visible surface indication of the presence and movement of the chum is called a slick. This is the oily surface of the water above a chum line, and it is also carried away from the boat and may or may not extend as far back as the underwater trail of chum. Usually the chum particles sink deeper as they are carried away from the initial drop point, and the slick portion of surface water dissipates at some distance from the boat.

Where the current is substantial, the chum line may extend a long distance, and particles may not sink very deep. In slack water, the chum line has much less distant movement and more vertical sinking. Many saltwater gamefish move in and out of areas or move widely in search of food, so if they are present in the area you chum, they will eventually detect the chum line. However, in some locations, particularly in shallow backwaters and marshes, and on reefs, the fish are more resident and wander less, and may require more concentrated chum rather than a long trail.

When chumming, you want to attract the fish you're seeking so that they will respond to a baited hook or to an artificial lure that is fished in the chum line or in the area being baited. However, if you chum too heavily, the fish often settle well back in the slick, gorging on the chum. On the other hand, if you chum too sparingly or fail to maintain a consistent flow of chum, the fish may show little interest and often move off. You have to maintain the right balance.

A good rule of thumb is to drop pieces of chum into the water at regular intervals. When fishing with a group of anglers, and especially aboard a boat, one person should be assigned the responsibility of maintaining the chum line, because in the excitement of catching fish the chumming is often forgotten, only to be remembered too late, after the fish have moved out of the area.

Offshore, Atlantic Canyons

Anglers seeking bigeye tuna, yellowfin tuna, and albacore in the offshore canyons and shelf areas of the eastern Atlantic often use a combination of chunks of fish and ground fish with excellent results. Boats either are anchored or drift along with the wind or current, usually along the edges of the dropoff, where an upwelling of currents causes baitfish to congregate and the larger gamefish to feed.

Forage species such as butterfish, mackerel, and herring are cut into pieces, usually about the size of your index finger. Five or six pieces from a butterfish, and eight or ten from a mackerel or herring, is about right. This is usually done before leaving for the fishing grounds to save the chore of doing it on the water. The chummer tosses three or four chunks into the water and watches as they drift away. When the chum is 30 to 40 feet from the boat, more pieces are tossed over.

After a dozen or more chunks have been deposited into the sea, a ladle full of "soup," which is a mixture of ground menhaden, mackerel, or herring and equal parts seawater, is deposited into the ocean. This mixture disperses in a cloud and

is carried along with the current. As fish detect the scent of the soup drifting along, they move toward its source, picking up tiny pieces of the ground fish and also the chunks. It's not unusual to attract a school of tuna and see the fish moving ever closer to the boat, as the fish vie for the offering drifting along.

Anglers fish with 4/0 through 7/0 O'Shaughnessy, beak, or circle hooks tied directly to a 5- to 6-foot-long fluorocarbon leader. A half or a whole butterfish is usually used, as are live squid, mackerel, spot, and porgy. The hooked bait should drift back with the chum unimpeded until it is 100 or more feet from the boat. Then reel in and repeat the procedure. As a rule, the angler who works at keeping the bait moving along with the chum will catch far more fish than the angler who locks the reel in gear and keeps it in one position. If you let the line hang in a fixed position, the current pushing against the bait will often push it toward the surface and spin it in a manner that is not as attractive to the fish as a drifting bait.

Some offshore anglers rely especially heavily on chunks of bait, which has come to be called chunking. This term refers to the use of pieces of fish meat, often in 2- to 3-inch cubes, especially for chumming yellowfin and bluefin tuna. The procedure is essentially the same as that described earlier, although heavy pieces sink deeper and faster than smaller chum and particles, so you have to be constantly attentive to the location and condition of your hooked chunk.

Inshore, Eastern U.S.

Chumming for inshore species, such as bluefish, striped bass, bonito, school bluefin tuna, Spanish mackerel, king mackerel, and little tunny, is similar to offshore chumming, although with lighter tackle and smaller chunks of chum. Small mullet, spearing, sand eels, and killies are all effective in a chum line, and chunks or strips of butterfish, mackerel, croaker, bluefish, spot, and menhaden are popularly used.

Menhaden is the preferred chum substance; it is commonly purchased in frozen blocks by private and charter boaters. A few operators, including some party boats, have large electrical grinders to mince fresh menhaden onboard—an operation that is noisy and messy. Some inshore menhaden chummers will ladle out chum; others like to put

A Chesapeake Bay rockfish angler, fishing near Kent Island, Maryland, uses a meat grinder to mash and periodically dispense bait, as well as a cutting board to produce chunks of menhaden.

the frozen chum in a covered plastic 5-gallon bucket that has been riddled with 1-inch holes, hanging it alongside the boat with a rope that has been run through a hole in the side and the top. Fifty pounds of chum is recommended for a full day of fishing, especially if the water is warm and the currents swift.

Arrive at your designated fishing spot before the top or bottom of the tide, and allow some time to anchor and get the chum line going. Use the frozen material for chumming, but bait up with fresh fish pieces. Fresh bait that has not been previously frozen works best and does not become as mushy on the hook. Although at times any piece of bait works well, strips may be more effective in moderate current and chunks in heavier current.

Inshore/Offshore, Western U.S

Anglers on the West Coast of the United States enjoy exciting chumming for a wide variety of species when they're able to obtain live anchovies as chum. Southern California boats that fish the inshore kelp beds, along with long-range boats that head far to sea for albacore and those who head off the Baja Peninsula for yellowfin tuna, rely on anchovies to bring gamefish within range.

These boats take on dipnets, popularly called "scoops," full of anchovies from bait barges anchored in coastal harbors. The anchovies are kept in livewells with circulating seawater to keep

them in perfect condition until the fishing grounds are reached.

When inshore fishing at kelp beds, boats anchor just off from the kelp, which is where baitfish seek sanctuary and gamefish roam nearby, occasionally making sorties into the kelp for a meal. It takes patience and skill to coax fish from the kelp. In brief, you remove several anchovies from the livewell with a dipnet and toss them into the air so they land midway between the boat and the kelp. The excited anchovies either seek the sanctuary of the kelp or hurriedly swim back to the boat to seek shelter beneath its stern. Gradually the anchovies get the gamefish excited, and it's not unusual to have yellowtail, white seabass, bonito, barracuda, and kelp bass vying for them.

Small No. 3 or 4 O'Shaughnessy, beak, or claw style hooks, tied directly to the end of the line, are hooked to the bait, which is only 3 to 5 inches long, and are then cast away from the boat and live-lined. An active anchovy will often swim about excitedly, and when gamefish are plentiful, the strikes come fast and furious. Always keep your rod tip pointed in the direction the line is moving; when a fish picks up the bait and moves off, lock your reel in gear and lift back smartly to set the hook.

Offshore anglers also chum with anchovies as well as with several small species of mackerel and jacks. Long-range boats usually sail with a supply of chum in the tanks but often stop on productive banks where anglers bring fish onboard to fill the live tanks with a supply of fish that can be used as live or dead chum.

In some cases, boats anchor over productive banks and kelp beds. Albacore anglers often troll until either albacore or bluefin tuna strike the trolled lures; while the trolled fish are being fought, the chumming begins and holds what is usually a school of albacore at the boat. The techniques used with other types of chumming are essentially the same, although tackle and hook size vary with the species sought.

Chunk bait has become a more popular chum when live anchovies are not available. Some of the largest yellowfin tuna are now caught by chunking, using pieces of mackerel, rainbow runners, jacks, or other common fish, burying the hook inside the pieces so that the point is buried and does not penetrate the skin. The most common hooks for this are 8/0 and 9/0 sizes, usually connected to a

150- to 200-pound-strength fluorocarbon leader, which in turn is connected to the fishing line via a 4/0 to 6/0 black barrel swivel.

Hooked chunks are changed frequently and observed closely as they drift with unhooked bait. Strong current and no current require a little more attention and finessing, the former keeping the bait up and the latter permitting it to sink. When chunks sink for two minutes, they should be retrieved and redropped.

More on Chumming with Live Fish

There is a lot of merit to chumming with live fish as bait, although this is usually a specialized affair with several requirements: a means to store and keep the fish lively, the ability to obtain or find copious amounts of the proper baitfish, the ability to catch large numbers of live baitfish in a short time period, and sometimes gamefish that are concentrated or visible. Some species are caught by using a cast net, a method that takes energy and effort, and is dependent on finding ample schools of baitfish, usually in fairly shallow water.

In South Florida, for example, charter boat captains developed a technique of using live pilchards for offshore fishing, especially dolphin and sailfish. They start by finding schools of pilchards via sonar in inshore environs, toss softball-size balls of sand into the water to attract the pilchards, then capture them with a large cast net. Offshore, they look for cruising sailfish or dolphin, pitch live pilchards individually in the vicinity of the dolphin or sailfish, then cast out a hooked live pilchard.

This live-bait chumming is very exciting; it may also be used to draw gamefish close enough

A chum depth charge can be made by placing one paper bag inside another and then layering the interior with sand on the bottom, pieces of bait on top of the sand, and rolled oats on top of the bait pieces. Twist the bag closed.

to the boat to take a cast offering of an artificial lure, usually a fly. It is a technique that should work well for some other species, inshore as well as offshore, although its success is hindered by a frequent inability to find ample live baitfish.

Other Chumming Techniques

In protected bays, rivers, and estuaries, anglers often chum with grass shrimp and pieces of crab. The preferred method of fishing is to anchor along the edge of a channel where gamefish move with the tide as they search for a meal. The same chum can be used when fishing from piers, bulkheads, docks, and bridges, where it is important to position yourself so you can dispense the chum and have it carried away by the current, along with your baited rig.

Bottom-feeding fish also respond to a chum line if you get and keep the chum on the bottom. You can accomplish this with a chum pot filled with frozen ground chum that is eased to the bottom with a strong line. As the chum thaws, it oozes from the pot and is carried along the bottom, and the fish move toward the source of the free meal. Ground menhaden, mussels, clams, conch, grass shrimp, and sea worms are popular in chum pots. Occasionally it pays to give the cord holding the chum pot a good yank, especially if there is little current around slack tide; this will send a cloud of chum streaming from the pot.

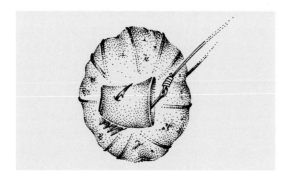

A chum ball consists of ground chum, rolled oats, and beach sand, with a baited hook placed inside; a leader is wrapped around the ball to hold it together while it settles to the bottom.

Chumming is also very effective for reef- and wreck-dwelling fish, but requires careful anchoring and boat positioning, and occasional repositioning depending on the flow of the current. Usually, frozen ground chum is placed in a mesh bag and hung over the side to ooze away. At the same time, large balls of sand and chum are dropped overboard, falling to the bottom and crumbling. In place of or in addition to these, small brown paper bags filled with sand and larger chunks of chum and rolled oats are dropped overboard to drift to the bottom and disperse, attracting fish from the reef to a point beneath the boat.

It is worth noting that shrimp trawling is a major business in some areas, and that anchored shrimp trawlers dispense large quantities of refuse, which is referred to as trash or bycatch. The trash consists of literally dozens of species of small fish, squid, crabs, and crushed or broken shrimp. When dropped into the sea, this smorgasbord sometimes attracts hordes of gamefish.

Sometimes anglers may get permission to tie up to the stern of the shrimper and take advantage of the chum slick that is established as the trash is shoveled over. Others often pull up to a shrimper and for a few dollars or some horse trading take aboard a couple of containers filled with trash. Some shrimpers retain the trash and sell it when they return to port. Shrimp trash can be used in both offshore and inshore waters for a variety of species.

Freshwater Chumming

Chumming in freshwater is not as widely practiced for a range of species as it is in saltwater, although it is a major component of fishing for carp, somewhat of a component for catfish and bullhead fishing, and of minor practice for other species, including panfish and trout. In Europe, however, it is a major component of fishing.

In North America, a general abundance of gamefish and their relative availability make it theoretically less necessary to "resort" to the use of feeding or chumming. To some extent, a low reliance on chumming in North America is due to the nature of the fish species or the aquatic conditions; sight-feeding, cover-relating fish like bass and pike, for example, would seem a less desirable target for chumming, although this is not an absolute. To some extent it is also due to attitudes; some freshwater anglers, for example, believe that chumming is either undignified or unfair. The low use of chumming is also due to laws; chumming is illegal in some places in North America.

Freshwater chumming is much different than saltwater chumming. There are few opportunities to obtain, by purchase or catch, large amounts of fish to use as ground-up chum, so chum availability is an inhibiting factor in many places. However, some rivers and large reservoirs support big populations of alewives, gizzard and threadfin shad, smelt, or herring, which conceivably could be used for chum if they could legally be obtained and retained in necessary quantities. Therefore, partially by default, and partially owing to the nature of some of the species that are most susceptible to chumming, most freshwater chumming is done with foods that are not naturally found in the water, or with commercially prepared attractants.

As with saltwater chumming, all the elements of freshwater chumming are mastered only after much experience; the angler must know a great deal about the targeted fish, including where it lives throughout the year and its feeding habits. Also like saltwater chumming, freshwater chumming aims to keep fish in the area you're fishing, or attract them to it, and then get them to inhale a hooked bait. After you start catching fish, you have to keep them interested; be careful not to underfeed or, worse, overfeed the fish in that area.

After much experience, you will develop an instinct for knowing how much and when to feed; the best advice in this respect is to chum little and often. By chumming modestly at the start, you will not overfeed; the worst thing that can happen when you are chumming is to see your chances ruined by a nearby angler who throws in a lot of chum (like a full can of corn). An abundance of chum discourages the fish from picking up your baited hook.

How you chum depends on whether the fish you seek are sight feeders or smell and/or touch feeders. Sight feeders include such species as bluegill, crappie, perch, bass, trout, and walleye. Smell and/or touch feeders include catfish, carp, drum, and suckers.

Chumming also varies by the type of waterway. Stillwaters and flowing waters are very different environments, and each affects the behavior of fish differently. Flowing-water fish, for example, can be drawn upstream hundreds of yards by scent, or by following particles upstream to where they are being introduced. Even stillwaters (especially larger bodies of water) have gentle current that moves in the opposite direction of any prevailing wind; it is possible that targeted fish could be above, below, or ahead of any chum drift you have created. Furthermore, targeted fish can literally be yards away from your scent trail, so they have no way of sensing that your bait is so close to them, unless they feel (via their lateral line) or hear other fish activity near them, or if the wind changes.

Stillwater Chumming

There are two methods of stillwater chumming: loose feeding and throwing in balls of chum, which is called balling.

Loose feeding is simple and inexpensive. Corn, chopped worms, or maggots are thrown into the water by hand for close fishing. For chumming at greater distances, anglers use a flat mesh pouch catapult (a special type of slingshot) to get loose feed 30 to 40 yards away, depending on the wind.

Loose feeding is highly effective because the idea is to attract fish with the same chumming bait that is used on the hook. Loose feeding of maggots is generally the best technique for bluegills, crappie, perch, catfish, carp, and shiners.

The balling method of chumming uses ground dried breadcrumbs, which have been carefully blended with water into a ball. The ball does not contain chunks of chum but is fine and unclogged. The best way to mix this chum is in a large bucket or bowl so that any chunks that form can be broken up and mixed in; the end result should be an evenly mixed, damp, fluffy bowl of breadcrumbs.

The basic chum mixture is rolled into a ball in two ways. One is by gently squeezing a ball of chum with one hand so that it just holds together; when this ball is lobbed gently into stillwater, it will explode and drift downward through the water in a cloud. This cloud is extremely attractive to many species of very small fish. In turn, the activity created by the small fish will attract larger species, such as bluegill, crappie, and others, and begin a literal chain reaction of feeding excitement. Since there is nothing of any substance to fill up the larger fish, they will be excited and looking for food, so a hookbait that is cast into the cloud produces action.

Balls of this chum can be thrown even farther than is possible using loose feeding and a catapult. Balls can be thrown as far as the angler can reach; if greater distance is needed, special catapults with cup pouches can fire chum up to 80 yards away.

The other way to feed the same stillwater mix of breadcrumbs is to squeeze it into a hard ball. When pitched into the water, the hard ball goes directly to the bottom with very little of it breaking off. Corn, chopped worms or minnows, maggots, or liver can be added to the hard ball of chum and will be carried directly to the bottom. This is a good idea for targeting such species as catfish, carp, buffalo, and drum.

Flowing-Water Chumming

In flowing water, a heavier mix of chum is necessary to get to the bottom quicker. This can be achieved by adding cornmeal and breadcrumbs that are much larger and coarser than stillwater cloud chum.

Mixing chum for flowing water takes more time than it does for stillwater. You must slightly overwet the chum mixture so it is very damp, but it must not clog up. The wet and mixed chum must be left for at least 30 minutes so that all the moisture is absorbed and it is very sticky. When you're ready to make a ball, mix in your chosen hookbait; the addition should never be more than 40 percent of the entire ball, or the ball will break up when it is thrown or when it hits the

A river angler fishing from the bank prepares chum to dispense in the water in front of him.

water. Squeeze the chum into a hard ball, and throw it a couple of yards upstream so it lands directly in front of you on the bottom.

Hundreds of baits and chums are successful for catching catfish and carp. A well-known favorite is Wheaties cereal soaked in strawberry soda; it makes a fantastic dough bait for carp and buffalo. There are dozens of effective stinkbaits that catch catfish, but a favorite when the fishing is really tough because of weather extremes is thin slivers of half-frozen liver; the chum here is the blood that leaches out and is carried downstream to those sensitive barbels of the catfish.

The major ingredients for most commercial chums and mixes made by professional competition anglers are breadcrumbs, cornmeal, and peanuts, although you can experiment with every other type of grain and seed to find a personal favorite. However, most angling activities only require different textures of breadcrumbs and cornmeal. In places having a lot of stocked fish (usually trout), ground-up fish pellets will be a very good attractant, because the fish will know the smell.

Only with experience will you learn how to correctly blend, wet, squeeze, and feed the chum in a precise spot.

26

Drift Fishing

Drift fishing from a boat appears to be about as lazy a fishing method as you can find, but there is more to it than meets the eye. In fact, drifting with bait or lures is sometimes more advantageous than moving under electric or outboard motor power; for example, when the fish appear to be spooked by motor noise, drift fishing is actually a smart strategy.

Drift fishing can be either haphazard or calculated. The haphazard drifters, who pay little regard to how deep they are fishing, where they are headed, and what they are using, are not likely to be as effective as those drifters who use carefully selected tackle and make calculated approaches that take into account careful boat positioning.

One of the keys to success is setting up your boat for it. Because of its design, the weight inside, the hull configuration, and a variety of factors, every boat has a tendency to move off a straight line even though wind direction would seem to dictate a certain path as long as you start at the right spot. To determine how your boat drifts, do it in a controlled situation with the outboard motor in the water and aligned straight with the keel. To counter the tendency to move off a straight line, turn the motor in the direction that the boat wants to head; the motor will act like a rudder and keep the boat in a proper attitude with the wind.

Freshwater

Drifting in freshwater occurs in both lakes and rivers. Certain factors affect success and make drifting less likely to be an aimless hit-or-miss activity.

When drift fishing with bait, for example, pay attention to the type of bait rig that you use and to the weight or sinker. Bank, dipsey, pencil lead, and split shot sinkers are commonly used in bait drifting. Split shot are often used for suspending bait at specific depths; the others are essentially used for keeping contact with the bottom and are good in deep water and cast well. Split shot are preferred for light tackle. Dipsey sinkers are also used with light to medium tackle and where bait is suspended off the bottom above the sinker.

A very popular freshwater baitfishing rig, used for drifting as well as for trolling, is a spinner rig, which features a small spinner ahead of a worm, with a fixed sinker or sliding sinker above it. A spinner rig is especially useful for perch, walleye, and bass. Another popular bottom-drifting bait rig features a three-way swivel with one lead going to a sinker and the other to a bait hook.

Bass anglers will find that a Carolina rig is a very good worm rig for bottom drifting. You need the right size weight to keep the worm down, of course, which will depend on wind and depth.

Some anglers who cast lures use a wind-aided drift to their advantage, in combination with occasional electric motor use, to help maintain a desired position. Be sure to cast ahead of the boat to cover the area you are approaching, especially when drifting over weeds. However, a fast wind-aided drift does not allow for proper retrieval of some lures that are cast downwind and retrieved upwind, and some strikes are missed because of decreased sensitivity. When jigging and worm fishing, you are better off fishing on the upwind side of the boat, letting the lures cover ground at the same pace as the boat.

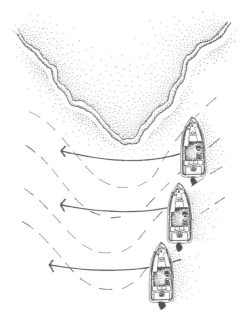

This fishing boat is using the wind to drift across an extended underwater point (note angle of motor to aid drift); several drifts are made to cover the water from shallow to deep.

A common bait rig for drift fishing uses a sinker on one lead and a bait hook on another.

If the wind is pushing you at such a clip that you cannot maintain contact with the bottom, you may need to use a heavier weight, or periodically reel in and lower your offering right beside the boat until it hits bottom. Another option is to cast it to the side and slightly ahead of the boat; this action gives the lure (or bait) the opportunity to reach the bottom by the time the boat is directly overhead, increasing the effective time that it stays in the likely area before swinging upward and having to be retrieved.

To properly drift over a particular stretch of water, you must plan the approach properly, taking wind and current into consideration. Preferably the boat is broadside to the wind, but this is not possible with some boats, although on smaller craft the use of a sea anchor can assure this. Note where you start a drift and have success so that you can return and redrift over productive stretches; also drift to the sides in order to cover all of a particular area. The longer you drift and the more the wind shifts, the harder it will be, especially in open-water environs, to return to the proper place or to achieve the desirable drift.

When making a long drift, you'll usually find that fish are caught sporadically rather than in one tight spot, but this may depend upon the species. Repeat this drift and focus on adjacent waters for similar drifts. Although the places to drift vary with species pursued, points are a universal possibility. Submerged weeds are good drifting locations for bass and pike, provided the weeds have enough depth and density.

One of the benefits of drifting, especially in shallow water and near shore, is that you are not creating noise, so try to use an electric motor, if you have one, sparingly to control drift or maintain position.

When drift fishing in a river, boaters use electric motors, outboard motors, or oars to effect a downstream boat movement at a pace much slower than the speed of the current. The slowed movement allows them to cast lures and baits and work them better or longer (or present them more often) in likely places. This drifting method is especially effective for salmon, steelhead, trout, bass, and walleye.

The most critical aspect of river drift fishing is proper bait or lure presentation through boat control. Slipping, which is a form of backtrolling, is the best way to achieve success in river drift fishing. It entails moving slowly backward downstream while in complete control of your craft, in such a way that you and the passengers can fish at ease. To do this, point the bow of your boat upstream and accelerate the outboard motor in forward gear. With the bow placed into the current, throttle down the motor to a point where your boat has begun to move backward downstream. The thrust of the motor is not enough to keep you going forward, and your boat slowly drifts backward, stern first. The boat moves very slowly, sometimes almost imperceptibly, and you have precise control over your position and rate of descent.

With the motor at a steady forward thrust, the boat backs downstream with ease as you cast and retrieve. Cast upstream and retrieve slowly downstream. The bow of the boat is always pointed into the current.

A similar outcome can be produced in moderate- to slow-flowing rivers by using an electric motor to position the bow facing into the current and wind, and then by drifting with bait or jigs. Maintaining pace with the current allows for a vertical presentation that aids hooksetting and gives

Controlling the path and speed of a drift, as these walleye anglers are doing, is usually essential to success.

the fish less of a chance to detect the offering. It also permits the use of lighter jigs, which are often more likely to be taken than a heavier product.

Most river anglers who fish from shore are drift fishing. The standard procedure for casting to nearly every river species, regardless of whether you're using lure, fly, or bait, is to cast across and upstream and then allow the offering to drift or swim naturally in the current.

Saltwater

Drift fishing in saltwater takes place in coastal bays, tidal rivers, and the open ocean, with movement caused by tide and wind. Because of tide, these places can be completely devoid of fish or activity at one stage of the tide, yet provide sterling action just hours later. Thus it's important to study each place you plan to fish, and determine how different wind and tide conditions affect the area. Above all, study coastal charts of the area, so you know the bottom conformation.

Canal Drifting

Canals are a favorite drifting spot because they are usually narrow, clearly defined, and rather restricted, with extremely swift currents, especially during moon tides. Their bottoms may be irregular, including flat areas, shallow spots, sandy areas, rocky areas, and deep holes. The water may run swift and silent in some spots or noisily with large waves in others. Each hour presents a different set of circumstances; by carefully studying the conditions, you can quickly adjust to the changing conditions, movements, and feeding habits of the fish, which can include a wide variety of species. Incidentally, many canals are best fished at night because of daytime boat traffic; dusk and daybreak, when the tides are right, are also good.

If the canal has swift current, flounder will bury themselves in the sand bottom sections; as the current slows, they begin to move about searching for food. They are most active from an hour before the change in tide to an hour after and readily take a bait drifted along the bottom. Another place to catch flounder is where the canal meets with a bay. The current carries plenty of food; on the flood tide it flows toward the bay, and fishing is productive where the waterway widens and empties into the bay.

If a canal has bulkheads, you may find species like sea bass, blackfish, and porgies close to the bulkheads, feeding on grass shrimp and mussels. Drifting a sinker along close to the bottom often results in snagging on debris, especially in the rocky bottom areas, so use a float rig that keeps the hooked bait just off the bottom yet within range of feeding fish. Drift close to the bulkhead, holding your rod tip as close to it as possible.

Some species avoid swift tidal flow and may stack up in deep holes. As the tide slows, usually an hour before, during, and after the change, they fan out searching for food. Live bait is good for these fish and is often very effective when drifting.

Open-Ocean Drifting

Drift fishing on the open expanse of ocean is totally different from that experienced in a confined area. On the surface the water is all the same as far as the eye can see. There is a difference on the bottom, however, because depressions, peaks, ridges, rocks, and reefs contribute to where bait congregates. Where the bait congregates is where you'll find larger game, so it's important to know the bottom conformation and the direction that your boat will drift, whether as a result of wind or tide. Through careful planning, your boat will

drift over the area most likely to be populated by feeding fish.

Sharks are a common drift-fishing catch, and the best way to score with them is while chumming and drifting. Position your drift so that tide or wind carries you across known wrecks, reefs, or irregular bottom conformations where fish known to attract feeding sharks are found. If you're well positioned, the drift can carry you several miles, with the chum leaving a shark-attracting trail behind the boat. It may take minutes or hours, but if you cover the grounds, chum correctly, and have your baits set at various depths, you'll have a great chance to score.

Bottom-feeding fish like snapper and grouper are also a common drift-fishing catch, located over rock and coral bottom. At intermediate depths around reefs and rocks, you may catch dolphin, king mackerel, Spanish mackerel, barracuda, wahoo, and little tunny. This combination is ideally suited to deep jigging from a drifting boat. Favored jigs are leadheads with either bucktail or plastic bodies.

The key to successful deep jigging while drifting is being intimately familiar with the bottom conformation. This can be accomplished by carefully studying charts of the area and then using sonar to view the reef, wreck, or ridge. The sonar lets you determine where the peaks and valleys exist and where the fish are holding. Then it's a matter of determining the direction of drift. If wind is lacking, you'll be moved by the tidal flow; if wind is present, it may overpower you and move you against the current.

Once you've made this determination, move to the high bottom spot and drop a marker buoy, moving farther away from the marker on each succeeding drift. The buoy allows you to bracket the area and also alerts you to avoid drifting from deep water into the peaks of the reef—where the line may snag and where a hooked fish may escape by diving into the coral and breaking off.

The most effective method is to move up to the marker buoy and shut down the motor. Allow the jig to settle all the way to the bottom. As soon as it touches down, lock the reel in gear promptly, lift back smartly with your rod tip, and begin reeling. Grouper and snapper cruising along the bottom often view the plummeting jig and then excitedly charge it as it leaps off the bottom and heads to the surface.

While retrieving, you can jig with your rod tip, smartly lifting it, which causes the jig to dart upward and then falter; keep repeating this until the jig reaches the surface. Many bottom feeders often strike the jig deep; intermediate cruisers will strike at midlevel, sometimes just as you're about to lift the jig from the water.

When you receive a strike, set back firmly and quickly attempt to get a few turns on the reel, lifting back smartly to get the fish away from the sharp coral. If you've positioned the drift properly, the movement of the boat away from the peaks of the reef will help put more distance between the fish and the bottom. In shallow water the positioning of your drift isn't as critical as it is when fishing offshore reefs.

You can catch various flatfish species when drift fishing over a sandy, soft, or mud bottom. When water clarity and temperature are to their liking, they vacate the sand bottom and move about aggressively searching for a meal. As flatfish move about, they may cruise along the perimeter of a rocky bottom, or where wrecks or artificial reefs litter the bottom. They'll often move to a broad expanse of relatively flat bottom, punctuated by a series of hills or lumps that rise to the surface, because forage is most plentiful here.

Open-water drift-fishing opportunities also exist in many bays, rivers, and creeks, where weedbeds can be fished for seatrout. This can be fine light-tackle sport, using a light popping rod or a spinning outfit with 10-pound line. Natural baits and artificials are both effective.

Perhaps the most relaxing tactic is using a cork and shrimp bait combination, which is designed to float a bait just off the bottom or above the weedbeds, or occasionally at intermediate levels.

As such, you must know the prevailing depths over which you'll be drifting.

A popping cork is slipped onto the line and held in position with a stopper that slides into the bottom of the cork. The popping cork is tapered at the bottom end, and is blunt and hollowed out at the other end, which is positioned facing the rod. Thus when you pull back smartly, the cork gurgles and pops. The seatrout is attracted to the area, at which time it observes and takes the bait, which can be any variety of live or dead shrimp, as well as a sandworm, or live spot. Casting and retrieving lures, especially jigs with plastic shrimplike tails, is also a possibility.

Leisurely drifting and chumming on a broad expanse of offshore water may bring great rewards, and there's excitement in not knowing what may strike your offering. With modern electronics you can cruise known haunts of pelagic species. Once a favorable temperature break is located, you'll often see schools of squid, mackerel, herring, and other types of forage. This can be exploited by shutting the motor, drifting, and establishing a chum line to attract the targeted species. You can jig, use live bait, or drift dead bait or strips in the chum.

While you're drifting along, if you stream a bait out 100 feet or more, the current will push it toward the surface; adding a rubber-core sinker to the leader will keep the hooked bait drifting along at the same depth as the chum. Conversely, in minimal current or wind, you may have to add an inflated balloon, cork, or Styrofoam float to the line to suspend the bait at the desired level. Otherwise, it might sink directly to the bottom while the light, partially suspended chum particles drift off at intermediate levels.

27

Trolling

Trolling is a common fishing method in both freshwater and saltwater for a wide range of species. In simplest terms, it is a method of presenting a lure or bait behind a power-driven boat. It is especially popular in wide-open waters for fish that are deep and/or nomadic and where there are few underwater obstructions, and it is an important means of searching conscientiously for concentrations of certain species.

Many anglers troll for some or most of their fish. Trolling is *the* way to catch trout and salmon on lakes and reservoirs; it is *the* method on some muskie waters. It is a valued technique for walleye, an overlooked method for black bass, and an important means of catching striped bass. In saltwater, trolling is a critical method for catching many pelagic species, especially billfish, and important for pursuing many inshore species, including kingfish, bluefish, and various jacks. There is plenty of science and drama involved, whether the quarry is blue marlin, chinook salmon, walleye, or dolphin.

Successful trollers must know exactly where their lures are and how those lures are acting, and they must make a calculated, determined effort to entice a fish. That means being able to do many things well, including rigging lines, reading sonar, setting lures, judging when to change lures or locations, knowing the proper speed at which to fish, and understanding how to manipulate a boat to effect the kind of presentation that attracts fish.

General Methods

Trolling can be broken down into the following basic methods:

1 Fishing an object on an unweighted monofilament, braided, or fly line. This method, known as flatlining, is popular for relatively shallow fishing in freshwater and saltwater because the depth achieved is entirely dependent on the weight or diving ability of the object being trolled. To know how deep you're fishing, you must know the depth that object will attain given boat speed, line size, current, trolling-line length, and so on. To avoid haphazard effort and sporadic success, you must learn to evaluate the depth that the trolled lures or baits actually attain.

High-speed surface flatlining is also practiced in some situations, primarily in saltwater for billfish. Here, lures are trolled quickly on top of the water or through the surface foam.

2 Fishing an object on a weighted line. Fishing an object on a weighted line involves using some type of weight to get a lure or bait deeper than it could be presented unaided. The problem of knowing the actual depth being fished is the same as with unweighted lines.

3 Fishing an object behind a lead core or wire line. Here, the weight of the line causes the object being trolled to sink. The depth of the lure or bait depends on how much line is let out. This can be a more precise method of fishing than flatlining when it is important to achieve a specific depth. To gauge distance, lead-core line is marked by different colors at intervals, and wire line is usually marked with tape by anglers. Although stronger than nylon or braided line, lead-core line is bulkier, and it dampens the fight of a fish. Wire, which has to be used on stout tackle, is subject to kinking, crimping, and spooling difficulties; although it transmits the actions of the fish well to the angler, wire line and the corresponding tackle also blunt the fight.

4 Fishing an object behind a diving planer. A diving planer is a device used on a fishing line for the purpose of getting lures deep without weight or other attachments. Because it pulls so hard when trolled, a diving planer is fished off a very stout rod and is used with fairly heavy line. Diving planers run deep on a relatively short line; the length of line trolled determines how deep the planer will dive. A planer releases when a fish strikes, so you don't have to fight it along with the fish; nevertheless, the planer may impede the fight and activity of the fish, and its size or presence may deter some fish from striking. You have to set the lure no more than 5 feet behind the planer in order to land a fish.

5 Fishing an object behind a releasable cannonball sinker. This is a deep-trolling system traditionally used for Pacific salmon fishing. A large, cannonball-shaped sinker gets the line down deep; the sinker is released and drops to the bottom when a fish strikes. You lose a lot of lead weight in this system, and you need stout, heavy tackle. Also, you don't often know the depth at which you're fishing when you're off the bottom. Present and future restrictions on lead usage and disposal may preclude this approach in some places.

6 Fishing an object behind a downrigger. A downrigger takes the burden of getting a line to a specific depth away from the fishing line. A lure attached to your fishing line is placed in the water and set at the desired distance to run behind your boat. The fishing line is placed in the release attached to the downrigger cable; the release frees the line when a fish strikes, and the angler plays the fish unencumbered. This affords the most controlled depth presentation possible, plus the use of lighter and more sporting tackle. It has relegated wire and lead-core line to minority status among regular and accomplished trollers, except in places where the lake or ocean floor is full of rocks and radical changes in depth. Downrigger trolling originated on the Great Lakes for trout and salmon fishing; it spread inland for muskies, stripers, and walleye, then to saltwater for inshore and offshore fishing.

Speed Considerations

Routinely successful trollers have a special understanding of the behavior of the fish they seek; of the size, color, and style of lure that appeals to those fish under various conditions; and of boat maneuvering techniques for proper presentation. They also have a keen awareness of how speed relates to these other elements.

The better guides and charter boat captains have a sixth sense about speed; they intuitively know if they are at the right speed, or they rely on an instrument to gauge it. Many anglers, however, fail to recognize that speed is an integral aspect of trolling and that they must be attentive to it. No matter what kind of fish you troll for, or what tackle and type of boat you use, you'll get more out of your lures or bait by paying close attention to the speed at which they are working.

One of the greatest mistakes made by trollers is to fish at the same boat speed when heading into the wind as when moving with the wind. On an otherwise still body of water, you will go faster with the wind than against it, assuming you never reposition the throttle. The same is true of current.

Boat speed, however, must be compatible with the lures fished. Trolling lures are designed to be fished within a certain range of speeds; there is a particular speed at which each lure exhibits its maximum action. Some lures work tolerably at slow or fast speeds, some can sustain action in a wide range of speeds, and others have a narrow range of workability.

Plugs that don't wobble, don't have a natural swimming action, don't track true, or that run on their sides, roll, or skip out of the water either need to be tuned to work properly or are being run too slow or too fast. Spoons that lie flat as they're trolled, have a lazy wobble, hang more vertically than horizontally, or spin furiously aren't working right. You may find that a spoon will swim perfectly at a certain boat speed, whereas a plug will hardly wobble at the same speed. The two should not be fished together.

Trollers should check the swimming action of every lure before it is put into the water, even a lure that they have recently fished successfully. Put the lure in the water, point the rod tip at the water or lower it into the water with the lure several feet behind the tip, and watch the lure swim at the boat's current speed. You can alter boat speed to get the lure to run well, but this might adversely affect the action of other lures that you already have out.

If you do a lot of trolling, it may be helpful to devise your own lure speed chart. Use a tachometer, an electronic speedometer, an incremental indicator, or whatever reference device you have. Spend the time to run your different lures in the water beside the boat to determine their ideal speed, and observe the range of speed they

will tolerate. That information will be valuable, especially when you want to mix lures or change boat speed.

Knowing the range of speed your lures will tolerate is very helpful when you want to find out which lure speed is preferred by fish on a given day. It is no accident that many fish are caught when boaters speed up or slow down and when they make turns. On a turn, the lure on the outside of the turn speeds up and the lure on the inside slows down, unless the turn is very long and gradual. These changes in lure behavior often trigger strikes and may indicate that your speed was previously incorrect for the lure to be successful or that you needed a change in speed to trigger a strike from a curious fish. Making frequent alterations in speed, either by decreasing or advancing the throttle or by turning, is a valuable trolling tactic—but you'll need to know whether your lures will work properly at the different speeds.

Effective trolling speed varies according to species and season. Few anglers have the problem of not being able to troll fast enough (except rowers and electric-motor trollers headed into a wind), but some encounter situations when they cannot troll slowly enough. Some boats simply cannot troll slowly enough even at the lowest throttle setting, particularly if they're headed downwind. To slow down, consider using a low-horsepower auxiliary motor if you have a big boat, or a trolling plate, which baffles the prop thrust and stymies forward propulsion, or a sea anchor, which is a bag that is dragged alongside or behind the boat.

To determine boat speed, you need some reference point. A tachometer shows engine revolutions per minute (rpm). Although rpm is not a perfect gauge of boat speed, you can use it to estimate speed when conditions are relatively calm. Stick with a certain setting if you're catching fish. You have to alter rpms, however, when wind, waves, or current impedes your forward movement.

Small-boat trollers, including those with tiller steering, may not have a tachometer, so they have to guess at relative speeds or use some type of measuring device. Some boaters fashion a speed indicator by attaching one end of a 3-foot wire or heavy monofilament leader to a l-pound lead weight and the other end to an arrowlike indicator, which pivots along a plate that has incremental measuring units marked on it. The weight is dropped in the water, and the arrow points to a spot on the plate; the arrow's position changes as boat speed is altered. Commercially made speed indicators work similarly.

The units of measurement on these devices do not correlate to actual speed in miles per hour or knots, but simply to relative speed. When you put a lure in the water and get it to work properly, note the position of the arrow and run the boat at a speed that keeps it there.

Precise indications of knots or miles per hour are obtained by using certain electronic instruments. These are connected to paddlewheels mounted on the transom; the paddle spins as the boat moves, relaying speed on a digital display. These units may read differently from one another, but they can be calibrated. Once you get accustomed to a particular unit, you'll learn to correlate the information it reveals to fishing conditions.

The best electronic device for calculating boat speed, and one with exceptional reliability and accuracy, is a GPS. This device calculates distance moved over time, is incorporated into many sonar units, and should be set to operate in the fastest update mode.

Most speedometers measure boat and lure speed at or near the surface. In many trolling situations, this speed will be the same, or nearly the same, as the speed of the lure at the level you are trolling. There are times, however, when surface speed has no relation to lure speed. Rivers, tidal creeks, the open ocean, and even some big lakes have deep current, which affects lure or bait presentation.

Deep current is usually so subtle that a visual inspection of the surface and measurements of speed at that level give no indication of it. In some places, there is such a strong current at 50 feet or deeper that it is detectable by watching the action of downrigger weights and cables: With the boat at a slow speed heading into the current, the weights and cables sway back; going with the current, the weights and cables hang nearly vertically.

Below-surface or deep-water currents affect the speed and action of trolling lures. It is possible for a boat to be moving at 2 mph while the lure is acting as if it were running faster. If you're flatlining under such circumstances, you may be able to detect the influence of current by watching your lines and rod tips, but most of the time this will not be an indicator. You can determine the presence of strong current by watching a downrigger cable, but even then you won't know how it is influencing your lures.

Electronic speed indicators can relay the speed of your lure or downrigger via sensors that attach to the downrigger cable above the weight and instantly transmit that speed to a readout. They also can indicate temperature at the depth of the sensor and at the water surface.

Flatlining

Trolling a lure or bait on an unweighted fishing line is known as flatlining. This is a popular technique for angling in relatively shallow water (1 to 25 feet), because the depth achieved is primarily dependent on the weight or diving ability of the object being trolled. Flatlines are used in freshwater and saltwater angling for a variety of species, and often in conjunction with planer boards or sideplaners.

Running a flatline is the simplest kind of trolling. Flatlines are set straight out behind the boat; there are no heavy sinkers, downrigger weights, diving planers, or other devices that influence the depth attained by the lure. Flatlines are sometimes referred to as high lines, usually when trolled in conjunction with some type of deep-diving lure. Anyone with a rod, reel, line, and lure can run a flatline.

The keys to flatline trolling productivity are the length of line and how you maneuver the boat to position the lures or bait. Generally, in freshwater the clearer the water, the shallower the fish, the spookier the fish, and the more boat activity there is, the longer the line you need. Long lines are particularly important in inland, clear-water trout and salmon

Flatline trolling for muskellunge on the French River, Ontario.

fishing, where it is not uncommon to troll lures 200 to 300 feet behind the boat. Long lines have also become more common in Great Lakes walleye trolling because of increasing water clarity.

Key elements of trolling success include altering the lure's path regularly by turning, by steering in an S-shaped pattern or other irregular way, or by altering the speed of the boat. These changes enhance presentation by affecting the speed and action of the lure and making it appear less "mechanical."

In making a flatline trolling presentation, you must consider where the fish are and how to get your lures close without alarming them. Fish in shallow water near shore, or close to the surface in open water, characteristically move out of the boat's path because they are especially wary.

After the boat has passed, the fish may continue to swim away, they may stay where they are once they have moved, or they may return to their original location. If your lure is trailing directly behind a straight-moving boat, the fish in the first two instances may never see your lure. If your line is too short, fish in the third instance may not see it if they are slow to return to their position, or they may see it but associate it with the boat. This illustrates why a lure should be fished on a long line for some types of fish and how proper boat maneuvering can bring lures into the range of fish that may not have been in the boat's path or that may have moved out of it.

A lot of shallow-holding fish can be caught by trolling. Correct line placement, lure presentation, and boat control are critical. The true test of shallow flatline trolling is making presentations in tight areas. Near shore, around reefs or shoals or islands, along grass lines and weed edges, and so forth, are hard places to troll effectively because maneuverability is limited. Thus you need to sweep in and out from shore and plan strategic approaches to points, sandbars, islands, shoals, channels, and the like. You may have to troll by these structures more than once and from different directions to cover the location effectively.

Flatline trolling is not just for shallow-water fishing, however; many anglers flatline both large and small deep-running plugs. When fishing deep water, though, you must know how deep your lures dive with various lengths and strengths of line, and you must pay attention to the depth beneath you and to the lures behind you while trolling. This applies equally to trolling weighted lures and medium- or deep-diving plugs.

When flatlining, either place lures or bait on a direct path behind the boat or place them to the side of the boat via sideplaners or outriggers. Those that are set off to the side are connected via releases to the line that is towing the sideplaner or extended along the outrigger. Those that are run directly behind the boat are often not placed in any release, so the line extends directly from the rod tip to the trailing lure or bait. For some

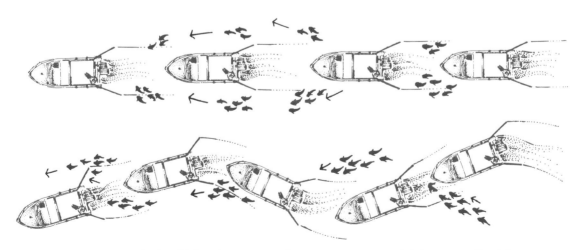

When using a long line (200 to 300 feet) in flatline trolling, you may intercept fish that move off and then return after the boat has passed by (top, right to left). It is often more productive to vary your course by making moderate or exaggerated S-turns, which allow lures to pass fish you might have missed otherwise (bottom, right to left).

situations, this latter method may be adequate; adjusting the position of the rod is important for avoiding tangles or getting lures deeper in the water. Tangles are more likely when the line rides high and when it is windy.

The higher the rod tip, the more the lure or bait tends to ride toward the surface; to get it deeper, position the rod tip closer to the water by angling it to the side of the gunwales. To get the lines lower or to aid in setting the hook upon a strike, you can also use a release clip that is attached to a low position on the transom of the boat.

Special Techniques

Trolling with Sideplaners

Trolling strategies and boat maneuvering techniques when using sideplaner boards are similar to those used for flatlining. When you turn, however, the outside board increases its speed and the inside one slows or stalls. Because the fishing lines are well separated, there is less chance of tangling when you turn, particularly if all the lines are nearly the same distance behind the boat, or if the inside lines are not as far back as the outside lines.

Be careful not to turn so sharply that the inside board stops dead in the water and the lures attached to it don't move; if you're in shallow water and using a sinking plug or a spoon, the motionless lure can settle to the bottom and hang up. The release on the tow line can also get tangled when the board picks up speed. Furthermore, many fish strike a lure on a turn. If your lure is floating upward or fluttering down and a fish strikes it, there may be no tension on either the fishing line or a tow rope line, meaning that the release cannot be snapped or the hook set, and you could potentially lose a fish. If you must make a sharp turn, be sure to keep the inside board moving slightly, which keeps tension on the line.

When fishing multiple lines off large sideplaner boards, you must pay close attention to how you have these spread apart on the tow rope line, and also that you have the setback distances staggered to avoid tangling and ease fish playing. This becomes more complicated when you use lures that dive to different depths.

Those who find sideplaner boards too much trouble simply run flatlines. But when it is necessary

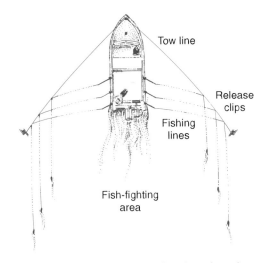

You may not fish this many lines, but this is how they would be arranged with sideplaners. Note that the setback distance is staggered on both sides. When a fish takes any lure, it is played in the middle ground behind the boat, and the other lines are moved outward along the tow line.

to get your lures away from the boat, when you want to cover a wide spread of water with each passage of your boat, or when you troll some hard-to-reach places, sideplaner boards will put your trolling lures over a lot of fish that you couldn't reach otherwise.

Trolling with Diving Planers

The key to fishing with diving planers is to make sure that they get to the right depth. To determine the depth that a diver will run, consult the chart supplied by the manufacturer. Because diving planers run deep and at sharp angles, you cannot estimate the amount of line let out; you must use the pull or pass method of line length determination. You have to let out a certain length of line to get to a specific depth. This varies with different diving planers and with the diameter of line being used.

Many diving planers have an adjustable tension screw release, and you need to set this just right for the strength of line you're using and the depth you'll fish. Diving planers pull awfully hard. If you want to retrieve one and the release won't trip (or, worse, if a small fish is on and the release won't trip), it's hard work bringing it in. There are a few planers that can be reset without retrieving the planer, although you still need to watch line length in order to get it to the desired depth.

A variety of lures can be fished successfully behind a diving planer. Spoons and cut plugs are especially favored because these devices are used primarily for trout and salmon trolling. Minnow plugs of various sizes also get the nod, as do dodger/fly or dodger/squid combinations. Diving plugs aren't usually worked unless they are very shallow runners and can withstand sometimes erratic planer action.

Set lures a short distance back because of the difficulty of netting a fish that is behind a diving planer; 3 to 5 feet is a common setback length. Leader strength should be as strong or stronger than the main fishing line, preferably 17 to 20 pounds if big fish are likely to be encountered, and perhaps 25 to 30 if a dodger is trolled.

The main fishing line should be strong, at least 14 pounds; most anglers use 20. High-tech braided lines can be very effective, but beware of pulling the hooks out of fish since these lines have no stretch and many strikes with diving planers are very sharp. Also, a 20-pound braided line with the same diameter as 8-pound monofilament slices through the water so easily that you have to completely reevaluate diving depth attainment.

Long, stout rods are necessary for diving planer use. On big boats, beefy 9- to 10-footers are used, and on smaller ones, beefy 7- or 8-footers are worked. Because diving planers pull so hard, a good rod holder is necessary, preferably an adjustable one that can take a lot of handle torque and that is easy to get the rod out of. It's better to place diving planer rods on the gunwale, several feet ahead of the transom, and at a low angle.

Mooching

The most common technique for catching salmon in Pacific Northwest coastal waters is "mooching," which involves the use of bait and is practiced in a way that includes a bit of drifting and subtle slow-trolling. A lot of mooching is done in areas where there is current—in rivers as well as in coastal areas where tides and eddies are prominent.

For mooching, anglers use herring, sometimes live, sometimes freshly killed and fished whole or cut, and sometimes fished as thawed/treated/cut bait. Cut bait is preferred in most areas, but the angle of the cut is important because it influences the speed of the roll as the bait is drifted or trolled. An angled cut is made behind the gills by the

pectoral fin; the innards are pulled or routed out. Snelled salmon hooks in two- or three-hook rigs are used. Positioning the hooks is important and varies according to the number of hooks used, the size of the bait, and the speed of the roll desired. In any case, the lead hook is impaled through the head, inserted inside the cavity behind several ribs, and hooked out through the top of the bait.

Tackle consists of a long rod, generally 10½ feet, and a reel capable of holding several hundred yards of line. In some locales, notably British Columbia, anglers are partial to so-called mooching reels, which are 1:1 direct-drive devices akin to large fly reels. Levelwind reels and fly reels are also used. The latter are used with lighter line, shorter rods, and smaller bait when smaller fish, especially coho salmon, are abundant.

Fairly heavy sinkers, from 2 to 6 ounces, are used; these are keel-shaped and fished several feet above the bait. A barrel swivel is used a few feet ahead of the sinker, and the length of the leader from swivel to bait is roughly equal to the length of the rod.

Boat control is very important. Tides, wind, and swells dictate positioning, but the object is to achieve a proper roll of the bait, as well as to keep it in the most advantageous locations. When trolling, or "motor mooching," the boat operator frequently (in some cases constantly) puts the tiller-steered motor in and out of gear, and sometimes may go backward a short distance to maneuver.

Although some strikes are vicious and result in instant hookups, many are soft—the fish may bump the bait—and the angler has to pay out line quickly to give the fish time to get the bait well into its mouth without feeling resistance. Most

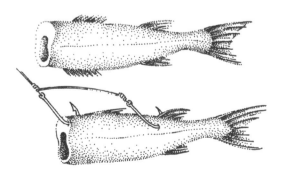

Plug-cut herring, shown here, mooch well if the proper cutting angle is achieved on the bait, and the hooks are correctly placed.

fish are hooked just inside the mouth and can be released without harm if that is desired.

Backtrolling

Backtrolling refers to two freshwater fishing techniques primarily used by walleye, steelhead, and salmon anglers. In both methods, the angler uses a small boat and precise boat-handling methods to manipulate the boat while presenting a lure or bait behind the boat in a systematic way, making a thorough, slow, and careful presentation. A backtroller can maintain position along specific depths, nearly hover over selected spots, and maneuver the boat using wind direction to ensure that the following bait remains in the proper place. This is especially vital when a school of fish is packed into one small spot.

In one form of backtrolling, the angler runs a small boat stern first, and the boat is typically outfitted with transom-mounted splash guards to keep wave action from dumping water into the boat. Using a tiller-steered outboard motor in reverse, or a transom-mounted electric motor (with the lower unit turned so that the stern goes backward when the motor is technically in a forward position), the angler maneuvers the boat very slowly to maintain precise position around points, reefs, weedlines, sandbars, and along dropoffs. This is a technique especially favored by bottom-fishing walleye anglers who slow-troll with worms, leeches, and small minnows.

A more common method of maintaining precise boat control and efficient lure or bait placement—one that is often used in rivers—is achieved by floating, drifting, or trolling slowly backward downcurrent. In some places this is called backtrolling or back bouncing, but in others it is called hotshotting (a derivative of the West Coast technique of using a tight-wiggling, deep-diving trolling plug) for river steelhead and salmon, or pulling plugs. In still other places, it is called slipping. In Europe, it is called harling.

The idea is to have the bow of your boat pointed upstream, using the motor or oars to control the downstream progression of the boat. The boat moves very slowly—it actually drifts—downstream and at times remains stationary in the current (some boaters anchor in the spot where they catch a fish) as lures are fished at varied distances (from a few feet to 75 feet) behind the boat.

The primary benefit of this technique is that the lures essentially dangle in front of fish that the boat has not yet passed over; in upstream trolling, the boat passes over the fish and alerts them to your presence and usually spooks them. Additionally, lures that are backtrolled downstream approach the head of fish instead of coming from behind and swimming past their head. Anglers usually fish backtrolled lures in channels and deep pools where bigger fish lie, and the lures waver in front of the fish much longer than they would if cast and retrieved or if trolled upstream and away from the fish.

Overall, this technique is highly effective in river fishing because the presentation is more natural and the fish are less likely to be disturbed by the lures before they see them.

In most downstream backtrolling, the angler uses diving plugs for fish that take them. Some fish, such as shad, don't take plugs; in that case, the preferred offerings are a shad dart (a type of jig) or tiny spoons fished behind a torpedo-shaped beadchain sinker. Others respond well to bait; winter-run steelhead, for example, are caught with pencil lead–weighted spawn sacks, single-hook salmon eggs, or worms. Many different attractions, including plugs, spoons, spinners, flies, and baits, are used as conditions and location dictate. Plugs are most often flatlined with or without a sinker, and some form of sinker is always used with baits. If a plug is to be effective, it must run straight and dive to the bottom.

When backtrolling, skilled boat maneuvering is a prerequisite to precise lure positioning. The

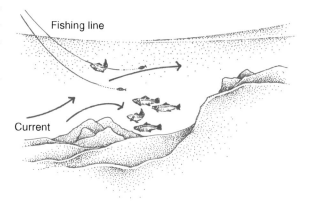

Depicted is the tail of a river pool and two lures that are being backtrolled downstream to approach fish facing upstream.

location and depth of the offering is critical to successful river fishing. Usually the lure must be on or close to the bottom, and only the appropriate amount of weight or lure design will achieve this.

Pools and deep runs are the areas in which backtrolling is most favored. Often the boat must be positioned far enough upriver so the lure works slowly from the head of a pool, or runs down through the tail of it. When backtrolling from side to side across the river, realize that it takes a while for a trailing lure to catch up to the boat's position.

Be sure to troll backward in a slow, controlled fashion. When you stop rowing or throttle back the motor, a floating plug rises, a spinner doesn't spin, weights sink, and so forth. This is caused by the sudden lack of pressure against those objects. Slow, controlled backward movement keeps lures working best and draws more strikes. Boat control is maintained with oars, especially in rafts, jonboats, and river drift boats, or with a small tiller-steered outboard motor. The bow of the boat is headed upstream and always above the area to be fished. It is important to move the boat just fast enough to hold even with the current.

Once in position and keeping pace with the current, if fishing a plug you should freespool or strip out line until the plug is the appropriate distance behind the boat; many plugs are fished 50 feet back. If you use several lures or several plugs, they should all be set out the same distance to avoid tangling and to thoroughly work the area downstream. The lure will dive when line movement stops; the stronger the current and the lighter the line, the deeper the lure will dive, so keep constant pressure on it. After a few minutes, the boat operator can slowly decrease forward momentum so that the boat always runs downstream at a slower pace than the river's natural speed. By drifting slower than the natural current, the slowly moving object is available longer and is more threatening and provocative, or simply an easier meal.

If necessary, in order to get lures into the right spots and to fish a hole without moving the boat over the entire run, anglers use a tactic called back bouncing. To do this, slowly lift the rod tip upward and feel the lure working, then drop it down till it hits bottom. Then either reel up a bit or lift and bounce back the plug or bait with the current flow as you drift. As it is alternately dropped back to hit the bottom and then lifted, the offering is always worked back toward the fish.

Constantly watch the rod tip for a strike and for the proper working action of a lure. Many anglers know how fast to run their boat by watching the action of their rod tips, especially when using hard-pulling plugs. A constantly pulsating rod tip, incidentally, also indicates that a lure is working properly.

28

Downrigger Fishing

Fishing with downriggers is all about making a controlled presentation, whether in deep water, as is usually the case, or in shallow. With downriggers, you can be versatile enough to cover a broad range of trolling situations, including river fishing, drifting, and live-bait fishing. Proper employment of downriggers begins with their installation on a boat.

Downriggers are primarily located on and across the transom, or near the transom on the gunwales. Transom-mounted downriggers extend straight back, perpendicular to the stern. The booms should be long enough to clear any trim tabs or swim platform and to enable the cable to clear the propeller when seas are rough or tight turns are made. A four-downrigger setup would have one unit on each corner, perpendicular to the gunwale, and one on each side of the motor, facing aft, to give a good horizontal spread to the weights and trolling lines.

On small boats, downriggers can be located wherever they are most convenient, especially if only one or two are used and it is easy to get to them, but close to the stern is usually best. If downriggers are mounted amidships and used for shallow fishing, the trailing line may be cut by the propeller in tight turns.

Deep trollers fish for salmon in the coastal waters of northern British Columbia near Dundas Island.

Whether you use pedestal mounts, swivel bases, trolling boards, or the like depends on the interior arrangement of your boat, the amount of freeboard it has, your budget, and your personal taste.

Fishing Depth

The depth that is trolled with downriggers can vary from just below the surface to as deep as the cable on your spool will allow. Determine desired fishing depth by checking temperature levels to see where the thermocline or preferred temperature of your quarry, or its bottom habitat, can be found. You can also pick what seems like an appropriate depth temporarily and wait until you find fish on sonar before making changes.

Sonar equipment is essential for downrigger fishing. Use it to find baitfish or gamefish and the levels at which they are located, as well as to determine the depth of the lake bottom or ocean floor and other aspects of the underwater terrain. Without sonar, you're just guessing, and you also run the risk of hanging up your downrigger weight if the depth gets shallower than the level at which it is being trolled.

Many downrigger anglers like to use a wide-angle (32 to 50 degrees) transducer to see their weights on sonar screens. This wide-angle view can be valuable, but it can also give false impressions. Its angle of view is very large at deeper levels, and sometimes the fish you see may not be directly below your boat. Nonetheless, a wide-angle display allows you to see more of what is around you.

Be aware that just because your downrigger line counter reads 50 feet, your lures may not be running at exactly 50 feet, for several reasons. One of these is swayback, which is the tendency of a downrigger cable and weight to angle backward due to significant forward motion or current. It becomes more pronounced if you increase boat speed, encounter underwater current, or fish in fast-flowing rivers. As a result, the weight does not run directly below the boat or at the level indicated by the depth counter, and you must allow for this.

Many anglers attach temperature- and speed-sensing probes to downrigger cables. These are usually part of lightweight, torpedo-shaped tubes set just above the weight. Such devices can present more drag and increase swayback; using heavier weights helps minimize this.

As with swayback, you must account for the extra depth achieved by diving plugs when you troll them behind a downrigger weight. If, for example, you want your lure to run at 20 feet and

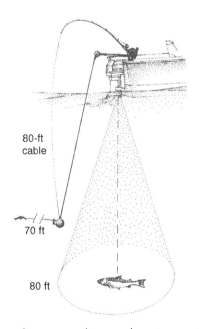

Because of certain conditions, a downrigger weight may not be at the vertical depth indicated on the cable counter. For example, if you set out 80 feet of cable to reach a fish that is 80 feet deep, the effects of swayback may cause the weight to be at the 70-foot level instead. Swayback has to be figured in setting the weight properly to put the lure in front of fish. This means letting out more cable, especially if the lure runs at the same depth as the weight.

you set a diving plug at the 20-foot level as indicated on the counter attached to the downrigger, that lure will be below the indicated level and will probably not be successful. If a diving plug runs 5 to 6 feet deep at a given speed and at the distance you have set it behind the downrigger weight, you must set the weight until the line counter reads 13 or 14 feet, no more.

Lure Distance (Setback)

How far back from the weight to set your lures varies from a few feet to 200 feet, depending on the depth being fished and the species being pursued. As a general rule, the deeper you fish, the less distance you need between weight and lure; the shallower you set the weights, the farther back you put the lines. This is only a general guideline, because at times some fish can be caught shallow on short lines. Determining the proper setback requires experimentation and analysis of different conditions. It is advantageous, though not always effective, to fish with the shortest setback possible (depending on water clarity, species, depth, and so forth), because a shorter line increases hooksetting efficiency, minimizes possible conflicts with other boats in heavy traffic areas, and makes boat maneuvering easier.

To determine the length of line paid out, you can use one of several systems. With levelwind reels, you can count the number of "passes" that the levelwind guide makes across the top of the reel. Measure the amount of line that comes off the spool for one pass; then multiply that amount by the number of passes to arrive at an approximate setback distance. Some reels have built-in line counters that calculate distance; these are preferred by many charter boat captains and big-water boaters.

Another method, used with levelwind reels possessing a line guide that locks in an open position, and with spinning and fly reels, is to count "pulls." Start with the lure or fly in the water, hold the rod in one hand, and grab the line just ahead of the reel with your other hand. Pull off line in set increments, either as far as your arm will reach or in 1- or 2-foot strips. Count the number of pulls to arrive at setback length.

A third method is to "sweep" by putting the lure in the water, pointing the tip at the lure, and sweeping the rod toward the bow of the boat for a measured length. As the boat moves ahead, bring the rod tip back and then sweep forward again. If your sweep is 6 feet, multiply that by the number of sweeps you make to approximate setback length. Sweeping is a bit less accurate than using pulls or passes.

You can estimate setback distance by sight when floating/diving plugs are fished. But rough water, glare, and hard-to-see lures make this tough, and sometimes inaccurate. Many people are not good at judging even short distances, however, and often grossly overestimate the distance that they have set a lure behind the boat; this misjudgment can sometimes be detrimental to angling success.

Once you've set the lures and lowered the weight, put the rod in a holder near or with the downrigger. Reel in all slack, then pull down on the line near the first rod guide while you turn the reel handle to bring the line as tight as possible, without pulling it out of the release. The rod should be well arched if properly set. Also check the reel drag for proper setting. The clicker should be on so that if a fish strikes and takes line before someone spots the rod tip bouncing, the clicker will alert you that a fish is on and taking line off the reel.

Line-Setting Patterns

The way you mount downriggers and the number you use determine the horizontal spread that can be achieved with lures. If you troll with only two downriggers, you needn't be too concerned with line-setting systems other than to keep the weights at different levels; also, try to vary setback lengths and to maximize your opportunities per line or per downrigger. The more 'riggers you employ, however, the more you should employ patterns or systems of operation, not only to cover the water well horizontally and vertically but also to facilitate landing fish, to minimize line crossing and tangling, and to make better presentations.

Boaters who fish large open waters with four to six downriggers can employ some variation of V patterns in terms of the depth of the weight and lure setback; such patterns will help prevent inconsistent, possibly confusing, and perhaps troublesome lure and line placement.

Regarding depth, a V-down pattern will have the inner weights set deepest, the weights adjacent to them set shallower, and the outside weights set shallowest. A V-up pattern is just the reverse. An equal-depth pattern will have all the weights set at the same level.

Regarding line-to-lure setback, a V-in pattern will set the inner lures closest to the weight, the lures next to them farther back, and the outside lures farthest back. A V-out pattern is the reverse. In an equal-length setback all the lures will be set at the same distance behind the downrigger weight.

A V-down depth system is preferred by many trollers because the deepest lines are directly below the boat; shallower lines are out of the boat's direct path, perhaps where fish that are spooked by the boat or the inner downriggers may have moved. The V-up system might be the best approach when you're after fish that are attracted to boat noise or prop wash. An equal-depth presentation may be useful when fish are being caught only at a specific level—such as when they occupy a narrow band near the thermocline—or when you don't need to scour all depth levels.

There is seldom much reason to use a V-out setback. The V-in pattern is favored for the different downrigger depth settings and also for flatlining and planer board trolling. When fish are falling regularly to lures trolled at a fairly specific midrange distance behind downrigger weights (especially when depths are nearly the same), there is little reason to stagger them much, so equal-length setbacks can be used. With the V-in system, the inner lures will run under the outer ones in turns, and fish directly below the boat may move up and out toward the lures set farther back. When used in combination with either the V-down or V-up depth settings, this setback system helps avoid line tangling when a fish strikes and pulls a deep line from the release.

Naturally, you have to experiment with these patterns and see which is best for your type of fishing and boat. (When you fish only one or two downriggers, this is all academic.) Such patterns are most useful when fishing in mid- to large-size boats; the most common pattern is a V-down/V-in combination.

Keep in mind that depth and setback distances are relative. A V-down system could set the shallowest depth trolled at 12 feet, the intermediate depth at 18, and the greatest depth at 24, which are not significant variations, or it could set the same

progression at 20, 40, and 60 feet. The same is true for setbacks. There are no limitations.

The reason why you should use some type of pattern is so that you always know relatively where your weights and lures are—and the more rigs you troll, the harder it is to keep track of things. When a large fish strikes and lines are cleared, you can easily forget which weight the successful lure was on, how deep that weight was, and how far the lure was set behind the release. When you use a pattern, you know these facts and can rerig immediately in a similar fashion.

Because outside lures speed up and inside lures slow down on a turn—and because the effects vary with the type of lure used (floating plugs rise while spoons and sinking plugs descend)—it is important to minimize the possibility of lines crossing and tangling. When setting out lines, try to keep the boat running straight, even if you're temporarily headed in a direction you don't want to go. A straight course while rigging minimizes line crossing and tangles.

A means of fishing with multiple rods/lines on a single downrigger, stacking is particularly useful for covering different depths when you're unsure how deep to troll. It is especially useful on boats equipped

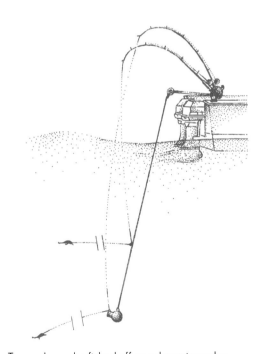

Two rods can be fished off one downrigger by stacking as shown, resulting in two lures being placed at different depths.

with just one or two downriggers and allows you to control the depth at which two lures are fished.

To employ a stacked system, set the first line as you would conventionally. Once the first line has been placed in the release next to the weight, lower the weight 10 feet and attach a stacker release to the downrigger cable. Put the second lure out the desired distance, and set the line in the stacker release. Place both reels in rod holders, and leave on the freespool clickers; then place the boom in the proper position (if applicable), and lower the weight to the desired depth. The two lines are now spaced 10 to 12 feet apart.

Be sure to place the rods in holders so that the lower line will not tangle with the upper line if a fish strikes and immediately comes toward the surface. The setback for the upper line should be shorter than for the lower line to minimize interference if a fish strikes the lower line.

The vertical distance between the two lines is optional, although it shouldn't be less than 10 feet to avoid tangling from erratic action or turns. Where very deep water is fished or where you're scouting at various depths, a difference of 30 to 50 feet may be useful. You might encounter this situation when trolling near the bottom for one species of fish (lake trout, for example) while running a second line off the same downrigger for a different species (such as chinook salmon) that might be considerably higher in the water column and near the thermocline.

Boat Manipulation and Lure Behavior

Line placement, lure presentation, and boat control are absolutely critical for sustained trolling success, and they work together. Downrigger fishing is usually combined with sonar to locate fish or suitable habitat, primarily the former. Many of the fish caught by downrigger trollers have not been spotted first on sonar, which means that the fish were out of the boat's path of travel and came to the lures, instead of the lures being swum past their noses.

Creative and intelligent boat maneuvering can bring lures into the range of fish that are out of the boat's path. To regularly alter the lure's course of travel, you can turn the boat, steer in an S-shaped pattern or other irregular way, or change the boat speed. A good tactic is to sweep in and out from shore and to plan strategic approaches to points, sandbars, islands, shoals, channels, and the like. To be successful in some situations, you must cover a lot of territory and make versatile presentations; in other situations, you need to keep covering the same area or keep following the fish.

Irregular maneuvering is a good downrigger trolling tactic because changes in a lure's behavior can precipitate a strike. Do whatever you can to make your offerings more attractive. Turning and altering speed are two basic activities.

Another way to alter a lure's behavior is by raising and lowering the weight periodically. Some electric downriggers can be programmed to oscillate automatically. It's worth doing this on your own, however, when fishing is slow and you want to trigger a strike from a fish that you've just spotted on sonar. Simply raise or lower the downrigger weight quickly to just above the level of the fish.

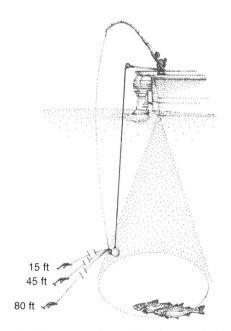

Lures should swim just above fish rather than below them or far above because most fish attack prey from below. When you are trolling a diving plug behind a downrigger weight, the depth at which the lure will run actually depends on the distance it is set behind the weight as well as the design of the lure's lip. Thus when you detect fish on sonar, the placement of the downrigger weight should take into account the diving ability of the lure.

If that doesn't work, wait a few moments for the lure to pass the fish; then take the rod out of its holder and pop the fishing line out of the release. Let the lure flutter down for a few seconds; then jig it once or twice. If nothing happens, retrieve the lure and reset the line. Often you'll catch fish in some stage of this operation.

Clearing Lines

You've got a whole bunch of lines set and you hook a fish. Do you keep moving? Do you pull in all the lines and raise all the weights?

Many big-boat trollers, particularly charter boat captains who fish a lot of lines, do not stop; they may slow down, but they don't really want to rerig everything and they hope to catch more fish in the same area. They try to maneuver the boat to land the fish without crossing lines, messing up the rigging pattern, and pulling everything in and resetting.

Small-boat trollers with only a few lines out don't have that problem and can usually pull in without too much trouble. Most anglers don't like to keep the boat moving, especially if they've hooked a good-size fish. After determining how large the fish is, they may clear everything, or may clear just one side of the boat and work the fish to that side for netting. This depends on the boat handler's skills, the angler's fish-playing abilities, the size of the fish, and the amount of gear in use.

With big fish, it's usually best to clear everything, put the boat in neutral, and maneuver the boat as necessary to maintain a desirable position on the fish. There is no question that you get more sport and satisfaction out of playing a fish from a still boat than from dragging it in while the boat is moving.

29

Inshore Fishing
from Boats

The term "inshore" is a generic one used by anglers to refer to coastal marine areas. Although the spot where inshore ends and offshore begins is not strictly defined, in general, inshore fishing refers to angling from a variety of boats for resident and migratory species in estuaries, rivers, bays, and nearshore ocean waters, whereas offshore fishing refers to blue-water fishing for pelagic species.

Inshore waters are popular for several reasons. Chief among these is the limited travel time required to reach the fishing grounds, which makes short outings feasible and facilitates a swift return to port for any reason, particularly stormy weather.

Another reason is that inshore waters hold a variety of popular fish species. This is partially due to the fact that coastal estuaries are important spawning and nursery grounds. With many species and varied environs comes the suitability of using a variety of angling methods. Even though drift and bottom fishing with bait may be the most popular methods overall, inshore anglers have opportunities to cast and jig for various species, troll for some species, and, in certain cases, stalk and sight-fish for their quarry. This wide variety opens up the game for many different types of equipment and approaches.

Generally, however, inshore fishing is well suited to light and medium tackle. The waters are protected and usually not very deep, and inshore species for the most part are relatively small, although heavyweight specimens of some species can test the angler's equipment and skill.

For maximum enjoyment, the choice of tackle should be appropriate to the quarry, so the angler isn't handicapped by tackle that is too light or too heavy. Those fishing out of private boats have more latitude in gear selection and more opportunities to use lighter equipment than those fishing out of party boats, where maneuverability is less and where more people of differing skill levels have to be accommodated.

Primary Species and Tactics

The following is a synopsis of the primary inshore species and the most popular methods of fishing for them.

Northeastern Flounder

The rock-studded coastline of Maine offers hundreds of rivers and bays that empty into the Atlantic. Many have mud, sand, or pebble bottoms where winter flounder take up residence. By anchoring on mud flats or along channel edges and chumming with a mixture of ground clams or crushed mussels sent to the bottom in a chum pot, these tasty flatfish are quickly attracted within range.

Small No. 8 or 9 Chestertown or wide-gap hooks baited with sandworms or bloodworms readily bring strikes from flounder, and sometimes harbor pollock or small codfish are caught on the same rigs, although most are immature fish that should be immediately released.

Much the same scene is repeated along the Massachusetts, Connecticut, Long Island, and New Jersey coasts, except that this region has many barrier islands, with broad bays separating them from the mainland, that provide winter flounder each spring and fall.

Atlantic Mackerel

Atlantic mackerel summer in the inshore waters of Maine, often traveling in huge schools. While mostly found in close-to-shore ocean waters, they'll often invade large coastal bays as they search for food. These provide fine light-tackle sport on tiny diamond jigs, bucktails, or tube teasers. Flies worked with a sinking line may draw strikes until the angler's arm is weary.

These fish usually winter off the Virginia Capes and provide boat anglers with fine action as they move north to the Maritime Provinces for the summer and then return again in early winter. Fun to catch, they're especially well suited to newcomers and youngsters because the action is often fast and furious when you locate a school.

East Coast Stripers and Bluefish

Both of these popular species frequent the same inshore waters of the Middle and North Atlantic coasts and are regularly targeted by anglers casting or trolling artificials, chumming, bottom fishing, drifting, and jigging.

Most of the stripers and blues that migrate north to New England have achieved respectable size. Many smaller fish are encountered along their midrange of Long Island and south to New Jersey and through the Chesapeake Bay area. Many of the youngsters of both clans spend their first few seasons in the bays, rivers, and creeks near where they were hatched. The inshore nursery grounds have an abundance of grass shrimp, spearing, sand lance, and other forage to satisfy their ravenous appetites.

Some of the fish are small but provide fine catch-and-release sport for anglers armed with light outfits. Both species are readily caught on plugs, plastic-tailed and bucktail-dressed leadheads, metal jigs, and streamer flies.

Inshore party boat fishing for both stripers and blues is popular throughout their range as well. The most popular lure-fishing technique for catching bass and blues is using a diamond or slab-sided chromed jig, with a plastic or feather teaser 18 to 24 inches ahead of it. The schools are often mixed, with stripers on or near the bottom and bluefish closer to the surface.

Tautog, Sea Bass, and Porgies

Inshore bottom feeders like tautog, black sea bass, and porgies are plentiful along the Middle Atlantic. They're found around most broken, irregular bottom, particularly rock ledges and artificial reefs, and frequent these areas because of abundant food and sanctuary from predatory species.

The most popular technique for catching all three of these bottom dwellers is to use a high-low rig, employing a pair of hooks snelled to a 12- to 18-inch leader. Virginia, Sproat, claw, or beak style hooks are most popular. Use a No. 8 or 10 hook for porgies, which often average from less than a pound to over 2 pounds, and a No. 4 or 6 hook for the generally larger sea bass. With tautog it's a matter of where you're fishing; in open ocean waters where they range in weight from 3 to 6 pounds or more, Nos. 2, 1, and even 1/0 hooks are preferred.

Small pieces of conch, clam, squid, or seaworm are preferred baits for porgies and sea bass, while tautog prefer green crabs and fiddler crabs, although they'll take the aforementioned baits as well.

When you find appropriate structure, such as artificial reefs or rockpiles or mussel beds in bays and the open ocean, anchor so your boat is positioned directly above the structure. All three species stick very close to the structure. Bait up, using sufficient sinker weight on your rig to hold bottom, and lower the rig to the bottom. These species are notorious bait stealers, so be alert and lift back smartly with your rod tip at the first tug on the bait.

Weakfish and Seatrout

The northerly weakfish and southerly seatrout provide a variety of inshore angling opportunities. These fish spend much of their time in the shallow reaches of bays and rivers, moving across eelgrass and weedbeds where forage is abundant. Often the water on the shallow flats ranges from 3 to 6 feet deep.

The techniques, habitat, and feeding patterns of these species are very similar. Both are creatures of habit and tend to be lazy when seeking a meal. As a result, they're easily attracted to a chum line of their favorite food, which includes the tiny grass shrimp so plentiful in coastal bays and rivers, as well as the larger shrimp that are targeted as table fare.

Many anglers find success fishing with bait under a float, suspending the bait just above the level of the weeds and using a small split shot or rubber-core sinker to help it drift along perpendicularly to the bottom. A cork or float with a scooped-out head, which emits a popping or gurgling sound as it is pulled through the water, helps attracts attention.

You can also catch weakfish by working a small bucktail jig or soft-tailed jig, as well as a

A spotted seatrout is landed in the Laguna Madre near Port Mansfield, Texas.

small swimming plug. Drifting across open bottom often brings strikes on an ebbing tide when these fish vacate the shallows. Here, a high-low bottom rig with a pair of hooks snelled to a 12- to 18-inch leader works fine. Use a bank or dipsey style sinker of sufficient weight to effortlessly glide along the bottom. Shrimp, strips of squid, spearing, and live killies are effective baits.

When weakfish and seatrout move out of estuaries, bays, and rivers into more open water they travel in huge schools, often moving close to the bottom and feeding on baitfish. Then they can be caught on diamond jigs and teasers, bucktails, or natural baits drifted along the bottom. Trolling with small plugs, bucktail jigs, or spoons takes many of both species, as the small-boat angler can cover a lot of water.

Southern Flatfish

Flounder spend a lot of time in the shallow environs of bays and estuaries, and they inhabit open reaches of the Atlantic and Gulf, generally close to shore. However, they often frequent humps or high bottom locations several miles from shore, especially when forage is plentiful there.

These flatfish move about while searching for a meal and are aggressive bottom feeders. However, during a cold snap, they will lie on the bottom for days without moving about or feeding.

As flounder rest on the bottom, their eyes extend upward, always alert for an unsuspecting baitfish, shrimp, or crab that happens by. They're extremely fast and will engulf the prey in an instant. As a result of this trait, successful flounder anglers find drifting to be the most successful fishing technique. Although chumming does produce strikes from flounder, as does fishing at anchor, you'll catch more flatfish if you leave the boat unanchored and cover known flounder grounds while drifting at the mercy of the current or wind.

The most popular flatfish rig is a simple setup with a small three-way swivel. Tie one end of the swivel directly to your line. To another end tie a 30- to 36-inch leader of 20-pound test, and then snell a No. 1/0 through 3/0 Carlisle, beak, claw, or wide-gap hook to that. To the remaining end of the swivel, tie a 6- to 8-inch piece of monofilament line with a loop in the end of it; slip a dipsey or bank style sinker of sufficient weight to hold the bottom onto the loop.

A variety of baits are effective when drifted along the bottom, including sand eels, spearing, crabs, shrimp, squid, and assorted live minnows, especially killies, or mummichogs.

Redfish

Redfish are a formidable target of anglers fishing inshore waters from the Virginia Capes south through Florida and across the Gulf Coast. Often called the southern counterpart to the striped bass, they frequent much the same waters and have very similar habits.

Much fishing for reds is done by seeking and casting to small groups or individuals in the shallows of bays, where they are feeding. These fish are often caught by stalking and making presentations to individual fish, especially with soft-tailed jigs. When the wind is blowing and the water is too deep or too roiled to visually spot fish, blind casting can be effective with the same lures, as well as with shallow-running plugs, walking-style topwater plugs, gold-colored weedless spoons, spinnerbaits, and shrimp bait.

An exciting method of catching redfish is to sight-cast to them when they are on the move and amongst larger schools. Schools present themselves in different ways. In open ocean waters, they often appear as a huge dark shadow or dark area while they cruise along, whereas in the shallows of bays and estuaries, their movement often disturbs the surface as the tightly packed schools mill about.

The key is positioning your boat upcurrent from the school and permitting wind or current to move you within casting range. Don't approach too closely while motoring in because you may spook the school. Once positioned, place your cast so it goes beyond and ahead of the fish; then work the lure back toward the school.

There are also opportunities to catch redfish on live shrimp, spot, pinfish, or grunts, or to troll for them using spoons.

Bonefish, Tarpon, and Permit

Bonefish, tarpon, and permit are among the most prized fish of inshore environs. Although they are usually associated with flats fishing and sight-casting activities, they may also be caught in bays and in the deeper holes of nearshore waters by using methods suited to fishing for nonvisible fish. All three of these species are caught by a variety of techniques, including fishing live baitfish at anchor, drift fishing, and in some cases deep jigging.

Unquestionably the most challenging, exciting, and popular technique is to move by pushpole or electric motor across shallow flats and sight-cast to fish as they move through water barely deep enough to cover their backs. All flats travelers are spooky, and care must be exercised to avoid approaching too closely. This may require getting into position and waiting until a sighted fish moves within range. In some cases, mainly bonefish on the shallowest flats, you can wade into position and cast to a fish slowly feeding across a flat.

Bonefish are fairly plentiful, and though they generally travel alone, they sometimes gather in small pods and even schools. Many anglers employ a single live shrimp on a 1/0 beak style hook and cast just ahead of the cruising fish. Tiny jigs also bring strikes, and fly fishing has become popular.

Permit are sometimes encountered on the flats, and they present a formidable challenge because of their wariness, greater size, and fast speed. Permit are also caught on shrimp; they can be taken on flies, although fly fishing for permit is more difficult than it is for bonefish. The most common offering is a small live crab.

Tarpon are a particularly good fly fishing species when they cruise the flats; they too may take shrimp and crab baits. In the channels between flats and islands, they are popularly caught on live mullet or pinfish. Fishing for big tarpon, particularly in the many passes emptying into the Gulf of Mexico, is usually a baitfishing proposition. Live crabs, pinfish, grunts, mullet, squirrel fish, and other small species are drifted through the area frequented by the tarpon, which move with the tides searching for a meal. Frequently, large pods of feeding tarpon are encountered on the surface and may be caught by casting a live bait to the cruising fish.

Grouper and Snapper

Many species of grouper and snapper are popular with inshore anglers from the Carolinas to Texas. They're found on nearly every patch of rock bottom, on myriad coral reefs, and around every shipwreck and ledge where food is abundant.

Inshore small-boat anglers fishing these various structures employ a variety of techniques for snapper and grouper. Anchoring and chumming adjacent to and above the structure is very effective for yellowtail snapper and porgies. Fishing live baits in the depths is also productive, particularly with big black grouper, red grouper, mutton snapper, and red snapper. Bottom fishing with a high-low rig produces all bottom dwellers.

An especially enjoyable method of catching all of these species is to drift and deep-jig the reef with bucktail jigs or plastic-bodied leadheads. When there is deep water and swift current or strong wind, you may need to use jigs weighing from 1 to 4 ounces in order to reach the bottom; then keep the jig perpendicular to the bottom as you retrieve. It often helps to quickly lift your rod tip so that the jig darts toward the surface, and continue reeling and jigging until it reaches the surface. If a strike isn't received, drop it back down and continue jigging and retrieving.

Bonus inshore catches are possible when you're deep-jigging the reefs. This includes species like crevalle jack, king mackerel, wahoo, Spanish and cero mackerel, dolphin, barracuda, and little tunny.

Cobia

Found in nominal quantities along the Atlantic coast from the Carolinas south, cobia come into their own along the Gulf Coast, where they're apt to be found cruising around channel markers, buoys, docks, and anchored boats. Many cobia are found in bays and passes.

One of the most popular methods of catching them is anchoring in a pass and using a sliding-egg sinker rig on the bottom with a live pinfish or grunt as bait. A more exciting approach is to cruise the passes, visiting buoys, channel markers, and dock areas; once a cobia is spotted, cast to it. Bucktail jigs and swimming plugs all bring strikes, but a live baitfish hooked just beneath the dorsal fin and cast within range of a hungry cobia will quickly bring an exciting surface strike.

Pacific Kelp

Some of the most enjoyable inshore action along the California coast is had while fishing waters adjoining enormous giant kelp beds. This mass of kelp provides sanctuary for anchovies, sardines, and a host of small fish and the fry of others, all of which often satisfy the appetites of bigger game.

Chumming is a popular method of fishing kelp. Boats generally anchor just off from the kelp, positioning the boat so that anglers are sufficiently close to cast their baits near to the kelp, or to permit the current to carry the lively baits, usually anchovies, along the edge of the kelp beds.

In this kind of fishing, you never know which species will take your bait, because there is variety galore cruising along the kelp searching for a meal. Pacific barracuda and Pacific bonito are two of the most popular, although somewhat smaller, of the targeted species. Pacific yellowtail and white seabass also call this habitat home and are among the prized catches. Kelp bass readily inhale a lively anchovy fished tight to the kelp.

Bottom fishing along the kelp also brings results. Although chumming usually entices strikes from fish that move through the midrange and surface layers, you can often score down on the bottom, too. When the other species mentioned aren't cooperating, many anglers add a weight to their lines, sending their bait down to the bottom for sand bass, California corbina, or Pacific halibut.

Silver Salmon and King Salmon

Inshore anglers have opportunities for silver salmon and king salmon from Northern California northward through the entire coast of British Columbia. Various forms of trolling are employed, especially downrigger fishing and mooching, the latter more prominent in Canadian than in American waters. Dodgers and flashers are often used along with anchovy- or herring-baited hooks.

This angling takes place in open waters not far from shore, and finding fish is of tantamount importance. At times, slow trolling for the big salmon is fast and furious. Frequently, though, you have to put in the time, searching with sonar for schools of baitfish and, once they're located, systematically slow-trolling the area until the bigger signals, indicating salmon, show up on the screen. When the season gets under way, the fish are usually concentrated.

In British Columbia, when bait is abundant and coho salmon runs are in full force, you can troll colorful streamer flies on the surface, using fly rods or other light tackle. Strikes are jolting and often immediately followed by a silvery blur cartwheeling out of the water.

Rockfish and Lingcod

Rockfish are regularly sought by inshore bottom anglers wherever there is a broken bottom of irregular rocks, and also well offshore in deep habitats. You can anchor over a productive area or drift, using chunk baits with a basic high-low rig having enough weight to hold bottom.

Lingcod, caught in many of the same areas, are commonly taken on live bait. Slack tides are especially favored, since they afford the best opportunity to work a bait or lure straight down to the rocky, scraggy bottoms while avoiding a snag.

Metal slab jigs that imitate smaller fish also work well, as do big leadhead jigs with soft plastic bodies or pork rind strips. Many bait anglers use herring, and live baits work much better than dead ones. The ultimate lingcod bait is a live greenling about 10 inches long, fished with a large, single hook through both lips. You need a sinker that is large enough to take the offering down, but exercise care in keeping it just off bottom or the bait will dodge into a hole and become snagged before a lingcod finds it.

Lingcod habitually dive for a rocky crevice when hooked, so try to turn them toward the surface and reel them as far off the bottom as possible after setting the hook. For this reason, you need fairly stout tackle and an abrasion-resistant leader.

Northwest Halibut

Impressive size, relative abundance, and brute strength make the Pacific halibut a popular quarry

Inshore waters that provide good fishing opportunity include estuary environs such as the California Delta near San Francisco, where this striped bass was taken.

from the southern Oregon coast northward, with larger specimens usually found in more remote waters of northern British Columbia and Alaska. These bottom dwellers are found wherever food is abundant, especially near islands and over banks and humps.

The key to fishing halibut successfully is to get a bait or lure down to them and keep it there long enough for a fish to find it. Most anglers prefer to use bait, especially large herring. Squid, octopus, and belly skin off halibut or salmon, as well as whole cod, greenling, or other small bottom fish, are also effective baits.

Halibut use their eyes, nose, and lateral line to locate a meal, so anglers often lift the bait well off the bottom to increase visibility and then drop it quickly to create a thumping vibration. Heavy tackle is generally preferred for halibut fishing because of the weight of the objects fished, the depth, and the size of the fish possible.

Fishing around Buoys

Some species of saltwater fish are attracted to buoys and channel markers, no matter how small the object or structure and its foundation or anchoring means might be. Cobia are often caught around these, as are tripletail, drum, snapper, amberjack, and on occasion other species.

Boaters should approach buoys and channel markers slowly, shutting the outboard motor off at a distance and allowing the boat to drift past the object or within reasonable casting distance of it. The shallower the water the more this is true. Engine noise will likely drive fish away. Consider the direction of wind and current in order to position the boat for a proper drift, and work the surface and near-surface water first, trying to draw an eager fish away from the buoy or marker. If you don't catch a fish immediately, try another drift or two, and try getting a little deeper, probably with a bucktail jig. If the water is deep and the current is too swift to make a good deep presentation while drifting, you may have to drop anchor well upcurrent to position the boat right next to the structure. Then you can fish a jig or bait.

Often when the tide or current runs hard there is little action at these locations. Keep trying. Sometimes buoys and channel markers produce fish when there is little or no water movement.

Fishing from Party Boats

The term "party boat" encompasses a variety of sportfishing vessels that are known by various local names, including drift boats, long-range boats, head boats, and day boats. A party boat is usually a large vessel that accommodates individual anglers, mostly on a nonreserved basis and with daily fares applied per head, generally paid upon boarding. Party boats offer an economical way for people of any skill level to spend a day fishing on a large body of water, sometimes for a variety of species.

Party boat anglers catch a full gamut of species, with most fish being small- to medium-sized inshore specimens. Bottom fishing is the hallmark of party boat angling. This may occur with the boat anchored over wrecks, reefs, or irregular broken bottom, or while drifting over smooth bottom. Some boats specialize in chumming, which may be employed at anchor or while drifting. Trolling is sometimes done, too, but this limits the number of anglers who can stream their lines from the stern. Jigging is popular and common on party boats, whether at anchor or while drifting.

Because sea conditions change frequently and the habits of fish change just as quickly, the party boat captain and his mates or deckhands quickly

Open to the public, party boats depart daily during the season from major ports; here, anglers prepare to board a party boat in Atlantic Highlands, New Jersey.

adapt. So although a boat may start the day by bottom fishing, if a school of surface-feeding fish is located, you could be switching gear and techniques to take advantage of a developing opportunity.

Equipment

Anglers who regularly fish on party boats have their own tackle and bring it with them, usually needing to be supplied only with bait. After you have made a few excursions on party boats and seen what veteran anglers have and what the boats provide, you'll probably want to outfit yourself and bring your own equipment. Until then you can rent equipment from the boat.

Much can be learned from veteran party boat anglers, as they have this type of fishing down to a science. Because time on the fishing grounds is often limited, the veteran is extremely well organized with his tackle, so not a moment is wasted. Many of the pros develop a personal party boat checklist to ensure that they have everything with them necessary for a successful day. This includes:

- Proper clothing, including rain gear and hat
- Ice chest with ice for fish, and a compartment for food and beverages
- Plastic bags in which to place cleaned fish on ice
- Deck shoes or slip-on boots to keep dry
- Pills for seasickness, headache, or pain relief

- Polarized sunglasses
- Folding toothbrush and toothpaste
- Sunscreen of SPF 25 or higher
- Sleeping bag for overnighters

These items ensure that you'll have an enjoyable trip, regardless of duration. Little things like a toothbrush to freshen your mouth after a night in a bunk, or an antacid tablet for indigestion, or especially sunscreen to prevent a burn, often make the difference in a trip's enjoyment. Regulars carry all of this gear with them and at least one completely rigged rod and reel. Since there is plenty of room on the bigger party boats, they also bring a spare outfit as insurance, and a tackle box loaded with essentials.

A party boat tackle box should be roomy, plastic, and waterproof, with all items easily accessible. It should contain:

- Sharp filleting knife
- Serrated knife for steaking, cutting bone
- Diamond knife sharpener
- Stainless steel dehooker
- Vise-grip cutting pliers in sheath
- Eight-inch broomstick for wrapping line around to pull free from bottom snags
- Sinkers for the type of fishing expected
- Terminal rigs for the type of fishing expected
- Jigs, spoons, feathers, and other lures and rigged leaders

As anglers become proficient on party boats, some expand their horizon from the species normally targeted to seek bigger game. For example, many boats chum for yellowtail snapper throughout their southern range. These average 2 to 4 pounds and are pursued with small hooks and light tackle. Frequenting the same grounds as yellowtails are big grouper and snapper, some weighing 50 pounds or more, which are targeted by anglers who bring heavy tackle and use big baits to catch these goliaths of the deep. Many anglers bring a pair of outfits aboard, one heavy and one light; they first make a catch of the smaller gamesters and then switch over to target the heavyweights, making for a fun-filled and well-rounded day.

Fishing and Rail Position

Upon boarding, most veterans discuss with the mates the exact method to be used on arrival at the fishing grounds, and the techniques that have proven most effective. They rig accordingly as the boat travels to the fishing grounds and wear their cutting pliers and bait knife in a sheath on their belt. Time on the fishing grounds is limited, so it's smart to be totally prepared.

Many party boat anglers wear a carpenter's tool apron in which they place a couple of extra sinkers and complete terminal rigs so they can quickly retie and get back in the water should they lose a rig. This saves time from rummaging through a tackle box or having to make up a rig or purchase one from a busy mate.

Included in the tool apron is the 8-inch piece of broomstick; this is a godsend when it's necessary to break off a snagged bottom rig. It prevents breaking costly tackle as you try to break off, and, more importantly, it keeps the line from cutting your hands.

Once the fishing grounds are reached, the captain either announces over the boat's loudspeaker that fishing will begin, or signals this by sounding the horn. At each fishing location along the rail, the mates will have placed a container of bait; if live bait is used, it is readily available at the circulating tanks. After you are baited up and fishing, it's a good practice to be aware of the actions of other anglers. Watch the first people to score, and don't hesitate to mimic their technique.

Rail position in certain types of party boat fishing can often put you at a decided advantage. In many types of reef and wreck fishing, the boat is anchored over sand bottom and the current holds the boat in position either close to or over the choice bottom. In this kind of situation, anglers along the stern have the best spots; as the fish are chummed, the first baited hooks they respond to are those of anglers positioned at the stern.

As a rule of thumb, it's difficult to beat the stern position for any kind of party boat fishing, and it's not unusual to see party boat regulars arrive extra early, even hours before boarding time, so they can place their outfit in a desired spot.

When drift fishing, the captain usually positions the boat so the lines of anglers on one side will stream away from the boat and the lines of those on the other side will drift under the boat. Every half hour or so the skipper will make a move over new bottom, and alternate the position of the boat, so the anglers whose lines drifted under the boat will stream away from it and vice versa for the other side. It is usually best to have your lines drift away from rather than under the boat.

The best position on boats that drift is the bow, where only two or three anglers can fish. In this way they can take advantage of their lines streaming away on either drift, and it enables them to cast out and away from the bow, which results in more bottom being covered.

When party boats are crowded, each angler has a spot at the rail, usually marked by a painted stripe on the rail, or where there is a piece of cord tied, to which you can attach your outfit. Some boats have rod holders at each position.

When the boat isn't crowded, it's much more comfortable and you can move about more readily. At such times, it's often wise to move away from where the anglers tend to cluster near the stern, and to situate yourself alone, which often results in more strikes and less chance of a tangle.

In some types of party boat fishing, the fish that are hooked are so large and strong that you just can't stand at the rail and bring the fish directly to you. At such times, it's necessary to follow the fish up and down the rail. Most party boat anglers are extremely courteous and when they hear the time-honored call, "Fish on, coming through," they'll clear the rail, and raise or lower their line to permit you to follow your fish. With a big fish, the mate frequently

accompanies the angler to make certain no tangles occur en route.

As a big fish is brought alongside, it's especially important to be alert to any last-minute runs. The mates are at the ready with a long-handled net or gaff (sometimes two gaffs are necessary, as with large yellowfin tuna), and as soon as the fish is within range they either net or gaff it. At this time, it's critical that the angler just reel the fish close enough for the mates to handle. Sometimes, in the excitement, anglers try to lift the fish, and with a big fish thrashing at boatside, this can often result in a broken line.

Stay calm, reel the fish within range, and let the mates show their skill. It's much easier for a fish to be gaffed or netted when it is a foot or so beneath the surface and not thrashing on the surface or with its head lifted from the water. As the fish is brought aboard, place your reel in freespool or open the bail on a spinning reel, so the mate can move away from the rail and other anglers can move freely as he unhooks your fish.

The Road to Success

It's worth noting that party boat regulars often become extremely proficient. It's not unusual to see veteran anglers aboard party boats consistently catching more and bigger fish than other anglers. This should never be construed as luck, although occasionally it may be, but more as an understanding of the species sought, its feeding habits, the weather conditions, speed of drift, current, water clarity, and a host of other factors.

It's often the little things that count. On a summer morning with a lazy drift, all of the anglers onboard may be catching summer flounders while using a 4-ounce sinker to hold bottom. As afternoon winds develop velocity, the boat's speed of drift accelerates, and at times it may take a full 16 ounces of sinker weight to keep a rig on the bottom. Those anglers who respond by changing weights continue to score, while those who continue using a light sinker actually have their baits drifting at midlevel, well above the bottom-feeding fish.

Always having a fresh bait on your hook, keeping the hooks sharp, using lightweight or fluorocarbon leaders less visible to fish, tying the correct knots, and, above all, being alert are just a few of the many small things that collectively make a big difference in success.

Anglers usually have a specific rail position on a party boat, but may move around when it's not crowded; the bow and stern are often preferred locations.

30

Coastal Pier, Bridge, and Dock Fishing

Perhaps the most leisurely type of fishing available to coastal anglers is fishing from the piers, bridges, docks, and bulkheads that are readily accessible along most areas of the seacoast. In certain places, some of the best publicly accessible nonboat angling is at these structures, which can be enjoyed at nominal cost compared with other types of fishing. In fact, although there is usually a fee to access piers built expressly for fishing, for the most part there is no cost associated with using structures.

Piers, bridges, docks, and bulkheads exist in tidal rivers, harbors, inlets, waterways, and marinas; in some cases they are also found in open bays or along otherwise unobstructed oceanfront. The diversity and productivity of the fishing opportunity offered by these structures varies with location, and is influenced by many factors, including water depth, water salinity, tides, current, season, size and location of the structure, amount of cover present, and, of course, species of fish.

Anglers fish from the pier at Atlantic Beach, North Carolina.

The species available at these structures range from large to tiny, from major gamefish to major table fish. Huge tarpon are regularly taken from bridges in the Florida Keys; snook and redfish are also common southern bridge catches. In South Carolina, which is known for its fishing piers, anglers may catch such larger game as cobia and king mackerel, and possibly sharks. Anglers casting from New Jersey piers often encounter big striped bass, bluefish, and weakfish, all of which strike a variety of lures and natural baits. In San Diego, it might be fast-moving Pacific bonito and barracuda, and in the Northwest it might be king salmon. However, while it is possible to catch such exciting gamefish at these structures, bottom feeders are the bread-and-butter quarry.

Fishing these structures is fairly easy to master and is especially suited to those who are prone to seasickness when boating. Because it is not very physically demanding (especially in the case of piers and large docks), it is accessible and enjoyable for those with physical limitations. These structures also provide an excellent opportunity for family fishing and offer an inexpensive means of introducing children to angling, especially when bottom-feeding species are available.

Rigs, Lures, and Gear

Bottom Rigs

While gear needs vary, all of the species sought around these structures are mostly attracted to them because they provide foraging opportunity. Forage species take up residence in and around these structures, and predators move in and out of them when tides and current make that forage more abundant or more vulnerable. As a result, the predominant activity is fishing with bait rigs, and also keeping your line relatively perpendicular to the bottom.

Many different bottom rigs can be used for fishing from these structures. The fishfinder bottom rig is a popular rig that may be used to present a natural bait to anything from a half-pound spot to a 100-pound tarpon. It's built around an egg-shaped sinker that has a hole through the middle. Slip a sinker of sufficient weight to hold bottom—usually ½ ounce to 4 ounces or more—onto your line. Next tie in a tiny barrel swivel, which will prevent the sinker from slipping off the line yet permit it to slide on the line ahead of the swivel. To the barrel swivel, tie a 12- to 36-inch-long leader of a size balanced to the hook and bait you're using. When pursuing winter flounder, spot, or croakers, use a No. 6 Claw or Beak style hook and 12 inches of 8-pound-test leader. If the target is redfish or snook, use a 5/0 or 7/0 Claw or Beak style hook and 36 inches of 30-pound-test leader material.

When this rig is adorned with bait and lowered from a structure, it rests on the bottom, and a feeding gamefish is able to pick up the bait and move off with it without feeling the weight of the sinker. This gives the fish an opportunity to get the bait well into its mouth before you set the hook, resulting in more hooked fish.

Another popular bottom rig is the single hook version, which is built around a three-way swivel. Tie the three-way swivel directly to the end of your line. Attach a snelled hook to one eye of the swivel; the hook should be appropriately sized for the targeted species and should be snelled to a length of leader. Finally, to the remaining eye of the swivel, either tie in your sinker or use a small duolock snap to attach it. Bait the hook and lower the rig into the water.

A high-low rig is a third type of bottom rig favored by many who fish from these structures. With the line perpendicular to the bottom, the high-low rig enables you to fish one bait directly on the bottom and a second (or high hook) bait 24 to 30 inches off the bottom. Many tackle shops have ready-made high-low rigs available, but you can tie up your own.

To make this rig, begin by using a Double Surgeon's Knot to tie a loop in the end of your line and attach the sinker to this loop. Tie in a dropper loop just a few inches up from the loop; when the loop is completed, it should extend approximately 10 to 12 inches from the standing part of the line, meaning in effect that you've used 20 to 24 inches of line in preparing the dropper loop. Next slip a Claw or Beak style hook (with a turned-down eye) onto the loop, looping the hook through the loop twice. If you loop it only once, it will slip and slide free, but putting it through twice will firm it up tight and, in effect, will result in a double leader leading to the hook. Repeat the same procedure where you want to place your high hook, which should be anywhere from 12 to 36 inches up from the low hook.

Lures and Other Gear

Most of the same lures employed in the surf and on jetties may be used effectively from bridges, piers, docks, and bulkheads. However, an important difference is that at the latter structures you usually fish from a greater height above the water. Although you may be fairly close to the water when fishing from bulkheads and docks, you're likely to be 30 feet or higher off the water when casting lures from bridges and piers. As a result, the techniques used from the surf or jetty simply don't apply when fishing from these structures.

The most popular items in the arsenal of lure casters are plugs, bucktail or plastic-tailed lead-head jigs, and metal squids and jigs. Lures ranging in weight from ½ ounce to 1½ ounces, which are sufficiently heavy to be easily cast from these structures, are among the most popular. Since they are relatively light, they don't require heavy tackle to make a good cast and presentation.

Unlike other kinds of fishing, pier fishing doesn't require a lot of gear beyond the basics. You will need a tackle box/satchel and bait container; for nighttime bridge casters, a miner's headlamp, worn loosely around the neck, may come in handy.

Many fish caught from these structures are of a size that can readily be reeled in with little difficulty. But if you have the good fortune of hooking a big striper, bluefish, or tarpon, landing it can present a problem. Sometimes you can walk it to shore and beach it with little difficulty, or bring it close enough for a companion with a long-handled net to capture. Other times, various obstructions make this impossible.

To help land heavy fish, many public piers have landing nets fabricated from a heavy round metal rod to which is attached a net bag and a length of $1/8$-inch cord. The net is lowered into the water, and the fish maneuvered above it; an assisting angler lifts the net, capturing the fish, and then lifts net and fish to the top of the structure.

Anglers fishing for snook and tarpon, which are often released, regularly crimp the barbs of the hooks on their lures. Once a fish is brought within what would be landing range, they give it slack line; usually the fish then either jumps or rolls, ridding itself of the hook and gaining its freedom. Thus the angler is not obliged to handle a fish that would have been released anyway.

Fishing with Bait

Casting Bait Away from Structure

In some instances it is good to cast a bait rig away from the structure. For certain species, a cast-and-retrieve approach is best; this is especially true when seeking summer flounder and weakfish, since they like to work shell beds that are located in the vicinity of structures. To fish effectively away from structure, cast as far as you can from the structure, let the rig settle to the bottom, and then lift your rod tip. This causes the rig to slide along the bottom, hesitate, and then slide forward again when retrieved. The fish spots the bait, which is usually a live minnow, sees it move and falter, and is often on it in a flash.

With some species, a motionless bait placed away from a structure gets the most strikes. This is particularly true with spot, croaker, rockfish, surf perch, and other species that move about searching for seaworms, shrimp, clams, and other forage on the bottom. The stage of the tide may have a bearing on whether you should fish away from a structure or close to it. When the current is strong, some fish, particularly flounder, are more likely to be away from the structure; when it is very slow or nonexistent, they may be under the structure or within a few feet.

Fishing Bait Close to Structure

Some species, like tautog and sheepshead, often feed extremely close to the pilings that support piers, bridges, and bulkheads. They search for crabs, shrimp, and other forage that cling to these structures, and they'll also use their teeth to rip mussels from the pilings. To score, you've got to present your bait just inches from the pilings or concrete.

Veteran pier and bridge anglers often move from piling to piling, carefully lowering their high-low rig and permitting it to rest motionless for a few minutes. If no hits are received, they move to the next piling and then the next until they get a strike. Both sheepshead and tautog are extremely fast, and you've got to strike immediately or they'll strip your bait from the hook.

Fishing Live Bait

Fishing from piers, bridges, docks, and bulkheads is very effective with a wide variety of live baits, which can easily be presented in a natural manner. There are many ways of fishing a live bait, though unquestionably the simplest technique is to tie a hook directly to the end of the line, bait it, and lower the bait into the water. As simple as this rig is to make and use, it is among the most effective of live-bait rigs.

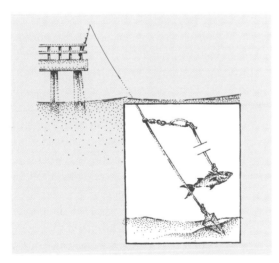

Shown here is a live-bait rig fished at a good distance from a pier. Setup begins by casting a pyramid sinker without bait and lodging it securely in the mud or sand; then live bait, which has been attached to a leader and snap swivel (inset), is placed on the fishing line. The bait slides down into the water and achieves a free-swimming position. This method allows the angler to make a distant presentation of live bait without having to actually cast the bait.

Anglers have especially good results on striped bass with it. They put a size 1/0 or 2/0 Claw or Beak bait-holder hook into the mouth of a single large sandworm, exiting about an inch down on the worm. This enables the angler to lower the worm into the water and drift it out with whatever current moves about the structure, where it swims enticingly and draws strikes.

This same rig is also effective for striped bass and weakfish when used with live eels, which are hooked through the lips and fished in the same manner. Live spot account for many big weakfish when used in this manner, and both grunts and pinfish are very effective baits when live-lined for snook and redfish; these baits are hooked either through the lips or eyes, or just forward of the dorsal fin, which permits them to swim about freely.

Because many live baits are small and invariably stay close to the structure you're fishing from, you might add a float to the line anywhere from a foot to several feet above the hook. Favored floats are those that can be easily snapped anywhere on the line to hold the bait at the desired depth. Float rigs are particularly effective for weakfish.

Buoy Rig for Live Bait

Large live baits stay very close to the structure you're fishing from, seeking sanctuary. Because big baits are difficult to cast and are easily ripped from the hook when the angler casts with force, many pier and bulkhead anglers employ a unique buoy rig approach to get the bait far from the structure from which they're fishing.

To prepare this rig, tie a 2- to 4-ounce pyramid sinker directly to the end of the line. Next tie a 36-inch-long piece of 20- or 30-pound-test leader material to a barrel swivel with a coastlock snap on it. Tie a Claw or Beak style live-bait hook, or a treble hook, to the end of the leader material.

Cast the pyramid sinker to the general area where you want your bait to be. Once the sinker is firmly secured into the sand or mud bottom, slip the coastlock snap over the line and close it so that it can slide on the line. A live baitfish, usually impaled through the back, is then placed on the hook and is permitted to slide down the line and into the water. Once the bait enters the water, it can swim only from its entry point down to the sinker; often it will move back and forth, perhaps excitedly fluttering on the surface and attracting striped bass, bluefish, snook, tarpon, redfish, king mackerel, barracuda, and other large gamefish. If sharp-toothed species, such as king mackerel, barracuda, and bluefish, are in an area, it's often wise to use a 6-inch-long piece of No. 8 or 9 stainless steel leader material between the hook and the monofilament leader, employing a tiny barrel swivel to join the two.

This method of fishing a live bait from piers and bulkheads often brings exciting strikes because the baitfish moves to the surface when being stalked by the quarry. Once the bait is taken, the hook is usually set as the fish mouths it, so you quickly reel up the sinker until it comes taut with the coastlock snap and then lift back to ensure that the hook is set.

Chumming

Used in concert with the techniques just discussed, chumming often enhances your fishing opportunities from these structures by attracting fish within range of your natural baits. Many operators of commercial fishing piers regularly chum from their structures. Ground menhaden is often used to attract baitfish and keep them in the vicinity of the pier, which in turn attracts a variety of species.

The time-proven technique of using a weighted chum pot, filled with ground menhaden, herring, mackerel, mussels, clams, or crabs, is regularly used to bring fish within range. Almost all bottom feeders will move toward the source of chum when it is carried along by the current.

Chumming with live grass shrimp readily attracts weakfish and seatrout to dock areas. Pacific bonito and rock bass will respond to small pieces of fish dispersed from structures. The same is true for bluefish, striped bass, snappers, and groupers. When an easily obtained meal is available, most bottom feeders and gamefish will take advantage of it, much to the benefit of the angler who employs any of the wide variety of chums.

Casting from Bridges and Piers

Both bridges and piers position you high off the water. Currents moving beneath these structures are most often caused by tidal flow but are affected by wind as well. As these currents reach the pilings, towers, or other structure that support the pier, they cause what are popularly called "dead spots" just before the structure, or

behind it as the current passes swiftly through. At both dead spots, the current separates and fish can take up station in quiet water, waiting for food to be swept along.

Many gamefish, especially weakfish, striped bass, tarpon, and snook, take up a feeding station in the quiet water facing the current. If the structure permits, position yourself so that you can cast your lure 20 or 30 feet up from where you expect the fish to be feeding. This enables you to work the lure and to swim it with the current to within range of the fish. Often this requires a faster rate of retrieve than you would employ elsewhere, since the current is pushing the lure. You've got to speed up the retrieve to give the plug a swimming action or to make the jig appear to be darting downcurrent and faltering as it moves along.

If you don't receive strikes casting directly upcurrent, move to the left or right of where you think the fish are holding. Cast up and across at a 45-degree angle, with the lure dropping in a spot past where the fish may be feeding. Work it across and downcurrent, within view of the fish. Sometimes you can work a swimming plug or leadhead bucktail or plastic-tailed jig so that it comes within the sight line of the feeding fish, which will often dart out to engulf it, right within view from your vantage on the bridge or pier.

Situations such as described often occur during the swiftest of tides with boiling currents that the fish prefer to avoid. Often, as the tide or current moderates, fish will expand their range, moving up and down along the structure looking for a meal, and you should adjust accordingly. Don't hesitate to move about. Most veterans look for spots devoid of anglers, so that they can work their lures through new territory, sometimes receiving strikes on their first presentation.

By crossing to the other side of the bridge you experience an entirely different set of circumstances. The current is running beneath the structure, often forming rips and eddies, with the same dead spots of minimal current where the fish like to hold and feed when the current is heavy. In this situation, you can often cast out a swimming plug and "swim" it in the current. If the current is sufficiently swift, only a very slow retrieve, or a twitching of the rod tip, is necessary to keep the plug working. Many anglers just walk the plug, moving it back and forth along the bridge or pier rail, permitting the lure to move in and out of the spots holding fish, much as a struggling baitfish would do in order to stem the current.

Leadhead jigs work effectively in this situation too. Lighter jigs will work near the surface, and the current will do tricks with them, permitting them to settle, be shifted to the side, and then swept toward the surface as they ease into the fast current. In this situation, add a strip of pork rind or a soft tail to the lure to enhance its action in the current. Twitch your rod tip and move it back and forth, ensuring that the lure resembles a struggling baitfish.

Don't hesitate to switch to a heavy jig that will get down in the current. The old adage that "if there's a fish feeding on the surface, there's a dozen down on the bottom" holds true with fishing these structures. A heavy jig, perhaps in the 1½-ounce range, can be worked deep while fishing either upcurrent or downcurrent. The key is using the current to your advantage and always maintaining control of the jig's movement. A heavy jig bouncing on the bottom is often observed as it's swept along; and just as the current, or the angler, works it off the bottom, it's taken by a hungry snook, striper, weakfish, or tarpon.

Fish It All

On all piers and bridges, it's important to thoroughly fish all the water surrounding the structure. Anglers tend to bunch up at the end of a pier or the middle of a bridge. Veteran anglers avoid the crowds and work the perimeter. This is especially true where a pier extends out from the beach. Often there are eelgrass beds, marsh grass, or reeds extending out from the beach that hold baitfish, and the fish know this and move in close. An ocean pier—along the surf line where the tumbling waves harbor baitfish or expose crabs, shrimp, and seaworms—is another spot often devoid of anglers, yet one certainly warranting several casts.

Work Shadow Lines

Although daytime sport is enjoyable, there is excitement on the night tides because many coastal species are more active nocturnal feeders and the success ratio is often far superior at night. A unique situation develops after dark on many structures. Illumination from bridge or pier lights, and even a bright moon, develops a shadow line, with the water close to the structure in total darkness and the water beyond the shadow line brightly illuminated.

With the water flowing toward the bridge or pier, which is popularly called the "front of the bridge," gamefish often take up station facing into the current in the darkness, with their noses tight to the shadow line. On the opposite side, or the "back of the bridge," the opposite occurs, with the fish in the brightly lit area, but still with their noses tight to the shadow line, facing into the current or darkness. It's not unusual to see 100-pound tarpon lined up side by side in the shadow line

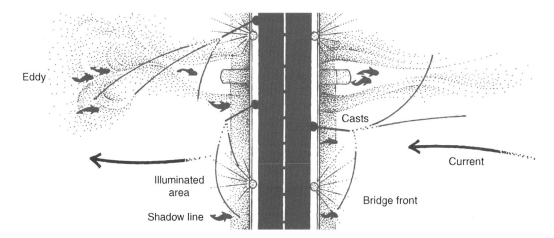

Depicted is a typical major bridge with walkways and with lights that illuminate the water beyond a shadow line at night. Feeding fish will locate in the shadow line on the bridge front and outside the shadow line on the back (downstream side) of the bridge, as well as in dead water ahead of and below bridge pilings and where the water eddies. Anglers fishing from the bridge should position themselves to make casts to these areas.

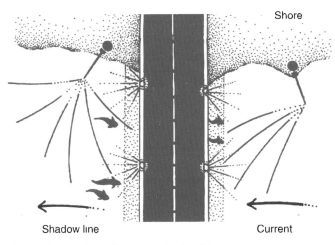

Shore

Shadow line

Current

Anglers fishing from shore at night should cast out and across the current to properly scour the area around a bridge. It is especially important to work the shadow lines above and below the bridge. Note the positions of fish near the bridge relative to overhead lights.

of the bridges in the Keys or to see striped bass doing the same in the waters of many bridges.

Use the same techniques described earlier: Either cast up into the current and retrieve your lure within the vision window of the fish, or cast at an angle and work the lure across and toward the shadow line where the fish are holding. The key with either plugs or leadhead jigs is to fish the lure parallel with the surface, whether working it near the surface or in the depths. Strikes often come as deep-running lures lift off the bottom at the conclusion of a retrieve.

If you observe fish holding on the backside of the bridge, waiting for forage such as crabs, shrimp, and small fish to be carried under the bridge toward them, you have to work extra hard to properly present a lure. Often the shadow line is tight to the bridge, and if you permit a lure to work in the rips and eddies, it is many yards behind the line of vision of the feeding fish. At such times, by pointing your rod tip downward and properly timing your cast by rocking the rod and flipping the lure up into the current beneath the bridge, you can then quickly take up the slack as the lure is swept along by the current and to the shadow line and waiting fish. At first this may seem awkward to do, but once you master the motion you'll find it rewards you with many strikes.

Work the Corners

Not to be overlooked are the corners where the structure meets land. Often you can fish from rock riprap that is adjacent to the bridge foundation. Sometimes this is a beach or shore, and sometimes it is a bulkhead. Frequently the bridge is located at a narrow point of a bay or river, so there is an open expanse of water funneling through beneath the bridge structure. This can cause back eddies, tidal rip lines, and currents of varying speed, which sometimes create miniature whirlpools that trap forage species and attract gamefish.

By positioning yourself in the corner, employing a bracket approach to present your lures, and using the tidal flow to your advantage, you can cover a lot of water and catch some beautiful fish. Corner spots often provide exciting tarpon, redfish, and snook angling in southern waters, and striped bass, bluefish, weakfish, and summer flounder in northern waters. All of these bunch up in corners where food is swept their way on a moving tide.

Casting from Docks and Bulkheads

Somewhat different techniques are brought into play when you're positioned fairly low to the water while fishing from docks and bulkheads. Both structures provide good fishing because they also offer sanctuary for forage. Shrimp tend to cling to bulkheads and dock pilings, and hungry fish regularly cruise along these structures. Crabs often cling to the pilings too, or can be observed at night in the area swimming beneath the dock lights. When there is a seaworm hatch, it's not unusual to observe literally millions of inch-long squirmers swimming just beneath the surface. At such times the water often boils as practically every species in residence gorges on the tiny yet plentiful food. Where there is abundant food around docks and bulkheads, there will be predators to catch.

Natural Drift

Under natural drift conditions, a single sandworm or bloodworm, impaled on a hook and drifted along with the current, quickly brings strikes. A plastic worm may also bring strikes. The key is presentation, with the most successful approach being to drift these items with the current as unimpeded as possible. Veteran bulkhead casters often "walk the worm," permitting the current to carry it along just inches from the bulkhead.

Work Tight to the Bulkhead

Plastic-tailed leadhead jigs also produce excellent results when worked tight to the bulkhead; often snook, redfish, striped bass, bluefish, seatrout, tarpon, ladyfish, snapper, and other species feed just inches from where you may be standing.

Tight to the bulkhead means just that, casting out and permitting the current to carry your jig as you walk along the bulkhead or dock, working your rod tip so that the jig darts ahead into the current, then falters and is swept along again, much like a struggling shrimp or tiny baitfish. Work the jig just 6 to 12 inches from the bulkhead or pilings and you'll be surprised by exciting strikes. Do not overlook the corners of these structures either.

Know the Tides

Depending on location, many dock and bulkhead areas come alive at or near slack tide. With swift currents, many gamefish take up station anywhere they can get out of the quick flow, which may be in the middle of a bay or river. As the current slows, they move about, searching for food; they know that the dock and bulkhead areas often have an abundance of forage.

To capitalize on this situation, try to time your visits to key locations an hour before to an hour after either the flood or the ebb tide. By timing your movements, you can often cover three or four spots in different areas, capitalizing on the slow-moving water in each location. As you gain experience, you'll no longer be surprised to see a spot having a 4-knot current and no fish life suddenly erupt with surface-crashing, feeding gamefish. Then, as the current begins to boil, the bonanza shuts off as quickly as it began.

Dead Spots and Shadow Lines

Some of the techniques employed by bridge casters have application for fishing from docks. As current flows to the pilings or supports of the dock, there is a dead spot in the current, as is the case on the downcurrent side of the dock. Work these spots diligently with swimming plugs and leadhead jigs.

The same can be said for a shadow line from the dock lights. The difference is that you're usually close to the water. Keep your rod tip low so that the plug or jig works parallel with the surface, and work the lure right up close to the pilings.

31

Jetty Fishing

The most commonly fished structures for many shorebound coastal anglers are the assorted formations of rock, concrete, wood, and rubble that protrude into the water. These include groins, inlet jetties, rockpiles, and accessible harbor breakwaters. Though slightly different, they are all commonly referred to as jetties and provide a wealth of angling possibilities. Fishing these jetties can be enjoyed at nominal cost, and can provide a wide range of species and angling experiences.

Jetty fishing is actually among the most physical types of angling you can experience, especially if you move about, visit several jetties during an outing, and work along the length of each of them. This is unlike other types of saltwater angling in that there is no comfortable platform or secure location to fish from.

Angling from jetties requires dexterity to move about the moss- and mussel-covered rocks, sometimes in darkness; an ability to present a lure or bait properly to gamefish; and the temerity to land fish from a promontory that is often cascaded with crashing waves and flying spray. Jetty fishing aficionados, known as "jetty jockeys," are a breed of anglers who find excitement, challenge, and reward in an activity that tests their skills every second they are on the rocks.

An angler fishes from the head of the jetty at Barnegat, New Jersey.

Fishing with Bait

Use a basic bottom-fishing bait rig for fishing natural bait around jetties, such as that described for pier and bridge fishing. Work such a rig on the bottom in the waters surrounding the structure you're fishing.

Assuming you're fishing from a rockpile that extends several hundred feet seaward, make your initial casts from along the side of the jetty just outside the surf line. Often the churning surf exposes sand fleas, crabs, shrimp, sand eels, and other forage, and the fish move in to feed. Patience is important, but if your bait rests on the bottom in prime water and doesn't receive a strike in 10 to 15 minutes, move farther out on the jetty and make another cast into new water. Keep repeating this procedure until you receive strikes; this way you're covering the entire bottom surrounding the structure.

It's usually not essential to cast great distances from a jetty or rockpile, since the natural forage is often in close. Rather, cast a nominal distance, perhaps 100 to 150 feet, and periodically reel in the bait several feet, thus bracketing the entire area.

Live baits are often used when targeting some bigger gamefish. These should be freelined without a sinker so that the bait can swim out and away from the jetty. For this, tie a tiny barrel swivel to the end of the line and then a 3- or 4-foot leader of 20- to 30-pound test. The leader is heavier than the main line because fish often ingest part of the leader when taking the bait, and this helps

prevent leader breakage. This basic terminal rig will work for the majority of species found around coastal jetties. The key is tailoring the size of the hook and bait to the species being sought. In some cases it may help to add a sliding float to the line, positioning it so that the bait works from 3 to 5 feet beneath the surface, with the float signaling precisely where the bait is.

Properly hooked, a live baitfish will swim about for a half hour or more, becoming excited as a large gamefish zeroes in on it. Live baits such as these are transported to jetties in 5-gallon buckets; place just a couple of baits in the bucket so that all of the oxygen in the water isn't quickly consumed. This is just about the only practical way to bring live bait onto jetties and departs from the rule that buckets should not be carried onto rockpiles. When the bait is no longer useful, save it and use it in chunks or strips later, after you've used up all your live ammunition.

Fishing with Lures

The most popular lures for jetty fishing are metal squids, plugs, and bucktail or soft-bodied jigs. Within these three lure categories are dozens of combinations.

Metal squids include the time-proven molded-block tin squids, hammered stainless steel jigs, chrome- and gold-plated jigs, and assorted variations of the diamond jig. Some of these are fished plain and others by adding a plastic tail or tube to the hook, or feathers, bucktail skirt, or pork rind strip. The lures are available in sizes ranging from ¼ ounce to 3 or 4 ounces. The key is matching lure size and color to the baitfish in residence.

Dozens of plugs also have merit around jetties. Perhaps the most popular one is the swimming minnow version. It's important to match the size to available forage. Other possibilities include an assortment of popping, darting, and skipping surface plugs. These work best when there's a lot of activity around and competition for food.

A bucktail or plastic-bodied jig may be the best all-around lure. Various sizes, colors, and soft body styles are possible. With the soft tails, you simply select the size and look that seems best and slip the tail onto the hook. The soft bodies replicate many baitfish, include such important jetty forage as sand eels, herring, and mullet.

Jetty fishing offers the opportunity to fish at various levels and with various techniques, depending on water conditions and likely species.

Jetty anglers regularly employ some of these lures in combination; they'll use a plug or metal squid as the primary lure at the end of the line and put a hooked soft-tailed bait 24 to 30 inches ahead of that as a teaser. This combination is deployed by tying a small barrel swivel to the end of your line, followed by a 30- to 36-inch leader for attaching the main lure. The teaser, which can also be a streamer fly or even just a strip of pork rind on a hook, is then tied off the barrel swivel on a 6-inch dropper line.

Sometimes the teaser gets strikes, and sometimes the primary lure. It's not unusual to hook a double, with a fish on each lure; this may happen when a lot of bluefish, seatrout, and striped bass are around.

Live eels are used effectively for striped bass, weakfish, cobia, and other species found around rockpiles, although many anglers employ dead rigged eels with great results. These common eels, ranging in length from 6 to 18 inches, are killed in salt brine, then rigged on metal squids designed expressly for this purpose. The metal squid's hook is placed in the head of the eel, and a second hook is run through the eel with a rigging needle so that it comes out near the eel's vent. Rigged in this manner, the eel is a combination lure and bait. It is cast and retrieved much the same as a plug or metal squid and is very effective.

Anglers generally keep six to a dozen eels rigged and stored in sea salt brine in wide-mouthed 1-gallon plastic jars. Rigged and stored in this manner, the eels are tough and keep for months at a time.

It's easy to make the mistake of carrying a massive lure selection with you and constantly changing. The better tactic is to select two or three lures of each basic type and build confidence in them, matching the lure to the specific situation. When the surf adjacent to the jetty is running high and the wind is onshore, for example, it's appropriate to break out a heavy metal squid to reach into the stiff wind, whereas on a calm, windless night a small swimming plug worked in close to the rocks may be just right.

Footwear and Other Gear

Safety underfoot is unquestionably the most important consideration when jetty fishing. You'll be walking on a variety of surfaces, all of which may be wet, covered with slippery marine growth, or sheathed in mussels. Be careful as you move about.

Do not wear ordinary footwear or even rubber-soled boots or waders, all of which are only practical when the jetty is high and dry, which is usually when the fishing is poor. A variety of jetty footwear is available, with the term "jetty creepers" often used to describe soles designed for secure footing. Ordinary golf soles, such as those found on golf shoes, which have replaceable aluminum cleats, are ideal. Manufactured strap-on creepers with spiked soles are also used, but are less desirable because the straps tend to bind and the creepers often are tough to put on and uncomfortable to wear.

Depending on where you fish and the type of structure you'll be fishing from, select basic footwear as light as you can go. Golf shoes are ideal, followed by knee boots if you'll be sloshing through ankle-deep water, followed by hip boots and waders, the latter as a last resort. You will need boots or waders on jetties or breakwaters where the surf has eroded the beaches, requiring that you wade through water to gain access. A good storm suit is also indispensable in most jetty fishing situations, where waves crash against the rocks, producing windblown spray.

Since mobility is essential while jetty fishing, keep tackle to a minimum and carry it with you only in a shoulder bag, not in a tackle box. Use plastic sealable pouches to keep gear in the bag readily accessible and dry. Many good shoulder bags are available, some compartmented with plastic tubing and sleeves for inserting lures. Store the bag in a well-ventilated spot after each jetty fishing excursion; if you place a wet shoulder bag in a damp place and come back a week later, your lures will be a rusty mess.

If you fish from jetties at night (which is often when the angling is superior as the fish move in close to feed), you'll need a headlamp. This can be strapped loosely around your collar, so that the light hangs under your chin. The headlamp makes changing lures, moving around the rocks, or putting your beam on a fish about to be landed relatively easy.

General Tactics

Tidal Influence

Tides play an important role when fishing from jetties. High tide may bring 8 or 10 feet of water where only a sand flat existed at low tide. At some jetties, the rockpile isn't accessible at high tide, and you can get onto the rocks only after the tide has ebbed for a couple of hours. Experience is the best teacher. Visit the spots you plan to fish; if you're new to an area, visit local tackle shops and ask their advice about tides.

There are no set rules, as many species move about with the tides, taking up station to feed for just a short while and then moving on. The key is learning which jetty locations produce results at a given tide stage and planning your strategy accordingly. It's not unusual to visit several jetties in the course of a tide, capitalizing on the movements of the fish.

Because erosion and the ravages of the ocean often displace rocks and tumble them away from the jetty, you'll sometimes get snagged on them. It's a good idea to pre-visit the jetties you plan to fish when the tide is low; then you can make a visual observation of spots to avoid later when the water is higher and more favorable for fishing. Often the fronts of jetties are in disarray; at high tide the jetty appears straight and intact, whereas on the ebb tide you'll notice that the front of the jetty actually has boulders tumbled about.

Cover It All

Fish are attracted to a jetty because forage species often seek the protection of the rocks. Since you don't know precisely where the fish will be feeding, it is very important that you thoroughly cover all the water surrounding the jetty.

This is best accomplished by making your first cast shortly after you walk out onto the jetty, placing your lure just outside the curl of the breakers working in toward the beach. Often the churning action of the waves there exposes sand fleas, crabs, and shrimp, and fish will move into the heavy water to feed. After several casts, move out onto the jetty and bracket your casts, making a cast in toward the beach, so that the retrieve almost parallels the jetty. Next place a cast at a 45-degree angle from where you're standing, then straight in front of you, out 45 degrees, and finally almost paralleling the jetty. Then move out and repeat the procedure.

As you approach the end of the jetty, you'll often find that the seas are crashing onto the rocks and that it's difficult to cast over the submerged rocks and to work your lure. But this is a spot where the fish often feed, so work it carefully.

Complete the circuit, and work the remaining side of the jetty to the beach. Over time you'll find that each jetty will produce strikes at different

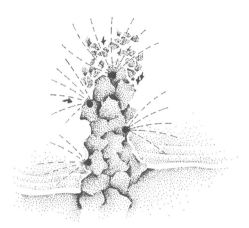

From each casting location on a jetty, an angler should bracket the area with casts to properly cover all water where fish may be feeding.

spots. Sometimes it's the location of submerged rocks and the way currents swirl around them that result in fish taking up station to feed. With experience, you'll accumulate a wealth of information about each jetty, and instead of working the entire rockpile you'll be able to concentrate your efforts in the spots, and with the lures, that regularly produce strikes.

Although casting away from the jetty works for most species, there are exceptions, for example, tautog (blackfish), sea bass, grunts, snapper, and sheepshead. These species often crowd the rocks, even swimming into crevices as they search for crabs and shrimp or rip mussels from the rocks. To catch them, you've got to present your baits in close, with the rig resting among the rocks. These fish will never find the bait if it's 10 or 15 feet from the jetty.

It's easy to snag your rig in the rocks, so when targeting these species simply tie a loop into the end of your line, onto which you slip a ½- or 1-ounce dipsey or bank sinker. Tie in a dropper loop a foot or so above the sinker, and put a 10- to 12-inch leader with a No. 1 or 2 Claw or Beak style hook on it. This is a small, compact rig that is less apt to get snagged than a multihook rig with a swivel.

Bait the hook with small pieces of seaworm, shrimp, squid, clam, mussel, snail, or cut mullet, and cast out just far enough that the bait rests on either the rocks or the sand immediately adjacent to the rocks where these species are searching for a meal. Most species that feed among jetty rocks

are quick to take a bait, so be alert and strike the fish immediately; delaying often results in a lost bait or a hooked fish that dives into a rocky crevice and cuts your line or leader.

Casting/Landing Tips

Try to make each cast count. If a fish is feeding in a pocket adjacent to a jetty, it will often strike on your first cast, since it is actively searching for a meal; as your lure comes into range, it's onto the lure in a flash.

Work every lure to the edge of the rocks before lifting it from the water. People often reel fast as their lure approaches the rocks to avoid getting fouled. This is a big mistake, because the greatest number of strikes will come in close. Sometimes the fish are feeding in close; more often they are attracted to and follow the lure and realize that it appears to be seeking the sanctuary of the rocks, so they make a last-second lunge to prevent it from getting away. Huge stripers, tarpon, and snook often startle anglers as they crash a lure within a rod's length, an exciting experience that gets the adrenaline moving.

When fishing for smaller fish, you can usually reel them within range of where you're standing and work them in close with the assistance of a wave, or you can simply lift them onto the rockpile. With bigger specimens, once the fish is hooked, permit it to move well away from the jetty, where it can't get the line caught on the rocks and mussels. Let the fish have its head, take drag, and tire itself out. As the fish tires, work it in close and position yourself so that you can get it within range of your gaff or, if someone is with you, within range of their position. Avoid spots where tumbled rocks or pilings or other debris are in front of you; this limits your control, especially when you have a big fish doing its best to get away.

Inlet Jetty Tactics

Technically, a jetty is a structure that extends from inlets and harbor mouths, although the word "jetty" is also commonly used to refer to coastal structures that extend from a beach where there is no inlet (these are actually groins).

The inlet entrance usually has a pair of parallel jetties or rockpiles on each side of it. These jetties may provide excellent fishing. However, the conditions at inlet jetties vary considerably from other coastal jetties. For one thing, the area between inlet jetties may be a couple of hundred feet wide and over a quarter-mile long. Where most coastal jetties have currents working up and down the beach adjacent to them, in the inlets the tidal flow, moving into bays and rivers or emptying into the ocean, presents a different set of conditions, requiring different tactics.

The tidal flow in and out of inlets ranges from just a few feet to 10 feet or more. As this water moves, strong currents develop, often carrying huge quantities of bait with it. This typically occurs on the ebbing tide, when forage species found in bays and rivers are carried along with the tide, as well as quantities of crabs, shrimp, and other food. Gamefish and bottom feeders often take up station in the inlets, usually along the bottom, in areas where they can place themselves out of the heaviest current and wait for a meal to be swept their way.

Often the currents are so swift that any lure, or the heaviest sinker and bottom rig, is just swept along. Therefore, the jetty angler who uses natural baits with a bottom rig must constantly cast out a rig, permit the current to carry it along, and then retrieve and cast again. Bottom fishing is usually best within an hour or so of either high or low tide; current moves with less velocity just before the slack, and the fish that have taken up station in the quiet water behind or ahead of rocks, ledges, or depressions in the bottom may begin to move about in search of a meal.

Many of the lightweight lures that are customarily fished from coastal jetties, especially surface and intermediate-depth plugs and metal squids, don't work as effectively in the swift and often deep water adjacent to inlet jetties. The single best lure in inlets is a leadhead jig, with either a bucktail or a soft plastic body, or a combination of both, perhaps also with a strip of pork rind. These lures get to the bottom quickly in even the heaviest current and can then be worked along the bottom as the current carries them along.

When you start lure fishing at an inlet jetty, position yourself low to the water on the rocks and cast out and across the current, beginning with a short cast of perhaps 25 to 40 feet. As the lure enters the water, permit it to settle on a slack

Inlet Jetty

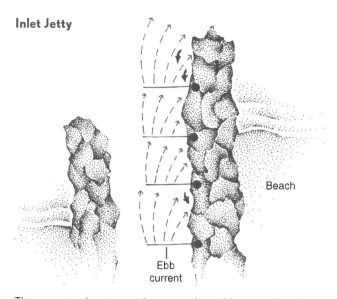

This scenario depicts an inlet jetty with an ebb current heading seaward. Jetty anglers here should work toward the end of the jetty; at each location begin with short casts and extend outward; then move 20 or 30 feet out and repeat.

line. As soon as the jig touches bottom, the line will pull taut, and you should close the bail or engage the gears. Let the lure be lifted off the bottom and carried by the current; it will often lift off the bottom again, move some more, and then bounce. As it moves along, it is being carried in toward the rocks; and as it nears the end of the swing, the current will sweep it off the bottom. This is where strikes most often occur. Frequently the strike feels as though you've snagged bottom, as a fish moves up and engulfs the jig as it lifts off the bottom.

Lengthen each succeeding cast by 15 or 20 feet, which enables the bucktail jig to bounce and sweep across a progressively longer stretch of bottom. Continue extending the distance of your casts as far as you can. If you receive no strikes, move out along the jetty rocks 20 or 30 feet and repeat the same procedure. In this way you'll cover all of the bottom. What often happens is that you'll receive the first strike and then you'll get multiple strikes on successive casts, as your jig works into an area where a pod of fish are schooled up, waiting for a meal to be carried to them.

Getting the feel of a bucktail jig bouncing bottom correctly is best accomplished by getting low to the water and keeping your rod tip pointed downward. Play it safe and don't get too close if a sea is running in the inlet. As the tide begins to slack, especially on the ebb—which is when the bulk of the forage is in the inlet—you'll find the jig moving more slowly. You can enhance its action by working your rod tip, causing the jig to dart ahead, then falter, and be again carried by the tide. At the end of the sweep, you can work the jig back to you, alternately lifting your rod tip, hesitating, then sweeping it upward, reeling, and repeating until you've completed the retrieve.

An occasional exception to this deep-fishing/deep-lure scenario occurs when the tide is swiftly ebbing and rips are formed to the seaward end of the inlet jetties. Tarpon, crevalle jack, snook, redfish, striped bass, weakfish, and bluefish may take up station in these rips and feed on the baitfish that become trapped in the whirlpool-like eddies. Often this activity is accompanied by seagulls and other seabirds picking baitfish from the water. This is when a big surface-swimming plug cast out into the rips and just held in the current, where it swims as the current pushes against it, may bring exciting surface strikes.

32

Surf Fishing

Fishing from the beach engenders a vision of an angler with a long rod, braving large breaking waves and casting a heavily weighted bait great distances over roiled and foamy water, mostly on a deserted stretch of beach, at dawn or at night. However, angling in or from the surf not only refers to this conventional view, but also to fishing accessible coastal beaches, in protected backwaters, or in locations where the surf ripples instead of pounds, with a variety of fishing equipment for any number of inshore species, at all times of the day.

The beach may be the venue of choice for anglers without boats or for those who prefer to be on (somewhat) solid ground. It may be preferred by those who simply like the sights, sounds, challenges, and camaraderie provided, notwithstanding some disadvantages in mobility. In any case, fishing along the beach pits angler against fish in a place where almost everything favors the fish. It is an act that requires total confidence in the ability to pick the exact spot along miles of coastline where a fish will find the angler's single offering.

Surf Tackle

While all surf anglers aspire to catch a trophy fish, most are happy with a bucketful of the various small species that are common along the surf line. And although specialized attention is devoted to some species, especially when fishing with lures, a majority of the effort is directed at catching anything that is available.

The average surf caster will carry some heavy artillery but will also have a variety of smaller outfits that in some cases are light enough to be at home on freshwater trout streams. Therefore, selecting a surf fishing outfit requires an examination of several factors, beginning with the size and strength of the individual. A big person can usually handle a much heavier outfit than someone small in stature. This does not mean that these two people couldn't fish side by side and have an equal chance of success; they just need tackle to match their physical capabilities.

Basic Outfits

Most rods used by surf anglers are longer than those used by anglers who fish from boats, because the length is needed to overcome the height of the waves and to attain greater casting distance. While long is good, longer is not necessarily better. Once a rod surpasses 12 to 13 feet in length, effectiveness drops off dramatically. Even 12-footers may be too much for some people, so this is where you need to evaluate rod length in relation to your own stature and strength.

The heaviest outfit in common use by today's surf caster is a 10- to 12-foot long rod designed to toss a 6- to 12-ounce sinker and a big chunk of cut bait into the teeth of a gale. Reels with a capacity of at least 300 yards of 20-pound line or 200 yards of 30-pound, and sporting ball bearings on the drive shaft, are very popular, and a 50- to 80-pound shock leader is often tied to the end of the main line.

A more practical outfit that will serve all but the most severe surf fishing is a 10- to 12-foot medium-action rod that will handle 4 to 6 ounces of weight. Conventional reels or spinning reels, filled with 15- to 20-pound line and matched to the rod, complete the package.

Although this is the conventional medium-weight tackle for surf fishing, some situations require slightly different approaches. For example, anglers who fish for snook in the surf in some parts of their range may use 7- to 9-foot rods equipped with medium-weight baitcasting reels and spooled with 12- to 17-pound line. These anglers are especially concerned with getting

some distance on their casts to place lures out into the proper depth of water and portion of the surf, as well as having some leverage for playing fish. They may use the same tackle inland or inshore for non–surf fishing activities. So surf tackle is relative to the situation, and some situations may dictate still lighter tackle yet.

In addition to the standard medium-action outfit, most surf anglers will also have at least one smaller setup. This will be used, for example, when working a slough for small bottom feeders or when tossing light lures for trout, blues, and drum.

A 7-foot rod matched to a reel holding 10- to 15-pound line will handle bottom fishing and will cast all but the smallest lures. Speckled trout anglers and anglers fishing for small stripers often toss small jigs or lightweight plugs, and they will step down to much lighter rods and reels using 6- to 8-pound line. These smaller outfits are also utilized by pompano anglers who cast light weights and small baits just beyond the surf line.

Shock Leaders

Shock leaders are required in most surf fishing situations. A shock leader absorbs the wear on the line created by constant casting with heavy weights or lures. It should be long enough to wrap two or three times around the spool while the lure or bait rig hangs close to the first guide up from the reel. This heavy leader also comes in handy when trying to pull a big fish in through the breakers.

As a general rule the shock leader should be twice as heavy as the running line. The knot is the

An angler fishes the surf at Montauk, New York.

weak link in the rig, so it must be tied properly, trimmed as closely as possible, and regularly checked for wear.

Accessories

Since fishing the surf without getting into the water is almost impossible, you'll need good-quality chest waders in cold water and cold weather. These must be worn with a tightened belt to seal off the top in case the angler takes a tumble in the surf. Without this protection, the waders can fill up, pulling the angler under the water. As an added precaution, and for additional protection against rain and surf spray, a foul-weather jacket is worn over the waders and is also belted at the waist.

Surf casters should always wear some type of protective footwear. "Wet shoes" (shoes made to be worn in water), an old pair of canvas deck shoes, or even a pair of high-sided rubber boots will work in warm conditions. Wading shoes or boots that cover the ankle and keep out sand are also good.

Because many surf outfits, especially those used with bait and heavy weights, are heavy, you'll need a rod holder, which in surf fishing is called a sand spike. These are 3 to 5 feet long and mostly made from heavy PVC pipe or very light plastic tubes.

To land fish that you plan to keep, a gaff is often indispensable. Beach anglers generally use a short-handled or release gaff placed under the fish's lower jaw.

For nighttime surf fishing, you need a small flashlight with a narrow beam that is usually held in the mouth when a light is needed to tie on new rigs or untangle lines. A miner's light worn around the head is another option. Bigger and brighter lights should be avoided, as you don't want to project light on the water, which will spook fish.

You'll also need a pair of high-quality fishing pliers for cutting line and leader, removing hooks, crimping wire leader sleeves, and other tasks; a stainless steel multipurpose tool for various unanticipated needs; and a knife for cutting bait or cleaning and filleting fish.

Fishing with Bait

In most surf fishing situations, bait outproduces artificial lures, but there is more to baitfishing than simply tossing out a hunk of meat. The angler who presents the proper bait in a natural manner will consistently have success. An effective presentation requires consideration of both the proper bait to use and the way to use it, as well as choice of bait rigs.

Bait Rigs

A typical surf bait rig consists of a hook and sinker held together by a leader. For big fish, such as trophy-size red drum or striped bass, you need 50- to 100-pound leaders. Small bottom fish, however, can be taken on leaders as light as 10 pounds.

Rigs can be purchased in local tackle shops, as can locally favored baits. When fishing an unfamiliar area, you should begin by purchasing local rigs to match whatever has been catching fish in that location even if you prefer to make up your own rig, as many surf anglers do. Effective bait rigs vary from one location to another, but most fall into one of three categories: top/bottom, single hook, and fishfinder.

The top/bottom rig, which is primarily used for small bottom fish, features a sinker and two hooks, spaced 5 to 12 inches apart, decorated with beads, spinner blades, bucktail hair, soft grubs, floats, or any other device that you believe will attract fish. Some species, such as pompano, prefer to take their bait from a plain hook.

In most applications, the drop from the leader to the hook will be quite short. Long leaders will foul when they're cast or as they're tossed about in the surf. Short leaders keep the hook close to the line for a better hookset. A top/bottom rig made from wire with 3- to 4-inch standoffs is popular

Top/Bottom Rig

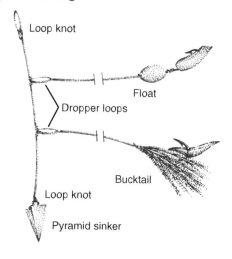

Loop knot

Float

Dropper loops

Bucktail

Loop knot

Pyramid sinker

Single-Hook Rig

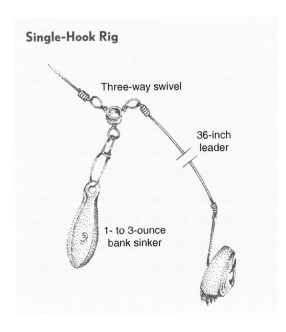

Three-way swivel

36-inch leader

1- to 3-ounce bank sinker

in a few areas. Snelled hooks are looped over the ends of the standoffs.

Single-hook rigs are used when seeking bigger fish. Leaders may be 12 inches or longer and are made from heavy nylon monofilament or braided wire; the latter is reserved for such toothy critters as big bluefish, and the monofilament is used in all other cases.

The heart of the single-hook rig is a three-way swivel. The leader is attached to one eye, a sinker snap to the second eye, and the running line to the third eye. In most cases, the hook is left undecorated, but a large cork float may be added when sight feeders are the target.

A fishfinder rig is a single-hook rig that moves along the line. The running line or shock leader is threaded through a sleeve, usually made from plastic, and then tied to a large swivel. The leader is tied to the other end of the swivel. A sinker snap is attached to the plastic sleeve to secure the sinker, which will rest on the bottom. When a fish picks up the bait, it can move away without feeling the weight of the sinker. This is important when using live baits or when the target species needs a bit of time to get the bait well into its mouth.

The length of the leader on a fishfinder rig is a matter of some disagreement. A long leader, up to 36 inches, is favored by some, but it is very difficult to cast. Short leaders of 12 inches or less are easier to cast but provide little protection to the

running line or shock leader. One variation is to put the plastic sleeve on the leader, which restricts the amount of line a fish can take but allows the sinker to slide down within 6 inches of the hook when casting.

Surf anglers seek all types and sizes of fish and utilize all types and sizes of hooks. The Chestertown is popular for small bottom feeders; the wide-gap Siwash works well on larger fish such as trout or flounder; and the offset beak is often used for big drum or striped bass. Circle hooks have gained popularity because they impale fish in the corner of the mouth and allow easy, unharmed release.

Sinkers are needed to anchor each of these rigs to the bottom. They basically are found in pyramid and bank styles, with the former more common along the beach. A pyramid sinker digs into the sand to hold the rig in place. A bank sinker does not dig into the sand or hold a rig in one location, so it is used to move the bait across the bottom as the angler slowly cranks the rig back to the beach.

Surf Bait Basics

The most important consideration for bait is its condition. Fresh bait is vital to success and must be selected with the same care used to buy fish for the table. Look at the gills of prospective baitfish; they should be red, and the eyes should be clear, not pink. The flesh should not be soft, and the fish should have a clean smell. Frozen fish will work as bait, but fresh (unfrozen) is preferable. Frozen shrimp and crabs are useless.

Fishfinder Rig

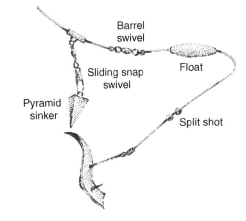

Barrel swivel

Sliding snap swivel

Float

Pyramid sinker

Split shot

Known as a fishfinder rig, this is a basic setup for surf fishing.

Frozen squid, however, seems to work as well as the fresh product.

Bait must be properly stored to stay in prime condition. A cooler should be dedicated just for bait and set up to keep bait and ice separated. Most bait will lose color and turn to mush when submerged in ice water. Plastic containers that seal out air and water are excellent for keeping bait in a cooler. They also separate the different types of bait you might use, making it convenient to find what you want in the bottom of a crowded cooler. While fishing, cut the bait into whatever size is appropriate, take what you need to put on the hook, and return the rest to the cooler.

Fish used for bait in surf angling come in all shapes and sizes. In most cases, fish are cut into pieces, but small specimens such as finger mullet may be used whole. Depending on the target species, fish bait is cut into fillets or chunks. Use chunks when you need a tougher bait for long casts or bigger fish. Use fillets when you want a thin bait that will move in current. Fillets may be whole or cut into strips. Strip baits are effective when trying to imitate small, thin baitfish, whereas whole fillets imitate larger species.

Fish baits should be cut with care. Make strips wide at the hook end and tapering down to a point. Cut fillets to the shape of a fish; a sharp knife will split the tail for a very lifelike presentation. Chunks should be cut from the back of the head to the tail. The size of the target species determines the size of the chunk. For some reason, many anglers discard the head and tail, forgetting that fish eat the whole thing. In all cases it's a good idea to remove the scales from fish bait; this is easy to do and makes hook insertion much easier.

Baits should be hooked through the thickest part, chunks through the back, fillets and strip baits through the wide end. Put the hook all the way through the bait and leave the point exposed. It is hard enough to drive a hook into the fish's mouth; you don't want to be driving it through the bait as well.

Squid is cut into strips or small pieces. Strips work well when small, thin baitfish are in the surf. Pieces are just right for bottom feeders. The head of a squid makes an excellent bait for larger gamefish, and the tentacles can be threaded onto a Chestertown hook in place of a worm.

Sea worms are great baits for a surprising number of fish. Striped bass and weakfish are very fond of worms, especially in the spring. Sea mullet and spot will take a worm in place of anything else. Whole worms are hooked through the head or tail and allowed to stream out in the current. At times you may need several worms on the same hook to attract attention. Worms cut into bite-size pieces and threaded onto the hook are the ticket for bottom feeders who suck the bait into their mouths. A bit of worm left dangling from the end of the hook will add some moving enticement to the bait.

Fresh shrimp may be fished whole or cut into small pieces. They are very expensive bait and are saved for situations where only shrimp are effective. Pompano and speckled trout prefer shrimp, but both will often take less expensive offerings.

Crabs come in hard and peeler stages. A hard crab has a hard outer shell; a peeler crab has a soft shell under a hard outer shell. A peeler, also called a shedder, is getting ready to shed the outer shell and emerge as a soft-shelled crab, a stage during which it is defenseless and an easy prey.

When fishing with either type of crab, remove the hard outer shell and cut the crab into sections with heavy-duty shears. Place the hook through a leg hole, not through the shell. Crabs do not stay on the hook very well and are often secured with rubber bands or dental floss.

Red drum are very fond of peeler crabs, especially in the spring when crabs are shedding.

Not all surf fishing requires heavy outfits; opportunities exist for using lighter tackle and casting with lures in the near-surf waters, as this angler is doing at Cape May Point, New Jersey.

Unfortunately, every fish in the ocean shares this craving for peeler crabs, and baits do not last long in the water.

Peelers are expensive, so try to get the largest ones you can, and cut them into as many pieces as possible. Trout will take a single section, but red drum require at least a quarter of a crab to attract their attention. A small piece of peeler on a bucktail will give the appearance of a larger bait.

Hard crab is a poor substitute when fish are feeding on peelers. The two baits evidently smell and taste different, because fish can certainly tell them apart. Hard crabs become more acceptable later in the season when peelers are scarce. Cut hard crabs in small sections for big fall-run spot and croaker, and use half of a crab for drum and striped bass.

Live bait is used by surf anglers, but it does require a special container to keep the bait alive. Carrying a large container full of water and bait is not practical for a walk-on angler. A four-wheel-drive vehicle is needed to move a heavy livewell and provide the power to aerate it.

Live baitfish are deployed with a fishfinder rig. When live bait is taken, the fish will swim off while turning the bait around to swallow it head-first. This process takes a few seconds, and the fish may drop the bait if it feels the weight of the sinker. Exactly how much time you should allow for the fish to have the bait before you take up the slack and set the hook depends on the size of the bait, the species of fish, and your own judgment, keeping in mind that a longer wait usually means a more deeply hooked fish, which is more difficult to release unharmed.

Fish used as bait are best hooked through the lips or eye sockets. This allows them to swim in a somewhat natural manner while anchored to the bottom or while being slowly retrieved. Eels are also fished alive but require different treatment and handling. Store eels in a small cooler with a mixture of ice and water. By keeping the eels as cold as possible, they will be much easier to handle when the time comes to put them on a hook. A damp rag will allow the eel to be handled without getting slime on the angler and the tackle.

Hook the eel through the lips or the eyes. Use a single-hook rig with a 3-foot leader tied to a drail heavy enough to cast the bait beyond the breakers. A slow retrieve back to the beach keeps the eel moving and prevents a seriously tangled leader.

Eels that are set on the bottom get into curled and line-wrapped mischief.

Salted eels are fished with a swimming lip. Although technically they are dead baits, rigged eels are worked like a lure. Cast them out and retrieve them so that they swim just above the bottom. A rigged eel is deadly on striped bass, especially at night or on overcast days.

Sitting versus Fishing

Most surf anglers leave their rods in a sand spike while their bait soaks somewhere offshore. Spiking the rod and soaking bait allows the angler to enjoy the social side of surf fishing while still catching the occasional fish.

In some cases, you want the bait to stay in one place, such as at the edge of a bar when you're waiting for a big drum to pass by. But if you want to catch more than the occasional fish, you need to work at it. Get your rod out of the sand spike and tend to business by replacing old bait with fresh bait, repositioning the bait, and covering various areas of the surf.

Certain situations clearly dictate a more active approach to surf angling. Flounder, for instance, prefer a moving target, so you must keep the bait moving over the bottom. Several fish species cruise the inshore side of an outer bar looking for food washed over by the wave action. The best way to capitalize on this is to cast a bait onto the bar and allow it to wash down the dropoff. It takes some practice to reel in just enough line to keep in touch with the rig while letting it drop in a natural manner. You don't do this once and then stop; you keep trying.

Using very light tackle and small rigs for pompano requires similar techniques. The small sinker will not hold bottom and will be swept along the beach. You must watch the angle of your line, moving it inshore while the current takes it parallel to the shore. The strike will come just beyond the breaker or in the whitewater after the wave breaks. Once the rig has passed these spots without notice, slowly reel in and try again.

Fishing with Lures

Although fishing with bait is generally preferred in the surf, lures are used in many locations on a wide variety of fish, and at certain times they outproduce live or dead baits. Some species, like Spanish mackerel, are seldom taken on bait but will hit a well-placed metal lure. When bluefish are blitzing the beach, a surf bait will work, but a big surface popper provides more exciting action.

Three basic types of lures are used in the surf: metal lures, plugs, and leadhead jigs. Each has a specific use, but most fish will take all three under varying conditions.

Metal Lures

Because surf fishing requires casting a good distance and letting a sinking lure settle into and work through roiling water, anglers often prefer a thick-bodied metal lure. These are straight, heavy-bodied products that are primarily used for casting, and work with either a fast or a slow retrieve. Thin and thick versions are used when you're matching thin or fat baitfish, respectively. Lead models also come in various sizes, with smaller ones working on Spanish mackerel and small bluefish, and larger ones on trout and striped bass.

Smaller metal lures are cast to breaking fish and retrieved rather quickly. The strike often comes as soon as the lure hits the water, so the reel must be engaged upon impact. If the fish fails to strike immediately, crank the lure quickly to keep it working close to the surface. At times a slight pause to let the lure drop a bit may induce a strike. Larger, heavier lures are fished along the bottom with a hopping, jigging action to imitate a sand eel. Sometimes it's good to let a lure sink into the sand and then jerk it out by quickly raising the rod tip.

Spoons are sometimes also used in the surf, but their wide surface area and generally light weight make them less aerodynamic and more difficult to cast. Under favorable conditions, the heavier, thicker metal spoons can be employed as is. Light-weight spoons can be effective when accompanied by a drail, which is tied 12 to 18 inches above the spoon to add the weight necessary to cast beyond the breakers. Allow the rig to sink, then use a moderate retrieve to keep the spoon just above the bottom. Trout, stripers, drum, and other bottom feeders may find this technique irresistible.

Plugs

A surf fishing plug must be heavy enough and have the proper shape to cast well, plus have a slow to moderate swimming action. Most surf plugs are shallow-swimming models; deep divers have little merit in the shallow intertidal zone of the surf.

Swimming plugs for surf use come in various styles. The most popular have a slow side-to-side action and can be worked in different sea conditions. Darting versions have a long, angled face and swim in a wide side-to-side motion. They can be very effective in a rip at the mouth of an inlet or at the end of a point or bar. Cast the plug upcurrent, and allow it to sweep past with little or no retrieve. The force of the current will cause the plug to work.

Breaking waves and crosscurrents will contribute to the action of most swimming lures, and you must adjust the retrieve to compensate for these factors. Plugs should be cast just beyond a wave that is about to break. As the wave rolls toward the beach, the plug is retrieved at the proper speed to keep it working in the whitewater but ahead of the next wave that would tumble it head over tail. The plug should give the impression of a baitfish caught up in or struggling against the waves and thus easy prey.

An exception to this retrieval tactic are needlefish-like plugs that are long and thin and without inherent action. These are slowly retrieved without any movement of the rod tip so that they come through the water in a straight line. These plugs are basically like a stick with hooks, but they have accounted for many big stripers. Some other straight-running plugs are used in the surf with a bit of rod-tip movement.

Surf anglers can also double up when using a plug by placing a second lure on a dropper line ahead of the plug. This second lure may be a small fly, soft grub, or small bucktail jig, each of which acts like a baitfish trying to avoid a predator (the plug). Quite often a strike will come on the dropper lure.

Crosscurrents or rips at the end of points leave eddies of slower-moving water where gamefish wait for bait to tumble past. A plug cast up and across the current will sweep by this eddy and may attract a strike. Slow-swimming lures that will work with little more than the pressure of the current are particularly effective in these rips. Plugs worked in the roiled surf along jetties, causeways, and pilings are also likely to bring strikes, since the flash of these lures where waves wash up and roil can be an attractant.

Occasionally a surface plug has merit in the surf, although this is usually when a school of gamefish has pinned a school of bait against the beach or is chasing bait to the surface. At such times, almost any lure that will reach the fracas will be effective, but a surface lure that pops, chugs, and spits water is most exciting to fish.

Leadhead Jigs

The most versatile weapon in the surf angler's arsenal is the leadhead jig, known to many simply as a leadhead. Dressed with bucktail hair, a soft-bait tail, or a strip of bait, this lure will imitate the food of most gamefish. The prudent angler will carry a selection of these lures in a wide variety of colors.

Leadheads come in a variety of head shapes, with the rounded, bullet, and Upperman styles very popular with surf casters. A surf jig must cast well and sink fast, and these particular shapes have low resistance to both air and water.

Turbulent surf waters make it difficult to maintain control of a jig. Light line will aid in both casting distance and control, with the jig tied directly to the main line without benefit of leader or hardware.

Select the size and color of the bucktail to match the size and color of local baitfish. Also consider contrast. A dark lure works better against a light background like sand, and a light color stands out more against a dark background like rocks. A bucktail with white hair and a red head is a popular all-around pattern.

Bucktails can be worked fast or slow, shallow or deep. A fast retrieve just below the surface can be deadly on Spanish mackerel or bluefish. Working it slowly along the bottom is good for speckled trout, flounder, or striped bass.

Threading a soft-tail bait onto the hook shank makes a leadhead jig even more versatile. Large soft-tail leadheads are effective on drum, striped bass, and flounder. Smaller versions are used for speckled trout, puppy drum, and a wide variety of other small bottom feeders.

The speed of retrieve is generally slower for soft-tailed jigs. A straight retrieve works best on swimming models, whereas a hop-and-skip action can make the straight runners come alive. Tying two jigs 8 to 10 inches apart improves casting distance and may make the package more appealing.

Always work a jig all the way through the surf line. Gamefish may follow it to the water's edge before deciding to eat, so an early end to the retrieve may take the lure out of the water too soon.

Sweetening a jig with some sort of natural bait is a common practice along the surf. Tough items such as squid or shark belly hold up well and may be added to a naked jig or one dressed with buck-tail hair or a soft tail. Pork rind can add life to any leadhead; the long, thin strips imitate such natural food as spearing, and they are deadly on flounder and trout. They also work for bluefish and hold up against their sharp teeth. White seems to be the favorite and most productive color in the surf, but pork rind is available in many hues.

Picking a Spot

The surf line is a constantly changing mix of sand, mud, rock, or any combination of materials. Surf anglers must use experience and knowledge to pick a spot where the fish will be active during their time on the beach. Most surf anglers are on foot and thus have limited mobility. While it is always possible that the inexperienced angler may stumble onto a fishing hotspot, those who study the surf and learn about tides and currents will know where to be and at what preferred times, and will do better over the long haul.

Sand makes up most of the beaches where surf anglers congregate, and it moves about with the tides and currents. This movement creates bars, sloughs, washouts, runouts, holes, channels, and other formations that may combine some or all of the above. The surf angler must look at the surface of the water and figure out exactly what lies underneath, be aware of the present stage of the tide and current, and have some knowledge of what the existing or predicted winds will do to the waves. It is also helpful to know when the target species is likely to stop by for a meal. This sounds like finding a needle in a haystack, but it is not that complicated.

According to oceanographers, a wave will break when the water below it is twice as deep as the wave is high. In other words, a 1-foot wave will break in 2 feet of water. Thus waves break in shallow water but hold together over deep water.

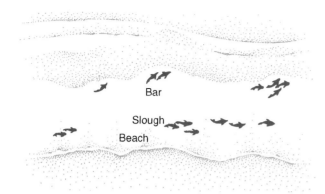

Where there is an outer bar that receives breaking waves, fish hold close to the inner side of the bar and also lurk in the deeper water of the slough.

A natural beach allows a wave to break gradually, dissipating its energy over some distance. As the wave rolls in, it begins to break offshore on the outer bar, churning sand from the bottom and pushing it back to the bar. A smaller wave now rides across the deeper water of the slough before breaking onshore. As this wave breaks on the beach, it scours out a dropoff at the edge of the whitewater. This dropoff moves in and out with the tide, but the outer bar remains somewhat stationary.

The distance from where the surf caster stands to the outer bar can vary considerably. In some places the bar will come to the beach forming a point, but a little farther up or down the shoreline the bar will be a distance of at least two and a half casting lengths offshore.

Deep holes form along the beach due to varying combinations of wind, tide, and current. Some may come and go on a single tide, and others stay around until the next big storm. Washouts, runouts, and breaks in the outer bar are channels created by currents moving back and forth on the tides. Not only are these channels deeper than the surrounding water, but they act as highways for fish and bait to move from offshore to inshore and back offshore.

Low tide is the best time to figure out what lies below the water. When the depth of the water is at its lowest point, the difference between shallow and deep water is apparent. Waves will be breaking on the shallow areas, some of which may be completely exposed. Deeper water will be calm and should appear blue or green rather than white.

A wind blowing toward the shore will create problems as it pushes more water toward the beach and increases the size of the waves. Deeper water and higher waves can disguise bottom structure; if the wind increases to more than 15 knots, the entire ocean may turn white.

Winds blowing offshore have a different effect. They push water away from land, exposing structure not seen on normal low tides. These winds also push the warm surface water offshore and can drop surf temperatures by 10° to 15°F. This sudden temperature drop is seldom beneficial to surf fishing.

If you crest the top of the dune line at low tide, you can survey a considerable stretch of beach. Look for waves breaking on an offshore bar that is close enough to be in casting range. A break in the bar or a place where the bar comes to the beach will funnel fish to you.

Set up a station close to the break or the point and you will be in position for some action on the rising tide. Walk-on anglers will stay in one area, but those with four-wheel-drive vehicles can move about looking for the best action. Drive slowly and stop often to watch wave action and water color. Birds feeding close to shore are a positive sign, especially if big fish are observed breaking under the birds.

Watch not only the water, birds, and fish, but other anglers. When everyone is sitting in chairs or leaning on their vehicles talking, the action is pretty slow. A tight group of anglers standing at the water's edge, holding rods without a sand spike in sight, indicates that someone recently caught something. If most of the rods are bent, you've found a good place to fish, and you better get started.

Every beach is a separate entity. Some are similar but none are exactly the same. A rocky coast in Maine or California fishes completely different from a sandy beach in North Carolina. The only way to learn how to read the beach where you fish

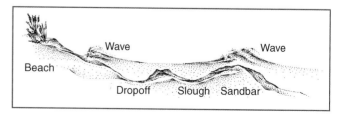

This cross-sectional view of the beach and surf helps to illustrate the features that affect site selection and fish presence.

is experience. The more time you put in, the more knowledge you'll gain. For example, you should learn when stripers stage on the end of a certain bar, or when pompano move over an outer bar, or at what stage of the tide you can expect to find flounder in a particular slough. No matter how much you read or how many old salts you talk to, the only way to learn how to read the beach is to get out there and fish.

Night Fishing

Many fish species move into the surf at night to feed when they feel safer in the shallow water. Striped bass, weakfish, and red drum are among the fish that are taken regularly after dark.

Fishing the surf at night is similar to fishing in daylight but does require a few modifications. Avoid bright lights at all cost. Fish have very sensitive eyes, and the beam from a flashlight, headlights, or searchlight will send them to deeper, darker water. Never approach a fishing site with the headlights on or scan the water with a flashlight or searchlight.

It's a good idea to arrive at the beach before dark to scout the waters and allow your eyes to adjust. Scouting out the situation in daylight will make the return trip easier and safer because you will have seen the territory earlier in the light. You should always be careful when wading in the surf but especially so after dark. An angler who is knocked down by a wave or who steps into a deep hole may go unnoticed until it is too late. A miner's light worn around the neck or on a hat helps surf anglers keep track of one another without shedding enough light on the water to spook the fish. The same light is also handy for close work when tying knots or unhooking fish.

Dress appropriately for night fishing because even the warmest summer day can turn into a chilly night. This is amplified when water temperatures are cold and the wind is blowing.

Casting into a totally dark ocean using the sound of breaking waves as a guide takes a bit of getting used to. Any available moonlight helps, as do permanent shore lights. Fortunately, the tops of breaking waves are white and reflect even the smallest amount of available light.

33

Offshore Fishing

The term "offshore" is largely a generic one used by saltwater anglers to refer to deep-water areas on the edges of ocean currents or to shelves commonly called blue water. The fish pursued in these areas are generally pelagic big-game species, particularly billfish, tuna, and dolphin.

Although offshore fishing is done at great distances from some mainland coasts, it can be done fairly close to other coasts if hydrographic contours and currents provide appropriate conditions suitable to the presence of big-game species. Thus offshore fishing may be enjoyed by anglers fishing from private sportfishing boats of various sizes, from charter boats, and, less commonly, from long-range party boats.

Generally, offshore fishing is done with medium- to heavy-duty conventional tackle or big-game tackle, even though some of these species, or smaller specimens, may be caught with other equipment where circumstances permit.

Trolling

Because of the expanse of water and the nature of pelagic species, offshore environs are primarily fished by trolling and by chumming while the boat is drifting or at anchor. Trollers use both lures and rigged natural baits, but some live-bait fishing occurs. The technique of chumming was covered separately, as were the general principles of trolling. However, offshore trolling for large gamefish is significantly more involved than other types of trolling, and requires separate review here.

In saltwater, there are many lures that are of use for trolling and which only have application for trolling. They are not designed to be cast, or jigged, or retrieved by some combination of rod movement and wrist action. They're too large, too hard-pulling, or too cumbersome for anything but trolling, and they often must be worked faster than would be prudent for any caster. The action they exhibit, the noise they produce, the water disturbance they make, and their passing resemblance to squid and flyingfish are important and intertwined elements—all of which are best accentuated when traveling at high rates of speed. Thus special trolling lures have evolved for roaming the vast ocean expanses and, in some cases, for use with the heavier tackle that is often demanded for saltwater bruisers.

The category of saltwater trolling lures includes a number of distinctive items and some that are closely related or fished in conjunction with others. Teasers, for example, can be fished hookless as an attractor ahead of a hard-headed offshore lure or can be fished as lures when rigged with hooks. While teasers are primarily used as attention-getting devices, they are relatively unique in fishing because they are only used in saltwater, only used on the surface, and only used for trolling.

Offshore lures are fished either on the surface or under but fairly close to the surface. A distinguishing characteristic is their ability and effectiveness—some would call it necessity—to be trolled at high speeds. High speeds in offshore fishing go way beyond the higher speeds that are used in most other forms of trolling, being on average in the 8 to 10 knots range, but on the low end starting at 5 knots and on the high end going into the upper teens (with some reports of offshore trolling lures catching fish up to 24 knots).

The principal key to success with offshore lures is that they must "look right." They must create maximum visibility while still tracking straight and not flying, and to do this it may be necessary to make numerous adjustments when first setting them out. This requires some experimentation and experience to accomplish.

There is a difference between looking good and looking perfect, and you really want them to be perfect. It's worth remembering that pelagic fish feed in certain ways and that their common foods behave in certain ways. Flyingfish, for example, exit the water sharply, and after gliding they dive back into the water and swim, but they don't skip. This is the action you want to imitate.

First, the boat speed must be adjusted to your choice of lures, or vice versa in the case of a boat with limited power, keeping in mind that you shouldn't mix lures that run best at different speeds. When boat speed is limited by power or design or by sea conditions, the choice of lure must be made accordingly. Flat- and slant-faced lures (with a shallow angle) have the widest range of application, while swimming lures are limited to slower trolling speeds. Concave straight runners work well over a broad range of boat speeds but tend to fly at the upper end or when seas are up. Weighted lures, pointy-headed styles, and doorknob styles can handle the highest speeds.

When seas are up, you must adjust, and your options include switching to weighted lures, slowing the boat speed and switching to lures that either swim erratically or create turbulence and smoke at slower speeds, or dropping the lures farther back behind the boat to keep them from flying out of the water.

In all cases, lures should ride the face of the wave for best action. Although there are many theories on placement, most pros prefer to set large lures out flat on the second to fourth wake wave behind the boat, and smaller lures on the fifth to seventh wave. Some put out a fifth line (called a "shotgun"), which is placed very short and center or very far back and center.

Offshore trolling lures are meant to create an attractive commotion on top of the water, as depicted here, just beneath the surface, or both, depending on design.

Wherever you place them, make sure that they are getting the proper action. Many people tend to troll at too slow a speed, and lure action suffers. Remember that most offshore lures are designed to run best at 8 to 10 knots, and some even higher; 8 to 10 knots is generally considered an optimum range for marlin, tuna, and wahoo.

Because action, as well as a tendency to fly, increases when the angle of the line where it hits the water increases, many experts use a tagline on their flatlines. The angle of entry of the long lines can usually be lowered by running the outrigger tagline lower. Reducing this angle can also help prevent lures from flying out of the water in rough seas.

A tagline is nothing more than a heavy cord fixed either to the outrigger poles or to a cleat at the transom. Fixed, nonrelease clips or waxed line-ties are secured to the end of the cord. A rubber band (No. 64 is the preferred size) is wrapped at least five times around the fishing line, then the two end loops in the rubber band are snapped into the clip or secured to the waxed-line ties by a quick-release loop. When a fish strikes, the rubber band stretches considerably before breaking, providing some initial give and helping to set the hook.

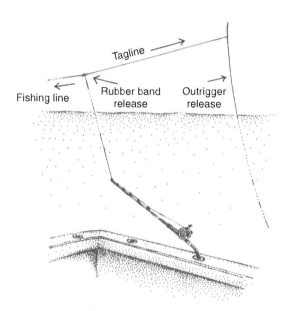

As shown, a tagline is a length of heavy cord or line between outrigger line and fishing line (or between boat and fishing line). A rubber band release, or spring tension release, is used to free the fishing line when a fish strikes the trolled lure or bait.

The size of the lure hook should be determined by the breaking strength of the line employed, and if possible the distance between barb and shank should be greater than the diameter of the lure head. Remember that heavy, thick hooks require heavier strike drags and hence heavier line.

Most pros rig two hooks with artificial lures, connecting them with a variety of materials from heavy monofilament (usually snelled), to heavy wire or cable. Even the experts argue between using stiff rigs versus loose-swinging "gaffer" rigs, but the beginner would do well to start with ready-made rigs. Many tackle shops sell prerigged lures, and that's a good way to start.

The second most important axiom for successful big-game fishing with offshore lures is paying close attention. When fishing offshore lures with tackle up to and including 50-pound-test class, the angler must set the hook and do so quickly. To accomplish this, he must be within a short step or two of the rods and watching the lures at all times. Besides, it's more fun to see the fish approach and strike the lure.

Although a good captain will hit the throttle the instant the rod bends and line begins to spill against the drag of the reel, the function of his action is simply to keep slack out of the line if the fish should charge toward the boat. With line of 50-pound test or less, this added momentum of the boat is not guaranteed to set the hooks for the inattentive angler. The angler must take the rod in hand and haul back hard and repeatedly to set the hook; failure to do so is the most frequent cause of "pulled hooks" and lost fish when using offshore lures, especially for big fish.

When fishing 80- to 130-pound-test tackle for marlin, the greater strike drag setting of the reel made possible by the heavier line does make it possible for the captain to set the hook by advancing the throttle. Although the method is not foolproof, the inattentive heavy-tackle angler can count on a high degree of success as long as he has a capable and attentive helmsman.

When using a soft-bodied offshore lure, leave the rod in a holder with the reel set at just enough drag to prevent line spilling from the pull of the lure being trolled through the water. Then, when a big fish strikes, it feels little or no tension on the "meal" it has just mouthed, and swims away with it. The angler has time to pull the rod from the holder and either adjust a stand-up harness or settle into a fighting chair before setting the hook. When the angler is ready, the drag lever is advanced to strike position, slack is quickly cranked back onto the reel, the rod tip is raised, and the hook is set hard. When done right, the technique delivers a high hookup percentage.

Spread

There is a lot of discussion among big-game anglers about offshore trolling lure spreads. A commonly employed standard marlin spread is as follows: Two giant concave-face lures are fished flat and very close to the boat, within 30 to 40 feet behind the transom. These lines are rubber-banded to taglines tied off at each corner of the transom. The outrigger-connected lines are either held directly by the outrigger clips, or taglined with rubber bands and trolled about 150 feet out, no farther from the boat than dead baits would be trolled. A fifth line is trolled either just behind the flatlines, dead center, or far away down the middle. The three farthest lures are either small teardrops or all-eyes with concave faces.

In all cases the lure distance from the boat is adjusted so that each lure rides on the face of one of the boat's wake waves. It's easy to tell when the placement is correct. The air-gathering action is considerably greater when the placement is just right; you can see the difference as you let out or bring in the lure ever so slightly, seeking just the right spot on the wave. Here again, standard placement on this wave or that is nothing more than a guideline: flatlines on third and fourth, outrigger lures on fifth and sixth, and so on. What matters most is that the lures look right—that is, they are smoking maximally, tracking well, and not flying.

Once a spread is set and looks just right, it's best to resist the urge to keep changing things simply because no fish has risen immediately. Offshore trolling is a waiting game, and once you have confidence in the spread, stick with it. Troll up-sea, then down-sea, preferably with slight S-curve course variations. By not always trolling in dead-straight lines, you will alternately speed up and slow down the port and starboard lures. This slight alteration in lure speed is more natural than constant throttle changes, and often incites fish interest.

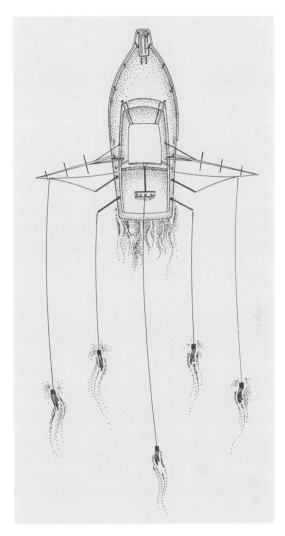

In a common spread for trolling offshore lures, the longest line is set down the middle off a rod placed in a holder on the flying bridge. The outrigger lines are about equal in length and deeper than the inside flatlines. The distance of lures relative to one another is proportionally greater than shown in this compressed depiction.

Using Teasers

No matter how big your lures or baits look to you, in the big water of the ocean they are really small. Visibility is the key to the trolling game, so the angler must do everything possible to draw attention to his small lures as they track across the boundless sea. That's what various types of teasers do.

It is well known that the vibrations produced by a boat in offshore waters—from the noise of the motor(s), the flash of the propeller(s), and the splashing sounds of the hull as it courses through

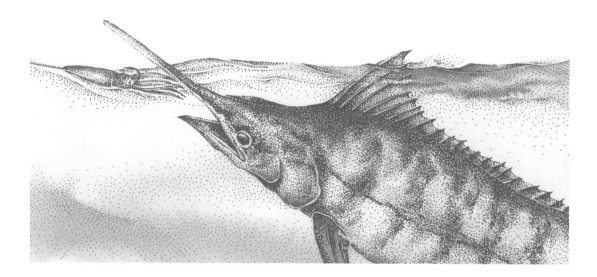

the water—are considerable and attractive to fish. Likewise, the churning wake created by the boat's propellers attracts attention and raises saltwater gamefish. The more attention that is drawn to the area directly behind the moving boat, the more likely it will be that gamefish will find and strike the relatively small baits and lures that are dragged there. Then the action and appearance of the baits or lures can do their job of drawing a strike. So teasers are an important part of the attraction element of offshore fishing.

There are numerous kinds of commonly recognized teasers, made from assorted materials and in varied shapes. In general such devices can be considered as one of several types: hard or soft conventional single teasers, trolling birds, and daisy chains. However, the entire category of lures known as teasers is rather broad and ill-defined. Conventional teasers are analogous to hard- and soft-headed offshore lures, which themselves can be used as teasers when run without a hook.

Teasers can be employed at any time when trolling offshore. There's nothing to lose, and little doubt that anything you can add to your spread of hooked baits or lures that may attract gamefish is worth setting out. That teasers attract gamefish is borne out by the fact that gamefish often attack the teaser first.

When you are using a single teaser and such attacks occur, the trick is to move a hooked bait or lure into the vicinity of the teaser, while at the same time removing the hookless attractor from the spot. To facilitate this action, some people simply drag the teaser from a long heavy rod, rather than from a heavy cord fixed to a cleat. The fish's attention must be drawn away from the teaser and toward the bait with the hook in it.

It's often not as difficult as it sounds. Indeed, the attacking or inspecting fish often will first strike the teaser, and then dart away and strike one of the other trolled offerings without any action on the part of the angler. The fish may simply be drawn within sight of the other baits or lures by the teaser itself and, once in the spread, may decide to inspect each of them. To cover both situations, troll at least one flatlined lure or bait just behind the churning teaser.

If the fish doesn't attack the nearby lure, you can take matters into your own hands by reeling the hooked lure or bait to a position in front of the fish, diverting its attention. Then "feed" the fish the hooked bait or lure, preferably with a rod-tip dropback when fishing lures. The rod-tip dropback is simply a maneuver in which the rod is held high above and behind the angler's head with a firm two-handed grip. When the fish grabs the bait or lure, the rod tip is instantly lowered to a position pointing at the fish, thus feeding the bait into its mouth. Then the rod tip is immediately raised hard several times in a stabbing motion to set the hook. If the hook pulls free, the lure is rapidly reeled back to the surface and the procedure is repeated.

An offshore trolling lure is unhooked from a Pacific sailfish.

An alternative move, used more often with baits than with lures, is to raise the rod tip with the reel in freespool mode and the spool held firmly by the thumb. When the fish strikes, thumb tension is eased and the line is freespooled briefly to allow the fish to swallow the bait, taking care not to allow the spool to overrun and create a bird's nest. Then the reel is shifted back into gear, and when the line comes taut the fish is struck by repeatedly and forcefully raising the rod tip.

You can, of course, also use hookless natural baits as single teasers. Single split-tail mullet and other baitfish, or strips cut from the shiny bellies of tuna or dolphin, have long been dragged by off-shore trollers. The manner of using these is usually to yank them away from an inspecting gamefish at the same instant that rigged natural baits, flies, or castable lures are presented. This is the classic bait-and-switch tactic.

Attracted by the natural teaser and then sub-sequently angered by its sudden disappearance, the gamefish is more likely to cast caution to the wind and strike the new offering with reckless abandon. Such teasers are preferred to artificial ones in many parts of the world and are the teaser of choice for many fly anglers.

For fly anglers, especially those who desire to catch a possible record fish, it is essential that cast-ing a fly to a teased fish be done from a nontrolling boat. Practicality (of hooking the fish) and record rules require this. Thus when a fish comes to eat a teaser (or string of teasers), it is imperative that the trolled offering be pulled rapidly toward the boat ahead of the searching billfish, until it is possible to cast a fly to it.

At that time, the boat is taken out of gear, the bait is rapidly yanked from the water, the fly is cast, and the billfish is allowed to pursue the fly. The aim is not only to get the billfish to take the fly, but for the angler to set the hook in the corner of the billfish's mouth as it makes a turn with the fly.

For billfishing, many experienced trollers favor soft teasers because the fish seem to hold on to them longer and are more likely to return to them because they feel like natural bait. While the objective is not to catch fish on these hookless teasers, the fact that they are soft is more likely to cause a fish that strikes one to return to take a hooked lure that is following in the spread. This is less of an issue with blue marlin, and more of one with white marlin and sailfish.

Multiple teasers, as used in a string, are usually attached to a flatline that is tied to the stern cleat; this is especially common on smaller boats. On larger boats, especially offshore charter boats, teasers are attached to lines that connect to reels mounted up on the bridge; this allows the captain to manipulate or retrieve them when necessary. Some of these are attached to electric reels or winches for fast retrieval; the line for these is run through glass eyes or locked-down release clips that are positioned low on the outriggers. Teasers can also be deployed via a rod and reel that is secured in a recessed gunwale or transom rod holder.

Large teasers are usually fixed close to the transom under the theory that they are easier to see in the frothy wake than smaller teasers, and that they are most likely to be the first thing that a billfish sees after it comes up to inspect a moving boat. This is especially so when trolling at fast speeds, such as 7 to 10 knots, for marlin. When fishing slower, smaller teasers can be fished close to the transom, and are more visible then because the area behind the boat is less disturbed.

Often billfish move away from the teaser and then inspect or strike one or more of the hooked lures that are pulled a few waves back. When they hit big teasers, the lures are pulled away from them by virtue of the motion of the boat or the action of the angler or mate, and this tends to make the fish mad and ready to pounce on the trailing lure.

Kite Fishing

Fishing with kites is a tactic employed in saltwater, primarily by offshore anglers fishing for sailfish. The main purpose is to work a live bait far from the boat, but kite fishing also offers the clear water advantage of presenting the bait without an obvious fishing line. Although baits fished off kites can be presented at various levels, they are typically fished on or close to the surface and are worked both while trolling or while drifting.

The principle of kite fishing is similar to that of trolling with sideplaners or planer boards in that the kite carries the fishing line and bait away from the boat at distances that can be varied and, via a release clip, the line is freed from the kite to allow an angler to play a fish unimpeded.

Kites for fishing come in versions suitable for different wind conditions, and they are attached by tow line to a retrieval device; this may be an old 6/0 or 9/0 conventional reel and short rod, or a large-wheeled direct-drive manual retriever with a swiveling clip, similar to the devices used for retrieving sideplaners. The tow line is usually Dacron, at least 50-pound strength, which may be subject to fraying but has the benefit of not stretching. When two kites are fished together, they are kept away from each other by attaching split shot to the kite edges (on opposite sides), and they may be labeled left or right fliers.

In operation the kite is set out a reasonable distance and the fishing line is attached to it via a release clip on the tow line (running it through a ceramic guide attached to the clip keeps the line in the right position). Multiple baits may be fished via multiple release clips, though few people fish more than two baits from one kite. Baits are fished so that they frantically circle near the surface, which attracts the attention of fish.

It's important to keep monitoring the kite lines to make sure that the baits are properly positioned; colorful markers on the line help make the position of the baits visible. If changes in the wind raise or lower the kite, the bait will be affected and the line has to be adjusted to keep the bait on the surface.

When a fish strikes, the angler grabs the appropriate rod, reels the line until it comes tight to the release clip, and then waits until the striking fish has swallowed the bait and moved enough to pull the line out of the release clip. The angler points the rod at the fish and reels in slack until the line gets tight, setting the hook several times.

Kites are used in drifting when there is ample wind, and in trolling when there is not enough wind, or even when there is wind in conjunction with trolling baits or lures on flatlines and off downriggers. In the latter scenario, kites help round out the offerings and the breadth of water covered.

Stand-Up Fishing

Stand-up fishing is a saltwater angling technique in which anglers stand up while utilizing relatively short rods and repeated short-pumping strokes to

With a short stand-up rod and quick-pumping motion, an angler can catch large fish without an overly long endurance contest. This angler is wrestling a large red snapper from the Gulf of Mexico.

fight offshore fish. It is differentiated from standard big-game or offshore fishing in which conventional rods are longer and the angler sits in a fighting chair equipped with a between-the-legs gimbal.

Stand-up tackle and fish-fighting methods evolved in the 1980s in response to the needs of Southern California offshore anglers who were primarily tangling with monstrous yellowfin tuna on long-range party boats. These boats were not equipped with fighting chairs, and dozens of anglers on a single long-range boat at anchor labored with heavy conventional big-game tackle and long rods while standing up to fight tuna and, occasionally, billfish.

An entire tackle and fishing system for these anglers emerged. This included short, sturdy quick-recovery rods with short butts; long foregrips; matching kidney harnesses in a variety of sizes and shapes and with sophisticated padding and bracing; and harnesses that allowed the gimbal belt to be clipped onto the harness itself.

Stand-up systems offer several advantages not afforded big-game anglers anchored to a chair. The most significant of these is mobility. The stand-up angler is able to rove about the cockpit whenever the fish surges or changes direction, which in turn increases the odds for successfully landing a powerful fish. This is especially true near the end of the fight. When a large billfish or tuna is brought to the boat, the seated angler can do little to prevent a cutoff if his quarry suddenly charges beneath the boat. The mobile angler can more easily handle any situation by following the fish around the cockpit, can keep the rod tip pointed at the fish more easily, and can often prevent catastrophe when a green fish is brought to the boat.

Many people feel that greater pressure can be exerted on a powerful gamefish with a short stand-up rod and a quick pumping action, which in turn reduces the fighting time. However, this is not necessarily the case; in some instances, using stand-up tackle to land big fish may take longer. This depends upon the physical condition of the angler, having the appropriate tackle, and properly employing effective technique.

Although stand-up tackle evolved originally for tuna anglers, it has broadened to a base that includes billfish and shark anglers as well, plus any small-skiff anglers without a chair. When fishing for billfish with 20- to 50-pound-class tackle,

an angler is not handicapped by using stand-up gear. Multiple hookups, which can often occur when seeking sailfish, are more easily handled by the stand-up angler.

Although the amount of pressure that can be applied to a fish is limited by the drag setting of the reel commensurate with the line strength (whether standing or sitting), many offshore anglers feel that they can more easily apply maximum pressure with a good stand-up system. In either case, the experienced angler usually increases the pressure on the line or spool with a gloved hand when the situation calls for it.

Those fish that are not truly monstrous in size are fair game for stand-up fishing, and this tackle is preferred by many people over heavier conventional gear used in fighting chairs. Thus stand-up tackle has become popular not only for midsize tuna and billfish, but also sharks, wahoo, amberjack, yellowtail, and large bottom fish, including halibut and lingcod.

Tackle

The rod and the gimbal harness are at the heart of the stand-up system. Most stand-up fishing, especially for deep- and hard-fighting species, is done with lever drag big-game reels and special stand-up rods, although some stand-up spinning tackle is available for lighter work. Stand-up rods are generally 5 to 6 feet in length because the pumping strokes (called short-stroking or short-pumping) that are most effective when standing are short and rely little on the recovery power of the rod. They need the strength of a strong butt. Short-stroke pumping gains line a little at a time; this, not the gradual recovery of the rod itself, is what whips the fish.

Much of the advantage of the short rod is lost if the harness and gimbal belt do not fit properly. When fighting a large fish with stand-up tackle, one is constantly on the edge of a fine balance. If the reel drag should grab, or if the harness straps are not adjusted properly, you may find yourself on the verge of going overboard as you rock back and forth to pump your fish. The harness must allow your center of gravity to be precisely where it should be, tipping you neither too far forward nor backward. If you have to lean forward all the time, you're in trouble. Just any old harness with a high-riding gimbal belt will not do.

The padded harness should fit snugly across your hips, not above the hip bones. It should definitely not be situated beneath your buttocks or across the back of your legs where it would force your center of gravity, under load, much too far back for safety.

Most stand-up anglers after big game prefer lever drag reels, and many use models with two-speed features. Star drag reels can do the job, but have the disadvantage of not being able to be readjusted accurately during the fight. On lever drag reels, however, the drag can be preset so that the angler can always return to his preset strike position and know how many pounds of drag tension the reel is exerting at a variety of settings.

Drag is an important element of this system, for obvious reasons. There is a lot of pressure applied on big fish, and when they surge it's essential that the drag not only be properly set but smooth. If it surges, the angler can lose balance and be in danger of falling. At the very least, it will hamper fishing efforts and increase the length of the fight.

Accessory tackle items that many stand-up anglers employ, especially those on long-range party boats where they fish over railings, is a forearm pad and knee pads. The forearm pad protects the arm when it brushes against the rail, and the knee pads protect the knees against railings and gunwales. On boats with high gunwales or rails, many anglers plant their feet squarely on the deck with their knees against these objects, so the pads provide some comfort.

Technique

There's a two-part component to stand-up technique that combines body motion as well as lifting technique. When using stand-up tackle on a deep fish, begin with your left hand on the rod near the top of the foregrip and right hand on the reel handle, and lift up. Some anglers lift up with their arms, but many prefer leg-hip-pelvis action in conjunction with the harness. When you use your arms you're putting a lot of stress on back and shoulder muscles; there is more power in your legs.

Stand with your feet well apart for comfort and stability, then make a dipping and pumping motion by bending your knees and thrusting the gimbal on your pelvis forward as you pump the rod upward. This is followed quickly by using your legs to rise up while lowering the rod a short distance and winding a few inches of line rapidly and evenly onto the reel spool. Lowering the rod only a short distance produces just a few inches of line at a time, but the idea is to keep this up and make many line-gaining strokes per minute, giving the fish no chance to get its head or have a moment of recovery.

In the real world of pitching decks and surging big gamefish, much has been made of this stand-up fishing technique, referred to by some as a "pump and grind" burlesque motion. No matter how it

This angler is using stand-up tackle with a properly adjusted rod belt and harness, and knee pads for bracing. Playing a fish begins with the left hand gripping the rod near the top of the foregrip (1). Working a deep fish requires lifting, which is best done by dipping the knees and hips and leaning back (2), then simultaneously lowering the rod and turning the handle to recover line (3). Continue this until the fish is brought to landing position. When a fish runs off and takes line during a battle, or when you need to rest briefly, maintain pressure by leaning slightly back to keep the rod tip up, and hold the rod in hand without pulling on it (4). Alternate hands for holding the rod if necessary, but recover line whenever the opportunity exists.

looks, when used sensibly it allows the angler to apply maximum pressure on a fish, especially when the fight is straight up and down (and close to that) or when the boat is backing down. If the feet are planted too far apart, or the angler exaggerates the pumping action to the point of leaning too far forward or backward at either end of the stroke, he can place himself in jeopardy.

This can be especially true when a fish is pulling hard far from the boat horizontally. At such times, the rod is bent less than when the fight is more up and down, and the chances are greater of pitching forward when the boat rolls or the fish suddenly surges harder, or of crashing backward if the line snaps or the hook pulls.

When a fish is close to the boat, with the rod sharply bent by a fish bulldogging below, you can maintain better balance while at the same time applying greater pressure. The leverage becomes greater because the fore grip-to-rod-tip distance is shorter when the rod takes a deep bend. It's also easier to maintain a steady balance when the pressure of the fish is down, rather than out.

It is important to realize that this short-rod/short-pumping technique avoids the long strokes from conventional tackle that often permit a fish to get its head on a downstroke even though it appears that the angler is making progress.

Called short stroking, the basic method of fighting a large fish on stand-up tackle is more than just a continuous series of short rod jerks. However, it does involve short rod lifts followed by rapid cranking of the handle, with attention paid to maximizing effort in the power zone and being careful not to lift the rod too high.

Bringing the rod tip up high (above horizontal in the case of stand-up fishing) places too much pressure on the rod tip and not enough on the butt. Properly designed stand-up rods have a fast rod-tip recovery, but gain most of their muscling ability from a powerful butt; the lower two-thirds of the rod provide great lifting ability, and this is diminished when the rod is raised above the horizontal level. Therefore, the correct technique is nonstop short cycles of lifting and retrieving line.

With the knees bent, the reel in low gear (assuming a two-speed reel), and the rod doubled over to the water, begin by raising the rod up to horizontal position; this is called the upstroke. You should start cranking the reel handle a fraction of a second before lowering the rod and continue until the downstroke is completed. The distance moved may be so slight that only a fraction of a turn of the handle is completed. As soon as the downstroke is completed, the upstroke begins, and the cycle is repeated. Most of the time, you make progress in short increments, but it is important with large fish that you keep it up. Keeping the short-stroking action up does not allow a fish to rest for a second, and directs its head upward.

It's best to maintain a steady rhythm when pumping fish using stand-up tackle and be careful not to overdo it. Rest when the fish is taking line, and cradle the rod in your hand rather than wrapping your thumb around it; this avoids the "death" grip and lessens hand cramping and fatigue. When there are swells, you can use the motion of the sea to your benefit, pulling on a fish as the boat lifts upward, and reeling in line as the boat descends.

Note that there are some physical limitations to this technique and that not everyone can do it. Stand-up fishing for large fish is not recommended for children or for adults with a bad back or in a physical condition that would prevent them from maintaining their balance and strength during the course of a fight. This does not mean that stand-up fishing is only for athletic muscle-bound gym rats. On the contrary, proper technique rather than plenty of muscle is the key, provided that you have the right equipment.

34

Other Situations

In the truest-to-angling sense, schooling is the phenomenon of gamefish actively feeding upon prey species and vulnerable to angling effort. Some species of gamefish forage together and prey upon schools of baitfish. Some gamefish species do not ordinarily school but will do so in a loose sense when there is ample feeding opportunity.

When gamefish are grouped and actively feeding upon large numbers of prey, they may be particularly vulnerable to angling. This may generate a high level of action and angler enthusiasm, although it is usually an occurrence of short duration.

Angling for Schooling Fish

The phenomenon of schooling does not occur everywhere and with all species. Some of the more popular fish that school in saltwater include dolphin, bluefish, striped bass, tuna, and sailfish. Tuna and sailfish are caught by trolling and baitfishing but rarely by casting; they are such fast movers that they are seldom appropriate for the casting type of school-fishing tactics that are characteristic of most other species, although trollers will judiciously maneuver around schools to place their following lures or baits amid or along a school of actively feeding fish.

At some times people actually depend on schooling fish behavior for the bulk of their deliberate angling activities. In many freshwater locales in the fall, striped bass, hybrid stripers, and white bass chase and consume pods of baitfish—usually threadfin or gizzard shad—and roam over a wide area as they keep up with the bait and maraud them. Often this phenomenon is best observed in early and late daylight hours. With white bass, it happens on points and along rocky shores as well as in open water, but with stripers it may happen anywhere. The key to finding it is observation.

Striper anglers usually motor to places where schooling fish are frequently observed or were seen the morning or evening before. They shut the outboard motor off, and watch and wait. When a sudden splashing occurs in the distance, and/or a flock of seagulls is seen hovering expectantly and diving to the water, that is a giveaway and also the signal to shift into breakneck gear.

The tactic is to race to the site of the commotion, glide to the outer edge of it, cut the motor, and cast into the melee. Sometimes nearly any lure will do; sometimes it must be close in size and shape to the baitfish being pummeled. Two or three anglers may get into fish this way; if the school moves on, you try to move with it, being careful not to put the fish down (which often happens anyway, because of the fish you catch or the intrusion of your boat or that of others) and trying not to lose their direction.

The same thing happens with striped bass and bluefish in saltwater, except that when bluefish

Striped bass are the quest of these anglers on Oklahoma's Lake Texonia; boats in the background are moving to keep up with the fast-traveling school of fish.

and bait are really thick, the blues are reasonably undisturbed by boats, and fish-catching can be fast for a longer period of time.

Likewise, bird activity in inshore or offshore waters can be an indication of feeding by schools of some species or several species, from mackerel to albacore to dolphin, and here the open waters may be conducive to trolling around the edges of the melee to pick off fish, as well as getting into position to cast lures or pitch out live bait.

Many offshore anglers will use the high vantage point of towers to spot dolphin schools near floating weedlines, and will pitch some unhooked live bait to them to start a flurry of feeding, then cast some hooked bait among the fray. It is also possible to use chum to get the fish into casting position with light spinning tackle or a fly rod, since the school will keep feeding toward the boat.

Some species of freshwater fish are known as "schooling" fish because they tend to be found in groups. Walleye, yellow perch, and crappie, for example, are usually clustered, albeit out of visual sight in deep water or on the bottom. In nearly any place that you catch one of these fish, there are usually others.

Panfish anglers well know that they can locate a school of fish, especially crappie, and catch them by the score with jigs or live bait as long as they are fishing at the proper depth. Crappie will school heavily in deep locales in summer and fall, and stay in one particular area. They require a presentation with some finesse, contrary to the slam-bang action that is associated with the frenzied behavior of other species. But at least with these fish, once you have found a concentration, you don't have to work to keep locating them.

More species of freshwater fish may cluster than what people think. And in places with little or no fishing pressure, this is more likely to be observed; the difference being that fish in highly pressured waters are wary and more likely to be spooked by any activity, whereas those in virgin or lightly pressured waters are more tolerant.

Northern pike and chain pickerel are great examples of fish that can be deceptively abundant, although not actually schooled per se. In northern Canadian waters, schools of 2- to 5-pound lake trout cruise shallow rocky shorelines on summer evenings to feed on bugs, and they are caught by stealthy anglers using flies and small jigs on light tackle, who cast to wandering pods of fish. If you're patient, you can sit and wait for these trout to come by; if not, you can intercept them by boat, shutting the motor off before getting to the fish, then casting to their midst as they cruise by.

These fish are in no way behaving like surface-busting striped bass would, yet they are cruising en masse and they are aggressive. In these shallow, clear waters, you can actually stalk the school, and several fish will charge your lure.

Walleye, charr, and lake trout may be found in heavy concentrations in those northern locales where there is a large inlet to a lake at various times of the season, and the fish seem to be secure because of the depth and heavy current present. Such a place can provide fast fishing for a while, but it may need to be rested when the action slows, perhaps for 30 to 60 minutes before you return and get into more fish.

This seems to be more likely for charr and lakers than for walleye, but it also seems to be because the fish come in to feed and then leave, rather than taking up permanent local residence. In any event, finding these types of situations—where there's an abundance of active schooling fish—can result in terrific action.

Largemouth bass, which are very oriented to cover for hiding and feeding purposes, do gather in loosely defined schools when there is ample open-water bait. The bait are primarily surface or near-surface feeding fish, usually detected by observation. Their appearance may be short-lived and may be fairly obvious to those close enough to be able to observe this behavior.

Bass that appear to be schooling generally herd baitfish, primarily shad but sometimes alewives, against some type of underwater structure, like a reef, hump, or weed edge. Keeping up with these fish is often difficult, and they are usually spooked easily by boats that get too close.

This is a liberal definition of schools and schooling behavior, however, since largemouth and smallmouth bass are generally not a schooling type of fish once they have passed the juvenile stage. Many anglers refer to bass schools when discussing an abundance of these fish in one particular location, but this is not a school nor is it true schooling behavior, just a lot of fish of the same species coexisting, usually in an area with plenty of cover and forage opportunity.

Fishing Tailwaters

A tailwater is the entire section of river below a dam whose flows are dependent upon dam releases. A tailwater is sometimes also called a tailrace, which is actually a component of the tailwater, being the often turbulent section of river immediately below a large dam, where water spews from the upstream impoundment. Tailwaters exist wherever rivers have been impounded, and flow for varied distances.

In North America, tailwaters offer excellent fishing opportunities for a host of species. Many tailwaters exist, and have the environment that they do, because natural rivers and their habitats and native species were flooded by dams. Those dams primarily support hydroelectric power generation, and downstream flows are dependent on water releases, which means that the species and fishing are likewise dependent on them.

In some tailwaters, erratic release schedules, meager flows, and warm water from reservoir surface discharges adversely impact the fisheries, and there have been long ongoing struggles with water regulators to achieve sustained flows of proper temperature to benefit fish and other downstream aquatic life.

In the southern United States, the most prominent tailwater species is striped bass, but significant fisheries exist in many tailwaters for trout, catfish, walleye, smallmouth bass, and white bass. In western states, trout are the primary fish; tailwaters there provide some of the best and most popular trout fishing known. Many of these species, particularly trout, feed well and grow to good, if not large, sizes but don't manage natural reproduction; their populations are supported through regular plantings in the river itself or in a downstream impoundment.

Water conditions and fishing are often different in the tailrace than they are through the rest of the tailwater. The tailrace is often very good for fishing because it has cooler and well-oxygenated water, an abundance of food, turbulent water that is conducive to aggressive feeding, and the concentration of upstream-migrating fish, which can go no farther than the dam.

When the water is moving swiftly, which often depends on releases, fishing is likely to be prime.

This is not unlike the movement of tides in coastal rivers and their influence on fish activity.

In swift tailraces, much fishing is done from boats, since shore fishing limits effectiveness and being situated on the bank has inherent danger when water levels rise suddenly. Anglers in boats cast with lures or drift bait, both while anchored or while drifting. Fishing with live bait, especially shad that have been caught by dipping or using a cast net, is highly popular.

The swift and well-oxygenated water in tailraces here lends itself very well to releasing fish unharmed. This is especially true for striped bass, which are often difficult to revive and release in good condition, especially in summer months. A drawback, however, is the extra safety precautions that must be taken in the turbulent below-dam environment. Rising water levels can sink improperly anchored boats, and extreme currents and roiling water can make boat operation very tricky.

Farther downriver, the tailwater becomes more like a normal river, except that water temperatures usually are constant, and there are often sudden increases in water level. In rivers that are waded, such increases can be especially dangerous; an unobservant angler may be quickly stranded on a rock with swift and rising cold water closing in.

The methods for fishing tailwaters vary with species and the rivers. In larger, heavier flows, a lot of fishing is done from power boats. Fishing is also carried out by floating in inflatable rafts, canoes, jonboats, or drift boats. Wading is prominent also, especially by trout anglers, and occurs whenever shallow water and pools or runs can feasibly be approached on foot; this is obviously in the smaller and shallow systems but also in the downstream reaches of larger tailwaters. Anglers who float down tailwaters often get out of their craft to fish some runs and pools.

For various species, a lot of fishing is done with bait. This includes live or cut shad or herring for stripers, assorted baits for catfish, minnows for walleye, and eggs and various processed baits for trout. Where stripers are found, live bait is best, but it usually has to be gathered, often by cast netting, and must be well cared for in proper wells. Jigs, assorted swimming plugs, jigging spoons, and bottom-bouncing bait rigs are among the mix as well.

Miles and miles of prime trout habitat exist in many tailwaters, and this opens up a range of fishing possibilities for primarily rainbow and brown trout. Bait is popular in many waters, but casting with spinners, small jigs, and small minnow plugs can be effective. Fly fishing is highly effective in many tailwater trout fisheries, and more common in western than southern rivers. The variety of food in downstream tailwaters—various types of baitfish, aquatic insects, terrestrial insects, aquatic worms, and crustaceans—means that a fly angler has a bulging vest in order to imitate everything that tailwater trout might feed upon.

For trout fishing, streamer flies are good when the water level is rising or falling, and baitfish may be a more prominent food item. The rising water will often bring fair numbers of terrestrial insects into the water, making it good for fishing with hoppers, beetles, crickets, and the like. Day in and day out, fly fishing in tailwaters, however, sees the use of mayfly and caddisfly imitations, various nymphs, and a variety of flies that imitate scuds, worms, and the like.

Fishing Brush

The term "brush" is a collective one pertaining to flooded bushes and small trees, the tops of large trees that have fallen into the water, and isolated piles of material that have been placed in the

The long, shallow runs of the White River in Arkansas provide some of North America's best tailwater trout fishing.

water to attract fish. Brush can provide excellent fishing opportunity for largemouth bass, and sometimes other species, depending on the depth and location.

Bushes are a common characteristic of many reservoirs, where they exist on flats, along tributaries, and in shallow locations subject to flooding during high water. Fallen treetops exist in all types of waters, but obviously near shore. This usually means that they are in shallow water, although in some places the bottom drops sharply away from a wooded shore and the water can be up to 20 feet deep where a treetop has fallen.

Fishing Bushes for Bass

Bushes or small trees showing in the water usually mean that the water level is high. High water causes more food in newly flooded areas for small fish—and thus more small fish for predators like bass, for whom bushes draw food and offer ambush cover.

In natural lakes, bushes may grow along shorelines or around the shore of islands. Bushes along mainland shorelines usually indicate that there are a couple of feet of water near the shore, and perhaps an undercut bank. The bass are close to the edge here because these bushes don't extend very far into the water. Usually they are just temporarily flooded. When fishing shore-based bushes, you may be able to get close if the water is turbid; but when it is clear, you have to stay a reasonable casting distance away. If you can get close, it pays to pitch a jig or plastic worm to the cover. If you have to stay back because of water clarity, a surface lure, especially one with subtle motion that doesn't move too far too fast, is a good bet.

If the fish are not aggressive and/or the water is clear, try a slow-moving lure like a soft jerkbait or Texas-rigged worm. These should be cast parallel to the cover rather than perpendicular to it because it is unlikely that a bass will come far out of the cover to get it. Work the lure as close to the cover as possible, for as long as possible; casting parallel accomplishes that.

Much of the same is true for bushes that are around an island or marshy hummock, although water may extend farther into this brush and thus bass may get back into this cover. Focus attention on the points of the island brush cover and on the pockets that indent the island. If the bass are not aggressive, perhaps because of cold water, a front, or angling pressure, they are likely to be deeper in this cover and tougher to coax into striking. Pinpoint presentations, and perhaps low-light approaches, may be necessary.

In reservoirs, bushes and small trees are usually found in patches near or away from the shoreline. High water often means a lot of bushes; the trick is figuring out which ones to fish. Bushes on points are an obviously important place to concentrate, and so are bushes along creek channels, in shallow bays, along flats, and in small coves or pockets. Isolated bushes are likely to have fish, as are bushes that stand out from others because they are on the points of a cluster or the edge of an opening; large bushes frequently harbor bigger bass.

Bushes may hold fish from springtime, when the water starts warming, through the fall. In midsummer, however, when the water is low and very warm in the shallows, the shallowest bushes are unlikely to be productive. On the other hand, shallow bushes may be very productive in the spring when the water is warming and bass are preparing to spawn. Thus, in spring, bushes in backwater areas are likely to be better than bushes along a mainland shoreline, but the reverse would be true later in the season. Bushes located along creeks would also be good in the summer.

Fishing Fallen Treetops for Bass

Fallen trees are a common bass cover, particularly on natural lakes and ponds, and in many places they remain as cover for a long time, regardless of water levels. They usually fall nearly perpendicular to the shoreline, or on enough of an angle from the shore to put all the upper branches into the water. These branches, limbs, and trunks provide cover for bass to ambush prey; in time these objects collect organisms that attract small fish, which attract other fish, and soon a food chain has developed around the tree.

Some trees attract numerous bass; others may hold just one or two. Those holding only one may hold the king of the pond. A fallen treetop on a point would be an exceptional place to find bass, but that seldom happens, although a tree close to the point or just around the corner can be just as attractive.

Fallen treetops near a creek channel, in a location also having other cover (like lily pads or

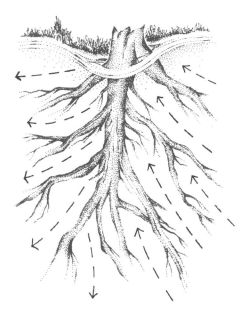

When fishing for bass among the snaggy cluster of a fallen tree, you must retrieve your soft worm, weedless jig, or spinnerbait through lanes and parallel to the limbs.

grass), in flooded backwater areas, and on rocky shorelines or banks with riprap are especially worthwhile. If the water is extremely shallow, the tree is unlikely to hold bass, except in spring at spawning time and in late fall. With a few feet of depth or more, and preferably some shade, the tree could attract bass throughout the season.

Not all fallen treetops are alike; some are much thicker than others. Recently fallen ones may be full of leaves, which offer cover and shade. Bass may be suspended in the limbs, underneath them in the deeper water, or back up near the trunk in the thickest part of the tree.

Fishing Brush for Panfish

It is common to find panfish around brush. Shallow flooded bushes provide spawning habitat in the spring for crappies, and fallen treetops can be a place to catch crappie, bluegills, and other panfish, especially if the treetop is thick and there is 5 to 10 feet of water at the end of the tree. These species are seldom fished in the same manner as bass in bushes or treetops, although large panfish will occasionally strike a spinnerbait or plug. This is rare but indicates the presence of fish of similar size.

If the water is turbid, panfish anglers can quietly get close to brush and sit near or on top of it. Small

jigs fished plain or tipped with a piece of worm, or such live bait as minnows, crickets, and worms, are the top choices. Use light wire hooks that can be straightened if they snag on the cover and freed (they can be rebent for continued use), and both jigs and bait can be fished beneath a small float. Fishing vertically is best to minimize snags; if you can't get close enough to the cover to do this, it may be necessary to use a long (perhaps cane or telescoping) pole for precise presentation.

In deeper water, submerged brush is often a target of anglers who seek panfish, and a lot of hidden brush in lakes and reservoirs is planted by anglers specifically for this purpose. Similar tactics, as well as the use of vertically fished jigging spoons, work in these places.

Fishing in Timber

Flooded timber is a form of natural cover that exists in many impoundments and in the flooded backwater of river systems. It can be important in fishing for largemouth bass, striped bass, and crappie. Fields of standing timber in relatively shallow water, or the remnant stumps that remain, are very obvious to anglers, but in many reservoirs timber is covered by water and not obvious to the eye. The latter occurs when the flooded land is left uncleared, so that live trees are flooded when the impoundment fills with water. They have a long life when submerged, and, though hazards to navigation, they can provide shelter and ambush-feeding opportunities for some gamefish.

Many anglers take a pretty haphazard approach to timber, but not every tree is the same. Where timber sticks out of the water, there can be visible clues to good places to fish. The most conspicuous is the leading edge of the timber, which many anglers treat like a shoreline, keeping their boat out from it and casting lures to the edge or just beyond the edge and by it. This may be occasionally productive in young reservoirs, but not where timber has stood for a long time and fish behavior is relatively stabilized.

Also conspicuous are timbered points. If a timbered point is being washed by wind, it could have a concentration of bait on it. Another prominent place in a stand of trees might be the edge of a clearing, which could be where an old pond existed.

Fishing among treetops is common in some reservoirs and in the backwaters of large rivers; this scene is at El Salto Lake, Mexico.

Where largemouth bass are the quarry, you frequently need to get into the trees and maneuver around, fishing deliberately in those places that are just a little different. This might be as simple as finding leaning trees rather than perpendicular ones. Leaning trees offer more shade and are more conducive to hiding than straight ones.

It might mean looking for the largest, widest trees, again for shade, but also because of the underwater protection they might afford. Large multilimbed trees eventually lose their limbs, which usually fall around the base of the tree. If enough fall and get stuck on lower below-water limbs, they form a canopy, which is a great hiding place.

Tight clumps of smaller trees can provide protection and may be a key spot in finding bass. A clump of trees on the edge of a creek channel is a particularly good spot.

A channel is one of the most important underwater terrain features to look for with sonar, with special emphasis on the outside bends, where it comes near a point or shore, and especially where two channels meet. A roadbed, a dropoff, and other features are worth looking for as well.

Sonar is absolutely invaluable for fishing completely submerged timber, where there are seldom visual clues to depth or tree conformations. In deep-submerged timber, fish are usually suspended, sometimes at the treetops and sometimes among the branches. To prevent fishing haphazardly, you have to know where you are and where your lure is.

You can vertically jig deep timber by using a fairly heavy lead jig or preferably a jigging spoon. Spoons have treble hooks, whereas jigs have a single hook. Single hooks get hung up less so you might try replacing trebles with singles.

Spoons have an O-ring between the body and the hook, and this allows for a bit of swiveling, which facilitates desnagging. In any event, lower the lure through the limbs, and retrieve by slowly jigging it; when it hits a limb, drop it down and then bring it back up over the limb. Keep jigging. As long as you haven't buried the hook, it will usually come free when the weight of the lure falls back on it. When it gets wedged in a crotch, however, you may not get it free.

Jigging is most effective when you use an electric motor for positioning, or when you are tied to a tree, and where there is no breeze. You have to be able to jig vertically, and when you move off

To fish deep in timber with minimal snagging, get directly over the tops of trees and fish vertically with jigs and jigging spoons (inset).

the vertical line you greatly increase the chance of hanging up. By jigging gently and using sensitive line with a fairly stiff-tipped rod, you can have a lot of excitement in the treetops with striped bass, hybrid stripers, or largemouths. Obviously, you need to be able to muscle a fish out of the branches and limbs very quickly.

Most of the angling done in trees is by casting, however, especially for largemouth bass and active schooling fish. Surface lures, when appropriate, are very productive. Because the water is usually stained or turbid in flooded timber, noise and action are important, so walking stickbaits, poppers, and buzzbaits are good choices.

A rattling, vibrating crankbait is also a good lure choice, worked just below the surface. So is a spinnerbait. Floating-diving crankbaits have merit at times as well, although there is a knack to working these just right; don't set the hook when you tick a limb, and let the plug float up to get over obstructions.

For conventional casting as well as flipping, a plastic worm (use a pegged slip sinker) is a prime lure for largemouths in timber, as is a weed-guard-protected jig with rubber tentacles and pork chunk. The latter is used for flipping in shallow to mid-depth water.

Be sure to take commonsense precautions while fishing in flooded trees. Watch where you put your hands, for example; ants, bees, snakes, tarantulas, and other creatures may be about. Tilt the outboard motor up when in use, and run only at low throttle. When standing in a boat, be aware of bumping into trees while off balance so you don't fall out.

Night Fishing

In terms of the overall number of anglers, fishing at night is not nearly as popular as fishing during the day. This is mainly because people are more comfortable fishing during daylight hours than at night. There are many places, and many species of fish, that could provide good night fishing experiences if anglers were more willing to try it. In some cases, less competition from other anglers, chances for larger fish, and sometimes opportunities for a better overall catch are clear incentives to be angling at night.

Some species of fish are very active at night and have physical adaptations that make them more prone than others to night activity. The large glossy white eyes of walleye, for example, are actually due to a special reflective layer in the retina of the eye known as the tapetum lucidum (this same layer is also found in the eyes of cats, raccoons, and deer). It gathers light that enters the eye, making it extremely sensitive to bright daylight intensities but also well adapted to nocturnal vision.

Species that have an especially well-tuned sense of smell, like catfish and sharks, are more nocturnal than others. And some species that are very reliant on their hearing abilities will use this sense, especially their lateral line, to detect food opportunities even when vision is limited.

Many fish, especially in midsummer when daylight is greatest, are more active in the low-light hours of dawn and dusk. This may be partly due to the fact that there is less human activity on the water at that time. The same can be said about fish activity at night. Places such as trout streams that tend to have a lot of human activity in the day may be more productive at night because the fish have found night feeding more

As the sun sets, a walleye angler gets busy on Lake Kesagami, Ontario.

advantageous, whether or not they are physiologically attuned to this.

Among the fish that are known to be nocturnally active and are typically fished for at night are largemouth bass, walleye, striped bass, catfish, trout, coho and chinook salmon, tuna, tarpon, snook, and swordfish. Ironically, a good amount of angling is carried out at night under the lights of bridges, roadways, and docks, because the light draws insects, baitfish, and larger predators; a host of species, in both freshwater and saltwater, may be attracted.

The methods used for after-dark fishing vary widely, from casting surface lures in the pitch black for largemouth bass to using glowing lures for deep salmon trolling, and from fishing live eels off a wave-whipped jetty for striped bass to sitting in a lantern-equipped boat while fishing deep bait for catfish or trout. One thing that can be said with certainty about fishing for all species of fish in the inky blackness of night is that you just don't fish like you would in daylight.

Naturally, anglers are accustomed to seeing what they're doing and watching the line or the lure, and this is seldom possible at night, although black lights make it possible to watch fluorescent lines very well. Therefore, intuition and a feel for the line become more important at night than in the daylight. Obviously, your vision is better on nights with moonlight than on dark or overcast nights. Keeping the use of lights to a minimum is a good idea for some types of fishing, though it is unnecessary for others. Indeed, when fishing offshore for tuna at night, boats direct powerful halogen beams into the water to attract baitfish. A small headlamp is a proper accessory for other types of night fishing, since it frees both hands and issues only a small amount of light.

Acclimating yourself to night fishing and to seeing in the blackness takes some adjustment, so you're smart to keep a couple of rods handy with different lures or baits on them in order to minimize the need to use a light and retie. If you're casting with a baitcasting outfit and get a bad backlash, you can put that rod aside and employ a different one. If you're prone to backlashes with baitcasting tackle, consider using spinning gear at night, especially if circumstances don't require accurate lure placement close to cover.

Be attentive to safety. Landing and unhooking fish caught on lures with multiple hooks is more of a problem in the darkness. Be careful about losing your balance while standing up in a boat at night; in daylight you often brace for a collision with objects, but in the dark you rarely see the objects and are jolted off balance when the boat bumps something. Don't leave things underfoot in a boat, especially hooked lures. When in a boat, keep a high-powered flashlight handy so you can warn an approaching motorboat about your presence. And when you're under power, have bow and stern lights on.

When fishing in pure darkness, you can do several things to enhance your success. Familiarize yourself with the place that you're fishing. It's best to slow down and work an area well rather than hustle all over.

In most situations, it helps to concentrate on quiet and stealth. Noise from operating the motor constantly, moving things around in the boat, chucking an anchor overboard, plunking the electric motor into position, and so on, is not helpful. In a boat, you should approach an area silently from afar as opposed to running up on it with motor on. Drifting quietly and working methodically all around a boat is effective in some situations.

Finally, have great respect for the water and the forces of nature, especially at night. If you get into some trouble, chances are that there will be few people around to help.

Ice Fishing

Fishing through the ice is a traditional activity in northern locations where the ice is thick enough for people to safely venture onto frozen lakes and ponds. In some places, a winter community develops, and ice houses, also known as shacks, shanties, and bobhouses, dot the surface.

Like open-water angling, ice fishing encompasses both passionate devotees and anglers who fish only occasionally. The most serious ice anglers work hard at trying to catch fish and learn new methods; other anglers enjoy just being outside in the winter and aren't overly concerned with success. Many people, of course, fall in between.

Ice fishing involves a range of approaches for successfully attracting and landing fish. The best ice anglers know they can't make the fish do what they want them to do, so they try to adjust to the fish and avoid being locked into fixed ideas about lures, baits, and locations. If you assume that, in general, fish are aggressive only a small percentage of the time, in a negative mood the majority of the time, and in a neutral mood for the remainder of the time, then your best approach is to finesse the situation, being a bit crafty and cautious. This approach will not alarm fish no matter what their disposition is. On the other hand, an aggressive approach, such as jigging a large spoon for perch, will probably scare or turn off most fish. Thus beginning with a tiny baited jig should bring better results.

When you're starting out, a companion who is an experienced ice angler is a great advantage. Ask questions and try to learn the basics. For catching panfish, you can start very simply with a jigging rod and a thin, small float about 1½ inches long and $^3/_{16}$ inch wide. The float is held in place on a light line (4-pound test is good) with two silicone tubes. Use two BB-size split shots (each of which is $^1/_{64}$ ounce) to balance your float, placed about 2½ inches above a No. 12 or 14 hook; switch to a smaller hook and lighter line if the fish are hard to catch. Carefully place one or two maggots or waxworms on the hook.

This approach will be effective during the first three to five weeks of the ice fishing season when panfish are normally close to the shore in shallow water that is 18 inches to 4 feet deep. Carefully lower your hooked bait in the hole, and watch for any movement of the float up, down, or sideways.

The float can fly down on a strike or move very slowly just a fraction of an inch. This is why a float is best if you are a beginner; you can see the entire range of bites and get accustomed to them. Sometimes it's better to jig without a float, but if you have had success seeing bites, you can easily learn straight jigging and imagine how the bites feel.

The approach just described is a good way to get started on ice fishing for bluegills, crappie, or perch. By using finesse, you can readily adapt to those easier times when fish are aggressive.

To be aggressive about catching fish you need to locate them. Using portable sonar and keeping on the move are important elements for locating fish. Make sure your sonar unit can shoot through the ice and can depict both the fish and the weeds where some species may be holding. You can facilitate the effectiveness of the sonar by squirting nontoxic antifreeze on the ice and then placing

A lake trout like this is a superb catch for any ice angler; this specimen was caught at Lake Simcoe, Ontario.

the transducer on the wet spot. Ice has to be fairly clear for this, but thickness is no problem. In heavily marbled or snow-saturated ice, make a hole and place the transducer in the hole.

Using sonar allows you to keep moving. When fish appear on the sonar screen, drill a hole and then carefully watch the fish on the screen as you jig. You can often see how the fish respond to your bait or lure and to the jigging action; you can even watch the fish take the bait. Jig at various levels for good coverage.

Lures/Bait

Minnows are the favorite live bait of ice anglers, especially when fished on a bait hook below a tip-up. They are most often hooked through the lips, which is the strongest location, and then behind the dorsal fin. They are also popularly fished on a jig hook. Bait anglers who use tip-ups also need an assortment of hooks, split shot weights, floats, and other terminal tackle, as well as small baits like maggots and grubs.

There are loads of jigs and jigging spoons suitable for ice fishing, depending on the target species, as well as some specialty ice fishing lures. Each behaves differently in the water, and the action is also influenced by the addition of bait. Generally, however, any jigging lure should be worked in a subtle manner for panfish and more dramatically for larger predators.

Different shapes of small ice jigs are used, as are different types of jigging spoons, most of which weigh from $^1/_8$ to $^1/_{12}$ ounce. Another choice is small leadhead jigs, which are dressed with soft lure bodies or tipped with bait. Balanced jigging lures, which lie horizontally and have a hook at each end as well as under the belly, swim in a unique manner due to a tail fin, and these lures are popular in different sizes for various fish.

Safety

Never take ice for granted and assume it is safe. Invisible underwater currents, springs, and heat-attracting debris in or on the ice can weaken it dramatically. Some well-frozen lakes develop pressure ridges that you should stay away from. As a rule, always fish with a companion, and test ice thickness before you travel on it.

Right after freeze-up, ice toward the middle of the lake is thinner than that along the shore-line. River ice and lake ice can vary in thickness throughout the winter and in different parts of the river or lake. Do not assume uniform thickness.

The thickness of the ice is not always an accurate measure of its strength. Cracking and sudden temperature drops can severely weaken ice. Heavy snow cover insulates ice, drastically reducing its growth; the snow may cause water to overflow around the edges, thus weakening the ice there.

As a guideline, the minimum ice thickness for certain loads is as follows: 4 inches for a person walking; 6 inches for a snowmobile; 8 inches for a vehicle weighing 3,500 pounds; and 12 inches for a vehicle weighing 8,000 pounds.

If you're fishing by yourself (which may not be wise) early in the season when the ice is thin, consider hanging ice picks around your neck. If you fall into the water, you'll have something with which you can grab on to the ice and pull yourself out. Carrying extra clothes—even if you leave them in your vehicle on shore—is a good idea, though you'll probably never need them if you're careful.

Always dress properly for ice fishing. The danger of developing hypothermia or frostbite is obvious.

Tuning Lures

All lures must swim true to be effective. If they don't have the right action, they will probably not be as effective as they were designed to be—in fact, they may be totally ineffective. Plugs, for example, must run straight on the retrieve, not lie on their side or run off at an angle; spoons must have the right wobble and should not lie flat or skip.

Some anglers take already serviceable lures and make minor adjustments—such as bending the lip or changing the hooks—that make the lures work exceptionally well, and it can be worthwhile to tinker with some lures to see whether they can be improved through modification. Tuning, however, means more than modifying a lure that already works; it's making minor adjustments to lures that are not swimming properly.

Lures don't always work just right, or as well as they could. Some that have been working properly may run awry after you catch fish on them, someone steps on them, or they get bashed against a hard object. Some lures work perfectly right out of the box, but others, especially diving plugs, do not. Moreover, you can buy a dozen identical lures and find that several need tuning to work right.

There are ways to tune lures to make them run true. The process is not difficult, but it does take a few minutes to accomplish, and it takes observation to know when to work on a lure to make it run better. Some plugs seem to need more frequent tuning than others, and some small lures need more frequent tuning than large ones. Others never get tuned exactly right. It is not uncommon to make many attempts to modify a new lure before you get it running to your satisfaction.

The majority of plugs have clear plastic bills of various lengths and shapes designed to make them dive. Into these bills are attached line-tie screws, and virtually all running problems involve the position of these little screws. When a plug runs awry, it is usually the fault of the line-tie. The line-tie screw must be placed perpendicularly to the plane of the bill of the lure. Because this screw eye is partially positioned by hand at the manufacturing plant, human error can be introduced. If the screw is placed a fraction of an inch out of position, the lure will not run true.

Besides the line-tie, other factors are at work as well. Plastic lures are molded in two halves that are joined and glued, and sometimes a change in the sealing of those halves, or some other aspect of mold design or construction, can affect a lure's performance. A few manufacturers tank-test each lure before they package it to ensure that it runs properly; however, most do not perform this labor-intensive activity.

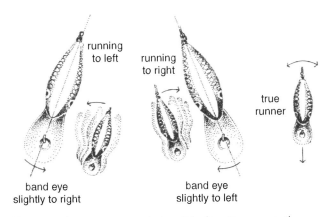

running
to left

running
to right

true
runner

band eye
slightly to right

band eye
slightly to left

To tune a plug to run properly, bend the line-tie screw in the opposite direction from which the lure is running astray. Do this incrementally until the plug runs straight ahead with a good side-to-side wobble.

A well-designed plug, with or without a lip, should have a good wiggling action. Some lures have a tight action, and some have more of a wide wobble. Whatever its action, a lure should come back in a straight line while swimming or diving. The body of a plug should swim on a vertical axis, like a real baitfish, not be canted off to either side; if it runs even a little bit off, it will have an unnatural action that will likely cost you fish. (This is not necessarily true for erratic-swimming and darting cut-plug lures that have no lip or bill. These lures appeal to fish, especially salmon, precisely because of their erratic movement.)

It is a good idea to check each plug before you fish it. Tie it on your line, drop a few feet of line from the tip of the rod to the lure, and then run the lure through the water next to your boat. If the lure does not run properly, adjust it immediately. If you can't tell by doing this, then cast the lure about 30 feet away, hold the rod tip out straight, and watch to see whether the lure runs off an imaginary straight line to either the right or the left.

To adjust a plug, you need a pair of pliers to bend the line-tie screw. Watch the lure swim. If the lure runs off to the right, bend the line-tie screw to the left; and if the lure runs left, bend the screw right. Tweak the screw in small steps, bending it slightly and checking its action in the water to see the change. Keep adjusting and checking until the lure runs perfectly. In serious cases, you may have to bend the line-tie screw far from its original position.

When bending the line-tie screw, be careful not to loosen it; the screw is epoxied in place, and loosening it may render the plug unusable. Sometimes you can take out the screw and reglue it, using clear, quick-setting epoxy. Also, make sure that you bend the eye, not twist it.

Before you tune a lure that seems to run awry, make sure you're not retrieving or trolling it too fast. All plugs have a top working speed beyond which they will not run properly. This speed is not the same for all lures. Some lures that run well at slower speeds will run awry at faster speeds, yet can be tuned to swim properly anyway.

Generally, swimming plugs do not run very well if a tight knot is tied directly to the screw eye. For this reason, it is best to use a split ring or rounded snap for connection. Most plugs are supplied with split rings or snaps, and your knot should be tied to this. Snap swivels may alter the action of these plugs, making tuning difficult, so avoid using these.

A new knot on a lure that was running fine may change the action because of the position of the knot. This is corrected by changing the position and alignment of the knot, or by retying the knot and snugging it tight. You may find that some plugs work best if you use a loop knot. With some deep-diving minnow plugs, tie a loop knot directly to the line-tie screw or the split ring.

Some of these comments about plugs and line-ties apply to other lures. Spinners usually don't pose much of a problem except for the occasional bent shaft, which can be corrected easily if not too severe. Streamers need to swim upright, and usually you simply adjust the knot location on the eye of the fly to achieve this. Heavy spoons don't usually get bent out of shape, but wafer-thin spoons do, and this sometimes requires adroit remodeling. A few thin flutter spoons can be bent at the tip and base, to the left or right, to modify their action.

It pays to experiment with such tuning, if for no other reason than to compare actions. Remember to watch for line twist with these lures; in the case of spoons or spinners, use a good-quality snap swivel to eliminate twist. In addition, be aware of the small things that might affect the way your lure swims. Some lures are sensitive to the slightest adornment. If you pull a lure through weeds and get a tiny confetti trailer on your hooks or line-tie, you'll feel the action of the lure change if you have the rod in your hand, or you may notice a change in the movement of your rod tip.

Unsnagging

Getting your lure stuck on some object in, on, under, or near the water is part of the fishing game. Many species of fish orient to bottom and to different types of structural cover, and, as the saying goes, if you aren't getting snagged occasionally, you're probably not angling where the fish are. Therefore, getting unsnagged is a practice you'll have to master unless you don't mind losing lures and breaking your line a lot.

An important point to realize about retrieving a snagged lure is that it doesn't pay to use brute strength and yank on a stuck lure unless you have very heavy line (and then you may straighten the hook) or you are stuck on something flimsy. You usually can't muscle that lure free. Moreover, in so doing you probably will sink the hook deeper into the snagged object; or you may break your line, meaning that you've probably lost the plug altogether; or you may free the bait but send it speeding perilously back to you.

Many lures will come free if you simply jiggle your rod a bit. Another tactic is to take line from the rod between the reel and first guide, pull back on the rod to get the line very taut, and then snap free the line in the other hand; this action may jolt the lure free, especially if it is a jig or single-hooked lure. This technique sometimes works when you are a distance away from an object that is fairly shallow and you don't want to go into the shallows to retrieve it. It is especially worth trying on a snagged lure that is deeper than the length of your rod, in which case you should position your boat directly over it.

Sometimes it pays to give the stuck lure slack line. A floating plug may float free, or another bait might fall back from the object it was hung on. In current, you can often free a lightly snagged lure by paying out 20 to 30 feet of line so that it drifts downcurrent, and then retrieve the slack line slowly. The force of the downstream current provides a different angle of pull that frequently frees the lure.

Generally, you need to change the angle of pull to retrieve many snagged lures, which simply

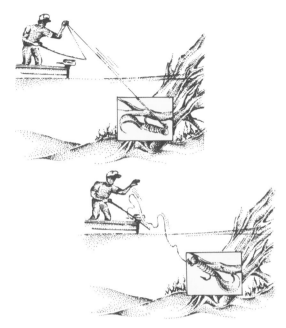

Before applying direct, hard-pulling pressure in an attempt to free a snagged lure, first try taking the line ahead of the rod tip, bringing it taut (top), and then making a snap release (bottom).

hang up by the lip or bill or head, usually by wedging into something. Changing position, whether that means walking down the bank or moving your boat to get a different angle of pull, usually does the job. In deeper water, position yourself 180 degrees from where you were when you got stuck and simply pull.

If your lure is stuck in water that is no deeper than the length of your rod, and will not come free by any other means, position your boat over the location, stick your rod tip into the water, reel up the slack line until the tip of the rod hits the lure, and then gently push or wiggle it free. You must be gentle when doing this so that you don't break the tip of the rod or jam the guide ring out of its retainer. Be especially careful when you're doing this around rocks. This technique is very effective when a lure is stuck on vegetation, dock pilings, or wood.

You might try using a long pole to poke a stuck lure free or to pull the lure free. Some of the telescoping pushpoles used in freshwater have a ring eye on one foot and a bent metal piece on the other. These are meant for reaching up to a stuck lure or for sliding down a fishing line to get to where a lure is snagged, and they are almost 100 percent effective for anything that can be reached within 10 to 15 feet.

For lures that are snagged deeper and can't be reached or snapped or jiggled free, you'll have to employ some type of retriever or knocker, which is a weight that slides down the fishing line and dislodges the stuck lure. This technique is most commonly used for plugs, which is why the knocker is often called a plug knocker, and also for jigging spoons. The knocker may be homemade or commercially manufactured. Sometimes an old sparkplug is used as a knocker by putting a split ring over the gap arm and pinching the arm to a closed position.

The trouble with these free-falling devices is that they sometimes don't work, especially if a lure has been pulled hard into an object (a deep stump, for example); later, when the line gets broken, you lose both the lure and the knocker. Leaving large weights (often lead) and sparkplugs on the bottom is akin to littering, and not environmentally sensitive.

There are, however, string- or cord-fastened retrievers, which are meant either to dislodge the snagged lure or to tangle on the hooks. When the lure is freed, you simply pull on the string to retrieve everything. These attach to the fishing line and slide down it also. They usually take some time to use, but if you have to retrieve a lure that is catching fish, or the last of its kind, or one that you paid premium dollars for, then it's probably worth the time. With either kind of device, position yourself over the top of it for best results.

When you can't get free by any of these means, then you have to try pulling up on the lure as a last resort. For last-chance unsnagging, tighten the drag and point the rod directly at the lure while reeling up all slack and pulling back. When a lure is deep, because of the distance of water between you and the lure, you don't have to worry about it rocketing back at you if you are successful in freeing it.

Beware of pulling on a lure that is stuck out of the water or close to the surface. Many people have been hit by multihooked lures, lead sinkers, and hard objects that suddenly pull free under great tension and fly back at them at the speed of light. It can be dangerous. Warn others in your boat to watch out before you pull on the lure if there is a chance of it coming back to the boat.

This direct pulling might break the line if it doesn't free the lure. If the line doesn't break, usually because it is very strong, then you should wrap the line over a shirt- or jacket-covered elbow or a piece of broomstick handle and pull on it. Do not wrap the line around your hand, because it can slice through the flesh.

After you've been stuck on an object, check the first few feet of line to make sure it isn't abraded. If it is, cut off the damaged section and tie a new knot.

PART FIVE

Practical Matters

35

Angling Etiquette

Trespass is probably the number one etiquette problem in freshwater fishing, and is actually a legal matter. Anglers must obtain permission to fish on private waters, to cross private property to access public or private waters, and, in some cases, even to stop briefly on private property while wading or navigating through public waters.

Courtesy and good manners are not legal issues, but they do apply to all aspects of angling. For example, if you're fishing a small stream and come upon an angler working a pool, you should pass that pool up or wait until the angler fishing it departs. Likewise, when fishing in a lake or reservoir, it is bad form to come into an area that another boat occupies. Allow a reasonable amount of space, and assume that they are, and will continue, working the area and not just the immediate spot where they're located. Crowded waters, however, make breaches of such reasonable etiquette too frequent. So do competitive fishing events.

While there is no formal established guide to proper conduct on the water for anglers, many of whom are also boaters, there are certain conventions that are followed in some places and by some groups of anglers. For example, many North American Atlantic salmon anglers gather at a river pool and take turns rotating through the pool, fishing from the head of the pool to the runout, with following anglers entering the water only when their predecessor has moved sufficiently downstream, depending on the size of the pool. This is one of the more civilized forms of angling behavior on crowded water, made bearable in part by a general lack of fish.

Although common sense prescribes that proper behavior is necessary when sharing waters with others, this becomes complicated when anglers don't realize the extent of the circumstances. For example, a person fishing along a saltwater flat by poling and stalking fish will generally be heading downtide to spot and cast to fish that will be moving or facing uptide. Another person who runs by downtide or who pulls up to start fishing downtide, even within a hundred yards, is more than inconsiderate; this action is likely to spoil a careful stalk by spooking fish. In such an instance the pre-positioned angler should be given a very wide berth by a passing boat, should be allowed his original course by the newly arrived angler moving uptide (like the Atlantic salmon river anglers), or should be asked by the newcomer where he can fish (only after approaching quietly from uptide or via radio communication) without interfering.

Most examples of proper etiquette involve common sense. For example, trollers shouldn't run their boats too close to other trollers or anchored boats to avoid cutting or hooking lines, and should stay well away from shore anglers; well away is out of casting range. Boaters who cast along a shoreline should swing away from shore anglers (or swimmers) and leave this area completely to their less mobile counterparts.

Boating anglers should always give the right of way to a boat that has a fish; pull in your own lines if necessary and swing far away from their area. Sometimes in crowded situations this requires quick action.

Most boating anglers don't think of themselves as being a problem for nonboaters, although they're very aware when they are on the receiving end of poor conduct by waterskiers, some pleasure boaters, and many operators of personal watercraft. However, the wake of fast-moving fishing boats, especially in narrow places like canals and nearshore areas, can cause people in a small boat

When waters are fringed with docks and boathouses, as this Ontario lake is, anglers should be mindful of private property and steer clear of those in use.

to grip the gunwales while the boat rocks, and does little to engender goodwill. Idling away from shore, observing no-wake zones and speed limits, and giving a wide berth to shores (100 to 150 feet is the minimum and a legal requirement in some waters), especially where there are homes and docks, are examples of good etiquette.

Boating anglers should be aware of others in a variety of not so immediately obvious ways. For example, boaters greatly interfere with duck hunters in the fall by getting anywhere near an active blind; sometimes it's difficult to know which blinds are currently in use, even if decoys are on the water, but boating or angling activity may too easily destroy the duck hunter's already limited chance of success.

Fishing around docks and boathouses, which are popular targets for bass anglers, requires commonsense courtesies as well. Those who don't have pinpoint casting control should avoid fishing around these objects, as owners do not appreciate having lures and hooks bounce off their property, get tangled in dock lines, or stuck on foam dock supports. Do not fish docks when they're being used, and leave the area politely if asked to do so, even though the surrounding water is public.

Boating anglers should also make sure that they spend minimal time launching and loading a boat from active or crowded access sites. Boat preparation for fishing, as well as unloading, should take place away from the launch ramp and the public dock. When fish are kept, they should never be cleaned on the beach or shore; do so in designated fish-cleaning areas at a launch site, or at home.

Anglers fishing while floating in canoes, kayaks, jonboats, or other craft need to steer clear of wading anglers. Sometimes this is not possible, and they wind up floating right in front of anglers and over the pool they're fishing. Where possible, it's best to go behind a wading angler, or directly in front of that person (if it is too shallow behind them) so as to minimize your impact on the pool or run. You may have to explain your intentions as you approach.

Although North American anglers are fortunate to have reasonably good access, and in some cases excellent access, to most bodies of water, they need to be mindful that their actions as anglers and as boaters may have an impact on future access for themselves and others. This is especially relevant with respect to coastal areas, and with surf anglers in particular.

For the most part, coastal beaches are controlled by federal, state, and municipal governments, as well as by private individuals, organizations, and corporations. In most cases, you must have permission to access a particular portion of beach. Many government agencies have established access points for a good deal of oceanfront. Most charge a fee to use a four-wheel-drive vehicle, if that is allowed at all (a special permit is usually issued, and it may require the holder to have a pail, tow rope or chain, shovel, fishing rod, and other items in the vehicle while on the beach). A few beaches are free for walk-on anglers, but very few have free and unrestricted access to the ocean for beach buggies.

As coastal areas become more populated and increasingly utilized, fishing space becomes a rarer commodity. The fate of all beaches is susceptible to many influences, and anglers may find it increasingly difficult to gain access to beaches or to convince policymakers that they are entitled to recreate there as well. Some angling organizations and surf fishing clubs have been able to hold their ground, but pressure to ban access has grown and is likely to continue.

Surf anglers must be aware of this problem and do what they can to establish and maintain a good image and a good rapport with others. Exercising common sense is important. Always leaving the beach as clean as, or cleaner than, you found it, even if this involves cleaning up someone else's mess, is a good way to start. Dispose of unused or discarded bait properly. Take off cleats or creepers when walking on wooden boardwalks or access lanes. Do not cross a strip of private property without permission simply because it is the easy way to get to a desirable fishing spot. If someone is swimming or surfing right in the middle of your favorite fishing spot, leave it and come back later.

Beach buggy owners must be particularly careful. Stay in designated areas, do not drive on or even near the dunes, and avoid nesting bird habitat, especially that of piping plovers. Don't take an unnecessary risk. If the sand looks a little soft, get out of the vehicle and walk across; if you sink, your beach buggy will go down to the axles, and it may put one more nail in the coffin for other vehicular users.

These are just a few examples of ways in which common sense dictates courteous, sensible, and practical behavior. The golden etiquette rule should always be: Do unto others as you would have them do unto you.

36

Ethical Fishing

Ethics, which is a system or code of morals, is different from laws. What is legal behavior may not be viewed by a majority of people as ethical, or may not fit an objective view of proper behavior. Sportsmanship is essential to any discussion of ethics because it is the notion of fair play, and angling by sporting means, that should separate the recreational angler from the commercial fisherman.

In angling today, and especially in North America, there is a lack of spoken and written attention to ethics. Many people, particularly fly anglers, believe that they adhere to a generally understood but seldom expressed code of ethics; most often this revolves around the act of harmlessly releasing fish (the catch-and-release ethic) or around the methodology (casting and/or fishing exclusively with flies or artificial lures, for examples, as ethics unto themselves).

Casting Lures

Casting with artificial lures (which includes flies) is a sportfishing methodology especially favored by many anglers, in some cases to the exclusion of various forms of bait presentation. Many people who cast artificial lures believe that doing so is more challenging, more interesting, or more sporting than fishing with any form of natural or processed bait or by means of trolling.

A majority of anglers prefer to catch fish by actively casting and retrieving an artificial lure and by always holding the rod in their hand. However, it is not feasible to fish exclusively by casting with artificial lures for all species and for all sizes of fish in all places where they're found (rivers, big lakes, ocean reefs, blue water, and so forth), although one can certainly argue that the means are more important than the results. Some environments and some species clearly lend themselves to casting, making a personal casting ethic for those species practical and not counterproductive.

The ethical issue of using artificial lures in lieu of natural or processed bait likewise involves the subject of practicality and incorporates questions about releasing fish. Many people who use only artificial lures (especially flies) assume moral superiority because of this, which is not necessarily justified. The artificial lure versus bait issue is one of many ethical concerns that has been addressed in specific instances by laws. The effects on fish caught with artificial lures and bait are addressed in chapter 37.

Fishing for Spawners

An ethical issue that is overlooked by much of the sporting media these days is that of angling for spawning largemouth and smallmouth bass, which are vulnerable to detection and capture when on their large and easily observed shallow nests in the spring. The consequences of deliberately or incidentally catching (and in many cases releasing) spawning bass have triggered a few scientific studies, and perceived potential negative effects from fishing during the spawning season are the main reason why a minority of fisheries agencies close the angling season during the spawning period. Such closures, however, are inconsistent among fisheries agencies, some with neighboring jurisdictions, which logically raises questions about validity.

Although the personal ethic of some anglers is that it is unsportsmanlike to deliberately angle for spawning bass, many anglers do so (it is legal in most states). Curiously, questions regarding the propriety and sportsmanship of angling for other species when they are spawning or specifically on their spawning migrations—such as salmon, steelhead, trout, charr, striped bass, shad, and tuna—are raised even less often, perhaps because of their generally brief availability.

Fishing/Catching to Excess

The propriety of keeping a limit or excessive number of fish each time an angler goes fishing, even if it is legal to do so and even if the fish will be consumed, raises ethical questions; this practice long ago gave rise to "game hog" and other derisive terms. Likewise, continuing to catch and release large numbers of fish when the angling is very good is viewed by some people as excessive, somewhat like running up the score in a lopsided athletic contest.

Receiving Assistance

One ethical issue sometimes concerns the very act of setting the hook on a fish and playing it. The International Game Fish Association long ago established ethical rules for catches that were acceptable as world records.

Anglers who do not set the hook themselves on a potential record catch, for example, and/or who allow someone else to handle their rod while playing or landing that fish, cannot receive a record, no matter how stupendous the fish is. Although the wisdom of this is widely supported, similar mandates do not exist in many state record programs and most anglers are generally unfamiliar with these principles. Many other aspects of the equipment used and means of fishing are covered by these record-establishing rules.

The generally accepted ethic, however, is that it is not fair for an angler to receive assistance in setting the hook or in landing the fish.

Foul Hooking

Many people view it as unsportsmanlike to catch or keep a fish that has not been hooked in the mouth, and some laws and fisheries agency regulations prohibit keeping a fish that has been foul-hooked, even if it occurred accidentally.

The legal foul hooking of fish, known as snagging, is a related and highly controversial matter, and one that was once advocated by fisheries agencies for some species and is still supported by a few. This has led to atrocious behavior by people who are unconscious of fair play ethics.

During the fall chinook salmon run, people crowd the Salmon River in New York, where the deliberate foul hooking of fish was once legal.

Using Mismatched Tackle

Many anglers fish with tackle that is either too light or too heavy for the intended species or common size of the species they seek. This includes rods and reels but especially the breaking strength of line used.

Ethics are called into question when anglers use heavy tackle on the off chance that they'll hook a huge fish, thereby ensuring that there is little contest in landing the much more plentiful smaller specimens. On the other hand, using extremely light tackle for some species, especially those that are hard, strong fighters, is also unfair if the fish will or must be released, because it is likely that the fish will have a harder time recovering and/or escaping its other predators when released.

Selling Fish

Some saltwater sportfish (especially tuna and dolphin) are legally sold by people who used recreational angling methods to capture the fish. The lack of ethics in this is pretty obvious, not to mention that commercial fishermen are rightly accused of overexploiting most ocean fisheries resources (particularly tuna) by the angling community at the same time that some of their own brotherhood are selling fish that have been caught on rod and reel.

Killing Fish

Anti-angling groups object to catch-and-release fishing because fish "are only let go to be hooked and tortured all over again," and the criticism is that even when fish are kept, most are not killed immediately; they're put in boxes where they slowly suffocate. Although British sporting magazines recommend that anglers carry a "priest," or club, to kill fish instantly and humanely, North American writers rarely broach the subject. Perhaps many people feel that the growing popularity of catch-and-release fishing is proof of its moral superiority, or that what isn't actually written into law is ethically acceptable.

Pollution

It is ironic that anglers—who have a lot to gain from clean environments and healthy fish populations—number among themselves people who discard trash on the shore or into the water. Used fishing line, for example, is especially harmful, as it can entangle birds or other animals, but there are many examples of ways in which some anglers (albeit a small minority) despoil the environment through their personal behavior, both while fishing and not.

Competitions and Equipment

Competitive fishing events are commonplace and, for a few people, raise ethical concerns that are rarely discussed or addressed because many of these events are important business and tourism tools. Concerns include the use of public resources for private gain, the philosophy of angling, the methodologies and equipment used by competitors, the handling and disposing of fish, interfering with and/or usurping the rights of the general public, and the well-being of fish that are caught/transported/handled/released.

The variety of equipment employed in recent decades has grown enormously, and much of it is profiled in some way within this book. Electronic product developments have led to some attempts to curb or eliminate by law their use; these have been unsuccessful but included proposed bans on sonar equipment and underwater viewing cameras. The use of some of these items has raised regionally isolated ethical debates concerning increasing commercialism and, of course, what constitutes fair play in the pursuit of sportfish species.

37

Catch-and-Release

C atch-and-release" is an action rooted in angling ethics and tradition and refers to the practice of catching game-fish by sporting methods and with sporting equipment and then releasing them alive. Catch-and-release has become very popular in many types of fishing, and is still evolving as more is learned about the factors affecting the survival of sport-caught fish that have been released and as anglers learn and practice the proper methods of landing, handling, and releasing their catches.

As a voluntary action, catch-and-release is a personal if not moral or ethical judgment, and some practitioners believe that its spirit has special meaning only when it is done by choice, especially with respect to fish that are notable for their size or scarcity. However, what was once primarily a voluntary action has increasingly become legally mandated for certain sizes, numbers, and species of fish. Thus catch-and-release has become both personal philosophy and governmental policy, and it is important that anglers understand what they must do to ensure the survival of fish that they must, or decide to, return to the water.

Although catch-and-release fishing has been touted by some as a panacea for improving fishing, this is not true for all species and in all situations. Moreover, some people have preached the concept so aggressively that one could get the impression that keeping any fish is wrong, even if the law allows otherwise.

Some fish, like this large Saskatchewan pike, need to be held stable in the water for a while until they can swim off on their own.

Some newcomers to angling, particularly fly fishing, have embraced total catch-and-release out of a sense of political correctness; this thinking puts them at odds with the many anglers for whom a meal of freshly caught fish is appropriate not only for nutritional reasons, but also for the satisfying conclusion to an angling experience that it represents.

Another issue concerns what to do with trophy fish. Some anglers deem it morally reprehensible to keep a particularly large fish. People who rarely keep fish might choose not to release a particularly large one and instead send it to a taxidermist. It is important to know that taxidermists can produce replica mounts from fiberglass or graphite molds that are as good as skin mounts, and longer-lasting. Thus, in the case of trophy fish, it's possible to experience the unique pleasure of releasing one of the rare members of a fish population and still have a representation to hang over the fireplace.

Compounding the acceptance of catch-and-release is that regulations vary widely, and what is acceptable on one body of water may not be on another. In certain situations, biologists have the challenging chore of convincing anglers to release small fish of a certain species at one lake, but keep them at another.

The amount of fishing done by individual recreational anglers varies widely, as do skill levels and success from novices to professionals. Thus the amount of fishing that an angler does, and the amount of success that the angler experiences, has to be part of the equation in developing a personal catch-and-release ethic.

Anglers who fish often and with a high degree of accomplishment are the most likely to have an entrenched interest in catch-and-release. However, they do not have a higher moral standing than those who fish only a few days a year, with relatively modest success, and who keep most of their legal catch to eat. Furthermore, there is some mortality among the fish that are released by all anglers; even anglers who live-release every fish they catch cannot claim to have no effect on the resource.

To effectively practice catch-and-release, whether by choice or by mandate, anglers must know how to properly release fish, and they must understand what factors contribute to unintended angling-related mortality.

Injury and Stress

The most logical question to ask about releasing fish is whether they will survive after being hooked, played, landed, handled, unhooked, and returned to the water. The answer is that many, but certainly not all, will survive, and that survival depends on many factors.

Numerous studies have been conducted by professional fisheries researchers on the survival rates of fish that are caught and released. Some general conclusions stand out in the collective body of scientific studies, chief among them that using bait is more detrimental to fish than using lures or flies, that barbless hooks cause slightly lower mortality than barbed hooks, that bleeding fish are unlikely to survive, and that deeply hooked fish are at much greater risk than those hooked around the edges of the mouth.

Fish primarily die before and after being released because of injury and stress. Some weakened or struggling fish may also die as a result of predation by other fish, birds, and some reptiles

Gill

Isthmus

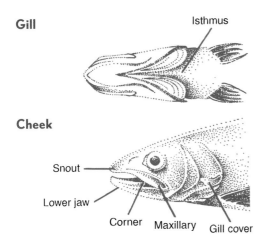

Cheek

Snout

Lower jaw

Corner   Maxillary   Gill cover

The least harmful hooking areas are the jaw, snout, corners of the mouth, maxillary, and cheek. The most harmful hooking areas are the eye, tongue, isthmus, and gills.

and mammals; this seldom accounts for a high mortality, although injury or stress may be an indirect factor. Death that occurs after release, usually out of sight of the angler and without the angler's knowledge, is called delayed mortality. Many fish that die from injury or stress do so within 24 hours after being released, the vast majority within 48 hours.

The response of fish to injury and stress varies among species, and even among individuals of the same species. Some species are more resistant to rough-handling stresses than others, and such variables as water temperature, season (spawning), and even size of the fish make a difference in how fish react to being caught and released. Thus, although one particular action may be identified as being harmful to a fish, or as causing stress, or as causing mortality, a number of actions may be collectively responsible.

Most of the stress-related problems center around the gills, the respiratory system, and the circulatory system.

Gills. The gills are an especially sensitive area of a fish. Bleeding can come from even a slight nick, and in itself is a high-stress factor.

A fish cannot breathe out of water; it gets oxygen from the water that passes over the gills. Keeping a fish out of the water, whether to unhook it, photograph it, or weigh it, increases the stress load. When oxygen is low, fish breathe faster, trying to pass more water over the gills. If held out of

the water for too long, a fish can suffocate. How long is too long? There is no stopwatch answer for this. The size and species of the fish, the temperature, and even humidity all play a role.

Lifting any fish by its gill flap, as many anglers do, is definitely harmful; it exposes the gill tissues to air and can result in tearing of the filaments. Touching and grabbing the gills can be very harmful. To reduce stress, anglers should minimize exposure of the gills to air, avoid touching them, and avoid grabbing a fish by the gills or lifting it by the gill cover.

Lactic acid buildup. Vigorous physical exertion causes lactic acid to accumulate in the fish's muscles. This occurs when the muscles are deprived of oxygen and the body incompletely metabolizes glucose. The same thing occurs in humans after strenuous exertion, and it produces the "oxygen debt" that long-distance runners and other athletes experience. When the exertion is over, if all other systems are functioning properly, the body metabolizes the lactic acid and restores the oxygen to appropriate levels. But this may not happen immediately; the more severe the lactic acid buildup, the longer it takes to return to normal.

Ordinarily, the metabolic process operates at a continuous balanced level, but there are natural times when lactic acid builds up. Chasing or escaping from predators, for example, is likely to temporarily build up lactic acid. The rigors of migration can produce moments of buildup.

The accumulation of lactic acid in a fish's muscles can lead to blood acidification and temporary disruption of many metabolic processes. If a captured fish is able to restore its blood acid (pH) level to normal or prestress levels, normal physiological processes return and the fish may survive after being released. If the blood chemistry balance is not restored, the fish will probably die. The volume of lactic acid generated is directly proportional to the duration of muscular activity.

Extended battles promote lactic acid buildup. In general it is advantageous to land a fish quickly if you intend to release it, unless it has been hooked in very deep water. Playing the fish until it is exhausted, or "belly up," may lead to lactic acid poisoning and death. This eventuality may be prevented not only by playing a fish quickly, but also by unhooking it carefully and releasing it as quickly as possible.

Experienced anglers know that lactic acid buildup and the resulting stress work differently in fish. A rainbow trout, for example, will put up more of a struggle than a bullhead catfish. The coolwater trout is more likely to build up lactic acid than the warmwater bullhead; and the trout will not endure long if kept out of the water, whereas the hardier bullhead may last a surprisingly long time.

Anglers should become acquainted with the fighting characteristics of the different species and should be able to recognize when certain fish need to be landed quickly and given more attention in the revival and release process. Some fish are so stressed after being landed (as well as handled for release), and their lactic acid level so high, that they have a greatly increased need for oxygen. This condition makes them harder to revive, and they may need more time to recover before they regain equilibrium and can swim off on their own.

Stress is the factor that initiates lactic acid buildup, and this is compounded by injury, either because of where the fish is hooked or how it is handled later on. Bringing a fish to boat quickly, for example, while generally recommended, can have a drawback if the fish is so frisky that the angler, in efforts to unhook and release it, causes internal or external injury. Putting a stressed fish into a livewell may not be helpful either if the well doesn't have sufficient aeration. In that case, the fish will struggle to get the oxygen it needs, thereby creating more stress rather than less. If the livewell is uncrowded, is properly aerated, and/or the water has been treated with conditioning agents, stress can be reduced.

Thus, in the various stages of contact with a sport-caught fish, anglers may compound or mitigate stress, and it is important to have an understanding of the impact of all actions.

How a Fish Is Hooked

A determining factor in the survival of a fish after release is where it is hooked. Many studies have proven that fish caught with bait suffer a much higher rate of mortality than those caught with lures or flies. The studies differ in the mortality percentage of bait-hooked fish, but they agree that the use of bait generally results in deeply hooked fish and a significantly higher mortality.

Note that the manner of fishing also effects deep hooking. Trolling with a lure or fly, for example, is unlikely to cause a deep-hooked fish. If an angler lets a fish run with either live or dead bait and waits to set the hook, the likelihood is great that the fish will swallow the bait, which will probably result in it being hooked deeply, especially in the esophagus or stomach. Removing a hook from these areas is usually difficult; it often cannot be done without taking the fish out of the water, and hook removal in this instance may cause internal damage. If the hook is swallowed so deeply that it punctures the heart, which is just behind the mouth, or the liver or kidney, the fish is going to die.

Although such deep hooking is often a result of fishing with bait, it can also happen with lures, which may be swallowed by fish if they are allowed to run with them. Deep swallowing of the lure can cause the same degree (if not more) of hooking mortality as bait swallowing. Indeed, some studies have shown that live bait has caused no significant difference in mortality over certain types of lures that were likely to be taken deeply. A study of live bait use compared with the use of Carolina-rigged plastic worms on largemouth bass, for example, showed a slightly higher mortality for the worms.

One way that anglers using bait can reduce harm to fish is to set the hook quickly. This is helpful, since most fish can inhale a piece of bait in an instant; however, it does not work for all species, and its success may depend on the type of

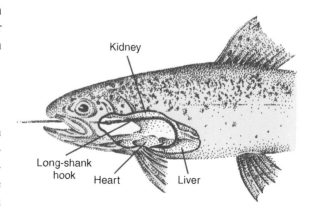

The kidney, heart, and liver are all vulnerable when a fishhook is lodged within the throat of a fish.

bait used or species sought. Some fish crush a bait and then turn it around to inhale; for those species, deep hooking can be avoided by being alert to a take and quickly reacting properly.

Incidentally, some baitfishing with treble hooks is actually better than baitfishing with single hooks, since the trebles are harder to swallow, although the bait may act less naturally with the treble and the fish may detect a treble hook sooner than a single one. In some saltwater fishing, the use of circle hooks has gained popularity for bait-fishing because these hooks usually catch in the corner of the mouth, causing less injury to a fish that will be released.

Most lures or flies are less likely to be taken deep than bait hooks, in part because they are usually moving and anglers react fairly quickly to a strike. As a result, most fish caught on lures or flies are hooked in body locations where the hook does not severely damage the fish. Fish suffer the lowest mortality when they are hooked in the jaw, the snout, the corner of the mouth, the maxillary, or the cheek. Hooking in the eye, the tongue, or the isthmus is more serious.

Being hooked in or near the gills is bad news because the hook may damage the gill filaments. This type of injury causes bleeding and decreases the fish's chance of survival.

Studies have shown that fish caught on flies have a slightly lower mortality rate than those caught on lures, but the difference is so small that it has virtually no impact on the overall mortality picture. This negligible impact is the reason why special-use regulations established by fisheries managers generally prohibit the use of bait but permit lures and flies, or specify single-hook lures and flies. Nevertheless, a belief persists among some anglers, primarily fly anglers, that people using lures, or "hardware," as it may derisively be called, cause more harm to the resource. Assuming that proper care is taken to unhook and release a fish, this is not so.

Another issue is the use of treble hooks versus single hooks. An evaluation of all studies on this topic concluded that there was no significant relationship between mortality and the number of hook points. However, treble hooks on average are more difficult to remove from fish, which means that doing so usually takes longer.

A lure with multiple treble hooks, such as many plugs, may have two or three sets of hooks. Fish are often impaled by two or three hook points on multiple-treble-hooked lures; unhooking them may take longer, or one hook may cause no damage (in the corner of the mouth, for example) but another may damage a vulnerable area (such as the eye or the gill). Therefore, a reasonable conclusion is that the probability of injury, although perhaps not mortality, to a fish is greater when a lure with multiple treble hooks is used.

In certain places, especially remote waters of northern Canada, the use of single hooks is either mandated by law or required as lodge or outfitter policy; and in some cases, those hooks must be barbless as well. The purpose of such policies is to minimize injury and permit quick release; these actions in turn help to maintain a large population of fish, all of which are slow-growing, and to increase the likelihood of big fish getting bigger.

A key issue in all these situations is the percentage of fish mortality. Studies of trout show mortalities of less than 5 percent for fish caught on lures and flies, and the rates decrease from there with single and barbless hooks.

All of this has to be kept in perspective, because a fish caught on a barbless hook may still be mortally wounded if the angler rips out the hook, squeezes the fish hard while holding it for release, drops it on the ground or boat floor, and so forth. The hooks used and the location of hooking are just part of the picture. How the angler plays, lands, handles, and releases fish is also very important.

Playing and Landing Fish

The technical aspects of how to play and land fish are discussed in chapter 18. The intent here is to particularly spotlight the effects of these activities upon fish that are to be released.

The issue of how you play the fish is central to what constitutes an exhausted fish, and it is admittedly a gray area. On the one hand, fish played to complete exhaustion may not survive. The key words are "may not." If complete exhaustion meant certain death for a fish, then it would mean death for every animal that exercises itself to exhaustion, including long-distance runners and racehorses. Obviously, exhaustion cannot equate entirely with death. Some large and strong fish that are played to exhaustion can be revived and set free. Some cannot.

The way that a fish is played may be the critical element. Playing a fish aggressively is more likely to result in breaking its spirit and saving its life. A tug-of-war can last longer and result in a "stubborn" fish that will not give up and cannot be resuscitated after capture. Fish of identical sizes can be played to identical times with different outcomes; one may be played aggressively by an experienced angler using light tackle and be successfully released, and the other may be played by an inexperienced angler using heavier tackle and be incapable of revival.

If you take the fight to the fish, no matter what the tackle, you often can convince it to give up. Anglers who fish for such powerful bruisers as tuna and billfish experience this frequently.

One of the critical areas affecting the well-being of fish to be released is how they are treated once they are caught. Mishandling results in injury and stress, and is an aspect of catch-and-release that every angler can do something about.

Whether or not a fish is tired, its chance of survival is best if it never leaves the water. In some instances, frisky and obviously unharmed fish can be shaken off at boatside by leaving some slack in the line and jiggling the rod tip. This is especially true if single-hooked and barbless lures are used. An angler who is having great success and catching many fish while using multihooked lures should consider using lures with a single hook or pinching the barbs, rather than continuing to catch fish on the original lures, especially if the fish are repeatedly small and frisky.

Wading anglers can accomplish the task of keeping a fish in the water easier than boat or bank anglers can; some fish, like steelhead, can be grabbed by the tail and held with one hand and unhooked with the other, all while staying in the water. Or the fish can be pinned against the angler's wet, wader-covered legs with one hand while the hook is removed.

Some fish can be unhooked in the water without handling. To do this, grasp the hook with needle- or long-nosed pliers and, without touching the fish (which may cause it to thrash about), quickly pull back and up on the point (in the opposite direction from which it is embedded) to free it. Once you have hold of the hook with the pliers, unhook the fish instantly in a quick wrist-twisting motion. This is usually, but not always,

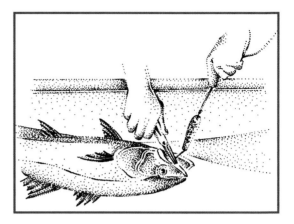

When fishing from a boat, you can easily release some fish without handling them by keeping the fish in the water at boatside and using pliers to free the hook.

a two-person operation; one angler holds the rod while the other reaches over (possibly holding the line lightly to steer the fish to an advantageous position) and, while the fish rests at the surface, uses pliers to quickly grab and free the hook. This is about as simple and as good a no-touch release as you can get. Unfortunately, this method isn't always possible because of the size or behavior of the fish, the number of hooks or how the fish is hooked, the distance from water to gunwale of the boat, or other factors.

When you can't release the fish in the water, you have to land it by grabbing the fish by hand,

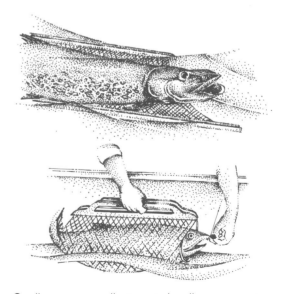

Cradles are an excellent way to handle some species of fish; a release cradle (top) provides optimal support for a long fish.

netting it, cradling it, or gaffing it in the jaw, taking precautions to minimize damage in the process. Netting is especially problematic if a multihooked lure is used. Such hooks inevitably grab the webbing of the net, and the fish thrashes and rips itself while pulling violently against the embedded hooks. If the fish rolls in the net with treble hooks, untangling becomes a real problem, and a good deal of time is lost before the fish can be unhooked. The situation is bad all around; some species may go into the net in good shape but come out with ripped skin, jaws, or eyes and be much worse off.

Hand-Landing

When you land a fish without a net or gaff, you have to hold it somehow. Big fish are difficult to hold, and when brought into a boat they are liable to be dropped or to squirm out of your hands and fall. Some fish, like a sailfish or big tarpon, might have to be held by two people in order to be properly subdued, supported, and unhooked. Nevertheless, both large and small fish are often brought into boats to be released, and therefore are handled. In fact, in some cases, there is no other choice.

The problem with physically handling a fish, as well as with letting it flop on the deck or floor of a boat or on the shore, is that the protective mucus coating may be removed, and the possibility increases of an infection that eventually may become grotesque and life-threatening. In addition, if the fish flops about while still hooked to a lure, the hooks on the lure may catch on some object (it might even be someone's leg or arm, which can be extremely serious) and cause further injury to the fish, which may also lead to infection.

Don't let a fish flop onshore or in a boat if you intend to release it. Wetting your hands before you hold a fish may help prevent removal of that protective mucus; however, many anglers maintain that wet hands make it harder to hold the fish, meaning that they have to grip it tighter. Using a sure-grip cotton glove that has been wetted is a good idea. However, don't grasp a small fish tightly around the middle of the body during unhooking, because you may cause internal damage.

Admittedly, it's a fine line between holding a fish tightly enough to keep it from squirming free, but not so tightly that the internal organs are compressed. Smaller fish, with less meat at the nape,

A good gripping tool such as this helps keep hands away from fish and hooks, and facilitates unhooking for release.

are more easily hurt by holding tightly there. Big freshwater fish, and many saltwater fish, can be held in that location without harm; for many, it is the best place to do so.

When holding and subduing larger fish, try placing a wet cloth or towel over the fish, at least over the head, which usually has a calming effect and is especially useful for fish that may be held for a longer period.

Of course, you can hand-land or securely hold some fish by the tail, or by the lower jaw; in the latter case, this may be by hand or with a jaw-gripping tool. Many fish cannot, or should not, be supported by the lower jaw whether you are holding the jaw by hand or with a gripping device, but they can be gripped there while they are still in the water or while the rest of the body is being supported.

Lifting fish up may or may not be a problem. The longer and heavier the fish, the more inappropriate lifting seems; yet lifting and briefly carrying fish, either headfirst or tailfirst, has not been harmful to many fish.

Keeping large fish in a horizontal position, in or out of the water, is more in their best interests

Like this walleye, many fish can be grasped behind the gills without injury, provided they aren't squeezed tightly.

than lifting them vertically. Smaller fish are less likely to be harmed when held vertically. Largemouth bass, which have been much studied, are commonly held vertically by anglers for unhooking and do not suffer from this position. However, most largemouth bass are small, and holding a 2-pound largemouth this way is not comparable to doing the same with a 40-pound striper.

Holding fish under the gills, as previously discussed, is not appropriate, nor is putting your fingers in their eye sockets. It was once fairly common to grab some species by the cavity of their eye sockets, but this sorry practice has become almost universally abandoned unless a fish is going to be kept. It causes obvious injury to the fish, and may lead to infections.

Keep in mind that a minimum amount of handling is desirable in all cases, particularly in warm water. If fish must be taken out of the water, as previously explained, be conscious of their inability to breathe and of the length of time that they are forced to forgo oxygen while being unhooked. Many of the fish that are held by anglers in the photographs in this book were released, even though they were held briefly out of water to take the photograph. When photographing fish, be prepared to take the photo quickly by having your camera available and ready to shoot. Of course, it helps if the fish are caught quickly and the water is cool.

As for weighing, lifting up a fish to weigh it is certainly not beneficial to the fish, and it prolongs the time spent out of water. Weighing occasionally leads to injury when a fish gets dropped, or when its gills are damaged from being touched or from the way it is hoisted for weighing.

Methods of estimating weight are detailed in chapter 19. If you absolutely have to weigh a fish, do so quickly, preferably with the assistance of someone else, and place the hook of the scale through the membrane behind the lower jaw, not under the gills or gill cover. Remember to be careful for your own sake as well as that of the fish.

Unhooking Fish

A hook should be removed carefully, not in a jerking or ripping manner that might cause injury. Tugging at a hook could rip the flesh inside the mouth or on the cheek or other location, which could prompt bleeding or lead to infection. Ripping out a hook could also tear the jaw or the maxillary. So the best action is to try to remove the hook without damaging the fish. Removal is usually easier with barbless hooks than with barbed ones, and in both cases it means backing the hook point out rather than just grabbing and pulling, which is sometimes difficult. Of course, hook removal should be done not just quickly for the sake of the fish but also carefully to avoid hooking yourself.

If you are removing the point of a hook from a fish with your fingers, be very careful; should the fish move or slip from your grasp, the potential for hooking yourself is great. People have been hooked in this manner, and one of the worst scenarios that you can imagine is getting a finger stuck on a hook that is still connected to the fish; this is definitely a possibility when using a multihooked lure or a treble hook. Whenever you're unhooking a fish or otherwise handling it, whether with your fingers or with some tool, be careful not to hurt yourself, since the gill covers, fin spines, and teeth are some of the body parts that can cause a nasty cut, which may become infected.

For grabbing and freeing many hooks, the most popular tool is a long-nosed or needle-nosed plier. It is especially useful for midsized hooks and treble hooks on lures, which make up the bulk of hooks used by anglers. With a tapered head, it fits well into a fish's mouth, or fairly deep into the mouth. For strictly small hooks and for flies that anglers would prefer not to crush (or to tear the dressing) during removal, a standard or angled-head hemostat works fairly well.

These tools may not be adequate for fish with big mouths and large or sharp teeth, but other unhooking devices, usually with long arms and a trigger to secure the grip on a hook, are available. Jaw spreaders, which keep the mouth of toothy fish open for unhooking work, help a lone angler unhook fish, but you have to use the proper size for the circumstances and be careful not to rip the fish with the ends.

Still another tool that is used in saltwater by anglers fishing with fairly heavy line or leader is simply called a hook puller by many. It looks a lot like an old hauling tool for ice blocks, except the business end is hooked and is used to grab around

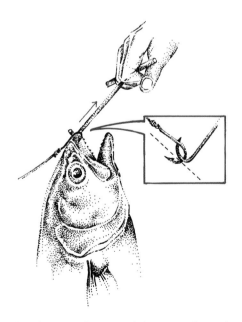

Small and intermediate-size fish, especially in saltwater, are often unhooked with a hook puller, a tool with a crooked end. When a fish is lifted up with heavy line or leader, the hook puller is looped over the bend of the fishhook (inset), the fish is quickly raised up, and the fishhook point is pulled in the opposite direction, allowing the fish to fall back into the water.

the bend of a hook when a fish is lifted up with a heavy line or leader. With one hand on the line close to the hook and with the hook puller looped over the bend of the hook, the angler quickly raises up the fish and pulls the hook point in the opposite direction. This works best when the hook is embedded within a few inches of the jaws, and when the fish is not so large that it can't be lifted by the line or leader.

Perhaps the most contentious aspect of catch-and-release is whether to remove the hook from a fish that has been deeply impaled. This has primarily been a baitfishing issue, and for a long time the standard advice was to cut the line or leader off and leave the hook in the fish rather than to try to remove it and risk causing internal injury and bleeding. Many studies have found greatly increased rates of survival—sometimes two and three times better—if the hook is left in.

However, hooks do corrode (depending on the type of hook, and they corrode faster in saltwater), and sometimes they are passed through the anal vent. Although leaving a hook in a fish may indeed be preferable to pulling it out, a deeply swallowed hook that is well into the stomach may nevertheless puncture vital organs; even if the fish is released, the damage is done. A hook left in the throat above the gills or the esophagus is not as serious. Whether or not to cut the line is usually a decision that anglers make based on circumstances at the exact moment and also on such factors as the condition of the fish, the length of the fight, and the tools available for unhooking.

Sometimes the difficulty of unhooking a deeply caught fish is increased because of the size of the fish's mouth, the strength of the fish, the presence of teeth, and other factors. If two anglers work on a fish, one holding and controlling the fish and/or keeping its mouth open and the other working to free the hook, the unhooking time can be shortened and the need for resuscitation lessened. So where a difficult situation exists, an angler should try to involve an extra pair of hands.

The Release

With the hook out, it's time for the final act. In many cases, especially with small fish and with fish that have been landed quickly, simply putting them back in the water and letting go is all that has to be done; the fish is lively, makes a thrust with

In a river, be sure to face a fish upstream so that water flows into its mouth, forcing oxygen over its gills; a chinook salmon is being released here.

its tail, and disappears. Many anglers release fish rather cavalierly. They may be standing in a boat and, after unhooking the fish, just toss it back in the water. For the most part, this does not seem to hurt a fish, but it can't be good for them. It is not asking too much for anglers to bend over and release fish into the water more gently.

If a fish has been kept out of water for a while, if it has struggled mightily, and if it is stressed, then just returning it to the water may not be enough, no matter how gently it is done. A stressed released fish often turns over on its side or back, being too weak to maintain its equilibrium.

To revive a fish, you need to keep it upright in the water. If you are in a river or a place with current, the fish should be headed into the current, not facing away from it. You should not let a stressed fish free in a swift current, even after it has been revived, because it may not have the strength to resist the current, which could carry it away and bounce it on the bottom or against objects. In a river, a stressed fish should be taken out of strong current and released where the current is less. Sometimes a fish released in the shallow backwaters of a river will rest there for a short while before moving, and it should not be rushed out before it is ready.

When reviving a fish, you can get oxygen to it by moving it forward to force water into its mouth and over the gills. A fish takes water into its mouth and forces it over the gills and out the external opening to take oxygen into the blood. It cannot do this by swimming backward or by facing

downstream. If you hold a fish facing downstream long enough in a strong current, it will die. That seems to indicate that moving water backward over a fish may not be helpful, and that you should only focus on moving the fish forward.

Moving a fish forward only is admittedly harder to do for fish that cannot be held by the mouth by hand; however, with the right gripping tool, it may be possible. Mouth-gripped fish can be led forward in a circular or figure-eight pattern, especially if they are not big, but other fish, and large individuals, are harder to lead like this. Boat anglers can aid some fish by moving the boat slowly forward under outboard or electric motor power, but such fish have to be held by the head, or supported by the head and forward part of the body. You can seldom hold a fish by the tail alone and move the boat forward, because the fish gets turned sideways or backward.

Cradling the fish with both hands is an alternative if you cannot move it forward. One hand holds the caudal peduncle, and the other supports the belly close to the pectoral fins. Hold the fish upright and keep it steady, perhaps moving it sideways if possible, until it recovers and can swim off on its own.

The key is keeping the fish upright and supporting it, and giving it time. Devote whatever time is necessary to reviving a fish and getting it to the point where it can swim off on its own. It is not uncommon to spend 20 minutes reviving a large fish, and some people have devoted an hour to a successful effort.

A fish is usually ready to go off on its own when it uses its tail muscles to try to swim. If it

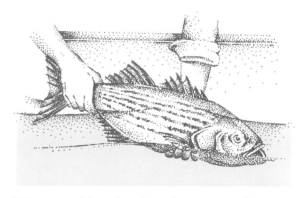

Before some fish can be released, you may need to revive them; this requires careful handling and moving the fish forward to pass oxygenated water over their gills.

does this forcefully enough, you may let go of the tail immediately and the fish will dart off or swim slowly but assuredly away. It sometimes helps to poke the fish in the tail; this action provokes the fish into a short flight away and forces a burst of water and oxygen into its system, perhaps aiding its recovery. If the fish swims off well on its own, this isn't necessary, but if it sits in one place and looks like it could be vulnerable to a predator's attack, then a slight poke with a rod tip, boathook, net handle, oar, or paddle might be worthwhile. Keep an eye on the fish as it swims off until you can no longer see it.

Special Circumstances

Certain aspects of releasing fish and of catch-and-release in general deserve special consideration and more detailed evaluation.

Releasing Deep-Water Fish

A general rule when releasing some fish and keeping others is to keep the ones that are caught in deep water rather than those caught in shallow water. Fish caught in deep water are usually harder to revive than those caught in shallow water, so being thoughtfully selective makes sense. However, if you do have to release deep-water fish, they should be appropriately cared for, since the deep water may cause a problem that is not experienced when fish caught in shallower water are released.

When some species of freshwater and saltwater fish are brought up from very deep water, they suffer a condition that is equivalent to what people know as "the bends," because pressure increases about 15 pounds every 33 feet in the water. This pressure has to be relieved; if it is not, the air bladder expands within the abdominal cavity, and the expansion may cause the stomach to protrude from the mouth. A fish in this condition, which is compounded by a sometimes drastic change in water temperature, will turn belly up if released and cannot recover until it has been "degassed."

Some species are able to belch the pressure away during retrieval, but in others it builds. Those in which it does not build have a pneumatic duct connected to the air bladder, allowing these fish to expel air and make more extensive vertical movements. Such fish include the various trout and salmon species, as well as carp and catfish. Those in which pressure builds lack this duct and cannot expel air; adjustment to pressure is slow, meaning that these fish cannot make rapid vertical movements. These species include largemouth and smallmouth bass, spotted bass, walleye, yellow perch, panfish species, striped bass, snapper, grouper, cod, hake, and black sea bass. Other fish, including lake trout and salmon, that have been brought up too quickly for their bodies to naturally adjust to the pressure changes, may still experience a problem, even though they have the natural means to overcome it.

How deep is deep enough to cause this depressurization? This is hard to say, but over 40 feet is generally thought to be enough to cause it in snapper and grouper, over 30 feet for walleyes, and over 60 feet for lake trout.

To relieve this pressure in trout and salmon, especially in lake trout, the fish can be "burped." Salmonids have an opening between the air bladder and esophagus that allows them to expel the air that bloats the air bladder. Burping is accomplished by holding the fish on its side or back and massaging or kneading the belly from the anal vent toward the head. This is sometimes difficult and may require a more active effort, actually squeezing the fish. A sound is made when the air is expelled. When the fish is ready to be released, hold it in the water at the surface with the head in the water, moving it forward or from side to side until it is fully recovered. To release it, there are two options. For fish that are large and too heavy to hold well, give the tail a quick squeeze to stimulate a vigorous dive. For fish that aren't so large and hard to hold, give the fish a vigorous shove or push headfirst and straight toward the bottom for a solid head start back down to the pressures and temperature from which it was taken. This thrusting tactic may also be helpful with other fish.

Burping is not suitable for other species because the air pressure cannot be naturally vented. It can still be expelled, however, using a technique that is called puncturing or venting by fisheries professionals and "fizzing" by some laypeople. Puncturing entails the insertion of a sharp object, usually a long needle, through the body wall of the fish to let the pent-up air escape through the puncture hole. The proper type of needle is a 16- to 20-gauge hypodermic needle obtained from medical or veterinary supply stores; a larger needle may be needed for very big fish. Where the needle is inserted into the fish may vary with the species. For walleye, the location is on either side of the fish approximately 1 inch above the anal vent; for snapper and grouper, it is just behind and above the base of the pectoral fin. The needle is inserted on a 45-degree angle under, not through, the scales, preferably when the fish is in a livewell. Hold the fish with its head slightly down and stroke the abdominal area to force air out. A sharpened pump needle also works, perhaps better because the air is quickly released through the hollow tube. If done correctly, the fish will be able to right itself in the livewell, and it then can be returned to the water.

It's a good idea to check with various fisheries agencies to get a more detailed review of this procedure. In general, puncturing is not recommended by most fisheries professionals because of concerns about inexpert handling by untrained anglers. The extra length of time that a fish would be held out of the water (where a livewell is not used) and the possibility of improper technique and perhaps further internal damage to the fish are other reasons why fisheries managers discourage the general public from this practice.

There is no direct evidence that puncturing or burping is effective against delayed mortality, and some research has indicated that untreated fish left on the surface of the water do recover on their own and return to deep water—unless they are discovered by seagulls or other predators. Those who would attempt puncturing should probably practice first on deep-caught fish that would be kept for eating anyway. The difficulties inherent in releasing fish caught from deep water lend some credence to the belief that catch-and-release is primarily a shallow-water proposition, although the definition of "deep" and "shallow" is open to vastly different interpretations.

Anglers can take two other courses of action to help a deep-dwelling fish survive. The first is to play a deeply caught fish on a moderate and steady retrieve, rather than trying to bring it in as quickly as possible. A fast retrieve, which is the usual recommendation in most situations, does not give the fish time to adjust to changes in pressure naturally. Avoiding a fast retrieve may make the fish more suitable for release without degassing

efforts. On the other hand, following this advice increases your chances of losing a fish because of the extra playing time, and there is no clear guide regarding how long a fish needs to adjust internal pressure. Moreover, in saltwater, bottom-dwelling fish, once they are initially hooked, often have to be played aggressively to keep them from diving into cover and cutting the line, and this aggressive fight carries through into the rest of the playing action.

The second course open to anglers is to give the fish a good start by thrusting it headfirst into the water when they release it. This is especially useful with lake trout or salmon, and is also useful for releasing tuna and amberjack that are small enough to be hand-lifted. To propel the fish forward, lift it by the tail and then thrust it headfirst into the water and as far as you can reach, as if you were stabbing a spear deep into the water. This quickly propels it downward.

Bleeding Fish

Another general rule when releasing some fish and keeping others is to keep a fish that is bleeding rather than one that is not; bleeders, particularly those hooked in the gills, are less likely to survive than unharmed fish. This is not an absolute, however. In professional studies, and in the results of tag-and-release efforts of anglers, some fish that were bleeding when released have survived and been well enough to live for a long time and be caught again. Cuts or tears in flesh that cause a minor amount of bleeding may not be fatal; many anglers have caught fish that had been recently attacked by other predators, enough to create an open wound with some signs of bleeding, and the fish survived.

Fish that are bleeding from the gills, however, receive an extra dose of stress, and this is most likely to be critical. If there is a lot of bleeding, regardless of the cause, the appropriate action is to keep the fish if you can legally do so, rather than to cause it to become a mortality statistic that doesn't serve a meal purpose (although it may be food for other aquatic creatures).

However, the biggest dilemma is what to do when you land a fish that is bleeding but cannot legally be kept. Some anglers feel that keeping such a fish is an ethically appropriate act, but good intentions are hard to prove when confronted by law enforcement officials. If you don't release a fish that is bleeding, it will surely die, but if you have to release one that is bleeding, it might just recover.

Replacing Treble Hooks with Singles

You can't completely avoid injuring fish, but in some fishing circumstances you can minimize the chance of this happening, especially when using plugs, almost all of which are supplied by manufacturers with multiple sets of treble hooks. To ensure individual safety and the well-being of fish that are released, you may use plugs with single rather than treble hooks. Generally this requires replacing the manufacturer-supplied trebles with separately purchased single hooks of an appropriate style and size.

Single-hook use is required in only a few places in North America, so using one is mostly a personal choice. By choice some anglers don't use live bait. Some won't troll. Some won't angle for various species during the spawning period. The issue of single hooks over treble hooks is also an individual choice, one that is based on your attitude. You don't have to take the treble hooks off all your lures, but there are times when a single hook is more appropriate than a treble for safety, fishing effectiveness, and the benefit of the resource.

Confining Fish

Fish that are to be released should not be kept on a stringer or cooped up in a warm, poorly oxygenated container or well; you're reducing their survival chances significantly by doing this. In a well or container, cool water and abundant oxygen are vital. Don't cull—that is, replace a fish on a stringer or in a well with another—unless you are keeping an injured fish and releasing a healthy one. In some places, once you have taken possession of a fish by confining it, culling by returning that fish to the water is illegal.

Generally a fish that has been confined is not as suitable for release as one that has been freshly caught. Livewells are very popular in freshwater and are especially geared for confining bass and walleye, although they are sometimes used to retain other fish. Although it is seldom beneficial to keep fish in these so-called livewells for later release (as opposed to instant, on-the-spot release), many people do this in freshwater,

particularly people who fish in bass and walleye tournaments.

If you do keep fish in a livewell, pay special attention to the water temperature and to the fish's need for frequent and ample aeration. In closed systems, the use of a stabilizing chemical, which decreases the fish's need for oxygen consumption and fights fungus infection and mucus loss, is beneficial. Using ice, noniodized salt, and some drugs (available from aquarium supply stores) are other measures that can be taken to aid fish that are detained for a long period prior to release, though this is something that relatively few anglers other than tournament anglers need to be concerned with.

Releasing Particular Species

Bass

Fortunately, largemouth and smallmouth bass, as well as their cousins, are fairly hardy fish. Except under unusual circumstances, bass do not put up an extremely long fight, and they are fairly easy to land. They are not too disturbed by moderately respectful handling. They can be grasped without harm to fish or angler—in fact, you have a greater likelihood of injury than the fish because of the sharp points of multihooked lures.

But bass are not immune to problems, and it is wise to avoid excessive or rough handling and excessive time held out of water. Try to minimize injury from multiple hooks, and avoid or minimize netting. Take special care of bass that are confined in livewells. Probably no fish are subjected to livewell containment more than largemouth bass, particularly by competitive anglers who retain the fish until weigh-in and then release them. Good handling, adequate water temperature, and ample oxygen are keys to their survival in livewells.

Bass are often hooked lightly and it is sometimes possible to free them from the hooks simply by letting them idle near the surface, lowering the rod tip, and putting slack in the line. You might try jiggling the rod tip. If this doesn't free the fish, then try freeing it while in the water using long-nosed pliers. If bass are not released in the water, it's best to grab them by the lower jaw. This hold provides the least possible physical contact and does the least damage.

Trout

If proper care is taken of trout that will be released, the survival rate is very high. The survival rate of trout that are released after being caught on live bait is about three times better if the hook is left in than if it is extracted. Thus anglers should snip the line and not try to extract a small hook. If bait is used, a larger hook is less likely to get caught in the stomach than a small one. Most lure- and fly-caught trout are hooked in the jaws and the edges of the mouth, a few on the tongue, so it is relatively easy to get the hook out. On those occasions when a lure or fly hook is swallowed or manages to lodge in the gills, don't even bother with a token attempt unless the job looks easy; snip the line or tippet as close to the lure or fly as possible.

The less you handle trout, the better, but that is not always possible. Small stream trout squirm like eels, and often the hook cannot be removed without grasping the fish to keep it still. Here you can keep the fish in the surface water, but grab it around the body by gripping it behind the head and between the dorsal fin, trying to keep finger pressure off the soft belly and avoid squeezing it. Small fish can be completely encircled with a wet hand. Turning the fish upside down seems to have a tranquilizing effect. Only larger stream trout should be netted. Moving to the edge of the current is a good idea for releasing a large and tired fish, but take care not to stir up the shallows so much that it adds to the fish's breathing hardship.

Bigger trout, like lakers, are easy fish to injure in the landing and handling stages. Large trout may be brought alongside a boat and held upright in the

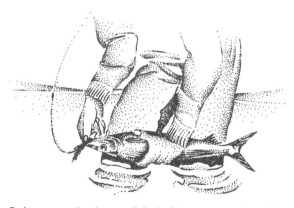

Before you unhook a small, frisky fish, try turning it upside down to tranquilize it.

water for hook removal. They should not be brought into the boat if you are going to release them.

Atlantic Salmon

Many of the advisements previously issued also apply to Atlantic salmon, but there are a few differences. Most Atlantic salmon fishing is done with flies, so there isn't much at issue regarding deeply hooked fish.

Atlantic salmon are fairly easily released if they haven't been played too long. They are taken in rivers, virtually all by wading anglers who should move to a quiet location if possible to play and land the fish. By using a tippet of medium to heavy strength, an angler should be able to land a fish fairly quickly. The Atlantic Salmon Federation recommends breaking the leader on a fish that is not landed in 15 to 20 minutes, and not using a tailer to land a fish that will be released. When being released, the salmon should be kept in the water, held gently in a supported horizontal and upright position, and revived gently facing upstream.

Marine Offshore Species

The National Marine Fisheries Service Game Fish Tagging Program advises anglers to simply tow such species as sharks and tuna slowly headfirst alongside the boat for tagging and before release. The forced flow of water over the gills will help revive the fish. The leader should be cut with cutting pliers as close to the hook as possible, allowing the revived fish to swim off. These fish can also be released by using a gaff as a dehooking tool. The technique requires the use of a V-notched stick or other device to depress the leader. The gaff hook is slipped over the hook, and simultaneously the leader is pressed down while the fishhook is popped back and out.

The same can be accomplished for billfish, although these species can be grabbed by the bill by one person while being tagged and unhooked by another. Holding the bill allows you to control the fish, which is very important. If you can reach far enough overboard (difficult if not impossible on many large sportfishing boats), hold the head of the billfish under the water, which in itself has a calming effect. When you grab the bill, place your hands so that the thumbs face each other; this position makes it easier to push the fish away if the fish thrashes. There are tools to slip over the bill for facilitating handling and hook removal.

38

Safety

Sportfishing is generally not a dangerous activity and seldom results in accidents. However, any activity that takes place on or around water; involves the operation of motorized vessels; causes people to come into contact with sharp objects like hooks, knives, and fish teeth; involves interaction with wild animals; and may be pursued in inclement weather can justly raise some safety concerns. Accidents may be rare, but they do happen.

The greatest concern for anyone who spends time around water is the possibility of drowning. The four major causes of drowning, in order, are: not wearing a personal flotation device; abuse of alcohol; lack of sufficient swimming skills; and hypothermia (chilling of the body because of exposure to cold). Two-thirds of the people who drown never had any intention or expectation of being in the water.

Anyone who cannot swim should be wearing a personal flotation device (PFD) when on or near the water. A PFD must be worn to be helpful, because it is almost always too difficult to put on once a person is in the water and in trouble.

People who spend time around water not only should develop a healthy respect for it, but should become comfortable with it. Learning to swim, at least to be able to float and tread water, means that if you do take an unexpected plunge, you know enough to somewhat help yourself. Small children, of course, need constant supervision around water.

Alcohol (and drugs) and water are a lethal mixture. More than half of the people who drown annually have consumed alcohol prior to their accident, so it is obvious that no one who is on or in the water should consume alcohol.

Being in cold water is much more of a concern than being in warm water, even if you know how to swim and are wearing a PFD. This can lead to hypothermia.

Wading Issues

Most anglers give little thought to safety while wading, until they fall when they least expect to or when they're washed down a turbulent stream with their waders perilously filling up with frigid water. The latter can be a frightening and possibly fatal experience, which most anglers can avoid through common sense and the correct equipment. By learning to read and judge waters, you'll become adept at sensing when to move forward and when to step back.

Swift flowage poses the most obvious difficulty, of course, and rivers that contain steep drops and whitewater are most dangerous and allow only edge wading (and maybe not even that). Likewise, some flows may have objects floating down them, such as ice chunks or logs, that you need to look out for, especially if you are not facing upstream (keep looking behind you).

Many rivers have some sections that are easy to wade, others that are difficult, and some that look easy but are actually not because their bottoms are slippery and put a lot of pressure on your feet. Surf anglers generally need waders so they can stand on the surf edge and gain extra casting distance without getting wet, but sometimes they need to wade out in the surf and beware of undertow. Thus wading differs depending on the circumstances. Nevertheless, there are some general guidelines to follow.

Wading is a skill. The more you do it, the better you become. Consideration should always be given to depth, water speed, bottom configuration, and whether it is prudent to wade through fast or deep areas at all. Many anglers have taken one step too many and found themselves slipping into deeper water over the top of their waders; in rivers, this may result in a floating trip though the rapids or pool, which is not worth the fish you might have caught.

Always respect water. Proceed slowly. Make sure that your foot is firmly planted and stable before taking the next step. Crablike steps are much better than reaching strides. Concentrate on the task at hand. Wearing polarized sunglasses helps make the trail under the water more visible, although the deeper you wade and the murkier the water, the less this helps. In clear water, polarized sunglasses are a great aid.

Scout an area that you intend to wade across before starting to do so. Often, you will find a better route, usually shallower, a little distance upstream or downstream; often the tail of a pool is best to cross because the water is shallower at the bottom lip and the velocity is less.

Do not cast and wade at the same time; better to get into position and then cast. Don't walk or leap from one large rock to another; don't wade in turbulent water upstream of a large rock; and beware of deep holes below large rocks. In tailwater rivers, beware of rising water; dam releases can suddenly raise the water level, and if you notice the water coming up, waste no time in getting to shore.

In swift, deep, or unfamiliar water, you should plan every step and take slow steps by sliding your foot along rather than lifting it. If you lift your feet in swift water, the current can push your leg away and throw you off balance. Also, place your feet between rocks instead of on top of them, which is an invitation to slipping or moving too deep with the next step.

In rivers, you should wade with your body and feet sideways to the flow. Even a slight turn in fast water can spin you or knock you over. Wade across at an angle, preferably slightly quartered upstream. Remember that the more you weigh, the easier it is to wade fast water; the lighter you are, the harder. A light person should draft below a heavier one if the two can cross swift water together; a better idea for two people in swift water may be to link elbows and cross slowly, having the stability of four feet on the bottom.

Use a wading staff or stick, which acts as a stabilizing third leg and is also valuable for probing depth and poking for rocks. Most people find that it's best to place the staff upstream.

Without a stick, you can use your fishing rod to help stabilize you in deep swift current, especially when you start to feel unbalanced or are about to stumble or fall. Hold the rod in your downstream hand and keep it pointed directly downstream. Place the tip section in the current to act as a stabilizer. Obviously, you need to have the rod in the proper hand to start with, so when you don't have a staff, start wading with the rod in your downstream hand. In the worst cases, use both a staff in your upstream hand and the rod in your downstream hand.

Once you get across a rough spot, or are about to leave the water, don't let up your concentration. Many people fall on their way out of the water by taking their last steps for granted. High and slippery stream banks are also a problem.

When you're getting out of a boat to wade, especially if you're not right on shore in shallow water, don't be fooled by the illusion of depth that comes with clear water. The water is often deeper than it looks.

If you start heading into especially soft-bottomed areas, do not keep going forward, as you may find your feet so deeply buried in muck that suction keeps your feet mired. If you start sinking into soft bottoms, retreat to firmer ground and find a better route.

When you hook a strong fish, gradually retreat from deep water and get to shore. You can follow a fish, if necessary, more easily from the shallows, where you have more maneuverability, and also can effect a higher rod angle.

If you do find yourself floating downriver in current while wearing chest waders, don't panic. Get your feet pointed downstream so they can be used to deflect your body, and especially head, from objects, and go with the flow on your back with your head up. Use your arms to try to maneuver toward the bank and water that is calm and

When wading across a river, to help maintain balance when footing is uncertain or the current is swift, lay the tip of your fishing rod into the water directly downstream of your position, and keep the rod in the water while wading across the flow.

shallow enough for you stand up in. Do not float headfirst or try to fight the current.

It is a good idea to test your waders at some point in a swimming pool or warm safe stream or lake to see what happens to them when they fill with water, and how you are able (or not able) to maneuver. A wet, fully clothed person in waders full of water is very heavy, barely able to move, and a candidate for drowning, so this is a matter to be taken very seriously.

Boat Operation Issues

It is especially important not to overload a boat (too much weight or too many people), to make sure that a properly fitting PFD is available for every passenger, and to have the required safety equipment (warning device, navigational lights, fire extinguisher, and so on) aboard and in functioning condition.

Other than reckless boat handling, the chief causes of boating safety concerns for anglers are dams, dangerous currents, navigational hazards, anchoring, and wind or storms. Most of these concerns can be minimized by prudent boat operation and good boat-handling skills, but it's important to learn to recognize situations that can present a problem and to not underestimate them. The force of current and the effects of strong converging currents, for example, are commonly not respected enough. The dangers inherent in improper anchoring are significant, especially in heavy winds or strong current, and many boaters run into problems by anchoring poorly or in unsafe places or circumstances.

River tailraces, for example, can be extremely dangerous because of the velocity and turbulence of discharged water, changing water levels, and unpredictable current patterns. In these places, anglers should not tie their boat to the dam or anchor at it; downstream anchoring should be done with a quick-release device, and the engine should always be kept running in fast water. It's important to be alert for rising water and to keep a safe distance from other boats as well.

When anchoring, as a general practice anchor rode should be attached only to the bow of the boat, and to a strong cleat, except under the absolute best of circumstances. It can be extremely dangerous to anchor stern first. Even when the surface of the water is calm, the wake of a passing boat could send a deluge of water over the stern of a boat, causing it to capsize. In a river, a boat anchored stern first is susceptible to being pulled down and into the water if another boat should drift over the exposed rode.

In large bodies of water and in big rivers, prudent navigation requires not just evaluating what lies ahead on the open water, but what may lie below. The water isn't like a highway, where everything is visible. Reefs, sandbars, rockpiles, and other objects are commonly present in many waters, and not necessarily marked; boaters must be sure of their path of travel, or proceed cautiously otherwise. The sudden striking of objects has unexpectedly and quickly sunk fishing boats, pitching occupants into the water.

Fishing and boating at night, which is common in summer for freshwater and saltwater anglers, brings added concerns for navigation and boat handling, and a greater concern for caution. This obviously applies to those who are moving under power, and not as obviously to those who are not; people in a boat that is anchored in a channel need to use lights to indicate their presence to others, or risk unintentionally being in harm's way.

Strong winds often cause problems for boaters. Sometimes, coping with the wind is not terribly prudent, and the sensible thing to do is head for port. This is especially so if the winds appear to be building; don't wait for the worst conditions to arrive.

The first concern when fishing in heavy wind—especially when the water is cold, the waves are high, the boat is small or tipsy or flat-hulled, or there is a far distance to go—should be safety. You must put on and fasten a proper-fitting PFD that will keep your fully clothed body afloat and your head upright.

When the wind and weather are rough, you have to consider whether you, and the boat you expect to use, are up to fishing. On the personal comfort level, taking a pounding by running through heavy waves is hard on the back and neck, particularly for older anglers. And though the fish may be biting like crazy, that is small comfort to a companion who gets seasick.

But the boat is another story. You have to realistically assess what your boat can handle, going forth only if you're are completely sure and prepared,

Safe fishing extends to the notion of wearing a proper-fitting PFD in certain circumstances, as this angler is doing while kayak fishing in the often choppy waters of Cape May Harbor, New Jersey, where large boats frequently create big wakes.

or turning back when good sense demands it. Of course, going out to fish under severe wind is much different than being on the water and angling when conditions change from calm to frothy.

Too many anglers push their luck each year, not noticing shifts in wind speed or direction, or thinking they can run themselves out of trouble. Sometimes they pay for it. Most people are guilty of not looking enough to the horizon for squalls and thunderstorms. That is one reason why on large bodies of water the wise angler has a VHF radio, handheld weather radio, or other device to stay informed of weather patterns, changes, and potential problems when in a locale where these devices function.

If the wind has picked up enough to put whitecaps on the water or, worse, a trail of foam, beware. It's already late, especially on large shallow lakes, which are among the most dangerous bodies of water because big waves build up quickly there. So are lakes with many reefs and shoals. Small boaters get caught in troughs, or get pushed up into shallows or shoals or boulders and bang up the outboard's lower unit or the boat hull, maybe even causing capsizing (especially watch out in a canoe). Recognize the dangers that lie ahead and be smart enough to avoid them so that you remain safe.

In addition, you need to be sure that nothing impedes your boat's progress when you're faced with strong winds and their accompanying waves. A crippled boat is very tough to handle properly in the worst conditions. You shouldn't be out there with a motor that isn't working well, for example. And make sure that any ropes aren't lying out where rough-water bouncing could cause them to be swept overboard. If so, the rope will be in the boat's propeller in an instant, probably seizing up the motor, and you'll be in a lot of trouble.

Thunderstorms

Although many weather events pose danger to anglers, a thunderstorm is the significant event most likely to be encountered by people who fish. Lightning is the leading cause of weather-related deaths and a prominent cause of weather-related injuries. Approximately one in four lightning strikes on humans happens to people involved in recreation; many such strikes are on or near water.

Whenever the slightest chance of a thunderstorm exists, the first safety precaution is to check the latest weather forecast and keep an eye on the sky. Recognize the signs of an impending storm: towering thunderheads, darkening skies, lightning, and increasing wind. Use whatever electronic device you have to get the latest weather information.

When a thunderstorm threatens, getting inside a home, large building, or all-metal automobile (not a convertible or the bed of a truck) is the best course of action. This is usually not possible for anglers unless they act well in advance of a storm. Many people put themselves in unnecessary danger by waiting too long to take action when a thunderstorm approaches.

Anglers who are wading or who are along the bank or shore need to get out of and away from the water. Anglers in boats should quickly get to a safe place on land whenever possible; if not possible, they may be able to get out of the storm's path by moving, but only if they act well ahead of its arrival. You cannot outrun a thunderstorm that is imminent. If the storm is still very distant, you can try to outrun it. To do so, you need to know what direction the storm is moving in. Thus running is effective only on large bodies of water and when storms do not cover wide expanses.

If you are caught outside on land, do not stand underneath an isolated tree, a telephone pole, or isolated objects, or near power lines or metal fences. Avoid projecting above the surrounding landscape. In a forest, seek shelter in a low area under a thick growth of small trees. In open areas, go to a low place, such as a ravine or valley. If you're in a group in the open, spread out, keeping people 5 to 10 yards apart. Stay away from metal vehicles and objects, and do not carry or raise any objects. Remove any metal objects from your hair or head, and remove metal-cleated boots.

Lightning may strike up to 10 miles from the center of the storm, so precautions should be taken even though the parent cloud is not directly overhead. If you are caught in the open, far from shelter, and if you feel your hair stand on end, lightning may be about to strike you. Drop to your knees and bend forward, putting your hands on your knees. Do not lie flat on the ground.

If you are stuck in a boat and the same thing happens, or your fishing rod begins to buzz or the line rises out of the water, lightning is about to strike. Immediately crouch down, lean forward, and put your hands on your knees, making sure not to touch anything else in the boat.

The reason behind these positions—and why you don't lie flat—is that when lightning strikes, it seeks the quickest way through the object it strikes. The more things that you touch or have

A thunderstorm threatens a summer day on Lake of the Woods on the Minnesota-Ontario border, making it a good time to be back at the dock.

contact with, the more lightning will travel through the body in an effort to seek a way out.

Many lightning strikes occur without the warning of thunder, so precautions are necessary even when there is no thunder. When there is both thunder and lightning, you can tell how many miles the lightning is from your position by counting the seconds between the sound of the thunder and the sight of the lightning, then dividing that by five. Scientists say that if you can hear thunder, then you are in range of being struck.

Thus, to avoid becoming a statistic, anglers should watch the sky for signs of an impending storm, get off the water early and especially if they hear thunder, and pick the proper places for refuge on land.

Glossary

alien species A species occurring in an area outside of its historically known natural range as a result of intentional or accidental dispersal; also known as exotic or introduced species.

all-tackle world record The largest individual of a singular species of sportfish caught on sporting tackle within the parameters established by the International Game Fish Association.

anadromous Fish that spend part of their lives in the ocean and move into freshwater rivers or streams to spawn.

angler A person who catches, or tries to catch, fish for personal use, fun, challenge, and leisure by using sporting equipment, essentially some type of rod, usually but not always equipped with a reel, to which a line and a hook or lure are attached, and by fair and sporting methods that afford the quarry an opportunity to avoid capture.

angling The act of catching, or trying to catch, fish for personal use, fun, challenge, and leisure using sporting equipment, essentially with some type of rod, usually but not always equipped with a reel, to which a line and a hook or lure is attached, and by sporting methods. The term is used interchangeably with "sportfishing" but has a more specific meaning than "fishing," although both words may connote the same thing when used in reference to the employment of sporting equipment. Angling is distinguished from commercial or recreational fishing by virtue of the equipment employed, an implicit understanding of fair chase, and the exercise of sportsmanship.

artificial fly An imitation of a natural aquatic or terrestrial insect, especially one consumed by fish.

artificial reef A man-made artificial structure that provides habitat for many kinds of fish.

attractor **1.** A type of trolling accessory that uses vibration or visual stimuli to get the attention of fish, and draws them to a trailing lure.
2. Cover, objects, or structures placed in the water that serve to attract prey and predatory fish, and which provide angling opportunities.

backing Reserve line that is connected to the main line on the spool of a reel for situations when greater line lengths are necessary.

backing down A boat manipulation tactic primarily used in offshore fishing to help an angler gain line when hooked up to a large and strong fish.

backlash The tangle of line that develops on the spool of a revolving-spool reel as a result of the differential between the speed of the line moving through the rod guides and the amount of line being made available to follow the lure by the spin imparted to the reel spool.

bag limit Synonymous with creel limit, bag limit means the legal quantity or number of fish of a species or group of species that may be taken, caught, or killed during a specified period. Bag limits may apply universally to many waters or may be site-specific.

bait-and-switch A saltwater angling tactic in which a trolled hookless teaser that has attracted a gamefish is quickly removed from the water while a hooked lure, bait, or fly is simultaneously presented.

baitfish Any fish species that are forage for predators.

big game Large and strong saltwater sportfish—especially billfish, shark, and tuna—that are customarily caught in offshore waters and with medium- to heavy-duty conventional tackle or big-game tackle.

bill-wrapped The wrapping of the bill of a marlin or sailfish with the leader or fishing line.

bite **1.** The strike of a fish, especially common to natural bait usage.

2. An expression for the state (slow or fast) of sportfishing activity.

3. A point of measurement on a hook.

black salmon Overwintering sea-run Atlantic salmon.

blackmouth Immature, resident chinook salmon.

blind casting   Fishing in circumstances in which the fish cannot be seen, and lures or flies are cast without firm knowledge that the quarry is present.

blue water   That portion of the open ocean that is blue in color and usually many miles from shore.

bottom   The floor underneath a body of water, such as the lakebed, riverbed, or seabed.

bottom bouncer   A bent wire-armed weighted bottom rig for trolling or drift fishing with bait or lures.

bottom rig   Any type of weighted terminal tackle configuration for fishing a bait, lure, or fly along the bed of a waterway.

breaking fish   Fish that are chasing baitfish, usually in open water, and herding them to the surface while feeding, with the result that the bait and/or the pursuing fish erupt on the surface in such a manner as to be visible from a distance.

breaking strength   The amount of pressure that must be applied to an unknotted line before the molecules part and the line breaks.

bright fish   Fresh, migratory anadromous fish that have recently entered and are ascending a tributary, and which do not yet exhibit their spawning coloration and markings.

carryover fish   Stocked fish, usually trout, that survive at least one winter in the wild; also known as holdover fish.

cast   To throw an object that is connected to a rod via fishing line; also, the distant placement of an object via line and rod in the water.

catadromous   Fish that migrate from freshwater to saltwater in order to spawn.

centrepin reel   A revolving-spool single-action reel with a large arbor, used in Europe for fishing with a float. Also known as a float reel, and similar in appearance to a fly reel, this item always has two handles and a 3- to 4-inch diameter, and a very sensitive and free-spinning spool.

charter boat   A sportfishing boat available for hire and capable of taking a limited number of anglers aboard on an exclusive basis, usually by advance reservation.

ciguatera   Poisoning caused by eating the flesh of fish toxic to humans. Found in many tropical reef fish, ciguatera is caused by a toxin found in certain algae eaten by reef fish. The poison accumulates when reef fish are eaten by larger fish and then by humans.

coarse fish   Freshwater species that are not considered game-fish; also known as rough fish.

coaster   A brook trout that leaves its natal stream and spends part of the year in large, deep, clear lakes, cruising close to the shore.

coldwater fish   Freshwater species whose optimum environment is cold and well-oxygenated water, usually under 60°F.

coolwater fish   Freshwater species whose optimum environment is water of intermediate temperature, approximately from 60° to 70°F.

cover   Any natural or man-made object that provides shelter and feeding opportunity, and which predatory fish use as a place from which to ambush prey.

creel limit   Synonymous with bag limit, creel limit means the quantity or number of fish of a species or group of species that may be taken, caught, or killed during a specified period.

culling   The replacement of a fish that has been caught or confined (in a basket, in a livewell, on a stringer) with a freshly caught fish.

dead bait   Whole dead fish or other natural organisms used to catch predatory fish, especially bottom scroungers.

deep-sea fishing   Fishing in the ocean, usually on charter and party boats, especially for bottom-dwelling species.

delayed mortality   The phenomenon in which a fish that is caught by an angler and released alive dies at some later time, usually because of injury or stress.

demersal   Fish that live on or near the seabed or water bottom; used synonymously with groundfish.

diadromous   Fish that migrate between freshwater and saltwater.

downrunner   Shad that have spawned and are migrating down-river to return to the sea.

drag-free drift   Presenting a fly in current so that it drifts naturally and without the movement that is created by fly line.

dropoff   A place where the bottom of a body of water slopes abruptly downward and the depth is significantly greater.

eddy   A countercurrent forming on the side of or within a main current.

epilimnion   The upper and warmer layer of water in a lake or pond that is stratified; the layer of water above the thermocline.

estuary   A body of water where freshwater from rivers and streams meets the saltwater of the sea; it may be called a bay, sound, or lagoon.

exotic species   Organisms introduced into habitats where they are not native.

finfish   All species of fish; used collectively to separate true fish from crustaceans and mollusks, which are collectively termed shellfish, and most common in reference to saltwater and anadromous species.

finning   A fish that is basking near the surface with dorsal and/or tail fins protruding from the water.

fisher   An archaic and non-gender-specific version of the word "fisherman" that does not distinguish between commercial, subsistence, or recreational fishing.

fisheries/fishery   All the activities involved in catching a species of fish or group of species; the place where a species or group of species is caught.

fisherman   A broad, general term for a person who catches or tries to catch fish, and which does not imply a distinction between commercial or recreational action or between the methods, techniques, or equipment employed.

fishing   The act of catching or trying to catch fish. The word has a general meaning with no explicit distinction between commercial or recreational action or the methods, techniques, or equipment employed. It is often used interchangeably with the words "angling" and "sportfishing," although these terms refer solely to recreational activity and the implied usage of sporting equipment.

fishing guide   A person hired to take people sportfishing, usually by boat, sometimes on foot, in freshwater and saltwater.

fishing pressure   The amount of fishing effort generated. Biologists express this in number of people, boats, hours, days, and other units of measurement, as well as some combination of these, that is applied to one species or group of species. Anglers use the term to broadly refer to the number and frequency of people fishing.

flasher   **1.** A type of sonar with a flashing light that indicates depth on a circular dial.

2. A type of attractor used in trolling to get the attention of deep fish.

flat   A long, level, and shallow part of a body of water adjacent to deeper water and/or channels.

fluke   A common name for summer flounder.

fly book   A flexible, easily stowed pouch, also known as a fly wallet, for holding artificial flies, especially streamers, when angling.

fly box   A light, compact storage device for artificial flies.

fly dressing   Materials that, when tied on a hook, form the appearance or pattern of an artificial fly.

forage fish   Prey or food species of predatory fish.

foul hook   To hook a fish accidentally in some part of its body other than its mouth.

freespool   The condition in which line is able to freely unwind from the spool of a fishing reel; the disengagement of gears. When the gears of a reel are disengaged to allow line to come off the spool, the reel is said to be "in freespool."

fresh-run fish   A fish that has recently entered a river for upstream migration; also known as a fresh fish.

gamefish   Freshwater and saltwater fish that are sought by recreational anglers and valued for their fighting virtues and willingness to take a lure, fly, or natural bait. In many localities, certain species are designated by law as gamefish, which prevents them from being captured commercially and prohibits their sale by anglers.

grilse   A salmon, usually male, that returns to freshwater rivers after one year at sea.

groin   A man-made structure, usually of concrete or stone, projecting into the water from the shore to protect a sandy beach from erosion; also known as a jetty.

groundfish   A species or group of fish that lives on or near the seabed; used synonymously with demersal.

hatch   The occasion when aquatic insects emerge from the water, shed a skin or case, mate, and deposit eggs on the water.

head boat   A sportfishing boat, also called a party boat, that takes anglers out for a per-person fee.

high-low rig   A two-hook bottom-fishing bait rig.

holdover fish   Stocked fish, usually trout, that survive through at least one winter in the wild; also known as carryover fish.

hump   A moderately elevated and generally isolated portion of an otherwise flat lakebed or seabed.

hybrid   The offspring of two individuals of different species.

hypolimnion   The lower and colder layer of water in a lake or pond that is stratified; the layer of water below the thermocline.

inlet   A tributary mouth to a lake or the sea, primarily the latter; an entry point to the sea from a bay, harbor, or estuary.

inshore   The waters from the shallower part of the continental shelf toward shore.

International Game Fish Association   A nonprofit membership association, also known by the acronym IGFA, that verifies and designates all freshwater and saltwater world record fish catches; creates and maintains the ethical standards and rules used in most fishing tournaments and for world record consideration; serves as an information source for the media, governments, scientists, and the general public; maintains an historical museum documenting the sport of fishing; has the world's largest and most current collection of angling literature; and is a leader in fisheries conservation issues.

jack   A young, sexually mature male salmon that returns to freshwater rivers during the spawning run.

jetty   A man-made structure, usually of concrete or stone, projecting into the water from the shore to protect a sandy beach from erosion, funnel current from an inlet, or protect a harbor or pier; also known as a groin.

jump fishing   Spotting, chasing, and fishing for schooling fish, particularly striped bass in freshwater, that are feeding on the surface.

keeper   A fish that meets legal length limits.

kelt   A sea-run Atlantic salmon that has overwintered in a river and returned to saltwater in the spring; also called black salmon.

landlocked   Anadromous fish that have adapted to a completely freshwater existence, spending the greater portion of their life in a lake and returning to natal rivers or streams to spawn.

lie   The station or home habitat used for rest or feeding by a fish, primarily salmonids, in a river or stream. Such a location provides feeding opportunity and often shelter.

limestone stream   A stream that flows through a bedrock of limestone or through land laced with varying degrees of limestone deposits; also known as a chalk stream.

limit   A restriction on the size or number of fish that can be taken, caught, or killed. Regulations pertaining to numbers of fish are called bag, creel, daily, and possession limits; regulations pertaining to size are called minimum length, total length, or slot limits.

line-class world record   The largest individual of a given species of sportfish that is caught on a specific breaking strength of line, and within parameters established by the International Game Fish Association.

live bait   Whole live fish or other natural organisms used to catch predatory fish in both freshwater and saltwater.

livewell   A containment device for keeping fish or bait alive; also called a baitwell when used exclusively for holding bait.

livies   Small live fish used as bait in saltwater.

long-range boat   A party boat that makes excursions lasting from several days to two weeks to distant fishing grounds.

lunker   A big fish of any of the larger species.

marker buoy   A small portable float, usually attached to a heavy weight, used by boating anglers to temporarily mark the location of underwater hydrographic features.

matching the hatch   The selection and use of artificial flies that exactly, or as closely as possible, mimic the look, size, and behavior of naturally occurring aquatic insects.

mate   A person who assists the captain on a charter boat or party boat.

migration   A regular journey made by a particular species of fish, on an annual or lifetime basis, usually associated with propagation patterns but also with the seasonal availability of food.

minimum length limit   A restriction pertaining to the minimum size of fish that may be kept.

mooching   A combination of drifting and slow motor trolling, this is a technique for catching salmon in Pacific Northwest coastal waters using a precisely cut bait, usually herring, with a moderate-weight sinker, and with a large-arbored 1:1 revolving-spool single-action reel that allows for minimal resistance when a fish takes the bait and moves off. Precise boat control is important; the objective is to get the cut bait to roll and keep it in a precise position, depending on current and tide.

mudding   The behavior of bottom-feeding fish, especially bonefish, in shallow water, which creates a mud trail as it roots while feeding, often with head down and the upper lobe of its tail out of the water.

mudline   The edge created in a large body of water by the influx of turbid current, usually a river.

nearshore   The shallow portion of inshore saltwaters adjacent to the shoreline.

nest   A visible bed, often circular, made by egg-laying fish on the bottom of a body of water for spawning.

no kill   A regulation for a portion of a body of water, usually a section of river or stream, where it is required that all fish that are caught be released alive and unharmed.

offshore   That portion of the water from which land is not visible; also, deep-water areas on the edge of ocean currents or shelves where big-game species, particularly billfish and tuna, are pursued.

overfishing   Harvesting fish at a rate that does not generate a desirable, sustainable, or "safe" population or stock level.

panfish   A nontechnical generic term for small freshwater fish that are widely utilized for food as well as sport.

parr   Small young anadromous fish, particularly salmon and trout, living in freshwater prior to migrating out to sea.

pattern   The particular appearance of an artificial fly, comprised of the parts that make up its likeness, the way they are incorporated onto the fly hook, and the colors.

pelagic fish   Free-swimming fish that inhabit the open sea and are independent of the seabed or water bottom.

pharyngeal   Bones in the throat of certain fish that are used like teeth to crush food. These bones are hard and strong and will crush such objects as clams, mussels, and snails.

pier   A raised structure that extends perpendicular from shore out into a body of water.

piscivorous   Fish-eating. Most predatory fish, and most of those considered sportfish, are piscivorous.

plankton   Passively floating or weakly swimming organisms in a body of water.

pocket water   A boulder-strewn or large rock-studded section of river or stream composed of fast and slow current, in which the commotion downstream of one rock meets another rock and so on, creating small pools or eddies downstream of the rocks. The creases or edges of the currents along these places hold trout.

pod   A small, tight group of fish swimming together.

point   A place where the land juts out in the water away from the shore and where the underwater bottom terrain usually continues to taper down and off.

poling   A method of propelling a boat silently in shallow water, common to angling on saltwater flats and some rivers.

pool   **1.** A section of any flowing waterway, usually deeper than other portions and without turbulence.

2. The capacity of an impoundment.

possession limit   A restriction on the total number of fish of a species or group of species that may be legally possessed by one person.

potamadromous   Fish that migrate within rivers or streams to spawn.

practice plug   A hookless, cylindrical, plastic- or rubber-coated weight used for practice casting with spinning, spincasting, and baitcasting tackle.

predator   A species that feeds on other species. Most of the fish species that are pursued by anglers are predators at or near the top of the food chain.

prey   A species that is fed upon by other species.

processed bait   Foodstuffs used to attract and catch fish even though they do not occur naturally in aquatic environments. This term differentiates such items from natural baits.

pumping   The act of systematically raising the rod tip, then quickly lowering it while simultaneously reeling in line, in order to tire a fish and bring it to the boat. This is a key component of fighting a large or strong fish.

quota   The maximum number of (primarily saltwater) fish that can be legally landed in a specified time period. This can apply to the total fishery (commercial and recreational catch) or to segments of the fishery.

raise (a fish)   When a targeted species is attracted to an angler's lure, fly, or bait and can be observed pursuing it, yet does not strike, or strikes and misses.

reading water   Watching water conditions to determine where fish may be located and how to present lures, flies, or bait to them.

record   The largest individual of a particular species of fish taken by anglers, according to the characteristics or type of equipment used, the body of water, the geographic or governmental region, or other method of classification.

redd   A pit or trough made by female salmon and trout in the gravel bottom of rivers or streams for spawning. Eggs are laid in the redd, which is sometimes also called a nest.

reef   A mass or ridge of rock or coral, often near the surface, in a body of freshwater or saltwater.

retrieving   The act of manipulating objects that have been cast or lowered into the water and that need to be worked by hand in order to impart fish-attracting action to them.

riffle   A hard-bottomed area of a creek, stream, or small river that is shallow and characterized by a choppy disturbed surface.

rig   **1.** An arrangement of terminal tackle.

2. The ready-to-fish final configuration of a lure and leader.

3. A ready-to-fish natural bait prepared with hook, weight, line (often wire), and other accessories.

riparian   Pertaining to the bank of a natural waterway, usually a river, sometimes a lake or tidewater. Riparian rights refer to the legal rights of the owner of property on a riverbank.

riprap   A collection of loose stones providing a foundation for, and to prevent erosion of, an embankment supporting a levee, dam, bridge, road, or similar man-made structure.

rise   The visible disturbance of the water's surface by a fish that is feeding, usually on insects that are on or just under the surface.

roe   The eggs of a female fish; also a female fish with eggs.

rough fish   Freshwater species that are not considered gamefish; also known as coarse fish.

run   **1.** A seasonal migration undertaken by fish.

2. A generally uniform section of a stream, creek, or small to midsize river that is deeper than a riffle and without the disturbed surface, yet not as deep and slow-flowing as a pool.

3. The behavior of a fish taking line off a reel under tension and swimming away from the angler.

runout   The site where shallow marsh ponds or swamps drain with falling tides or receding floodwaters into deeper canals and bayous.

salmonid   Any member of the Salmonidae family; this includes the various trout, salmon, charr, whitefish, and grayling.

salter   A sea-run brook trout. This fish is not truly anadromous but may go to saltwater for short periods to feed or for temperature reasons.

school   A closely spaced collection of fish that swim in association with one another. Fish in a school are often of the same species and of similar size, but species may intermingle and vary in size.

schoolies   Small fish that run together.

schooling   **1.** The behavioral grouping of fish, usually of the same or related species, which move together as a unit and exhibit a specific geometrical relationship.

2. The phenomenon of gamefish actively feeding upon prey species and vulnerable to angling effort.

seamount   A mountain rising 1,000 meters or more from the seafloor with a relatively small summit.

season   **1.** A time period with opening and closing dates for commercial and recreational fishing for certain fish or groups of fish.

2. The time when migratory species of fish are present.

setback   The distance that a lure or bait is placed behind the boat, or behind an object such as a sideplaner.

shadow line   The sharp edge between water that is illuminated at night and that which is not, as created by overhead light.

shellfish   A popular general designation for crustaceans and mollusks, but not including finfish.

shoal   **1.** A shallow part of a body of water representing a submerged ridge, bar, or bank that consists of or is covered by mud, sand, or gravel.

2. A school of fish, usually at the surface or in shallow water.

skirt   A dressing of synthetic material, hair, or rubber attached to a hook shank or lure body.

slot limit   A regulation prohibiting anglers from keeping fish that are either outside of a specified range or within a specified range.

slough   A marshy backwater; also a small, fingerlike dead-end channel off a river, lake, or tidal creek.

smolt   A young silvery salmon migrating from freshwater to the sea.

snag   **1.** An obstruction on which a lure is likely to get stuck.

2. To hook a fish in some part of its body other than the inside of its mouth.

spearing   Taking fish with a handheld prong, harpoonlike device, or spear, any of which may also be known as a gig.

species   A group of similar fish that can freely interbreed; similar species make up a genus.

specimen   A large or trophy-size representative of a particular species.

spool   **1.** The part of a reel that holds fishing line.

2. A storage device (usually round and with a large arbor) that holds fresh line for use on a fishing reel.

3. The act of putting line on a fishing reel.

4. Depleting line on a reel when accomplished by the actions of a large and powerful fish.

sportfish   Freshwater and saltwater fish sought by recreational anglers using sporting equipment.

sportfisherman   **1.** A person who catches or tries to catch fish for personal use, fun, challenge, and leisure by using sporting methods and sporting equipment, essentially some type of rod, usually but not always equipped with a reel, to which a line and a hook or lure are attached. The term is used interchangeably with "angler"; although it has a masculine gender, it is often used in a generic sense.

2. A large boat, also referred to as a sportfishing boat or off-shore boat, that is usually over 35 feet long, outfitted with big-game fishing equipment and set up for angling, and capable of cruising many miles offshore in the primary pursuit of pelagic species.

sportfishery   All aspects of catching or trying to catch fish for personal use, fun, challenge, and leisure by using sporting equipment, provided that the proceeds are released or kept for personal use and not sold. This term includes fisheries resources, anglers, and businesses providing goods and services.

sportfishing   The act of catching or trying to catch fish for personal use, fun, challenge, and leisure by using sporting methods and sporting equipment, essentially some type of rod, usually but not always equipped with a reel, to which a line and a hook or lure are attached. The term is used interchangeably with "angling."

standard length   The length of a fish as measured from the tip of its snout to the hidden base of the tailfin rays.

stillfishing   Any activity in which the angler fishes from a sta-tionary position, usually with bait and float or bobber.

stocking   The introduction of fish (and other organisms) into a body of water.

stratification   The temperature layering of lakes in temperate climates.

strike   **1.** The actual or attempted assault of a lure, fly, or hooked natural bait by a fish; also called a "bite" with reference to natural bait.

2. The reaction of an angler when a fish takes the lure, fly, or bait, generally known as "setting the hook" but also referred to as "striking the fish."

3. A preset drag position on a lever drag reel.

strike indicator   **1.** Any small object, usually one that floats, that is used to indicate a bite, or strike, by a fish on some form of natural bait.

2. A visible object that is attached to the leader when fly fishing to show leader movement when a fly has been taken by a fish in moving water.

strip bait   A strip of meat from a fish, clam, squid, or other bait impaled on a fishhook.

structure   Any object that provides shelter or feeding oppor-tunity to gamefish.

subspecies   A recognizable subpopulation of a single species, usually with a particular geographic distribution.

surface   The uppermost part of a body of water.

suspending   The habit of some fish, mainly freshwater species, to hold steady in midwater; this is distinguished from species that normally live in midwater levels, cruising in pursuit of baitfish.

tackle   Man-made equipment used almost exclusively for sportfishing; commonly called fishing tackle and with fun-damental reference to rods, reels, lines, leaders, and assorted terminal gear.

tagging   A method of marking fish for identification pur-poses.

tailer   A nooselike device that slips over the tail of a fish and cinches down on the caudal peduncle for landing; also called a tail rope or loop.

tailing   **1.** A method of landing a fish by grabbing it around the caudal peduncle, either by hand or with a tailer.

2. The phenomenon of a fish's fin, usually the upper tail fin, sticking above the surface of the water when the fish is feed-ing in shallow water.

tailrace   The disturbed and often turbulent section of river directly below a large dam, where water from the upstream impoundment is released.

tailwater   The entire section of river below a dam whose flows are dependent upon dam releases.

take   A strike by a fish.

teaser   An attractor used on the surface in offshore trolling.

terminal rig   An arrangement of terminal tackle items as a fishing unit; this usually involves some type of sinker, swivel, and hook or lure, plus a leader.

terminal tackle   The individual and collective equipment used at the end of a fishing line.

thermal bar   A sharp distinction between temperatures off-shore, primarily a phenomenon of large lakes.

thermocline   The layer of water containing rapid temperature change in a stratified lake or pond; the layer below the epilimnion and above the hypolimnion.

tidal rip   A spot where two or more currents collide or where a swift deep current confronts a shoal.

tide line   The line of debris that often collects along the edge of a tidal rip.

tipping   Placing live or dead natural bait on the hook of a lure, primarily a jig.

topwater   **1.** The surface of a water body, usually a pond or lake.

2. Lures fished on the surface.

3. Surface fishing tactics.

total length   The length of a fish as measured from the tip of its snout to the tip of its tail.

trolling motor   **1.** A fuel-powered motor, usually of low horsepower, used for slow movement in trolling.

2. A common term for an electric motor, whether used for trolling purposes or for positioning while casting or bottom fishing.

trophy fish   A large specimen of gamefish, usually above an arbitrary size deemed notable by common consensus or one that exceeds the minimum requirements of an award or recognition program.

turbidity   The amount of suspended particles in the water column. Turbid water is clouded with sediment and in extreme cases may be muddy.

turnover   The complete mixing of all the water in a lake, resulting in the temperature temporarily being the same from the surface to the bottom.

tyee   A chinook salmon 35 pounds or larger.

upstream fishing   Facing, casting, and fishing upstream in flowing water.

upwelling   A rise in water from a lower level to a higher level, usually induced by current and wind, most prevalent in the ocean where current pushes water up and over a prominent seafloor structure.

venue   A particular fishing site or location, be that a river, lake, reservoir, canal, or other place.

wade fishing   Fishing by means of wading in the water.

warmwater fish   Freshwater species whose optimum environment contains warm water, usually over 70°F, and that can tolerate warm and even turbid or poorly oxygenated water during summer.

wingdam   A man-made arrangement of rocks in a river that extends from shore a variable distance perpendicular to the river and is intended to deflect current and prevent bank erosion.

year-class   The fish spawned and hatched in a given year, also referred to as a "generation" of fish.

zooplankton   Minute suspended animals in the water column of seas and lakes.

Index

NOTE: Page references in *italics* refer to photos and illustrations.